THE COMEDY OF

Neil Simon

THE COMEDY OF

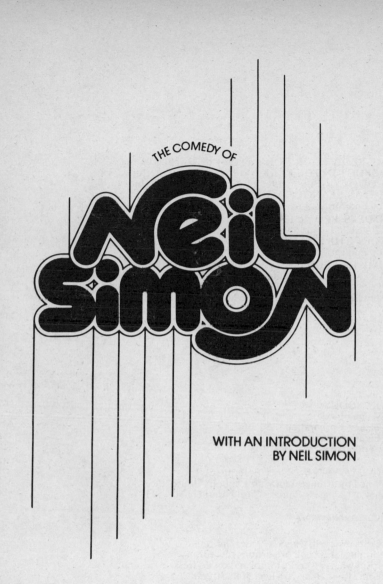

NEIL SIMON

WITH AN INTRODUCTION
BY NEIL SIMON

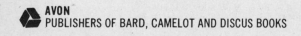

AVON
PUBLISHERS OF BARD, CAMELOT AND DISCUS BOOKS

AVON BOOKS
A division of
The Hearst Corporation
959 Eighth Avenue
New York, New York 10019

Copyright © 1971 by Nancy Enterprises, Inc.
Published by arrangement with Random House, Inc.
Library of Congress Catalog Card Number: 70-159374.

ISBN: 0-380-00789-4

First Avon Printing, June, 1973.

AVON TRADEMARK REG. U.S. PAT. OFF. AND
OTHER COUNTRIES—MARCA REGISTRADA,
HECHO EN U.S.A.

Printed in the U.S.A.
10 9 8 7

All for Joan

Contents

The
COMEDY
of Neil Simon

Introduction

Portrait of the Writer
as a Schizophrenic

Not long after we were married, my wife and I stood toe
to toe in the kitchen, exchanging verbal punches that were
as devastating and as painful as any thrown in a champion-
ship heavyweight match. Each accusation, each emotional
blow found its mark, and we both reeled from the awesome
destructive power of the truths we hurled. Then suddenly,
because there were no adequate words left to express her
hurt, frustration and anger, my wife did what now seems
to be the only sensible and rational thing she could have
done. She picked up a frozen veal chop recently left out on
the table to defrost, and hurled it at me, striking me just
above the right eye. I was so stunned I could barely react;
stunned not by the blow nor the intent, but by the absurd-
ity that I, a grown man, had just been hit in the head with
a frozen veal chop. I could not contain myself, and a faint
flicker of a smile crossed my face. Suddenly the anger and
hostility drained from me and I found myself outside the
situation looking in, no longer involved as a man in conflict,
but as an observer, an audience so to speak, watching two
people on a stage, both of whom cared for each other, but
were unable or unwilling to yield or to submit without
having first gained some small vicious victory. Add to the
scene the fact that, like the two policemen in a Roald Dahl
short story who ate the frozen mutton leg murder instrument for dinner, thus depriving themselves of their single
piece of evidence, I would soon be eating the object that
nearly destroyed my marriage. And I hate veal chops.

The marriage survived and is still prospering, despite
occasional rematches of our earlier, more successful fights.
On these occasions, I again find myself subtly extricating
myself from the scene of battle, and taking a seat at a higher
and safer vantage point, viewing the struggle much like
Lord Cardigan and Lord Raglan in the Crimean War, con-

cerned about the outcome, but at the same time making notes for future use. A strange phenomenon, this two-headed monster who finds himself totally involved in situations, and then suddenly and without warning steps back to watch the proceedings. There is evidence that this phenomenon is prevalent among that strange breed called writers, but it is even more prevalent among that stranger breed called comic writers. It is one thing for a writer to understand this; it is another to live with it. Like the werewolf, that half-man, half-beast, I have had to come to grips with the frightening but indisputable truth: I am a creature controlled by some cruel fate that had twisted and warped my personality so that at the first sign of personal involvement, I became transformed from human being into the most feared and dangerous beast on earth, the observer-writer. Like Lon Chaney's portrayal of Lawrence Talbot, the monster-turned-back-into-man, the writer-once-more-human suffers great pangs of guilt the mornings after his transformations, but is powerless to do anything about it. He is cursed. He tries to go about his normal life—until he feels the transformation beginning again, and he knows what lies ahead.

I wasn't always like that. In the beginning, I was a boy. A plain boy. A nice, plain boy. I went to school, I ate breakfast, I listened to *The Shadow*, I dreamt of being Joe DiMaggio, I went to the movies a lot and once was thrown out of a theater for laughing too loud at Chaplin in *Modern Times*. No sinister signs, no black omens. A nice, plain boy . . . Well, perhaps a few telltale hints to a discerning eye. I would go with my parents to visit a "distant" relative, distant in those days meaning a forty-minute trolley ride across the river to the Bronx, and once there, I imagined myself invisible. No earthly creature could see me because no earthly creature talked to me for hours at a time, save for grown-ups, when they offered me a cookie or a nice apple. I refused, hoping this would discourage them from further contact, enabling me to mask myself again in a cloak of obscurity. Hours would go by. They would talk, I would listen. I got to know them better by listening than if I had engaged them in conversation myself. On the trolley going home I realized again that I could not be seen by the human eye. People talked to each other, not to me. They looked at each other, not at me. Unobserved, unnoticed, unheeded, I could go about my curious business, storing up vast amounts of valuable information like accents, hair styles; those who shined their shoes and those who did not, nose blowers, nose wipers, nose leakers and those with various other nose habits too indelicate to mention. Occasionally I would be noticed, invariably by another young boy my own age and alone with his parents. I would have to be careful. If the other boy noticed what I was doing, I would be exposed. I stared at the Wrigley Chewing Gum sign above the heads of the occupants on the other side, hoping and praying the interloper would get off before I did. Success at last. There he goes. Stubby arms and a fat behind. Bad athlete, good student, and probably gets an allowance. Oh, terrific, his underwear constantly sticks in his crotch and he pulls at it in a really ridiculous way. I have him now. Let him dare to threaten to expose me, to reveal to the world my existence, and I shall shame him with vivid descriptions of how he gets off a trolley. Home to bed and dreams of victory and triumph. The Shadow knows.

I grow. An inch here, an inch there, a crack in the voice, a stubble on the chin, a passing shot at puberty, a glancing blow at sex and Shazam, I'm a man. If not a man, at least a tall boy. Would you accept an enormous child? My dreams, my goals, my ambitions are to be like Them, the Others. Accepted, Respected and Noticed. Not an impossible dream to fulfill if one works zealously, passionately and tirelessly. But at what? Business? No interest. Sports? No talent. Doctor? Lawyer? Engineer? No college degree, no talent, no interest.

My dreams and ambitions suddenly seem to be unreachable. How can you be Accepted, Respected and Noticed, when you are Unseen, Unobserved and Unheeded? Dichotomy. A Division in two. Split right down the old middle. May I make a suggestion? How about a blending of the two? If you remain Unseen, Unobserved and Unheeded, and write down for others to read what you see, observe and heed, you might become Accepted, Respected and Noticed.

Marriage, a home, a child here, a child there, Manhood at last. But the breach widens, the rift expands. The Unseen Eye observes, the Unseen hand writes—but it doesn't live comfortably alongside normal human functions. How can one be a husband, a father, a friend, a person, by withdrawing? How does one become an Observer, a Listener, if one is engaged, involved? The two continue to grow, to mature, but separately, apart . . . Until finally the split is complete. They can and do exist by themselves, housed in the same shell, but functioning as single and independent entities. A Monster is born.

The Human Being is a rather dull fellow. He doesn't smoke, is a moderate social drinker, dresses neatly but conservatively, watches his weight, his receding hairline and long-legged girls in short skirts, like the millions of faceless and fairly undistinguished members of his class and generation. He is often mistaken for looking like a grocery clerk —often *by* grocery clerks. He enjoys sports and indulges in childhood fantasies. He throws a pass, catches a long fly or hits a smashing backhand and envisages some shrewd sports promoter standing on the sidelines, cigar in mouth, asking, "Who's the new kid? Tell him I want to see him in my office." He drives rented Avis cars, always within the speed limits, his reading habits fluctuate somewhere between the Classics and *Variety*, and he would skip a seven-course meal in a three-star French restaurant for a corned beef on a seeded roll anytime. He watches his children perform in school plays, leaving in the middle on some pretext of an important business appointment and later regretting it, and sometimes stays to the bitter end, and regrets that too. He is kind to his mother, respectful to his mother-in-law, and is politically liberal, dove-ish, active and incredibly naive. He is an ecologist who believes in trees and grass and fresh air and the freedom of all animals, and has been seen on more than one occasion kicking his dog in the kidneys to get the mutt off the bed. He is a childish optimist. He thinks that justice will always prevail, that the meek shall inherit the earth, that bigotry and prejudice will not go unpunished and that the New York Football Giants, the Mets and the Knicks all will finish first next season. He is a dreamer and a realist, not acknowledging pain and defeat in his life but accepting it when it comes. He is a sensitive man and a sentimentalist; he reveres *Jules and Jim* for its classic beauty and cries at *Love Story*. Some would say, an ordinary man.

A look, the sound of a voice, a stranger passing on the street—and in an instant the transformation takes place. The mild-mannered Human Being suddenly dashes for cover behind his protective cloak called skin and peers out, unseen, through two tiny keyholes called eyes. He stands there undetected, unnoticed, a gleeful, malicious smirk on his face watching, penetrating, probing the movements, manners and absurd gestures of those ridiculous creatures performing their inane daily functions. "How laughably that woman dresses . . . How pathetically that man eats . . . How forlornly that couple walks . . . " The writer is loose!

The lenses are constantly adjusted, more distance for wider observations of physical behavior and characteristics; close range for deep probing and psychological motivations. But wait. Look there. A familiar face approaches. Quick. Look the other way. Don't risk discovery. There's important work to be done, this is no time for social amenities. Too late. He's spotted you. A fast Hello, How's your wife, Why don't we have dinner next week? He's gone. Relax. Nice fellow, but who's he kidding with that mustache? Compensating for a height deficiency. Did you notice how his eyes kept avoiding yours, constantly looking at the traffic as he talked? What's he afraid of? What's he done? Who is he looking for? When is he—Stop it! Stop it! Behave yourself. Leave that poor fellow with his short legs alone. He's your friend. You like him. He's a decent man. So his eyes avoid yours, does that make him guilty of a criminal act? Perhaps he just likes to watch traffic when he talks. You really must call him next week and say you'd like to have dinner.

The Human Being, having asserted his position and being satisfied with his own decency and humane behavior, relaxes into his reveries. If the Knicks can just get by Baltimore, and Willis Reed's knee can hold out just a little longer—what's that? There's a crazy lady who's talking to her dog. She's not crazy because she's talking to him but because she expects an answer. "Why did you do that, Teddy? Don't pull away from me, you naughty dog. You tell Mommy, why you did that." She will not be satisfied until Teddy answers, which Teddy will not, which means she will never be satisfied, which she is not, which is why she is a little old lady living by herself, which is why—Oh, God, shut up! Shut up, will you? Leave the poor woman alone. She's lucky she's got a Teddy. I am bored with your probing and prying. Stop looking at everyone. It's a beautiful spring day. Can't we just walk and enjoy the sun, for God's sakes?

The warmth of the sun passes through his body, pleasing him and comforting him. Is life not wonderful? Is nature not divine? Are God's creatures not truly wonderful? Is a hot dog with sauerkraut and a cold Pepsi in the park not one of mankind's greatest joys? His pleasure is not long lasting. A man and an attractive woman are walking slowly in front of him, talking in muted but heated words. He loves her but this can't go on. What can't go on? Their marriage? Their affair? Their business partnership? Their dance team? Damn that loud bus, I missed what she said. They're stopping. She's tired, she wants to sit on the bench. What do I do? Sit on the other end of the bench and pretend to read my newspaper? Fool, I have no newspaper. I could read the contents on my Pepsi bottle but how long would that take? Surely they'll suspect and move on . . . How about letting them alone and permitting them to live their lives in privacy? Monster, Monster, leave the world alone, it's none of your business.

Not content to pray on his fellow creatures, the Monster eventually turns on his alter ego, the Human Being, and dissects him unmercifully. In one play he has a newlywed accuse her husband of a week of being a stuffed shirt. "You're very proper and dignified. Even when you're drunk. You sit in a restaurant looking unhappy and watching your coat." It's true. He does. He tries to protect and defend himself. "The only reason I was watching my coat was because I saw someone else watching my coat." But the Monster will not be put off. He knows a stuffed shirt when he sees one, and he cuts even deeper. He uses the newlywed as the instrument to voice the feelings he has about the young husband. "You can't even walk into a candy store and ask for a Tootsie Roll. You've got to point to it and say to the lady, 'I'll have that thing in the brown and white wrapper.'" The Human-Being-Young-Husband fights back feebly. The Monster turns on the newlywed. He accuses her of being immature, adolescent, childishly romantic. Words echoing a real-life encounter that ended with a flying frozen veal chop. Is nothing sacred? Are there no secrets to be kept? But the Monster has observed, and what he has observed, he will reveal. Even the truth about himself. The young bride points another accusing finger: "Do you know what you are? You're a Watcher. There are Watchers in this world and there are Do-ers. And the Watchers sit around watching the Do-ers do. Well, tonight you watched and I did." Damn you, Monster, they're just a couple of nice kids starting out in life. Give them a break, will you?

The transformation begins to take place more often, more easily, sometimes almost going unnoticed, not realizing it's even happening. The distinguishing characteristics that separated them slowly become faded and muted until finally it is difficult to tell one from the other. Who is that now, looking back at me in the glass? If it's the Monster, why does the face look so benign, so innocent, so content with the world? If it's the Human Being, why does he look into the eyes so deeply, with such disgust and self-contempt? It is night. The battle for sleep rages. The human is tired, but the writer is restless with ideas, characters, conflicts, situations. "Shut up, damn you," screams the gentle self, "and let a person get some sleep." After a fitful night, morning comes and it's the Human who pays the price, who bears the baggy-eyed scars of a sleepless night. The Monster is bright, alert, ready to go to work. The man drags his weary body into the kitchen and force-feeds himself so that the Beast can live for another day, to pry and probe and eventually to leave the remains of his victims spread out on a typewritten page with their names disguised, but their identities known to the world, exposed for all to see, to examine, to jeer at, to sympathize and identify with, and hopefully to laugh with, at and for—all under the soon-to-be disparaged, cheered, ignored and overpraised title of ————"A New Comedy by . . . "

NEIL SIMON
New York City
March 10, 1971

COME
BLOW
YOUR
HORN

Act One

At rise: ALAN BAKER, *in a short Italian suede ski jacket is standing in the doorway being his charming, persuasive best in attempting to lure* PEGGY EVANS *into his bachelor apartment.* PEGGY *is in a ski outfit that fits her so snugly it leaves little room for skiing.* ALAN *puts down his valise, then slides* PEGGY'S *overnight bag out of her hand without her even noticing it and places it on the floor.* ALAN *is very adept at this game. Being good-looking, bright, thirty-three and single against* PEGGY'S *twenty-two years of blissful ignorance and eagerness to please, it appears that* ALAN *has all the marbles stacked on his side.*

PEGGY   Alan, no!

ALAN   Come on, honey.

PEGGY   Alan, no.

ALAN (*Taking off her ski jacket*)   Just five more minutes. Come on.

PEGGY   Alan, no. Please.
(*He pulls her into the living room*)

ALAN   But you said you were cold.

PEGGY   I am.

ALAN (*Embracing her*)   I'll start a fire. I'll have your blood going up and down in no time.

PEGGY   Alan, I want to go upstairs and take a bath. I've got about an inch of the New York Thruway on me.

ALAN   Honey, you can't go yet. We've got to have one last drink. To cap the perfect weekend.

PEGGY   It was four days.

ALAN   It's not polite to count . . . Don't you ever get tired looking sensational?

PEGGY   Do you think I do?

ALAN   You saw what happened at the ski jump. They were looking at you and jumping into the parking lot . . . Come here.
(*He bites her on the neck*)

PEGGY   Why do you always do that?

ALAN   Do what?

PEGGY   Bite me on the neck.

ALAN   What's the matter? You don't think I'm a vampire, do you?

PEGGY   Gee, I never thought of that.

ALAN   If it'll make you feel safer, I'll chew on your ear lobe.
(*He does*)

PEGGY (*Giggles*)   Kiss me.

ALAN   I'm not through with the hors d'oeuvres yet.
(*He kisses her*)

PEGGY (*Sighs and sits on sofa*)   Now I feel warm again.

ALAN   Good.

PEGGY   Thank you for the weekend, Alan. I had a wonderful time.

ALAN   Yeah, it was fun.
(*Crossing toward bar*)

PEGGY   Even though he didn't show up.

ALAN (*Stops and turns*)   Who?

PEGGY   Your friend from M-G-M.

ALAN (*Continuing to bar. Quickly*)   Oh, Mr. Manheim. Yeah . . . Well, that's show biz.

PEGGY   Did it say when he expects to be in N⸱⸱⸱⸱ ⸱k again?

ALAN   Did what?
(*Picks up carton containing scotch* ⸱

PEGGY   The telegram. From Hollywood.

ALAN   Oh! Didn't I tell you? Next week. Early part.

PEGGY   It's kind of funny now that you think of it, isn't it?

ALAN   What is?

PEGGY   Him wanting to meet me in a hotel.

ALAN (*Taking bottle out of carton*)   It was a ski lodge.

PEGGY   Was it? Anyway, it was nice. I've never been to New Hampshire before.

ALAN   It was Vermont.
        (*Putting down carton*)

PEGGY   Oh. I'm terrible with names. I can't imagine why an important man like that wants to travel all the way up there just to meet me.

ALAN (*Puts bottle back on bar*)   I explained all that. Since this picture he's planning is all about a winter carnival, he figured the best place to meet you would be against the natural setting of the picture. To see how you photograph against the snow. That makes sense . . . (*Not too sure*) Doesn't it?
        (*Crosses right*)

PEGGY   Oh, sure.

ALAN   Sure.
        (*Pulls* PEGGY *up from couch and embraces her*)

PEGGY   We ought to go again sometime when it's not for business. Just for fun.

ALAN   *That* should be a weekend.

PEGGY   Maybe next time I could learn to ski.

ALAN   I wouldn't be surprised.

PEGGY   It's a shame we were cooped up in the room so long.

ALAN   Yes. Well, I explained, we had that bad break in the weather.

PEGGY   You mean all that snow.

ALAN Exactly . . . But you make the cutest little Saint
Bernard . . .
(*He is just about to kiss her when the buzzer rings*)

PEGGY That's the lobby.

ALAN I don't hear a thing.

PEGGY Maybe it's for me.

ALAN *My* buzzer? You live up in the penthouse.

PEGGY I know. But I'm always here.
(*He looks at her quizzically, then goes to wall phone and
picks it up*)

ALAN (*Into phone*) Yes? . . . Who? . . . Buddy? . . . Hi, kid
. . . Now? . . . Well, sure. Sure, if it's important. You know
the apartment. (*He hangs up*) My kid brother.

PEGGY Oh. I'd better go.

ALAN (ALAN *reaches for her again*) This is the seventh floor.
We still have over a minute.

PEGGY (*Eluding him*) I want to go up and change anyway.
(*She picks up her parka and goes to him, then says invitingly*)
You think he'll be here long?

ALAN Not when you ask me like that.

PEGGY Why don't you come up in twenty minutes?

ALAN Why don't you come down in nineteen?

PEGGY All right. 'By, Alan.

ALAN 'By, Connie.

PEGGY Peggy!
(*She breaks from him*)

ALAN What?

PEGGY Peggy! That's the third time this weekend you
called me Connie.

ALAN I didn't say Connie. I said Honey!

PEGGY Oh!

ALAN Oh!

PEGGY   Sorry.
(ALAN *opens door. She smiles and exits.* ALAN *breathes a sigh of relief. Picks up suitcase and goes into bedroom as the doorbell rings*)

ALAN (*Off stage*)   Come on in, it's open.
(BUDDY BAKER, *his younger brother, enters with a valise in hand. Buddy is the complete opposite of Alan. Reserved, unsure, shy*)

BUDDY   Hello, Alan . . . Are you busy?
(*Enters apartment and looks around*)

ALAN (*Off stage*)   No, no. Come on in, kid. (ALAN *on*) What's up? (ALAN *sees suitcase*) What's in there?

BUDDY   Pajamas, toothbrush, the works.

ALAN   You're kidding.

BUDDY   Nope.

ALAN   You mean you left? (BUDDY *nods*) Permanently?

BUDDY   I took eight pairs of socks. For me, that's permanently.

ALAN   I don't believe it. You can't tell me you actually ran away from home.

BUDDY   Well, I cheated a little. I took a taxi.
(*Takes off coat and places it on suitcase*)

ALAN   You're serious. You mean my baby brother finally broke out of prison?

BUDDY   We planned it long enough, didn't we?

ALAN   Yes, but every time I brought it up you said you weren't ready. Why didn't you say something to me?

BUDDY   When? You weren't at work since Thursday.

ALAN   Hey, did Dad say anything? About my being gone?

BUDDY   Not at the office. But at home he's been slamming doors. The chandelier in the foyer fell down. Where were you?

ALAN   Vermont.

BUDDY   Skiing?

ALAN   Only during the day.
        (*Sits on sofa and lights cigarette*)

BUDDY   I don't know how you do it. If I'm at work one
        minute after nine, he docks my pay . . . and I get less to
        eat at home.

ALAN   Because he expects it from you. From me he says he
        expects nothing, so that's what I give him.

BUDDY   You're better off. At least you're not treated like a
        baby. You can talk with him.

ALAN   We don't talk. We have heart to heart threatening
        . . .

BUDDY   That's better than the subtle treatment I get. Last
        night I came home three o'clock in the morning. He
        didn't approve. What do you think he did? (ALAN *shakes his
        head*) As I passed his bedroom door, he crowed like a
        rooster. Cock-a-doodle-doo.

ALAN   You're kidding. What'd you say?

BUDDY   Nothing. I wanted to cluck back like a chicken but
        I didn't have the nerve.

ALAN   Oh, he's beautiful.

BUDDY   And then yesterday was my birthday. (*Sits on
        sofa*) Twenty-one years old.

ALAN   Oh, that's right. Gee, I'm sorry I wasn't there,
        Buddy. Happy birthday, kid.
        (*He shakes* BUDDY's *hand warmly*)

BUDDY   Thanks.

ALAN   I even forgot to get you a present.

BUDDY   I got one. A beaut. From Mom and Dad.

ALAN   What was it?

BUDDY   A surprise party. Mom, Dad, and the Klingers.

ALAN   Who are the Klingers?

BUDDY   Oh, the Klingers are that lovely couple the folks
        met last summer at Lake Mahopac.

ALAN   Why? They're not your friends.

BUDDY   Think. Why would they have the Klingers to meet me?

ALAN   They've got a daughter.

BUDDY   Oh, have they got a daughter.

ALAN   You mean they brought her with them?

BUDDY   In a crate.

ALAN   Let me guess. Naomi?

BUDDY   Close. Renee.

ALAN   Not much on looks but brilliant.

BUDDY   A genius. An I.Q. of 170. Same as her weight.

ALAN   And of course they had her dressed for the kill. They figured what she couldn't do, maybe Bergdorf could.

BUDDY   Nothing could help. So I spent the night of my twenty-first birthday watching a girl devour an entire bowl of cashew nuts.

ALAN   Oh, I'm sorry, kid.

BUDDY   (Rises, crosses right center)   It's been getting worse and worse. He looks in my closets, my drawers. He listens to my phone calls. I don't know what it is I've done, Alan, but I swear he's going to turn me in.

ALAN   Well, it's simple enough. He's afraid you're going to follow in my footsteps.

BUDDY   I did. I thought it over all day and realized I had to leave . . . Well–here I am.

ALAN   Oh, I'm so proud of you, Buddy. If you weren't twenty-one, I'd kiss you.

BUDDY   You really think I did the right thing?

ALAN   What did you do, rob a bank? You're only going to be living four subway stations away. You're still working for him, *aren't you?*

BUDDY   Well, there's going to be trouble there too.

ALAN   What do you mean?

BUDDY I know I'm going to be struck by lightning for saying this . . . but I'm thinking of leaving the business.

ALAN . . . On the level?

BUDDY I'm not happy there, Alan. I'm not like you. You're good in the business . . . I'm not.

ALAN It's just that you're inexperienced.

BUDDY It's not only that. It just doesn't interest me. Gee whiz, there's a million more important things going on in the world today. New countries are being born. They're getting ready to send men to the moon. I just can't get excited about making wax fruit.

ALAN Why not? It's a business like anything else.

BUDDY It's different for you, Alan. You're hardly ever there. (*He sits*) You're the salesman, you're outside all day. Meeting people. Human beings. But I'm inside looking at petrified apples and pears and plums. They never rot, they never turn brown, they never grow old . . . It's like the fruit version of *The Picture of Dorian Gray*.

ALAN (*Follows*) You know why you feel that way? Because you never get a chance to take the chains off. During the day it's all right. But at night you've got to bite into the *real* fruit of life, Buddy, not wax.

BUDDY Yeah, I guess so.

ALAN But that's all behind you now, right?

BUDDY (*Crosses downstage left*) Well . . . (*He looks at his watch*) In a few minutes anyway.

ALAN (*Crosses downstage left*) What do you mean?

BUDDY Dad should be coming home soon.

ALAN You mean you didn't tell him you were leaving?

BUDDY I couldn't, Alan.

ALAN Why not? Were you scared?

BUDDY You bet I was. With you out of work these last few days he hasn't been all smiles . . . And besides . . . I just didn't want to hurt him . . . Sure he's stubborn and old-fashioned . . . but he means well.

ALAN   I know, kid. I understand.

BUDDY   I left him at the plant and came home early tonight. Then I wrote him a long letter explaining how I felt and left it on his bed. And in the morning, I think I'll be able to reason with him. Don't you?
(*Crosses to* ALAN *right*)

ALAN   Frankly no, but what's the difference? I'm proud of you. You walked out of Egypt, kid. How about a drink? To celebrate. Scotch or bourbon?
(*He crosses to bar*)

BUDDY (*Sits on sofa*)   Sure . . .

ALAN   Scotch, bourbon?

BUDDY   Scotch.

ALAN   Scotch it is.

BUDDY   And ginger ale.

ALAN (*Stops*)   Scotch and ginger ale? . . . They must know you in every bar in town. (*He makes drinks*) Hey, how did Mom take all this?

BUDDY (*Crosses and sits sofa*)   Oh, she's upset, of course. The most important thing to her is peace in the family.

ALAN   *And* a clean apartment.

BUDDY (*Smiles*)   And a clean apartment.

ALAN   By the way, how is the Museum of Expensive Furniture?

BUDDY   Oh, the living room is still closed to the public!

ALAN   Living room? I don't remember ever seeing a living room.

BUDDY   Sure you did. The one that had the lamp shades wrapped in cellophane for the past twenty years.

ALAN (*Placing drinks on coffee table*)   Oh, yes. I was outlawed from that room years ago for putting a cigarette in an ash tray.

BUDDY   . . . But you know why I really left home. I don't want to have milk and cake standing over the sink any more. I want to sit in a chair and eat like real people.

ALAN Whoa, boy. You've got to start easy otherwise you'll get the bends. Maybe tonight you can hang your coat on the doorknob. Then maybe in a few days you'll be ready for bigger things . . . like leaving your socks on the floor.

BUDDY (*Swings around right*) Oh, it's going to be wonderful, just the two of us, Alan. (*He looks around*) Hey, I never realized it before, but this is a great apartment.

ALAN Yeah. It comes a little high, but you pay for the atmosphere.

BUDDY Oh, I almost forgot. How much is my rent?

ALAN What rent?

BUDDY For my share? I won't stay here unless I can pay my share.

ALAN All right, sport. Give me thirty dollars.

BUDDY Who are you kidding? This place is no sixty dollars a month.

ALAN Look, that's your rent. Thirty dollars. When the old man starts paying you more, you can pay *me* more.

BUDDY Well, just to start with. But we split everything else. The food and gas and electricity and everything. Agreed?

ALAN (*Crosses right to* BUDDY, *bringing a drink*) Agreed. (*Hands* BUDDY *a drink*) Here. You owe me seventy-five cents. (*Raising his glass*) Well, here's to the Baker Brothers. The dream we've planned for years . . . You take all the girls on the West Side, I'll take the East Side . . . and I'll get in trouble afore ye. (*He winks affectionately at* BUDDY. BUDDY *drinks,* ALAN *watches*) How is it?

BUDDY (*Not very happy*) Different.

ALAN It should be. You just invented it. (*The phone rings*) Ten to one it's a gorgeous girl. (*Phone rings again. He picks up phone*) Hello? . . . Oh, Mom! . . . How are you, gorgeous? . . . We were just talking about you . . . Yes, about ten minutes ago . . . He's fine . . . Of course I'm going to take care of him . . . All right, sweetheart. (*He holds phone out to* BUDDY) It's the Curator of the Museum.

BUDDY (*He takes the phone anxiously and sits on sofa.* ALAN *goes to bar for refill*)   Hello, Mom? . . . How are you? . . . Fine . . . Fine . . . No, no. I'll have dinner soon . . . I don't know, some place in the neighborhood . . . Mom . . . Did Dad read the letter yet? . . . Oh, still at the plant. (ALAN *crosses to* BUDDY. BUDDY *breathes a little easier*) What? . . . Mom, I don't want you to hide the letter . . . I *want* him to read it . . . He what? . . . Oh, boy!

ALAN   What's wrong?

BUDDY   Well, I know that just makes it worse, Mom, but I can't–Mom! . . . Mom! . . . Mom! . . .

ALAN   She's crying?
   (*Nods*)

BUDDY   She's crying.

ALAN   Crying.

BUDDY (*Back into phone*)   Mom, please calm down . . . No, Mom, that's not fair of you to ask me that

ALAN   What does she want you to do, come home?

BUDDY (*Jumping up*)   Mom, don't tear up the letter. I can't come home.

ALAN (*Crossing downstage left in front of table*)   Let me talk to her.

BUDDY   But what about my life?

ALAN   Let me talk to her.

BUDDY   Mom, please-don't-tear-up-the-letter!

ALAN (*Reaching for phone*)   Give me the phone.

BUDDY (*Turns away*)   Alan, will you wait a minute. (*Back into phone*) All right, Mom. Let me think about it. I will. I'll call you back . . . Later . . . I promise . . . All right . . . Don't tear up the letter . . . Good-by.
   (*He hangs up*)

ALAN   You'll think about what?

BUDDY   Dad called Mom about ten minutes ago from the plant. Screaming. Some customer is angry at you! Because you didn't show up for a meeting today?

ALAN   Oh, my gosh, Mr. Meltzer, I forgot.

BUDDY   Anyway, Mom's afraid when he finds out that I left on top of this he'll go to pieces.

ALAN   All right, all right. One thing has nothing to do with the other. I'll straighten him out.

BUDDY   But he's going to let this all out on Mom. And you know when he starts to yell. You could get killed just from the fall-out.

ALAN   Well, what do you want to do?

BUDDY   I don't know. Maybe I should go home.
   (*Picks up coat and suitcase*)

ALAN   Go home? Why?

BUDDY   Why should Mother get the blame for something we've done?

ALAN (*Follows*)   Don't ask me. I don't crow like a rooster at three o'clock in the morning.

BUDDY   What am I supposed to do?

ALAN   Grow up. Be a man. You're twenty-one years old.
   (*Takes his suitcase and coat and puts them down by sofa*)

BUDDY   You mean just forget about it?

ALAN   Buddy, how long do you want to wait until you start enjoying life? When you're sixty-five you get social security, not girls.

BUDDY   I don't know how we got all twisted around. I'm on your side. I want to leave. It's Dad who's against it.

ALAN   Buddy, I know he means well. But he'll just never understand that things in life change. He's been in the wax-fruit business too long. *You've* changed.

BUDDY   I know, but—

ALAN You're twenty-one years old now. You're ripe. Come on, kid. You've got one shoe off. Kick the other one off.

BUDDY (*Looks at* ALAN *a moment, then shrugs*) I—I guess you're right.

ALAN Then you'll stay?

BUDDY (*Nods*) Yeah . . . Why not?

ALAN (*Puts arm around him*) That's the kid brother I love and adore. Now go put your stuff in the bedroom.

BUDDY You sure I won't be in your way here or anything?
  (*Picking up his coat and suitcase*)

ALAN Of course not. We just may have to work out a traffic system. I've got a girl coming down in a few minutes.

BUDDY A girl? Why didn't you say so? Whenever you want to be alone, just say the word. I'll go out to a movie.

ALAN Don't worry. With my schedule, you won't miss a picture this year. (*The doorbell rings*) You hear that? She's here ten minutes ahead of time.
  (*The doorbell rings again*)

BUDDY I'd better put this in here and go.
  (*Goes into bedroom*)

ALAN No, no. I want you to see her first. (*He crosses to door*) Ready for the thrill of your life? (*He opens the door a crack as he says:*) . . . and my third wish, O Geni, is that when I open the door, the most beautiful girl in the world will be standing there. (*He motions* BUDDY *to come out of bedroom. As he opens the door, there stands his* FATHER, *scowling disgustedly*) Dad!!
  (BUDDY *enters and immediately goes back into bedroom closing door quietly behind him*)

FATHER (*Steps in and looks at* ALAN *and nods disgustedly. He walks into the room.* ALAN *looks after him, dismayed, and seems puzzled when he doesn't see* BUDDY. *The* FATHER *examines the room. It is obvious he approves of nothing in the apartment*)

ALAN (*Meeting him downstage center*) Gee, Dad . . . this is a . . . pleasant . . . surprise. (*The* FATHER *looks at him as if to say, "I'll bet"*) How . . . how are you?

FATHER How am I? . . . I'll tell you sometime . . . That's how I am.
> (*He continues his inspection*)

ALAN I've redecorated the place . . . How do you like it?

FATHER Fancy . . . Very fancy . . . You must have some nice job.
> (*Sniffs highball glass*)

ALAN I just got in, Dad. I was about to call you.

FATHER The phone company shouldn't have to depend on your business.

ALAN I wanted to explain what happened to me. Why I wasn't in the last two days.

FATHER There's nothing to explain.

ALAN Yes, there is, Dad.

FATHER Why? I understand. You work very hard two days a week and you need a five-day weekend. That's normal.

ALAN Dad, I'm not going to lie. I was up in Vermont skiing. I intended to be back Sunday night, but I twisted my bad ankle again. I couldn't drive. I thought it was broken.

FATHER I'll send you a get-well card.

ALAN I'm sorry, Dad. I really am.

FATHER You're sorry. I can't ask more than that.

ALAN I'll be in the office first thing in the morning.

FATHER That's good news. You know the address, don't you?

ALAN Yes, Dad. I know the address.

FATHER See. I always said you were smart. So I'll see you in the morning.

ALAN Right!
> (ALAN *starts upstage*)

FATHER (*Stops*) Oh, by the way . . . How's the Meltzer account going?

ALAN   The Meltzer account?
(ALAN *comes back*)

FATHER   From Atlantic City? The one you bragged about was all wrapped up?

ALAN   Oh . . . er . . . fine.

FATHER   Fine? . . . I'm glad to hear that . . . Because he called today.

ALAN (*Surprised*)   Oh? . . . About an order?

FATHER   Yes. About an order.

ALAN (*A little skeptical*)   . . . Did . . . did we get one?

FATHER   Yes . . . We got one.

ALAN   . . . How much?

FATHER   How much?—guess

ALAN   Well, Dad I—

FATHER   Guess! Guess how much we got from Meltzer.

ALAN   . . . Nothing?

FATHER   Bingo! Right on the button! . . . Bum!

ALAN   Dad, wait a minute . . .

FATHER   Did you have a nice weekend, bum? Do you know what it costs to go skiing for four days? Three thousand dollars a day? Bum!

ALAN   I tried to call him. I couldn't get a line through.

FATHER   On skis you tried to call him? You should be in the Olympics.

ALAN (*Crossing to phone*)   I'll call him right back. I'll explain everything.

FATHER   Where you gonna call him?

ALAN   In Atlantic City.

FATHER   Who're you going to talk to? The Boardwalk? He's here!

ALAN   In New York?

FATHER In the Hotel Croyden. For two days he's sitting waiting while you're playing in the snow.

ALAN Dad, I promise you. I won't lose the account.

FATHER Why? This would be the first one you ever lost? You want to see the list? You could ski (*gestures*) down your cancellations.

ALAN I couldn't get back in time, Dad. Skiing had nothing to do with it.

FATHER I'm sorry. I forgot. I left out golf and sailing and sleeping and drinking and women. You're terrific. If I was in the bum business I would want ten like you.

ALAN That's not true. I put in plenty of time in the business.

FATHER Two years. In six years you put in two years. I had my bookkeeper figure it out.

ALAN Thank you.

FATHER My own son. I get more help from my competitors.
(*Starts to sit*)

ALAN Well, why not? You treat me like one.

FATHER (*Jumping up*) *I* treat you? Do *I* wander in at eleven o'clock in the morning? Do *I* take three hours for lunch . . . in night clubs? . . . When are you there?

ALAN What do you mean, when?

FATHER When? When? You take off legal holidays, Jewish holidays, Catholic holidays . . . Last year you took off Hallowe'en.

ALAN I was sick.

FATHER When you came back to work you were sick. When you were sick you were dancing.

ALAN In the first place, it's not true. And in the second place, what good does it do coming in? You don't need me. You never ask my advice about the business, do you?

FATHER What does a skier know about wax fruit?

ALAN You see? You see? You won't even listen.

FATHER (*He sits*) Come in early. I'll listen.

ALAN I did. For three years. Only then I was "too young" to have anything to say. And now that I've got my own apartment, I'm too much of a "bum" to have anything to say. Admit it, Dad. You don't give me the same respect you give the night watchman.

FATHER At least I know where he is at night.

ALAN . . . You know where I am, too. Having fun. What's wrong with it? I think what I do at night should be my business.

FATHER Not when it's nighttime four days in a row. Listen, what do I care? (*He rises and crosses right*) Do whatever you want. Go ahead and live like a bum.

ALAN Why am I a bum?

FATHER Are you married?

ALAN No.

FATHER Then you're a bum!

ALAN Give me a chance. I'll get married.

FATHER I heard that for years. When you were twenty-six, twenty-seven, twenty-eight, even twenty-nine, you were a bachelor. But now you're over thirty and you're still not married, so you're a bum and that's all there is to it.
(*Turns away*)

ALAN Who made thirty the closing date? All I want to do is have a little fun out of life like any other healthy, normal American boy.

FATHER Healthy you are, American you are, normal you're not.

ALAN What do you mean?

FATHER Look at your brother, that's what I mean. That's normal. He'll be something, that kid. He'll never be like you. Not in a million years.

ALAN Really? He might surprise you.

FATHER   That I'll bet my life on. He's in the plant the first thing in the morning, he puts in a whole day's work. No, that's one son I'll never have to worry about.

ALAN   Have you read your mail lately?

FATHER   What?

ALAN   Nothing.

FATHER   All right, I don't want to discuss anything more. I want to see you in the office tomorrow morning at eight o'clock.

ALAN   Eight o'clock? There's no one there then.

FATHER   You'll be there. And you'll be there two nights a week and Saturdays, holidays, birthdays, and vacations. I'm sick and tired of being the father. From now on I'm the boss.

ALAN   All right, Dad, but eight o'clock is silly. I have nothing to do until nine.

FATHER (*Crossing up to foyer*)   You play solitaire all day anyway. You can get in three more games.

ALAN   Okay. Okay, I'll be there.

FATHER   *With* the Meltzer account. If you haven't got it signed and in your pocket . . . you can ski (*gesturing*) right into the unemployment office.

ALAN   I'll try, Dad. I'll really do my best.

FATHER   With your best, we're in trouble. From you I need a miracle. (ALAN *sits downstage right center chair*) Eight o'clock with the Meltzer account . . .

ALAN   Yes, Dad.

FATHER   The day your brother becomes like you, I throw myself in front of an airplane.
        (*And with that he exits. As front door slams,* BUDDY *comes rushing out of the bedroom door in a state of shock*)

BUDDY   Did you hear that? I told you, Alan. I told you what he'd do.

ALAN (*Crosses to phone*)   What hotel did he say, the Croyden?

BUDDY   Wait'll he reads that letter. He'll kill himself. He'll kill all of us. Like those stories in the Daily *News*. Alan, give me the phone.
>   (ALAN *dials 411*)

ALAN   Take it easy, will you. I've got to call Meltzer.

BUDDY   Meltzer? We've got to get to Mom before he gets home. She's got to tear up that letter.

ALAN   Will you relax. He's not going to kill anyone until he's had his supper . . . I'll straighten everything out.

BUDDY   How?

ALAN   All I've got to do is get Meltzer to sign. (*Into phone*) I'd like the number of the Hotel Croyden please.

BUDDY   Suppose you don't?

ALAN   There's no problem. He came to New York because I promised him a party . . . (*Into phone*) What was that? Thank you.
>   (*Dials number*)

BUDDY   I sure picked a rotten time to leave. It's going to be murder up there. (*Starts to go*) I'm going home.

ALAN   You walk out that door, I don't want you back.

BUDDY (*Coming back*)   Alan, why don't you help me?

ALAN (*Into phone*)   Mr. Martin Meltzer, please . . . Thank you. (*To* BUDDY) I'm doing more than helping you. I'm saving you. It took you two years to get this far. Next time it'll take you five. (*Into phone and rises*) Hello? Mr. Meltzer? Hi? Alan Baker! . . . Where was I? . . . I'm too embarrassed to tell you . . . You ready? . . . Atlantic City . . . Yes. I thought you wanted me to come *there* . . . I just didn't think . . . Sure, I had the girls with me . . .

BUDDY   You're a lunatic!

ALAN (*Covers phone quickly*)   Will you shut up? (*Back into phone*) What? . . . Well, can't you take the morning train back? . . . Can I still get in touch with the girls? . . . They're here with me right now.

BUDDY   Where?

ALAN (*Covers phone again quickly*)   I'll shove you in the closet.
(*Back into phone*) What was that? . . . Yes . . . That was one
of the girls you heard . . . Pretty? (*He laughs. Turns head
slightly from phone*) Honey, he wants to know if you're
pretty . . . Mr. Meltzer, did you ever see an ugly girl in
the Copacabana line? . . . No, they're off this week . . . Yes,
they're dying to . . . Your hotel. Room 326 . . . Half hour?
You have the drinks ready, I'll bring the drinkers. (*He
laughs a phony laugh into the phone and hangs up*) I hate
myself.
     (*He picks up book and thumbs through it quickly*)

BUDDY   I never saw anyone like you. Is it like this every
night?

ALAN   Well, it's always slow before Christmas. (*Reading
from book*) "Married . . . Married . . . Europe . . . Pregnant
. . ." (*Finds something in book*) Ahhh, here we are. Chickie
Parker.
     (*He dials*)

BUDDY   Chickie Parker?

ALAN   And she looks just like she sounds. (*Into phone*) Hello?
. . . Chickie? Don't you know you could be arrested for
having such a sexy voice? . . . Alan . . . How could I? I just
got in from Europe an hour ago . . . Switzerland . . . A
specialist there told me if I don't see you within a half an
hour, I'll die . . . Yes, tonight . . . A friend of mine is
having a little party . . . Wonderful guy . . . Hundred
laughs . . . Hey, Chickie, is your roommate free? The
French girl? . . . Wonderful. Yes. Bring her . . . No, I can't.
I've got to get the pretzels. Can you meet me there? The
Hotel Croyden, Room 326, Marty Meltzer . . . A half hour
. . . Marvelous. I just love you . . . What? . . . Yes, Alan
Baker. (*He bangs up*) *Voilà!*

BUDDY (*He's flabbergasted*)   And it took me three months to
get a date for my prom.

ALAN   I'd better get going. (*He starts for bedroom when the
buzzer rings. He stops*) Now what? (*He crosses quickly to inter-
com and speaks into it*) . . . Hello? . . . Who? (*Big surprise*)
Connie!! . . . What are you doing here? . . . No, honey, no

. . . Now? . . . Well, sure . . . sure, come on. (*He hangs up*) Of all the nights.

BUDDY   Who's that?

ALAN   A girl.

BUDDY   Another one? Is she coming up?
   (ALAN *nods*)

ALAN (*Half to himself*)   She wasn't due back in town till tomorrow. What a time to show up.

BUDDY   Then why are you seeing her?

ALAN   Oh, I can't give this girl the brush.

BUDDY   I thought that part would be easy.

ALAN   You don't understand. This girl is different. She's not like . . . well, she's different

BUDDY   You mean this one's for serious?

ALAN   Who said serious? I just said different.

BUDDY   Oh boy, would that solve everything at home if you got married. You know Mom's had an open line to the caterers for three years now.

ALAN   Married? Me? With all this? Are you crazy?

BUDDY   Well, I just thought—since she's a *nice* girl . . .

ALAN   She's the *nicest* . . . but I'm working on it . . . Listen, you'd better blow. I want to see her alone.
   (*Doorbell rings*)

BUDDY   Okay.
   (*He starts for the door*)

ALAN   Oh! Hey, go out the service entrance in the kitchen . . . Come back in a few minutes.

BUDDY (*He nods and goes to kitchen door*)   Boy, no wonder you come in at eleven o'clock in the morning!
   (*He exits*)
   (ALAN *crosses quickly to the door and opens it about an inch and says aloud:*)

ALAN   And my third wish, O Geni, is that when I open my eyes, the most beautiful girl in the world will be standing there.
(*He opens door, turns and looks*)
(CONNIE *is standing there, holding an octagonal hat box*)
(ALAN *crossing downstage right*)

O Joy! My third wish has been granted. Enter, beautiful lady.
(CONNIE *enters*)

CONNIE   Well, I guess it's safe as long as you've used up the other two wishes.

ALAN   How are you, Connie?

CONNIE   Fine . . . now that I'm back.

ALAN (*He embraces her*)   Mmm. How does a girl get to smell like that?

CONNIE   She washes occasionally.
(*Holding package between them*)

ALAN   Come here. I've been thinking about this moment for two whole weeks. (*He tries to get closer*) Will you put down that package.

CONNIE (*She presents it to him*)   After you open it.

ALAN (*He takes it*)   What is it?

CONNIE   A present.

ALAN   For me? Why?

CONNIE (*She shrugs*)   I like you! . . . And I missed you.

ALAN   Well, I did too, but I didn't get you a present.

CONNIE   Well, don't get upset about it. I just like you six dollars and ninety-eight cents more than you like me . . . Open it.
(*Unbuttons jacket*)
(*He opens it*)

ALAN (*He looks in box. He is overwhelmed*)   Connie! . . . My ski hat!
(*He takes it out of box*)

CONNIE   It's like the one you lost, isn't it?

ALAN (*He is really quite thrilled with it*)   It's the same thing.
(*He looks inside at the label*) It's the identical one I bought
in Switzerland. I've looked all over New York for this.
Where (*Puts box on fireplace chair*) did you ever get it?

CONNIE   In Montreal . . . It wasn't hard. Up there the news-
stand dealers wear (*He puts hat on—She puts jacket on sofa*)
them.

ALAN   It even fits. How did you know my head size?

CONNIE   I've got an imprint on my neck.

ALAN (*Throws hat on sofa*)   Connie, you're wonderful. Only
you would think of a thing like this.

CONNIE   Well, I *thought* of a watch, but I could afford this
better.

ALAN   Come here you.
(*He takes her in his arms*)

CONNIE (*Coyly*)   Ah, the pay-off.

ALAN   Thank you very much.
(*He kisses her*)

CONNIE   You're welcome—very much.
(ALAN *moves to embrace her. She backs away*)

CONNIE   Alan relax.

ALAN   I'm not through yet.
(*She crosses left*)

CONNIE   I've just come eight hundred miles in a prehistoric
train and I'm tired, hungry, and too weak to be chased
around the sofa.

ALAN (*Crosses to Connie*)   I'll carry you. We'll save lots of
time and energy.
(*He moves after*)

CONNIE   Alan, please don't take advantage. I've got enough
handicaps as it is.

ALAN   Like what?

CONNIE (*Wilting*)   Like being on your side. (*He grabs her and she swings around right of him*) It isn't fair. You and me against me is not fair. What is it you've got?

ALAN   I don't know. Am I terribly good-looking?

CONNIE   Oh, God, no. You've got just enough things wrong with your face to make you very attractive . . . It's something else. Some strange power you have over me. But beware. The day I find out what it is, I'll have a gypsy destroy the spell with a dead chicken.

ALAN   You little fool. Nothing can stop the Phantom Lover.
   (*He starts after her*)

CONNIE   Alan, no!
   (*Backs right*)

ALAN (*Stalking her*)   One kiss. If it leaves you cold, I'll stop. But if it gets you all crazy, we play house rules.

CONNIE (*Moves so chair right is between them*)   Now, Alan, play fair.

ALAN   I'll keep my hands behind my back. I'll spot you a five-point lead. I'll only be permitted to use my upper lip.
   (*Steps up on chair*)

CONNIE   Alan, not now. Please. I haven't got the strength to put up an interesting fight. I just wanted to see you before I fell into bed for the next week and a half.

ALAN   Okay. (*He pecks her*) A rough tour, heh?
   (ALAN *gets down off chair*)

CONNIE   This was the roughest.
   (*Sits on right arm of chair*)

ALAN (*He laugh*)   You poor kid. When does the show go out again?

CONNIE   *They* leave in two weeks.

ALAN   They? . . . Not you?

CONNIE (*Smiles*)   Not me.

ALAN   Why not?

CONNIE I just suddenly decided to quit.

ALAN Oh. Well, have you got another show lined up?

CONNIE Well . . . it's not just the show I quit . . . It's show business.

ALAN (*He looks at her*) . . . Are you serious?

CONNIE (*She nods. She doesn't want to make a big thing of it now*) I'll tell you all about it tomorrow. (*Starts left*) Will you call me, darling? . . . In the afternoon?

ALAN Wait a minute. I want to hear about this.

CONNIE There's nothing to tell.

ALAN Nothing to tell? You're giving up your career and there's nothing to tell?

CONNIE (*She laughs*) Oh, Alan, darling . . . what career?

ALAN What do you mean, what career? You're a singer, aren't you?

CONNIE Well, I wouldn't invest in it.

ALAN I don't get it. Things are going so well for you . . . All those musicals you do.

CONNIE (*Sits sofa*) They're not musicals. They're industrial shows. Two-hour commercials completely uninterrupted by entertainment.

ALAN (*Sits sofa and puts hat on table behind sofa*) I'm serious.

CONNIE I'm dead serious. This past month we did a show for the Consolidated Meat Packers. Have you any idea what it's like singing "Why not take all of me"* dressed as a sausage?

ALAN (*He smiles*) It sounds funny.

CONNIE Maybe to you. But I've seen butchers sit there and cry.

ALAN All right, so it's not *My Fair Lady*. You don't expect it to come easy, do you?

*Line from "All of Me" by Seymour Simons and Gerald Marks. © Copyright 1931 Bourne, Inc., New York, N.Y. Copyright renewed. Used by permission.

CONNIE I don't expect it to come at all. Not now. Alan
. . . (*Breaks left*) I'd work my throat to the bone if I
thought I had a chance . . . or if I wanted it that much.
But somehow lately I don't care any more . . . I guess it
started when I met you.
(*Sits left arm*)

ALAN Honey, everyone gets discouraged. But you don't
suddenly throw away a promising career.

CONNIE Promising? Even you once said I was a lousy
singer.

ALAN No, I didn't. I said you had a lousy voice. There's a
big difference.

CONNIE There is?

ALAN Of course. You've got looks, personality. That's all
you need in the music business today. Hockey players are
making albums.

CONNIE It's *not* enough, Alan. You've got to have talent
too.

ALAN Only if you want to be good. Not if you want to be
a star.

CONNIE Well, it's pretty evident I'm not going to be either.

ALAN I just don't understand your attitude.

CONNIE I don't understand *yours*. The world isn't losing
one of its great artists.

ALAN What suddenly brought all this on?

CONNIE (*Sits left of him*) It's very simple. I just got tired of
being away from you so long.

ALAN (*Withdrawing slightly*) . . . Oh! . . . Well . . . if that's
what you want.

CONNIE That's it. No more traveling. No more buses and
trains and long-distance phone calls. (*She moves closer*) I
don't want to be more than a thirty-five cent taxi ride
away from you.

ALAN (*Getting a little jittery*) You . . . seem to have made up your mind.

CONNIE Yes. And what a relief it is.

ALAN Well . . . What will you do now?

CONNIE I'll manage. (ALAN *rises—drifts right of center*) Girls are doing it every day. I'll maybe do a little modeling or become a secretary . . . or . . . a housewife.

ALAN (*Turns to face her*) What?

CONNIE Housewife. You know . . . sleep-in maids.

ALAN (*Serious*) What do you mean?

CONNIE It was a joke . . . You didn't get it.

ALAN (*Deadpan*) Yeah, I get it . . . It's funny. (*Looks at his watch*) Holy mackerel, look at the time. (*Starts upstage left*) Honey, I'm awfully sorry but I've got an important business appointment. Can I call you later?

CONNIE No. I want to finish talking.

ALAN About what?

CONNIE Housewives.

ALAN What about them?

CONNIE You act as if you never heard of them.

ALAN Sure I did. My mother's a housewife. Connie, sweetheart . . . This is serious talk. Let's set aside a whole night for it. But right now I've really got to run.
(*Holds her jacket out for her*)

CONNIE How far?

ALAN What?

CONNIE I must have touched a nerve or something.

ALAN That's not true. We've discussed marriage before, haven't we?

CONNIE Yes. On this very couch. Or were they just campaign promises?

ALAN What difference did it make? I didn't win the election, did I?

CONNIE The returns aren't all in yet.

ALAN (*He looks at his watch nervously*) Connie, honey. *You're* tired and I've got a business appointment . . .
   (*Holds jacket out again*)

CONNIE At seven o'clock?

ALAN It won't take long. I can be through by ten.

CONNIE I'll bet you can.

ALAN What do you mean?

CONNIE Oh, Alan, I'm a big girl. You've got a date.

ALAN It's a business appointment . . . And besides, I didn't expect you back until tomorrow.

CONNIE You know, something just occured to me. (*Rises*) A few minutes ago I couldn't understand why you were fighting so hard to keep me in show business. It's suddenly very clear.

ALAN What is?

CONNIE It's not *my* career you're worried about. It's *yours!*

ALAN *My* career??

CONNIE As a lover. (*Grabs jacket and crosses right center*) That's why you want me to stay out on the road.

ALAN Why? I'm crazy about you.

CONNIE Yes . . . when I'm here. The minute I leave . . . substitution. Oh, it's beautiful. A bachelor's dream. The two-platoon system.
   (*Putting on jacket*)

ALAN What are you talking about?

CONNIE You'll never grow stale, Alan. Or bored. Not as long as you keep rotating the crops every two weeks.

ALAN You're not being fair. (*Crossing downstage left*) I never said I didn't want to get married. But you come in here and make it sound like an emergency.

CONNIE   For some strange reason I thought you felt the same as I did. These past six months were . . .

ALAN   They were wonderful. That's why I hate to see them end.

CONNIE   END! Getting married is the end?

ALAN   I didn't mean it that way. Connie, you've got to understand, in a way a thirty-three-year-old guy is a lot younger than a twenty-four-year-old girl. That is, he may not be ready for marriage yet.

CONNIE   Let's leave the third person out of this. You mean you.

ALAN   The point is, I didn't actually start my bachelor fling until late in life. And to tell the truth, I don't know if I'm flung out yet.

CONNIE   You would be if you were in love with me.

ALAN   I am. Very much in love . . . only . . . I don't know. I'm like a kid with a few chocolates left in the box. I want to finish them first.

CONNIE   Will you stop twisting thoughts. Now you're making it sound as if I'm taking candy from a baby.
        (*Crosses right and sits*)

ALAN   No, I'm not. I'm leveling with you. Sure I see other girls. I'm only human but (*Crossing toward bar*) you must admit although these past six months were wonderful and exciting, I *have* made certain sacrifices that go against the very nature of man. (*Turns to her*) And you know from whence I speak.

CONNIE   The subject hasn't exactly been taboo.

ALAN (*Crosses left*)   True it was discussed. But it never got off the drawing board. If it were another girl, I'd be in Tahiti painting by now. But here I am. Still battling it out.

CONNIE   The war would be over if I knew just what it was we were fighting for.

ALAN   I don't think I follow that.

CONNIE   All right, then, Alan, let's have the truth. Either you've said to yourself, "I'm going to marry this girl," or, "I'm going to have an affair with her." All I ask is that you let me in on your decision. If marriage is out just say so. I won't run. I'll stay and fight for my honor the way a girl who's been properly brought up should. And I can truthfully tell you I'll lose the battle before long, because, damn it, I'm in love with you. But if you're really in love with me, you've got to tell me and be prepared to back it up with the rest of your life. (*Rises*) Well, which is it going to be, Alan? Do we march down the aisle or into the bedroom?

ALAN   (*He stares at her unbelievingly a few seconds*)   That's the lousiest thing I ever heard . . . What am I supposed to say?
     (*Starts right*)

CONNIE   Say what you really feel.

ALAN   You mean if I want to make love to you all I have to do is speak up?

CONNIE   Loud and clear.

ALAN   You're a nut. (*Breaks left*) A sweet, beautiful nut!

CONNIE   I'm waiting, Alan.

ALAN   (*Turning to her*)   For what? If I say I want you, you're mine. If I say I love you, I'm yours.

CONNIE   It's that simple.

ALAN   Well, I'm not going to play. (*Crosses left*) It's more dangerous than Russian roulette.

CONNIE   It's just being honest with each other, Alan. That's what you're afraid of. You won't even be honest with yourself.

ALAN   How can I be? I don't know what I want yet.

CONNIE   I didn't say you *had* to love me. I just want to know if you do.

ALAN   (*Crossing right to center*)   If I want you I don't have to love you, but if I love you I shouldn't want you—I . . . I don't know. You've got to be an I.B.M. machine to figure out this affair.

CONNIE   I guess so. I forgot to make room for human failing.

ALAN   Boy oh boy, for an innocent little girl you sure play rough.

CONNIE   I didn't choose the game, Alan.
(*She starts to go*)

ALAN   Where are you going?
(*He stops her*)

CONNIE   I'd say you needed a chance to think.

ALAN   No, I don't.

CONNIE   You mean you've made up your mind?

ALAN   Yes . . . Yes, I've made up my mind.

CONNIE   . . . Well?

ALAN   You mean, no matter what I say, you'll go along with it?

CONNIE   To the letter.

ALAN   Okay . . . Okay, then . . . We march into the bedroom.

CONNIE (*Stares at him*)   That's the lousiest thing I ever heard.

ALAN   Uh huh. You see. You see. It's not so much fun when the *dentist* is sitting in the chair is it? You don't like it when I hold the drill.

CONNIE   I'm not complaining, Alan. I asked for it.

ALAN   Oh, that you did. And I called your little bluff, didn't I?

CONNIE   You certainly did.
(*She goes up to door*)

ALAN   Where are you going?

CONNIE   Back to my hotel.

ALAN (*Crossing up left of her*)   All right, wait a second, Connie. The joke is over. You're embarrassed because I made you lose face. I'm sorry. But when you pushed me into a corner like that I had no choice.

CONNIE   Oh, my face is still all there, Alan. I just figure if I'm going into business here I might as well get the rest of my merchandise.
(*She goes blowing him a kiss.* ALAN *stares after her*)

ALAN   . . . No . . . Never happen . . . Not her . . . (*The doorbell rings.* ALAN *rushes to it. He opens it expectantly. It's* BUDDY) Oh, it's you.

BUDDY   Hey, was that her?

ALAN   Where'd you go?

BUDDY   Downstairs for a sandwich. Now that's what I call a pretty girl.
(ALAN *gets coat from closet*)

ALAN   You stay away from that kind. They're nothing but trouble.

BUDDY   How did it go?

ALAN   Oh, fine. Fine.

BUDDY   I thought maybe the other girl walked in.

ALAN   What other girl?

BUDDY   The one you were expecting. From upstairs. Didn't you call her?

ALAN   Peggy! O, my gosh, I forgot.
(*He crosses quickly to telephone. Throwing coat over sofa back*)

BUDDY (*Crosses downstage right center*)   You ought to get one of those maps with the stick pins so you know where they are all the time.

ALAN (*Dialing*)   I don't know what I'm doing tonight. What's that number again?

BUDDY   Is she as pretty as the one that just left?

ALAN   Peggy? Prettier. With none of the disadvantages.`

BUDDY   Boy, what a great place to live. And all for thirty bucks a month.
(*Sits right center chair*)

ALAN (*Hangs up*) Hey, that's right. I forgot we're sharing everything. How would you like to meet her?

BUDDY Who?

ALAN Peggy. From upstairs.

BUDDY (*Jumps up*) Me? Are you kidding?

ALAN Why? She's coming down anyway. No sense in sending her home empty-handed.

BUDDY But she's expecting you.

ALAN Turn the lights down low. She won't figure it out till she's going back up in the elevator.

BUDDY You're crazy.

ALAN No. That's how I met her. She rang the wrong bell one night. There's some poor guy in this building waiting for her since last July.

BUDDY You're not serious, Alan. She probably baby-sits for boys like me.

ALAN No. She's only twenty-two.

BUDDY I'm talking about experience, not age. I didn't realize it until I got here tonight, but I've been living in a convent all my life.

ALAN Buddy, trust me. She'll be crazy about you.

BUDDY (*Crossing away left*) No, she won't. I don't want to meet her, Alan.

ALAN (*Crossing to him*) I don't get you. Where's your spirit of adventure? You sound like an old man.

BUDDY An old man?

ALAN Sure, look at the way you dress. Why does a young boy like you wear a black suit?

BUDDY It's not black. It's charcoal gray.

ALAN Whatever it is, you look like Herbert Hoover.

BUDDY I'm sorry. I'll buy an all-white suit tomorrow.

ALAN   Buddy, I don't do this for everyone. Just brothers I love.

BUDDY   I'd like to, Alan, but gee, I had other plans.
        (*Break away left*)

ALAN   What other plans?

BUDDY   They've got that emergency UN meeting on television tonight, I'd really like to see it.

ALAN (*Crossing to him*)   The UN? Buddy, if I offered this to the Security Council, the meeting would be off tonight.

BUDDY   Look, maybe you're not interested in what's going on in the world, but I am.

ALAN   I'm interested in what's going on with you. What is it? Are you afraid?

BUDDY   Yes—I mean, no.

ALAN   You mean, yes.

BUDDY   No, I don't.

ALAN   You know, something just occurred to me. Is it possible that—

BUDDY   You're going to be late, Alan.

ALAN   I figured you were in the Army, overseas. Paris. I took it for granted—

BUDDY (*Crosses up left of sofa*)   I got around.

ALAN   Where? In a sightseeing bus?

BUDDY   What are you making such a fuss about? What's so damn important about it, anyway?

ALAN (*Crosses upstage right of sofa*)   It's plenty important.

BUDDY (*Evades him crossing downstage right*)   I'll get around to it soon enough.

ALAN   Buddy, baby, why didn't you tell me? (*Crosses right to* BUDDY)   That's what big brothers are for. This is the answer to your problem.

BUDDY   I haven't got a problem.

ALAN   You haven't, huh?

BUDDY   Look, there's a big difference between the way you and I operate. If I get a handshake from a girl I figure I had a good night.

ALAN   With Peggy, all you have to do is say "Hello." From there on it's downhill.

BUDDY   It can't be that easy. I know. I've tried.

ALAN   Look kid, I wanted to get you a birthday present anyway. Now I found something you haven't got.

BUDDY   I don't want it. I'm happy the way I am.

ALAN   Buddy, please. If not for your sake, then for mine.

BUDDY   For yours?

ALAN   Ever since I moved out, I felt I haven't really been looking after you . . . the way a big brother should. I want to make it up to you, kid.

BUDDY   I'm not complaining. You've been fine.

ALAN   It would really give me pleasure, Buddy, to do this for you . . . It's something a father could never do.

BUDDY   I'll say.

ALAN   But brothers, well, it's different, Buddy . . . I feel that it's my duty and privilege to help you at this very important time of your life. What do you say, Buddy? . . . Please!

BUDDY   Well . . . if it'll make you happy, all right.

ALAN   Thanks, kid. (BUDDY *shrugs.* ALAN *crosses to phone and dials—*BUDDY *crosses right*) You'll see. This'll be set up so perfectly, you won't even have to say a word to her . . .
     (*Hums "In a Little Spanish Town"*)
     (*Into phone*)
Hello? Peggy? . . . Yeah . . . No, no, wait a minute . . . (*He rises*) I have good and bad news . . . First the bad news. I've got to go out . . . No, most of the evening. Important business . . . You ready for the good news? . . . He's here . . . Manheim!

BUDDY   Who?

ALAN   (*Into phone*) Oscar Manheim, the producer from M-G-M.

BUDDY (*Runs left of center*) What?????

ALAN   Just as you left . . . He's staying in my apartment tonight . . . He wants to meet you.

BUDDY   I gotta get out of here.
  (*He starts to go*)

ALAN (*Into phone*) Yes, now . . . I told him all about you.

BUDDY   Please, Alan.

ALAN (*Into phone*) Ten minutes? . . . Fine . . . Oh, don't dare thank me, honey. I'm really doing *him* the favor. (*He hangs up*) The ball's over the fence, kid. All you've got to do now is run the bases.

BUDDY   Are you out of your mind? Me? A producer?

ALAN   You want to be a director? I'll call her back.
  (*Motions to phone*)

BUDDY   But why did you tell her that?

ALAN   Just to make it easier for you.

BUDDY   Easier?

ALAN   Now the pressure's off you. It's all on her.

BUDDY   What are you talking about?

ALAN   She's got a bug about getting into pictures. Now's her chance to prove how really talented she is.

BUDDY   How would I know?

ALAN   Because you're a big producer from M-G-M, Oscar Manheim.

BUDDY   Doesn't she know what he looks like?

ALAN   No. I made him up. Sounds real, huh?

BUDDY   Made it up? But she could call M-G-M and check.

ALAN   *She doesn't know how to dial.* Look. She's been auditioning for years without making a picture. She's got more money than M-G-M. She's having too much fun being discovered.

BUDDY   What am I supposed to do, make her a star?

ALAN   No. Just give her a small part in the picture.

BUDDY   *What picture??*

ALAN   *I Was a Teen-age Producer.* I don't know. Can't you make up a picture?

BUDDY (*Breaking away right*)   No. Right now I can't even think of my own name.

ALAN (*Gets ready to leave*)   You're my brother. When the chips are down, you'll come through.

BUDDY   A twenty-one-year-old movie producer. Holy cow! (*Crosses left to sofa*)

ALAN   Well, I'd better get going.

BUDDY   Wait a minute. When is she going to be here?

ALAN   Ten minutes. She just lives upstairs.

BUDDY   Ten minutes? I don't feel so good.

ALAN   Look, if you're really too scared I'll call her back and cancel it.

BUDDY   No. No, never mind.

ALAN   You won't admit it, but you're glad I called. Is there anything you need?

BUDDY   Yeah. A drink.

ALAN   Here you are. (*Hands drink to him. Then picks up trench coat*)

BUDDY   Well, here's to Oscar Wilhelm.

ALAN   *Manheim.*

BUDDY   Oh, jeez. (*He drinks it all quickly*)

ALAN   Hey, take it easy with that stuff. (*Crossing up to foyer; puts on trench coat*)

BUDDY   Can you imagine if I drop dead and she calls the police. They'll bury me in Hollywood.

ALAN   It's going to be the greatest night of your life. You'll thank me for it some day. (*He's at the door*)

BUDDY   Alan!

ALAN   Yes?

BUDDY   Will you call before you come home?

ALAN   I'll call, I'll ring the doorbell and I'll cough loud as soon as I'm within two blocks of the house. (*He opens the door*) So long, kid. And happy birthday! (*And he's gone*)
(BUDDY *stares after him a minute*)

BUDDY   Happy birthday! . . . Why couldn't he get me a tie like everyone else? . . . How'd I get talked into this? (*He rubs his stomach as he apparently just got a twinge of nervousness. He picks up both glasses and puts them on bar. Starts right, gets a thought, looks at his own jacket. Runs up to hall closet, takes out jacket, looks at it, puts it back. Then he takes out a bright blue smoking jacket, runs down to sofa, takes off his jacket, throws it on sofa, throws hanger on sofa table and puts on smoking jacket. Picks up cigarette holder from coffee table, inserts cigarette and starts to light it. As he does so doorbell rings. He stands paralyzed with fear. Screams*) Oh! . . . Just a sec . . . (*He looks around in a panic. He starts upstage, sees his jacket on sofa and throws it under back of sofa. Then he runs to the door and stops quickly to compose himself. He straightens himself up. Hell, he's going to go through with it. He opens the door. A small, rather harassed woman in her late fifties stands there*) (*Yells*) Mom!

WOMAN (*Curtain falls as she speaks crossing downstage right*) Oh, darling, I'm so glad you're here.

BUDDY (*Follows—in a state of shock*)   Mom! . . .

Curtain

Act Two

COME BLOW

YOUR HORN

The same.

At Rise: BUDDY *is frantically pacing back and forth. Buddy is about to have his first experience and here sits his mother.*

MRS. BAKER *is a woman who has managed to find a little misery in the best of things. Sorrow and trouble are the only things that can make her happy. She was born in this country, dresses in fine fashion and in general her speech and appearance are definitely American. But she thinks Old World. Superstitions, beliefs, customs still cling to her. Or rather she clings to them. Because of this, we can't take her hysterics too seriously.*

BUDDY   Mom, are you feeling all right?

MOTHER   Darling, can I have a cold glass of water? I almost fainted on the subway.

BUDDY   Mom, what are you doing here?

MOTHER   I got such a dizzy spell. I never thought I'd get here.

BUDDY   Mom . . . what did you want?

MOTHER   A glass of water, sweetheart.

BUDDY   No, I meant—
   (*But maybe the water would be quicker. He rushes to the bar and pours a glass of water*)

MOTHER   I've got no luck. I never had any and I never will.

BUDDY (*Rushes back with glass*)   Here, Mom.

MOTHER (*Takes a sip*)   That just makes me nauseous. (*He takes glass and puts it on fireplace bench left*) Let me catch my breath.

BUDDY   Maybe you need some fresh air, Mom. Outside?

MOTHER (*Rises*) Just let me sit a few minutes . . . Where's Alan?

BUDDY Out. On business. Do you feel any better?

MOTHER When did I ever feel better?

BUDDY Mom, I hope you understand, but I've got this appointment tonight.

MOTHER Did you have dinner yet?

BUDDY What? Dinner? Yes. Yes, I had a sandwich.

MOTHER A sandwich? For supper? That's how you start the minute you're away?

BUDDY I'm not hungry, Mom. You see, I've got this appointment . . .

MOTHER What'd you have, one of those greasy hamburgers?

BUDDY No. Roast beef. I had a big roast beef sandwich.

MOTHER That's not enough for you. Let me make you some eggs.

BUDDY I don't want any eggs.

MOTHER Look at this place. Look at the dirt.

BUDDY It's all right, Mom.

MOTHER Sure. Boys. I'll bet no one's been in here to clean in a year.

BUDDY (*He might as well tell her*) Mom, will you listen to me. I'm . . . I'm . . . I'm expecting a girl here in a few minutes.

MOTHER To clean?

BUDDY (*Exasperated*) No, not to clean . . . She's a friend of mine.

MOTHER From our neighborhood?

BUDDY No, you don't know her. She's . . . er . . . a girl I knew in school. We're writing a story together.

MOTHER   Then let me make you some appetizers.

BUDDY   We don't want any appetizers.

MOTHER   Buddy, I've got to talk to you about your father.

BUDDY   Can't we do it tomorrow? She's going to be here any second.

MOTHER   What's the matter? She's more important than me?

BUDDY   Mom, no one's more important than you.

MOTHER   How can you say that when you worry me like this? I know you. You won't eat unless the food's in front of you.

BUDDY   *No one* eats unless the food's in front of them. Mom, I haven't got time . . .

MOTHER (*Hurt*)   You want me to go, I'll go.

BUDDY   Mom, please don't be hurt. I didn't want to have this meeting. It came up unexpectedly. But I have to go through with it.

MOTHER   Buddy, your father's going to be home in a few minutes. You should have heard him on the phone before about Alan. If the operator was listening, there'll be a man there in the morning to rip it off the wall.

BUDDY   I can't discuss this with you now.

MOTHER   No, but for girls you've got time.
(*Sits right center chair*)

BUDDY   It's not a girl. It's . . . a . . . meeting. About a story we're writing. It may go on till two o'clock in the morning.

MOTHER   Without appetizers?

BUDDY   *We don't need appetizers!*

MOTHER (*Crosses to him*)   Wait'll he reads that letter. Wait'll he finds out you're gone. Remember what he did when Alan left?

BUDDY   I know, Mom. He was very upset.

MOTHER   Upset? I'll never forget it. He came home from work at three o'clock, went into his room, put on his pajamas and got into bed to die . . . Four days he stayed in bed. He just laid there waiting to die.

BUDDY   But he didn't die, Mom. He put on weight.

MOTHER   Don't think he wasn't disappointed . . . He was plenty hurt by Alan leaving, believe me. He thought by now Alan would be married, have a grandchild. Who knows if he'll ever get married. And now you.

BUDDY   Mom, please—

MOTHER   I know what he's going to say tonight. He'll blame it all on me. He'll say I was too easy with the both of you. He'll say, "Because of you my sister Gussie has two grandchildren and all I've got is a bum and a letter" . . . I know him.

BUDDY   Look, Mom. How about if I come home tomorrow night for dinner? And I'll have a long talk with Dad about everything. Okay?

MOTHER   Tomorrow? By tomorrow he'll be in bed again writing out his will. He'll be on the phone saying good-by to his family.

BUDDY   He won't, Mom. He just gets very dramatic sometimes.

MOTHER   Maybe I am too easygoing. Maybe if I were like some mothers who forbid their children to do everything, I'd be better off today.

BUDDY   No, Mom. You're the best mother I ever had . . . Do you feel any better?

MOTHER   How do I know? I feel too sick to tell.

BUDDY   Really, a good night's sleep and you'll feel wonderful. Take something before you go to bed. Some warm milk.

MOTHER   Who buys milk now that you're not there.

BUDDY   Then buy some.

MOTHER   Maybe I'll be better off if I take a hot bath.

BUDDY   That's the girl.

MOTHER   I'll probably pass out right in the tub.

BUDDY   No you won't. Why do you get so emotional all the time?

MOTHER   I don't look for it, believe me, darling.

BUDDY   Mom, everything's going to be all right. (*He half lifts her to her feet*) Sleep tight.
        (*He kisses her forehead*)

MOTHER   I feel better knowing at least you'll be there tomorrow.

BUDDY   For dinner. I promise.
        (*He starts upstage*)

MOTHER (*She stops*) . . . What'll I make?

BUDDY (*Coming down to her*)   What?

MOTHER   For dinner? What do you want to eat?

BUDDY   Anything. I don't care. Good night, Mom.

MOTHER   I want to make something you like now that you're not home.

BUDDY   I like everything. Roast beef, okay?

MOTHER   All right, good. (*He starts upstage. She starts, then stops*) You had roast beef tonight.
        (*He comes back*)

BUDDY (*Beside himself with anxiety*)   I can eat it again.

MOTHER   I could get a turkey. A big turkey.

BUDDY   Okay! Turkey! Wonderful!

MOTHER   It doesn't really pay for one night.

BUDDY (*He can't take it any more. He practically screams*)
        Mom, for Pete's sakes, it doesn't matter.

MOTHER (*Near tears*)   What are you yelling? I'm only trying to make you happy. Who do I cook for, myself? I haven't eaten anything besides coffee for ten years.

BUDDY   I'm sorry, Mom.

MOTHER   Oh, I've got that stick in the heart again.
(*Sits right center chair*)

BUDDY   You're just upset.

MOTHER   No. I ate lamb chops tonight. They never agree with me.

BUDDY   Oh, boy.

MOTHER   Darling, do you have an Alka-Seltzer?

BUDDY   Alka-Seltzer? I don't know . . . Wait a minute. I'll look in the kitchen.
(*He rushes off madly to the kitchen right*)

MOTHER   (*She rubs her stomach*)   She wished it on me. His sister Gussie wished it on me.
(BUDDY *comes running back out*)

BUDDY   There isn't any here.

MOTHER   Sure. Boys. You wouldn't have water if you didn't have a faucet.

BUDDY   Mom, make anything you want. Turkey. Roast beef. I'll be home tomorrow night. Now why don't you go home and relax. Take a cab.

MOTHER   It's starting to rain. Where am I going to get a cab?

BUDDY   I'll get you one, okay?

MOTHER   All right. Let me sit a few minutes.

BUDDY   A few minutes? (*He can't wait any longer*) Mom, I'll get the doorman to get you a cab. (*Runs up to door*) Do you want to wait in the lobby?

MOTHER   You don't have to run out.

BUDDY   I'll be right back. In two minutes.
(*And he is gone in a flash*)

MOTHER   Don't get overheated . . . Who am I talking to?
(*She looks around the apartment and shakes her head disapprovingly. Puts bag on chair, unbuttons coat . . . She gets up, crosses to the coffee table, empties one ash tray into the other. Then starts to cross with the refuse into the kitchen when the phone rings. She*

turns and goes to the phone) (*Into phone*) Hello? . . . Who?
. . . No, he isn't. To whom am I speaking to, please?
Meltzer? Martin Meltzer . . . No, this is Alan's mother
. . . What? . . . Why should I kid about a thing like that?
. . . No, I'm positive he's not here . . . A message? . . . Wait.
I'll get a pencil. (*She looks for a pencil. There is none on the
table, so she runs quickly to the left cabinet, then upstage cabinet,
sofa, table and looks frantically for a pencil. There is none to be
found. She runs back quickly to the phone*) Go on, I'll remember. Talk fast so I could write it down as soon as you're
finished . . . "Extremely important. Your wife just came
in unexpectedly from Atlantic City and is on her way to
the Hotel Croyden so Alan should be sure *not* to come
with those certain parties." Yes, I have it . . . I do . . . I
can't repeat it to you, I'm trying to remember it . . . Mr.
Meltzer, Hotel Croyden . . . Yes . . . Don't talk any more,
I'm going to write it down quick. Good-by. (*She hangs
up*) Some message. That's a book, not a message. (*She starts
to look for a pencil again*) Where's a pencil? They don't have
Alka-Seltzer, they're gonna have a pencil? (*She crosses right
toward counter*) (*The phone rings*) Suddenly I'm an answer-
ing service. (*She answers phone*) Hello? . . . No, he isn't
. . . This is Alan's mother . . . Why should I kid about a
thing like that? . . . To whom am I speaking to please?
. . . Who? . . . Chickie? . . . That's a name? . . . Chickie
Parker . . . You forgot whose hotel? . . . Mr. Meltzer's?
Where do I know that name from? . . . Oh, for God sakes,
he just called. With a message to Alan. Something about
Atlantic City. I think he said Alan shouldn't go there
. . . I don't know what it means either. I'm not a secretary.
I'm a mother . . . without a pencil . . . The hotel? . . . Yes,
he did mention it . . . I think it was the Parker . . . Oh,
that's *your* name . . . Wait. Oh, yes. The Croyden . . . A
message for Alan? I can only try, darling . . . "Chickie was
detained but she's on her way to the Croyden now." Yes.
You're welcome. Good-by. (*She hangs up. She crosses upstage
to desk area, looking for a pencil*) There must be some carrying on here. Their father should only know . . . A busi-
nessman and a college boy and they don't have a pencil.
(*She starts right and the phone rings again*) Oh, for God's
sakes. (*The phone rings again*) All right, all right, what do
you want from me? (*She rushes quickly to the phone and picks
it up*) Yes? . . . Who? . . . Who did you want, please? . . .

No, he's out. This is Alan's mother . . . Listen, don't start that with me . . . Who is this? . . . Connie what? . . . Again with a message . . . Miss, can't you write it down, I don't have a pencil . . . You what? . . . Yes . . . Yes . . . Yes . . . You're welcome . . . Good-by. (*She hangs up*) Good-by, go home, good luck, who knows what she said. (*Sits sofa and cries*) Who tells him to have so many phone calls? . . . It's disgusting. (*The phone rings. She screams*) What do you want from my life? (*She just stares at the phone. It continues to ring*) I wouldn't pick it up now if it stood on its head. (*It continues to ring*) Oh, I'm so nauseous. (*She can't stand it any longer. She picks it up, but she yells at it angrily*) Hello? . . . What do you want? . . . Who is this? . . . Alan who? . . . Oh, Alan . . . (*She starts to cry*) It's Mother. (*She sits*) What am I doing here? . . . I'm answering your phone calls . . . He's outside getting me a subway . . . I mean a taxi . . . No, there's no one else here . . . Who called? . . . The whole world called . . . First a man called . . . Meltzer? . . . No, it didn't sound like that . . .

(*The door opens and* BUDDY *rushes in*)

BUDDY Okay, Mom.

MOTHER (*Into phone*) Oh, I've got to go now. Buddy is here with the cab. Talk to Buddy.

BUDDY I've got the cab. It's waiting outside.

MOTHER Here.
(*Hands him phone*)

BUDDY Who is that?

MOTHER Alan. (*She gets up and hands phone to* BUDDY *and crosses right to get bag*) Here!

BUDDY (*Taking phone*) Hello, Alan? . . . What's wrong? I don't know who called, I was outside. (*To* MOTHER) Mom, did someone call?

MOTHER I gave all the messages to Alan. I don't want to keep the taxi waiting. Good-by, sweetheart.
(*She starts to door*)

BUDDY Mom, who called? A girl?

MOTHER   Yes, darling. Good-by.

BUDDY   What did she say?

MOTHER   I don't remember.
   (*She opens door*)

BUDDY   Why didn't you write it down?

MOTHER   Don't *you* start with me . . . This must be costing a fortune. I only hope I don't pass out in the taxi!
   (*She goes*)

BUDDY   Mom, wait . . . (*Into phone*) Hello, Alan . . . I don't know. I can't make head or tail out of her . . . Where are you? . . . No, she didn't get here yet . . . Lousy, that's how I feel . . . I already had a drink. It doesn't help . . . Hey, wait a minute. Who am I again? . . . Oscar *Wol*heim? . . . *Manheim!* Oscar Manheim . . . Oh, boy . . . Look, Alan. I changed my mind. I can't go through with it I'm going out. Yes. Now. Well . . . I'll leave her a note from you . . . I'm sorry. Good-by. (*He hangs up*) That's it. I'll leave her a note. That's all. (*He quickly starts to search for a pencil and paper. He looks in the shelves under downstage left cabinet and takes out container with two dozen pencils*) Eight thousand pencils and no paper. (*He crosses to table behind sofa and finds piece of paper. He sits on sofa and starts to write and repeats aloud*) "Dear Peggy . . . More bad news . . . Paul . . . (*Momentarily forgets name*) Manheim . . . is . . . dead! . . . Love . . . Alan"
   (*He puts down pencil, then crosses to door. Reads letter again as he bends down to leave it under door. The front bell rings. He gasps. The bell rings again. He throws up his hands in despair and then opens door.* PEGGY *stands there ravishingly dressed. She looks utterly fantastic*)

PEGGY   Hi. I'm Peggy Evans. (*She walks in. He closes door*) I'm not disturbing you or anything, am I?

BUDDY (*He looks at her, overwhelmed by her pulchritude, follows her downstage*)   No . . . not at all.
   (*He is in a state of semi-shock*)

PEGGY (*Sitting on sofa*)   Alan said you wanted to meet me. I hope you forgive the way I look. I've been in a car all day . . . I must be a mess.

BUDDY   No . . . You look . . . very neat.
         (*He tears up the note and puts pieces in his pocket*)

PEGGY   Thanks . . . Coming from you, that's something.
         (*She crosses to him*) It's a shame you couldn't get up to the
         ski lodge.

BUDDY   What ski lodge?

PEGGY   In New Hampshire. Or Vermont. I'm not very
         good at names. In fact, I'm afraid I've forgotten yours.

BUDDY   Oh . . . It's . . . *Man*heim.

PEGGY   That's right. Mr. Manheim.

BUDDY   Jack Man—heim . . . No, not Jack.

PEGGY   That's right, Jack.

BUDDY   Yes, Jack . . . won't you sit down?
         (*Indicating right center chair*)

PEGGY   Thank you . . . (*She sits on sofa*) I understand you had
         some problem at the studio.

BUDDY   Oh, yes . . . we did.

PEGGY   What was it?
         (*She takes a cigarette and lights it*)

BUDDY   It was . . . er . . . (*He sees flame*) Er . . . we had a . . . fire.

PEGGY   Who?

BUDDY   I beg your pardon?

PEGGY   Who did you have to fire?

BUDDY   No, no. *A* fire. Part of the studio burned down.

PEGGY   Oh? Was anyone hurt?

BUDDY   No . . . just a few extras . . . Say, would you like a
         drink?

PEGGY   Oooh, like a transfusion. I don't mind admitting it,
         but I'm nervous.

BUDDY   *You're* nervous? What would you like?

PEGGY   What are you having?

BUDDY (*This one is easy. He tosses it off grandly*)   Oh . . . scotch and ginger ale.

PEGGY   Oh, that's cute. I mean what are you *really* having?

BUDDY (*Embarrassed*)   I don't know. What are you having?

PEGGY   Grand Marnier.

BUDDY   Grandma who?

PEGGY   Grand Marnier. It's French. You know, a liquoor.

BUDDY   Oh . . . (*He crosses up to bar and looks for it. He picks up a scotch bottle*) No, I don't see any.

PEGGY   Oh, scotch'll be fine. (*He pours drinks*) I suppose you've heard it before, but you look awfully young for a producer.

BUDDY (*Crossing left of her*)   Oh, do I?

PEGGY   To look at you I'd say you were only about twenty-six, but I bet I'm way off.

BUDDY   Oh, way off. (*Hands her drink and sits left of her*) Well, here we are.

PEGGY   What should we drink to?

BUDDY   Anything you like.

PEGGY   Let's make a silent toast.

BUDDY   Okay.
(*They both close their eyes, take a beat, she opens hers, nudges him, he opens his eyes, clink glasses and drink*)

PEGGY (*Makes herself comfortable, puts down glass and snuffs out cigarette*)   Well, now . . . down to business.

BUDDY   Huh?

PEGGY   I suppose you want to know what I've done.

BUDDY   Not necessarily.

PEGGY   I'll be perfectly frank with you. I've never been in a picture before.

BUDDY   Is that so?

PEGGY But I'm not totally inexperienced.

BUDDY So Alan told me.

PEGGY Last summer when I was on the Coast I did an "Untouchables."

BUDDY No kidding?

PEGGY I was a dead body. They fished me out of the river.

BUDDY I think I saw that.

PEGGY Lots of people did. I got loads of work from it. But it's not what I really want to do. That's why I'm taking acting class. With Felix Ungar. He lives in this building. Right under this apartment. In fact *that's* how I met Alan. (*She puts her hand on his right knee*) I rang the wrong bell one night.
    (BUDDY *looks down at his knee and laughs almost hysterically*)

BUDDY How about that?

PEGGY And look how it turned out. Through a silly mistake, I'm being auditioned by one of the biggest producers (*taking hand off knee*) in the business. Life is funny, isn't it?

BUDDY (*Puts drink down and rises crossing right*) Hysterical.

PEGGY (*Rises—crosses below coffee table*) Well, is there anything you'd like me to do?

BUDDY What?

PEGGY Do. Read a scene? Or kind of take on a character like in class. Or is just talking like this enough?

BUDDY Oh, it's plenty. To tell the truth, I'm a little tired. (*Sits right center chair*)

PEGGY Oh, from the trip. Would you like me to massage your think muscle?

BUDDY Huh?

PEGGY Here! (*She indicates her temple. She goes to where he's sitting, and stands over him*) Just close your eyes and put your head back.

BUDDY   I don't think . . .

PEGGY   I'm very good at this. Now just relax . . . (*He does*) . . . and try and forget about the picture business. (*She massages*) No, I can feel it. You're still thinking about the studio.

BUDDY   No, I'm not. I swear I'm not.
        (*The phone rings. He jumps up*)

PEGGY   Are you expecting anyone?

BUDDY   Me? No! No! (*It rings again, angrily*) No, I'll get it. I'll get it. (*He crosses to phone quickly and picks it up. Into phone*) Hello! . . . *Dad!!!* . . . I'm sorry. I didn't mean to yell . . . What? . . . now? . . . Look, Dad, I'll come downstairs, okay? . . . Dad? . . . Dad? . . . Oh, boy!
        (*He hangs up*)

PEGGY   Is anything wrong?

BUDDY   What? Oh, yeah . . . It's . . . it's someone I don't want to see . . . A writer. . .

PEGGY   Dad? It sounded like it was your father.

BUDDY   Oh! Oh, no. That's just a nickname. Dad. You know, like Ernest Hemingway is Poppa.

PEGGY   Oh! Is Dad coming up?

BUDDY   Yeah, Dad's coming up . . . Look would you do me a big, big favor? I've got to be alone with him for a few minutes . . . To talk about script changes.

PEGGY   I understand. I could go up and get that bottle of Grand Marnier.

BUDDY   (*That's inspirational*)   That's it. Would you do that?

PEGGY   Of course.
        (*She starts for the door*)

BUDDY   (*He stops her*)   Not that way!

PEGGY   What?

BUDDY   I don't want him to know I'm auditioning someone else. He's already got someone in mind.

PEGGY   Oh, I appreciate that. Thanks an awful lot, Mr. Manheim.

> (*She kisses him and exits through the kitchen door. He starts right to make sure she has gone. He looks at his jacket, unbuttons it, takes it off, throws it into bedroom and closes door. He runs downstage grabs the two glasses from coffee table and puts them on bar. He starts right, stops, looks at glasses. Picks one up and examines it for lipstick, takes out his handkerchief, wipes lipstick off, puts glass on bar. As he wipes his own mouth with handkerchief, doorbell rings. He frantically tries to jam handkerchief into pocket and can't. Doorbell rings again. Panicky, he throws handkerchief out window left. He grabs a large book from upstage bookshelf, opens it, goes to door, book in hand, composes himself as if he had been reading all evening and opens door. There stands his* FATHER, *with the letter in his hand*)

BUDDY   Hello, Dad. (*The* FATHER *walks in, holds up the letter to* BUDDY'S *face, to indicate he got it, then he walks into the apartment.* BUDDY *follows left of him*) Are you all right, Dad? . . . Is anything wrong? (*The* FATHER *stares ahead speechless. He has taken letter out of envelope and now holds it in front of* BUDDY'S *face*) I—I didn't think you'd be coming down tonight . . . I was going to have a long talk with you in the morning . . . at the plant . . . and then I told Mother I'd be home for dinner tomorrow night . . . so you and I could sit down and talk some more . . . and I could explain how I . . . Dad, you're angry, aren't you? . . .

FATHER   Me? Angry. Why should I be angry?

BUDDY   About the letter.

FATHER   (*Looks at him*)   What letter?

BUDDY   This letter. The letter I wrote you.

FATHER   No, no. You didn't write this letter. Someone I don't know wrote this letter. Not you. You, I know. This person I never met.

BUDDY   Dad, don't you think it would be better if we waited until tomorrow, when we're both—calmer? Dad, I meant to have a long talk with you about this.

FATHER Talk? What's there to talk about? (*He still holds up letter*) It's signed, sealed and delivered. The Declaration of Independence . . . What's there to talk about?

BUDDY Dad, I think you're too upset now to discuss this logically.

FATHER Oh, I expected it. (*Puts letter in envelope*) You hang around your brother long enough it was bound to happen. So what's the windup. My sister Gussie has two grandchildren and I have a bum and a letter.

BUDDY Dad, this didn't suddenly happen. I tried to explain how I felt the other night. But you wouldn't listen.

FATHER (*He starts to sit and jumps up*) Don't try and tell me I wouldn't listen. That's all I did was listen.
    (*Crosses left*)

BUDDY But every time I would start to say something, you would walk out of the room.

FATHER If you showed me a little respect, then maybe I would listen.

BUDDY Dad, you're not making any sense.

FATHER *I'm* not making sense? Very nice. Very nice talk to a father.

BUDDY What do you want me to say?

FATHER I want to hear from your own lips . . . nicely . . . why such a young boy can't live at home with his parents.

BUDDY Young boy?

FATHER (*Holding up a warning finger*) Nicely!

BUDDY Dad, I'm twenty-one.

FATHER (*Noncommittal*) You're twenty-one.

BUDDY You say it as if you don't believe me. I was twenty-one yesterday, wasn't I?

FATHER (*Shrugs*) Whatever you say.

BUDDY   What do you mean whatever I say?

FATHER (*Finger up again*)   Nicely!

BUDDY   All right. I *say* I was twenty-one. That's old enough to make your own decision in life. When *you* were twenty-one, you were already married, weren't you?

FATHER   You were there?

BUDDY   No, I wasn't there. You told me yourself.

FATHER   Those days were altogether different. (*Crosses away left*) I was working when I was eleven years old. (*Turns to him*) *I* didn't go to camp.

BUDDY   *What's camp got to do with all this???*

FATHER (*Threatening*)   I'll walk right out of here!

BUDDY   Dad, all right. I don't mean to be disrespectful, but your answers never match my questions.

FATHER (*Crossing above and right of Buddy*)   Oh, that too? I don't talk fancy enough for you like your brother and his show business friends.

BUDDY   That's what I mean. Who said anything about show business?

FATHER   Well, that's where he is all day, isn't he? Backstage at some burlesque house.

BUDDY   They haven't had burlesque in New York in twenty years.

FATHER   He hasn't put in a day's work in twenty years. And now I suppose I can expect that of you.

BUDDY   No, Dad. I'll work there as long as you want me to . . . No matter how I feel about it.

FATHER   What do you mean, no matter how you feel?

BUDDY   Well, Dad, I never had a chance to try anything else. I had two years of college, then the Army, and then right into the business. Maybe it's not the right field for me.

FATHER   Not the right field? (*He addresses an imaginary lis-*
tener in right center chair) I give the boy the biggest artificial
fruit manufacturing house in the East, he tells me *not the*
right field. Ha!
         (*He sits right center chair*)

BUDDY   I don't know if I've got any talent . . . but . . . I've
always toyed with the idea of becoming a writer.

FATHER   A writer? What kind of writer? Letters? (*He holds*
up letter) Letters you write beautiful. I don't know who's
going to buy them, but they're terrific.

BUDDY   But supposing I'm good? I'm not even getting a
chance to find out. Supposing I could write plays . . . for
television or the theater?

FATHER   Plays can close. (*Crossing to him*) Television you
turn off. Wax fruit lays in the bowl till you're a hundred.

BUDDY   But business doesn't stimulate me, Dad. I don't
have fun.

FATHER   You don't have fun? I'll put in music, you can
dance while you work.

BUDDY   Dad, forget about the business for now. I'll stay. All
I want now is your permission for me to live here on my
own.

FATHER (*Puts letter in coat pocket*)   All right, let me ask you
a question. If you were in my place, if you were my
father, with conditions in the world as they are today,
with juvenile delinquency, with the stories you read in
the papers about the crazy parties that go on, the drinking
and whatnot . . . would you let *your* son leave home?

BUDDY   Yes!

FATHER   That's no answer!

BUDDY   Dad, it just doesn't seem as if we're ever going to
understand each other.

FATHER   How can we? You listen to your brother more
than you listen to me.

BUDDY   That's not true.

FATHER   Do you deny that he's the one who put this bug in your mouth about leaving home?

BUDDY   In your ear, Dad.

FATHER   What?

BUDDY   Bug in your ear.

FATHER   Excuse my ignorance, Mr. Writer.

BUDDY   I wasn't making fun of you.

FATHER   Why not? Your brother does.

BUDDY   No, he doesn't.

FATHER   He doesn't, heh? I can imagine the things he must tell you. You'll learn plenty from him, believe me, plenty. At least you I had hopes for. Alan I could never talk to. But you, you were always good. I could take you anywhere. I could take you visiting, you would sit on a chair for three hours, you wouldn't hear a peep out of you. I remember I used to say, give Aunt Gussie a kiss. You'd go right over and give Aunt Gussie a kiss. But the older one. I chased him all over Brooklyn one day because he wouldn't give Aunt Gussie a kiss . . . What was so terrible to give Aunt Gussie a kiss?

BUDDY   I guess it was that hat she wore. You always had to kiss her through a veil.

FATHER   You see how you take his side.

BUDDY   I wasn't taking his side.

FATHER   No, heh? What's the use talking to you. You'll do what he says in the end anyway. If you want to become a bum like him, that's your affair.

BUDDY   Why is Alan a bum?

FATHER   Is he married?

BUDDY   No.

FATHER   Then he's a bum!

BUDDY   Dad, you really never had any problems with me before, have you? Won't you trust me now?

FATHER (*He sighs*)   All right, you want trust. I'll give you trust.

BUDDY   What do you mean?

FATHER   There's a disagreement here. A dispute. We'll arbitrate.

BUDDY   That's all I've been asking of you.

FATHER   I've heard your side. You've heard my side. If you want, we'll give it a six-month trial period. Fairer than that, I can't be.

BUDDY   I think that's very fair, Dad. Six months is fine. (*Crossing left*)

FATHER   Then it's settled. You'll come home and live for six months . . .

BUDDY   Come home? (*Shouts, crossing to him*) You don't want to give me a trial. You don't want to be fair . . . You just —just—

FATHER (*Rises and shakes upstage hand*)   Don't you raise your voice. You're not too big to get a good slap across the face.

BUDDY   I'm sorry, Dad.

FATHER   I never thought I'd live to see this day. That a son would talk to his father like this. I've been some terrible father to you, haven't I?

BUDDY   No, Dad. You've been a wonderful father. Just meet me halfway. Please . . . What do you say?

FATHER (*Crosses left of him*)   I'll . . . I'll let you know.

BUDDY   What do you mean, you'll let me know?

FATHER   I'm not rushing into any decision pell mell . . . I'll go home and think about it. If you want, you can stay here tonight, I won't argue. But tomorrow, you'll come home for dinner and we'll see what we'll see.

BUDDY   All right, that'll be fine. Good night, Dad. (*He starts upstage*)

FATHER   You need any money?

BUDDY   No, I've got plenty.
(*Comes back*)

FATHER   Where are you going to sleep?

BUDDY   On the sofa.

FATHER   That's some place to sleep.

BUDDY   Dad, I'll be all right. I'll see you tomorrow. I promise.

FATHER   You don't have to promise. You say you'll be there, I trust you.

BUDDY   Thanks, Dad. Good night.
(*Starts up again*)

FATHER (*Just about to leave, when he stops and turns*)   Oh, wait a minute.

BUDDY   What's the matter?

FATHER   I want to call your mother. Tell her everything's all right. I know she's worried.
(*He crosses to phone*)

BUDDY (*Crossing and sits down center chair*)   Oh, boy!
(*The* FATHER *dials, sighing, in* BUDDY'S *direction*)

FATHER (*Into phone*)   Hello? . . . Jezebel? . . . Is Mrs. Baker home? . . . Oh! I wonder where she is? . . . Listen, Jezebel, before you go home, I want you to write down a message for her . . . All right, get a pencil . . .
(*Suddenly* PEGGY *comes out from the kitchen. She wears a topcoat.* BUDDY *rises as she enters*)

PEGGY   Excuse me, but I'm all out of Grand Marnier too, I'll run down to the liquor store and get some. (*To* FATHER) Hello, Dad!
(*She goes back out kitchen door*)
(*The* FATHER *stares after her dumfounded.* BUDDY *is in a state of shock. The* FATHER *turns slowly back to the phone*)

FATHER   Hello, Jezebel? . . . Tell Mrs. Baker I'm with the bum! . . . The twenty-one-year-old bum! (*He slams the phone down, turns and points an accusing finger at* BUDDY) Bum!

BUDDY   Dad . . .

FATHER   Bum!

BUDDY   Let me explain . . .

FATHER   Bum!

BUDDY   Please . . .

FATHER   Twenty-one years old! You're a bigger bum than
your brother is right now and you've still got twelve
years to go!

BUDDY   Dad, please.
        (*The front door suddenly opens.* ALAN *walks in and sees the*
        FATHER.)

ALAN   Dad!!

FATHER   Ah, the other bum. Come on in. We're having a
party.

ALAN   What are you doing here?

FATHER   I was invited to dinner. That's some cook you have
in there.

ALAN   Where?

BUDDY (*Defeated*)   In the kitchen.

ALAN   What? . . . (*To* BUDDY) Well, didn't you explain? That
she was waiting for me?

FATHER   I don't need you to make up stories. (*Crosses to*
BUDDY) I've got Tennessee Williams for that.
        (*The phone rings.* FATHER *starts out*)

ALAN   Dad, wait. I want to talk to you.
        (*He crosses quickly to the phone*)

FATHER   I've heard enough.
        (*He starts to go*)

ALAN (*Into phone*)   Hello? . . . Oh, Mr. Meltzer.

FATHER (*Stops*)   Meltzer? What does he want?

ALAN (*Into phone*)   Now, please. Calm down. I tried to explain. There was a mixup somewhere.

FATHER   What's wrong?

ALAN   Nothing, Dad. Nothing. (*Into phone*) What? . . . Well, how should I know your wife was coming in? . . . I didn't get any message from my mother.

FATHER (*Crosses to him*)   What are you talking about?

ALAN (*Into phone*)   If I can just talk to your wife . . . Mr. Meltzer, there's no need for a lawsuit.

FATHER   Lawsuit? What lawsuit?

ALAN   Dad, wait a minute . . . (*Into phone*) Mr. Meltzer . . .

FATHER   Give me that phone. (*Grabs phone and brightly says*) Hello? Meltzer? This is Mr. Baker, senior. What's the trouble?

ALAN   He's hysterical, Dad. Don't listen to him.

FATHER   Your wife and *who* rang the doorbell together? What French girl? . . . But who arranged such a thing? . . . I see . . . (*Turns to* ALAN) I see . . . Good-by.
(*He hands phone to* ALAN, *who hangs up, and starts for door.* ALAN *follows*)

ALAN   Dad, if you'd just listen for five minutes . . . Dad!!!!! Dad, Dad . . . please say something!
(*The* FATHER *crosses past them in silence. He turns on raised foyer and speaks calmly*)

FATHER   May you and your brother live and be well. God bless you, all the luck in the world, you should know nothing but happiness. If I ever speak to either one of you again, my tongue should fall out!
(*He opens the door and goes*)
(*The two brothers stand there looking at each other helplessly*)

BUDDY (*Crosses right to fireplace*)   I knew it. I knew this would happen.

ALAN (*Concerned*)   Do you think he means it?
(ALAN *takes off coat and puts it on left handrail*)

BUDDY   Means it? In ten minutes he'll be home, giving the rest of my clothes to the janitor.

ALAN (*Crosses downstage right of sofa*)   I never saw him this mad. (*Crossing down*) Not since the day he chased me all over Brooklyn when I wouldn't give Aunt Gussie a kiss.

BUDDY   Oh, he's mad all right. And he means it. (*Crosses left to him*) We're *fired*.

ALAN (*Musing*)   But how can he get along without us?

BUDDY   And he was almost out the door. And then that fruitcake walks in and says, "Hello, Dad" . . . His mustache almost fell off.

ALAN (*Sits sofa*)   I'm sorry, kid. I didn't mean to get you involved.

BUDDY   It's not your fault.

ALAN   I thought I was doing you a favor . . . Well, it's over with anyway.

BUDDY   What's over? She's coming back with a French bottle to do silly little things.

ALAN   She is?

BUDDY   She gets me all crazy. Suppose I do something nutty, like signing her to a five-year contract? . . . (*Doorbell rings*) I can't face her again, Alan. Please.

ALAN   All right, never mind. I'll take over. Go on out to a movie.

BUDDY (*Grabs his coat from under sofa*)   That's a great idea. Maybe one of my pictures is playing around.
   (*Doorbell rings again. He exits through kitchen right.* ALAN *opens door;* CONNIE *stands there with valise*)

ALAN   Connie!
   (*Closes door. She puts down case and gives Alan long kiss interrupting his* "*Wha . . .*" *then when she releases him*)

CONNIE   Me no Connie. Me Jane. You Tarzan. Jane come to swing with Tarzan in tree.

ALAN   What's in that suitcase?

CONNIE   The rest of my merchandise.
   (*She takes off her coat. Puts it on right handrail*)

ALAN You're drunk.
(*Crossing away right*)

CONNIE On one martini?

ALAN You get loaded just ordering one.

CONNIE Now, then, the bedroom. It's in that direction, isn't it?
(*She picks up suitcase and starts for bedroom*)

ALAN You stay out of there. What's come over you?

CONNIE Nothing, darling. I gave you a choice and you made it.

ALAN What?

CONNIE Wonderful service, isn't it? You don't even have to pick it up. We deliver.

ALAN You're not drunk. You're crazy.

CONNIE (*Puts down suitcase and crosses right stalking him as he backs away*) Just think of it, darling? We're going to live together, love together. Fun, fun, fun. Sin, sin, sin.

ALAN Connie, you're scaring the hell out of me.

CONNIE You don't even have to say you love me. And when you get bored, just kick me out and give me a letter of recommendation.

ALAN Will you cut it out? It's not funny any more.
(*Breaks away left*)

CONNIE I don't understand, Alan. Isn't this what you want? Isn't this what you asked for?

ALAN No.

CONNIE No?

ALAN That's right, no. I said I could see nothing wrong for two young people who were very fond of each other to have a healthy, normal relationship. But I see no reason to turn this affair into a . . . foreign art movie.

CONNIE Good heavens, sir. I must be in the wrong apartment.

ALAN   Look, I told you before. I'm not denying anything. Six nights a week I'm Leonard Lover. But with you . . . well, you're different.

CONNIE   Careful, Alan. You're on the brink of committing yourself.

ALAN   Who's keeping it a secret? I love you.

CONNIE   You weren't very sure.

ALAN   I am now. If I can turn down an offer like this with a girl like you, I must be in love.

CONNIE   Well, then . . . where does that leave us?

ALAN   . . . I don't know.

CONNIE (*Sits right arm of right center chair*)   You don't know?

ALAN (*Crossing to her*)   Look honey, you've got to give me a chance to think. A lot of things have happened tonight. I just lost my job.

CONNIE   I thought you worked for your father.

ALAN   We must be in a hell of a recession. He just let two sons go . . . Oh, Connie, don't you see . . .

CONNIE   No, I don't see. You love me but you won't marry me, and you love me too much to live with me.

ALAN (*Crosses around chair to right of it*)   I know. I can't figure it out either.

CONNIE (*Angry*)   I see. Well, I'm sorry, Alan, but I can't spend the rest of my life waiting in the hallway.
(*She gets up and crosses to center*)

ALAN   Wait a minute.

CONNIE   For what? I either come in or go out. You want me or you don't. Yes or no.

ALAN   Why can't things be like they were before?

CONNIE   It's too late. We've raised the stakes.

ALAN   Who made you the dealer all of a sudden?

CONNIE   If the game is too big, Alan, get out.

ALAN   I see. A brilliant maneuver, General. You've got me cornered. Very well, I surrender.

CONNIE   I don't take prisoners.
          (*She goes to foyer*)

ALAN (*Angry*)   I mean it. If that's what you want, I'll marry you.

CONNIE (*Grabs coat. Puts over left arm*)   If that's the way you'll marry me, I don't want it.

ALAN (*Crossing to her*)   Connie, wait. Where are you going?

CONNIE (*Putting on coat*)   Right now I want to be about a thirty-five-*dollar* taxi ride away from you.

ALAN (*Sincerely. Crossing to her*)   Connie, wait . . . I don't want you to leave.

CONNIE (*She's made up her mind*)   I'm sorry.

ALAN   You mean I won't see you again?

CONNIE   I don't know. Maybe if you get lonely enough. (*The phone rings*) You probably won't have much chance tonight. Start in the morning.
          (*Phone rings again. Picks up suitcase*)

ALAN   Connie, wait.

CONNIE   Answer your phone, Alan. It's the second platoon.
          (*Phone rings again*)

ALAN (*He picks up phone*)   Hello . . . Oh, Mom. (*To* CONNIE) Connie, it's my mother.

CONNIE   Your mother? Oh, come on, Alan.
          (*She opens door*)

ALAN   Why should I kid about a thing like that?

CONNIE   Good-by.
          (*And she's gone closing door behind her*)

ALAN   Connie . . . Connie, wait. (*Back into phone. He sits*) Hello, Mom? . . . What's wrong? Did Dad get home yet? . . . Aunt Gussie's? . . . Well, don't worry about it. He'll probably just sleep there tonight. He'll be home tomorrow when he calms down . . . Mom, please don't cry

. . . All right, look, I'll come up and sleep there tonight . . . Yes, in my old room . . . I don't feel like being alone either . . . What? . . . No, not yet . . . Mom, please, I'm very upset . . . I've got a lot on my mind . . . I can't decide that now . . . Mom, I don't care—lamb chops, turkey, chicken salad, anything . . .

Curtain

Act Three

Three weeks later.

At Rise: BUDDY *has* ALAN'S *sports jacket in his arms, one sleeve draped over his shoulder. The jacket is putting in extra duty as* BUDDY'S *dancing partner.*

This is a different BUDDY *from the one we've seen before. In a few weeks he seems to have blossomed. He now has the assurance and self-confidence that comes with independence. He has a bounce and vitality we haven't seen before.*

He dances and chants his own rhythm.

BUDDY ... One, two, cha-cha-cha ... Very good, cha-cha-cha ... And turn, cha-cha-cha ... (*The telephone rings on* "*turn*") Answer phone, cha-cha-cha ... Very good, cha-cha-cha ... (*He places coat on sofa saying "Excuse me, my dear." He picks up phone*) Hello? ... Snow? (*He sits on sofa*) ... Don't you know you could get arrested for having such a sexy voice ... No ... I'm still trying to get tickets for the Ionesco play that's opening tonight ... They're supposed to call me. Then I thought we might go up to the Palladium ... for a little ... cha-cha-cha. Oh, say ... could you pick me up here? It would be easier. Wonderful ... 42 East 63rd Street. About seven? ... Make it five to. I'm only human. Good-by. (*He hangs up, slaps his hands, and gives a little giggle of joy. Then he resumes*) Do it right, cha-cha-cha ... Tonight's the night, cha-cha-cha ... (*The phone rings. He picks it up. Sits on upstage end of coffee table*) Hello?

(*At this moment, the door opens and* ALAN *enters. Or better, he drags in. This is not the* ALAN *of two weeks ago. He looks bedraggled. He seems to have lost a great deal of cockiness, his self-assurance. He hangs trench coat in closet and crosses downstage right to counter*)

BUDDY Yes, it is ... Yes? ... Oh, wonderful ... That's two tickets for tonight ... Yes, I'll pick them up at the box office . . . In Alan Baker's name . . . Thank you very much. Good-by. (*He hangs up. He sees* ALAN) Oh, hi, Aly. I didn't hear you come in. Gee, what a break. Your broker just got me two tickets for the Ionesco play tonight. I used your name. Is it all right?

ALAN (*Staring ahead*)   Why not? I'm not using it any more. (BUDDY *gets up, picks up his dancing partner, and resumes*)

BUDDY   And again, cha-cha-cha . . . To the right, cha-cha-cha . . .(*He keeps on dancing*) Where were you today?

ALAN (*Staring ahead*)   At the Polo Grounds waiting for the Giants to come back . . . Anyone call?

BUDDY (*He's still dancing*)   Yeah . . . a Mr. Copeland . . . and a Mr. Sampler . . . cha-cha-cha . . .

ALAN (*Looks at him*)   What'd they say?

BUDDY   Nice and easy, cha-cha-cha . . .

ALAN (*Angry*)   Hey, Pupi, I'm talking to you.

BUDDY (*He stops*)   What's wrong?

ALAN   I'd like to hear one sentence without the rhythm in it. What'd they say?

BUDDY   Who?

ALAN (*Crossing to him*)   Copeland and Sampler, cha-cha-cha!

BUDDY   Nothing. They'll call back later. What's eating you, Alan?
(*Pats* ALAN'S *shoulder and puts coat on sofa and sits*)

ALAN   It's just a little annoying to have to wait until the dance is over to get my messages.
(*He takes coat off sofa, brushes it and hangs it in closet upstage*)

BUDDY   Boy, you're jumpy lately. You've got a case of nerves, old boy.

ALAN (*Crossing downstage to right center chair*)   Thank you, doctor, is my hour up?

BUDDY   What do you do all day, anyway? You're gone from ten to six. You come home bushed. You keep getting strange calls all day. What's all the mystery?

ALAN   There's no mystery.

BUDDY (*Accusingly*)   Have you got a job?

ALAN   No, I haven't got a job. Are you sure no one else called?

BUDDY   You mean Connie?

ALAN (*Expectantly*)   Connie? Why? Did she . . . ?

BUDDY   No, but you talk about her in your sleep.

ALAN (*Sits right center chair*)   Me? You're crazy.

BUDDY   Last night you even walked in your sleep. You stretched out your arms and said, "Oh, Connie, darling" . . . I'm going to have to start locking my door.

ALAN   Are you ribbing me?

BUDDY   Why don't you call her, Alan?

ALAN   What for? I'm not interested . . . Besides . . . she checked out of her hotel.

BUDDY   Oh! Where'd she go?

ALAN   How should I know. I didn't ask them.

BUDDY   Maybe she left a forwarding address.

ALAN   There's no forwarding address.

BUDDY   How do you know?

ALAN   I asked them . . . Look, will you forget about Connie.

BUDDY   Subject closed. (ALAN *rises and* BUDDY *crosses to bar*) How about a drink?

ALAN   I don't want a drink. (BUDDY *pours one.* ALAN *looks at him*) What are you drinking for?

BUDDY   I like one at night now. Helps me unwind.
         (*Crossing right of center. He drinks*)

ALAN   What do *you* have to unwind from?

BUDDY   Oh, the little everyday problems of life.

ALAN (*Rises and crosses to him*)   Problems? You never had it
so good. You sleep till twelve o'clock. Lounge around
until two. You go out every night. How do you fill up the
rest of the day?

BUDDY   Well, that's one of the little problems I have to
unwind from. (ALAN *turns away right disgustedly*) I'm just
having a little fun. What's wrong, Alan?

ALAN (*Changing his attitude. Turns upstage*)   Nothing. Nothing, I'm sorry, kid. I don't know what's wrong with me
lately. Listen, I don't feel like sitting in again tonight.
You want to go to a movie? Just the two of us?

BUDDY (*Puts glass on sofa table*)   Oh, gee, I'd like to, Alan, but
I've got a date.

ALAN   Again? That's four times this week. Who's on tonight?

BUDDY   This one's a dancer. Modern jazz. Her name is
Snow.

ALAN   Snow?

BUDDY (*Crosses to* ALAN)   Snow Eskanazi¹

ALAN   Sounds like an Italian Eskimo.

BUDDY   She's a real weirdo. Wears that white flour on her
face like the Japanese Kabuki dancers. But I've got a
hunch underneath she's very pretty.

ALAN   Take her out in a strong wind, maybe you'll find out
. . . Where do you collect these girls, anyway?

BUDDY   I met Snow at that party I went to in the Village
last Saturday.

ALAN   The one you took the Greek interpreter to?

BUDDY   Yeah. Snow was with an Indian exchange student.
I was sitting on the floor next to her and she leans over
and gives me her phone number. Just like that.

ALAN   How did Sabu feel about all this?

BUDDY   He loaned her the pencil. Besides, he made a date with the Greek interpreter.

ALAN   (*Sits right center chair*)   No wonder they have emergency sessions at the UN.

BUDDY   Like a jerk I went and left early. You know what I hear they played at three o'clock in the morning?

ALAN   What?

BUDDY   Strip Scrabble!

ALAN   Strip Scrabble?? . . . I suddenly feel eight years old. Are you sure you're the same boy who was eating milk and cake over a sink three weeks ago?

BUDDY   How about that, what's happened to me, Alan? You've given me a new lease on life. Three weeks here with no one telling me what to do and when to come home. Well, I'm a different person, aren't I?

ALAN   Different? You're going to need identification before I let you in here again.

BUDDY   That's why I hate to see you moping around like this. (*Crosses to him*) You're a different person too. It's not like you to let yourself go.
   (*Pats his knee*)

ALAN   (*Indignant*)   What do you mean?

BUDDY   Well, you've been sitting home every night, you haven't called a girl in three weeks, you're even getting to look seedy. Why don't you call Rocco tomorrow?
   (*Crosses away left*)

ALAN   Rocco?

BUDDY   My barber.

ALAN   (*Rises and crosses to him*)   *Your* barber? What do you mean, *your* barber? *I* sent you there. He's *my* barber.

BUDDY   I know. It was just a figure of speech. I didn't mean anything. You can have him back.
   (*Fixes* ALAN'S *tie*)

ALAN   I don't want him back. I just want it clear that you only go there. But Rocco is *my* barber.
(*Turns away right, unfixes his tie*)

BUDDY   Sure, Alan, sure . . . Anyway, cheer up. (*He pats* ALAN'S *shoulder patronizingly*) Things'll get better. (ALAN *sits right center chair*) (*the doorbell rings*) That can't be Snow. It's too early. (*He hops over to door and opens it. It's* PEGGY *in another crazy outfit*) Oh, hello.

PEGGY   Hello, Mr. Manheim.

BUDDY   Come on in. You know Alan Baker.
(*He no longer fears the masquerade*)

PEGGY   Oh, sure. Hi! (*Waves*) I heard you were back. Is everything all right in Hollywood?

BUDDY   Oh, great. We're just about ready to roll on the picture.

PEGGY   I never got a call. I guess you found someone else for my part.

BUDDY   Not at all. We just have the male lead set. We're still looking for the girl.

PEGGY   Oh? Who did you get?

BUDDY   For what?

PEGGY   The male lead.

BUDDY   Oh. Someone new. An Italian actor.

ALAN   Rocco La Barber.

PEGGY   Oh, sure. I've heard of him.

BUDDY   Well . . . if you'll excuse me, I've got to get dressed. I've got to look over some locations tonight.

PEGGY   Of course.

BUDDY   I'll call you. I'm still very interested. (*Looks at his watch and shoots his cuff*) Great Scot, it's nearly seven.
(*Smiles at* ALAN *and prances into the bedroom*)

PEGGY   So young and so brilliant.

ALAN   Eight colleges are after his brain.

PEGGY (*Crosses above* ALAN)   I can understand why *he* hasn't called. What's your excuse?

ALAN (*Rises and starts left*)   No excuse. I've just been busy.

PEGGY (*Stepping downstage*)   And I've been lonely, Alan . . . really lonely . . .

ALAN   I haven't been doing much either.

PEGGY (*Crosses to him*)   You haven't called in nearly three weeks. You never answered my messages.

ALAN   I'm sorry.

PEGGY (*Swings him around*)   Prove it. Let's go to Connecticut this weekend.

ALAN   What's in Connecticut?

PEGGY (*Putting arm around him*)   The ski lodge.

ALAN   It's Vermont.

PEGGY   I don't care. As long as we're together. How about it?

ALAN (*Breaking left*)   Well, Peggy . . . I'm not working any more. I don't have much time for skiing.

PEGGY (*Angry. Crosses stage up right of him*)

ALAN (*Stops her*)   Peggy, wait. It's nothing personal. I'm still crazy about you . . . All right, look. We'll go this weekend.

PEGGY   That's more like my Alan. (*She puts his arm around her*) Bite me on the neck.

ALAN   What?

PEGGY   Bite me on the neck like you used to.

ALAN   Well, Peggy, I don't really feel . . .

PEGGY   Oh, come on.
          (ALAN *shrugs and bites her*)

PEGGY   Ow! You bit me. (*She breaks up to foyer, turns*) You really *must* be a vampire.

(*She opens door and exits.* ALAN *crosses back down to sofa and sits*)
(BUDDY *returns wearing a sports jacket. It's one of those multicolored jobs that they advertise every Sunday in the* Times *but no one ever really buys*)

BUDDY (*He turns around, modeling it*)   Well? How do you like the sports jacket?

ALAN   I like the lining. What's the jacket like?

BUDDY   How do you think this will go at Sardi's?

ALAN   What are you doing, going to Sardi's?

BUDDY   I thought I'd make an impression on Snow. Hey, that reminds me. I'd better make a reservation.
(BUDDY *picks up phone, and dials*)

ALAN (*Exaggeratively swings legs on sofa out of* BUDDY'S *way*) You certainly have blossomed into the Young Man about Town. The theater, the latest styles, Sardi's. I've created an Ivy League Frankenstein.

BUDDY (*Into phone*)   Hello? I'd like to reserve a table for two for tonight, please. Seven-thirty . . . Oh, you are? (*He covers phone with his hand*) He says they're all booked up. (*He snaps his fingers, back into phone*) Are you sure you don't have a reservation for me? Manheim? I'm with M-G-M.
(ALAN *throws up his hands*)

BUDDY (*Into phone*)   Yes, it was probably an oversight . . . Would you? I'd appreciate that . . . Thanks, so much. Good-by! (*He hangs up*) Voilà!

ALAN (*Looks up to heaven*)   What have I done?

BUDDY (*Starts upstage and stops*)   You think he believed me?

ALAN   Why not? I did.

BUDDY   I'd better get moving. (*Starts for foyer and stops and comes downstage right of* ALAN) Oh, by the way, Alan. What are you doing about eleven-thirty tonight?

ALAN   I'll be sitting in a shawl reading the Bible. Why?

BUDDY   I hear there's a great picture at the Paris. Why don't you catch the last show. I think it lets out about one.

ALAN I don't want to be let out about one.

BUDDY Well, you see, I thought later on I might drop back here with Snow . . . for a nightcap.

ALAN You what?

BUDDY I hate to ask you, Alan, but this may be my night to conquer Mount Everest. You don't mind going to a movie, do you?

ALAN (*Rises. Seething*) You're damned right I mind!

BUDDY What's wrong, Alan? That was our arrangement, wasn't it? If one fellow had a girl—

ALAN That was *my* arrangement. I did the arranging and *you* went to the movies. Where do you get this *our* stuff?

BUDDY (*Quite innocently*) I thought we were splitting everything fifty-fifty?

ALAN We were, until you got all the fifties. (*Crosses right of him and turns*) Boy, what nerve. We're not splitting anything any more. Is that understood?

BUDDY Sure, Alan.

ALAN Except the rent. From now on your rent is a hundred forty-two dollars a month.

BUDDY Okay.

ALAN (*Crosses right to counter*) I think I've been bighearted long enough.

BUDDY Alan, I never . . .

ALAN And buy your own food too. I'm sick and tired of bringing home cookies and watching you finish them reading *my* magazines and watching *my* television.

BUDDY You're kidding!

ALAN (*Picks up box and shakes it at him*) The hell I am. Just keep away from my Fig Newtons!

BUDDY (*Half chuckles at the ridiculousness of the situation*) I don't understand. I always give you some of my Yankee Doodles.

ALAN (*But he's not kidding. Crossing to him*)   And stop eating them all over the rug with your crumbs. I never saw anything like it. Clothes lying all over the place. It's disgusting.

BUDDY   Alan, what's eating you? Is it because of this girl?

ALAN (*Crossing upstage left*)   Connie? She's got nothing to do with this.

BUDDY (*Sits sofa*)   Well, something's bothering you. I'd like to know what.

ALAN   Oh, you would, heh? Well, there's plenty bothering me. I happen to think you're pretty ungrateful.

BUDDY   Ungrateful!

ALAN (*Crossing right of* BUDDY *behind sofa*)   Yes, ungrateful. I took you in here, taught you how to dress and walk and talk. Now look at you. You're a big man.

BUDDY   What's wrong, Alan? You said youself I should grow up and become a man.

ALAN   I said become a man. (*Points to himself*) Not this man. Don't take my place in life.

BUDDY   How have I taken your place?

ALAN   I run the water for a bath and five minutes later I hear you splashing in there. You're using my barber, my restaurants, my ticket broker, my apartment, and my socks. How's it going, kid, am I having fun?

BUDDY   You're the one who suggested I do all these things. You said I should start having some fun.

ALAN   I said fun. Have a good time. I didn't say anything about carrying on like this.
      (*Crosses right of center*)

BUDDY   Like what?

ALAN (*Turns*)   Like a bum!

BUDDY (*Jumps up*)   A *bum???*

ALAN   You heard me. What kind of crows are you running around with? (*Crosses to him*) Intellectual delinquents . . .

Strip Scrabble! . . . You're lucky Interpol didn't rush in there and raid the joint.

BUDDY   What kind of girls do you know? When did that kook upstairs get out of the Girl Scouts?

ALAN   I'm talking to *you!* Where were you until four o'clock the other morning?

BUDDY   What's the difference?

ALAN   (*Crosses and sits right center chair*)   I want to know where you were until four o'clock in the morning?

BUDDY   Cocka-doddle-doo! What's with you?

ALAN   (*Jumps up*)   Don't cocka-doddle-doo me.

BUDDY   When did you suddenly switch sides? (*Crosses to him*) When I moved in here you were carrying on like every night was New Year's Eve.

ALAN   We're not talking about a thirty-three-year-old bum. We're talking about a twenty-one-year-old bum.

BUDDY   Oh, you mean it's all right for you.

ALAN   I mean, it's not all right for you. (*Crosses left to coffee table*) Three weeks ago you came in here heartsick over the fate of the world. When was the last time you picked up a newspaper or a book without a phone number in it? What happened to our young hope for a brave new world? We're losing half of South America and you're doing the cha-cha.

BUDDY   What's dancing got to do with it?

ALAN   (*Crosses to him*)   And what about looking for a job?

BUDDY   I have been.

ALAN   Since when is the employment office in an espresso joint in the Village? You're nothing but a clean-shaven beatnik.

BUDDY   I haven't asked you for anything.

ALAN   You'd have starved to death if Mom hadn't been smuggling pot-roast sandwiches through the enemy lines.

BUDDY I didn't notice you throwing yours in the garbage can.

ALAN At least I call her now and then. You're too busy to worry about her. And have you thought once of how Dad is getting along with the business without either of us there now?

BUDDY What brought all this on?

ALAN I'm seeing you for the first time.

BUDDY You mean you're seeing yourself for the first time. I'm just a carbon copy of you.

ALAN Well, whoever it is, I don't like it.

BUDDY Why do *I* get the blame? You go around committing murder and I get the chair.

ALAN (*He raises his arm threateningly*) Don't get smart with me. You're not too big yet to get a good slap across the face.

BUDDY Holy mackerel, I got two fathers!

ALAN Cut that out. I'm nothing like him. Nothing at all. (*Turns away left*)

BUDDY Well, you certainly don't sound like yourself.

ALAN (*Turns to him*) How can I? *You're* myself now.

BUDDY Well, maybe there's one too many of you around here.

ALAN Maybe there is. Which one of me is leaving?

BUDDY It's your apartment. In the meantime, I've got to shave. (*Crosses to bedroom door and* ALAN *crosses downstage center as* BUDDY *goes up to door.* BUDDY *stops and turns*) By the way, which is my water, the hot or the cold?
     (*He stalks out of the room*)

ALAN How do you like the nerve of that kid? Well, we'll see how big an operator he is without me to supply him with everything. (*Crossing left to bar and pours himself a drink. Tips glass to his mouth and realizes there's nothing in it. He picks up bottle and sees it's empty*) A whole bottle of scotch! (*He* takes empty bottle, crosses angrily to bedroom door, waves empty bottle and shouts*) Bum! (*He starts to bar and the doorbell rings. Puts bottle on sofa table*) Ah, that must be Nanook of the North! . . . This I've got to see. (*He crosses to door and opens it. The* MOTHER *stands there with a heavy valise*) Mom! Mom, what are you doing here?

MOTHER (*She trudges into the room*)   I'm lucky I'm here at all. Six blocks I had to lug this from the subway. You'd think a stranger would help a woman.
        (*She puts down valise and flops in a chair*)

ALAN (*Follows left of her*)   Mom, what are you doing with a suitcase? Where are you going?

MOTHER   I'm not going any more. I'm here.

ALAN   Here? Why?

MOTHER   For the same reason Buddy's here . . . I've run away from home.

ALAN   Mom, you're not serious?

MOTHER   Don't think I'm not ashamed. A woman of my age running away from home. I was so humiliated. A woman from my building saw me in the subway with the suitcase. I had to lie to her. I said I was going to visit my brother in California. Then at 125th Street I had to change to a local to come here. She's not so dumb. For California you don't change at 125th Street. I should worry. My life is over anyway.

ALAN   Why, Mom? What happened?

MOTHER   What happened? Ask America what happened? In Alaska they must have heard how that man has been carrying on with me. For three weeks now. Three weeks.

ALAN   All right, Mom, he's very upset. But he'll get over it. He always does.

MOTHER   No, not this time. This time it's different. There's no making up now. I thought maybe there was a chance this morning. I was going to show him I could be bigger than he was. I wanted to show him *I* didn't forget.

ALAN   Forget what?

MOTHER   Today. It's our thirty-seventh anniversary.

ALAN (*Kneels left of her*) Oh, that's right. Happy anniversary, Mom.
>   (*He kisses her*)

MOTHER Thank you, darling. Anyway, I went over to him. I swear to you, I had a big smile on my face, like this: (*She gives a big smile. Then goes back to her sorrow*) And then as nice as I could possibly say it, I said, "Happy Anniversary, darling. I wish you all the happiness in the world." (*She sobs*) And what do you think he said to me?

ALAN What?

MOTHER "Thank you . . . and I wish you what you wish me." (*She sobs*) For what? What did I do he should say such a thing?

ALAN But how do you know he meant anything wrong by that?

MOTHER Because he knows what I was wishing him.
>   (*She cries*)

ALAN (*Throws up his hands in futility. Crossing up right of her*) Oh, boy!

MOTHER All because of you two. He keeps blaming me. "Your bums. Your two bums!"
>   (BUDDY *comes out of the bedroom*)

BUDDY (*Crosses to left of* MOTHER; *leaves jacket on desk*) Mom? What are you doing here?

MOTHER (*Crosses right to* BUDDY. *She starts right in on him*) I'm lucky I'm here at all. Six blocks I had to lug this from the subway.

BUDDY Whose suitcase is that?

ALAN My new roommate's! . . . Mom, will you listen to me. You're just being emotional. You know you can't live here.

BUDDY Here?

MOTHER Where else have I got to go? A hotel? Maybe I should move in with his sister Gussie? I'll join the Army first.

ALAN Mom, it's not that I don't want you. But you wouldn't be comfortable here. It's a small bachelor apartment.

MOTHER So what am I now? I'm a bachelor too. (*She feels terribly sorry for herself*) A bachelor with two grown sons. (*The doorbell rings*)

BUDDY (*Runs up to door*) Oh, that's probably Snow.

MOTHER You're expecting company? (*She picks up suitcase and starts to bedroom*) I won't be in your way. I'll go in the bedroom with my sewing.

ALAN Mom, you don't have to do that.

MOTHER You wouldn't hear me. I'll be like a dead person.

ALAN Mom, you don't need your suitcase.

MOTHER (*Stopping at bedroom right door and turns*) It's all right. I want to unpack my Alka-Seltzer. Oh, I'm so nauseous.
    (*She holds her stomach and goes into the bedroom. The doorbell rings again twice*)

ALAN (*Crossing to counter right. To* BUDDY) Well, answer it, lover.
    (BUDDY *crosses to door quickly and opens it. The* FATHER *stands there, steaming*)

BUDDY Dad!

FATHER (*He storms in on foyer. To* BUDDY) Where is she? I know she's here. (*To* ALAN) Where's their mother?

ALAN (*Weakly*) In the bedroom.

FATHER Oh, they're hiding them in the bedroom now. What's the matter, the kitchen's being painted? (*He crosses to bedroom and opens door. He looks in*) Very nice. Very nice for a mother.
    (BUDDY *crosses downstage and sits on sofa*)

MOTHER (*From off stage*) What do you want?

FATHER What is she doing in there?

MOTHER (*Off stage*) She's drinking Alka-Seltzer.

FATHER (*Crossing downstage below coffee table. Turns away*)   I thought I'd find her in here.

> (*The* MOTHER *comes out with a glass in her hand. Crossing downstage center*)

MOTHER   Where else should I be? They're still my children.

FATHER   She should be home. I'm still her husband.

MOTHER   Not when you treat your own children the way you do.

FATHER   This is something I will not discuss in front of strangers.

MOTHER   They're your sons.

FATHER (*Crossing right center*)   They're *your* sons! They're my strangers! . . . Is she coming home?

MOTHER   She's home. This is where she lives now.

FATHER   This is where she lives? With bums?

MOTHER   That's right. So that makes me a bum too. All right? Now you're happy? Now you've got three bums.

ALAN   Dad, can I say something?

FATHER   Who's he talking to? I'm not even here.

BUDDY (*Crossing downstage left of* FATHER)   Can *I* say something?

FATHER   Write it in a play. I'll be there opening night.

ALAN   All right, Dad, please calm down. Will you talk to me for one minute?

FATHER (*Crossing left below coffee table*)   Is she coming?

ALAN   Dad, please. It's important.

FATHER   Did the woman hear what I said?

ALAN   All right, don't answer me directly. If you understand, blink your eyes once for "yes" and twice for "no."

FATHER (*To* MOTHER)   Did she listen to that? If I were here, I'd slap him in the mouth . . . Is she coming?

BUDDY   Dad, we can't go on like this forever.

FATHER   Forever is over. They'll have no more parents to bother them. They should be very happy.

ALAN (*Crosses left*)   What do you mean, no more parents?

FATHER (*To* MOTHER)   Tell him. Four months we'll be gone. I've got the tickets in my pocket.

MOTHER   You bought the tickets? I told you, I'm not going. Not until everything is all right with you and the boys.

ALAN   Going where?

FATHER   Around the world. (*Crosses right center*) Tell him around the world we're going. Ask him if that's far enough?

MOTHER   I'm not going around any worlds.

FATHER   She's going. I've got the tickets in my pocket.

ALAN   Do you mean it? Are you really going?

FATHER (*Takes ticket out of pocket and holds it up*)   Here! In three weeks we'll be in China. They'll be here bumming around in peace, and we'll be in China . . . in the middle of a revolution. They'll worry a lot.

ALAN (*One step to* FATHER)   But how can you leave for four months? Who's going to take care of the business?

FATHER   What business? Tell him? Is she coming around the world . . . (*Crossing left below coffee table*) or do I take my sister Gussie?

MOTHER   I told you, I'm not going pleasure cruising with aggravation still on my heart.

ALAN (*Crosses left to center*)   Dad, what about the business???

FATHER   Is she coming?

MOTHER   Answer him!

FATHER   I answered him. Tomorrow there'll be no business. I'm selling the business. Is that an answer?

ALAN   Selling the business?

BUDDY   Are you serious?

FATHER   Look who's suddenly so shocked. The skier and the Pulitzer Prize winner.

ALAN (*Crossing left to him*)   Why are you selling it?

FATHER   Who should I save it for, his children?

BUDDY   But who did you sell it to, Dad?

FATHER   Who? To Chiang Kai-shek. That's why I'm going to China.
(*Crosses right to counter*)

ALAN (*Following*)   Why, Dad. Are you selling because of us?

FATHER   You? You think I need you two? I did bigger business in the three weeks you were gone than in the six years you were there.
(*The doorbell rings*)

BUDDY   Oh, boy!

FATHER (*To* MOTHER)   I'm not waiting any more. If she wants, I'll meet her in Hong Kong.

ALAN   Dad, wait. I've got to talk to you about this.
(*Doorbell rings*)

BUDDY (*Looking upstage anxiously*)   Can't you talk later?
(*The doorbell rings again*)

MOTHER   Buddy, the doorbell.

BUDDY   Alan, what'll I do?

ALAN   Will you take that girl and get out of here?
(BUDDY *starts upstage*)

FATHER (*Crossing to* BUDDY)   Girl? What girl??

BUDDY   Just a girl, Dad. Do you think you could finish this conversation in the bedroom?

FATHER (*He can't take any more*)   The bedroom? I'll break every bone in his body.
(*He raises his arm to hit* BUDDY)

MOTHER (*Crossing downstage left*)   Harry!

FATHER (*Follows imitating*)   Harry, Harry.

BUDDY (*Backing away*) Dad, wait . . .
(*Suddenly the door opens and* CONNIE *enters*)

CONNIE (*On foyer*) Oh, hello!

ALAN (*Crosses upstage to right of* CONNIE. *Stunned*) Connie!

MOTHER Harry, please, don't say anything.

FATHER Don't *say* anything? No, I'll sit here and applaud.

ALAN Connie, where have you been?

CONNIE Cincinnati.

ALAN Cincinnati?

CONNIE (*Crossing downstage right to counter*) With the Electrical Appliance Dealers of America.
(ALAN *follows her*)

FATHER I don't have to listen to this kind of talk.
(*He starts for door left above sofa.* BUDDY *stops him*)

BUDDY Dad, wait a minute, please.

ALAN You mean you did another industrial show?

CONNIE I was Miss Automatic Toaster. I popped up and sang . . . And after the show three salesmen tried to butter me.

ALAN But why did you take the job? You said you were quitting.

CONNIE You changed my mind for me. Look, Alan, this doesn't seem to be the time to discuss this . . .

ALAN No, no. This is only my mother and father.

FATHER *Only??*

CONNIE (*Looks at her and says to* MOTHER) Oh, hello.

MOTHER (*Sweetly*) How do you do?

FATHER (*Crossing to left of her below sofa. To* MOTHER) Are you crazy, "How do you do?"

ALAN What do you mean, I changed your mind?

CONNIE   You were right, Alan. I'm much too talented to quit. Besides, I'm beginning to enjoy my work.

ALAN   What work?

FATHER   What do you think, what work? (*To* MOTHER) You're going to stay here while this is going on?

BUDDY (*Takes his arm*)   Dad, you don't know what you're saying.

FATHER (*Lifts arm from shoulder exaggerating movement*) Pushing? A father you're pushing?

MOTHER (*Starts upstage behind sofa table*)   Harry, come in the bedroom.

CONNIE (*Moves as if to go*)   Alan, call me later.

ALAN (*Stops her*)   No, tell me what you're talking about.

CONNIE   Well, I really came to say good-by.

ALAN   Good-by?

CONNIE   The Electrical Dealers want me to go to Europe. With all expenses paid.

FATHER (*Shrugs*)   She's not ashamed to say it

CONNIE (BUDDY *and* FATHER *exchange places*)   It's a wonderful opportunity, Alan. And after all, it's about time I had a "fling."

ALAN   A *fling??*

CONNIE   You know how it is with a twenty-four-year-old girl. She's really not ready to settle down yet.

ALAN   Connie, listen to me.
(*The phone rings*)

FATHER (*Points to phone. Says to* MOTHER)   You hear? That's the cook. She'll be coming to work soon.
(*Phone rings*)

CONNIE   I don't leave until Thursday. Call me, Alan.

BUDDY (*Grabs* FATHER'S *arm*)   Dad, please come inside and talk to me.

FATHER   Again he's pushing.
    (*The phone keeps ringing*)

ALAN   Connie, you can't go to Europe. I won't let you.
    (*Phone rings*)

MOTHER   Alan, your phone.

CONNIE   You won't *let* me?

ALAN   Connie, I need you. (*Phone rings*) I didn't realize it
    until you were out of my life for three weeks. I couldn't
    stand it. I love (*phone rings*) you, sweetheart.

MOTHER (*Crosses to right of center*)   Alan, your phone.

CONNIE   Alan, we've been through those words before.

ALAN   I didn't really feel (*phone rings*) this way before.
    You've got to believe me. It's all over. I have flung!
    (*Ring*)

MOTHER (*Crosses left to coffee table*)   Buddy, the phone.

BUDDY   Dad . . .

FATHER (*To* BUDDY)   If he pushes me once more, he'll bleed
    from the nose.

BUDDY   I wasn't pushing you.
    (*The phone rings*)

MOTHER   Maybe I'm crazy. No one hears a phone.
    (*She picks it up*)

CONNIE   Alan, are you sure?

MOTHER (*Into phone*)   Hello?

CONNIE   Are you really sure?

ALAN   I was never so sure of anything in my life.

MOTHER   Alan, it's for you.

ALAN   I'm busy, Mom. Take a message.

MOTHER   Again with a message.

BUDDY   Who is it, Mom?

MOTHER   Do I know? Do I have a pencil?

BUDDY   All right, don't get excited.

FATHER   That's right. Yell at your mother. Push *her!*

BUDDY (*Crosses upstage above sofa table*)   I wasn't pushing!

MOTHER   Alan, it's a Mr. Kaplan or Koplon . . . Oh, I'm so nauseous.

FATHER   Copeland? From Begley's Department Store in Texas? . . . Give me that.
          (*He grabs phone*)

ALAN (*Crossing left*)   No, Dad—

FATHER (*Into phone*)   Hello? . . . Mr. Copeland of Texas? . . . How do you do, sir . . . To what do I owe the honor of this phone call? . . . Order? What order? . . . Yes, of course it's Mr. Baker . . . No, his father . . . Oh . . . just a minute. (*He is bewildered. He looks front hut hands him phone*) It's for him.

ALAN (*Into phone*)   Hello, Mr. Copeland . . . You what? . . . Oh, wonderful . . . The same order we talked about today? . . . Yes, I've got it. You'll have the shipment the first of the month . . . Not at all . . . Have a nice trip back . . . and thank you . . . Good by.
          (*He hangs up*)

FATHER (*Stares at him*)   How does he come to know Copeland of Texas?

ALAN   I heard he was in town. I called him and took him out to lunch a few times . . . alone. (*He takes out paper from his pocket*) I guess *you'd* better take care of this order, Dad.
          (FATHER *takes paper and looks at it in disbelief*)

FATHER   Four years I'm after Copeland of Texas.

BUDDY (*Crosses downstage right of* ALAN)   So that's what you've been doing every day. Working. And all those phone calls from Copeland and Sampler.

FATHER   Sampler too? . . . I just got a telegram for a big order tonight. For transparent grapes.

ALAN   I thought I owed you that much, Dad.

FATHER (*To* ALAN)   Owed me? (*Then crosses left*) He owes me nothing. I don't need his orders.
    (*Puts invoice in pocket*)

ALAN (*Crosses left to him*)   Dad, please. Even if you don't want me to work for you, can't we at least be friends?

FATHER (*Angry. Away from* ALAN)   I don't need a bum for a friend.

ALAN   Why am I bum?

FATHER   Is he married?

ALAN   Yes!

FATHER   Then he's a bu— (*He stops short and turns to* ALAN) What????

ALAN   That is . . . I will be if Connie says yes. (*He crosses right to* CONNIE *who steps to him*) Connie, I'll wake up a judge tonight. I'll get down on both knees. I'll do anything, but please . . . won't you marry me?

CONNIE   Oh, darling. (*They kiss*)
    (CONNIE *nudges him*)

ALAN   Huh! (*Turns to others*) Mom, I guess you can call the caterers . . : This is Connie Dayton. The girl I'm going to marry.

BUDDY   No kidding?
    (CONNIE *crosses left to* MOTHER. *They meet right center*)

MOTHER   Oh, darling.
    (*She and* CONNIE *embrace*)

BUDDY (*Crosses to* MOTHER)   Gee, congratulations.
    (*They all look at* ALAN *who then looks for approval from the* FATHER. *They all turn and look at* FATHER)

ALAN   Dad—
    (*The* FATHER *turns away from them*)

MOTHER   Harry, your son is going to get married.

FATHER   No one tells me nothing. All I get is pushed.

ALAN (*Crosses left to* FATHER)   Dad, I don't know how to say this to you . . . but . . . well, you were right about so many things. (FATHER *nods . . . huh . . . huh*) I was a bum. (FATHER

nods . . . huh . . . huh) I guess every boy's got to be a bum even for a little while. I just ran into overtime. (FATHER *nods . . . huh . . . huh*) There's a lot more I want to say to you, Dad, but not now. Look, why don't we all go out to celebrate? To a night club.
(*Crosses right to* CONNIE)

FATHER   He hasn't got a job, he's going to night clubs.

MOTHER   Harry, the children want to take us out.

FATHER   Let them save their money for furniture.

ALAN (*Afraid things are going to start all over again*)   Oh, Dad, can't you just once—

CONNIE   No, Alan, Alan. (*Leaping into the breach. Crosses left to* FATHER) Mr. Baker is right. It's impossible to talk in night clubs anyway. And tonight I'd like to talk. After all, I suddenly have a new family. (*To* MR. BAKER, *tenderly*) Please Mr. Baker . . . why don't we all have dinner together.

FATHER (*He turns slowly to see who this girl is. She looks "nice." "Very nice." And suddenly he has no more sons. Now he's got a daughter. He smiles. Removes hat and places it over his heart and bows*)   Well . . . Maybe just for a cup of coffee.

ALAN (*Crosses left to* CONNIE)   Thanks, Dad.

FATHER (*To* ALAN . . . *warning*)   But we come home early. You've got to be at the plant eight o'clock in the morning and I don't want any excuses.

ALAN   Do you mean that? Do you really want me back?

FATHER   No, I'm going to put the night watchman in charge while I'm in China.

ALAN (*Laughs—starts upstage taking* CONNIE)   Come on, everybody.

CONNIE (*On way up stops at* BUDDY)   Good night, Buddy.
(*She kisses him and continues to foyer*)

BUDDY   Good night, Connie.

MOTHER (*Crosses to* BUDDY)   Buddy, darling, you do whatever you want, sweetheart. You're not a baby any more.

BUDDY   Thanks, Mom.
   (*He kisses her*)

MOTHER   But be up for dinner Friday night.

BUDDY   I will.

MOTHER   And bring your laundry.
   (*Crosses to bedroom to get valise and coat*)

BUDDY (*As* FATHER *starts toward door*)   Well, Dad, you still
   haven't said anything. Is it OK to leave home?

FATHER (*Stops*)   No.

BUDDY   Oh, Dad.

FATHER (*Crosses to* BUDDY)   So what are you asking me? (ALAN
   crosses left of FATHER *behind sofa*) If I say "no" it's "yes"
   anyway. There was a time when my "no" was "no," but
   now you're twenty-one and "no" is "yes." So it's "yes"
   and forget the "no." (ALAN *and* BUDDY *exchange puzzled
   looks*)
      (*He takes valise from* MOTHER *who has come out of bedroom
      and they all start out*)

BUDDY (*As* FATHER *goes off*)   Thanks, Dad.

ALAN (*Has put on coat*)   See you back here later? . . . About
   twelve?

BUDDY   Make it one.

ALAN (*Smiles*)   Right, Mr. Manheim. (*He goes to door and turns*)
   So long . . . bum! (*He exits*)
      (BUDDY *looks after him, crosses to upstage left desk and gets
      jacket. Puts jacket on and looks around room. He crosses
      now to sofa and arranges pillows. Doorbell rings.* BUDDY
      crosses to downstage left lamp and turns it out)

BUDDY   Coming, my Snowflake! (*He goes to door, composes
   himself, then opens it. A* WOMAN *in her fifties stands there*)
   Aunt Gussie!
      (*Curtain starts down*)

WOMAN (*She walks into room as curtain falls*)   I was in the
   neighborhood, so I thought I'd say hello.

Curtain

Barefoot
in the Park

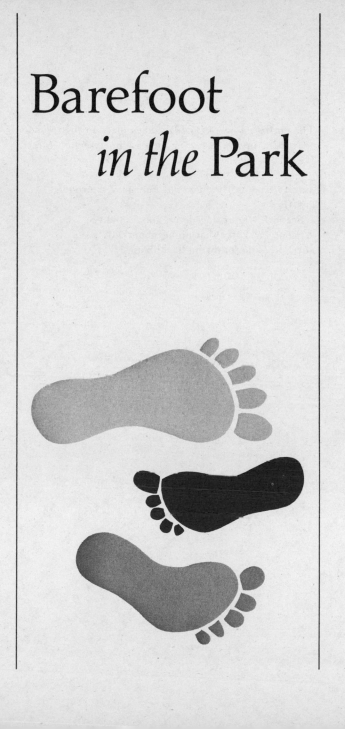

Act One

A large one-room apartment on the top floor of an old brownstone on East Forty-eighth Street off Third Avenue. The room is barren. A ladder, a canvas drop cloth, and a couple of empty paint cans stand forlornly in the center of the room. There is a huge skylight which pours the bright February sunshine glaringly into the room. Through the skylight we can see the roofs and windows of brownstones across the street and the framework of a large building under construction. Crests of clinging snow can be seen in the two windows under the skylight. At stage right, there is the entrance door, a step below the apartment itself. At stage left, four steps lead to a raised area from which two doors open, the upstage one leading to a bathroom, the other to the bedroom. We will soon learn that the latter is not really a bedroom, but a small dressing room. The bathroom has only a shower and a sink and what-have-you. On another raised section up right is the kitchen. It's not really a kitchen, but just an old stove, an older refrigerator, and a chipped sink standing nakedly between them. Upstage left of this area is another platform on which stand a steamer trunk and a few suitcases. The room has just been freshly painted—not carefully, maybe not professionally, but painted. There is a small Franklin stove downstage left below the platform, and an open closet downstage right. Completing the furnishings of the room are a railing that runs downstage of the entrance wall, and a radiator that sits high on the upstage left wall. For all the room's drabness and coldness, there is great promise here. Someone with taste, imagination, and personality can make this that perfect love nest we all dream about. That person is now putting the key in the door.

It opens and CORIE BRATTER *enters. She is lovely, young, and full of hope for the future. She enters the apartment, looks around, and sighs as though the world were just beginning. For her, it is. She is wearing Levis and a yellow top under a large, shaggy white fur coat; she carries a bouquet of flowers. After rapturously examining the room, she takes the small paint can, fills it with water, and puts in the flowers, throwing the wrapping on the floor. The first bit of color in the room. As she crosses to put the "vase" on top of the Franklin stove, the doorbell buzzes. She puts the flowers down, crosses to the door, buzzes back, and then opens the door and shouts down:*

CORIE   Hello?
  (*From the depths, possibly from the bottom of the earth we hear a voice shout up*)

VOICE   Bratter?

CORIE   (*Yelling back*)   Yes. Up here! . . . Top floor!
  (*She crosses to the suitcases, opens the medium-sized one and takes out a large bottle of champagne which she puts into the refrigerator*)

VOICE   (*From below, this time a little closer*)   Hello?

CORIE   (*Rushes to the door again and shouts down*)   Up here! You have another floor to go.
  (*Crossing back to the open suitcase she takes out three small logs and carries them to the Franklin stove. As she drops them in front of the stove, the owner of the voice appears at the door: a tall, heavy-set man in his mid-thirties, in a plaid wool jacket and baseball cap. He is breathing very, very hard*)

TELEPHONE MAN   Tel—(*He tries to catch his breath*)— Telephone Company.

CORIE   Oh, the phone. Good. Come on in.
  (*He steps in, carrying a black leather repair kit*)

TELEPHONE MAN   That's quite a—(*Gasp, gasp*)—quite a climb.

CORIE   Yes, it's five flights. If you don't count the front stoop.

TELEPHONE MAN   I *counted* the front stoop. (*Gasp, gasp . . . he looks at his notebook*) Paul Bratter, right?

CORIE   *Mrs.* Paul Bratter.

TELEPHONE MAN (*Still checking the book*) Princess phone?

CORIE The little one? That lights up? In beige?

TELEPHONE MAN The little one . . . (*Gasp, gasp*) That lights up . . . (*Gasp, gasp*) In beige . . . (*Gasp, gasp. He swallows hard*)

CORIE Would you like a glass of water?

TELEPHONE MAN (*Sucking for air, nods*) Please!

CORIE (*Crosses to the sink*) I'd offer you soda or a beer but we don't have anything yet.

TELEPHONE MAN A glass of water's fine.

CORIE (*Suddenly embarrassed*) Except I don't have a glass either.

TELEPHONE MAN Oh!

CORIE Nothing's arrived yet . . . You could put your head under and just schlurp.

TELEPHONE MAN No, I'm okay. Just a little out of shape. (*As he climbs stiffly up the step out of the well, he groans with pain. After looking about*) Where do you want the phone?

CORIE (*Looks around*) The phone . . . Let me see . . . Gee, I don't know. Do you have any ideas?

TELEPHONE MAN Well, it depends what you're gonna do with the room. You gonna have furniture in here?

CORIE Yes, it's on its way up.

TELEPHONE MAN (*He looks back at the stairs*) Heavy furniture?

CORIE I'll tell you what. (*She points to the telephone junction box on the wall left of the stairs*) Just put it over there and give me a long extension cord. If I can't find a place, I'll just hang it out the window.

TELEPHONE MAN Fair enough. (*He crosses to the junction box, coughing and in pain*) Whoo!

CORIE Say, I'm awfully sorry about the stairs.
(*Taking the large suitcase, she starts to drag it into the bedroom*)

TELEPHONE MAN (*On his knees; he opens his tool box*) You're really gonna live up here, heh? . . . I mean, every day?

CORIE Every day.

TELEPHONE MAN You don't mind it?

CORIE (*Stopping on the stairs*) Mind it? . . . I love this apartment . . . besides (*she continues into the bedroom*) it *does* discourage people.

TELEPHONE MAN What people?

CORIE (*Comes out of the bedroom and starts for the other suitcases*) Mothers, friends, relatives, mothers. I mean no one just pops in on you when they have to climb five flights.

TELEPHONE MAN You're a newlywed, right?

CORIE Six days. What gave me away?

TELEPHONE MAN I watch "What's My Line" a lot.
(*The doorbell buzzes*)

CORIE Oh! I hope that's the furniture.

TELEPHONE MAN I don't want to see this.

CORIE (*Presses the buzzer and yells down the stairs*) Helloooo! Bloomingdale's?
(*From below, a voice*)

VOICE   Lord and Taylor.

CORIE   Lord and Taylor? (*Shrugs and takes the now empty suitcase and puts it into the closet*) Probably another wedding gift . . . From my mother. She sends me wedding gifts twice a day . . .

TELEPHONE MAN   I hope it's an electric heater.
   (*He blows on his hands*)

CORIE (*Worried, she feels the steam pipe next to the closet*) Really? Is it cold in here?

TELEPHONE MAN   I can't grip the screwdriver. Maybe the steam is off.

CORIE   Maybe that's it.
   (*She gets up on the stairs and tests the radiator*)

TELEPHONE MAN   Just turn it on. It'll come right up.

CORIE   It *is* on. It's just not coming up.

TELEPHONE MAN   Oh! . . . Well, that's these old brownstones for you.
   (*He zips up his jacket*)

CORIE   I prefer it this way. It's a medical fact, you know, that steam heat is very bad for you.

TELEPHONE MAN   Yeah? In February?
   (*Suddenly the* DELIVERY MAN *appears in the door, carrying three packages. He is in his early sixties and from the way he is breathing, it seems the end is very near. He gasps for air*)

CORIE (*Crossing to him*)   Oh, hi . . . Just put it down . . . anywhere.
   (*The* DELIVERY MAN *puts the packages down, panting. He wants to talk but can't. He extends his hand to the* TELEPHONE MAN *for a bit of compassion*)

TELEPHONE MAN   I know. I know.

CORIE   I'm awfully sorry about the stairs. (*The* DELIVERY MAN *takes out a pad and pencil and holds them out limply toward* CORIE) What's this?

TELEPHONE MAN   I think he wants you to sign it.

CORIE   Oh, yes. (*She signs it quickly*) Wait, just a minute. (*She picks up her bag from where she had left it in the kitchen area and takes out some change*) Here you go . . . (*She puts it in his hand. He nods weakly and turns to go*) Will you be all right? . . . (*And for the first time he gets out some words. They are: "Argh, argh." He exits*)

CORIE (*Closes the door behind him*)   It's a shame, isn't it? Giving such hard work to an old man.
        (*She takes two of the packages and puts them with the remaining suitcases*)

TELEPHONE MAN   He's probably only twenty-five. They age fast on this route. (*He dials the phone and then talks into it*) Hello, Ed? Yeah . . . On . . . er . . . Eldorado five, eight, one, nine, one . . . Give me a straight check.

CORIE (*Moving to* TELEPHONE MAN)   Is that my number? Eldorado five, eight, one, nine, one (*The* TELEPHONE MAN *nods*) It has a nice sound, hasn't it?

TELEPHONE MAN (*Why fool with a romantic*)   Yeah, it's a beautiful number. (*The phone rings. He answers it, disguising his voice*) Hello? . . . (*He chuckles over his joke*) Good work, Mr. Bell, you've done it again. (*He hangs up, and turns to* CORIE) Well, you've got your phone. As my mother would say, may your first call be from the Sweepstakes.

CORIE (*Takes the phone*)   My very own phone . . . Gives you a sense of power, doesn't it? Can I make a call yet?

TELEPHONE MAN (*Putting the cover back on the junction box*)   Your bill started two minutes ago.

CORIE   Who can I call? . . . I know.
(She starts to dial)

TELEPHONE MAN   Oh, by the way. My name is Harry Pepper. And if you ever have any trouble with this phone, please, do me a favor, don't ask for Harry Pepper. (CORIE hangs up, a look of disappointment on her face) What's the matter, bad news?

CORIE   (Like a telephone operator)   It is going to be cloudy tonight with a light snow.

TELEPHONE MAN   (He looks up at the skylight)   And just think, you'll be the first one in the city to see it fall.
(The doorbell buzzes. CORIE puts down the phone, and rushes to the door)

CORIE   Oh, please, let that be the furniture and not Paul so Paul can see the apartment with furniture. (She buzzes, opens the door, and yells downstairs) Yes?

VOICE FROM BELOW   It's me!

CORIE   (Unhappily)   Oh, hi, Paul. (She turns into the room) Well, I guess he sees the apartment without the furniture.
(She takes the remaining package and places it with the others on the landing under the windows)

TELEPHONE MAN   (Gathering up his tools)   How long d'ja say you were married?

CORIE   Six days.

TELEPHONE MAN   He won't notice the place is empty until June. (He crosses to the door) Well, Eldorado five, eight, one, nine, one . . . Have a nice marriage . . . (He turns back into the room) And may you soon have many extensions. (He turns and looks at the climb down he has to make and moans) Ooohh!
(He is gone. CORIE quickly starts to prepare the room for PAUL's entrance. She gathers up the canvas drop cloth and throws it into the closet)

PAUL'S VOICE   Corie? . . . Where are you?

CORIE (*Rushes back to the door and yells down*)   Up here, hon . . . Top floor . . . (*The phone rings*) Oh, my goodness. The phone. (*She rushes to it and answers it*) Hello? . . . Yes? . . . Oh, yes, he is . . . I mean he's on his way up . . . Can you hold on for two more floors? (*She puts down the receiver and yells*) Paul. Hurry up, darling!

PAUL'S VOICE   Okay. Okay.

CORIE (*Into the phone*)   Hello. He'll be with you in one more flight. Thank you. (*She puts the phone on the floor and continues to get the apartment ready. Rushing up the stairs, she closes the bedroom and bathroom doors. Surveying the room, she sees the wrapping from the flowers on the floor of the kitchen and the wadded-up newspapers on top of the stove. Quickly gathering them up, she stuffs them into the nearest hiding place—the refrigerator. Then dashing into the hall and closing the door behind her, she re-enters to make one more survey of her apartment. Satisfied with what she sees, she turns back to the open door, and yells down*) Now honey, don't expect too much. The furniture didn't get here yet and the paint didn't come out exactly right, but I think it's going to be beautiful . . . Paul? . . . Paul, are you all right?

PAUL'S VOICE   I'm coming. I'm coming.

CORIE (*Runs back to the phone and speaks into it*)   He's coming. He's coming. (*She puts down the phone and looks at the door.* PAUL *falls in through the doorway and hangs on the rail at the entrance to the apartment.* PAUL *is twenty-six but breathes and dresses like fifty-six. He carries a heavy suitcase and an attaché case and all the dignity he can bear. He drops the attaché case at the railing*) Hi, sweetheart. (*She smothers him with kisses but all he can do is fight for air*) . . . Oh, Paul, darling. (PAUL *sucks for oxygen*) . . . Well? (*She steps back*) Say something.

PAUL (*Breathing with great difficulty, he looks back down the stairs*) It's six flights . . . Did you know it's six flights?

CORIE It isn't. It's five.

PAUL (*Staggers up the step into the room, and collapses on the suitcase*) What about that big thing hanging outside the building?

CORIE That's not a flight. It's a stoop.

PAUL It may *look* like a stoop but it climbs like a flight. (*Gasp, gasp*)

CORIE Is that *all* you have to say?

PAUL (*Gasping*) I didn't think I'd get that much out. (*He breathes heavily*) It didn't seem like six flights when I first saw the apartment. (*Gasp*) Why is that?

CORIE You didn't see the apartment. Don't you remember, the woman wasn't home. You saw the third-floor apartment.

PAUL Then that's why.

CORIE (*Crossing above* PAUL) You don't like it. You really don't like it.

PAUL I *do* like it. (*He squints around*) I'm just waiting for my eyes to clear first.

CORIE I expected you to walk in here and say, "Wow." (*She takes his hand*)

PAUL I will. (*He takes a deep breath*) Okay. (*He looks around, then says without enthusiasm*) "Wow."

CORIE Oh, Paul. (*She throws herself onto* PAUL'*s knee*)

It'll be beautiful, I promise you. You just came home too soon.
> (*She nuzzles him*)

PAUL   You know I missed you.

CORIE   Did you really?

PAUL   Right in the middle of the Monday morning conference I began to feel sexy.

CORIE   That's marvelous. (*They kiss*) Oh, boy. Let's take a cab back to the Plaza. We still have an hour before check-out time.

PAUL   We can't. We took a towel and two ash trays. We're hot.
> (*He kisses her*)

CORIE   My gosh, you still love me.

PAUL   After six days at the Plaza? What's the trick?

CORIE (*Gets up and moves away*)   But that was a honeymoon. Now we're on a regular schedule. I thought you'd come home tonight, and we'd shake hands and start the marriage.
> (*She extends her hand to him*)

PAUL (*Rises*)   "How do you do? . . ."
> (*They shake hands. Then* CORIE *throws herself into his arms and kisses him*)

CORIE   My turn to say "Wow" . . . For a lawyer you're some good kisser.

PAUL (*With hidden import*)   For a kisser I'm some good lawyer.

CORIE   What does that mean? . . . Something's happened? . . . Something wonderful? . . . Well, for pete's sakes, what?

PAUL   It's not positive yet. The office is supposed to call and let me know in five minutes.

CORIE (*Then she remembers*) Oh! They called!

PAUL What . . . ?

CORIE I mean they're calling.

PAUL When . . . ?

CORIE Now . . . They're on the phone now.

PAUL (*Looking around*) Where . . . ?

CORIE (*Points to the phone*) There . . .

PAUL (*Rushes to the phone*) Why didn't you tell me?

CORIE I forgot. You kissed me and got me all crazy.

PAUL (*Into the phone*) Frank? . . . Yeah! . . . Listen, what did—oh, very funny. (*Looks to* CORIE) "For a lawyer, I'm some good kisser" . . . Come on, come, tell me? . . . Well? . . . (*A big grin.* CORIE *feeling left out, sneaks over and tries to tickle him*) You're kidding? The whole thing? Oh, Frank, baby. I love you . . . What do you mean, nervous? . . . I passed the bar, didn't I? . . . Yes, I'll go over everything tonight. (CORIE *reacts to* "*tonight*" *and slowly moves to the ladder*) I'll meet you in Schrafft's at eight o'clock in the morning. We'll go over the briefs . . . Hey, what kind of a tie do I wear? I don't know. I thought maybe something flowing like Oliver Wendell Holmes . . . Right. (*He stands up. He is bubbling with joy.* CORIE *has now climbed up the ladder*) Did you hear? . . . Did you hear?
(*He moves up the ladder to* CORIE)

CORIE What about tonight?

PAUL I've got to be in court tomorrow morning . . . *I've got my first case!*

CORIE What about tonight?

PAUL I'll have to go over the briefs. Marshall has to be in Washington tomorrow and he wants me to take over

. . . with Frank . . . but it's really my case. (*He hugs* CORIE) Oh, Corie, baby, I'm going to be a lawyer.

CORIE   That's wonderful . . . I just thought we were going to spend tonight together.

PAUL   We'll spend tomorrow night together. (*He crosses to railing and gets his attaché case*) I hope I brought those affidavits.

CORIE   *I* brought a black lace nightgown.
(*She crosses to the small suitcase*)

PAUL   (*Looks through affidavits from the case; his mind has now turned completely legal*) Marshall had everything laid out when I was at the office . . . It looks simple enough. A furrier is suing a woman for nonpayment of bills.

CORIE   (*Taking the nightgown out of the suitcase*)   I was going to cook you spaghetti with the white clam sauce . . . in a bikini.

PAUL   We're representing the furrier. He made four specially tailored coats for this woman on Park Avenue. Now she doesn't want the coats.

CORIE   (*Takes off her sweatshirt, and slipping her arms through the nightgown straps, she drapes it over her*) Then I found this great thing on Eighth Street. It's a crossword puzzle with dirty words.

PAUL   But the furrier can't get rid of the coats. She's only four-foot-eight. He'd have to sell them to a rich little girl.

CORIE   . . . then I was going to put on a record and do an authentic Cambodian fertility dance.

PAUL   The only trouble is, he didn't have a signed contract . . . (CORIE *begins her "fertility dance" and ends up collapsing on the bottom step of the ladder*) What are you doing?

CORIE I'm trying to get you all hot and bothered and you're summing up for the jury. The whole marriage is over.

PAUL (*Moves to* CORIE) Oh, Corie, honey, I'm sorry. (*He puts his arms around her*) I guess I'm pretty excited. You want me to be rich and famous, don't you?

CORIE During the day. At night I want you to be here and sexy.

PAUL I will. Just as soon as Birnbaum versus Gump is over . . . I'll tell you what. Tomorrow night is your night. We'll do whatever you want.

CORIE Something wild, insane, and crazy?

PAUL I promise.

CORIE (*Her eyes wide open*) Like what?

PAUL Well . . . I'll come home early and we'll wallpaper each other.

CORIE Oh, Paul, how wonderful . . . Can't we do it tonight?

PAUL No, we can't do it tonight, because tonight I've got to work. (*He rises, and looks around*) Except where do I sit?

CORIE The furniture will be here by five. They promised.

PAUL (*Drops the affidavits into the attaché case, and looks at his watch*) Five? . . . It's five-thirty. (*He crosses to the bedroom stairs*) What do we do, sleep in Bloomingdale's tonight?

CORIE They'll be here, Paul. They're probably stuck in traffic.

PAUL (*Crossing up to the bedroom*) And what about to-

night? I've got a case in court tomorrow. Maybe we should check into a hotel?
(*He looks into the bedroom*)

CORIE (*Rises and moves toward* PAUL.) We just checked *out* of a hotel. I don't care if the furniture *doesn't* come. I'm sleeping in my apartment *tonight*.

PAUL Where? Where? (*He looks into the bathroom, closes the door, and starts to come back down the steps*) There's only room for *one* in the bathtub. (*He suddenly turns, goes back up the steps and opens the door to the bathroom*) Where's the bathtub?

CORIE (*Hesitantly*) There is no bathtub.

PAUL No bathtub?

CORIE There's a shower . . .

PAUL How am I going to take a bath?

CORIE You won't take a bath. You'll take a shower.

PAUL I don't like showers. I like baths. Corie, how am I going to take a bath?

CORIE You'll lie down in the shower and hang your feet over the sink . . . I'm sorry there's no bathtub, Paul.

PAUL (*Closes the door, and crosses down into the room*) Hmmmm . . . Boy, of all the nights . . . (*He suddenly shivers*) It's freezing in here. (*He rubs his hands*) Isn't there any heat?

CORIE Of course there's heat. We have a radiator.

PAUL (*Gets up on the steps and feels the radiator*) The *radiator's* the coldest thing in the room.

CORIE It's probably the boiler. It's probably off in the whole building.

PAUL (*Putting on his gloves*)   No, it was warm coming up the stairs. (*He goes out the door into the hall*) See . . . It's nice and warm out here.

CORIE   Maybe it's because the apartment is empty.

PAUL   The *hall* is empty too, but it's warm out here.

CORIE (*Moves to the stove*)   It'll be all right once I get a fire going.

PAUL (*Goes to the phone*)   A fire? You'd have to keep the flame going night and day . . . I'll call the landlord.

CORIE (*Putting a log into the stove*)   He's not home.

PAUL   Where is he?

CORIE   In Florida! . . . There's a handyman that comes Monday, Wednesday, and Fridays.

PAUL   You mean we freeze on Tuesdays, Thursdays, and Saturdays?

CORIE   He'll be here in the morning.

PAUL   (*Moving to the windows*)   And what'll we do tonight? I've got a case in court in the morning.

CORIE (*Moves to* PAUL)   Will you stop saying it like you always have a case in court in the morning. This is your first one.

PAUL   Well, what'll we do?

CORIE   The furniture will be here. In the meantime I can light the stove and you can sit over the fire with your law books and a shawl like Abraham Lincoln.
(*She crosses to the Franklin stove and gets matches from the top of it*)

PAUL   Is that supposed to be funny?
(*He begins to investigate the small windows*)

CORIE   No. It was supposed to be nasty. It just came out funny. (*She strikes a match and attempts to light the log in the stove.* PAUL *tries the windows*) What are you doing?
        (*She gives up attempting to light the log*)

PAUL   I'm checking to see if the windows are closed.

CORIE   They're closed. I looked.

PAUL   Then why is it windy in here?

CORIE   (*Moves toward* PAUL)   I don't feel a draft.

PAUL   (*Moves away from the windows*)   I didn't say draft. I said wind . . . There's a brisk northeasterly wind blowing in this room.

CORIE   You don't have to get sarcastic.

PAUL   (*Moving up into the kitchen area*)   I'm not getting sarcastic, I'm getting chapped lips. (*Looking up, he glimpses the hole in the skylight*)

CORIE   How could there be wind in a closed room?

PAUL   How's this for an answer? There's a hole in the skylight.
        (*He points up*)

CORIE   (*Looks up, sees it, and is obviously embarrassed by it*)   Gee, I didn't see that before. Did you?

PAUL   (*Moves to the ladder*)   I didn't see the *apartment* before.

CORIE   (*Defensively. She crosses to the railing and gets her coat*)   All right, Paul, don't get upset. I'm sure it'll be fixed. We could plug it up with something for tonight.

PAUL   (*Gets up on the ladder*)   How? How? That's twenty feet high. You'd have to fly over in a plane and *drop* something in.

CORIE (*Putting on her coat*)   It's only for one night. And it's not that cold.

PAUL   In February? Do you know what it's like at three o'clock in the morning? In February? Ice-cold freezing.

CORIE   It's not going to be freezing. I called the Weather Bureau. It's going to be cloudy with a light s—
(*She catches herself and looks up*)

PAUL   What? (CORIE *turns away*) What? . . . A light what?

CORIE   Snow!

PAUL (*Coming down the ladder*)   Snow?? . . . It's going to snow tonight? . . . In here?

CORIE   They're wrong as often as they're right.

PAUL   I'm going to be shoveling snow in my own living room.

CORIE   It's a little hole.

PAUL   With that wind it could blow six-foot drifts in the bathroom. Honestly, Corie, I don't see how you can be so calm about all this.

CORIE   Well, what is it you want me to do?

PAUL   Go to pieces, like me. It's only natural.

CORIE (*Goes to him and puts her arms around him*)   I've got a better idea. I'll keep you warm . . . And there's no charge for electricity . . .
(*She kisses him*)

PAUL   I can see I haven't got much of a law career ahead of me.

CORIE   Good. I hope we starve. And they find us up here dead in each other's arms.

PAUL   "Frozen skinny lovers found on Forty-eighth Street."
(*They kiss*)

CORIE   Are we in love again?

PAUL   We're in love again.
(*They kiss again, a long passionate embrace. The doorbell buzzes*)

The COMEDY

of Neil Simon

CORIE   (*Breaking away*)   The bed. I hope it's the bed. (*She buzzes back, and then opens the door and yells down*) Helllooooo! Bloomingdale's? (*From below, a female voice: Surprise!* CORIE *turns to* PAUL) Oh, God.

PAUL   What's wrong.

CORIE   Please, let it be a woman delivering the furniture.

PAUL   A woman?

VOICE   Corie?

CORIE   But it's my mother.

PAUL   Your mother? Now?

CORIE   (*Taking off the nightgown and slipping into her top*)   She couldn't wait. Just one more day.

PAUL   Corie, you've got to get rid of her. I've got a case in court tomorrow.

CORIE   It's ugly in here without furniture, isn't it. She's just going to hate it, won't she?

VOICE   Corie? Where are you?

CORIE   (*Crosses to the door and yells down the stairs*)   Up here, Mom. Top floor.

PAUL   (*Hides the attaché case in a corner to the left of the windows*)   How am I going to work tonight?

CORIE She'll think this is the way we're going to live. Like gypsies in an empty store. (*Attempting to button her top*)

PAUL (*Throwing the nightgown and lingerie into a suitcase*) Maybe I ought to sleep in the office.

CORIE She'll freeze to death. She'll sit there in her fur coat and freeze to death.

PAUL (*Helps her button her top*) I don't get you, Corie. Five minutes ago this was the Garden of Eden. Now it's suddenly Cannery Row.

CORIE She doesn't understand, Paul. She has a different set of values. She's practical. She's not young like us.

PAUL (*Gathers up the suitcase with lingerie and takes it into the bedroom*) Well, I'm twenty-six and cold as hell.

VOICE (*Getting nearer*) Corie?

CORIE (*Yells down at the door*) One more flight, Mother . . . Paul, promise me one thing. Don't tell her about the rent. If she asks, tell her you're not quite sure yet.

PAUL (*Crossing to the door with his coat collar up around his face*) Not sure what my rent is? I *have* to know what my rent is. I'm a college graduate.

CORIE (*Stopping PAUL*) Can't you lie a little? For me? You don't have to tell her it's a hundred and twenty-five.

PAUL All right. How much is it?

CORIE Sixty?

PAUL What?

CORIE Sixty-five?

PAUL Corie—

CORIE Seventy-five, all right? Seventy-five dollars and sixty-three cents a month. Including gas and electricity. She'll believe that, won't she?

PAUL *Anyone* would believe that. It's the hundred and twenty-five that's hard to swallow.
(*He combs his hair*)

CORIE She's taking a long time. I hope she's all right.

PAUL I can't lie about the stairs. She's going to figure out it's six floors all by herself.

CORIE Shh. Shh, she's here.
(*She starts to open the door*)

PAUL (*Grabs her*) Just promise *me* one thing. Don't let her stay too long because I've got a . . .

CORIE (*With him*) . . . case in court in the morning . . . I know, I know . . . (*She opens the door and goes into the hall*) . . . Mother!
(MOTHER *shoots by her into the room and grabs the rail to keep from falling. She is in her late forties, pretty, but has not bothered to look after herself these past few years. She could use a permanent and a whole new wardrobe*)

PAUL (*Rushes to support her*) Hello, Mom.
(MOTHER *struggles for air*)

MOTHER Oh! . . . Oh! . . . I can't breathe.

CORIE Take it easy, Mom.
(*Holding her other arm*)

MOTHER I can't catch my breath.

PAUL You should have rested.

MOTHER I did . . . But there were always more stairs.

CORIE Paul, help her.

PAUL Come on, Mom. Watch the step.
(*He starts to lead her up the step into the room*)

MOTHER More stairs?
(*She steps up and* CORIE *and* PAUL *lead her toward*
PAUL's *suitcase, still standing near the wall*)

CORIE You want some water?

MOTHER Later. I can't swallow yet.

PAUL Here, sit down.
(*She sits on the suitcase*)

MOTHER Oh, my.

CORIE It's not *that* high, Mother.

MOTHER I know, dear. It's not bad really . . . What is it,
nine flights?

PAUL Five. We don't count the stoop.

MOTHER I didn't think I'd make it . . . If I'd known the
people on the third floor I'd have gone to visit them . . .
(PAUL *sits on the bottom step of the ladder*)

CORIE This is a pleasant surprise, Mother.

MOTHER Well, I really had no intention of coming up,
but I had a luncheon in Westchester and I thought,
since it's on my way home, I might as well drop in for a
few minutes . . .

CORIE On your way home to New Jersey?

MOTHER Yes. I just came over the Whitestone Bridge and
down the Major Deegan highway and now I'll cut across
town and onto the Henry Hudson Parkway and up to
the George Washington Bridge. It's no extra trouble.

PAUL   Sounds easy enough.

MOTHER   Yes . . .

CORIE   We were going to ask you over on Friday.

MOTHER   Friday. Good. I'll be here Friday . . . I'm not going to stay now, I know you both must be busy.

PAUL   Well, as a matter of fact . . .

CORIE   (*Stopping him*)   No, we're not, are we, Paul?
       (*He kills her with a glance*)

MOTHER   Besides, Aunt Harriet is ringing the bell for me in ten minutes . . . Just one good look around, that's all. I'm not sure I'm coming back.

CORIE   I wish you could have come an hour later. After the furniture arrived.

MOTHER   (*Gets up, looks, and stops cold*)   Don't worry. I've got a marvelous imagination.

CORIE   Well . . . ?

MOTHER   (*Stunned*)   Oh, Corie . . . it's . . . beautiful.

CORIE   You hate it . . .

MOTHER   (*Moves toward windows*)   No, no . . . It's a charming apartment. (*She trips over the platform*) I love it.

CORIE   (*Rushes to her*)   You can't really tell like this.

MOTHER   I'm crazy about it.

CORIE   It's not your kind of apartment. I knew you wouldn't like it.

MOTHER   (*Moves down to* PAUL)   I love it . . . Paul, didn't I say I loved it?
       (*She takes his hand*)

PAUL   She said she loved it.

MOTHER   I knew I said it.

CORIE (*To* MOTHER)   Do you really, Mother? I mean are you absolutely crazy in love with it?

MOTHER   Oh, yes. It's very cute . . . And there's so much you can do with it.

CORIE   I told you she hated it.

MOTHER (*Moves toward the bedroom landing*)   Corie, you don't give a person a chance. At least let me see the whole apartment.

PAUL   This *is* the whole apartment.

MOTHER (*Cheerfully*)   It's a nice, large room.

CORIE   There's a bedroom.

MOTHER   Where?

PAUL   One flight up.

CORIE   It's four little steps. (*She goes up the steps to the bedroom door*) See. One-two-three-four.

MOTHER (*To* PAUL)   Oh. Split-level. (*She climbs the steps*) And where's the bedroom? Through there?

CORIE   No. *In* there. That's the bedroom . . . It's really just a dressing room but I'm going to use it as a bedroom.

MOTHER (*At the bedroom door*)   That's a wonderful idea. And you can just put a bed in there.

CORIE   That's right.

MOTHER   How?
    (PAUL *moves to the steps*)

CORIE   It'll fit. I measured the room.

MOTHER   A double bed?

CORIE   No, an oversized single.

MOTHER   Oh, they're nice. And where will Paul sleep?

CORIE   With me.

PAUL (*Moves up on the landing*)   In an oversized single?

MOTHER   I'm sure you'll be comfortable.

CORIE   I'm positive.
(PAUL *moves back down the stairs and glumly surveys the room*)

MOTHER   It's a wonderful idea. Very clever . . .

CORIE   Thank you.

MOTHER   Except you can't get to the closet.

CORIE   Yes you can.

MOTHER   Without climbing over the bed?

CORIE   No, you *have* to climb over the bed.

MOTHER   That's a good idea.

CORIE (*Leaves the bedroom, crosses to the ladder, and climbs up*)   Everything's just temporary. As they say in *McCall's*, it won't really take shape until the bride's own personality becomes more clearly defined.

MOTHER   I think it's *you* right now. (*She turns to the other door*) What's in here? . . . (*She opens the door and looks in*) The bathroom . . . (*She closes the door*) No bathtub . . . You really have quite a lot here, for one room. (*She moves down the steps*) And where's the kitchen? (*She sees the stove and refrigerator, stops in horror, and then crosses toward the kitchen*) Whoo, there it is . . . Very cozy. I suppose you'll eat out a lot the first year.

CORIE We're never eating out. It's big enough to make spaghetti and things.

MOTHER What "things"?

CORIE It's a dish I make called "Things." Honestly, Mother, we won't starve.

MOTHER I know, dear. (*Under the skylight*) It's chilly in here. Do you feel a draft?

PAUL (*Looks up*) Uh, stand over here, Mom.
(*He moves her away from the hole to near the steam pipe next to the railing*)

CORIE What you need is a drink. Paul, why don't you run down and get some Scotch?

PAUL Now?

MOTHER (*Crossing toward the Franklin stove*) Oh, not for me. I'm leaving in a few minutes.

PAUL Oh. She's leaving in a few minutes.

CORIE She can stay for one drink.
(PAUL *quietly argues with* CORIE *at the ladder*)

MOTHER There's so much you can do in here. Lots of wall space. What color are you going to paint it?

CORIE It's painted.

MOTHER Very attractive.

PAUL (*Looks at his watch*) Wow. Nearly six.

MOTHER I've got to go.

CORIE Not until you have a drink . . . (*To* PAUL) Will you get the Scotch?
(*He continues to argue with her*)

MOTHER   All right. I'll stay for just one drink.

PAUL   Good. I'll get the Scotch.
(*He starts for the door*)

MOTHER   Button up, dear. It's cold.

PAUL   I've noticed that.

CORIE   And get some cheese.
(PAUL *is gone*)

MOTHER   Paul! (PAUL *reappears at the door, and* MOTHER
extends her arms) I just want to give my fella a kiss. And
wish him luck. (PAUL *comes back in and crosses all the
way over to* MOTHER. *She kisses him*) Your new home is
absolutely beautiful. It's a perfect little apartment.

PAUL   Oh . . . thanks, Mom.

MOTHER   Then you *do* like it?

PAUL   Like it? (*He looks at* CORIE *and starts to exit*)
Where else can you find anything like this . . . for
seventy-five sixty-three a month?
(*He exits, leaving* CORIE *and* MOTHER *alone.* CORIE
*climbs down the ladder, and looks for some sign of
approval from* MOTHER)

CORIE   Well?

MOTHER   Oh, Corie, I'm so excited for you.
(*They embrace*)

CORIE   It's not exactly what you pictured, is it, Mother?

MOTHER   Well, it is *unusual*—like you. (*She crosses right*)
I remember when you were a little girl you said you
wanted to live on the moon. (*She turns back to* CORIE)
I thought you were joking . . . What about Paul? Is he
happy with all this?

CORIE   He's happy with me. I think it's the same thing.
Why?

MOTHER   I worry about you two. You're so impulsive. You jump into life. Paul is like me. He looks first.
  (*She sits down on the suitcase*)

CORIE   He doesn't look. He stares. That's the trouble with both of you . . . (*She places a paint can next to* MOTHER *and sits on it*) Oh, Mother, you don't know how I dreaded your coming up here. I was sure you'd think I was completely out of my mind.

MOTHER   Why should you think that, dear?

CORIE   Well, it's the first thing I've ever done on my own. Without your help . . .

MOTHER   If you wanted it, I'm sure you would have asked for it . . . but you didn't. And I understand.

CORIE   I hope you do, Mother. It's something I just had to do all by myself.

MOTHER   Corie, you mustn't think I'm hurt. I'm not hurt.

CORIE   I'm so glad.

MOTHER   You mustn't think I'm hurt. I don't get hurt over things like that.

CORIE   I didn't think you would.

MOTHER   *Other* things hurt me, but not that . . .

CORIE   Good . . . Hey, let's open my presents and see what I've got. And you try to act surprised.
  (*She gets the presents and brings them to the paint can*)

MOTHER   You won't let me buy you anything . . . Oh, they're just a few little things.

CORIE   (*Sitting down and shaking the smallest box vigorously*)   What's in here? It sounds expensive.

MOTHER   Well, *now* I think it's a broken clock.

CORIE (*Opens the box, and throws wrappings and tissue paper on the floor*) I'll bet you cleaned out Saks' gift department. I think I'm a regular stop on the delivery route now.

(*She looks at the clock, replaces it in the box and puts it aside, and begins to open the largest box*)

MOTHER Aunt Harriet was with me when I picked it out. (*She laughs*) She thinks I'm over here every day now.

CORIE You know you're welcome, Mother.

MOTHER I said, "Why, Harriet? Just because I'm alone now," I said. "I'm not afraid to live alone. In some ways it's better to live alone," I said. (CORIE *examines the blanket she finds in the package; then she closes the box, puts it aside, and begins to open the final package.* MOTHER *picks up a piece of tissue paper and smoothes it out on her lap*) But, you can't tell her that. She thinks a woman living alone, way out in New Jersey, is the worst thing in the world . . . "It's not," I told her. "It's not the *worst* thing" . . .

CORIE (*She has opened the package and now takes out the dismantled parts of a coffee pot*) Hey, does this come with directions?

MOTHER If I knew about this kitchen, it would have come with hot coffee.

(*She laughs*)

CORIE (*Picks up the box with the clock and takes it with the parts of the coffee pot up into the kitchen*) Mother, you're an absolute angel. But you've got to stop buying things for me. It's getting embarrassing. (*She puts the clock on the refrigerator and the coffee pot on the sink*) If you keep it up I'm going to open a discount house . . .

(*She takes the blanket and places it with the suitcase near the windows*)

MOTHER It's my pleasure, Corie. (*She begins to gather up wrappings and tissue paper and place them in the box which contained the coffee pot*) It's a mother's greatest joy to be able to buy gifts for her daughter when she gets married. You'll see someday. I just hope your child doesn't deprive *you* of that pleasure.

CORIE I'm not depriving you, Mother.

MOTHER I didn't say you were.

CORIE (*Moves down to* MOTHER) Yes, you did.

MOTHER Then why are you?

CORIE Because I think you should spend the money on yourself, that's why.

MOTHER Myself? What does a woman like me need? Living all alone . . . Way out in New Jersey.
  (*She picks up the box with wrappings in it and places it outside the front door*)

CORIE (*Follows* MOTHER) It's only been six days. And you're five minutes from the city.

MOTHER Who can get through that traffic in five minutes?

CORIE Then why don't you move into New York?

MOTHER Where . . . ? Where would I live?

CORIE Mother, I don't care where you live. The point is, you've got to start living for yourself now . . . (MOTHER *moves back into the room*) Mother, the whole world has just opened up to you. Why don't you travel? You've got the time, the luggage. All you need are the shots.

MOTHER (*Sits on the suitcase*) Travel! . . . You think it's so easy for a woman of my age to travel alone?

CORIE You'll meet people.

MOTHER I read a story in the *Times*. A middle-aged woman traveling alone fell off the deck of a ship. They never discovered it until they got to France.

CORIE (*Moves left and turns back to* MOTHER) I promise
you, Mother, if *you* fell off a ship, *someone* would know
about it.

MOTHER I thought I might get myself a job.

CORIE (*Straws in the wind*) Hey, that's a great idea.
(*She sits on the paint can*)

MOTHER (*Shrugs, defeated*) What would I do?

CORIE I don't know what you would do. What would you
like to do?

MOTHER (*Considers*) I'd like to be a grandmother. I think
that would be nice.

CORIE A grandmother??? . . . What's your rush? You
know, underneath that Army uniform, you're still a
young, vital woman . . . Do you know what I think you
really need?

MOTHER Yes, and I don't want to hear it.
(*She gets up and moves away*)

CORIE (*Goes to her*) Because you're afraid to hear the
truth.

MOTHER It's not the truth I'm afraid to hear. It's the *word*
you're going to use.

CORIE You're darn right I'm going to use that word . . .
It's love!

MOTHER Oh . . . Thank you.

CORIE A week ago I didn't know what it meant. And then
I checked into the Plaza Hotel. For six wonderful days
. . . And do you know what happened to me there?

MOTHER I promised myself I wouldn't ask.

CORIE I found *love* . . . spiritual, emotional, and physical
love. And I don't think anyone on earth should be without it.

MOTHER I'm not. I have you.

CORIE I don't mean *that* kind of love. (*She moves to the ladder and leans against it*) I'm talking about late at night in . . .

MOTHER (*Quickly*) I *know* what you're talking about.

CORIE Don't you even want to discuss it?

MOTHER Not with *you* in the room.

CORIE Well, what are you going to do about it?

MOTHER I'm going back to New Jersey and give myself a Toni Home Permanent. Corie, sweetheart, I appreciate your concern, but I'm very happy the way I am.

CORIE I'll be the judge of who's happy.
(*They embrace. The door flies open and* PAUL *staggers in with the bottle of Scotch. He closes the door behind him and wearily leans his head against it, utterly exhausted*)

MOTHER Oh, Paul, you shouldn't have run . . . Just for me. (*The doorbell buzzes,* AUNT HARRIET's *special buzz*) . . . Ooh, and there's Harriet. I've got to go.
(*She picks up her purse from next to the suitcase*)

CORIE Some visit.

MOTHER Just a sneak preview. I'll see you on Friday for the World Première . . . (*To* PAUL) Good-bye, Paul . . . I'm so sorry . . . (*To* CORIE) Good-bye, love . . . I'll see you on Friday . . . (PAUL *opens the door for her*) Thank you . . . (*She glances out at the stairs*) Geronimo . . . !
(*She exits.* PAUL *shuts the door and, breathing hard, puts the bottle down at the foot of the ladder. He moves left, turns, and glares at* CORIE)

CORIE What is it? . . . The stairs? (PAUL *shakes his head "No"*) The hole? (PAUL *shakes his head "No"*) The bathtub? (PAUL *shakes his head "No"*) Something new? (PAUL *nods his head "Yes"*) Well, what? . . .

PAUL (*Leaning against the left wall*) Guess!

CORIE Paul, I can't guess. Tell me.

PAUL Oh, come on, Corie. Take a wild stab at it. Try something like, "All the neighbors are crazy."

CORIE *Are* all the neighbors crazy?

PAUL (*A pitchman's revelation*) I just had an interesting talk with the man down in the liquor store . . . Do you know we have some of the greatest weirdos in the country living right here, in this house?

CORIE Really? Like who?
         (*She puts the bottle on the kitchen platform*)

PAUL (*Gathering his strength, he paces to the right*) Well, like to start with, in apartment One-C are the Boscos . . . Mr. and Mrs. J. Bosco.

CORIE (*Moving to the ladder*) Who are they?

PAUL (*Paces to the left*) Mr. and Mrs. J. Bosco are a lovely young couple who just happen to be of the same sex and no one knows which one that is . . . (*He moves up to left of the windows*) In apartment Three-C live Mr. and Mrs. Gonzales.

CORIE So?

PAUL (*Moves right above the ladder*) I'm not through. Mr. and Mrs. Gonzales, Mr. and Mrs. Armandariz, and Mr. Calhoun . . . (*He turns back to* CORIE) who must be the umpire. (*He moves left to left of the ladder, very secretively*) No one knows who lives in apartment Four-D. No one has come in or gone out in three years except every morning there are nine empty cans of tuna fish outside the door . . .

CORIE No kidding? Who do you think lives there?

PAUL Well, it sounds like a big cat with a can opener

. . . (*He gets his attaché case from the corner, and turns to* CORIE) Now there *are* one or two normal couples in the building, but at this rent *we're* not one of them.

CORIE   Well, you've got to pay for all this color and charm.

PAUL   Well, if you figure it that way, we're getting a bargain . . . (*He starts to go up the stairs, then turns back*) Oh, yes. I forgot. Mr. Velasco. Victor Velasco. He lives in apartment Six-A.

CORIE   Where's Six-A? (PAUL *points straight up*) On the roof?

PAUL   Attic . . . It's an attic. (*He crosses up onto the bedroom landing*) He also skis and climbs mountains. He's fifty-eight years old and he's known as "The Bluebeard of Forty-eighth Street."

CORIE (*Moves to the stairs*)   What does that mean?

PAUL (*Turns back to* CORIE)   Well, it either means that he's a practicing girl-attacker or else he's an old man with a blue beard. (*He moves to the bedroom*) I'll say this, Corie. It's not going to be a dull two years.

CORIE   Where are you going?

PAUL (*Turns back at the bedroom door*)   I'm going to stand in the bedroom and work. I've got to pay for all this color and charm. If anything comes up, like the furniture or the heat, let me know. Just let me know. (*Bows off into the bedroom and slams the door*)

CORIE (*After a moment of thought, she begins to fold up the ladder and put it against the left wall*)   Can't I come in and watch you? . . . Hey, Paul, I'm lonesome . . . (*There is a knock at the door*) . . . and scared! (*As* CORIE *puts the ladder against the wall,* VICTOR VELASCO, *fifty-eight and not breathing very hard, opens the door and enters. It's not that he is in such good shape. He just doesn't think about getting tired. There are too many other things to do in the world. He wears no topcoat. Just a sport jacket, an ascot, and a Tyrolean hat.* CORIE *turns and is startled to find him in the room)*

VELASCO   I beg your pardon. (*He sweeps off his hat*) I hope I'm not disturbing you. I don't usually do this sort of thing but I find myself in a rather embarrassing position and I could use your help. (*He discreetly catches his breath*) My name is Velasco . . . Victor Velasco.

CORIE   (*Nervously*)   Oh, yes . . . You live in the attic.

VELASCO   Yes. That's right . . . Have we met?

CORIE   (*Very nervously*)   No, not yet.

VELASCO   Oh. Well, you see, I want to use your bedroom.

CORIE   My bedroom?

VELASCO   Yes. You see, I can't get into my apartment and I wanted to use your window. I'll just crawl out along the ledge.

CORIE   Oh, did you lose your key?

VELASCO   No. I have my key. I lost my money. I'm four months behind in the rent.

CORIE   Oh! . . . Gee, that's too bad. I mean it's right in the middle of winter . . .

VELASCO   You'll learn, as time goes by in this middle-income prison camp, that we have a rat fink for a landlord . . . (*He looks about the room*) You don't have any hot coffee, do you? I'd be glad to pay you for it.

CORIE   No. We just moved in.

VELASCO   Really? (*He looks about the barren room*) What are you, a folksinger?

CORIE   No. A wife . . . They didn't deliver our furniture yet.

VELASCO (*Moves toward* CORIE) You know, of course, that you're unbearably pretty. What's your name?

CORIE Corie . . . *Mrs.* Corie Bratter.

VELASCO (*Takes it in stride*) You're still unbearably pretty. I may fall in love with you by seven o'clock. (*Catching sight of the hole in the skylight*) I see the rat fink left the hole in the skylight.

CORIE Yes, I just noticed that. (*She crosses right, and looks up at the hole*) But he'll fix it, won't he?

VELASCO I wouldn't count on it. My bathtub's been running since 1949 . . . (*He moves toward* CORIE) Does your husband work during the day?

CORIE Yes . . . Why? . . .

VELASCO It's just that I'm home during the day, and I like to find out what my odds are . . . (*He scrutinizes* CORIE) Am I making you nervous?

CORIE (*Moving away*) Very nervous.

VELASCO (*Highly pleased*) Good. Once a month, I try to make pretty young girls nervous just to keep my ego from going out. But, I'll save you a lot of anguish . . . I'm fifty-six years old and a thoroughly nice fellow.

CORIE Except I heard you were fifty-eight years old. And if you're knocking off two years, I'm nervous all over again.

VELASCO Not only pretty but bright. (*He sits down on the paint can*) I wish I were ten years older.

CORIE Older?

VELASCO Yes. Dirty old men seem to get away with a lot more. I'm still at the awkward stage . . . How long are you married?

CORIE Six days . . .

VELASCO In love? . . .

CORIE Very much . . .

VELASCO Damn . . .

CORIE What's wrong?

VELASCO Under my present state of financial duress, I was hoping to be invited down soon for a free meal. But, with newlyweds I could starve to death.

CORIE Oh. Well, we'd love to have you for dinner, as soon as we get set up.

VELASCO (*Gets up, and stepping over the suitcase, moves to* CORIE) I hate generalizations. When?

CORIE When? . . . Well, Friday? Is that all right?

VELASCO Perfect. I'll be famished. I hadn't planned on eating Thursday.

CORIE Oh, no . . . wait! On Friday night my mo— (*She thinks it over*) Yeah. Friday night will be fine.

VELASCO It's a date. I'll bring the wine. You can pay me for it when I get here . . . (*He moves to the stairs*) Which reminds me. You're invited to my cocktail party tonight. Ten o'clock . . . You do drink, don't you?

CORIE Yes, of course.

VELASCO Good. Bring liquor. (*He crosses to* CORIE *and takes her hand*) I'll see you tonight at ten.

CORIE (*Shivering*) If I don't freeze to death first.

VELASCO Oh, you don't know about the plumbing, do you? Everything in this museum works backward. (*Crosses to the radiator on the wall*) For instance, there's a little knob up there that says, "Important—Turn right" . . . So you turn left.
(*He tries to reach it but can't*)

CORIE   Oh, can you give me a little boost? . . .

VELASCO   With the greatest of physical pleasure. One, two, three . . . up . . . (*He puts his arms around her, and lifts her to the radiator*) Okay? . . .

CORIE (*Attempting to turn the knob*)   I can't quite reach . . .

PAUL (*Comes out of the bedroom with an affidavit in his hand and his coat up over his head. He crosses to the head of the stairs*)   Hey, Corie, when are they going to get here with—
(*He stops as he sees* CORIE *in* VELASCO'S *arms.* VELASCO *looks at him, stunned, while* CORIE *remains motionless in the air*)

VELASCO (*Puts* CORIE *down*)   I thought you said he works during the day.

CORIE   Oh, Paul! This is Mr. Velasco. He was just showing me how to work the radiator.

VELASCO (*Extending his hand*)   Victor Velasco! I'm your upstairs neighbor. I'm fifty-eight years old and a thoroughly nice fellow.

PAUL (*Lowers his coat, and shakes hands weakly*)   Hello . . .

CORIE   Mr. Velasco was just telling me that all the plumbing works backwards.

VELASCO   That's right. An important thing to remember is, you have to flush "up." (*He demonstrates*) With that choice bit of information, I'll make my departure. (*He crosses up onto the bedroom landing*) Don't forget. Tonight at ten.

PAUL (*Looks at* CORIE)   What's tonight at ten?

CORIE (*Moves to the bottom of the stairs*)   Oh, thanks, but I don't think so. We're expecting our furniture any minute . . . Maybe some other time.

PAUL   What's tonight at ten?

VELASCO   I'll arrange it all for you in the morning. I'm also a brilliant decorator. (*He pats* PAUL *on the shoulder*) I insist you come.

CORIE   Well, it's really very nice of you.

VELASCO (*Crossing to the bedroom door*)   I told you. I'm a very nice person. *À ce soir* . . .
(*He exits into the bedroom*)

PAUL (*To* CORIE)   What's tonight at ten? . . . (*He suddenly realizes*) Where's he going? . . .
(*He crosses to the bedroom*)

CORIE (*Yelling after* VELASCO)   Don't forget Friday . . .

PAUL (*To* CORIE)   What's he doing in the bedroom? . . . What about Friday?
(*He goes into the bedroom*)

CORIE (*Rushes to the phone and dials*)   He's coming to dinner. (*Into the phone*) Hello, Operator?

PAUL (*Comes out of the bedroom*)   That nut went out the window.
(*He looks back into the bedroom*)

CORIE   I'm calling West Orange, New Jersey.

PAUL (*Crosses down the stairs to* CORIE)   Corie, did you hear what I said? There's an old nut out on our ledge.

CORIE (*Into the phone*)   Two, oh, one, seven, six, five, three, four, two, two.

PAUL   Who are you calling?

CORIE   My mother. On Friday night, she's going to have dinner with that old nut. (VELASCO *appears on the skylight, and carefully makes his way across.* CORIE *speaks*

into the phone) Hello, Jessie . . . Will you please tell
my mother to call me just as soon as she gets in!
  (PAUL *turns and sees* VELASCO. VELASCO *cheerfully waves and continues on his way*)

Curtain

Act Two

Scene One

Four days later. Seven o'clock, Friday evening.

The apartment is no longer an empty room. It is now a home. It is almost completely furnished, and the room, although a potpourri of various periods, styles, and prices, is extremely tasteful and comfortable. No ultramodern, clinical interior for CORIE. Each piece was selected with loving care. Since CORIE's greatest aim in life is to spend as much time as possible alone with PAUL, she has designed the room to suit this purpose. A wrought-iron sofa stands in the middle of the room, upholstered in a bright striped fabric. It is flanked by two old-fashioned, unmatched armchairs, one with a romantically carved wooden back; the other, a bentwood chair with a black leather seat. A low, dark, wooden coffee table with carved legs is in front of the sofa, and to the right is a small, round bentwood end table, covered with green felt. Under the windows, a light-wood, Spanish-looking table serves as a desk, and in front of it is a bamboo, straight-backed chair. A large wicker basket functions as the wastebasket. A dark side table with lyre-shaped legs fills the wall under the radiator, and below the bedroom landing an open cane side table serves as a bar and telephone stand. To the right of the windows stands a breakfront with shelves above and drawers below. The kitchen area is now partially hidden by a four-fold bamboo screen that has been backed by fabric, and potted plants have been placed in front of the screen. Straight-backed bentwood chairs stand downstage right and left. The closet has been covered by a drapery, the small windows by café curtains, and the skylight by a large, striped Austrian curtain. Books now fill the bookcase left of the kitchen, pictures and decorations have been tastefully arranged on the walls, and lamps placed about the room. The bedroom landing is graced with a bentwood washstand complete with pitcher and basin which is filled with a

*plant. In the bathroom a shower curtain and towels have
been hung, and the bedroom boasts a bed.*

AT RISE: *There is no one on stage. The apartment is
dark except for a crack of light under the bedroom door,
and faint moonlight from the skylight. Suddenly the front
door opens and* CORIE *rushes in, carrying a pastry box and
a bag containing two bottles. After switching on the lights
at the door, she puts her packages on the coffee table, and
hangs her coat in the closet.* CORIE *wears a cocktail dress
for the festivities planned for tonight, and she sings as she
hurries to get everything ready. She is breathing heavily
but she is getting accustomed to the stairs. As she takes a
bottle of vermouth and a bottle of gin out of the bag, the
doorbell buzzes. She buzzes back, opens the door, and yells
down the stairs.*

CORIE (*Yells*) Paul? (*We hear some strange, incoherent
sound from below*) Hi, love . . . (*She crosses back to
the coffee table, and dumps hors d'oeuvres from the
pastry box onto a tray*) Hey, they sent the wrong lamps
. . . but they go with the room so I'm keeping them.
(*She crosses to the bar, gets a martini pitcher and brings
it back to the coffee table.*) . . . Oh, do you have an Aunt
Fern? . . . Because she sent us a check . . . Anyway,
you have a cheap Aunt Fern . . . How you doing? (*We
hear a mumble from below.* CORIE *opens both bottles
and pours them simultaneously into the shaker so that
she has martinis made with equal parts of gin and vermouth*) . . . Oh, and your mother called from Philly
. . . She and Dad will be up a week from Sunday . . .
And your sister has a new boy friend. From Rutgers
. . . He's got acne and they all hate him . . . including
your sister. (*She takes the shaker and while mixing the
cocktails she crosses to the door*) . . . Hey, lover, start
puckering your lips 'cause you're gonna get kissed for
five solid minutes and then . . . (*She stops*) Oh, hello,
Mr. Munshin. I thought it was my husband. Sorry. (*A
door slams. She shrugs sheepishly and walks back into
the room, closing the door behind her. As she goes up
into the kitchen, the door opens and* PAUL *enters, gasping. He drops his attaché case at the railing, and collapses on the couch.* CORIE *comes out of the kitchen with*

the shaker and ice bucket) It was you. I thought I heard your voice.

(*She puts the ice bucket on the bookcase and the shaker on the end table*)

PAUL (*Gasp, gasp*) Mr. Munshin and I came in together. (CORIE *jumps on him and flings her arms around his neck; he winces in pain*) Do you have to carry on— a whole personal conversation with me—on the stairs?

CORIE Well, there's so much I wanted to tell you . . . and I haven't seen you all day . . . and it takes you so long to get up.

PAUL Everyone knows the intimate details of our life . . . I ring the bell and suddenly we're on the air.

CORIE Tomorrow I'll yell, "Come on up, Harry, my husband isn't home." (*She takes the empty box and bag, and throws them in the garbage pail in the kitchen*) Hey, wouldn't that be a gas if everyone in the building thought I was having an affair with someone?

PAUL Mr. Munshin thinks it's *him* right now.

CORIE (*Crossing back to the couch*) Well?

PAUL Well what?

CORIE What happened in court today? Gump or Birnbaum?

PAUL Birnbaum!

CORIE (*Jumps on his lap again. He winces again*) Oh, Paul, you won. You won, darling. Oh, sweetheart, I'm so proud of you. (*She stops and looks at him*) Well, aren't you happy?

PAUL (*Glumly*) Birnbaum won the protection of his good name but no damages. We were awarded six cents.

CORIE Six cents?

PAUL   That's the law. You have to be awarded something, so the court made it six cents.

CORIE   How much of that do you get?

PAUL   Nothing. Birnbaum gets the whole six cents . . . And I get a going-over in the office. From now on I get all the cases that come in for a dime or under.

CORIE *(Opening his collar and rubbing his neck)* Oh, darling, you won. That's all that counts. You're a good lawyer.

PAUL   Some lawyer . . . So tomorrow I go back to sharpening pencils.

CORIE   And tonight you're here with me. *(She kisses his neck)* Did you miss me today?

PAUL   No.

CORIE *(Gets off his lap and sits on the couch)* Why not?

PAUL   Because you called me eight times . . . I don't speak to you that much when I'm home.

CORIE *(Rearranging the canapés)* Oh, you're grouchy. I want a divorce.

PAUL   I'm not grouchy . . . I'm tired . . . I had a rotten day today . . . I'm a little irritable . . . and cold . . . and grouchy.

CORIE   Okay, grouch. I'll fix you a drink. *(She crosses to the bar and brings back three glasses)*

PAUL *(Crosses to the closet, takes off his overcoat and jacket, and hangs them up)* I just couldn't think today. Couldn't think . . . Moving furniture until three o'clock in the morning.

CORIE   Mr. Velasco moved. You complained.
(She pours a drink)

PAUL   Mr. Velasco *pointed! I* moved! . . . He came in here, drank my liquor, made three telephone calls, and ordered me around like I was one of the Santini Brothers.

(*He takes the drink from* CORIE, *and crosses to the dictionary on the table under the radiator. He takes a gulp of his drink and reacts with horror. He looks at* CORIE, *who shrugs in reply*)

CORIE   Temper, temper. We're supposed to be charming tonight.

PAUL   (*Taking off his tie*)   Yeah, well, I've got news for you. This thing tonight has "fiasco" written all over it.

CORIE   (*Moves to the mirror on the washstand on the bedroom landing*)   Why should it be a fiasco? It's just conceivable they may have something in common.

PAUL   (*Folding his tie*)   Your mother? That quiet, dainty little woman . . . and the Count of Monte Cristo? You must be kidding.
(*He puts the tie between the pages of the dictionary, and slams it shut*)

CORIE   Why?
(*She puts on a necklace and earrings*)

PAUL   (*Crosses to the closet and gets another tie*)   You saw his apartment. He wears Japanese kimonos and sleeps on rugs. Your mother wears a hairnet and sleeps on a board.

CORIE   What's that got to do with it?

PAUL   (*Crossing back to the mirror under the radiator and fixing his tie*)   Everything. He skis, climbs mountains, and the only way into his apartment is up a ladder or across a ledge. I don't really think he's looking for a good cook with a bad back.

CORIE   The possibility of anything permanent never even occurred to me.

PAUL Permanent? We're lucky if we get past seven o'clock . . .

    (The doorbell buzzes and PAUL *crosses to the door)*

CORIE That's her. Now you've got me worried . . . Paul, did I do something horrible?

PAUL *(Buzzing downstairs)* Probably.

CORIE Well, do something. Don't answer the door. Maybe she'll go home.

PAUL Too late. I buzzed. I could put a few Nembutals in his drink. It won't stop him but it could slow him down. *(He opens the door and yells downstairs)* Mom?

MOTHER'S VOICE *(From far below)* Yes, dear . . .

PAUL *(Yelling through his hands)* Take your time. *(He turns back into the room)* She's at Camp Three. She'll try the final assault in a few minutes.

CORIE Paul, maybe we could help her.

    (She comes down the stairs)

PAUL *(Getting his blazer out of the closet)* What do you mean?

CORIE *(Behind the couch)* A woman puts on rouge and powder to make her face more attractive. Maybe we can put some make-up on her personality.

PAUL *(Puts his attaché case on the bookcase)* I don't think I want to hear the rest of this.

CORIE All I'm saying is, we don't have to come right out and introduce her as "my dull fifty-year-old housewife mother."

PAUL *(Crosses to the bar and pours a drink of Scotch)* Well, that wasn't the wording I had planned. What did you have in mind?

CORIE *(Moves around the couch and sits on the right side of the couch)* Something a little more glamorous . . . A former actress.

PAUL Corie—

CORIE Well, she *was* in *The Man Who Came to Dinner.*

PAUL Your mother? In *The Man Who Came to Dinner?* . . . Where, in the West Orange P. T. A. show? *(He moves to the couch)*

CORIE No! . . . On Broadway . . . And she was in the original company of *Strange Interlude* and she had a small singing part in *Knickerbocker Holiday.*

PAUL Are you serious?

CORIE Honestly. Cross my heart.

PAUL Your mother? An actress? *(He sits next to CORIE)*

CORIE Yes.

PAUL Why didn't you ever tell me?

CORIE I didn't think you'd be interested.

PAUL That's fascinating. I can't get over it.

CORIE You see. *Now* you're interested in her.

PAUL It's a lie?

CORIE The whole thing.

PAUL I'm going to control myself. *(He gets up and crosses back of the couch)*

CORIE *(Gets up and crosses to him at right of the couch)* What do you say? Is she an actress?

PAUL No.
(*He moves toward the door*)

CORIE A fashion designer. The brains behind Ann Fogarty.

PAUL (*Points to the door*) She's on her way up.

CORIE A mystery writer . . . under an assumed name.

PAUL Let's lend her my trench coat and say she's a private eye.

CORIE You're no help.

PAUL I didn't book this act.

CORIE (*Moves to* PAUL) Paul, who is she going to be?

PAUL She's going to be your mother . . . and the evening will eventually pass . . . It just means . . . that the Birdman of Forty-eighth Street, is not going to be your father. (*He opens the door*) Hello, Mom.
(MOTHER *collapses in and* PAUL *and* CORIE *rush to support her. They quickly lead her to the armchair at right of the couch*)

CORIE Hello, sweetheart, how are you? (*She kisses* MOTHER, *who gasps for air*) Are you all right? (MOTHER *nods*) You want some water?
(MOTHER *shakes her head "No" as* PAUL *and* CORIE *lower her into the chair. She drops her pocketbook on the floor*)

MOTHER Paul . . . in my pocketbook . . . are some pink pills.

PAUL (*Picks up her bag, closes the door, and begins to look for the pills*) Pink pills . . .
(CORIE *helps* MOTHER *take off her coat*)

MOTHER I'll be all right . . . Just a little out of breath . . .

(CORIE *crosses to the coffee table and pours a drink*)
I had to park the car six blocks away . . . then it started
to rain so I ran the last two blocks . . . then my heel got
caught in the subway grating . . . so I pulled my foot
out and stepped in a puddle . . . then a cab went by
and splashed my stockings . . . if the hardware store
downstairs was open . . . I was going to buy a knife and
kill myself.
      (PAUL *gives her a pill, and* CORIE *gives her a drink*)

CORIE Here, Mom. Drink this down.

PAUL Here's the pill . . .
      (MOTHER *takes the pill, drinks, and coughs*)

MOTHER A martini? To wash down a pill?

CORIE It'll make you feel better.

MOTHER I *had* a martini at home. It made me sick . . .
That's why I'm taking the pill . . .
      (CORIE *puts the drink down on the table*)

PAUL (*Sitting on the end table*) You must be exhausted.

MOTHER I'd just like to crawl into bed and cry myself to
sleep.

CORIE (*Offering her the tray of hors d'oeuvres*) Here,
Mom, have an hors d'oeuvre.

MOTHER No, thank you, dear.

CORIE It's just blue cheese and sour cream.

MOTHER (*Holds her stomach*) I wish you hadn't said that.

PAUL She doesn't feel like it, Corie . . . (CORIE *puts the
tray down and sits on the couch.* PAUL *turns to*
MOTHER) Maybe you'd like to lie down?

CORIE (*Panicky*) Now? She can't lie down now.

MOTHER Corie's right. I can't lie down without my board

... (*She puts her gloves into a pocket of her coat*) Right now all I want to do is see the apartment.

PAUL (*Sitting on the couch*) That's right. You haven't seen it with its clothes on, have you?

MOTHER (*Rises and moves to the left*) Oh, Corie ... Corie ...

CORIE She doesn't like it.

MOTHER (*Exhausted, she sinks into the armchair at left of the couch*) Like it? It's magnificent ... and in less than a week. My goodness, how did you manage? Where did you get your ideas from?

PAUL We have a decorator who comes in through the window once a week.

CORIE (*Crossing to the bedroom*) Come take a look at the bedroom.

MOTHER (*Crossing to the bedroom*) Yes, that's what I want to do ... look at the bedroom. Were you able to get the bed in? (*She looks into the room*) Oh, it just fits, doesn't it?

PAUL (*Moves to the stairs*) Just. We have to turn in unison.

MOTHER It looks very snug ... and did you find a way to get to the closet?

CORIE Oh, we decided not to use the closet for a while.

MOTHER Really? Don't you need the space?

PAUL Not as much as we need the clothes. It flooded.

MOTHER The closet flooded?

CORIE It was an accident. Mr. Velasco left his bathtub running.

MOTHER (*Moving down the stairs*) Mr. Velasco . . . Oh, the man upstairs . . .

PAUL (*Taking her arm*) Oh, then you know about Mr. Velasco?

MOTHER Oh, yes. Corie had me on the phone for two hours.

PAUL Did you know he's been married three times?

MOTHER Yes . . . (*She turns back to* CORIE) If I were you, dear, I'd sleep with a gun. (*She sits in the bentwood armchair*)

PAUL Well, there's just one thing I want to say about this evening . . .

CORIE (*Quickly, as she crosses to the coffee table*) Er . . . not before you have a drink. (*She hands* MOTHER *the martini*) Come on, Mother. To toast our new home.

MOTHER (*Holding the glass*) Well, I can't refuse that.

CORIE (*Making a toast*) To the wonderful new life that's ahead of us all.

PAUL (*Holds up his glass*) And to the best sport I've ever seen. Your mother.

MOTHER (*Making a toast*) And to two very charming people . . . that I'm so glad to be seeing again tonight . . . your mother and father.
        (CORIE *sinks down on the sofa*)

PAUL (*About to drink, stops*) My what?

MOTHER Your mother and father.

PAUL What about my mother and father?

MOTHER Well, we're having dinner with them tonight, aren't we? . . . (*To* CORIE) Corie, isn't that what you said?

PAUL (*Sits next to* CORIE *on the sofa*) Is that right, Corie? Is that what you said?

CORIE (*Looks helpless, then plunges in*) Well, if I told you it was a blind date with Mr. Velasco upstairs, I couldn't have blasted you out of the house.

MOTHER A blind date . . . (*She doesn't quite get it yet*) With Mr. Velasco . . . (*Then the dawn*) The one that . . . ? (*She points up, then panics*) Good God! (*She takes a big gulp of her martini*)

PAUL (*To* CORIE) You didn't even tell your mother?

CORIE I was going to tell her the truth.

PAUL (*Looks at his watch*) It's one minute to seven. That's cutting it pretty thin, isn't it?

MOTHER Corie, how could you do this to me? Of all the people in the world . . .

CORIE (*Gets up and moves to* MOTHER) I don't see what you're making such a fuss about. He's just a man.

MOTHER My *accountant's* just a man. You make him sound like Douglas Fairbanks, Junior.

CORIE He looks *nothing* like Douglas Fairbanks, Junior, . . . does he, Paul?

PAUL No . . . He just jumps like him.

MOTHER I'm not even dressed.

CORIE (*Brushing her* MOTHER's *clothes*) You look fine, Mother.

MOTHER For Paul's parents I just wanted to look clean . . . *He'll* think I'm a nurse.

CORIE Look, Mother, I promise you you'll have a good time tonight. He's a sweet, charming, and intelligent man. If you'll just relax I *know* you'll have a perfectly nice evening. (*There is a knock on the door*) Besides, it's too late. He's here.

MOTHER Oh, no . . .

CORIE All right, now don't get excited.

MOTHER (*Gets up and puts her drink on the coffee table*) You could say I'm the cleaning woman . . . I'll dust the table. Give me five dollars and I'll leave.
(*She starts up the stairs to the bedroom*)

CORIE (*Stops* MOTHER *on the stairs*) You just stay here . . .

PAUL (*Going to* MOTHER) It's going to be fine, Mom.
(*He crosses to the door*)

CORIE (*Leads* MOTHER *back to the sofa*) And smile. You're irresistible when you do. And finish your martini.
(*She takes it from the table and hands it to* MOTHER)

MOTHER Do you have a lot of these?

CORIE As many as you need.

MOTHER I'm going to need a lot of these.
(*She downs a good belt*)

PAUL Can I open the door?

CORIE Paul, wait a minute . . . Mother . . . your hair . . . in the back . . .

MOTHER (*Stricken, she begins to fuss with her hair*) What? What's the matter with my hair?

CORIE (*Fixing* MOTHER'*s hair*) It's all right now. I fixed it.

MOTHER (*Moves toward* PAUL) Is something wrong with my hair?

PAUL (*Impatient*) There's a man standing out there.

CORIE   Wait a minute, Paul . . . (PAUL *moves back into the room and leans against the back of the armchair.* CORIE *turns* MOTHER *to her*) Now, Mother . . . The only thing I'd like to suggest is . . . well . . . just try and go along with everything.

MOTHER   What do you mean? Where are we going?

CORIE   I don't know. But wherever it is . . . just relax . . . and be one of the fellows.

MOTHER   One of what fellows?

CORIE   I mean, don't worry about your stomach.
        (*There is another knock on the door*)

MOTHER   Oh, my stomach.
        (*She sinks down on the couch*)

PAUL   Can I open the door now? . . .

CORIE   (*Moving to the right of the couch*)   Okay, okay . . . open the door.
        (PAUL *nods gratefully, then opens the door.* VE-LASCO *stands there, looking quite natty in a double-breasted, pin-striped blue suit. He carries a small covered frying pan in a gloved hand*)

PAUL   Oh, sorry to keep you waiting, Mr. Velasco. Come on in . . .

VELASCO   (*Moving into the well, to* PAUL)   Ah! Ho si mah ling . . .

PAUL   No, no . . . It's Paul.

VELASCO   I know. I was just saying hello in Chinese . . .

PAUL   Oh . . . hello.

VELASCO   (*To* CORIE)   Corie, rava-shing . . .

CORIE   (*Enthralled*)   Oh . . . What does that mean?

VELASCO Ravishing. That's English.

CORIE (*Taken aback*) Oh . . . Ah, Paul . . . Would you do the honors?

PAUL Yes, of course. Mr. Velasco, I'd like you to meet Corie's mother, Mrs. Banks . . . (CORIE *steps back, unveiling* MOTHER *with a gesture*) Mother, this is our new neighbor, Mr. Velasco . . .

MOTHER How do you do?

VELASCO (*Sweeps to* MOTHER, *takes her hand, and bows ever so slightly*) Mrs. Banks . . . I've been looking forward so to meeting you. I invite your daughter to my cocktail party and she spends the entire evening talking of nothing but you.
   (CORIE *moves up to left of the couch, taking it all in with great pleasure*)

MOTHER Oh? . . . It must have been a dull party.

VELASCO Not in the least.

MOTHER I mean if she did nothing but talk about me . . . *That* must have been dull. Not the party.
   (PAUL *moves behind the couch to the coffee table and gets his drink*)

VELASCO I understand.

MOTHER Thank you . . .

CORIE (*To the rescue*) Oh, is that for us?

VELASCO Yes . . . I couldn't get the wine . . . my credit stopped . . . so instead . . . (*He puts the pan down on the end table and with a flourish lifts the cover*) . . . Knichi!

MOTHER Knichi?

CORIE   It's an hors d'oeuvre. Mr. Velasco makes them himself. He's a famous gourmet.

MOTHER   A gourmet . . . Imagine!

VELASCO   This won second prize last year at the Venice
Food Festival.

MOTHER   Second prize . . .

CORIE   Mr. Velasco once cooked for the King of Sweden,
Mother.

MOTHER   Really? Did you work for him?

VELASCO   No . . . We belong to the same club.

MOTHER   (*Embarrassed*)   The same club . . . Of course.

VELASCO   It's a Gourmet Society. There's a hundred and
fifty of us.

MOTHER   All gourmets . . .

VELASCO   That includes the King, Prince Phillip, and
Darryl Zanuck.

MOTHER   Darryl Zanuck, too.

VELASCO   We meet once every five years for a dinner that
we cook ourselves. In 1987 they're supposed to come to
my house. (*He looks at his watch*) We have another
thirty seconds . . .

PAUL   Until what?

VELASCO   Until they're edible. (*He takes the cover off the
pan, and puts it on the end table*) Now . . . the last
fifteen seconds we just let them sit there and breathe . . .

CORIE   (*Moves to the right*)   Gee, they look marvelous.

VELASCO   When you eat this, you take a bite into history. Knichi is over two thousand years old . . . Not this particular batch, of course.
(*He laughs, but* MOTHER *laughs too loud and too long*)

CORIE (*Again to the rescue*)   Wow, what a great smell . . . (*To* VELASCO) Mr. Velasco, would you be a traitor to the Society if you told us what's in it?

VELASCO (*Secretively*)   Well, if caught, it's punishable by a cold salad at the dinner . . . but since I'm among friends, it's bits of salted fish, grated olives, spices, and onion biscuits . . . (MOTHER *reacts unhappily to the list of ingredients.* VELASCO *looks at his watch once more*) Ah, ready . . . Five, four, three, two, one . . . (*He holds the pan out to* MOTHER) Mrs. Banks?

MOTHER (*Tentatively*)   Oh . . . thank you.
(*She takes one and raises it slowly to her mouth*)

CORIE   What kind of fish?

VELASCO   Eel!

PAUL   Eel?

MOTHER (*Crumples with distaste*)   Eel??
(*She doesn't eat it*)

VELASCO   That's why the time element is so essential. Eel spoils quickly. (MOTHER *crumples even more*) Mrs. Banks, you're not eating.

MOTHER   My throat's a little dry. Maybe if I finish my martini first . . .

VELASCO   No, no . . . That will never do. The temperature of the knichi is very important. It must be now. In five minutes we throw it away.

MOTHER   Oh! . . . Well, I wouldn't want you to do that.
(*She looks at the knichi, then starts to take a nibble*)

VELASCO Pop it!

MOTHER I beg your pardon?

VELASCO (*Puts down the pan and takes off his cooking glove*) If you nibble at knichi, it tastes bitter. You must pop it. (*He takes a knichi, tosses it from hand to hand three or four times and then pops it into his mouth*) You see.

MOTHER Oh, yes.
        (*She tosses a knichi from hand to hand a few times and then tries to pop it into her mouth. But she misses and it flies over her shoulder.* VELASCO *quickly offers her another. Although this time she succeeds in getting it into her mouth, she chokes on it*)

CORIE (*Sitting next to her*) Mother, are you all right?

MOTHER (*Coughing*) I think I popped it back too far.

CORIE (*Takes* PAUL's *drink from him and hands it to* MOTHER) Here . . . Drink this.

MOTHER (*Drinks, gasps*) Ooh . . . Was that my martini?

PAUL (*Gets up and retrieves his drink*) No. My Scotch.

MOTHER Oh, my stomach.

VELASCO (*Moving left behind the couch*) The trick is to pop it right to the center of the tongue . . . Then it gets the benefit of the entire palate . . . Corie?
        (*He offers her the dish*)

CORIE (*Takes one*) Well, here goes. (*She tosses it back and forth, then pops it perfectly*) How about that?

VELASCO Perfect. You're the prettiest epicurean I've ever seen . . . (*He offers the knichi to* PAUL) Paul?

PAUL   Er, no thank you. I have a bad arm.

CORIE   You can *try* it. You should try everything, right, Mr. Velasco?

VELASCO   As the French say, "At least once" . . . (PAUL *pulls up his sleeve, takes a knichi . . . then bites into it*) Agh . . . Bitter, right?

CORIE   You know why, don't you?

PAUL   I didn't pop! I nibbled!

CORIE   Try another one and pop it.

PAUL   I don't want to pop another one. Besides, I think we're over the five-minute limit now, anyway.

VELASCO   (*Crossing to* MOTHER *behind the couch, he leans over to her very confidentially*)   Taste is something that must be cultivated.

MOTHER   (*Almost jumps*)   Er, yes, I've often said that . . .

CORIE   Well, are we ready to go out to dinner?

MOTHER   (*Nervously*)   You mean we're going out?

CORIE   We had a fire in our stove.

MOTHER   What happened?

PAUL   Nothing. We just turned it on.

CORIE   Mother, are you hungry?

MOTHER   Not terribly . . . no.

CORIE   Paul, you're the host. Suggest someplace.

PAUL   Well . . . er . . . how about Marty's on Forty-seventh Street?

CORIE   Marty's? That barn? You get a cow and a baked
potato. What kind of a suggestion was that?

PAUL   I'm sorry. I didn't know it was a trick question.

CORIE   Tonight has to be something special. Mr. Velasco,
you must know someplace different and unusual . . .

VELASCO (*Leaning against the end table*)   Unusual? Yes,
I know a very unusual place. It's the best food in New
York. But I'm somewhat hesitant to suggest . . .

CORIE   Oh, please. (*To* MOTHER)   What do you say,
Mother? Do you feel adventurous?

MOTHER   You know me, one of the fellows.

CORIE   (*To* VELASCO)   There you are. We place the evening in your hands.

VELASCO   A delightful proposition . . . For dinner, we go
to the Four Winds.

PAUL   Oh! The Chinese Restaurant? On Fifty-third
Street?

VELASCO   No . . . The Albanian restaurant on Staten
Island.

MOTHER (*Holds her stomach*)   Staten Island?

CORIE   Doesn't it sound wild, Mother?

MOTHER   Yes . . . wild.

CORIE   I love it already.
(*As she sweeps past* PAUL *on her way to the
bedroom, she punches him on the shoulder*)

VELASCO (*Sitting next to* MOTHER)   Don't expect anything lavish in the way of decor. But Uzu will take care
of the atmosphere.

MOTHER Who's Uzu?

VELASCO It's a Greek liqueur . . . Deceptively powerful. I'll only allow you one.

MOTHER Oh . . . thank you.

CORIE (*Coming out of the bedroom with her coat and purse*) It sounds perfect . . . Let's go.

PAUL It'll be murder getting a cab now.

VELASCO I'll worry about the transportation. All you have to do is pick up the check.

CORIE (*Back of the couch*) Mother has her car.

VELASCO (*Rises, and turns to* PAUL) You see? My job is done. Mrs. Banks . . .
          (*He holds up her coat.* PAUL *crosses to the closet and gets his overcoat*)

MOTHER (*Putting on her coat*) Mr. Velasco, don't you wear a coat?

VELASCO Only in the winter.

MOTHER It's thirty-five.

VELASCO (*Taking a beret out of his pocket*) For twenty-five I wear a coat . . . For thirty-five . . . (*He puts the beret on, and crosses to the door taking a scarf out of his pocket with a great flair.* PAUL *watches with great distaste and then crosses into the bedroom and opens the door*) Ready? . . . My group stay close to me. If anyone gets lost, we'll meet at the United States Embassy.
          (*He flings the scarf about his neck and exits.* MOTHER *desperately clutches* CORIE'S *arm, but* CORIE *manages to push her out the door*)

CORIE (*Turning back for* PAUL) What are you looking for?

PAUL *(Comes out of the bedroom)* My gloves . . .

CORIE *(With disdain)* You don't need gloves. It's only thirty-five.
　　(She sweeps out)

PAUL That's right. I forgot. *(Mimicking* VELASCO, *he flings his scarf around his neck as he crosses to the door)* We're having a heat wave. *(He turns off the lights and slams the door shut)*

Curtain

(In the dark we hear the splash of waves and the melancholy toots of foghorns in the harbor sounding almost as sad as PAUL *and* MOTHER *must be feeling at this moment)*

About 2:00 A.M.

*The apartment is still dark. We hear laughter on the
stairs. The door opens and* CORIE *rushes in. She is breath-
less, hysterical, and wearing* VELASCO's *beret and scarf.*

CORIE   Whoo . . . I beat you . . . I won.
(*She turns on the lights, crosses to the couch, and
collapses on it.* VELASCO *rushes in after her, breath-
less and laughing*)

VELASCO   (*Sinking to the floor in front of the couch*)
It wasn't a fair race. You tickled me.

CORIE   Ooh . . . Ooh, I feel good. Except my tongue keeps
rolling up. And when I talk it rolls back out like a noise-
maker.

VELASCO   That's a good sign. It shows the food was sea-
soned properly.

CORIE   Hey, tell me how to say it again.

VELASCO   Say what?

CORIE   "Waiter, there's a fly in my soup."

VELASCO   Oh. "Poopla . . . sirca al mercoori."

CORIE   That's right. "Sirca . . . poopla al mercoori."

VELASCO   No, no. That's "Fly, I have a waiter in my
soup."

CORIE   Well, I did. He put in his hand to take out the fly.

(*She rises to her knees*) Boy, I like that singer . . . (*She sways back and forth as she sings*) "Shama . . . shama . . . ela mal kemama" . . . (*She flings her coat onto the couch.* VELASCO *rises to a sitting position, crosses his legs, and plays an imaginary flute*) Hey, what am I singing, anyway?

VELASCO (*Stretches prone on the floor*) It's an old Albanian folk song.

CORIE (*Impressed with her own virtuosity*) "Shama shama . . ."? No kidding? What does it mean?

VELASCO "Jimmy cracked corn and I don't care."

CORIE Well, I don't. (*She feels her head*) Oh, boy . . . How many Zuzus did I have? Three or four?

VELASCO *U*zus! . . . Nine or ten.

CORIE Then it was ten 'cause I thought I had four . . . How is my head going to feel in the morning?

VELASCO Wonderful.

CORIE No headaches?

VELASCO No headache . . . But you won't be able to make a fist for three days.
    (*He raises his hands and demonstrates by not being able to make a fist*)

CORIE (*Holds out both hands and looks at them*) Yeah. Look at that. Stiff as a board. (*She climbs off the couch, and moves onto the floor next to* VELASCO) What do they put in Uzu anyway?

VELASCO (*Holding up stiff hands*) I think it's starch.

CORIE (*Looks at her two stiff hands*) . . . Hey, how about a game of ping-pong? We can play doubles.
    (CORIE *swings her two stiff hands at an imaginary ball*)

VELASCO   Not now. (*He sits up*) We're supposed to do something important. What was it?

CORIE   What was it? (*She ponders, then remembers*) Oh! . . . We're supposed to make coffee.
(CORIE *places the shoes she has taken off under the sofa and moves toward the kitchen*)

VELASCO (*Following her*)   I'll make it. What kind do you have?

CORIE   Instant Maxwell House.

VELASCO (*Crushed*)   Instant coffee?
(*He holds his brow with his stiff hands. He and* CORIE *disappear behind the screened kitchen continuing their babbling. Suddenly we hear scuffling in the hallway and* PAUL *struggles in through the door carrying* MOTHER *in his arms. From* PAUL's *staggering we'd guess that* MOTHER *must now weigh about two thousand pounds. He makes it to the sofa, where he drops her, and then sinks in utter exhaustion to the floor below her. They both stare unseeing, and suck desperately for air.* CORIE *and* VELASCO, *who carries a coffee pot, emerge from the kitchen*)

CORIE (*Crosses to* MOTHER)   Forgot the stove doesn't work. Upstairs, everyone . . . for coffee. (CORIE *pulls* MOTHER's *coat but there is no reaction from* MOTHER *or* PAUL) Don't you want coffee?
(PAUL *and* MOTHER *shake their heads* "No")

VELASCO (*Going to the door*)   They'll drink it if we make it . . .

CORIE (*Following him*)   Don't you two go away . . .
(CORIE *and* VELASCO *exit, both singing* "Shama, shama." PAUL *and* MOTHER *stare silently ahead. They appear to be in shock, as if having gone through some terrible ordeal*)

MOTHER (*Finally*)   . . . I feel like we've died . . . and gone to heaven . . . only we had to climb up . . .

PAUL (*Gathering his strength*) . . . Struck down in the prime of life . . .

MOTHER . . . I don't really feel sick . . . Just kind of numb . . . and I can't make a fist . . .
    (*She holds up a stiff hand*)

PAUL You want to hear something frightening? . . . My teeth feel soft . . . It's funny . . . but the best thing we had all night was the knichi.

MOTHER Anyway, Corie had a good time . . . Don't you think Corie had a good time, Paul?

PAUL (*Struggling up onto the couch*) Wonderful . . . Poor kid . . . It isn't often we get out to Staten Island in February.

MOTHER She seems to get such a terrific kick out of living. You've got to admire that, don't you, Paul?

PAUL I admire anyone who has three portions of poofla-poo pie.

MOTHER (*Starts*) What's poofla-poo pie?

PAUL Don't you remember? That gook that came in a turban.

MOTHER I thought that was the waiter . . . I tried, Paul. But I just couldn't seem to work up an appetite the way they did.

PAUL (*Reassuring her*) No, no, Mom . . . You mustn't blame yourself . . . We're just not used to that kind of food . . . You just don't pick up your fork and dig into a *brown* salad . . . You've got to play around with it for a while.

MOTHER Maybe I *am* getting old . . . I don't mind telling you it's very discouraging . . . (*With great difficulty, she manages to rouse herself and get up from the couch*) Anyway, I don't think I could get through coffee . . . I'm all out of pink pills . . .

PAUL   Where are you going?

MOTHER   Home . . . I want to die in my own bed. (*Exhausted, she sinks into a chair*)

PAUL   Well, what'll I tell them?

MOTHER   Oh, make up some clever little lie. (*She rallies herself and gets up*) Tell Corie I'm not really her mother. She'll probably never want to see me again anyway . . . Good night, dear. (*Just as* MOTHER *gets to the door, it opens and* CORIE *and* VELASCO *return*) Oh, coffee ready?
      (*She turns back into the room.* VELASCO *crosses to the bar as* CORIE *moves to behind the couch*)

CORIE   I was whistling the Armenian National Anthem and I blew out the pilot light.

VELASCO (*Puts four brandy snifters he has brought in down on the bar, and taking a decanter from the bar begins to pour brandy*) Instead we're going to have flaming brandy . . . Corie, give everyone a match.
      (CORIE *moves to the side table*)

MOTHER   I'm afraid you'll have to excuse me, dear. It *is* a little late.

CORIE (*Moves toward* MOTHER) Mother, you're not going home. It's the shank of the evening.

MOTHER   I know, but I've got a ten-o'clock dentist appointment . . . at nine o'clock . . . and it's been a very long evening . . . What I mean is it's late, but I've had a wonderful time . . . I don't know what I'm saying.

CORIE   But, Mother . . .

MOTHER   Darling, I'll call you in the morning. Good night, Paul . . . Good night, Mr. Velasco . . .

VELASCO (*Putting down the brandy, he crosses to* CORIE) Good night, Paul . . . Good night, Corie . . .

CORIE   Mr. Velasco, you're not going, too?

VELASCO   (*Taking his beret and scarf from* CORIE *and putting them on*)   Of course. I'm driving Mrs. Banks home.

MOTHER   (*Moves away in shock*)   Oh, no! . . . (*She recovers herself and turns back*)   I mean, oh, no, it's too late.

VELASCO   (*To* MOTHER)   Too late for what?

MOTHER   The buses. They stop running at two. How will you get home?

VELASCO   Why worry about it now? I'll meet that problem in New Jersey.
       (VELASCO *moves to the door and* CORIE *in great jubilation flings herself over the back of the couch*)

MOTHER   And it's such a long trip . . . (*She crosses to* CORIE)   Corie, isn't it a long trip?

CORIE   Not really. It's only about thirty minutes.

MOTHER   But it's such an inconvenience. Really, Mr. Velasco, it's very sweet of you but—

VELASCO   Victor!

MOTHER   What?

VELASCO   If we're going to spend the rest of the evening together, it must be Victor.

MOTHER   Oh!

VELASCO   And I insist the arrangement be reciprocal. What is it?

MOTHER   What is what?

CORIE   Your name, Mother. (*To* VELASCO)   It's Ethel.

MOTHER   Oh, that's right. Ethel. My name is Ethel.

VELASCO   That's better . . . Now . . . are we ready . . . Ethel?

MOTHER   Well . . . if you insist, Walter.

VELASCO   Victor! It's Victor.

MOTHER   Yes. Victor!

VELASCO   Good night, Paul . . . Shama shama, Corie.

CORIE   Shama shama!

VELASCO (*Moves to the door*)   If you don't hear from us in a week, we'll be at the Nacionál Hotel in Mexico City . . . Room seven-oh-three! . . . Let's go, Ethel!
(*And he goes out the door.* MOTHER *turns to* CORIE *and looks for help*)

MOTHER (*Frightened, she grabs* CORIE'S *arm*)   What does he mean by that?

CORIE   I don't know, but I'm dying to find out. Will you call me in the morning?

MOTHER   Yes . . . about six o'clock!
(*And in a panic, she exits*)

CORIE (*Takes a beat, closes the door, smiles, and turns to* PAUL)   Well . . . how about *that*, Mr. "This is going to be a fiasco tonight"? . . . He's taking her all the way out to New Jersey . . . at two o'clock in the morning . . . That's what I call "The Complete Gentleman" . . . (PAUL *looks at her with disdain, rises and staggers up the stairs into the bedroom*) He hasn't even given a thought about how he's going to get home . . . Maybe he'll sleep over . . . Hey, Paul, do you think . . . ? No, not my mother . . . (*She jumps up onto the couch*) Then again anything can happen with Rupert of Henzau . . . Boy, what a night . . . Hey! I got a plan. Let's take the bottle of Scotch downstairs, ring all the bells and yell "Police" . . . Just to see who comes out of whose apartment . . . (*There is no answer from the bedroom*) . . . Paul? . . . What's the matter, darling? . . . Don't you feel well?

PAUL (*Comes out of the bedroom, down the stairs, and crosses to the closet. He is taking his coat off and is angry*) What a rotten thing to do . . . To your own mother.

CORIE What?

PAUL Do you have any idea how she felt just now? Do you know what kind of a night this was for her?

CORIE (*Impishly*) It's not over yet.

PAUL You didn't see her sitting here two minutes ago. You were upstairs with that Hungarian Duncan Hines . . . Well, she was miserable. Her face was longer than that trip we took tonight.
(*He hangs up his coat in the closet*)

CORIE She never said a thing to me.

PAUL (*Takes out a hanger and puts his jacket on it*) She's too good a sport. She went the whole cockeyed way . . . Boy, oh boy . . . dragging a woman like that all the way out to the middle of the harbor for a bowl of sheep dip.
(*He hangs his jacket up and crosses to the diction-ary on the side table under the radiator. He takes his tie off and folds it neatly*)

CORIE (*Follows him to the table*) It was Greek bean soup. And at least *she* tasted it. She didn't jab at it with her knife, throwing cute little epigrams like, "Ho, ho, ho . . . I think there's someone in there."

PAUL (*Puts the tie between pages of the dictionary*) That's right. That's right. At least I was honest about it.

You ate two bowls because you were showing off for Al Capone at the next table.

(PAUL *searches for his wallet unsuccessfully*)

CORIE   What are you so angry about, Paul?

PAUL   (*Crossing to the closet*)   I just told you. I felt terrible for your mother.
(*He gets the wallet out of his jacket pocket*)

CORIE   (*Following after him to the front of the couch*) Why? Where is she at this very minute? Alone with probably the most attractive man she's ever met. Don't tell me *that* doesn't beat hell out of hair curlers and the "Late Late Show."

PAUL   (*Crossing onto bedroom landing*)   Oh, I can just hear it now. What sparkling conversation. He's probably telling her about a chicken cacciatore he once cooked for the High Lama of Tibet and she's sitting there shoving pink pills in her mouth.

CORIE   (*Taking her coat from the couch and putting it on the armchair at right*)   You never can tell what people talk about when they're alone.

PAUL   I don't understand how you can be so unconcerned about this.
(*He goes into the bedroom*)

CORIE   (*Moving to the stairs*)   Unconcerned . . . I'm plenty concerned. Do you think I'm going to get one wink of sleep until that phone rings tomorrow? I'm scared to death for my mother. But I'm grateful there's finally the opportunity for something to be scared about . . . (*She moves right, then turns back*) What I'm really concerned about is *you!*

PAUL   (*Bursts out of the bedroom, nearly slamming through the door*)   Me? Me?

CORIE I'm beginning to wonder if you're capable of *having* a good time.

PAUL Why? Because I like to wear my gloves in the winter?

CORIE No. Because there isn't the least bit of adventure in you. Do you know what you are? You're a Watcher. There are Watchers in this world and there are Do-ers. And the Watchers sit around watching the Do-ers do. Well, tonight you watched and I did.

PAUL (*Moves down the stairs to* CORIE) Yeah . . . Well, it was harder to watch what you did than it was for you to *do* what I was watching.
  (*He goes back up the stairs to the landing*)

CORIE You won't let your hair down for a minute? You couldn't even relax for one night. Boy, Paul, sometimes you act like a . . . a . . .
  (*She gets her shoes from under the couch*)

PAUL (*Stopping on the landing*) What . . . ? A stuffed shirt?

CORIE (*Drops the shoes on the couch*) I didn't say that.

PAUL That's what you're implying.

CORIE (*Moves to the right armchair and begins to take off her jewelry*) That's what you're anticipating. I didn't say you're a stuffed shirt. But you are extremely proper and dignified.

PAUL I'm proper and dignified? (*He moves to* CORIE) When . . . ? When was I proper and dignified?

CORIE (*Turns to* PAUL) All right. The other night. At Delfino's . . . You were drunk, right?

PAUL Right. I was stoned.

CORIE There you are. I didn't know it until you told me in the morning. (*She unzips her dress and takes it off*) You're a funny kind of drunk. You just sat there looking unhappy and watching your coat.

PAUL I was watching my coat because I saw someone else watching my coat . . . Look, if you want, I'll get drunk for you sometime. I'll show you a slob, make your hair stand on end.
   (*He unbuttons his shirt*)

CORIE (*Puts her dress on the chair*) It isn't necessary.

PAUL (*Starts to go, turns back*) Do you know . . . Do you know, in P. J. Clarke's last New Year's Eve, I punched an old woman . . . Don't tell me about drunks.
   (*He starts to go*)

CORIE (*Taking down her hair*) All right, Paul.

PAUL (*Turns back and moves to behind the couch*) When else? When else was I proper and dignified?

CORIE Always. You're always dressed right, you always look right, you always say the right things. You're very close to being perfect.

PAUL (*Hurt to the quick*) That's . . . that's a *rotten* thing to say.

CORIE (*Moves to PAUL*) I have never seen you without a jacket. I always feel like such a slob compared to you. Before we were married I was sure you slept with a tie.

PAUL No, no. Just for very *formal* sleeps.

CORIE You can't even walk into a candy store and ask the lady for a Tootsie Roll. (*Playing the scene out, she moves down to right side of the couch*) You've got to walk up to the counter and point at it and say, "I'll have that thing in the brown and white wrapper."

PAUL (*Moving to the bedroom door*) That's ridiculous.

CORIE And you're not. That's just the trouble. (*She crosses to the foot of the stairs*) Like Thursday night. You wouldn't walk barefoot with me in Washington Square Park. Why not?

PAUL (*Moving to the head of the stairs*) Very simple answer. It was seventeen degrees.

CORIE (*Moves back to the chair and continues taking down her hair*) Exactly. That's very sensible and logical. Except it isn't any fun.

PAUL (*Moves down the stairs to the couch*) You know maybe I *am* too proper and dignified for you. Maybe you would have been happier with someone a little more colorful and flamboyant . . . like the Geek!
(*He starts back to the bedroom*)

CORIE Well, he'd be a lot more laughs than a stuffed shirt.

PAUL (*Turns back on the landing*) Oh, oh . . . I thought you said I wasn't.

CORIE Well, you are now.

PAUL (*Reflectively*) I'm not going to listen to this . . . I'm not going to listen . . . (*He starts for the bedroom*) I've got a case in court in the morning.

CORIE (*Moves left*) Where are you going?

PAUL To sleep.

CORIE *Now?* How can you sleep now?

PAUL (*Steps up on the bed and turns back, leaning on the door jamb*) I'm going to close my eyes and count knichis. Good night!

CORIE You can't go to sleep now. We're having a fight.

PAUL *You* have the fight. When you're through, turn off the lights.
(*He turns back into the bedroom*)

CORIE Ooh, that gets me insane. You can even control your emotions.

PAUL (*Storms out to the head of the stairs*) Look, I'm just as upset as you are . . . (*He controls himself*) But when I get hungry, I eat. And when I get tired, I sleep. You eat and sleep, too. Don't deny it, I've seen you . . .

CORIE (*Moves right with a grand gesture*) Not in the middle of a crisis.

PAUL What crisis? We're just yelling a little.

CORIE You don't consider this a crisis? Our whole marriage hangs in the balance.

PAUL (*Sits on the steps*) It does? When did that happen?

CORIE Just now. It's suddenly very clear that you and I have absolutely *nothing* in common.

PAUL Why? Because I won't walk barefoot in the park in winter? You haven't got a case, Corie. Adultery, yes. Cold feet, no.

CORIE (*Seething*) Don't oversimplify this. I'm angry. Can't you see that?

PAUL (*Brings his hands to his eyes, peers at her through imaginary binoculars, and then looks at his watch*) Corie, it's two-fifteen. If I can fall asleep in about half an hour, I can get about five hours' sleep. I'll call you from court tomorrow and we can fight over the phone.
(*He gets up and moves to the bedroom*)

CORIE You will *not* go to sleep. You will stay here and fight to save our marriage.

PAUL (*In the doorway*) If our marriage hinges on breathing fish balls and poofla-poo pie, it's not worth saving . . . I am now going to crawl into our tiny, little, single bed. If you care to join me, we will be sleeping from left to right tonight.
(*He goes into the bedroom and slams the door*)

CORIE You won't discuss it . . . You're *afraid* to discuss it . . . I married a coward!! . . .
(*She takes a shoe from the couch and throws it at the bedroom door*)

PAUL (*Opens the door*) Corie, would you bring in a pail? The closet's dripping.

CORIE Ohh, I hate you! I hate you! I really, really hate you!

PAUL (*Storms to the head of the stairs*) Corie, there is one thing I learned in court. Be careful when you're tired and angry. You might say something you will soon regret. I-am-now-tired-and-angry.

CORIE And a coward.

PAUL (*Comes down the stairs to her at right of the couch*) And I will now say something I will soon regret . . . Okay, Corie, maybe you're right. Maybe we have nothing in common. Maybe we rushed into this marriage a little too fast. Maybe Love isn't enough. Maybe two people should have to take more than a blood test. Maybe they should be checked for common sense, understanding, and emotional maturity.

CORIE (*That hurt*) All right . . . Why don't you get it passed in the Supreme Court? Only those couples bearing a letter from their psychiatrists proving they're well-adjusted will be permitted to be married.

PAUL You're impossible.

CORIE You're unbearable.

PAUL You belong in a nursery school.

CORIE It's a lot more fun than the Home for the Fuddy Duddies.

PAUL (*Reaches out his hand to her*) All right, Corie, let's not get . . .

CORIE Don't you touch me . . . Don't you touch me . . .

(PAUL *very deliberately reaches out and touches her.* CORIE *screams hysterically and runs across the room, away from him. Hysterically*) I don't want you near me. Ever again.

PAUL (*Moves toward her*) Now wait a minute, Corie—

CORIE No. (*She turns away from him*) I can't look at you. I can't even be in the same room with you now.

PAUL Why?

CORIE I just can't, that's all. Not when you feel this way.

PAUL When I feel what way?

CORIE The way you feel about me.

PAUL Corie, you're hysterical.

CORIE (*Even more hysterically*) I am not hysterical. I know exactly what I'm saying. It's no good between us, Paul. It never will be again.

PAUL (*Throwing up his hands and sinking to the couch*) Holy cow.

CORIE I'm sorry, I— (*She fights back tears*) I don't want to cry.

PAUL Oh, for pete's sakes, cry. Go ahead and cry.

CORIE (*At the height of fury*) Don't you tell me when to cry. I'll cry when I want to cry. And I'm not going to have my cry until you're out of this apartment.

PAUL What do you mean, "out of this apartment"?

CORIE Well, you certainly don't think we're going to live here together, do you? After tonight?

PAUL Are you serious?

CORIE Of course I'm serious. *I want a divorce!*

PAUL (*Shocked, he jumps up*) A *divorce?* What?

CORIE (*Pulls herself together, and with great calm, begins to go up the stairs*) I'm sorry, Paul, I can't discuss it any more. Good night.

PAUL Where are you going?

CORIE To bed.
(*She turns back to* PAUL)

PAUL You can't. Not now.

CORIE You did before.

PAUL That was in the middle of a fight. This is in the middle of a divorce.

CORIE I can't talk to you when you're hysterical. Good night.
(*She goes into the bedroom*)

PAUL Will you come here? . . . (CORIE *comes out on the landing*) I want to know why you want a divorce.

CORIE I told you why. Because you and I have absolutely nothing in common.

PAUL What about those six days at the Plaza?

CORIE (*Sagely*) Six days does not a week make.

PAUL (*Taken aback*) What does *that* mean?

CORIE I don't know what it means. I just want a divorce.

PAUL You know, I think you really mean it.

CORIE I *do!*

PAUL You mean, every time we have a little fight, you're going to want a divorce?

CORIE (*Reassuring*) There isn't going to be any more

little fights. This is it, Paul! This is the end. Good night. (*She goes into the bedroom and closes the door behind her*)

PAUL Corie, do you mean to say— (*He yells*) Will you come down here?!

CORIE (*Yells from the bedroom*) Why?

PAUL (*Screams back*) Because I don't want to yell. (*The door opens and* CORIE *comes out. She stands at the top of the stairs. He points to his feet*) All the way.

CORIE (*Seething, comes all the way down and stands where he pointed*) Afraid the crazy neighbors will hear us?

PAUL You're serious.

CORIE Dead serious.

PAUL You mean the whole thing? With signing papers and going to court, shaking hands, good-bye, finished, forever, divorced?

CORIE (*Nodding in agreement*) That's what I mean . . .

PAUL I see . . . Well . . . I guess there's nothing left to be said.

CORIE I guess not.

PAUL Right . . . Well, er . . . Good night, Corie. (*And he goes up the stairs*)

CORIE Where are you going?

PAUL (*Turns back on the landing*) To bed.

CORIE Don't you want to talk about it?

PAUL At two-thirty in the morning?

CORIE   I can't sleep until this thing is settled.
(*She moves to the couch*)

PAUL   Well, it may take three months. Why don't you at least take a *nap?*

CORIE   You don't have to get snippy.

PAUL   Well, dammit, I'm sorry, but when I plan vacations I'm happy and when I plan divorces I'm snippy. (*He crosses to the bookcase and grabs his attaché case*) All right, you want to plan this thing, let's plan it. (*He storms to the coffee table and sweeps everything there onto the floor with his hand*) You want a quick divorce or a slow painful one?

CORIE   (*Horrified*)   I'm going to bed.
(*She goes up the stairs*)

PAUL   (*Shouts*)   You stay here or you get no divorce from me.

CORIE   (*Stops on the landing*)   You can try acting civilized.

PAUL   (*Putting down the attaché case*)   Okay, I'll be civilized. But charm you're not going to get. (*He pushes a chair toward her*) Now sit down! . . . Because there's a lot of legal and technical details to go through.
(*He opens the attaché case*)

CORIE   Can't you do all that? I don't know anything about legal things.

PAUL   (*Wheels on her and in a great gesture points an accusing finger at her*)   Ah, haa . . . Now *I'm* the Do-er and *you're* the Watcher! (*Relentlessly*) Right, Corie? Heh? Right? Right? Isn't that right, Corie?

CORIE   (*With utmost disdain*)   . . . So this is what you're *really* like!

PAUL   (*Grimacing like the monster he is*)   Yes . . . Yes . . .

CORIE (*Determined she's doing the right thing. She comes down the stairs, and sits, first carefully moving the chair away from* PAUL)   All right, what do I have to do?

PAUL   First of all, what grounds?
(*He sits on the couch*)

CORIE (*Not looking at* PAUL)   Grounds?

PAUL (*Taking a legal pad and a pencil out of the case*)
That's right. Grounds. What is your reason for divorcing me? And remember, my failure to appreciate knichis will only hold up in a Russian court.

CORIE   You're a scream, Paul. Why weren't you funny when we were happy?

PAUL   Okay . . . How about incompatible?

CORIE   Fine. Are you through with me?

PAUL   Not yet. What about the financial settlement?

CORIE   I don't want a thing.

PAUL   Oh, but you're entitled to it. Alimony, property? Supposing I just pay your rent. Seventy-five sixty-three a month, isn't it?

CORIE   Ha-ha . . .

PAUL   And you can have the furniture and the wedding gifts. I'd just like to keep my clothes.

CORIE (*Shocked, she turns to* PAUL)   I hardly expected bitterness from you.

PAUL   I'm not bitter. That's a statement of fact. You're always wearing my pajamas and slippers.

CORIE   Only after you go to work.

PAUL   Why?

CORIE   Because I like the way they—never mind. It's stupid. (*She begins to sob, gets up and goes up the steps to the bedroom*) I'll sign over your pajamas and slippers.

PAUL   If you'd like, you can visit them once a month.

CORIE (*Turns back on the landing*)   That's bitter!

PAUL   You're damned right it is.

CORIE (*Beginning to cry in earnest*)   You have no right to be bitter.

PAUL   Don't tell me when to be bitter.

CORIE   Things just didn't work out.

PAUL   They sure as hell didn't.

CORIE   You can't say we didn't try.

PAUL   Almost two whole weeks.

CORIE   It's better than finding out in two *years*.

PAUL   Or twenty.

CORIE   Or fifty.

PAUL   Lucky, aren't we?

CORIE   We're the luckiest people in the whole world.

PAUL   I thought you weren't going to cry.

CORIE   Well, I am! I'm going to have the biggest cry I ever had in my life. And I'm going to enjoy it. (*PAUL drops the pencil and pad into the attaché case, and buries his head in a pillow from the couch*) Because I'm going to cry so loud, I'm going to keep you awake all night long. Good night, Paul! . . . I mean, *good-bye!*
     (*She goes into the bedroom and slams the door, and we hear her crying. PAUL angrily slams his*

attaché case shut, gets up, and moves toward the stairs. At this moment, the bedroom door opens and CORIE *throws out a blanket, sheet, and pillow which land at* PAUL's *feet. Then she slams the door shut again. Again we hear crying from the bedroom.* PAUL *picks them up and glares at the door)*

PAUL (*Mimicking* CORIE) . . . all night long . . . work like a dog for a lousy six cents . . . (*Seething,* PAUL *throws the bedding on the end table, and begins to try to make up the sofa with the sheet and blanket, all the while mumbling through the whole argument they have just had. As he puts the blanket over the sofa, he suddenly bursts out)* . . . Six days does not a week make.

(*The phone rings. For a moment,* PAUL *attempts to ignore it, but it keeps on ringing and he finally 'orms over to it and rips the cord from the wall. Then, still mumbling to himself, he crosses to the light switch near the door and shuts off the lights. Moonlight from the skylight falls onto the sofa.* PAUL *gets into his makeshift bed and finally settles down. And then . . . it begins to snow. Through the hole in the skylight it falls, down onto* PAUL's *exposed head. He feels it and, after a quick moment, rises up on his knees and looks up at the hole. Soundlessly, he crumples into a heap)*

Curtain

Act Three

The following day. About 5:00 P.M.

CORIE *is at the couch picking up the towels she has put down on the floor and the arm of the couch to soak up the water left by the previous night's snow. She picks up the towels with great distaste and uses one to rub off the arm. She looks up at the hole in the skylight, rolls the couch downstage so that it will not be under the skylight, and takes the towels up into the bathroom. As she disappears into the bathroom, the front door opens and* PAUL *comes in, collapsing over the railing. He looks haggard and drawn, not just from the stairs, but from a lack of sleep and peace of mind. Also, he has a cold, and as he leans there, he wearily blows his nose. He carries his attaché case and a newspaper. The doorbell buzzes, and as he presses the buzzer,* CORIE *comes out of the bathroom. They look silently at one another and then they both move, crossing each other wordlessly;* PAUL *goes up the steps to the bedroom and* CORIE *crosses up to the kitchen. Just before he gets to the bedroom door,* PAUL *sneezes.*

CORIE (*About to go behind the screen, coldly, without looking at him*) God bless him!

> (PAUL *goes into the bedroom and slams the door.* CORIE *goes into the kitchen. She comes out with two plates, two knives and forks, and a napkin. Crossing to the table under the radiator, she puts down a plate with a knife and fork. Then putting the other setting down on the end table, she moves it all the way to the other side of the room. She goes back into the kitchen and emerges with two glasses. One she places on the side table and as she crosses toward the other table, our old friend Harry Pepper the* TELEPHONE MAN, *appears at the door. He is breathing as hard as ever. She sees him*)

CORIE Oh, hi!

TELEPHONE MAN (*Not too thrilled*) Hello again.

CORIE How have you been?

TELEPHONE MAN Fine. Fine, thanks.

CORIE Good . . . The telephone's out of order.

TELEPHONE MAN I know. I wouldn't be here for a social call.

CORIE Come on in . . .
(*He steps up into the apartment.* CORIE *closes the door behind him, and goes up into the kitchen to fill her glass with water*)

TELEPHONE MAN (*Looking around*) Hey! . . . Not bad . . . Not bad at all . . . you did a very nice job.

CORIE (*Speaking from the kitchen*) Thanks. You know anyone who might want to rent it?

TELEPHONE MAN You movin' *already?*

CORIE (*Picking up the salt and pepper shakers*) I'm looking for a smaller place.

TELEPHONE MAN (*Looks around with disbelief*) Smaller than this? . . . They're not easy to find.

CORIE (*Coming out of the kitchen*) I'll find one.
(*She places the glass of water and the shakers on the end table*)

TELEPHONE MAN (*Moves to the phone*) Well, let's see what the trouble is. (*The* TELEPHONE MAN *picks up the receiver, jiggles the buttons, and listens, while* CORIE *moves the straight-backed bentwood chair to back of the end table. He puts down the receiver*) It's dead.

CORIE I know. My husband killed it.
(*She crosses to the side table under the radiator, and takes a candlestick and candle, and a small vase with a yellow rose*)

TELEPHONE MAN *(Puzzled)* Oh! *(He looks down and notices that the wire has been pulled from the wall. He kneels down, opens his tool box, and cheerfully begins to replace the wire)* So how do you like married life?

CORIE *(Puts the candlestick and vase down on her table; blandly)* Very interesting.
(She goes up into the kitchen)

TELEPHONE MAN Well, after a couple of weeks, what's not interesting? Yeah, it's always nice to see two young kids getting started. With all the trouble today, you see a couple of newlyweds, you figure there's still hope for the world. *(As CORIE comes out of the kitchen with a pot of food, a ladle, and a pot holder, PAUL, still in his overcoat and with his attaché case and newspaper, comes out of the bedroom and slams the door behind him. Both CORIE and the TELEPHONE MAN stop. PAUL goes into the bathroom and slams that door hard. CORIE grimaces and the TELEPHONE MAN is shocked. Puzzled)* Who's that?

CORIE *(Rising above it)* Him!

TELEPHONE MAN Your husband?

CORIE *(Going to the bathroom door)* I suppose so. I wasn't looking. *(She pounds on the door with the ladle, and yells)* Dinnah—is served!
(She crosses to the side table and begins to ladle food onto the plate. The bathroom door opens, and PAUL comes out)

PAUL *(Nods at the TELEPHONE MAN and then moves down the stairs to the couch)* I have my own dinner, thank you.
(He sits on the couch, puts his attaché case on the table, and opens it)

CORIE *(Ignoring PAUL, crosses to the TELEPHONE MAN and offers him the plate)* . . . Would you like some goulash?

TELEPHONE MAN *(Embarrassed, he looks at PAUL)* Er,

no, thanks. We're not allowed to accept tips. (*He laughs at his small joke.* CORIE *takes the plate to the kitchen and drops the goulash, plate and all, into the garbage can. She then moves to her table and ladles goulash onto her plate.* PAUL, *meantime, has taken a small bag out of his attaché case. It contains a small bunch of grapes which he carefully places on top of his case.* CORIE *places the pot on the floor, and taking a book of matches from her apron pocket, she lights the candle. While she does this she sings to herself . . . "Shama, shama" . . .* PAUL *buries himself in his paper and begins to eat his grapes.*)

TELEPHONE MAN (*Taking all this in*) I'll be out of here as fast as I can.
(*He dives back to his work*)

CORIE (*Sitting down to eat*) Take your time. No one's rushing you.
(*The* TELEPHONE MAN *begins a nervous, tuneless hum as he works.* PAUL *continues to eat and read wordlessly. There is a long pause*)

PAUL (*Without looking up*) Is there any beer in the house? (CORIE *does not answer. The* TELEPHONE MAN *stops humming and looks at her, hoping she will . . . There is a pause . . .* PAUL *is still looking at his newspaper*) I said, is there any beer in the house?
(*There is no answer*)

TELEPHONE MAN (*He can't stand it any longer*) Would you like me to look?

CORIE There is *no* beer in the house.
(PAUL *throws down his paper and storms toward the* TELEPHONE MAN, *who draws back in fright.* PAUL *stops at the bar and pours himself a drink*)

TELEPHONE MAN (*With great relief, and trying to make conversation because no one else will*) That's *my* trouble . . . beer . . . I can drink ten cans in a night . . . of beer.
(PAUL *goes back to the couch and his newspaper. Not having eased the tension any, the* TELEPHONE

MAN *goes back to his work and again begins his
nervous humming*)

PAUL (*After another pause, still looking at his newspaper*)
Did my laundry come back today?

CORIE (*With food in her mouth, she takes her own sweet
time in answering*) Hmph.

PAUL (*Looks at her*) What does that mean?

CORIE It meant your laundry came back today . . . They
stuffed your shirts beautifully.
(*Having watched this exchange, the* TELEPHONE
MAN *desperately begins to whistle a pointless and
innocuous tune*)

PAUL (*Stung, takes a drink, then becoming aware of the*
TELEPHONE MAN) Would you like a drink? (*There is
no answer. The* TELEPHONE MAN *continues to work*)
I said, would you like a drink?

TELEPHONE MAN (*Startled, he looks up from his work*)
Who?

PAUL You!

TELEPHONE MAN Me?

PAUL Yes!

TELEPHONE MAN OH! . . . NO!

PAUL Right.
(*He goes back to his newspaper*)

TELEPHONE MAN (*Dives back to his work*) One more
little screw should do it . . . There! (*Turns the screw,
then says loud and elatedly*) I'm finished! I'm finished!
(*He throws the tools quickly back into his kit*) That
wasn't too long, was it?

CORIE No. Thank you very much.

TELEPHONE MAN (*Getting up and crossing to the door*) It's A. T. and T.'s pleasure.
> (*He nearly drops the kit, and in a panic rushes to the door. He is anxious to leave this scene*)

CORIE (*Picks up the pot from the floor and moves to him at the door*) I'm sorry to keep bothering you like this.

TELEPHONE MAN Oh, listen. Anytime.

CORIE (*Very confidingly*) I don't think we'll be needing you again.

TELEPHONE MAN Well, I wouldn't be too sure . . . Phones keep breaking down now and then but er . . . (*He looks at* CORIE *as if trying to get some secret and personal message across to cheer her up*) . . . somehow, they have a way of getting fixed. You know what I mean . . . (*He winks at her to indicate "Chin up." As he's winking,* PAUL *lowers his paper, turns around, and sees him. The* TELEPHONE MAN *is terribly embarrassed. So he winks at* PAUL. *Then, pulling himself together*) Well . . . 'bye.
> (*And he rushes out of the door.* CORIE *closes the door behind him and goes up into the kitchen with the pot and ladle. As soon as she is safely behind the screen,* PAUL *puts down his paper and runs to her table, where he swipes a mouthful of goulash. Dashing back to the couch, he is once more hidden behind his newspaper when* CORIE *comes out of the kitchen. She is now carrying a plate on which rests a small iced cake. She sits down, and pushing her plate aside, begins to eat her cake*)

CORIE Are you going to stay here again tonight?

PAUL I haven't found a room yet.

CORIE You've had all day to look.

PAUL (*Using the nasal spray he had taken out of the attaché case with the bag of grapes*) I've been very busy. I work during the day, you know.

CORIE   You could look during your lunch hour.

PAUL   I *eat* during my lunch hour. I'll look during my looking hour.
(*He puts down the spray and takes another drink*)

CORIE   You could look tonight.

PAUL   I intended to. (*He goes back to reading his paper*) But I'm coming down with a cold. I thought I'd just take a couple of aspirins and get right into the sofa.

CORIE   I'm sure you can find *some* place . . . Why don't you sleep at your club?

PAUL   It's not *that* kind of a club. It's a locker room and a handball court . . . and to sleep there I'd have to keep winning the serve. (*He looks at* CORIE) Look, does it bother you if I stay here another couple of days?

CORIE   It's your apartment, too. Get out whenever you want to get out. (*The phone rings. When* PAUL *makes no move to answer it,* CORIE, *with great resignation, crosses to the phone and picks it up*) Hello? . . . Who? . . . Yes, it is. (CORIE *suddenly acts very feminine, in a somewhat lower, more provocative and confidential voice, even laughing at times as though she were sharing some private little joke. She seems to be doing this all for* PAUL's *benefit. Into the phone*) . . . Oh, isn't that nice . . . Yes, I'm very interested . . . (*Takes the phone and moves away from* PAUL) Thursday night? . . . Well, I don't see why not . . .

PAUL (*Doesn't like the sound of this*)   Who is that?

CORIE (*Ignores him and laughs into the phone*) . . . What's that? . . . Eight o'clock? . . . It sounds perfect.

PAUL   Who are you talking to?

CORIE (*Still ignoring him*) . . . I see . . . But how did you get my number? . . . Oh, isn't that clever . . .

PAUL (*Crosses angrily and grabs the receiver*) Give me that phone.

CORIE (*Struggling with him for it*) I will not. Get away from here, Paul. It's for me.

PAUL I said give me that phone. (*Takes the receiver and its cradle from her.* CORIE *storms across to her table with great indignation, blows the candle out, and begins to take her setting into the kitchen.* PAUL, *into the phone*) Hello? . . . Who is this? . . . Who? . . . (*He looks at* CORIE *incredulously*) No, madam, we're *not* interested in Bossa Nova lessons. (PAUL *hangs up and stares at* CORIE *as she comes out of the kitchen.* CORIE *does not look at him as she finishes clearing the table and takes the plates into the kitchen.* PAUL *moves back to the couch and sits*) I'm glad we didn't have children . . . because you're a crazy lady.

CORIE (*Moves the chair back to the right, and carries the table back to the right of the couch*) I'll go where I want and do what I want. And I'm not going to stay in this house at nights as long as you're here.

PAUL (*Putting down the paper*) I see . . . Okay, Corie, when do you want me out?

CORIE I want you out now. Tonight.

PAUL (*Crossing to the closet*) Okay! Fine! (*He gets his suitcase and puts it on top of the end table*) I'll be out of here in five minutes. Is that soon enough for you?

CORIE Not if you can make it in two.

PAUL (*Opening the suitcase*) You can't wait, can you? You just can't wait till I'm gone and out of your life.

CORIE Right. When do I get it?

PAUL Get what?

CORIE My divorce. When do I get my divorce?

PAUL   How should I know? They didn't even send us our marriage license yet.

CORIE   I'll get your Jockey shorts.
(*She goes up into the bedroom*)

PAUL (*Moves to the coffee table and takes his drink*)   You can leave the suits. I'll pick them up in the spring when they're dry.

CORIE (*In the bedroom*)   You'd better ring the bell. 'Cause I'm buying a big dog tomorrow.

PAUL (*Finishing his drink*)   A dog . . . Fine, fine . . . Now you'll have someone to walk barefoot in the park with. (*The phone rings.* CORIE *comes out of the bedroom with a pile of Jockey shorts which she throws on the couch. She crosses to answer the phone*) If that's Arthur Murray, say hello.
(*He gathers up the Jockey shorts and puts them in the suitcase*)

CORIE (*Picks up the phone*)   Hello . . . Yes, Aunt Harriet . . . What? . . . No, mother's not with me . . . I'm positive   She left about two in the morning . . . What's wrong? . . . *What?*

PAUL (*Crossing to the closet and getting a pair of pants*)   What is it?

CORIE   (*Terribly frightened*) Mother??? . . . *My* Mother??? . . . Are you *sure?*

PAUL (*Putting the pants in the suitcase*)   What is it?

CORIE (*Into the phone, now very nervous*)   No, my phone's been out of order all day . . . (*She gives* PAUL *a dirty look*) No, I don't know *what* could have happened.

PAUL (*Blowing his nose*)   What's the matter?

CORIE   All right, Aunt Harriet, don't get excited . . . Yes
. . . Yes, I'll call as soon as I hear.
(*She hangs up*)

PAUL   (*Moves to* CORIE)   What happened to your
mother?

CORIE   She didn't come home last night. Her bed wasn't
slept in. Maybe I should call the police.
(*She starts to pick up the phone*)

PAUL   All right, take it easy, Corie . . .

CORIE (*Turns back to* PAUL)   Don't you understand? Jessie looked. She was not in her bedroom this morning.
(*She picks up the phone*)

PAUL (*Groping*)   Well . . . well, maybe her back was
bothering her and she went to sleep on the ironing
board.

CORIE   You stupid idiot, didn't you hear what I said? My
mother's been missing all night! . . . *My* mother!

PAUL (*The Chief of Police*)   All right, let's not crack up.

CORIE (*Seething*)   Will you go 'way. Get out of my life
and go away! (*She slams the receiver down and crosses
to the door*) I don't want to see you here when I get
back.

PAUL   Where are you going?

CORIE   Upstairs to find out what happened to my mother.
(*She opens the door*) *And don't be here when I get
back!*
(*She goes out and slams the door.* PAUL *goes to the
door*)

PAUL   Oh, yeah? . . . Well, I've got a big surprise for
you . . . (*He opens the door and yells after her*) I'm not
going to be here when you get back . . . (*Crossing to
the dictionary on the side table*) Let's see how you like
living alone . . . (*He pulls ties out of the dictionary*

and throws them in the suitcase) A dog . . . Ha! That's a laugh . . . Wait till she tries to take him out for a walk . . . He'll get one look at those stairs and he'll go right for her throat. (*Crossing into the bedroom*) You might as well get a parakeet, too . . . So you can talk to him all night. (*Mimicking* CORIE) "How much can I spend for bird seeds, Polly? Is a nickel too much?" (*He comes out of the bedroom with shirts and pajamas*) Well, fortunately, I don't need anyone to protect me. (*Putting the clothes in the suitcase*) Because I am a man, sweetheart . . . An independent, mature, self-sufficient man. (*He sneezes as he closes the suitcase*) God bless me! (*Feeling sorry for himself, he feels his head*) I probably got the flu. (*Crossing to the bar, he takes a bottle and glass*) Yeah, I'm hot, cold, sweating, freezing. It's probably a twenty-four-hour virus. I'll be all right . . . (*He looks at his watch*) . . . tomorrow at a quarter to five. (*He pours another drink, puts down the bottle, and drinks. As he drinks, he notices the hole in the skylight. Stepping up onto the black leather armchair*) Oh! . . . Oh, thanks a lot, pal. (*He holds the glass up in toast fashion*) "And thus it was written, some shall die by pestilence, some by the plague . . . and one poor schnook is gonna get it from a hole in the ceiling." (*Getting down, he puts the drink on the side table*) Well, I guess that's it. (*He gets the bottle of Scotch from the bar, and glances at the bedroom*) Good-bye, leaky closet . . . (*To the bathroom*) Good-bye, no bathtub . . . (*Taking the attaché case from the coffee table, he looks up at the hole*) Good-bye, hole . . . (*Getting his suitcase*) Good-bye, six flights . . . (*As* PAUL *moves to the door,* CORIE *comes in. She holds her apron to her mouth, and is very disturbed*) Good-bye, Corie . . . (PAUL *stops in the doorway as* CORIE *wordlessly goes right by him and starts to go up the stairs to the bedroom*) Don't I get a good-bye? . . . According to law, I'm entitled to a good-bye!

CORIE (*Stops on the stairs and slowly turns back to* PAUL, *in a heart-rending wail*) Good-bye . . .
   (*She goes into the bedroom and collapses on the bed*)

PAUL   Corie . . . Now what is it? (*Alarmed, he drops the*

suitcase and attaché case, and puts the bottle on the end table) Is it your mother? . . . Was it an accident? . . . (*He crosses to the bedroom*) Corie, for pete's sakes, what happened to your mother?

(*Suddenly* MOTHER *rushes in through the open door. She is now dressed in a man's bathrobe many sizes too big for her. Over-sized man's slippers flap on her bare feet. But she is holding her pocketbook. Desperately clutching the bathrobe, she crosses to the bedroom*)

MOTHER   Corie, please, listen! . . . It's not the way it looks at all!

PAUL (*Looks at her in amazement*)   Mother???

MOTHER (*Stops momentarily*)   Oh, good morning, Paul. (*She goes up the stairs*) Corie, you've got to talk to me. (CORIE *slams the door to the bedroom shut*) There's a perfectly good explanation. (*Hysterical, in front of the closed door*) Corie, please . . . You're not being fair . . . (*She turns to* PAUL) Paul, make her believe me.

PAUL (*Goes up the stairs and pounds on the bedroom door*)   Now, you see . . . Now are you satisfied? . . . (*He turns to* MOTHER, *being very forgiving*) It's all right, Mother, I understand.
    (*He starts for his suitcase*)

MOTHER (*Shocked*)   No! . . . *You don't understand!!!* (*She goes to* PAUL) You don't understand at all!! . . .

PAUL (*Picking up the suitcase, attaché case, and bottle*)   As long as you're all right, Mother.
    (*He looks at her, sadly shakes his head and exits*)

MOTHER (*Trying to stop him*)   No, Paul . . . You've got to believe me . . . (*But* PAUL *is gone*) Oh, this is awful . . . Somebody believe me.
    (*The bedroom door opens and* CORIE *comes out*)

CORIE   Paul! Where's Paul? . . .

MOTHER (*Putting her bag down on the end table*) Corie, I'm going to explain everything. The bathrobe, the slippers . . . It's all just a big mistake.

CORIE (*Rushing to the front door*) Did he go? Did Paul leave?

MOTHER (*Going to* CORIE) It happened last night . . . when I left with Mr. Velasco . . .

CORIE (*Closing the door*) He was right . . . Paul was right.
(*She moves to the couch and sits*)

MOTHER (*Following her*) It must have been the drinks. I had a great deal to drink last night . . . (*She sits next to* CORIE) I had Scotch, martinis, coffee, black bean soup, and Uzus . . .

CORIE You don't have to explain a thing to me, Mother.

MOTHER (*Horrified*) But I want to explain . . . When I got outside I suddenly felt dizzy . . . and I fainted . . . Well, I passed out. In the slush.

CORIE I should have listened to him . . . It's all my fault.

MOTHER (*Desperately trying to make her see*) Then Victor picked me up and carried me inside. I couldn't walk because my shoes fell down the sewer.

CORIE (*Deep in her own misery*) You hear about these things every day.

MOTHER He started to carry me up here but his beret fell over his eyes, and he fell down the stairs . . . He fell into apartment Three-C. I fell on his foot . . . They had to carry us up.

CORIE I thought we'd have a nice sociable evening, that's all.

MOTHER . . . Mr. Gonzales, Mr. Armandariz, and Mr. Calhoun . . . (*She sags in defeat*) They carried us up . . .

CORIE Just some drinks, dinner, and coffee . . . That's all . . .

MOTHER And then they put us down. On the rugs . . . Oh, he doesn't have beds . . . just thick rugs, and then I fell asleep . . .

CORIE Paul was right. He was right about so many things . . .

MOTHER And then when I woke up, Victor was gone. But I was there . . . in his bathrobe. (*She pounds the couch with her fist*) I swear that's the truth, Corie.

CORIE (*Turns to* MOTHER) You don't have to swear, Mother.

MOTHER But I want you to believe me. I've told you everything.

CORIE Then where are your clothes?

MOTHER *That* I can't tell you.

CORIE Why not?

MOTHER Because you won't believe me.

CORIE I'll believe you.

MOTHER You won't.

CORIE I will. Where are your clothes?

MOTHER I don't know.

CORIE I don't believe you.
(*She gets up and moves toward* MOTHER)

MOTHER Didn't I say you wouldn't believe me? I just

don't know where they are . . . (*She gets up and moves to the right*) Oh, Corie, I've never been so humiliated in all my life . . .

CORIE   Don't blame yourself . . . It's all my fault. *I* did it. I did this to you.
(*She leans on the bar, holding her head*)

MOTHER   And I had horrible nightmares. I dreamt my fingers were falling off because I couldn't make a fist. (*She paces and catches sight of herself in the mirror*) Oh, God! I look like someone they woke up in the middle of the night on the *Andrea Doria!*
(*She breaks into hysterical laughter, and then there is a pounding on the door*)

VELASCO'S VOICE   Hello. Anyone home? . . .

MOTHER (*Terror-stricken*)   It's him . . . (*She rushes to* CORIE) Corie, don't let him in. I can't face him now . . . not in his bathrobe.
(*There is another pounding at the door*)

VELASCO'S VOICE   Somebody, please!

CORIE (*Moving past* MOTHER)   All right, Mother. I'll handle this. Go in the bedroom . . .

MOTHER (*Moving to the stairs*)   Tell him I'm not here. Tell him anything.
(*The door opens and* VELASCO *steps in. He is now supporting himself with a cane and his foot is covered by a thick white stocking. As* VELASCO *enters,* CORIE *sinks into the armchair at right of the couch*)

VELASCO (*Hobbling up the step and moving to the couch*) I'm sorry but I need some aspirins desperately. (*He catches sight of* MOTHER *who is furtively trying to escape up the stairs to the bedroom*) Hello, Ethel.

MOTHER (*Caught, she stops and tries to cover her embarrassment*)   Oh, hello, Victor . . . Mr. Victor . . . Mr. Velasco.

VELASCO (*To* CORIE) Did you hear what happened to us last night? (*To* MOTHER) Did you tell her what happened to us last night?

MOTHER (*Horrified*) Why . . . ? What happened to us last night? (*She composes herself*) Oh, you mean what happened to us last night. (*With great nonchalance, moving down the stairs*) Yes . . . Yes . . . I told her.

VELASCO (*At the couch*) Did you know my big toe is broken?

MOTHER (*Smiles*) Yes . . . (*She catches herself*) I mean no . . . Isn't that terrible?

VELASCO I'll have to wear a slipper for the next month . . . Only I can't find my slippers . . . (*He sees them on* MOTHER'*s feet*) Oh, there they are . . .

MOTHER (*Looks down at her feet, as if surprised*) Oh, yes . . . There's your slippers.

VELASCO (*Sitting on the sofa and putting his foot up on the coffee table*) It took me forty minutes to walk up the stairs . . . I'll have to hire someone to pull me up the ladder. (*To* CORIE) Corie, could I please have about three hundred aspirins?
  (CORIE *crosses to the stairs*)

MOTHER (*Appealing to* CORIE) A broken toe . . . Isn't that awful!
  (CORIE *ignores her and goes into the bathroom*)

VELASCO That's not the worst of it. I just had a complete examination. Guess what else I have?

MOTHER What?

VELASCO An ulcer! From all the rich food . . . I have to take little pink pills like you.

MOTHER Oh, dear . . .

VELASCO You know something, Ethel . . . I don't think I'm as young as I think I am.

MOTHER   Why do you say that?

VELASCO   Isn't it obvious? Last night I couldn't carry you
up the stairs. I can't eat rich foods any more . . . (*Very
confidentially*) . . . and I dye my hair.

MOTHER (*Moves to the couch*) Oh . . . Well, it looks
very nice.

VELASCO   Thank you . . . So are you . . .

MOTHER (*Sitting next to* VELASCO) Oh . . . Thank you.

VELASCO   I mean it, Ethel. You're a very unusual woman.

MOTHER   Unusual? . . . In what way?

VELASCO (*Reflectively*) It's funny, but I can hardly feel
my big toe at all now.

MOTHER (*Insistent*) Unusual in what way?

VELASCO   Well, I took a look at you last night . . . I took
a long, close look at you . . . Do you know what you
are, Ethel?

MOTHER (*Ready for the compliment*) What?

VELASCO   A good sport.

MOTHER   Oh . . . A good sport.

VELASCO   To have gone through all you did last night. The
trip to Staten Island, the strange food, the drinks, being
carried up to my apartment like that. And you didn't say
one word about it.

MOTHER   Well, I didn't have much chance to . . . I did a
lot of fainting.

VELASCO   Yes . . . As a matter of fact, we both did . . . If
you remember . . .
    (*Remembering, he begins to laugh*)

MOTHER   Yes . . . (*She joins in. It is a warm, hearty laugh shared by two friends. After the laugh gradually dies out, there is a moment of awkward silence and then with an attempt at renewed gaiety,* MOTHER *says*) Mr. Velasco . . . Where are my clothes?

VELASCO   Your clothes . . . ? Oh, yes . . . (*He takes a piece of paper out of his pocket*) Here.
    (*He gives it to her*)

MOTHER   I'm sure I wore more than that.

VELASCO   It's a cleaning ticket. They're sending them up at six o'clock.

MOTHER (*Taking the ticket*)   Oh, they're at the cleaner's . . . (*After a moment's hesitation*) When did I take them off?

VELASCO   You didn't . . . You were drenched and out cold. Gonzales took them off.

MOTHER (*Shocked*)   Mr. Gonzales??

VELASCO   Not Mister! . . . *Doctor* Gonzales!

MOTHER (*Relieved*)   Doctor . . . Oh, *Doctor* Gonzales . . . Well, I suppose that's all right. How convenient to have an M.D. in the building.

VELASCO (*Laughing*)   He's not an M.D. He's a Doctor of Philosophy.

MOTHER (*Joins in the laughter with great abandon*)   Oh, no . . .
    (CORIE *comes out of the bathroom with aspirin and a glass of water, and watches them laughing with bewilderment*)

CORIE (*Goes behind the couch*)   Here's the aspirins.

VELASCO   Thank you, but I'm feeling better now.

MOTHER   *I'll* take them.
    (*Takes an aspirin and a sip of water*)

VELASCO (*Gets up and hobbles to the door*) I have to go.
I'm supposed to soak my foot every hour . . .

MOTHER Oh, dear . . . Is there anything I can do?

VELASCO (*Turns back*) Yes . . . Yes, there is . . . Would
you like to have dinner with me tonight?

MOTHER (*Surprised*) Me?

VELASCO (*Nods*) If you don't mind eating plain food.

MOTHER I love *plain* food.

VELASCO Good . . . I'll call the New York Hospital for a
reservation . . . (*He opens the door*) Pick me up in a
few minutes . . . We'll have a glass of buttermilk before
we go.
    (*He exits*)

MOTHER (*After a moment, she turns to* CORIE *on the stairs
and giggles. Takes the grapes from the coffee table*)
You know what? . . . I'll bet I'm the first woman ever
asked to dinner wearing a size forty-eight bathrobe.

CORIE (*Lost in her own problem*) Mother, can I talk to
you for a minute?

MOTHER (*Puts down the bunch of grapes, gets up, and
moves right*) I just realized. I slept without a board
. . . For the first time in years I slept without a board.

CORIE Mother, will you listen . . .

MOTHER (*Turns to* CORIE) You don't suppose Uzu is a
Greek miracle drug, do you?
    (*She flips a grape back and forth and pops it into
    her mouth like a knichi*)

CORIE Mother, before you go, there's something we've got
to talk about.

MOTHER (*Moving to* CORIE) Oh, Corie, how sweet . . .
You're worried about me.

CORIE I am *not* worried about you.

MOTHER (*Looks in the mirror*) Oh, dear. My hair. What am I going to do with my hair?

CORIE I don't *care* what you do with your hair.

MOTHER If *he* can dye it, why can't I? Do you think black would make me look too Mexican?

CORIE Mother, why won't you talk to me?

MOTHER (*Moving back of the couch*) Now? . . . But Victor's waiting . . . (*She turns back to* CORIE) Why don't you and Paul come with us?

CORIE That's what I've been trying to tell you . . . Paul isn't coming back.

MOTHER What do you mean? Where'd he go?

CORIE I don't know. Reno. Texas. Wherever it is that men go to get divorced.

MOTHER *Divorced???*

CORIE That's right. Divorced. Paul and I have split up. For good.

MOTHER I don't believe it.

CORIE Why don't you believe it?

MOTHER You? And Paul?

CORIE Well, you just saw him leave here with his suitcase. What did you think he had in there?

MOTHER I don't know. I know how neat he is. I thought maybe the garbage.

CORIE Mother, I believe *you*. Why won't you believe me?

MOTHER (*Moves left to the bentwood chair and sits facing* CORIE) Because in my entire life I've never seen two people more in love than you and Paul.

CORIE (*Tearfully*) Well, it's not true. It may have been yesterday but it sure isn't today. It's all over, Mother. He's gone.

MOTHER You mean he just walked out? For no reason at all? . . .

CORIE He had a perfectly *good* reason. I *told* him to get out. *I* did it. Me and my big stupid mouth.

MOTHER It couldn't have been all your fault.

CORIE No? . . . No?? Because of me you're running around without your clothes and Paul is out there on the streets with a cold looking for a place to sleep. Who's fault is that?

MOTHER Yours! . . . But do you want to know something that may shock you? . . . I still love you.

CORIE You do? . . .

MOTHER Yes, and Paul loves you, too.

CORIE And I love him . . . Only I don't know what he wants. I don't know how to make him happy . . . Oh, Mom, what am I going to do?

MOTHER That's the first time you've asked my advice since you were ten. (*She gets up and moves to* CORIE) It's very simple. You've just got to give up a little of you for him. Don't make everything a game. Just late at night in that little room upstairs. But take care of him. And make him feel important. And if you can do that, you'll have a happy and wonderful marriage . . . Like two out of every ten couples . . . But you'll be one of the two, baby . . . (*She gently strokes* CORIE's *hair*) Now get your coat and go on out after him . . . I've got a date. (*She crosses to the coffee table and picks up her handbag*) Aunt Harriet isn't going to believe a word of this . . . (*Flourishing her bathrobe, she moves to the door and opens it*) I wish I had my Polaroid camera . . .

(She pauses, blows CORIE *a kiss, and exits.* CORIE *thinks a moment, wipes her eyes, and then rushes to the closet for her coat. Without stopping to put it on, she rushes to the door and opens it. As the door opens,* PAUL *is revealed at the doorway. He greets* CORIE *with a loud sneeze. His clothes are disheveled, his overcoat is gone, and he is obviously drunk, but he still is carrying his suitcase)*

CORIE   Paul! . . . Paul, are you all right? . . .

PAUL *(Very carefully crossing to the coffee table)*   Fine . . . Fine, thank you . . .
   (He giggles)

CORIE *(Moves to him)*   I was just going out to look for you.

PAUL *(Puts the suitcase on the floor and starts to take out his clothes)*   Oh . . . ? Where were you going to look? . . .

CORIE   I don't know. I was just going to look.

PAUL *(Confidentially)*   Oh . . . ! Well, you'll never find me.
   (He throws a handful of clothes into the closet. He is apparently amused by some secret joke)

CORIE   Paul, I've got so much to say to you, darling.

PAUL *(Taking more clothes out of the suitcase)*   So, have I, Corie . . . I got all the way downstairs and suddenly it hit me. I saw everything clearly for the first time. *(He moves up left to behind the couch)* I said to myself, this is crazy . . . Crazy! . . . It's all wrong for me to run like this . . . *(He turns to* CORIE*)* And there's only one right thing to do, Corie.

CORIE *(Moving to him)*   Really, Paul? . . . What? . . .

PAUL *(Jubilantly)*   You get out!
   (He breaks into hysterical laughter)

CORIE   What? . . .

PAUL   Why should I get out? I'm paying a hundred
twenty-five a month . . . (*He looks about the apartment*) . . . for this . . . You get out.
   (*He stuffs clothes into the dictionary*)

CORIE   But I don't want to get out!

PAUL   (*Crossing back to the suitcase and getting another
handful of clothes*)   I'm afraid you'll have to . . . The
lease is in my name . . . (*He moves to the stairs*) I'll
give you ten minutes to pack your goulash.

CORIE   (*Moves to him*)   Paul, your coat! . . . Where is
your coat?

PAUL   (*Draws himself up in indignation*)   Coat? . . . I
don't need a coat . . . It's only two degrees . . .
   (*He starts to go up the stairs, slips and falls*)

CORIE   (*Rushing to him*)   Paul, are you all right? . . .

PAUL   (*Struggling up*)   You're dawdling, Corie . . . I
want you out of here in exactly ten minutes . . .

CORIE   (*Holding him*)   Paul, you're ice cold . . . You're
freezing! . . . What have you been doing?

PAUL   (*Pulls away from her and moves to a chair*)   What
do you think I've been doing? (*He puts his foot up
on the seat*) I've been walking barefoot in the Goddamn park.

CORIE   (*Pulls up his pants leg, revealing his stockingless
foot*)   Where's your socks? . . . Are you crazy?

PAUL   No . . . No . . . But guess what I am.

CORIE   (*Looks at him*)   You're drunk!

PAUL   (*In great triumph, he moves right*)   Ah . . . ! You
finally noticed!!

CORIE   Lousy, stinkin' drunk!

PAUL   Ah, gee . . . Thanks . . .

CORIE   (*Moves to him and feels his forehead*)   You're burning up with fever.

PAUL   How about that?

CORIE   You'll get pneumonia!

PAUL   If that's what you want, that is what I'll get.

CORIE   (*Leads him to the couch*)   I want you to get those shoes off . . . They're soaking wet . . .
(*She pushes him down onto the couch*)

PAUL   I can't . . . My feet have swellened . . .

CORIE   (*Pulling his shoes off*)   I never should have let you out of here. I knew you had a cold.
(*She puts the shoes on the side table*)

PAUL   (*Getting up and moving to the doorway*)   Hey! Hey, Corie . . . Let's do that thing you said before . . . Let's wake up the police and see if all the rooms come out of the crazy neighbors . . . (*He opens the door and shouts into the hall*) All right, everybody up . . .

CORIE   (*Runs to him and pulls him back into the room*)   Will you shut up and get into bed . . . (*As she struggles with him, she tickles him, and* PAUL *falls to the floor behind the couch.* CORIE *closes the door behind her*) Get into bed . . .

PAUL   You get in first.

CORIE   You're sick.

PAUL   Not *that* sick . . .
(*He lunges for her and she backs away against the door*)

CORIE   Stop it, Paul . . .

PAUL   Come on, Corie. Let's break my fever . . .
(*He grabs her*)

CORIE   I said stop it! (*Struggling to get away*) I mean it,
damn you . . . Stop it!
(*She gives him an elbow in the stomach and dodges
away through the kitchen*)

PAUL   Gee, you're pretty when you're mean and rotten.

CORIE   Keep away from me, Paul . . . (PAUL *moves toward her*) I'm warning you . . . I'll scream.
(CORIE *keeps the couch between her and* PAUL)

PAUL (*Stops*)   Shh . . . ! There's snow on the roof. We'll
have an avalanche! . . .

CORIE (*Dodging behind the chair*)   You shouldn't be
walking around like this. You've got a fever . . .

PAUL (*Moving to the chair*)   Stand still! The both of
you!

CORIE (*Running up the stairs to the bathroom*)   No, Paul
. . . ! I don't like you when you're like this.
(*She barricades herself in the bathroom*)

PAUL (*Chasing her and pounding on the door*)   Open
this door!

CORIE (*From the bathroom*)   I can't . . . I'm scared.

PAUL   Of me?

CORIE   Yes.

PAUL   Why?

CORIE   Because it's not you anymore . . . I want the old
Paul back.

PAUL   That fuddy duddy?

CORIE   He's not a fuddy duddy. He's dependable and he's strong and he takes care of me and tells me how much I can spend and protects me from people like you . . . (PAUL *suddenly has a brain storm and with great glee sneaks off into the bedroom*) And I just want him to know how much I love him . . . And that I'm going to make everything here exactly the way he wants it . . . I'm going to fix the hole in the skylight . . . and the leak in the closet . . . And I'm going to put in a bath-tub and if he wants I'll even carry him up the stairs every night . . . Because I want him to know how much I love him . . . (*Slowly and cautiously opening the door*) Can you hear me, darling? . . . Paul? . . . (PAUL *appears on the skylight. He is crawling drunkenly along the ledge.* CORIE, *having gotten no answer, comes out of the bathroom and goes into the bedroom searching for* PAUL) Paul, are you all right?
      (*She comes out of the bedroom and crosses toward the front door. When she is beneath him,* PAUL *taps on the skylight and stands up.* CORIE, *looking up, sees him and screams*)

CORIE   (*Screams*)   Paul . . . You idiot . . . Come down . . . You'll kill yourself.

PAUL   (*Teetering on the ledge, yelling through the skylight*)   I want to be a nut like everyone else in this building.

CORIE   (*Up on her knees on the couch, yelling back*)   No! No, Paul! . . . I don't want you to be a nut. I want you to come down.

PAUL   I'll come down when you've said it again . . . Loud and clear.

CORIE   What? . . . Anything, Paul . . . Anything!

PAUL   My husband . . .

CORIE   "My husband . . ."

PAUL   Paul Bratter . . .

CORIE   "Paul Bratter . . ."

PAUL   . . . rising young attorney . . .
    (*He nearly falls off the ledge*)

CORIE   (*Screaming in fright*) ". . . rising young attorney . . ."

PAUL   . . . is a lousy stinkin' drunk . . .

CORIE   ". . . is a lousy stinkin' drunk." . . . And I love him.

PAUL   And I love you, Corie. Even when I didn't like you, I loved you.

CORIE   (*Crossing to* PAUL) Then please, darling . . . Please, come down.

PAUL   I . . . I can't . . . Not now.

CORIE   Why not?

PAUL   I'm going to be sick . . .
    (*He looks around as if to find a place to be sick*)

CORIE   Oh, no!

PAUL   Oh, yes!

CORIE   (*Paces back and forth*) Paul . . . Paul . . . Don't move! I'll come out and get you.

PAUL   (*Holding on desperately*) Would you do that, Corie? Because I'm getting panicky!

CORIE   Yes . . . Yes, darling, I'm coming . . .
    (*She runs off into the bedroom*)

PAUL   Corie . . . Corie . . .

CORIE (*Dashing out of the bedroom and down the stairs*) What, Paul? . . . What???

PAUL   Don't leave me . . .

CORIE   You'll be all right, darling. Just hold on tight. And try to be calm . . .

PAUL   How? What should I do?

CORIE (*Ponders*)   What should he do? (*To* PAUL) Sing, Paul!

PAUL   Sing??

CORIE   Sing . . . Keep singing as loud as you can until I come out there. Promise me you'll keep singing, Paul . . .

PAUL   Yes, yes . . . I promise . . . I'll keep singing . . .

CORIE (*Moving to the stairs*)   But don't stop until I come out . . . I love you, darling . . . Keep singing, Paul . . . Keep singing!
(*She runs off into the bedroom*)

PAUL (*Calling after her in desperation*)   Corie, Corie, what song should I sing?? . . . Oh, God . . . (*He pulls himself together*) "Shama, shama. . . ."

Curtain

The
Odd Couple

Act One

It is a warm summer night in OSCAR MADISON's *apartment. This is one of those large eight-room affairs on Riverside Drive in the upper eighties. The building is about thirty-five years old and still has vestiges of its glorious past —high ceilings, walk-in closets and thick walls. We are in the living room with doors leading off to the kitchen, a bedroom and a bathroom, and a hallway to the other bedrooms.*

Although the furnishings have been chosen with extreme good taste, the room itself, without the touch and care of a woman these past few months, is now a study in slovenliness. Dirty dishes, discarded clothes, old newspapers, empty bottles, glasses filled and unfilled, opened and unopened laundry packages, mail and disarrayed furniture abound. The only cheerful note left in this room is the lovely view of the New Jersey Palisades through its twelfth-floor window. Three months ago this was a lovely apartment.

As the curtain rises, the room is filled with smoke. A poker game is in progress. There are six chairs around the table but only four men are sitting. They are MURRAY, ROY, SPEED *and* VINNIE. VINNIE, *with the largest stack of chips in front of him, is nervously tapping his foot; he keeps checking his watch.* ROY *is watching* SPEED *and* SPEED *is glaring at* MURRAY *with incredulity and utter fascination.* MURRAY *is the dealer. He slowly and methodically tries to shuffle. It is a ponderous and painful business.* SPEED *shakes his head in disbelief. This is all done wordlessly.*

SPEED (*Cups his chin in his hand and looks at* MURRAY) Tell me, Mr. Maverick, is this your first time on the riverboat?

MURRAY (*With utter disregard*) You don't like it, get a machine.

(*He continues to deal slowly*)

ROY Geez, it stinks in here.

VINNIE (*Looks at his watch*) What time is it?

SPEED   Again what time is it?

VINNIE (*Whining*) My watch is slow. I'd like to know what time it is.

SPEED (*Glares at him*) You're winning ninety-five dollars, that's what time it is. Where the hell are you running?

VINNIE   I'm not running anywhere. I just asked what time it was. Who said anything about running?

ROY (*Looks at his watch*) It's ten-thirty.
        (*There is a pause.* MURRAY *continues to shuffle*)

VINNIE (*After the pause*) I got to leave by twelve.

SPEED (*Looks up in despair*) Oh, Christ!

VINNIE   I told you that when I sat down. I got to leave by twelve. Murray, didn't I say that when I sat down? I said I got to leave by twelve.

SPEED   All right, don't talk to him. He's dealing. (*To* MURRAY) Murray, you wanna rest for a while? Go lie down, sweetheart.

MURRAY   You want speed or accuracy, make up your mind.
        (*He begins to deal slowly.* SPEED *puffs on his cigar angrily*)

ROY   Hey, you want to do me a really big favor? Smoke toward New Jersey.
        (SPEED *blows smoke at* ROY)

MURRAY   No kidding, I'm really worried about Felix. (*Points to an empty chair*) He's never been this late before. Maybe somebody should call. (*Yells off*) Hey, Oscar, why don't you call Felix?

ROY (*Waves his hand through the smoke*) Listen, why don't we chip in three dollars apiece and buy another window. How the hell can you breathe in here?

MURRAY   How many cards you got, four?

SPEED   Yes, Murray, we all have four cards. When you give us one more, we'll all have five. If you were to give us two more, we'd have six. Understand how it works now?

ROY (*Yells off*)   Hey, Oscar, what do you say? In or out?
(*From offstage we hear* OSCAR's *voice*)

OSCAR (*Offstage*)   Out, pussycat, out!
(SPEED *opens and the others bet*)

VINNIE   I told my wife I'd be home by one the latest. We're making an eight o'clock plane to Florida. I told you that when I sat down.

SPEED   Don't cry, Vinnie. You're forty-two years old. It's embarrassing. Give me two . . .
(*He discards*)

ROY   Why doesn't he fix the air conditioner? It's ninety-eight degrees, and it sits there sweating like everyone else. I'm out.
(*He goes to the window and looks out*)

MURRAY   Who goes to Florida in July?

VINNIE   It's off-season. There's no crowds and you get the best room for one-tenth the price. No cards . . .

SPEED   Some vacation. Six cheap people in an empty hotel.

MURRAY   Dealer takes four . . . Hey, you think maybe Felix is sick? (*He points to the empty chair*) I mean he's never been this late before.

ROY (*Takes a laundry bag from an armchair and sits*)   You know, it's the same garbage from last week's game. I'm beginning to recognize things.

MURRAY (*Throwing his cards down*)   I'm out . . .

SPEED (*Showing his hand*)   Two kings . . .

VINNIE   Straight . . .
(*He shows his hand and takes in the pot*)

MURRAY   Hey, maybe he's in his office locked in the john again. Did you know Felix was once locked in the john overnight. He wrote out his entire will on a half a roll of toilet paper! Heee, what a nut!
(VINNIE *is playing with his chips*)

SPEED (*Glares at him as he shuffles the cards*)   Don't play with your chips. I'm asking you nice; don't play with your chips.

VINNIE (*To* SPEED) I'm not playing. I'm counting. Leave me alone. What are you picking on me for? How much do you think I'm winning? Fifteen dollars!

SPEED Fifteen dollars? You dropped more than that in your cuffs!

(SPEED *deals a game of draw poker*)

MURRAY (*Yells off*) Hey, Oscar, what do you say?

OSCAR (*Enters carrying a tray with beer, sandwiches, a can of peanuts, and opened bags of pretzels and Fritos*) I'm in! I'm in! Go ahead. Deal!

(OSCAR MADISON *is forty-three. He is a pleasant, appealing man who seems to enjoy life to the fullest. He enjoys his weekly poker game, his friends, his excessive drinking and his cigars. He is also one of those lucky creatures in life who even enjoys his work—he's a sports-writer for the New York* Post. *His carefree attitude is evident in the sloppiness of his household, but it seems to bother others more than it does* OSCAR. *This is not to say that* OSCAR *is without cares or worries. He just doesn't seem to have any*)

VINNIE Aren't you going to look at your cards?

OSCAR (*Sets the tray on a side chair*) What for? I'm gonna bluff anyway. (*Opens a bottle of Coke*) Who gets the Coke?

MURRAY I get a Coke.

OSCAR My friend Murray the policeman gets a warm Coke.

(*He gives him the bottle*)

ROY (*Opens the betting*) You still didn't fix the refrigerator? It's been two weeks now. No wonder it stinks in here.

OSCAR (*Picks up his cards*) Temper, temper. If I wanted nagging I'd go back with my wife. (*Throws them down*) I'm out. Who wants food?

MURRAY What have you got?

OSCAR (*Looks under the bread*) I got brown sandwiches and green sandwiches. Well, what do you say?

MURRAY What's the green?

OSCAR It's either very new cheese or very old meat.

MURRAY I'll take the brown.
(OSCAR *gives* MURRAY *a sandwich*)

ROY (*Glares at* MURRAY) Are you crazy? You're not going to eat that, are you?

MURRAY I'm hungry.

ROY His refrigerator's been broken for two weeks. I saw milk standing in there that wasn't even in the bottle.

OSCAR (*To* ROY) What are you, some kind of a health nut? Eat, Murray, eat!

ROY I've got six cards . . .

SPEED That figures—I've got three aces. Misdeal.
(*They all throw their cards in.* SPEED *begins to shuffle*)

VINNIE You know who makes very good sandwiches? Felix. Did you ever taste his cream cheese and pimento on date-nut bread?

SPEED (*To* VINNIE) All right, make up your mind poker or menus. (OSCAR *opens a can of beer, which sprays in a geyser over the players and the table. There is a hubbub as they all yell at* OSCAR. *He hands* ROY *the overflowing can and pushes the puddle of beer under the chair. The players start to go back to the game only to be sprayed again as* OSCAR *opens another beer can. There is another outraged cry as they try to stop* OSCAR *and mop up the beer on the table with a towel which was hanging on the standing lamp.* OSCAR, *undisturbed, gives them the beer and the bags of refreshments, and they finally sit back in their chairs.* OSCAR *wipes his hands on the sleeve of* ROY's *jacket which is hanging on the back of the chair*) Hey, Vinnie, tell Oscar what time you're leaving.

VINNIE (*Like a trained dog*) Twelve o'clock.

SPEED (*To the others*) You hear? We got ten minutes before the next announcement. All right, this game is five card stud. (*He deals and ad libs calling the cards, ending with* MURRAY's *card*) . . . And a bullet for the policeman. All right, Murray, it's your bet. (*No answer*) Do something, huh.

OSCAR (*Getting a drink at the bar*) Don't yell at my friend Murray.

MURRAY (*Throwing in a coin*) I'm in for a quarter.

OSCAR (*Proudly looks in* MURRAY's *eyes*) Beautiful, baby, beautiful.
>   (*He sits down and begins to open the can of peanuts*)

ROY Hey, Oscar, let's make a rule. Every six months you have to buy fresh potato chips. How can you live like this? Don't you have a maid?

OSCAR (*Shakes his head*) She quit after my wife and kids left. The work got to be too much for her. (*He looks on the table*) The pot's shy. Who didn't put in a quarter?

MURRAY (*To* OSCAR) You didn't.

OSCAR (*Puts in money*) You got a big mouth, Murray. Just for that, lend me twenty dollars.
>   (SPEED *deals another round*)

MURRAY I just loaned you twenty dollars ten minutes ago.
>   (*They all join in a round of betting*)

OSCAR You loaned me *ten* dollars *twenty* minutes ago. Learn to count, pussycat.

MURRAY Learn to play poker, chicken licken! Borrow from somebody else. I keep winning my own money back.

ROY (*To* OSCAR) You owe everybody in the game. If you don't have it, you shouldn't play.

OSCAR All right, I'm through being the nice one. You owe me six dollars apiece for the buffet.

SPEED (*Dealing another round of cards*) Buffet? Hot beer and two sandwiches left over from when you went to high school?

OSCAR What do you want at a poker game, a tomato surprise? Murray, lend me twenty dollars or I'll call your wife and tell her you're in Central Park wearing a dress.

MURRAY You want money, ask Felix.

OSCAR He's not here.

MURRAY Neither am I.

ROY (*Gives him money*) All right, here. You're on the books for another twenty.

OSCAR   How many times are you gonna keep saying it?
(*He takes the money*)

MURRAY   When are you gonna call Felix?

OSCAR   When are we gonna play poker?

MURRAY   Aren't you even worried? It's the first game he's
missed in over two years.

OSCAR   The record is fifteen years set by Lou Gehrig in
1939! I'll call! I'll call!

ROY   How can you be so lazy?
(*The phone rings*)

OSCAR   (*Throwing his cards in*)   Call me irresponsible,
I'm funny that way.
(*He goes to the phone*)

SPEED   Pair of sixes . . .

VINNIE   Three deuces . . .

SPEED   (*Throws up his hands in despair*)   This is my last
week. I get all the aggravation I need at home.
(OSCAR *picks up the phone*)

OSCAR   Hello! Oscar the Poker Player!

VINNIE   (*To* OSCAR)   If it's my wife tell her I'm leaving at
twelve.

SPEED   (*To* VINNIE)   You look at your watch once more
and you get the peanuts in your face. (*To* ROY) Deal the
cards!
(*The game continues during* OSCAR's *phone conversation, with* ROY *dealing a game of stud*)

OSCAR   (*Into the phone*)   Who? Who did you want,
please? *Dabby?* Dabby who? No, there's no Dabby
here. Oh, *Daddy!* (*To the others*) For crise sakes, it's my
kid. (*Back into the phone, he speaks with great love and
affection*) Brucey, hello, baby. Yes, it's Daddy! (*There
is a general outburst of ad libbing from the poker players. To the others*) Hey, come on, give me a break,
willya? My five-year-old kid is calling from California.
It must be costing him a fortune. (*Back into the phone*)
How've you been, sweetheart? Yes, I finally got your
letter. It took three weeks. Yes, but next time you tell
Mommy to give you a stamp. I know, but you're not
supposed to draw it on. (*He laughs. To the others*) You
hear?

SPEED   We hear. We hear. We're all thrilled.

OSCAR   (*Into the phone*) What's that, darling? What goldfish? Oh, in your room! Oh, sure. Sure, I'm taking care of them. (*He holds the phone over his chest*) Oh, God, I killed my kid's goldfish! (*Back into the phone*) Yes, I feed them every day.

ROY   Murderer!

OSCAR   Mommy wants to speak to me? Right. Take care of yourself, soldier. I love you.

VINNIE   (*Beginning to deal a game of stud*) Ante a dollar . . .

SPEED   (*To* OSCAR) Cost you a dollar to play. You got a dollar?

OSCAR   Not after I get through talking to this lady. (*Into the phone with false cheerfulness*) Hello, Blanche. How are you? Err, yes, I have a pretty good idea why you're calling. I'm a week behind with the check, right? *Four* weeks? That's not possible. Because it's not possible. Blanche, I keep a record of every check and I *know* I'm only *three* weeks behind! Blanche, I'm trying the best I can. Blanche, don't threaten me with jail because it's not a threat. With my expenses and my alimony, a prisoner takes home more pay than I do! Very nice, in front of the kids. Blanche, don't tell me you're going to have my salary attached, just say goodbye! Goodbye! (*He hangs up. To the players*) I'm eight hundred dollars behind in alimony so let's up the stakes.
    (*He gets his drink from the poker table*)

ROY   She can do it, you know.

OSCAR   What?

ROY   Throw you in jail. For nonsupport of the kids.

OSCAR   Never. If she can't call me once a week to aggravate me, she's not happy.
    (*He crosses to the bar*)

MURRAY   It doesn't bother you? That you can go to jail? Or that maybe your kids don't have enough clothes or enough to eat?

OSCAR   Murray, *Poland* could live for a year on what my kids leave over from lunch! Can we play cards?
    (*He refills his drink*)

ROY But that's the point. You shouldn't *be* in this kind of trouble. It's because you don't know how to manage anything. I should know; I'm your accountant.

OSCAR (*Crossing to the table*) If you're my accountant, how come I need money?

ROY If you need money, how come you play poker?

OSCAR Because I need money.

ROY But you always lose.

OSCAR That's why I need the money! Listen, *I'm* not complaining. *You're* complaining. I get along all right. I'm living.

ROY Alone? In eight dirty rooms?

OSCAR If I win tonight, I'll buy a broom.
       (MURRAY *and* SPEED *buy chips from* VINNIE. *and* MURRAY *begins to shuffle the deck for a game of draw*)

ROY That's not what you need. What you need is a wife.

OSCAR How can I afford a wife when I can't afford a broom?

ROY Then don't play poker.

OSCAR (*Puts down his drink, rushes to* ROY *and they struggle over the bag of potato chips. which rips, showering everyone. They all begin to yell at one another*) Then don't come to my house and eat my potato chips!

MURRAY What are you yelling about? We're playing a friendly game.

SPEED Who's *playing?* We've been sitting here talking since eight o'clock.

VINNIE Since *seven*. That's why I said I was going to quit at *twelve*.

SPEED How'd you like a stale banana right in the mouth?

MURRAY (*The peacemaker*) All right, all right, let's calm down. Take it easy. I'm a cop, you know. I could arrest the whole lousy game. (*He finishes dealing the cards*) Four . . .

OSCAR (*Sitting at the table*) My friend Murray the Cop is right. Let's just play cards. And please hold them up; I can't see where I marked them.

MURRAY   You're worse than the kids from the PAL.

OSCAR   But you still love me, Roy, sweety, right?

ROY (*Petulant*)   Yeah, yeah.

OSCAR   That's not good enough. Come on, say it. In front of the whole poker game. "I love you, Oscar Madison."

ROY   You don't take any of this seriously, do you? You owe money to your wife, your government, your friends . . .

OSCAR (*Throws his cards down*)   What do you want me to do, Roy, jump in the garbage disposal and grind myself to death? (*The phone rings. He goes to answer it*) Life goes on even for those of us who are divorced, broke and sloppy. (*Into the phone*) Hello? Divorced, Broke and Sloppy. Oh, hello, sweetheart. (*He becomes very seductive, pulls the phone to the side and talks low, but he is still audible to the others, who turn and listen*) I told you not to call me during the game. I can't talk to you now. You *know* I do, darling. All right, just a minute. (*He turns*) Murray, it's your wife.

> (*He puts the phone on the table and sits on the sofa*)

MURRAY (*Nods disgustedly as he crosses to the phone*) I wish you *were* having an affair with her. Then she wouldn't bother *me* all the time. (*He picks up the phone*) Hello, Mimi, what's wrong?

> (SPEED *gets up, stretches and goes into the bathroom*)

OSCAR (*In a woman's voice, imitating* MIMI)   What time are you coming home? (*Then imitating* MURRAY) I don't know, about twelve, twelve-thirty.

MURRAY (*Into the phone*)   I don't know, about twelve, twelve-thirty! (ROY *gets up and stretches*) Why, what did you want, Mimi? "A corned beef sandwich and a strawberry malted!"

OSCAR   Is she pregnant again?

MURRAY (*Holds the phone over his chest*)   No, just fat! (*There is the sound of a toilet flushing, and after* SPEED *comes out of the bathroom,* VINNIE *goes in. Into the phone again*) What? How could you hear that? I had the phone over my chest. Who? Felix? No, he didn't show up tonight. What's wrong? You're kidding! How should I know? All right, all right, goodbye. (*The toilet flushes again, and after* VINNIE *comes out of the bathroom,* ROY *goes in*) Goodbye, Mimi. Goodbye. (*He hangs up. To the others*) Well, what did I tell you? I knew it!

ROY   What's the matter?

MURRAY (*Pacing by the couch*)   Felix is missing!

OSCAR   Who?

MURRAY   Felix! Felix Ungar! The man who sits in that chair every week and cleans ashtrays. I told you something was up.

SPEED (*At the table*)   What do you mean, missing?

MURRAY   He didn't show up for work today. He didn't come home tonight. No one knows where he is. Mimi just spoke to his wife.

VINNIE (*In his chair at the poker table*)   Felix?

MURRAY   They looked everywhere. I'm telling you he's missing.

OSCAR   Wait a minute. No one is missing for one day.

VINNIE   That's right. You've got to be missing for forty-eight hours before you're missing. The worst he could be is lost.

MURRAY   How could he be lost? He's forty-four years old and lives on West End Avenue. What's the matter with you?

ROY (*Sitting in an armchair*)   Maybe he had an accident.

OSCAR   They would have heard.

ROY   If he's laying in a gutter somewhere? Who would know who he is?

OSCAR   He's got ninety-two credit cards in his wallet. The minute something happens to him, America lights up.

VINNIE   Maybe he went to a movie. You know how long those pictures are today.

SPEED (*Looks at* VINNIE *contemptuously*)   No wonder you're going to Florida in July! Dumb, dumb, dumb!

ROY   Maybe he was mugged?

OSCAR   For thirty-six hours? How much money could he have on him?

ROY   Maybe they took his clothes. I knew a guy who was mugged in a doctor's office. He had to go home in a nurse's uniform.
(OSCAR *throws a pillow from the couch at* ROY)

SPEED   Murray, you're a cop. What do you think?

MURRAY   I think it's something real bad.

SPEED   How do you know?

MURRAY   I can feel it in my bones.

SPEED (*To the others*)   You hear? Bulldog Drummond.

ROY   Maybe he's drunk. Does he drink?

OSCAR   Felix? On New Year's Eve he has Pepto-Bismal. What are we guessing? I'll call his wife.
(*He picks up the phone*)

SPEED   Wait a minute! Don't start anything yet. Just 'cause we don't know where he is doesn't mean somebody else doesn't. Does he have a girl?

VINNIE   A what?

SPEED   A girl? You know. Like when you're through work early.

MURRAY   Felix? Playing around? Are you crazy? He wears a vest and galoshes.

SPEED (*Gets up and moves toward* MURRAY)   You mean you automatically know who has and who hasn't got a girl on the side?

MURRAY (*Moves to* SPEED)   Yes, I automatically know.

SPEED   All right, you're so smart. Have I got a girl?

MURRAY   No, you haven't got a girl. What you've got is what *I've* got. What you *wish* you got and what you *got* is a whole different civilization! *Oscar* maybe has a girl on the side.

SPEED   That's different. He's divorced. That's not on the side. That's in the middle.
(*He moves to the table*)

OSCAR (*To them both as he starts to dial*)   You through? 'Cause one of our poker players is missing. I'd like to find out about him.

VINNIE   I thought he looked edgy the last couple of weeks. *(To* SPEED*)* Didn't you think he looked edgy?

SPEED   No. As a matter of fact, I thought *you* looked edgy. *(He moves down to the right)*

OSCAR *(Into the phone)*   Hello? Frances? Oscar. I just heard.

ROY   Tell her not to worry. She's probably hysterical.

MURRAY   Yeah, you know women.
  (He sits down on the couch)

OSCAR *(Into the phone)*   Listen, Frances, the most important thing is not to worry. Oh! *(To the others)* She's not worried.

MURRAY   Sure.

OSCAR *(Into the phone)*   Frances, do you have *any* idea where he could be? He what? You're kidding? Why? No, I didn't know. Gee, that's too bad. All right, listen, Frances, you just sit tight and the minute I hear anything I'll let you know. Right. G'bye.
  (He hangs up. They all look at him expectantly. He gets up wordlessly and crosses to the table, thinking. They all watch him a second, not being able to stand it any longer)

MURRAY   Ya gonna tell us or do we hire a private detective?

OSCAR   They broke up!

ROY   Who?

OSCAR   Felix and Frances! They broke up! The entire marriage is through.

VINNIE   You're kidding!

ROY   I don't believe it.

SPEED   After twelve years?
  *(*OSCAR *sits down at the table)*

VINNIE   They were such a happy couple.

MURRAY   Twelve years doesn't mean you're a *happy* couple. It just means you're a *long* couple.

SPEED   Go figure it. Felix and Frances.

ROY   What are you surprised at? He used to sit there every Friday night and tell us how they were fighting.

SPEED   I know. But who believes Felix?

VINNIE   What happened?

OSCAR   She wants out, that's all.

MURRAY   He'll go to pieces. I know Felix. He's going to try something crazy.

SPEED   That's all he ever used to talk about. "My beautiful wife. My wonderful wife." What happened?

OSCAR   His beautiful, wonderful wife can't stand him, that's what happened.

MURRAY   He'll kill himself. You hear what I'm saying? He's going to go out and try to kill himself.

SPEED   (*To* MURRAY)   Will you shut up, Murray? Stop being a cop for two minutes. (*To* OSCAR) Where'd he go, Oscar?

OSCAR   He went out to kill himself.

MURRAY   What did I tell you?

ROY   (*To* OSCAR)   Are you serious?

OSCAR   That's what she said. He was going out to kill himself. He didn't want to do it at home 'cause the kids were sleeping.

VINNIE   Why?

OSCAR   Why? Because that's Felix, that's why. (*He goes to the bar and refills his drink*) You know what he's like. He sleeps on the window sill. "Love me or I'll jump." 'Cause he's a nut, that's why.

MURRAY   That's right. Remember he tried something like that in the army? She wanted to break off the engagement so he started cleaning guns in his mouth.

SPEED   I don't believe it. Talk! That's all Felix is, talk.

VINNIE   (*Worried*)   But is that what he said? In those words? "I'm going to kill myself?"

OSCAR   (*Pacing about the table*)   I don't know in what words. She didn't read it to me.

ROY   You mean he left her a note?

OSCAR   No, he sent a telegram.

MURRAY A *suicide telegram?* Who sends a suicide telegram?

OSCAR Felix, the nut, that's who! Can you imagine getting a thing like that? She even has to tip the kid a quarter.

ROY I don't get it. If he wants to kill himself, why does he send a telegram?

OSCAR Don't you see how his mind works? If he sends a note, she might not get it till Monday and he'd have no excuse for not being dead. This way, for a dollar ten, he's got a chance to be saved.

VINNIE You mean he really doesn't want to kill himself? He just wants sympathy.

OSCAR What he'd really like is to go to the funeral and sit in the back. He'd be the biggest crier there.

MURRAY He's right.

OSCAR Sure I'm right.

MURRAY We get these cases every day. All they want is attention. We got a guy who calls us every Saturday afternoon from the George Washington Bridge.

ROY I don't know. You never can tell what a guy'll do when he's hysterical.

MURRAY Nahhh. Nine out of ten times they don't jump.

ROY What about the tenth time?

MURRAY They jump. He's right. There's a possibility.

OSCAR Not with Felix. I know him. He's too nervous to kill himself. He wears his seatbelt in a drive-in movie.

VINNIE Isn't there someplace we could look for him?

SPEED Where? Where would you look? Who knows where he is?
        (*The doorbell rings. They all look at* OSCAR)

OSCAR Of course! If you're going to kill yourself, where's the safest place to do it? With your friends!
        (VINNIE *starts for the door*)

MURRAY (*Stopping him*) Wait a minute! The guy may be hysterical. Let's play it nice and easy. If *we're* calm, maybe *he'll* be calm.

ROY (*Getting up and joining them*) That's right. That's how they do it with those guys out on the ledge. You talk nice and soft.
(SPEED *rushes over to them, and joins in the frenzied discussion*)

VINNIE What'll we say to him?

MURRAY We don't say nothin'. Like we never heard a thing.

OSCAR (*Trying to get their attention*) You through with this discussion? Because he already could have hung himself out in the hall. (*To* VINNIE) Vinnie, open the door!

MURRAY Remember! Like we don't know nothin'.
(*They all rush back to their seats and grab up cards, which they concentrate on with the greatest intensity.* VINNIE *opens the door.* FELIX UNGAR *is there. He's about forty-four. His clothes are rumpled as if he had slept in them, and he needs a shave. Although he tries to act matter-of-fact, there is an air of great tension and nervousness about him*)

FELIX (*Softly*) Hi, Vin! (VINNIE *quickly goes back to his seat and studies his cards.* FELIX *has his hands in his pockets, trying to be very nonchalant. With controlled calm*) Hi, fellas. (*They all mumble hello, but do not look at him. He puts his coat over the railing and crosses to the table*) How's the game going? (*They all mumble appropriate remarks, and continue staring at their cards*) Good! Good! Sorry I'm late. (FELIX *looks a little disappointed that no one asks "What?" He starts to pick up a sandwich, changes his mind and makes a gesture of distaste. He vaguely looks around*) Any Coke left?

OSCAR (*Looking up from his cards*) Coke? Gee, I don't think so. I got a Seven-Up!

FELIX (*Bravely*) No, I felt like a Coke. I just don't feel like Seven-Up tonight!
(*He stands watching the game*)

OSCAR What's the bet?

SPEED You bet a quarter. It's up to Murray. Murray, what do you say? (MURRAY *is staring at* FELIX) Murray! Murray!

ROY (*To* VINNIE)   Tap his shoulder.

VINNIE (*Taps* MURRAY's *shoulder*)   Murray!

MURRAY (*Startled*)   What? What?

SPEED   It's up to you.

MURRAY   Why is it always up to me?

SPEED   It's not always up to you. It's up to you now. What do you do?

MURRAY   I'm in. I'm in.
   (*He throws in a quarter*)

FELIX (*Moves to the bookcase*)   Anyone call about me?

OSCAR   Er, not that I can remember. (*To the others*) Did anyone call for Felix? (*They all shrug and ad lib "No"*) Why? Were you expecting a call?

FELIX (*Looking at the books on the shelf*)   No! No! Just asking.
   (*He opens a book and examines it*)

ROY   Er, I'll see his bet and raise it a dollar.

FELIX (*Without looking up from the book*)   I just thought someone might have called.

SPEED   It costs me a dollar and a quarter to play, right?

OSCAR   Right!

FELIX (*Still looking at the book, in a sing-song*)   But, if no one called, no one called.
   (*He slams the book shut and puts it back. They all jump at the noise*)

SPEED (*Getting nervous*)   What does it cost me to play again?

MURRAY (*Angry*)   A dollar and a quarter! *A dollar and a quarter!* Pay attention, for crise sakes!

ROY   All right, take it easy. Take it easy.

OSCAR   Let's calm down, everyone, heh?

MURRAY   I'm sorry. I can't help it. (*Points to* SPEED) He makes me nervous.

SPEED   I make *you* nervous. You make *me* nervous. You make *everyone* nervous.

MURRAY (*Sarcastic*) I'm sorry. Forgive me. I'll kill my-self.

OSCAR Murray!
(*He motions with his head to* FELIX)

MURRAY (*Realizes his error*) Oh! Sorry.
(SPEED *glares at him. They all sit in silence a mo-ment, until* VINNIE *catches sight of* FELIX, *who is now staring out an upstage window. He quickly calls the others' attention to* FELIX)

FELIX (*Looking back at them from the window*) Gee, it's a pretty view from here. What is it, twelve floors?

OSCAR (*Quickly crossing to the window and closing it*) No. It's only eleven. That's all. Eleven. It says twelve but it's really only eleven. (*He then turns and closes the other window as* FELIX *watches him.* OSCAR *shivers slightly*) Chilly in here. (*To the others*) Isn't it chilly in here?
(*He crosses back to the table*)

ROY Yeah, that's much better.

OSCAR (*To* FELIX) Want to sit down and play? It's still early.

VINNIE Sure. We're in no rush. We'll be here till three, four in the morning.

FELIX (*Shrugs*) I don't know; I just don't feel much like playing now.

OSCAR (*Sitting at the table*) Oh! Well, what *do* you feel like doing?

FELIX (*Shrugs*) I'll find *something.* (*He starts to walk to-ward the other room*) Don't worry about me.

OSCAR Where are you going?

FELIX (*Stops in the doorway. He looks at the others who are all staring at him*) To the john.

OSCAR (*Looks at the others, worried, then at* FELIX) Alone?

FELIX (*Nods*) I always go alone! Why?

OSCAR (*Shrugs*) No reason. You gonna be in there long?

FELIX (*Shrugs, then says meaningfully, like a martyr*) As long as it takes.

*(Then he goes into the bathroom and slams the
door shut behind him. Immediately they all jump
up and crowd about the bathroom door, whispering
in frenzied anxiety)*

MURRAY Are you crazy? Letting him go to the john
alone?

OSCAR What did you want me to do?

ROY Stop him! Go in with him!

OSCAR Suppose he just has to go to the john?

MURRAY Supposing he does? He's better off being embarrassed than dead!

OSCAR How's he going to kill himself in the john?

SPEED What do you mean, how? Razor blades, pills. Anything that's in there.

OSCAR That's the kids' bathroom. The worst he could do
is brush his teeth to death.

ROY He could jump.

VINNIE That's right. Isn't there a window in there?

OSCAR It's only six inches wide.

MURRAY He could break the glass. He could cut his
wrists.

OSCAR He could also flush himself into the East River.
I'm telling you he's not going to try anything!
(He moves to the table)

ROY *(Goes to the doorway)* Shhh! Listen! He's crying.
(There is a pause as all listen as FELIX *sobs)* You hear
that. He's crying.

MURRAY Isn't that terrible? For God's sakes, Oscar, do
something! Say something!

OSCAR What? What do you say to a man who's crying in
your bathroom?
(There is the sound of the toilet flushing and ROY
makes a mad dash back to his chair)

ROY He's coming!
(They all scramble back to their places. MURRAY
gets mixed up with VINNIE *and they quickly
straighten it out.* FELIX *comes back into the room.
But he seems calm and collected, with no evident
sign of having cried)*

FELIX I guess I'll be running along.
(*He starts for the door.* OSCAR *jumps up. So do the others*)

OSCAR Felix, wait a second.

FELIX No! No! I can't talk to you. I can't talk to anyone.
(*They all try to grab him, stopping him near the stairs*)

MURRAY Felix, please. We're your friends. Don't run out like this.
(FELIX *struggles to pull away*)

OSCAR Felix, sit down. Just for a minute. Talk to us.

FELIX There's nothing to talk about. There's nothing to say. It's over. Over. Everything is over. Let me go!

(*He breaks away from them and dashes into the stage-right bedroom. They start to chase him and he dodges from the bedroom through the adjoining door into the bathroom*)

ROY Stop him! Grab him!

FELIX (*Looking for an exit*) Let me out! I've got to get out of here!

OSCAR Felix, you're hysterical.

FELIX Please let me out of here!

MURRAY The john! Don't let him get in the john!

FELIX (*Comes out of the bathroom with* ROY *hanging onto him, and the others trailing behind*) Leave alone. Why doesn't everyone leave me alone?

OSCAR All right, Felix, I'm warning you. Now cut it out!
(*He throws a half-filled glass of water, which he has picked up from the bookcase, into* FELIX'S *face*)

FELIX It's *my* problem. I'll work it out. Leave me alone. Oh, my stomach.
(*He collapses in* ROY'S *arms*)

MURRAY What's the matter with your stomach?

VINNIE He looks sick. Look at his face.
(*They all try to hold him as they lead him over to the couch*)

FELIX I'm not sick. I'm all right. I didn't take anything, I swear. Ohh, my stomach.

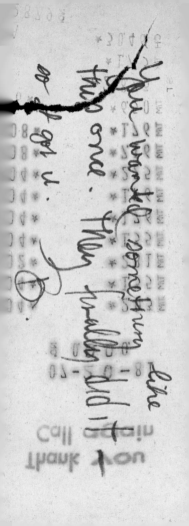

You wanted something like this one. They mailed; Did I get it. o

Thank you
Call again

07-20-81
NO. 0.000.

04 *	*2.03 T/M
04 *	*1.35 T/M
02 *	*2.81 T/M
04 *	*1.35 T/M
04 *	*1.76 T/M
04 *	*1.76 T/M
04 *	*2.25 T/M
08 *	*7.16 T/M
08 *	*1.76 T/M
	*6.50 T/M
06 *	*28.73 ST
	*1.73 CH TX
	*30.46 CH ST

A
287.9 NO.

OSCAR   What do you mean you didn't take anything? What did you take?

FELIX   (*Sitting on the couch*)   Nothing! Nothing! I didn't take anything. Don't tell Frances what I did, please! Oohh, my stomach.

MURRAY   He took something! I'm telling you he took something.

OSCAR   What, Felix? *What?*

FELIX   Nothing! I didn't take anything.

OSCAR   Pills? Did you take pills?

FELIX   No! No!

OSCAR   (*Grabbing* FELIX)   Don't lie to me, Felix. Did you take pills?

FELIX   No, I didn't. I didn't take anything.

MURRAY   Thank God he didn't take pills.
        (*They all relax and take a breath of relief*)

FELIX   Just a few, that's all.
        (*They all react in alarm and concern over the pills*)

OSCAR   He took pills.

MURRAY   How many pills?

OSCAR   What kind of pills?

FELIX   I don't know what kind. Little green ones. I just grabbed anything out of her medicine cabinet. I must have been crazy.

OSCAR   Didn't you look? Didn't you see what kind?

FELIX   I couldn't see. The light's broken. Don't call Frances. Don't tell her. I'm so ashamed. So ashamed.

OSCAR   Felix, how many pills did you take?

FELIX   I don't know. I can't remember.

OSCAR   I'm calling Frances.

FELIX   (*Grabs him*)   No! Don't call her. Don't call her. If she hears I took a whole bottle of pills . . .

MURRAY   A whole bottle? *A whole bottle of pills?* (*He turns to* VINNIE) My God, call an ambulance!
        (VINNIE *runs to the front door*)

OSCAR (*To* MURRAY)   You don't even know what *kind!*

MURRAY   What's the difference? He took a whole bottle!

OSCAR   Maybe they were vitamins. He could be the healthiest one in the room! Take it easy, will you?

FELIX   Don't call Frances. Promise me you won't call Frances.

MURRAY   Open his collar. Open the window. Give him some air.

SPEED   Walk him around. Don't let him go to sleep.
(SPEED *and* MURRAY *pick* FELIX *up and walk him around, while* ROY *rubs his wrists*)

ROY   Rub his wrists. Keep his circulation going.

VINNIE (*Running to the bathroom to get a compress*)   A cold compress. Put a cold compress on his neck.
(*They sit* FELIX *in the armchair, still chattering in alarm*)

OSCAR   One doctor at a time, heh? All the interns shut the hell up!

FELIX   I'm all right. I'll be all right. (*To* OSCAR *urgently*) You didn't call Frances, did you?

MURRAY (*To the others*)   You just gonna stand here? No one's gonna do anything? I'm calling a doctor.
(*He crosses to the phone*)

FELIX   No! No doctor.

MURRAY   You *gotta* have a doctor.

FELIX   I don't need a doctor.

MURRAY   You gotta get the pills out.

FELIX   I got them out. I threw up before! (*He sits back weakly.* MURRAY *hangs up the phone*) Don't you have a root beer or a ginger ale?
(VINNIE *gives the compress to* SPEED)

ROY (*To* VINNIE)   Get him a drink.

OSCAR (*Glares angrily at* FELIX)   He threw them up!

VINNIE   Which would you rather have, Felix, the root beer or the ginger ale?

SPEED (*To* VINNIE)   Get him the drink! Just get him the drink.

(VINNIE *runs into the kitchen as* SPEED *puts the compress on* FELIX's *head*)

FELIX   Twelve years. Twelve years we were married. Did you know we were married twelve years, Roy?

ROY (*Comforting him*)   Yes, Felix. I knew.

FELIX (*With great emotion in his voice*)   And now it's over. Like that, it's over. That's hysterical, isn't it?

SPEED   Maybe it was just a fight. You've had fights before, Felix.

FELIX   No, it's over. She's getting a lawyer tomorrow. *My* cousin. She's using *my* cousin! (*He sobs*) Who am I going to get?
(VINNIE *comes out of the kitchen with a glass of root beer*)

MURRAY (*Patting his shoulder*)   It's okay, Felix. Come on. Take it easy.

VINNIE (*Gives the glass to* FELIX)   Here's the root beer.

FELIX   I'm all right, honestly. I'm just crying.
(*He puts his head down. They all look at him helplessly*)

MURRAY   All right, let's not stand around looking at him. (*Pushes* SPEED *and* VINNIE *away*) Let's break it up, heh?

FELIX   Yes, don't stand there looking at me. Please.

OSCAR (*To the others*)   Come on, he's all right. Let's call it a night.
(MURRAY, SPEED *and* ROY *turn in their chips at the poker table, get their coats and get ready to go*)

FELIX   I'm so ashamed. Please, fellas, forgive me.

VINNIE (*Bending to* FELIX)   Oh, Felix, we—we understand.

FELIX   Don't say anything about this to anyone, Vinnie. Will you promise me?

VINNIE   I'm going to Florida tomorrow.

FELIX   Oh, that's nice. Have a good time.

VINNIE   Thanks.

FELIX (*Turns away and sighs in despair*)   We were going to go to Florida next winter. (*He laughs. but it's a sob*)

Without the kids! Now they'll go without me.

(VINNIE *gets his coat and* OSCAR *ushers them all to the door*)

MURRAY (*Stopping at the door*)   Maybe one of us should stay?

OSCAR   It's all right, Murray.

MURRAY   Suppose he tries something again?

OSCAR   He won't try anything again.

MURRAY   How do you *know* he won't try anything again?

FELIX (*Turns to* MURRAY)   I won't try anything again. I'm very tired.

OSCAR (*To* MURRAY)   You hear? He's very tired. He had a busy night. Good night, fellows.

(*They all ad lib goodbyes and leave. The door closes, but opens immediately and* ROY *comes back in*)

ROY   If anything happens, Oscar, just call me.

(*He exits, and as the door starts to close, it reopens and* SPEED *comes in*)

SPEED   I'm three blocks away. I could be here in five minutes.

(*He exits, and as the door starts to close, it reopens and* VINNIE *comes back in*)

VINNIE   If you need me I'll be at the Meridian Motel in Miami Beach.

OSCAR   You'll be the first one I'll call, Vinnie.

(VINNIE *exits. The door closes and then reopens as* MURRAY *comes back*)

MURRAY (*To* OSCAR)   You're sure?

OSCAR   I'm sure.

MURRAY (*Loudly to* FELIX, *as he gestures to* OSCAR *to come to the door*)   Good night, Felix. Try to get a good night's sleep. I guarantee you things are going to look a lot brighter in the morning. (*To* OSCAR, *sotto voce*) Take away his belt and his shoe laces.

(*He nods and exits.* OSCAR *turns and looks at* FELIX *sitting in the armchair and slowly moves across the room. There is a moment's silence*)

OSCAR (*He looks at* FELIX *and sighs*) Ohh, Felix, Felix, Felix, Felix!

FELIX (*Sits with his head buried in his hands. He doesn't look up*) I know, I know, I know, I know! What am I going to do, Oscar?

OSCAR You're gonna wash down the pills with some hot, black coffee. (*He starts for the kitchen, then stops*) Do you think I could leave you alone for two minutes?

FELIX No, I don't think so! Stay with me, Oscar. Talk to me.

OSCAR A cup of black coffee. It'll be good for you. Come on in the kitchen. I'll sit on you.

FELIX Oscar, the terrible thing is, I think I still love her. It's a lousy marriage but I still love her. I didn't want this divorce.

OSCAR (*Sitting on the arm of the couch*) How about some Ovaltine? You like Ovaltine? With a couple of fig newtons or chocolate mallomars?

FELIX All right, so we didn't get along. But we had two wonderful kids, and a beautiful home. Didn't we, Oscar?

OSCAR How about vanilla wafers? Or Vienna fingers? I got everything.

FELIX What more does she want? What does *any* woman want?

OSCAR I want to know what *you* want. Ovaltine, coffee or tea. Then we'll get to the divorce.

FELIX It's not fair, damn it! It's just not fair! (*He bangs his fist on the arm of the chair angrily, then suddenly winces in great pain and grabs his neck*) Oh! Ohh, my neck. My neck!

OSCAR What? What?

FELIX (*He gets up and paces in pain. He is holding his twisted neck*) It's a nerve spasm. I get it in the neck. Oh! Ohh, that hurts.

OSCAR (*Rushing to help*) Where? Where does it hurt?

FELIX (*Stretches out an arm like a halfback*) Don't touch me! Don't touch me!

OSCAR I just want to see where it hurts.

FELIX   It'll go away. Just let me alone a few minutes. Ohh! Ohh!

OSCAR   (*Moving to the couch*)   Lie down; I'll rub it. It'll ease the pain.

FELIX   (*In wild contortions*)   You don't know how. It's a special way. Only Frances knows how to rub me.

OSCAR   You want me to ask her to come over and rub you?

FELIX   (*Yells*)   No! No! We're getting divorced. She wouldn't want to rub me anymore. It's tension. I get it from tension. I must be tense.

OSCAR   I wouldn't be surprised. How long does it last?

FELIX   Sometimes a minute, sometimes hours. I once got it while I was driving. I crashed into a liquor store. Ohhh! Ohhh!
   (*He sits down, painfully, on the couch*)

OSCAR   (*Getting behind him*)   You want to suffer or do you want me to rub your stupid neck?
   (*He starts to massage it*)

FELIX   Easy! Easy!

OSCAR   (*Yells*)   Relax, damn it: relax!

FELIX   (*Yells back*)   Don't yell at me! (*Then quietly*) What should I do? Tell me nicely.

OSCAR   (*Rubbing the neck*)   Think of warm jello!

FELIX   Isn't that terrible? I can't do it. I can't relax. I sleep in one position all night. Frances says when I die on my tombstone it's going to say, "Here Stands Felix Ungar." (*He winces*) Oh! Ohh!

OSCAR   (*Stops rubbing*)   Does that hurt?

FELIX   No, it feels good.

OSCAR   Then say so. You make the same sound for pain or happiness.
   (*Starts to massage his neck again*)

FELIX   I know. I know. Oscar—I think I'm crazy.

OSCAR   Well, if it'll make you feel any better, I think so too.

FELIX   I mean it. Why else do I go to pieces like this?

Coming up here, scaring you to death. Trying to kill myself. What is that?

OSCAR That's panic. You're a panicky person. You have a low threshold for composure.
(*He stops rubbing*)

FELIX Don't stop. It feels good.

OSCAR If you don't relax I'll break my fingers. (*Touches his hair*) Look at this. The only man in the world with clenched hair.

FELIX I do terrible things, Oscar. You know I'm a cry baby.

OSCAR Bend over.
(FELIX *bends over and* OSCAR *begins to massage his back*)

FELIX (*Head down*)   I tell the whole world my problems.

OSCAR (*Massaging hard*)   Listen, if this hurts just tell me, because I don't know what the hell I'm doing.

FELIX It just isn't nice, Oscar, running up here like this, carrying on like a nut.

OSCAR (*Finishes massaging*)   How does your neck feel?

FELIX (*Twists his neck*)   Better. Only my back hurts.
(*He gets up and paces, rubbing his back*)

OSCAR What you need is a drink.
(*He starts for the bar*)

FELIX I can't drink. It makes me sick. I tried drinking last night.

OSCAR (*At the bar*)   Where *were* you last night?

FELIX Nowhere. I just walked.

OSCAR All night?

FELIX All night.

OSCAR In the rain?

FELIX No. In a hotel. I couldn't sleep. I walked around the room all night. It was over near Times Square. A dirty, depressing room. Then I found myself looking out the window. And suddenly, I began to think about jumping.

OSCAR   (*He has two glasses filled and crosses to* FELIX)
What changed your mind?

FELIX   Nothing. I'm still thinking about it.

OSCAR   Drink this.
         (*He hands him a glass, crosses to the couch and sits*)

FELIX   I don't want to get divorced, Oscar. I don't want to suddenly change my whole life. (*He moves to the couch and sits next to* OSCAR) Talk to me, Oscar. What am I going to do? What am I going to do?

OSCAR   You're going to pull yourself together. And then you're going to drink that Scotch, and then you and I are going to figure out a whole new life for you.

FELIX   Without Frances? Without the kids?

OSCAR   It's been done before.

FELIX   (*Paces around*)   You don't understand, Oscar. I'm nothing without them. I'm—*nothing!*

OSCAR   What do you mean, nothing? You're something! (FELIX *sits in the armchair*) A person! You're flesh and blood and bones and hair and nails and ears. You're not a fish. You're not a buffalo. You're *you!* You walk and talk and cry and complain and eat little green pills and send suicide telegrams. No one else does that, Felix. I'm telling you, *you're the only one of its kind in the world!* (*He goes to the bar*) Now drink that.

FELIX   Oscar, you've been through it yourself. What did you do? How did you get through those first few nights?

OSCAR   (*Pours a drink*)   I did exactly what you're doing.

FELIX   Getting hysterical!

OSCAR   No, drinking! *Drinking!* (*He comes back to the couch with the bottle and sits*) I drank for four days and four nights. And then I fell through a window. I was bleeding but I was forgetting.
         (*He drinks again*)

FELIX   How can you forget your kids? How can you wipe out twelve years of marriage?

OSCAR   You can't. When you walk into eight empty rooms every night it hits you in the face like a wet glove. But those are the facts, Felix. You've got to face it. You can't spend the rest of your life crying. It annoys people in the movies! Be a good boy and drink your Scotch.

(*He stretches out on the couch with his head near* FELIX)

FELIX I can imagine what Frances must be going through.

OSCAR What do you mean, what *she's* going through?

FELIX It's much harder on the woman, Oscar. She's all alone with the kids. Stuck there in the house. She can't get out like me. I mean where is she going to find someone now at her age? With two kids. Where?

OSCAR I don't know. Maybe someone'll come to the door! Felix, there's a hundred thousand divorces a year. There must be *something* nice about it. (FELIX *suddenly puts both his hands over his ears and hums quietly*) What's the matter now?

(*He sits up*)

FELIX My ears are closing up. I get it from the sinus. It must be the dust in here. I'm allergic to dust.

(*He hums. Then he gets up and tries to clear his ears by hopping first on one leg then the other as he goes to the window and opens it*)

OSCAR (*Jumping up*) What are you doing?

FELIX I'm not going to jump. I'm just going to breathe. (*He takes deep breaths*) I used to drive Frances crazy with my allergies. I'm allergic to perfume. For a while the only thing she could wear was my after-shave lotion. I was impossible to live with. It's a wonder she took it this long.

(*He suddenly bellows like a moose. He makes this strange sound another time.* OSCAR *looks at him dumbfounded*)

OSCAR What are you doing?

FELIX I'm trying to clear my ears. You create a pressure inside and then it opens it up.

(*He bellows again*)

OSCAR Did it open up?

FELIX A little bit. (*He rubs his neck*) I think I strained my throat.

(*He paces about the room*)

OSCAR Felix, why don't you leave yourself alone? Don't tinker.

FELIX I can't help myself. I drive everyone crazy. A marriage counselor once kicked me out of his office. He wrote on my chart, "Lunatic!" I don't blame her. It's impossible to be married to me.

OSCAR It takes two to make a rotten marriage.
(*He lies back down on the couch*)

FELIX You don't know what I was like at home. I bought her a book and made her write down every penny we spent. Thirty-eight cents for cigarettes; ten cents for a paper. Everything had to go in the book. And then we had a big fight because I said she forgot to write down how much the book was. Who could live with anyone like that?

OSCAR An accountant! What do I know? We're not perfect. We all have faults.

FELIX Faults? Heh! Faults. We have a maid who comes in to clean three times a week. And on the other days, Frances does the cleaning. And at night, after they've both cleaned up, I go in and clean the whole place again. I can't help it. I like things clean. Blame it on my mother. I was toilet-trained at five months old.

OSCAR How do you remember things like that?

FELIX I loused up the marriage. Nothing was ever right. I used to recook everything. The minute she walked out of the kitchen I would add salt or pepper. It's not that I didn't trust her, it's just that I was a better cook. Well, I cooked myself out of a marriage. (*He bangs his head with the palm of his hand three times*) God damned idiot!
(*He sinks down in the armchair*)

OSCAR Don't do that; you'll get a headache.

FELIX I can't stand it, Oscar. I hate me. Oh, boy, do I hate me.

OSCAR You don't hate you. You love you. You think no one has problems like you.

FELIX Don't give me that analyst jazz. I happen to know I hate my guts.

OSCAR Come on, Felix; I've never *seen* anyone so in love.

FELIX (*Hurt*) I thought you were my friend.

OSCAR That's why I can talk to you like this. Because I love you almost as much as *you* do.

FELIX Then help me.

OSCAR (*Up on one elbow*) How can I help you when I can't help myself? You think *you're* impossible to live with? Blanche used to say, "What time do you want dinner?" And I'd say, "I don't know. I'm not hungry." Then at three o'clock in the morning I'd wake her up and say, "Now!" I've been one of the highest paid sportswriters in the East for the past fourteen years, and we saved eight and a half dollars—in pennies! I'm never home, I gamble, I burn cigar holes in the furniture, drink like a fish and lie to her every chance I get. And for our tenth wedding anniversary, I took her to see the New York Rangers-Detroit Red Wings hockey game where she got hit with a puck. And I *still* can't understand why she left me. That's how impossible *I* am!

FELIX I'm not like you, Oscar. I couldn't take it living all alone. I don't know how I'm going to work. They've got to fire me. How am I going to make a living?

OSCAR You'll go on street corners and cry. They'll throw nickels at you! You'll work, Felix; you'll work.
(*He lies back down*)

FELIX You think I ought to call Frances?

OSCAR (*About to explode*) What for?
(*He sits up*)

FELIX Well, talk it out again.

OSCAR You've *talked* it all out. There are no words left in your entire marriage. When are you going to face up to it?

FELIX I can't help it, Oscar; I don't know what to do.

OSCAR Then listen to me. Tonight you're going to sleep here. And tomorrow you're going to get your clothes and your electric toothbrush and you'll move in with me.

FELIX No, no. It's your apartment. I'll be in the way.

OSCAR There's eight rooms. We could go for a year without seeing each other. Don't you understand? I *want* you to move in.

FELIX   Why? I'm a pest.

OSCAR   I *know* you're a pest. You don't have to keep telling me.

FELIX   Then why do you want me to live with you?

OSCAR   Because I can't stand living alone, that's why! For crying out loud, I'm proposing to you. What do you want, a ring?

FELIX (*Moves to* OSCAR)   Well, Oscar, if you really mean it, there's a lot I can do around here. I'm very handy around the house. I can fix things.

OSCAR   You don't have to fix things.

FELIX   I want to do *something*, Oscar. Let me do something.

OSCAR (*Nods*)   All right, you can take my wife's initials off the towels. Anything you want.

FELIX (*Beginning to tidy up*)   I can cook. I'm a terrific cook.

OSCAR   You don't have to cook. I eat cold cuts for breakfast.

FELIX   Two meals a day at home, we'll save a fortune. We've got to pay alimony, you know.

OSCAR (*Happy to see* FELIX's *new optimism*)   All right, you can cook.
(*He throws a pillow at him*)

FELIX (*Throws the pillow back*)   Do you like leg of lamb?

OSCAR   Yes, I like leg of lamb.

FELIX   I'll make it tomorrow night. I'll have to call Frances. She has my big pot.

OSCAR   *Will you forget Frances!* We'll get our own pots. Don't drive me crazy before you move in. (*The phone rings.* OSCAR *picks it up quickly*) Hello? Oh, hello, Frances!

FELIX (*Stops cleaning and starts to wave his arms wildly. He whispers screamingly*)   I'm not here! I'm not here! You didn't see me. You don't know where I am. I didn't call. I'm not here. I'm not here.

OSCAR (*Into the phone*)   Yes, he's here.

FELIX (*Pacing back and forth*)   How does she sound? Is

she worried? Is she crying? What is she saying? Does she want to speak to me? I don't want to speak to her.

OSCAR (*Into the phone*)   Yes, he is!

FELIX   You can tell her I'm not coming back. I've made up my mind. I've had it there. I've taken just as much as she has. You can tell her for me if she thinks I'm coming back she's got another think coming. Tell her. Tell her.

OSCAR (*Into the phone*)   Yes! Yes, he's fine.

FELIX   Don't tell her I'm fine! You heard me carrying on before. What are you telling her that for? I'm not fine.

OSCAR (*Into the phone*)   Yes, I understand, Frances.

FELIX (*Sits down next to* OSCAR)   Does she want to speak to me? Ask her if she wants to speak to me?

OSCAR (*Into the phone*)   Do you want to speak to him?

FELIX (*Reaches for the phone*)   Give me the phone. I'll speak to her.

OSCAR (*Into the phone*)   Oh. You don't want to speak to him.

FELIX   She doesn't want to speak to me?

OSCAR (*Into the phone*)   Yeah, I see. Right. Well, goodbye.
(*He hangs up*)

FELIX   She didn't want to speak to me?

OSCAR   No!

FELIX   Why did she call?

OSCAR   She wants to know when you're coming over for your clothes. She wants to have the room repainted.

FELIX   Oh!

OSCAR (*Pats* FELIX *on the shoulder*)   Listen, Felix, it's almost one o'clock.
(*He gets up*)

FELIX   Didn't want to speak to me, huh?

OSCAR   I'm going to bed. Do you want a cup of tea with Fruitanos or Raisinettos?

FELIX   She'll paint it pink. She always wanted it pink.

OSCAR   I'll get you a pair of pajamas. You like stripes, dots, or animals?
(*He goes into the bedroom*)

FELIX She's really heartbroken, isn't she? I want to kill
myself, and she's picking out colors.

OSCAR (*In the bedroom*) Which bedroom do you want?
I'm lousy with bedrooms.

FELIX (*Gets up and moves toward the bedroom*) You
know, I'm glad. Because she finally made me realize—it's
over. It didn't sink in until just this minute.

OSCAR (*Comes back with pillow, pillowcase, and pajamas*)
Felix, I want you to go to bed.

FELIX I don't think I believed her until just now. My
marriage is *really* over.

OSCAR Felix, go to bed.

FELIX Somehow it doesn't seem so bad now. I mean, I
think I can live with this thing.

OSCAR Live with it tomorrow. Go to bed tonight.

FELIX In a little while. I've got to think. I've got to start
rearranging my life. Do you have a pencil and paper?

OSCAR Not in a little while. Now! It's my house; I make
up the bedtime.
(*He throws the pajamas to him*)

FELIX Oscar, please. I have to be alone for a few minutes.
I've got to get organized. Go on, you go to bed. I'll—I'll
clean up.
(*He begins picking up debris from the floor*)

OSCAR (*Putting the pillow into the pillowcase*) You don't
have to clean up. I pay a dollar fifty an hour to clean up.

FELIX It's all right, Oscar. I wouldn't be able to sleep with
all this dirt around anyway. Go to bed. I'll see you in the
morning.
(*He puts the dishes on the tray*)

OSCAR You're not going to do anything big, are you, like
rolling up the rugs?

FELIX Ten minutes, that's all I'll be.

OSCAR You're sure?

FELIX (*Smiles*) I'm sure.

OSCAR No monkey business?

FELIX   No monkey business. I'll do the dishes and go right
to bed.

OSCAR   Yeah.
(*Crosses up to his bedroom, throwing the pillow
into the downstage bedroom as he passes. He closes
his bedroom door behind him*)

FELIX (*Calls him*)   Oscar! (OSCAR *anxiously comes out of
his bedroom and crosses to* FELIX) I'm going to be all
right! It's going to take me a couple of days, but I'm
going to be all right.

OSCAR (*Smiles*)   Good! Well, good night, Felix.
(*He turns to go toward the bedroom as* FELIX *begins to plump up a pillow from the couch*)

FELIX   Good night, Frances.
(OSCAR *stops dead.* FELIX, *unaware of his error,
plumps another pillow as* OSCAR *turns and stares at*
FELIX *with a troubled expression*)

Curtain

Act Two

The COMEDY
of Neil Simon

*Two weeks later, about eleven at night. The poker game
is in session again.* VINNIE, ROY, SPEED, MURRAY *and* OSCAR
are all seated at the table. FELIX's *chair is empty.*

*There is one major difference between this scene and
the opening poker-game scene. It is the appearance of the
room. It is immaculately clean. No, not clean. Sterile!
Spotless! Not a speck of dirt can be seen under the ten
coats of Johnson's Glo-Coat that have been applied to the
floor in the last three weeks. No laundry bags, no dirty
dishes, no half-filled glasses.*

Suddenly FELIX *appears from the kitchen. He carries a
tray with glasses and food—and napkins. After putting the
tray down, he takes the napkins one at a time, flicks them
out to full length and hands one to every player. They
take them with grumbling and put them on their laps. He
picks up a can of beer and very carefully pours it into a tall
glass, measuring it perfectly so that not a drop spills or over-
flows. With a flourish he puts the can down.*

FELIX (*Moves to* MURRAY) An ice-cold glass of beer for
Murray.

(MURRAY *reaches up for it*)

MURRAY Thank you, Felix.

FELIX (*Holds the glass back*) Where's your coaster?

MURRAY My what?

FELIX Your coaster. The little round thing that goes under
the glass.

MURRAY (*Looks around on the table*) I think I bet it.

OSCAR (*Picks it up and hands it to* MURRAY) I knew
I was winning too much. Here!

FELIX Always try to use your coasters, fellows. (*He picks*

up another drink from the tray) Scotch and a little bit of water?

SPEED *(Raises his hand)* Scotch and a little bit of water. *(Proudly)* And I have my coaster.
(*He holds it up for inspection*)

FELIX *(Hands him the drink)* I hate to be a pest but you know what wet glasses do?
(*He goes back to the tray and picks up and wipes a clean ashtray*)

OSCAR *(Coldly and deliberately)* They leave little rings on the table.

FELIX *(Nods)* Ruins the finish. Eats right through the polish.

OSCAR *(To the others)* So let's watch those little rings, huh?

FELIX *(Takes an ashtray and a plate with a sandwich from the tray and crosses to the table)* And we have a clean ashtray for Roy *(Handing* ROY *the ashtray)* Aaaaand—a sandwich for Vinnie.
(*Like a doting headwaiter, he skillfully places the sandwich in front of* VINNIE)

VINNIE *(Looks at* FELIX, *then at the sandwich)* Gee, it smells good. What is it?

FELIX Bacon, lettuce and tomato with mayonnaise on pumpernickel toast.

VINNIE *(Unbelievingly)* Where'd you get it?

FELIX *(Puzzled)* I made it. In the kitchen.

VINNIE You mean you put in toast and cooked bacon? Just for me?

OSCAR If you don't like it, he'll make you a meat loaf. Takes him five minutes.

FELIX It's no trouble. Honest. I love to cook. Try to eat over the dish. I just vacuumed the rug. *(He goes back to the tray, then stops)* Oscar!

OSCAR *(Quickly)* Yes, sir?

FELIX I forgot what you wanted. What did you ask me for?

OSCAR Two three-and-a-half-minute eggs and some petit fours.

FELIX (*Points to him*) A double gin and tonic. I'll be right back. (FELIX *starts out, then stops at a little box on the bar*) Who turned off the Pure-A-Tron?

MURRAY The what?

FELIX The Pure-A-Tron! (*He snaps it back on*) Don't play with this, fellows. I'm trying to get some of the grime out of the air.
(*He looks at them and shakes his head disapprovingly, then exits. They all sit in silence a few seconds*)

OSCAR Murray, I'll give you two hundred dollars for your gun.

SPEED (*Throws his cards on the table and gets up angrily*) I can't take it any more. (*With his hand on his neck*) I've had it up to here. In the last three hours we played four minutes of poker. I'm not giving up my Friday nights to watch cooking and housekeeping.

ROY (*Slumped in his chair, head hanging down*) I can't breathe. (*He points to the Pure-A-Tron*) That lousy machine is sucking everything out of the air.

VINNIE (*Chewing*) Gee, this is delicious. Who wants a bite?

MURRAY Is the toast warm?

VINNIE Perfect. And not too much mayonnaise. It's really a well-made sandwich.

MURRAY Cut me off a little piece.

VINNIE Give me your napkin. I don't want to drop any crumbs.

SPEED (*Watches them, horrified, as* VINNIE *carefully breaks the sandwich over* MURRAY'S *napkin. Then he turns to* OSCAR) Are you listening to this? Martha and Gertrude at the Automat. (*Almost crying in despair*) What the hell happened to our poker game?

ROY (*Still choking*) I'm telling you that thing could kill us. They'll find us here in the morning with our tongues on the floor.

SPEED (*Yells at* OSCAR) Do something! Get him back in the game.

OSCAR (*Rises, containing his anger*) Don't bother me with your petty little problems. You get this one stinkin' night a week. I'm cooped up here with Dione Lucas twenty-four hours a day.
(*He moves to the window*)

ROY It was better before. With the garbage and the smoke, it was better before.

VINNIE (*To* MURRAY) Did you notice what he does with the bread?

MURRAY What?

VINNIE He cuts off the crusts. That's why the sandwich is so light.

MURRAY And then he only uses the soft, green part of the lettuce. (*Chewing*) It's really delicious.

SPEED (*Reacts in amazement and disgust*) I'm going out of my mind.

OSCAR (*Yells toward the kitchen*) Felix! Damn it, Felix!

SPEED (*Takes the kitty box from the bookcase, puts it on the table, and puts the money in*) Forget it. I'm going home.

OSCAR Sit down!

SPEED I'll buy a book and I'll start to read again.

OSCAR Siddown! Will you siddown! (*Yells*) Felix!

SPEED Oscar, it's all over. The day his marriage busted up was the end of our poker game. (*He takes his jacket from the back of the chair and crosses to the door*) If you find some real players next week, call me.

OSCAR (*Following him*) You can't run out now. I'm a big loser.

SPEED (*With the door open*) You got no one to blame but yourself. It's all your fault. You're the one who stopped him from killing himself.
(*He exits and slams the door*)

OSCAR (*Stares at the door*) He's right! The man is absolutely right.
(*He moves to the table*)

MURRAY (*To* VINNIE) Are you going to eat that pickle?

VINNIE   I wasn't thinking of it. Why? Do you want it?

MURRAY   Unless you want it. It's your pickle.

VINNIE   No, no. Take it. I don't usually eat pickle.
(VINNIE *holds the plate with the pickle out to MUR-RAY.* OSCAR *slaps the plate, which sends the pickle flying through the air*)

OSCAR   Deal the cards!

MURRAY   What did you do that for?

OSCAR   Just deal the cards. You want to play poker, deal the cards. You want to eat, go to Schrafft's. (*To* VINNIE) Keep your sandwich and your pickles to yourself. I'm losing ninety-two dollars and everybody's getting fat! (*He screams*) Felix!
(FELIX *appears in the kitchen doorway*)

FELIX   What?

OSCAR   Close the kitchen and sit down. It's a quarter to twelve. I still got an hour and a half to win this month's alimony.

ROY   (*Sniffs*) What is that smell? Disinfectant! (*He smells the cards*) It's the cards. *He washed the cards!*
(*He throws down the cards, takes his jacket from the chair and moves past the table to put his money into the kitty box*)

FELIX   (*Comes to the table with* OSCAR's *drink, which he puts down; then he sits in his own seat*) Okay. What's the bet?

OSCAR   (*Hurrying to his seat*) I can't believe it. We're gonna play cards again. (*He sits*) It's up to Roy. Roy, baby, what are you gonna do?

ROY   I'm going to get in a cab and go to Central Park. If I don't get some fresh air, you got yourself a dead accountant.
(*He moves toward the door*)

OSCAR   (*Follows him*) What do you mean? It's not even twelve o'clock.

ROY   (*Turns back to* OSCAR) Look, I've been sitting here breathing Lysol and ammonia for four hours! Nature didn't intend for poker to be played like that. (*He crosses to the door*) If you wanna have a game next week

(*He points to* FELIX) either Louis Pasteur cleans up *after* we've gone, or we play in the Hotel Dixie! Good night!

> (*He goes and slams the door. There is a moment's silence.* OSCAR *goes back to the table and sits*)

OSCAR   We got just enough for handball!

FELIX   Gee, I'm sorry. Is it my fault?

VINNIE   No, I guess no one feels like playing much lately.

MURRAY   Yeah. I don't know what it is, but something's happening to the old gang.

> (*He goes to a side chair, sits and puts on his shoes*)

OSCAR   Don't you know what's happening to the old gang? It's breaking up. Everyone's getting divorced. I swear, we used to have better games when we couldn't get out at night.

VINNIE   (*Getting up and putting on his jacket*) Well, I guess I'll be going too. Bebe and I are driving to Asbury Park for the weekend.

FELIX   Just the two of you, heh? Gee, that's nice! You always do things like that together, don't you?

VINNIE   (*Shrugs*) We have to. I don't know how to drive! (*He takes all the money from the kitty box and moves to the door*) You coming, Murray?

MURRAY   (*Gets up, takes his jacket and moves toward the door*) Yeah, why not? If I'm not home by one o'clock with a hero sandwich and a frozen éclair, she'll have an all-points out on me. Ahhh, you guys got the life.

FELIX   Who?

MURRAY   (*Turns back*) Who? You! The Marx Brothers! Laugh, laugh, laugh. What have you got to worry about? If you suddenly want to go to the Playboy Club to hunt Bunnies, who's gonna stop you?

FELIX   I don't belong to the Playboy Club.

MURRAY   I know you don't, Felix, it's just a figure of speech. Anyway, it's not such a bad idea. Why don't you join?

FELIX   Why?

MURRAY   Why! Because for twenty-five dollars they give

you a key—and you walk into Paradise. *My* keys cost thirty cents—and you walk into corned beef and cabbage. (*He winks at him*) Listen to me.

(*He moves to the door*)

FELIX   What are you talking about, Murray? You're a happily married man.

MURRAY   (*Turns back on the landing*)   I'm not talking about *my* situation. (*He puts on his jacket*) I'm talking about *yours!* Fate has just played a cruel and rotten trick on you, so enjoy it! (*He turns to go, revealing "PAL" letters sewn on the back of his jacket*) C'mon, Vinnie.

(*VINNIE waves goodbye and they both exit*)

FELIX   (*Staring at the door*)   That's funny, isn't it, Oscar? They think we're happy. They really think we're enjoying this. (*He gets up and begins to straighten up the chairs*) They don't know, Oscar. They don't know what it's like.

(*He gives a short, ironic laugh, tucks the napkins under his arm and starts to pick up the dishes from the table*)

OSCAR   I'd be immensely grateful to you, Felix, if you didn't clean up just now.

FELIX   (*Puts dishes on the tray*)   It's only a few things. (*He stops and looks back at the door*) I can't get over what Murray just said. You know I think they really envy us. (*He clears more stuff from the table*)

OSCAR   Felix, leave everything alone. I'm not through dirtying-up for the night.

(*He drops some poker chips on the floor*)

FELIX   (*Putting stuff on the tray*)   But don't you see the irony of it? Don't you see it, Oscar?

OSCAR   (*Sighs heavily*)   Yes, I see it.

FELIX   (*Clearing the table*)   No, you don't. I really don't think you do.

OSCAR   Felix, I'm telling you I see the irony of it.

FELIX   (*Pauses*)   Then tell me. What is it? What's the irony?

OSCAR   (*Deep breath*)   The irony is—unless we can come

to some other arrangement, I'm gonna kill you! That's the irony.

FELIX What's wrong?
      (*He crosses back to the tray and puts down all the glasses and other things*)

OSCAR There's something wrong with this system, that's what's wrong. I don't think that two single men living alone in a big eight-room apartment should have a cleaner house than my mother.

FELIX (*Gets the rest of the dishes, glasses and coasters from the table*) What are you talking about? I'm just going to put the dishes in the sink. You want me to leave them here all night?

OSCAR (*Takes his glass, which* FELIX *has put on the tray, and crosses to the bar for a refill*) I don't care if you take them to bed with you. You can play Mr. Clean all you want. But don't make *me* feel guilty.

FELIX (*Takes the tray into the kitchen, leaving the swinging door open*) I'm not asking you to do it, Oscar. You don't have to clean up.

OSCAR (*Moves up to the door*) That's why you make me feel guilty. You're always in my bathroom hanging up my towels. Whenever I smoke you follow me around with an ashtray. Last night I found you washing the kitchen floor, shaking your head and moaning, "Footprints, footprints!"
      (*He paces around the room*)

FELIX (*Comes back to the table with a silent butler. He dumps the ashtrays, then wipes them carefully*) I didn't say they were yours.

OSCAR (*Angrily sits down in the wing chair*) Well, they *were* mine, damn it. I have feet and they make prints. What do you want me to do, climb across the cabinets?

FELIX No! I want you to walk on the floor.

OSCAR I appreciate that! I really do.

FELIX (*Crosses to the telephone table and cleans the ashtray there*) I'm just trying to keep the place livable. I didn't realize I irritated you that much.

OSCAR I just feel *I* should have the right to decide when my bathtub needs a going over with Dutch Cleanser. It's the democratic way!

FELIX (*Puts the silent butler and his rag down on the coffee table and sits down glumly on the couch*) I was wondering how long it would take.

OSCAR How long *what* would take?

FELIX Before I got on your nerves.

OSCAR I didn't say you get on my nerves.

FELIX Well, it's the same thing. You said I irritated you.

OSCAR *You* said you irritated me. *I* didn't say it.

FELIX Then what *did* you say?

OSCAR I don't know *what* I said. What's the difference what I said?

FELIX It doesn't make any difference. I was just repeating what I thought you said.

OSCAR Well, don't repeat what you *thought* I said. Repeat what I *said!* My God, that's irritating!

FELIX You see! You *did* say it!

OSCAR I don't believe this whole conversation.
(*He gets up and paces by the table*)

FELIX (*Pawing with a cup*) Oscar, I'm—I'm sorry. I don't know what's wrong with me.

OSCAR (*Still pacing*) And don't pout. If you want to fight, we'll fight. But don't pout! Fighting *I* win. Pouting *you* win!

FELIX You're right. Everything you say about me is absolutely right.

OSCAR (*Really angry, turns to* FELIX) And don't give in so easily. I'm *not* always right. Sometimes *you're* right.

FELIX You're right. I do that. I always figure I'm in the wrong.

OSCAR Only this time you *are* wrong. And I'm right.

FELIX Oh, leave me alone.

OSCAR And don't sulk. That's the same as pouting.

FELIX I know. I know. (*He squeezes his cup with anger*)

Damn me, why can't I do one lousy thing right?

(He suddenly stands up and cocks his arm back, about to hurl the cup angrily against the front door. Then he thinks better of it, puts the cup down and sits)

OSCAR *(Watching this)* Why didn't you throw it?

FELIX I almost did. I get so insane with myself sometimes.

OSCAR Then why don't you throw the cup?

FELIX Because I'm trying to control myself.

OSCAR Why?

FELIX What do you mean, why?

OSCAR Why do you have to control yourself? You're angry, you felt like throwing the cup, why don't you throw it?

FELIX Because there's no point to it. I'd still be angry and I'd have a broken cup.

OSCAR How do you *know* how you'd feel? Maybe you'd feel *wonderful*. Why do you have to control every single thought in your head? Why don't you let loose *once* in your life? Do something that you *feel* like doing—and not what you *think* you're supposed to do. Stop keeping books, Felix. Relax. Get drunk. Get angry. C'mon, *break the goddamned cup!*

(FELIX suddenly stands up and hurls the cup against the door, smashing it to pieces. Then he grabs his shoulder in pain)

FELIX Oww! I hurt my arm!

(He sinks down on the couch, massaging his arm)

OSCAR *(Throws up his hands)* You're hopeless! You're a hopeless mental case!

(He paces around the table)

FELIX *(Grimacing with pain)* I'm not supposed to throw with that arm. What a stupid thing to do.

OSCAR Why don't you live in a closet? I'll leave your meals outside the door and slide in the papers. Is that safe enough?

FELIX *(Rubbing his arm)* I used to have bursitis in this arm. I had to give up golf. Do you have a heating pad?

OSCAR How can you hurt your arm throwing a cup? If it had coffee in it, that's one thing. But an empty cup . . . (*He sits in the wing chair*)

FELIX All right, cut it out, Oscar. That's the way I am. I get hurt easily. I can't help it.

OSCAR You're not going to cry, are you? I think all those tears dripping on the arm is what gave you bursitis.

FELIX (*Holding his arm*) I once got it just from combing my hair.

OSCAR (*Shaking his head*) A world full of room-mates and I pick myself the Tin Man. (*He sighs*) Oh, well, I suppose I could have done worse.

FELIX (*Moves the rag and silent butler to the bar. Then he takes the chip box from the bar and crosses to the table*) You're darn right, you could have. A *lot* worse.

OSCAR How?

FELIX What do you mean, how? How'd you like to live with ten-thumbs Murray or Speed and his complaining? (*He gets down on his knees, picks up the chips and puts them into the box*) Don't forget I cook and clean and take care of this house. I save us a lot of money, don't I?

OSCAR Yeah, but then you keep me up all night counting it.

FELIX (*Goes to the table and sweeps the chips and cards into the box*) Now wait a minute. We're not always going at each other. We have some fun too, don't we?

OSCAR (*Crosses to the couch*) Fun? Felix, getting a clear picture on Channel Two isn't my idea of whoopee.

FELIX What are you talking about?

OSCAR All right, what do you and I do every night? (*He takes off his sneakers and drops them on the floor*)

FELIX What do we do? You mean after dinner?

OSCAR That's right. After we've had your halibut steak and the dishes are done and the sink has been Brillo'd and the pans have been S.O.S.'d and the leftovers have been Saran-Wrapped—what do we do?

FELIX (*Finishes clearing the table and puts everything on top of the bookcase*) Well, we read, we talk . . .

OSCAR (*Takes off his pants and throws them on the floor*)
No, no. I read and *you* talk! I try to work and you talk.
I take a bath and you talk. I go to sleep and you talk.
We've got your life arranged pretty good but I'm still
looking for a little entertainment.

FELIX (*Pulling the kitchen chairs away from the table*)
What are you saying? That I talk too much?

OSCAR (*Sits on the couch*)   No, no. I'm not complaining.
You have a lot to say. What's worrying me is that I'm
beginning to listen.

FELIX (*Pulls the table into the alcove*)   Oscar, I told you
a hundred times, just tell me to shut up. I'm not
sensitive.
(*He pulls the love seat down into the room, and
centers the table between the windows in the alcove*)

OSCAR   I don't think you're getting my point. For a husky
man, I think I've spent enough evenings discussing tomorrow's menu. The night was made for other things.

FELIX   Like what?
(*He puts two dining chairs neatly on one side of
the table*)

OSCAR   Like unless I get to touch something soft in the
next two weeks, I'm in big trouble.

FELIX   You mean women?
(*He puts the two other dining chairs neatly on the
other side of the table*)

OSCAR   If you want to give it a name, all right, women!

FELIX (*Picks up the two kitchen chairs and starts toward
the landing*)   That's funny. You know I haven't even
thought about women in weeks.

OSCAR   I fail to see the humor.

FELIX (*Stops*)   No, that's really strange. I mean when
Frances and I were happy, I don't think there was a girl
on the street I didn't stare at for ten minutes. (*He
crosses to the kitchen door and pushes it open with his
back*) I used to take the wrong subway home just following a pair of legs. But since we broke up, I don't
even know what a woman looks like.
(*He takes the chairs into the kitchen*)

OSCAR Well, either I could go downstairs and buy a couple of magazines—or I could make a phone call.

FELIX (*From the kitchen, as he washes the dishes*) What are you saying?

OSCAR (*Crosses to a humidor on a small table and takes out a cigar*) I'm saying let's spend one night talking to someone with higher voices than us.

FELIX You mean go out on a date?

OSCAR Yah . . .

FELIX Oh, well, I—I can't.

OSCAR Why not?

FELIX Well, it's all right for you. But I'm still married.

OSCAR (*Paces toward the kitchen door*) You can *cheat* until the divorce comes through!

FELIX It's not that. It's just that I have no—no *feeling* for it. I can't explain it.

OSCAR Try!

FELIX (*Comes to the doorway with a brush and dish in his hand*) Listen, I intend to go out. I get lonely too. But I'm just separated a few weeks. Give me a little time.
(*He goes back to the sink*)

OSCAR There isn't any time left. I saw *TV Guide* and there's nothing on this week! (*He paces into and through the kitchen and out the kitchen door onto the landing*) What am I asking you? All I want to do is have dinner with a couple of girls. You just have to eat and talk. It's not hard. You've eaten and talked before.

FELIX Why do you need me? Can't you go out yourself?

OSCAR Because I may want to come back here. And if we walk in and find you washing the windows, it puts a damper on things.
(*He sits down*)

FELIX (*Pokes his head out of the kitchen*) I'll take a pill and go to sleep.
(*He goes back into the kitchen*)

OSCAR Why take a pill when you can take a girl?

FELIX (*Comes out with an aerosol bomb held high over his head and circles around the room, spraying it*) Because

I'd feel guilty, that's why. Maybe it doesn't make any sense to you, but that's the way I feel.

(*He puts the bomb on the bar and takes the silent butler and rag into the kitchen. He places them on the sink and busily begins to wipe the refrigerator*)

OSCAR Look, for all I care you can take her in the kitchen and make a blueberry pie. But I think it's a lot healthier than sitting up in your bed every night writing Frances' name all through the crossword puzzles. Just for one night, talk to another girl.

FELIX (*Pushes the love seat carefully into position and sits, weakening*) But who would I call? The only single girl I know is my secretary and I don't think she likes me.

OSCAR (*Jumps up and crouches next to* FELIX) Leave that to me. There's two sisters who live in this building. English girls. One's a widow; the other's a divorcée. They're a barrel of laughs.

FELIX How do you know?

OSCAR I was trapped in the elevator with them last week. (*Runs to the telephone table, puts the directory on the floor, and gets down on his knees to look for the number*) I've been meaning to call them but I didn't know which one to take out. This'll be perfect.

FELIX What do they look like?

OSCAR Don't worry. Yours is very pretty.

FELIX I'm not worried. Which one is mine?

OSCAR (*Looking in the book*) The divorcée.

FELIX (*Goes to* OSCAR) Why do I get the divorcée?

OSCAR I don't care. You want the widow?
(*He circles a number on the page with a crayon*)

FELIX (*Sitting on the couch*) No, I don't want the widow. I don't even want the divorcée. I'm just doing this for you.

OSCAR Look, take whoever you want. When they come in the door, point to the sister of your choice. (*Tears the page out of the book, runs to the bookcase and hangs it up*) I don't care. I just want to have some laughs.

FELIX   All right. All right.

OSCAR (*Crosses to the couch and sits next to* FELIX) Don't
say all right. I want you to promise me you're going to
try to have a good time. Please, Felix. It's important.
Say, "I promise."

FELIX (*Nods*) I promise.

OSCAR Again!

FELIX I promise!

OSCAR And no writing in the book, a dollar thirty for the
cab.

FELIX No writing in the book.

OSCAR No one is to be called Frances. It's Gwendolyn
and Cecily.

FELIX No Frances.

OSCAR No crying, sighing, moaning or groaning.

FELIX I'll smile from seven to twelve.

OSCAR And this above all, no talk of the past. Only the
present.

FELIX And the future.

OSCAR That's the new Felix I've been waiting for. (*Leaps
up and prances around*) Oh, is this going to be a night.
Hey, where do you want to go?

FELIX For what?

OSCAR For dinner. Where'll we eat?

FELIX You mean a restaurant? For the four of us? It'll cost
a fortune.

OSCAR We'll cut down on laundry. We won't wear socks
on Thursdays.

FELIX But that's throwing away money. We can't afford
it, Oscar.

OSCAR We have to eat.

FELIX (*Moves to* OSCAR) We'll have dinner here.

OSCAR *Here?*

FELIX I'll cook. We'll save thirty, forty dollars.
(*He goes to the couch, sits and picks up the phone*)

OSCAR What kind of a double date is that? You'll be in
the kitchen all night.

FELIX No, I won't. I'll put it up in the afternoon. Once
I get my potatoes in, I'll have all the time in the world.
(*He starts to dial*)

OSCAR (*Pacing back and forth*) What happened to the
new Felix? Who are you calling?

FELIX Frances. I want to get her recipe for London broil.
The girls'll be crazy about it.
(*He dials as* OSCAR *storms off toward his bedroom*)

Curtain

It is a few days later, about eight o'clock.

No one is on stage. The dining table looks like a page out of House and Garden. *It is set for dinner for four, complete with linen tablecloth, candles and wine glasses. There is a floral centerpiece and flowers about the room, and crackers and dip on the coffee table. There are sounds of activity in the kitchen.*

The front door opens and OSCAR *enters with a bottle of wine in a brown paper bag, his jacket over his arm. He looks about gleefully as he listens to the sounds from the kitchen. He puts the bag on the table and his jacket over a chair.*

OSCAR (*Calls out in a playful mood*) I'm home, dear! (*He goes into his bedroom, taking off his shirt, and comes skipping out shaving with a cordless razor, with a clean shirt and a tie over his arm. He is joyfully singing as he admires the table*) Beautiful! Just beautiful! (*He sniffs, obviously catching the aroma from the kitchen*) Oh, yeah. Something wonderful is going on in that kitchen. (*He rubs his hands gleefully*) No, sir. There's no doubt about it. I'm the luckiest man on earth. (*He puts the razor into his pocket and begins to put on the shirt.* FELIX *enters slowly from the kitchen. He's wearing a small dish towel as an apron. He has a ladle in one hand. He looks silently and glumly at* OSCAR, *crosses to the armchair and sits*) I got the wine. (*He takes the bottle out of the bag and puts it on the table*) Batard Montrachet. Six and a quarter. You don't mind, do you, pussycat? We'll walk to work this week. (FELIX *sits glumly and silently*) Hey, no kidding, Felix, you did a great job. One little suggestion? Let's come down a little with the lights (*He switches off the wall brackets.*) —and up very softly with the music. (*He crosses to the* stereo set in the bookcase and picks up some record albums) What do you think goes better with London broil, Mancini or Sinatra? (FELIX just stares ahead) Felix? What's the matter? (He puts the albums down) Something's wrong. I can tell by your conversation. (He goes into the bathroom, gets a bottle of after-shave lotion and comes out putting it on) All right, Felix, what is it?

FELIX (Without looking at him) What is it? Let's start with what time do you think it is?

OSCAR What time? I don't know. Seven thirty?

FELIX Seven thirty? Try eight o'clock.

OSCAR (Puts the lotion down on the small table) All right, so it's eight o'clock. So?
(He begins to fix his tie)

FELIX So? You said you'd be home at seven.

OSCAR Is that what I said?

FELIX (Nods) That's what you said. "I will be home at seven" is what you said.

OSCAR Okay, I said I'd be home at seven. And it's eight. So what's the problem?

FELIX If you knew you were going to be late, why didn't you call me?

OSCAR (Pauses while making the knot in his tie) I couldn't call you. I was busy.

FELIX Too busy to pick up a phone? Where were you?

OSCAR I was in the office, working.

FELIX Working? Ha!

OSCAR Yes. Working!

FELIX I called your office at seven o'clock. You were gone.

OSCAR (Tucking in his shirt) It took me an hour to get home. I couldn't get a cab.

FELIX Since when do they have cabs in Hannigan's Bar?

OSCAR Wait a minute. I want to get this down on a tape recorder, because no one'll believe me. You mean now I have to call you if I'm coming home late for dinner?

FELIX (*Crosses to* OSCAR) Not *any* dinner. Just the ones I've been slaving over since two o'clock this afternoon—to help save *you* money to pay your wife's alimony.

OSCAR (*Controlling himself*) Felix, this is no time to have a domestic quarrel. We have two girls coming down any minute.

FELIX You mean you told them to be here at eight o'clock?

OSCAR (*Takes his jacket and crosses to the couch, then sits and takes some dip from the coffee table*) I don't remember what I said. Seven thirty, eight o'clock. What difference does it make?

FELIX (*Follows* OSCAR) I'll tell you what difference. You told me they were coming at seven thirty. You were going to be here at seven to help me with the hors d'oeuvres. At seven thirty they arrive and we have cocktails. At eight o'clock we have dinner. It is now eight o'clock. *My London broil is finished!* If we don't eat now the whole damned thing'll be *dried out!*

OSCAR Oh, God, help me.

FELIX Never mind helping *you.* Tell Him to save the meat. Because we got nine dollars and thirty-four cents worth drying up in there right now.

OSCAR Can't you keep it warm?

FELIX (*Pacing*) What do you think I am, the Magic Chef? I'm lucky I got it to come out at eight o'clock. What am I going to do?

OSCAR I don't know. Keep pouring gravy on it.

FELIX What gravy?

OSCAR Don't you have any gravy?

FELIX (*Storms over to* OSCAR) Where the hell am I going to get gravy at eight o'clock?

OSCAR (*Getting up*) I thought it comes when you cook the meat.

FELIX (*Follows him*) When you *cook the meat?* You don't know the first thing you're talking about. You have to make gravy. It doesn't come!

OSCAR You asked my advice, I'm giving it to you.
(*He puts on his jacket*)

FELIX Advice? (*He waves the ladle in his face*) You didn't
know where the kitchen was till I came here and showed
you.

OSCAR You wanna talk to me, put down the spoon.

FELIX (*Exploding in rage, again waving the ladle in his
face*) Spoon? You dumb ignoramus. It's a ladle. You
don't even know it's a ladle.

OSCAR All right, Felix, get a hold of yourself.

FELIX (*Pulls himself together and sits on the love seat*)
You think it's so easy? Go on. The kitchen's all yours.
Go make a London broil for four people who come a
half hour late.

OSCAR (*To no one in particular*) Listen to me. I'm argu-
ing with him over gravy.
(*The bell rings*)

FELIX (*Jumps up*) Well, they're here. Our dinner guests.
I'll get a saw and cut the meat.
(*He starts for the kitchen*)

OSCAR (*Stopping him*) Stay where you are!

FELIX I'm not taking the blame for this dinner.

OSCAR Who's blaming you? Who even *cares* about the
dinner?

FELIX (*Moves to* OSCAR) I care. I take *pride* in what I do.
And you're going to explain to them exactly what happened.

OSCAR All right, you can take a Polaroid picture of me
coming in at eight o'clock! Now take off that stupid
apron because I'm opening the door.
(*He rips the towel off* FELIX *and goes to the door*)

FELIX (*Takes his jacket from a dining chair and puts it on*)
I just want to get one thing clear. This is the last time
I ever cook for you. Because people like you don't even
appreciate a decent meal. That's why they have TV
dinners.

OSCAR You through?

FELIX   I'm through!

OSCAR   Then smile. (OSCAR *smiles and opens the door. The girls poke their heads through the door. They are in their young thirties and somewhat attractive. They are undoubtedly British*) Well, hello.

GWENDOLYN (*To* OSCAR) Hallo!

CECILY (*To* OSCAR) Hallo.

GWENDOLYN   I do hope we're not late.

OSCAR   No, no. You timed it perfectly. Come on in. (*He points to them as they enter*) Er, Felix, I'd like you to meet two very good friends of mine, Gwendolyn and Cecily . . .

CECILY (*Pointing out his mistake*) Cecily and Gwendolyn.

OSCAR   Oh, yes. Cecily and Gwendolyn . . . er (*Trying to remember their last name*) Er . . . Don't tell me. Robin? No, no. Cardinal?

GWENDOLYN   Wrong both times. It's Pigeon!

OSCAR   Pigeon. Right. Cecily and Gwendolyn Pigeon.

GWENDOLYN (*To* FELIX) You don't spell it like Walter Pidgeon. You spell it like "Coo-Coo" Pigeon.

OSCAR   We'll remember that if it comes up. Cecily and Gwendolyn, I'd like you to meet my room-mate, and our chef for the evening, Felix Ungar.

CECILY (*Holding her hand out*) Heh d'yew dew?

FELIX (*Moving to her and shaking her hand*) How do you do?

GWENDOLYN (*Holding her hand out*) Heh d'yew dew?

FELIX (*Stepping up on the landing and shaking her hand*) How do you do you?
     (*This puts him nose to nose with* OSCAR, *and there is an awkward pause as they look at each other*)

OSCAR   Well, we did that beautifully. Why don't we sit down and make ourselves comfortable?
     (FELIX *steps aside and ushers the girls down into the room. There is ad libbing and a bit of confusion and milling about as they all squeeze between the armchair and the couch, and the* PIGEONS *finally*

seat themselves on the couch. OSCAR *sits in the arm-chair, and* FELIX *sneaks past him to the love seat. Finally all have settled down)*

CECILY This is ever so nice, isn't it, Gwen?

GWENDOLYN (*Looking around*) Lovely. And much nicer than our flat. Do you have help?

OSCAR Er, yes. I have a man who comes in every night.

CECILY Aren't you the lucky one?
(CECILY, GWENDOLYN *and* OSCAR *all laugh at her joke.* OSCAR *looks over at* FELIX *but there is no response*)

OSCAR (*Rubs his hands together*) Well, isn't this nice? I was telling Felix yesterday about how we happened to meet.

GWENDOLYN Oh? Who's Felix?

OSCAR (*A little embarrassed, he points to* FELIX) He is!

GWENDOLYN Oh, yes, of course. I'm so sorry.
(FELIX *nods that it's all right*)

CECILY You know it happened to us again this morning.

OSCAR What did?

GWENDOLYN Stuck in the elevator again.

OSCAR Really? Just the two of you?

CECILY And poor old Mr. Kessler from the third floor. We were in there half an hour.

OSCAR No kidding? What happened?

GWENDOLYN Nothing much, I'm afraid.
(CECILY *and* GWENDOLYN *both laugh at her latest joke, joined by* OSCAR. *He once again looks over at* FELIX, *but there is no response*)

OSCAR (*Rubs his hands again*) Well, this really is nice.

CECILY And ever so much cooler than our place.

GWENDOLYN It's like equatorial Africa on our side of the building.

CECILY Last night it was so bad Gwen and I sat there in nature's own cooling ourselves in front of the open fridge. Can you imagine such a thing?

OSCAR Er, I'm working on it.

GWENDOLYN   Actually, it's impossible to get a night's sleep. Cec and I really don't know what to do.

OSCAR   Why don't you sleep with an air conditioner?

GWENDOLYN   We haven't got one.

OSCAR   I know. But we have.

GWENDOLYN   Oh, you! I told you about that one, didn't I, Cec?

FELIX   They say it may rain Friday.
   (*They all stare at* FELIX)

GWENDOLYN   Oh?

CECILY   That should cool things off a bit.

OSCAR   I wouldn't be surprised.

FELIX   Although sometimes it gets hotter after it rains.

GWENDOLYN   Yes, it does, doesn't it?
   (*They continue to stare at* FELIX)

FELIX   (*Jumps up and, picking up the ladle, starts for the kitchen*)   Dinner is served!

OSCAR   (*Stopping him*)   No, it isn't!

FELIX   Yes, it is!

OSCAR   No, it isn't! I'm sure the girls would like a cocktail first. (*To the girls*) Wouldn't you, girls?

GWENDOLYN   Well, I wouldn't put up a struggle.

OSCAR   There you are. (*To* CECILY) What would you like?

CECILY   Oh, I really don't know. (*To* OSCAR) What have you got?

FELIX   London broil.

OSCAR   (*To* FELIX)   She means to drink. (*To* CECILY) We have everything. And what we don't have, I mix in the medicine cabinet. What'll it be?
   (*He crouches next to her*)

CECILY   Oh, a double vodka.

GWENDOLYN   Cecily, not before dinner.

CECILY   (*To the men*)   My sister. She watches over me like a mother hen. (*To* OSCAR) Make it a *small* double vodka.

OSCAR A small double vodka! And for the beautiful mother hen?

GWENDOLYN Oh, I'd like something cool. I think I would like to have a double Drambuie with some crushed ice, unless you don't have the crushed ice.

OSCAR I was up all night with a sledge hammer. I shall return!
    (*He goes to the bar and gets bottles of vodka and Drambuie*)

FELIX (*Going to him*) Where are you going?

OSCAR To get the refreshments.

FELIX (*Starting to panic*) Inside? What'll *I* do?

OSCAR You can finish the weather report.
    (*He exits into the kitchen*)

FELIX (*Calls after him*) Don't forget to look at my meat!
    (*He turns and faces the girls. He crosses to a chair and sits. He crosses his legs nonchalantly. But he is ill at ease and he crosses them again. He is becoming aware of the silence and he can no longer get away with just smiling*) Er, Oscar tells me you're sisters.

CECILY Yes. That's right.
    (*She looks at* GWENDOLYN)

FELIX From England.

GWENDOLYN Yes. That's right.
    (*She looks at* CECILY)

FELIX I see. (*Silence. Then, his little joke*) We're not brothers.

CECILY Yes. We know.

FELIX Although I am a brother. I have a brother who's a doctor. He lives in Buffalo. That's upstate in New York.

GWENDOLYN (*Taking a cigarette from her purse*) Yes, we know.

FELIX You know my brother?

GWENDOLYN No. We know that Buffalo is upstate in New York.

FELIX Oh!
    (*He gets up, takes a cigarette lighter from the side table and moves to light* GWENDOLYN'S *cigarette*)

CECILY   We've been there! Have you?

FELIX   No! Is it nice?

CECILY   Lovely.

> (FELIX *closes the lighter on* GWENDOLYN's *cigarette and turns to go back to his chair, taking the cigarette, now caught in the lighter, with him. He notices the cigarette and hastily gives it back to* GWENDOLYN, *stopping to light it once again. He puts the lighter back on the table and sits down nervously. There is a pause*)

FELIX   Isn't that interesting? How long have you been in the United States of America?

CECILY   Almost four years now.

FELIX   (*Nods*) Uh huh. Just visiting?

GWENDOLYN   (*Looks at* CECILY)   No! We live here.

FELIX   And you work here too, do you?

CECILY   Yes. We're secretaries for Slenderama.

GWENDOLYN   You know. The health club.

CECILY   People bring us their bodies and we do wonderful things with them.

GWENDOLYN   Actually, if you're interested, we can get you ten per cent off.

CECILY   Off the price, not off your body.

FELIX   Yes, I see. (*He laughs. They all laugh. Suddenly he shouts toward the kitchen*) Oscar, where's the drinks?

OSCAR   (*Offstage*)   Coming! Coming!

CECILY   What field of endeavor are you engaged in?

FELIX   I write the news for CBS.

CECILY   Oh! Fascinating!

GWENDOLYN   Where do you get your ideas from?

FELIX   (*He looks at her as though she's a Martian*)   From the news.

GWENDOLYN   Oh, yes, of course. Silly me . . .

CECILY   Maybe you can mention Gwen and I in one of your news reports.

FELIX   Well, if you do something spectacular, maybe I will.

CECILY Oh, we've done spectacular things but I don't think we'd want it spread all over the telly, do you, Gwen?

(*They both laugh*)

FELIX (*He laughs too, then cries out almost for help*) Oscar!

OSCAR (*Offstage*) Yeah, yeah!

FELIX (*To the girls*) It's such a large apartment, sometimes you have to shout.

GWENDOLYN Just you two baches live here?

FELIX Baches? Oh, bachelors! We're not bachelors. We're divorced. That is, Oscar's divorced. I'm *getting* divorced.

CECILY Oh. Small world. We've cut the dinghy loose too, as they say.

GWENDOLYN Well, you couldn't have a *better* matched foursome, could you?

FELIX (*Smiles weakly*) No, I suppose not.

GWENDOLYN Although technically I'm a widow. I was divorcing my husband, but he died before the final papers came through.

FELIX Oh, I'm awfully sorry. (*Sighs*) It's a terrible thing, isn't it? Divorce.

GWENDOLYN It can be—if you haven't got the right solicitor.

CECILY That's true. Sometimes they can drag it out for months. I was lucky. Snip, cut and I was free.

FELIX I mean it's terrible what it can do to people. After all, what is divorce? It's taking two happy people and tearing their lives completely apart. It's inhuman, don't you think so?

CECILY Yes, it can be an awful bother.

GWENDOLYN But of course, that's all water under the bridge now, eh? Er, I'm terribly sorry, but I think I've forgotten your name.

FELIX Felix.

GWENDOLYN Oh, yes. Felix.

CECILY Like the cat.

(FELIX *takes his wallet from his jacket pocket*)

GWENDOLYN   Well, the Pigeons will have to beware of the cat, won't they?
(*She laughs*)

CECILY (*Nibbles on a nut from the dish*)   Mmm, cashews. Lovely.

FELIX (*Takes a snapshot out of his wallet*)   This is the worst part of breaking up.
(*He hands the picture to* CECILY)

CECILY (*Looks at it*)   Childhood sweethearts, were you?

FELIX   No, no. That's my little boy and girl. (CECILY *gives the picture to* GWENDOLYN, *takes a pair of glasses from her purse and puts them on*) He's seven, she's five.

CECILY (*Looks again*)   Oh! Sweet.

FELIX   They live with their mother.

GWENDOLYN   I imagine you must miss them terribly.

FELIX (*Takes back the picture and looks at it longingly*)   I can't stand being away from them. (*Shrugs*) But— that's what happens with divorce.

CECILY   When do you get to see them?

FELIX   Every night. I stop there on my way home! Then I take them on the weekends, and I get them on holidays and July and August.

CECILY   Oh! Well, when is it that you miss them?

FELIX   Whenever I'm not there. If they didn't have to go to school so early, I'd go over and make them breakfast. They love my French toast.

GWENDOLYN   You're certainly a devoted father.

FELIX   It's Frances who's the wonderful one.

CECILY   She's the little girl?

FELIX   No. She's the mother. My wife.

GWENDOLYN   The one you're divorcing?

FELIX (*Nods*)   Mm! She's done a terrific job bringing them up. They always look so nice. They're so polite. Speak beautifully. Never, "Yeah." Always, "Yes." They're such good kids. And she did it all. She's the kind of woman who— Ah, what am I saying? You don't want to hear any of this.
(*He puts the picture back in his wallet*)

CECILY Nonsense. You have a right to be proud. You have two beautiful children and a wonderful ex-wife.

FELIX (*Containing his emotions*) I know. I know. (*He hands* CECILY *another snapshot*) That's her. Frances.

GWENDOLYN (*Looking at the picture*) Oh, she's pretty. Isn't she pretty, Cecy?

CECILY Oh, yes. Pretty. A pretty girl. Very pretty.

FELIX (*Takes the picture back*) Thank you. (*Shows them another snapshot*) Isn't this nice?

GWENDOLYN (*Looks*) There's no one in the picture.

FELIX I know. It's a picture of our living room. We had a beautiful apartment.

GWENDOLYN Oh, yes. Pretty. Very pretty.

CECILY Those are lovely lamps.

FELIX Thank you! (*Takes the picture*) We bought them in Mexico on our honeymoon. (*He looks at the picture again*) I used to love to come home at night. (*He's beginning to break*) That was my whole life. My wife, my kids—and my apartment.
(*He breaks down and sobs*)

CECILY Does she have the lamps now too?

FELIX (*Nods*) I gave her everything. It'll never be like that again. Never! I—I— (*He turns his head away*) I'm sorry. (*He takes out a handkerchief and dabs his eyes.* GWENDOLYN *and* CECILY *look at each other with compassion*) Please forgive me. I didn't mean to get emotional. (*Trying to pull himself together, he picks up a bowl from the side table and offers it to the girls*) Would you like some potato chips?
(CECILY *takes the bowl*)

GWENDOLYN You mustn't be ashamed. I think it's a rare quality in a man to be able to cry.

FELIX (*Puts a hand over his eyes*) Please. Let's not talk about it.

CECILY I think it's sweet. Terribly, terribly sweet.
(*She takes a potato chip*)

FELIX You're just making it worse.

GWENDOLYN (*Teary-eyed*) It's so refreshing to hear a

man speak so highly of the woman he's divorcing! Oh, dear. (*She takes out her handkerchief*) Now you've got me thinking about poor Sydney.

CECILY Oh, Gwen. Please don't.
(*She puts the bowl down*)

GWENDOLYN It was a good marriage at first. Everyone said so. Didn't they, Cecily? Not like you and George.

CECILY (*The past returns as she comforts* GWENDOLYN) That's right. George and I were never happy. Not for one single, solitary day.
(*She remembers her unhappiness, grabs her handkerchief and dabs her eyes. All three are now sitting with handkerchiefs at their eyes*)

FELIX Isn't this ridiculous?

GWENDOLYN I don't know what brought this on. I was feeling so good a few minutes ago.

CECILY I haven't cried since I was fourteen.

FELIX Just let it pour out. It'll make you feel much better. I always do.

GWENDOLYN Oh, dear; oh, dear; oh, dear.
(*All three sit sobbing into their handkerchiefs. Suddenly* OSCAR *bursts happily into the room with a tray full of drinks. He is all smiles*)

OSCAR (*Like a corny M.C.*) Is ev-rybuddy happy? (*Then he sees the maudlin scene.* FELIX *and the girls quickly try to pull themselves together*) What the hell happened?

FELIX Nothing! Nothing!
(*He quickly puts his handkerchief away*)

OSCAR What do you mean, nothing? I'm gone three minutes and I walk into a funeral parlor. What did you say to them?

FELIX I didn't say anything. Don't start in again, Oscar.

OSCAR I can't leave you alone for five seconds. Well, if you really want to cry, go inside and look at your London broil.

FELIX (*He rushes madly into the kitchen*) Oh, my gosh! Why didn't you call me? I told you to call me.

OSCAR (*Giving a drink to* CECILY) I'm sorry, girls. I forgot to warn you about Felix. He's a walking soap opera.

GWENDOLYN   I think he's the dearest thing I ever met.

CECILY (*Taking the glass*)   He's so sensitive. So fragile. I just want to bundle him up in my arms and take care of him.

OSCAR (*Holds out* GWENDOLYN's *drink. At this, he puts it back down on the tray and takes a swallow from his own drink*)   Well, I think when he comes out of that kitchen you may have to.
(*Sure enough,* FELIX *comes out of the kitchen onto the landing looking like a wounded puppy. With a protective kitchen glove, he holds a pan with the exposed London broil. Black is the color of his true love*)

FELIX (*Very calmly*)   I'm going down to the delicatessen. I'll be right back.

OSCAR (*Going to him*)   Wait a minute. Maybe it's not so bad. Let's see it.

FELIX (*Shows him*)   Here! Look! Nine dollars and thirty-four cents worth of ashes! (*Pulls the pan away. To the girls*) I'll get some corned beef sandwiches.

OSCAR (*Trying to get a look at it*)   Give it to me! Maybe we can save some of it.

FELIX (*Holding it away from* OSCAR)   There's nothing to save. It's all black meat. Nobody likes black meat!

OSCAR   Can't I even look at it?

FELIX   No, you can't look at it!

OSCAR   Why can't I look at it?

FELIX   If you looked at your watch before, you wouldn't have to look at the black meat now! Leave it alone!
(*He turns to go back into the kitchen*)

GWENDOLYN (*Going to him*)   Felix! Can we look at it?

CECILY (*Turning to him, kneeling on the couch*)   Please? (FELIX *stops in the kitchen doorway. He hesitates for a moment. He likes them. Then he turns and wordlessly holds the pan out to them.* GWENDOLYN *and* CECILY *inspect it wordlessly, and then turn away sobbing quietly. To* OSCAR) How about Chinese food?

OSCAR   A wonderful idea.

GWENDOLYN   I've got a better idea. Why don't we just make pot luck in the kitchen?

OSCAR   A *much* better idea.

FELIX   I used up all the pots!
   (*He crosses to the love seat and sits, still holding the pan*)

CECILY   Well, then we can eat up in *our* place. We have tons of Horn and Hardart's.

OSCAR   (*Gleefully*)   That's the best idea I ever heard.

GWENDOLYN   Of course it's awfully hot up there. You'll have to take off your jackets.

OSCAR   (*Smiling*)   We can always open up a refrigerator.

CECILY   (*Gets her purse from the couch*)   Give us five minutes to get into our cooking things.
   (GWENDOLYN *gets her purse from the couch*)

OSCAR   Can't you make it four? I'm suddenly starving to death.
   (*The girls are crossing to the door*)

GWENDOLYN   Don't forget the wine.

OSCAR   How could I forget the wine?

CECILY   And a corkscrew.

OSCAR   *And* a corkscrew.

GWENDOLYN   And Felix.

OSCAR   No, I won't forget Felix.

CECILY   Ta, ta!

OSCAR   Ta, ta!

GWENDOLYN   Ta, ta!
   (*The girls exit*)

OSCAR   (*Throws a kiss at the closed door*)   You bet your sweet little crumpets, "Ta, Ta!" (*He wheels around beaming and quickly gathers up the corkscrew from the bar, and picks up the wine and the records*) Felix, I love you. You've just overcooked us into one hell of a night. Come on, get the ice bucket. Ready or not, here we come.
   (*He runs to the door*)

FELIX (*Sitting motionless*) I'm not going!

OSCAR What?

FELIX I said I'm not going.

OSCAR (*Crossing to* FELIX) Are you out of your mind? Do you know what's waiting for us up there? You've just been invited to spend the evening in a two-bedroom hothouse with the Coo-Coo Pigeon Sisters! What do you mean you're not going?

FELIX I don't know how to talk to them. I don't know what to say. I already told them about my brother in Buffalo. I've used up my conversation.

OSCAR Felix, they're crazy about you. They told me! One of them wants to wrap you up and make a bundle out of you. You're doing better than I am! Get the ice bucket.
(*He starts for the door*)

FELIX Don't you understand? I cried! I cried in front of two women.

OSCAR (*Stops*) And they *loved* it! I'm thinking of getting hysterical. (*Goes to the door*) Will you get the ice bucket?

FELIX But why did I cry? Because I felt guilty. Emotionally I'm still tied to Frances and the kids.

OSCAR Well, untie the knot just for tonight, will you!

FELIX I don't want to discuss it any more. (*Starts for the kitchen*) I'm going to scrub the pots and wash my hair. (*He goes into the kitchen and puts the pan in the sink*)

OSCAR (*Yelling*) Your greasy pots and your greasy hair can wait. You're coming upstairs with me!

FELIX (*In the kitchen*) I'm not! *I'm not!*

OSCAR What am I going to do with two girls? Felix, don't do this to me. I'll never forgive you!

FELIX I'm not going!

OSCAR (*Screams*) All right, damn you, I'll go without you! (*And he storms out the door and slams it. Then it opens and he comes in again*) Are you coming?

FELIX (*Comes out of the kitchen looking at a magazine*)
No.

OSCAR   You mean you're not going to make any effort to change? This is the person you're going to be—until the day you die?

FELIX (*Sitting on the couch*)   We are what we are.

OSCAR (*Nods, then crosses to a window, pulls back the drapes and opens the window wide. Then he starts back to the door*)   It's twelve floors, not eleven.
    (*He walks out as* FELIX *stares at the open windows*)

Curtain

Act Three

The next evening about 7:30 P.M. *The room is once again set up for the poker game, with the dining table pulled down, the chairs set about it, and the love seat moved back beneath the windows in the alcove.* FELIX *appears from the bedroom with a vacuum cleaner. He is doing a thorough job on the rug. As he vacuums around the table, the door opens and* OSCAR *comes in wearing a summer hat and carrying a newspaper. He glares at* FELIX, *who is still vacuuming, and shakes his head contemptuously. He crosses behind* FELIX, *leaving his hat on the side table next to the armchair, and goes into his bedroom.* FELIX *is not aware of his presence. Then suddenly the power stops on the vacuum, as* OSCAR *has obviously pulled the plug in the bedroom.* FELIX *tries switching the button on and off a few times, then turns to go back into the bedroom. He stops and realizes what's happened as* OSCAR *comes back into the room.* OSCAR *takes a cigar out of his pocket and as he crosses in front of* FELIX *to the couch, he unwraps it and drops the wrappings carelessly on the floor. He then steps up on the couch and walks back and forth mashing down the pillows. Stepping down, he plants one foot on the armchair and then sits on the couch, taking a wooden match from the coffee table and striking it on the table to light his cigar. He flips the used match onto the rug and settles back to read his newspaper.* FELIX *has watched this all in silence, and now carefully picks up the cigar wrappings and the match and drops them into* OSCAR's *hat. He then dusts his hands and takes the vacuum cleaner into the kitchen, pulling the cord in after him.* OSCAR *takes the wrappings from the hat and puts them in the butt-filled ashtray on the coffee table. Then he takes the ashtray and dumps it on the floor. As he once more settles down with his newspaper,* FELIX *comes out of the kitchen carrying a tray with a steaming dish of spaghetti. As he crosses behind* OSCAR *to the table, he indicates that it smells delicious and passes it close to* OSCAR *to make sure* OSCAR *smells the fantastic dish he's missing. As* FELIX *sits and begins to eat,* OSCAR *takes a can of aerosol spray from the bar, and circling the table, sprays all around* FELIX, *then puts the can down next to him and goes back to his newspaper.*

FELIX (*Pushing the spaghetti away*) All right, how much longer is this gonna go on?

OSCAR (*Reading his paper*) Are you talking to me?

FELIX That's right, I'm talking to you.

OSCAR What do you want to know?

FELIX I want to know if you're going to spend the rest of your life not talking to me. Because if you are, I'm going to buy a radio. (*No reply*) Well? (*No reply*) I see. You're not going to talk to me. (*No reply*) All right. Two can play at this game. (*Pause*) If you're not going to talk to me, I'm not going to talk to you. (*No reply*) I can act childish too, you know. (*No reply*) I can go on without talking just as long as you can.

OSCAR Then why the hell don't you shut up?

FELIX Are you talking to me?

OSCAR You had your chance to talk last night. I begged you to come upstairs with me. From now on I never want to hear a word from that shampooed head as long as you live. That's a warning, Felix.

FELIX (*Stares at him*) I stand warned. Over and out!

OSCAR (*Gets up, takes a key out of his pocket and slams it on the table*) There's a key to the back door. If you stick to the hallway and your room, you won't get hurt.
(*He sits back down on the couch*)

FELIX I don't think I gather the entire meaning of that remark.

OSCAR Then I'll explain it to you. Stay out of my way.

FELIX (*Picks up the key and moves to the couch*) I think you're serious. I think you're really serious. Are you serious?

OSCAR This is my apartment. Everything in my apartment is mine. The only thing here that's yours is you. Just stay in your room and speak softly.

FELIX Yeah, you're serious. Well, let me remind you that I pay half the rent and I'll go into any room I want.
(*He gets up angrily and starts toward the hallway*)

OSCAR Where are you going?

FELIX I'm going to walk around your bedroom.

OSCAR (*Slams down his newspaper*) You stay out of there.

FELIX (*Steaming*) Don't tell me where to go. I pay a hundred and twenty dollars a month.

OSCAR That was off-season. Starting tomorrow the rates are twelve dollars a day.

FELIX All right. (*He takes some bills out of his pocket and slams them down on the table*) There you are. I'm paid up for today. Now I'm going to walk in your bedroom.
   (*He starts to storm off*)

OSCAR Stay out of there! Stay out of my room!
   (*He chases after him.* FELIX *dodges around the table as* OSCAR *blocks the hallway*)

FELIX (*Backing away, keeping the table between them*) Watch yourself! Just watch yourself, Oscar!

OSCAR (*With a pointing finger*) I'm warning you. You want to live here, I don't want to see you, I don't want to hear you and I don't want to smell your cooking. Now get this spaghetti off my poker table.

FELIX Ha! Ha, ha!

OSCAR What the hell's so funny?

FELIX It's not spaghetti. It's linguini!
   (OSCAR *picks up the plate of linguini, crosses to the doorway and hurls it into the kitchen*)

OSCAR Now it's garbage!
   (*He paces by the couch*)

FELIX (*Looks at* OSCAR *unbelievingly: what an insane thing to do*) You are crazy! I'm a neurotic nut but *you* are crazy!

OSCAR *I'm* crazy, heh? That's really funny coming from a fruitcake like you.

FELIX (*Goes to the kitchen door and looks in at the mess. Turns back to* OSCAR) I'm not cleaning that up.

OSCAR Is that a promise?

FELIX Did you hear what I said? I'm not cleaning it up.

It's your mess. (*Looking into the kitchen again*) Look at it. Hanging all over the walls.

OSCAR (*Crosses to the landing and looks in the kitchen door*) I like it.
(*He closes the door and paces around*)

FELIX (*Fumes*) You'd just let it lie there, wouldn't you? Until it turns hard and brown and . . . Yich, it's disgusting. I'm cleaning it up.
(*He goes into the kitchen.* OSCAR *chases after him. There is the sound of a struggle and falling pots*)

OSCAR Leave it alone! You touch one strand of that linguini—and I'm gonna punch you right in your sinuses.

FELIX (*Dashes out of the kitchen with* OSCAR *in pursuit. He stops and tries to calm* OSCAR *down*) Oscar, I'd like you to take a couple of phenobarbital.

OSCAR (*Points*) Go to your room! Did you hear what I said? *Go to your room!*

FELIX All right, let's everybody just settle down, heh?
(*He puts his hand on* OSCAR'S *shoulder to calm him but* OSCAR *pulls away violently from his touch*)

OSCAR If you want to live through this night, you'd better tie me up and lock your doors and windows.

FELIX (*Sits at the table with a great pretense of calm*) All right, Oscar, I'd like to know what's happened.

OSCAR (*Moves toward him*) What's *happened?*

FELIX (*Hurriedly slides over to the next chair*) That's right. Something must have caused you to go off the deep end like this. What is it? Something I said? Something I did? Heh? What?

OSCAR (*Pacing*) It's nothing you said. It's nothing you did. It's *you!*

FELIX I see. Well, that's plain enough.

OSCAR I could make it plainer but I don't want to hurt you.

FELIX What is it, the cooking? The cleaning? The crying?

OSCAR (*Moving toward him*) I'll tell you exactly what it is. It's the cooking, cleaning and crying. It's the talking in your sleep, it's the moose calls that open your ears at two o'clock in the morning. I can't take it any more, Felix. I'm crackin' up. Everything you do irritates me. And when you're not here, the things I know you're gonna do when you come in irritate me. You leave me little notes on my pillow. I told you a hundred times, I can't stand little notes on my pillow. "We're all out of Corn Flakes. F.U." It took me three hours to figure out that F.U. was Felix Ungar. It's not your fault, Felix. It's a rotten combination.

FELIX   I get the picture.

OSCAR   That's just the frame. The picture I haven't even painted yet. I got a typewritten list in my office of the "Ten Most Aggravating Things You Do That Drive Me Berserk." But last night was the topper. Oh, that was the topper. Oh, that was the ever-loving lulu of all times.

FELIX   What are you talking about, the London broil?

OSCAR   No, not the London broil. I'm talking about those two lamb chops. (*He points upstairs*) I had it all set up with that English Betty Boop and her sister, and I wind up drinking tea all night and telling them *your* life story.

FELIX   (*Jumps up*)   Oho! So *that's* what's bothering you. That I loused up your evening!

OSCAR   After the mood you put them in, I'm surprised they didn't go out to Rockaway and swim back to England.

FELIX   Don't blame me. I warned you not to make the date in the first place.
         (*He makes his point by shaking his finger in OS-CAR's face*)

OSCAR   Don't point that finger at me unless you intend to use it!

FELIX   (*Moves in nose to nose with OSCAR*)   All right, Oscar, get off my back. Get off! Off!
         (*Startled by his own actions, FELIX jumps back from OSCAR, warily circles him, crosses to the couch and sits*)

OSCAR   What's this? A display of temper? I haven't seen you really angry since the day I dropped my cigar in your pancake batter.
         (*He starts toward the hallway*)

FELIX (*Threateningly*) Oscar, you're asking to hear something I don't want to say. But if I say it, I think you'd better hear it.

OSCAR (*Comes back to the table, places both hands on it and leans toward* FELIX) If you've got anything on your chest besides your chin, you'd better get it off.

FELIX (*Strides to the table, places both hands on it and leans toward* OSCAR. *They are nose to nose*) All right, I warned you. You're a wonderful guy, Oscar. You've done everything for me. If it weren't for you, I don't know what would have happened to me. You took me in here. gave me a place to live and something to live for. I'll never forget you for that. You're tops with me, Oscar.

OSCAR (*Motionless*) If I've just been told off, I think I may have missed it.

FELIX It's coming now! You're also one of the biggest slobs in the world.

OSCAR I see.

FELIX And completely unreliable.

OSCAR Finished?

FELIX Undependable.

OSCAR Is that it?

FELIX And irresponsible.

OSCAR Keep going. I think you're hot.

FELIX That's it. I'm finished. *Now* you've been told off. How do you like that?
(*He crosses to the couch*)

OSCAR (*Straightening up*) Good. Because now I'm going to tell *you* off. For six months I lived alone in this apartment. All alone in eight rooms. I was dejected, despondent and disgusted. Then *you* moved in—my dearest and closest friend. And after three weeks of close, personal contact—I am about to have a nervous breakdown! Do me a favor. Move into the kitchen. Live with your pots, your pans, your ladle and your meat thermometer. When you want to come out, ring a bell and I'll run into the bedroom. (*Almost breaking down*) I'm asking you nicely, Felix—as a friend. Stay out of my way!
(*And he goes into the bedroom*)

FELIX (*Is hurt by this, then remembers something. He calls after him*) Walk on the paper, will you? The floors are wet. (OSCAR *comes out of the door. He is glaring maniacally, as he slowly strides back down the hallway.* FELIX *quickly puts the couch between him and* OSCAR) Awright, keep away. Keep away from me.

OSCAR (*Chasing him around the couch*) Come on. Let me get in one shot. You pick it. Head, stomach or kidneys.

FELIX (*Dodging about the room*) You're gonna find yourself in one sweet law suit, Oscar.

OSCAR It's no use running, Felix. There's only eight rooms and I know the short cuts.
(*They are now poised at opposite ends of the couch.* FELIX *picks up a lamp for protection*)

FELIX Is this how you settle your problems, Oscar? Like an animal?

OSCAR All right. You wanna see how I settle my problems. I'll show you. (*Storms off into* FELIX's *bedroom. There is the sound of falling objects and he returns with a suitcase*) I'll show you how I settle them. (*Throws the suitcase on the table*) There! That's how I settle them!

FELIX (*Bewildered, looks at the suitcase*) Where are you going?

OSCAR (*Exploding*) Not me, you idiot! You. You're the one who's going. I want you out of here. Now! Tonight!
(*He opens the suitcase*)

FELIX What are you talking about?

OSCAR It's all over, Felix. The whole marriage. We're getting an annulment! Don't you understand? I don't want to live with you any more. I want you to pack your things, tie it up with your Saran Wrap and get out of here.

FELIX You mean actually move out?

OSCAR Actually, physically and immediately. I don't care where you go. Move into the Museum of Natural History. (*Goes into the kitchen. There is the crash of falling pots and pans*) I'm sure you'll be very comfortable there. You can dust around the Egyptian mummies to your heart's content. But I'm a human, living person. (*Comes out with a stack of cooking utensils which he throws into the open suitcase*) All I want is my freedom Is that too much to ask for? (*Closes it*) There, you're all packed.

FELIX   You know, I've got a good mind to really leave.

OSCAR   (*Looking to the heavens*) Why doesn't he ever listen to what I say? Why doesn't he hear me? I know I'm talking—I recognize my voice.

FELIX   (*Indignantly*)   Because if you really want me to go, I'll go.

OSCAR   Then go. I want you to go, so go. When are you going?

FELIX   When am I going, huh? Boy, you're in a bigger hurry than Frances was.

OSCAR   Take as much time as she gave you. I want you to follow your usual routine.

FELIX   In other words, you're throwing me out.

OSCAR   Not in other words. Those are the perfect ones. (*Picks up the suitcase and holds it out to* FELIX) I am throwing you out.

FELIX   All right, I just wanted to get the record straight. Let it be on *your* conscience.
        (*He goes into his bedroom*)

OSCAR   What? What? (*Follows him to the bedroom doorway*) Let what be on my conscience?

FELIX   (*Comes out putting on his jacket and passes by* OSCAR)   That you're throwing me out. (*Stops and turns back to him*) I'm perfectly willing to stay and clear the air of our differences. But you refuse, right?

OSCAR   (*Still holding the suitcase*)   Right! I'm sick and tired of you clearing the air. That's why I want you to leave!

FELIX   Okay, as long as I heard you say the words, "Get out of the house." Fine. But remember, what happens to me is your responsibility. Let it be on *your* head.
        (*He crosses to the door*)

OSCAR   (*Follows him to the door and screams*)   Wait a minute, damn it! Why can't you be thrown out like a decent human being? Why do you have to say things like, "Let it be on your head"? I don't want it on my head. I just want you out of the house.

FELIX What's the matter, Oscar? Can't cope with a little guilt feelings?

OSCAR (*Pounding the railing in frustration*) Damn you. I've been looking forward to throwing you out all day long, and now you even take the pleasure out of that.

FELIX Forgive me for spoiling your fun. I'm leaving now—according to your wishes and desires.
    (*He starts to open the door*)

OSCAR (*Pushes by* FELIX *and slams the door shut. He stands between* FELIX *and the door*) You're not leaving here until you take it back.

FELIX Take what back?

OSCAR "Let it be on your head." What the hell is that, the Curse of the Cat People?

FELIX Get out of my way, please.

OSCAR Is this how you left that night with Frances? No wonder she wanted to have the room repainted right away. (*Points to* FELIX's *bedroom*) I'm gonna have yours dipped in bronze.

FELIX (*Sits on the back of the couch with his back to* OSCAR) How can I leave if you're blocking the door?

OSCAR (*Very calmly*) Felix, we've been friends a long time. For the sake of that friendship, please say, "Oscar, we can't stand each other; let's break up."

FELIX I'll let you know what to do about my clothes. Either I'll call—or someone else will. (*Controlling great emotion*) I'd like to leave now.
    (OSCAR, *resigned, moves out of the way.* FELIX *opens the door*)

OSCAR Where will you go?

FELIX (*Turns in the doorway and looks at him*) Where? (*He smiles*) Oh, come on, Oscar. You're not really interested, are you?
    (*He exits.* OSCAR *looks as though he's about to burst with frustration. He calls after* FELIX)

OSCAR All right, Felix, you win. (*Goes out into the hall*) We'll try to iron it out. Anything you want. Come back, Felix. Felix? *Felix?* Don't leave me like this—you louse! (*But* FELIX *is gone.* OSCAR *comes back into the room closing the door. He is limp. He searches for something to ease his enormous frustration. He throws a pillow at the door, and then paces about like a caged lion*) All right, Oscar, get a hold of yourself! He's gone! Keep saying that over and over. He's gone. He's really gone! (*He holds his head in pain*) He did it. He put a curse on me. It's on my head. I don't know what it is, but something's on my head. (*The doorbell rings and he looks up hopefully*) Please let it be him. Let it be Felix. Please give me one more chance to kill him.

    (*Putting the suitcase on the sofa, he rushes to the door and opens it.* MURRAY *comes in with* VINNIE)

MURRAY (*Putting his jacket on a chair at the table*)   Hey, what's the matter with Felix? He walked right by me with that "human sacrifice" look on his face again.
    (*He takes off his shoes*)

VINNIE (*Laying his jacket on the love seat*)   What's with him? I asked him where he's going and he said, "Only Oscar knows. Only Oscar knows." Where's he going, Oscar?

OSCAR (*Sitting at the table*)   How the hell should I know? All right, let's get the game started, heh? Come on, get your chips.

MURRAY   I have to get something to eat. I'm starving. Mmm, I think I smell spaghetti.
    (*He goes into the kitchen*)

VINNIE   Isn't he playing tonight?
    (*He takes two chairs from the dining alcove and puts them at the table*)

OSCAR   I don't want to discuss it. I don't even want to hear his name.

VINNIE   Who? Felix?

OSCAR   I told you not to mention his name.

VINNIE   I didn't know what name you meant.
    (*He clears the table and places what's left of* FELIX's *dinner on the bookcase*)

MURRAY (*Comes out of the kitchen*)   Hey, did you know there's spaghetti all over the kitchen?

OSCAR Yes, I know, and it's not spaghetti; it's linguini.

MURRAY Oh. I thought it was spaghetti.
(*He goes back into the kitchen*)

VINNIE (*Taking the poker stuff from the bookcase and putting it on the table*) Why shouldn't I mention his name?

OSCAR Who?

VINNIE Felix. What's happened? Has something happened?
(SPEED *and* ROY *come in the open door*)

SPEED Yeah, what's the matter with Felix?
(SPEED *puts his jacket over a chair at the table.* ROY *sits in the armchair.* MURRAY *comes out of the kitchen with a six-pack of beer and bags of pretzels and chips. They all stare at* OSCAR *waiting for an answer. There is a long pause and then he stands up*)

OSCAR We broke up! I kicked him out. It was my decision. I threw him out of the house. All right? I admit it. Let it be on my head.

VINNIE Let what be on your head?

OSCAR How should I know? *Felix put it there!* Ask him!
(*He paces around to the right*)

MURRAY He'll go to pieces. I know Felix. He's gonna try something crazy.

OSCAR (*Turns to the boys*) Why do you think I did it?
(MURRAY *makes a gesture of disbelief and moves to the couch, putting down the beer and the bags.* OSCAR *moves to him*) You think I'm just selfish? That I wanted to be cruel? I did it for you—I did it for all of us.

ROY What are you talking about?

OSCAR (*Crosses to* ROY) All right, we've all been through the napkins and the ashtrays and the bacon, lettuce and tomato sandwiches. But that was just the beginning. Just the beginning. Do you know what he was planning for next Friday night's poker game? As a change of pace. Do you have any idea?

VINNIE What?

OSCAR A Luau! An Hawaiian Luau! Spareribs, roast pork and fried rice. They don't play poker like that in Honolulu.

MURRAY One thing has nothing to do with the other. We all know he's impossible, but he's still our friend, and he's still out on the street, and I'm still worried about him.

OSCAR (*Going to* MURRAY) And I'm not, heh? I'm not concerned? I'm not worried? Who do you think sent him out there in the first place?

MURRAY Frances!

OSCAR What?

MURRAY Frances sent him out in the first place. *You* sent him out in the second place. And whoever he lives with next will send him out in the third place. Don't you understand? It's Felix. He does it to himself.

OSCAR Why?

MURRAY I don't know why. *He* doesn't know why. There are people like that. There's a whole tribe in Africa who hit themselves on the head all day long.
(*He sums it all up with an eloquent gesture of resignation*)

OSCAR (*A slow realization of a whole new reason to be angry*) I'm not going to worry about him. Why should I? He's not worrying about me. He's somewhere out on the streets sulking and crying and having a wonderful time. If he had a spark of human decency he would leave us all alone and go back to Blanche.
(*He sits down at the table*)

VINNIE Why should he?

OSCAR (*Picks up a deck of cards*) Because it's his wife.

VINNIE No, Blanche is your wife. His wife is Frances.

OSCAR (*Stares at him*) What are you, some kind of wise guy?

VINNIE What did I say?

OSCAR (*Throws the cards in the air*) All right, the poker game is over. I don't want to play any more.
(*He paces around on the right*)

SPEED Who's playing? We didn't even start.

OSCAR (*Turns on him*)   Is that all you can do is complain? Have you given one single thought to where Felix might be?

SPEED   I thought you said you're not worried about him.

OSCAR (*Screams*)   I'm not worried, damn it! I'm not worried. (*The doorbell rings. A gleeful look passes over* OSCAR's *face*) It's him. I bet it's him! (*The boys start to go for the door.* OSCAR *stops them*) Don't let him in; he's not welcome in this house.

MURRAY (*Moves toward the door*)   Oscar, don't be childish. We've got to let him in.

OSCAR (*Stopping him and leading him to the table*)   I won't give him the satisfaction of knowing we've been worrying about him. Sit down. Play cards. Like nothing happened.

MURRAY   But, Oscar . . .

OSCAR   Sit down. Everybody. Come on, sit down and play poker.
(*They sit and* SPEED *begins to deal out cards*)

VINNIE (*Crossing to the door*)   Oscar . . .

OSCAR   All right, Vinnie, open the door.
(VINNIE *opens the door. It is* GWENDOLYN *standing there*)

VINNIE (*Surprised*)   Oh, hello. (*To* OSCAR) It's not him, Oscar.

GWENDOLYN   How do you do.
(*She walks into the room*)

OSCAR (*Crosses to her*)   Oh, hello, Cecily. Boys, I'd like you to meet Cecily Pigeon.

GWENDOLYN   Gwendolyn Pigeon. Please don't get up. (*To* OSCAR) May I see you for a moment, Mr. Madison?

OSCAR   Certainly, Gwen. What's the matter?

GWENDOLYN   I think you know. I've come for Felix's things.
(OSCAR *looks at her in shock and disbelief. He looks at the boys, then back at* GWENDOLYN)

OSCAR   Felix? My Felix?

GWENDOLYN   Yes. Felix Ungar. That sweet, tortured man

who's in my flat at this moment pouring his heart out to my sister.

OSCAR (*Turns to the boys*)   You hear? I'm worried to death and he's up there getting tea and sympathy.

(CECILY *rushes in dragging a reluctant* FELIX *with her*)

CECILY   Gwen, Felix doesn't want to stay. Please tell him to stay.

FELIX   Really, girls, this is very embarrassing. I can go to a hotel. (*To the boys*) Hello, fellas.

GWENDOLYN (*Overriding his objections*)   Nonsense. I told you, we've plenty of room, and it's a very comfortable sofa. Isn't it, Cecy?

CECILY (*Joining in*)   Enormous. And we've rented an air conditioner.

GWENDOLYN   And we just don't like the idea of you wandering the streets looking for a place to live.

FELIX   But I'd be in the way. Wouldn't I be in the way?

GWENDOLYN   How could you possibly be in anyone's way?

OSCAR   You want to see a typewritten list?

GWENDOLYN (*Turning on him*)   Haven't you said enough already, Mr. Madison? (*To* FELIX) I won't take no for an answer. Just for a few days, Felix.

CECILY   Until you get settled.

GWENDOLYN   Please. Please say, "Yes," Felix.

CECILY   Oh, please—we'd be so happy.

FELIX (*Considers*)   Well, maybe just for a few days.

GWENDOLYN (*Jumping with joy*)   Oh, wonderful.

CECILY (*Ecstatic*)   Marvelous!

GWENDOLYN (*Crosses to the door*)   You get your things and come right up.

CECILY   And come hungry. We're making dinner.

GWENDOLYN (*To the boys*)   Good night, gentlemen; sorry to interrupt your bridge game.

CECILY (*To* FELIX) If you'd like, you can invite your friends to play in our flat.

GWENDOLYN (*To* FELIX) Don't be late. Cocktails in fifteen minutes.

FELIX I won't.

GWENDOLYN Ta, ta.

CECILY Ta, ta.

FELIX Ta, ta.
> (*The girls leave.* FELIX *turns and looks at the fellows and smiles as he crosses the room into the bedroom. The five men stare dumbfounded at the door without moving. Finally* MURRAY *crosses to the door*)

SPEED (*To the others*) I told you. It's always the quiet guys.

MURRAY Gee, what nice girls.
> (*He closes the door.* FELIX *comes out of the bedroom carrying two suits in a plastic cleaner's bag*)

ROY Hey, Felix, are you really gonna move in with them?

FELIX (*Turns back to them*) Just for a few days. Until I find my own place. Well, so long, fellows. You can drop your crumbs on the rug again.
> (*He starts toward the door*)

OSCAR Hey, Felix. Aren't you going to thank me?

FELIX (*Stopping on the landing*) For what?

OSCAR For the two greatest things I ever did for you. Taking you in and throwing you out.

FELIX (*Lays his suits over the railing and goes to* OSCAR) You're right, Oscar. Thanks a lot. Getting kicked out twice is enough for any man. In gratitude, I remove the curse.

OSCAR (*Smiles*) Oh, bless you and thank you, Wicked Witch of the North.
> (*They shake hands. The phone rings*)

FELIX Ah, that must be the girls.

MURRAY (*Picking up the phone*) Hello?

FELIX They hate it so when I'm late for cocktails. (*Turning to the boys*) Well, so long.

MURRAY It's your wife.

FELIX (*Turning to* **MURRAY**) Oh? Well, do me a favor, Murray. Tell her I can't speak to her now. But tell her I'll be calling her in a few days, because she and I have a lot to talk about. And tell her if I sound different to her, it's because I'm not the same man she kicked out three weeks ago. Tell her, Murray; tell her.

MURRAY I will when I see her. This is Oscar's wife.

FELIX Oh!

MURRAY (*Into the phone*) Just a minute, Blanche.
(**OSCAR** *crosses to the phone and sits on the arm of the couch*)

FELIX Well, so long, fellows.
(*He shakes hands with the boys, takes his suits and moves to the door*)

OSCAR (*Into the phone*) Hello? Yeah, Blanche. I got a pretty good idea why you're calling. You got my checks, right? Good. (**FELIX** *stops at the door, caught by* **OSCAR**'s *conversation. He slowly comes back into the room to listen, putting his suits on the railing, and sitting down on the arm of the armchair*) So now I'm all paid up. No, no, I didn't win at the track. I've just been able to save a little money. I've been eating home a lot. (*Takes a pillow from the couch and throws it at* **FELIX**) Listen, Blanche, you don't have to thank me. I'm just doing what's right. Well, that's nice of you too. The apartment? No, I think you'd be shocked. It's in surprisingly good shape. (**FELIX** *throws the pillow back at* **OSCAR**) Say, Blanche, did Brucey get the goldfish I sent him? Yeah, well, I'll speak to you again soon, huh? Whenever you want. I don't go out much any more.

FELIX (*Gets up, takes his suits from the railing and goes to the door*) Well, good night, Mr. Madison. If you need me again, I get a dollar-fifty an hour.

OSCAR (*Makes a gesture to stop* **FELIX** *as he talks on the phone*) Well, kiss the kids for me. Good night, Blanche. (*Hangs up and turns to* **FELIX**) Felix?

FELIX (*At the opened door*) Yeah?

OSCAR How about next Friday night? You're not going to break up the game, are you?

FELIX Me? Never! Marriages may come and go, but the game must go on. So long, Frances.
     (*He exits, closing the door*)

OSCAR (*Yelling after him*) So long, Blanche. (*The boys all look at* OSCAR *a moment*) All right, are we just gonna sit around or are we gonna play poker?

ROY We're gonna play poker.
     (*There is a general hubbub as they pass out the beer, deal the cards and settle around the table*)

OSCAR (*Standing up*) Then let's play poker. (*Sharply, to the boys*) And watch your cigarettes, will you? This is my house, not a pig sty.
     (*He takes the ashtray from the side table next to the armchair, bends down and begins to pick up the butts. The boys settle down to play poker*)

Curtain

The Star-Spangled Girl

Act One

The curtains open on a duplex studio apartment over-looking the bay in San Francisco—it's not as nice as it sounds. It's a wood-shingled building about fifty years old. It was probably once the large Victorian home of a wealthy family, and in due course fell to its present state, an apart-ment and furnished-room multiple dwelling. Still, it's not without its charm.

The apartment is shared by two young men, ANDY HO-BART and NORMAN CORNELL. However, at first glance, one can see that their "home" has a double function. It also serves as their place of business, the offices of their small magazine Fallout. On the first level the entrance to the apartment is stage center, at the top of three stairs. Stage right center is a long kitchen bar.

It's late afternoon, in early summer. The door opens and ANDY HOBART enters. He is about twenty-six, but has the worried look of a man twice his age. ANDY is a dedicated, idealistic cynic charged with the energy of an angry genera-tion. He wears an old tan sports jacket over his khaki trou-sers, a checked shirt and no tie. He carries a briefcase that has seen better days. As he enters, he looks over at the desk and seems amazed and annoyed not to see anyone sitting there.

ANDY Norman . . . ? You home? I take it by your silence
that you're not home . . . (*He crosses to a tape recorder on the desk*) So where are you?
(*He turns the machine on, and puts his briefcase down*)

NORMAN'S VOICE (*Offstage*) I'm up on the roof stealing
laundry . . . You may be wearing a pink housecoat to-morrow, but at least it'll be clean. How about those fin-ished pages on the desk? (ANDY *picks them up and looks through them*) I've been pounding the typewriter for

nine straight hours. I am now capable of committing the perfect crime because I no longer have fingerprints . . . Mr. Franklyn telephoned five times. I repeat, five times. He said we owe him six hundred dollars in printing bills and fifty cents for five telephone calls. He also said if he doesn't get his money by Saturday, he's going to send over his two sons to break our four legs. I told him I'm just a writer and *you* take care of all bills, so they're going to break your legs and just sprain my ankles. I am now finished talking so please turn me off.

(ANDY *turns off the tape recorder as the telephone rings. He answers it*)

ANDY   *Fallout* magazine . . . Who's calling, please? Mr. Franklyn? One moment, Mr. Franklyn, I'll give you our billing department . . . (*He presses a button and uses a Titus Moody voice. He sits on the pole table*) Billing department . . . Yes . . . ? Oh, Mr. Franklyn. Yes, I got your five messages . . . You mean you haven't received our check . . . ? I can't understand that . . . Why just yesterday . . . (*He presses down on the receiver and cuts off the call. He looks over* NORMAN'S *pages. The telephone rings again. He picks it up*) Fallout magazine . . . Oh, Mr. Franklyn. I guess you got cut off. Sorry. I'll give you our billing department. (*He presses the button and resumes a Titus Moody voice*) Billing department . . . Oh, yes, Mr. Franklyn. Well—(*Again he deliberately clicks off. He hangs up and waits. The phone rings again.* ANDY *uses the nasal voice of a telephone operator*) . . . And a fifty percent chance of showers today. Tomorrow morning, clearing with patches of fog—(*He winces as* FRANKLYN *hangs up hard*) I don't know what you're so sore about, Franklyn. You may not be getting your money, but at least you know it's going to rain. (*The telephone rings again.* ANDY *turns on the tape machine and records*) . . . Hey, Luigi, how about a little service? (*The telephone rings again and he records that too. He turns off the machine, picks up phone and takes it to the desk. Then, with an Italian accent, he answers it*) Luigi's Restaurant . . . Who? No, is no magazine. Is Luigi's Restaurant . . .

(*He turns on the tape and plays it back*)

ANDY'S VOICE   Hey, Luigi, how about a little service?

ANDY (*Still in Italian accent*)   Sí, sí, I'm-a coming. (*The phone's ringing is heard on the tape recorder*) 'Scusa, my other phone, she's-a ringing. (*He hangs up and rubs his hands with satisfaction*) I can keep this up as long as you can, Franklyn.
(*The roof door opens and* NORMAN *comes down the ladder carrying a basket of laundry.* NORMAN *is about the same age as* ANDY. *Although he is the brain, the intellect behind* Fallout, *when he is away from the typewriter he is an incorrigible adolescent*)

NORMAN (*On the balcony*)   I just saved us eight dollars in laundry bills. And I found you your blue shirt.

ANDY   I didn't lose one.

NORMAN   I didn't say you did. I just said I found you one.

ANDY   Did you have lunch today?

NORMAN (*Comes down the steps to the landing*)   Certainly. I had one sardine on a frozen waffle.

ANDY   Why?

NORMAN   Because that's all there was.

ANDY   You mean there's nothing else to eat in the refrigerator?

NORMAN   There's three ice cubes and a light bulb. I'm saving them for tomorrow. (*At the center table, he puts the basket down. Then he holds up a shirt*) I'll put this in the freezer. We don't have any more starch.
(*He takes the shirt into the kitchen*)

ANDY (*Sitting on the pole table*)   Norman, it's just occurred to me that being poor is very boring. We really wouldn't have to worry about money if you would let me do what I suggested.

NORMAN (*Comes out of the kitchen and goes down right to the table between the sofas*)   What was that?

ANDY   Selling you to a medical school.

NORMAN   Never mind me, how about selling the magazine? How'd you do today?

ANDY   If selling two subscriptions is good, we only did
fair. (NORMAN *picks up an empty box of cookies*) Somehow I don't think the average San Francisco housewife
is ready for a politically controversial magazine that is
definitely anti-American . . . Is there any mail?

NORMAN   (*Throws down the empty box*)   In the wastebasket. (*He walks to the center table*) I'm so hungry.
(*He puts the clothesbasket on the floor, downstage
of the left chair. Then he eats crumbs from a plate
on the table*)

ANDY   (*He picks up the wastebasket, puts it on the pole
table and goes through the bills*)   Printing bills, typewriter repair bills, rent bills, electric bills, food bills, gas
bills. This is a bill for the waste paper basket.

NORMAN   (*Running his finger around the empty jam jar in
search of food*)   And we owe the lady from the pet shop
eighty cents.

ANDY   The pet shop? What for?

NORMAN   She gave me a haircut today.

ANDY   (*He returns the wastebasket to left of desk*)   Let
me worry about the bills, Norman, you write the magazine. I need your blue jacket. I've got to go out tonight.
(*He goes up left and gets the blue jacket hanging
upstage of a bulletin board*)

NORMAN   Business?

ANDY   Why else would I do the Monkey until three o'clock
in the morning at the Velvet Cucumber?

NORMAN   Who are you going with?

ANDY   Who do I go with every night? Our landlady, Mrs.

Mackininee. (*He takes the jacket to the sofa, where he lifts up the top mattress and lays the jacket between the mattress and springs. He drops the mattress down.* NORMAN *looks for food in the drawers of the slant-top desk*) Norman, you have no idea what I go through to keep us from being thrown out on the street. (ANDY *kneels on top of the mattress—he puts all his weight on it—to press the suit*) Not only is she totally lacking in rhythm, but she has no sense of direction. Last night she Watusied out the door and into the parking lot.

(*He rises and gets a dumbbell. Then rolls it over the mattress*)

NORMAN (*Good-naturedly, at slant-top desk eating from a small cereal box he has found*) It'll go down as one of the great sacrifices in journalistic history.

ANDY You don't think it's humiliating to sit in a night club with a dark-haired widow who wears blonde braids and picks up the bill?

NORMAN She likes you, doesn't she? Why don't you take her to the beach for the weekend so we can have the apartment painted?
(*He sits at the desk*)

ANDY You think I want to fall off her motorcycle the way her husband did?

NORMAN Listen, anytime you want to change places I'm perfectly willing.
(*The telephone rings.* NORMAN *gets up hurriedly and motions to* ANDY *to answer it as he goes to the chair left of the center table. He then sits and begins to fold clean socks.* ANDY *crosses left, above the table, to answer the phone*)

ANDY (*Into phone, Titus Moody voice again*) Billing department . . . ! (*Changes to his normal voice*) Oh, Mrs. Mackininee . . . No, no, I wasn't trying to sound older. I think I caught a cold last night. Yes, on the back of the motorcycle . . . You really are a wonderful driver . . . Did you ever find your other braid? Oh, too bad. I feel kind of responsible . . . Well, I do—I mean I felt myself slipping off and it was the first thing I grabbed . . . Yes, I'll pick you up at eight o'clock . . . Oh, that sounds wonderful. I can't wait to see them. 'Bye.

NORMAN You can't wait to see what?

ANDY Her new gold-sequined goggles. You can imagine how they look with her silver-lamé jumpsuit . . . Promise me one thing.

NORMAN What?

ANDY If there's a crash and they find my body next to hers, tell my mother and father I was kidnapped.
  (ANDY *goes and pulls the suit from under the sofa and walks to the stairs with it*)

NORMAN Listen, when you come home tonight, I want to hear everything that happened. I don't care what time it is, wake me up and tell me.

ANDY All right, Norman.

NORMAN Don't say all right. Promise me. You'll wake me up and you'll tell me everything. Don't leave anything out.

ANDY (*Leans over the balcony. He looks at* NORMAN *with concern*) Norman, I think you've been working too hard lately. Why don't you take the night off and go see a sexy movie?

NORMAN How can I take the night off? We've got a magazine to get out here.

ANDY You've got five days to finish three articles. You can do that with two fingers. Why don't you call up a girl?

NORMAN You can't just call up a girl. You have to know her first.

ANDY Well, call up a girl you know.

NORMAN   I don't like any of the girls I know. I only like the girls *you* know.

ANDY   All right, call up one of my girls.

NORMAN   I can't. I don't know them.
(NORMAN *rises and takes the clothesbasket into the kitchen. He returns and goes to the desk*)

ANDY   Norman, I'm as dedicated to this magazine as you are. Maybe even more. You put your talent into it; I put in my blood. And it's my job to preserve that talent and keep it in perfect working order. That's why I want you to relax once in a while. If you don't, you're going to get a bubble on your head.

NORMAN (*Seated at the desk*)   I'll go out as soon as this issue is finished.

ANDY   Who will you go out with?

NORMAN   A beautiful, gorgeous blonde will move into the empty apartment next door and I'll fall madly in love. All right?

ANDY   All right, Norman, if you're happier working, then I'm happy. Work all night and enjoy yourself.
(*He goes into the room and closes the door.* NORMAN *sits at the typewriter and picks up the clippings. He talks aloud to himself*)

NORMAN   I don't know how he expects me to finish a magazine if I don't sit down and finish it : . . Things do not get written by themselves—unless he believes in elves and gnomes . . . And they don't write magazines, they repair shoes . . .
(*He begins to type. The doorbell rings. He gets up, crosses to the door and opens it.* SOPHIE RAUSCH-MEYER, *a lovely young blonde, stands there. She is everything* NORMAN *has described. She is the proto-type of the all-American girl. If she had a few freckles on her nose it would be perfect. Her com-pact, solid form and freshly scrubbed face tell us*)

*that this is a purely physical creature. What she
can't do with an intellectual problem, she more than
makes up for with her strong backstroke or her
straight back when astride a horse. The Arkansas
drawl doesn't add to her image as an intellect either.
And best of all, she smells good)*

SOPHIE *(With a big, warm smile)* Excuse me. Mah name
is Sophie Rauschmeyer. Ah just moved into the empty
apartment next door. Ah know people in big cities don't
usually do this, but Ah promised mah folks Ah would
make mah akwaitance with mah neighbors so Ah just
want to say it's a pleasure meetin' you and hope Ah see
you again. Real soon. 'Bye!
*(She gives him a big smile. She turns, closes the
door and goes. NORMAN has not flinched a muscle
since she appeared. He now seems to be frozen to
the spot and stands motionless for what seems to be
an hour and a half)*

ANDY *(Comes out of his room, wearing the blue jacket, no
shoes)* Did someone just ring the bell . . . ? Norman,
did someone just come in?
(He leans down and taps NORMAN on his head)

NORMAN What? What? *(Quickly)* No! No! No one came
in. There's no one here. Go back to your room.

ANDY What's the matter, Norman?

NORMAN There's nothing the matter. Leave me alone. Go
back to your room. Can't you see I'm busy working.

ANDY At the door?

NORMAN I needed some air.

ANDY Why don't you open the window?

NORMAN I don't want fresh air. I want plain air . . . will
you please go back to your room?

ANDY All right, Norman. Don't tense up. Relax. Try and
relax. *(He is about to go back into his room when the*

doorbell rings again. ANDY *stops and looks at* NORMAN, *who doesn't move)* Now I hear a bell.

NORMAN   All right, so you hear a bell. People ring bells all day long. It's no reason for you to loiter on top of the stairs all night.
(*The doorbell rings again*)

ANDY   Are you going to answer that or am I?

NORMAN   *I'm* going to answer it. Stay up there.
(*He looks at* ANDY, *hoping he'll go away. But he knows he won't so* NORMAN *opens the door.* SOPHIE *stands there again. She has a cake in her hands*)

SOPHIE (*Big smile again*)   Excuse me again . . . Ah was just unpackin' and mah friends back home sent me this fruit cake with rum in it which Ah'm not allowed to eat 'cause Ah'm in trainin', and Ah'd hate to see it go to waste so Ah'd appreciate it if you'd accept it with mah compliments. (*She gives him the cake*) Nice seein' you again. 'Bye.
(*She pulls the door shut and exits.* NORMAN *gives a long look at the door*)

ANDY   Who's that, Norman?

NORMAN   Never mind who it is, I saw her first.

ANDY   All right, you saw her first. Who is she?

NORMAN (*Turns front*)   Her name is Sophie Rauschmeyer and she just moved into the empty apartment next door and she just gave me a fruit cake with rum in it and I love her. (*Running left, right, and all over the room*) Wahoo! Did you see what moved into this building? Next door to where I live! (*He puts the cake on the pole table*) It's for me. All for me. God loves me and He gave me something wonderful.
(*He stands with arms outstretched*)

ANDY (*Happy for* NORMAN, *on the bottom step*)   I was going to get you one for Christmas.

NORMAN (*He is now dancing all over the room*) Did you smell her? Did you get one whiff of that fragrance? Did you open your entire nose and smell that girl?

ANDY (*Comes down onto the stage floor and goes stage left*) I was upstairs, she didn't smell that far . . . I need your dancing shoes.
  (ANDY *picks up the cake, gives it to* NORMAN, *and then pushes him onto the pole table*)

NÓRMAN Didn't smell that far? It's all over the room. (ANDY *pulls the director's chair left, sits down and starts pulling off* NORMAN'S *shoes*) It's even out in the hall. I'll bet she's inundated the whole lousy neighborhood. They're gonna start raising rents. And you stay away from her.

ANDY No contest. She's not my type.

NORMAN Well, she's my type. (*He takes the cake to the kitchen—in stocking feet*) How do you know what type she is?

ANDY (*He pulls the chair back to the center table and gets the rubber stamp*) Norman, when it comes to girls, I have extrasensory perception. (*He applies the stamp to the pad, then to the shoes*) She's the all-outdoor type. Enormously strong from the neck down.

NORMAN (*He returns from the kitchen, and goes to the right of the center table*) Who cares what her I.Q. is? I'm not giving out any Fulbrights. I just want to smell her and touch her.

ANDY All right. Go ring her doorbell and say you want to smell her and touch her.

NORMAN Are you crazy, didn't you hear the way she talked? "Ah'm glad to make yo' akwaitance"—she comes from Rhett Butler country. The only way to make it with a girl like that is with romance, big gestures.

ANDY   All right. Go out and burn down Atlanta. She'll be crazy about you.

NORMAN (*Going left, downstage of the table*)   You think I wouldn't do it if I could get to nibble on her chin for an hour?

ANDY   I was right. You've been working much too hard lately.
(*He rises and goes right to the stairs*)

NORMAN (*Follows* ANDY)   Wait a minute. Talk to me. (ANDY *stops on the stairs and gets the tie hanging on the landing balustrade*) Help me. I've got to plan this all very carefully. I mustn't jump into anything. One wrong move and I can blow the entire love affair . . . Flowers? What about flowers? Flowers every morning. Flowers twice a day . . . No. No. That's not big enough.

ANDY (*Still on the stairs, he puts on the tie*)   How about trees?

NORMAN   Maybe it shouldn't be big. Maybe it should be small. Something with thought. Something personal. What could I do for her that's very small and very personal?

ANDY   How about brushing her teeth?

NORMAN   Get outa here! You're killing everything. You have no idea how to treat a girl like that.

ANDY   Personally I wouldn't try, but if she excites your nasal passages, Norman, I'm with you.

NORMAN   I got it! I got it! Where's the paint can? I need a can of green paint.
(*He goes stage left and gets the paint can from under the table*)

ANDY   What are you going to do?

NORMAN (*Goes to* ANDY) I'm going to paint the stairs. One letter on each step. So that when she comes home at night and goes up the stairs, it's going to read (*He indicates with his finger pointing up the stairs*) . . . I-love-you-Sophie-Rauschmeyer.

ANDY But she's already upstairs. When she goes down in the morning it's going to say Reymshaur-Ephos-Ouvlie!

NORMAN (*Goes down right*) Why do I bother talking to you?

ANDY I'm going to meet Mrs. Mackininee. (*Crosses to the door*) If I'm still alive, I'll be back at two A.M. . . . If not, about three-thirty.
(*He exits. Blackout*)

The lights come up. It is three days later. The room is empty. The door opens and ANDY *enters carrying his briefcase, having just returned from another grueling afternoon of selling.*

ANDY   Hi, Norman, how's it going? (*He stops and looks at the desk, but* NORMAN *isn't there. He walks into the room—he looks upset. He puts down his briefcase upstage of the radiator and crosses to the tape recorder*) All right, Norman, where the hell are you? (*The telephone rings.* ANDY *doesn't answer it. It rings again. He pushes the receiver into the waste paper basket. Then he picks it up*) Hello . . . ? Oh, Mr. Franklyn . . . I'm sorry I didn't answer the phone sooner, but I couldn't find it. I still have the bandages on my eyes—oh, didn't I tell you? Well, the doctor says my only chance is to have the operation. The only trouble is, it's six hundred dollars . . . Yes, the same amount I owe you . . . But I'm determined to pay your bill rather than have the operation—unless you have another suggestion . . . You like the first one best . . .
     (*We hear a pounding on the front door*)

NORMAN'S VOICE (*Offstage*)   Andy, hurry up. Open the door. I forgot my key.
          (ANDY *crosses to the door and opens it.* NORMAN *rushes in with a large package of groceries*)

ANDY   Where've you been all day?

NORMAN (*Taking the groceries to the center table*)   In love. Don't talk to me now. I'm busy.
          (*He crosses to the desk, takes off his jacket, and puts it on the desk-chair*)

ANDY I know you've been busy, but you haven't been working. I just looked on the desk; there are no new pages.

NORMAN (*Goes upstairs to his room for a fancy basket*) I've got plenty of time. Plenty of time.

ANDY Not anymore we don't. We have three days. Three days to finish three articles.

NORMAN I'm thinking all the time. I've got everything up here.
    (*He points to his head and starts downstairs*)

ANDY One! Give me one article. Give me one title you've thought of since the day that Arkansas frangipani checked in here and you painted love letters up and down the staircase . . . Let's hear one title!

NORMAN "The Real Case Against Fluoridation. Is Tooth Cancer Next?"

ANDY Write it. Sit down and write it. Now!

NORMAN Don't coerce me. I can't work under coercion.

ANDY How about under savage beating? I got a life savings and three years of work tied up in this venture. And I'm not going to see something good and vital and worthwhile go down the drain because you can't think of anything else but that corn-fed Minnie Mouse next door. What's in that package?

NORMAN Groceries.

ANDY I buy the groceries. Its for her, isn't it? What have you got in there?

NORMAN (*Indignantly picks up the bag*) None of your business. It's private groceries.

ANDY (*Looks at the package which* NORMAN *is holding*) The United Nations Gourmet Shoppe?

NORMAN They always have a big sale before Lent.

ANDY (*Snaps his fingers and points to the table.* NORMAN *obeys and puts the bag down.* ANDY *starts to take out some of the cans and jars and examines them*) Miniature watermelon . . . ? Baby Siberian herring filets . . . ? Tiny kumquats . . . ? Who's coming for dinner, a couple of midgets?

NORMAN I had a yen for some delicacies.
  (*He goes left, below the table, to the desk*)

ANDY Delicacies? You haven't eaten anything fancier than a banana and peanut-butter sandwich since the day I met you. (*Puts the jars back. He reaches in the bag and takes out the bill—he is shocked*) Twenty-two dollars?? You spent twenty-two dollars for *toy food?*

NORMAN Take it out of my share of the profits.

ANDY Your share of the profits can't pay for your banana and peanut-butter sandwiches. Are you out of your mind?

NORMAN I'm giving her a gift. You gave your mother a gift on Mother's Day, didn't you?

ANDY I gave her a year's subscription to our magazine. You hardly even know this girl.

NORMAN I know her. (*Goes to the telescope.* ANDY *crosses to the desk for glue and dummy magazine*) I know she works like a dog six days a week. I watch her through the telescope running after that bus every morning. I watch her coming home every night. Tired. Hungry. (*Goes left to* ANDY) That sweet, beautiful girl coming home to nothing better for dinner than a can of Broadcast Corned Beef Hash.

ANDY How do you know that?

NORMAN I check her garbage every afternoon.

ANDY All right, Norman, get a hold of yourself.
  (*He sits on the pole table*)

NORMAN Get a hold of myself? Are you kidding? My functioning days are over. I've become an animal. I've developed senses no man has ever used before. I can smell the shampoo in her hair three city blocks away. I can have my radio turned up full blast and still hear her taking off her stockings! Don't you understand, SHE TURNS ME ON! From my head to my toes, I take one look at her and I light up. This month alone my personal electric bill will be over two hundred dollars . . .

(*He starts putting the jars and cans into the basket*)

ANDY (*Glues a clipping onto the page of the dummy magazine*) You know, when I first met you in high school, I thought you were eccentric. When we worked on the journal together in college, I thought you were a very promising fruit cake. The last couple of years I decided you were a tremendously talented bedbug. Now I know what you are . . . (*He rises, and goes a few steps right*) *You are the unhatched egg of an illiterate looney bird!* We've got three days to get out a magazine and you spend your time buying pygmy cucumbers for a girl with strong shampoo?

NORMAN I'm going to let that pass. I am also not going to waste time trying to explain something that cannot be explained. Because it would be a waste of time.

ANDY You've already cornered the waste of time market. Explain it to me.

NORMAN Did you ever hear of physical attraction? Pure, unadulterated physical attraction?

ANDY I have.

NORMAN What is it?

ANDY It's when one hippopotamus likes another hippopotamus with no questions asked.

NORMAN Exactly. Now it's five-thirty and my hippopotamus will be getting off her bus. Now leave me alone because I've got work to do.

(*He takes the cans and jars out of the bag and puts them on the table*)

ANDY   All right . . . Look, I'll put the kumquats in the basket and you finish the article.

NORMAN   Who are you, Miles Standish? I'll put my own kumquats in the basket. (*He goes left, upstage of* ANDY) A ribbon! I need a red ribbon. You got a red ribbon?

ANDY   Do I have a red ribbon?

NORMAN   Either you have a red ribbon or you don't. If you have a red ribbon, I'd like it for my basket, please.

ANDY   I'm not going to discuss red ribbons with you at this time.

NORMAN   In other words, you're not going to give me your red ribbon!

ANDY   That's right. Out of the *thousands* I have saved in my closet, I'm not going to give you a red ribbon.

NORMAN   (*He goes up the stairs to the landing*) That's one I owe you, Andy. From now on I'm keeping score. (*He glances out the window*) There's her bus. (*He looks through the telescope*) I almost missed her bus account of you.

ANDY   Get away from that window.

NORMAN   Are you crazy? And miss Sophie getting off the bus? You know I wait for this all day.
(*He looks through the telescope, focusing it*)

ANDY   (*He takes a few steps right*)   Norman, write me two more articles and I'll buy you a bigger telescope. You'll be able to zoom right into her shoes. What do you say?

NORMAN   (*Looking through the telescope*)   I could have missed her bus. Sophie is on that bus and I almost missed it.

ANDY   (*He crosses up the stairs to the window and puts his hand over the lens, covering it*)   Damn you, Norman, answer me!

NORMAN (*Still looking through the telescope. He screams*) *Oh, my God! Sophie!* (*He looks up and sees that* ANDY *has his hand covering the opening*) You idiot! I thought her bus fell into a hole. Get your hand off my lens opening!

ANDY   My hand stays on your opening until you make me a promise.

NORMAN   I promise! I promise! Now get out of the way. (ANDY *comes down the stairs*) *There she is!* Oh, Mother in Heaven, will you look at that girl! Look at her! Just look at that girl!

ANDY   All right, let me see.

NORMAN (*Screams*)   Stay away from here. (ANDY *hangs up his jacket on the bulletin-board hook, then sits on the pole table*) I'm looking at her. Oh, you wonderful crazy Sophie. She has got without a doubt the most magnificent earlobes on the face of the earth. (*He looks out the window, straight down*) She's in the building. She'll be upstairs any minute. (*He runs down the steps, picks up the basket from the table and goes to the desk*) You're not going to give me your red ribbon, right?

ANDY   Who do you think I am, Fanny Farmer?

NORMAN   That's two I owe you.
        (*He sits at the typewriter, puts the basket on the floor and rips the paper out of the machine. Then he puts in another piece and begins to type*)

ANDY   What are you doing? Are you working . . . ? Norman, sweetheart, what are you writing? (*Rises and goes to peer over his shoulder. He then reads aloud*) . . . *Adomis terra amorta eternos* . . . What is that, a prescription?

NORMAN   It's "I worship the ground you walk on" in Latin. It goes with the groceries. (*He rises and puts the note in the basket, then faces* ANDY) Now get out of my way or you get Alberta peaches in brandy right between the eyes.

(ANDY *moves and* NORMAN *starts to the door as the telephone rings*)

ANDY (*Calls after* NORMAN) Norman, you've got three minutes to deliver your Care package. (*Picks up the phone*) United Nations Gourmet Shoppe . . . Oh, hello, Mrs. Mackininee, how are you . . . ? The beach this weekend? Gee, I don't know. I've developed this awful cough . . . Yes, I'm disappointed too.

NORMAN (*Rushes in*) She's got it! She's got the basket! (*He runs back to the door*)

ANDY (*Into the phone*) Yes, I agree it would be a lot more fun than staying home and collecting rents. What time do you want to go?

NORMAN (*Holding the door open and peeking through the crack*) She's reading the note.

ANDY (*Into the phone*) How?

NORMAN She's moving her gorgeous lips and reading the note.

ANDY (*Into the phone*) You mean I hold onto you and the surfboard at the same time? Won't that be a problem going through tunnels?

NORMAN She's looking over here . . . Here she comes! (*Closes the door and runs screaming to the center table*) Clean the apartment! Hurry up! (*He takes the grocery bag to upstage of bar*) Clean the apartment! (ANDY *hangs up the phone*) I'm shaking. (*Rushes left to* ANDY) Look at that hand shaking. Andy, I'm scared to death.

ANDY *You're* scared? I'm going surfing tomorrow with a daredevil landlady. They'll find me washed up in Hawaii. (*The doorbell rings*)

NORMAN   Open the door! Open the door! (*The doorbell rings again.* ANDY *turns to go*) *Where are you going?*

ANDY   To open the door.

NORMAN   Don't open the door. I'm not ready yet. (NORMAN *puts his jacket around his shoulders and gets a pipe from the slant-top desk, which he puts in his mouth—upside down. Then he sits above the desk and poses*) Open it! Open it!
          (ANDY *opens the door and* SOPHIE *enters carrying the basket. She seems quite upset*)

SOPHIE (*To* ANDY)   Excuse me. (*To* NORMAN) Mr. Cornell, Ah have tried to be neighborly, Ah have tried to be friendly and Ah have tried to be cordial . . . Ah don't know what it is that you're tryin' to be. That first night Ah was appreciative that you carried mah trunk up the stairs . . . The fact that it slipped and fell five flights and smashed to pieces was not your fault . . . Ah didn't even mind that personal message you painted on the stairs. Ah thought it was crazy, but sorta sweet. However, things have now gone too far . . . (*Goes down to the pole table*) Ah cannot accept gifts from a man Ah hardly know . . . (*Puts the basket on the pole table*) Especially canned goods. And Ah read your little note. Ah can guess the gist of it even though Ah don't speak Italian. (ANDY *sits on the stool below the kitchen bar*) This has got to stop, Mr. Cornell. Ah can do very well without you leavin' little chocolate-almond Hershey bars in mah mailbox—they melted yesterday, and now Ah got three gooey letters from home with nuts in 'em—and Ah can do without you sneakin' into mah room after Ah go to work and paintin' mah balcony without tellin' me about it. Ah stepped out there yesterday and mah slippers are still glued to the floor. And Ah can do without you tying big bottles of eau de cologne to mah cat's tail. The poor thing kept swishin' it yesterday and nearly beat herself to death . . . And most of all, Ah can certainly do without you watchin' me get on the bus every day through that high-powered telescope. You got me so nervous the other day Ah got on the wrong bus. In short, Mr. Cornell, and Ah don't want to have to say this again, *leave me ay-lone!*
          (*She turns and starts to go*)

NORMAN   Aside from that, is there any chance of your falling in love with me?
(SOPHIE *turns*)

SOPHIE   You are crackers, you know that, don't you? (*To* ANDY) Did you know your roommate is crackers?
(ANDY *crosses down right*)

ANDY   Yes, but I didn't know the exact medical term.

SOPHIE (*To* NORMAN)   Didn't you listen to one solitary word Ah said to you?

NORMAN   Yes, I'm listening . . . (*The jacket comes off his shoulders as he rises and goes above the pole table to* SOPHIE) I'm listening, I'm looking, and I'm smelling.
(*He sniffs*)

SOPHIE (*Yells and backs right*)   Ah don't want to be smelled! (NORMAN *follows and sniffs again. She moves right. To* ANDY) Tell him to stop smelling me.

ANDY (*Quietly*)   Norman, stop smelling her.
(*He sits on the sofa*)

SOPHIE (*To* NORMAN)   Ah am going to repeat this to you once more and for the last time. Ah am ingaged to be married to First Lieutenant Burt Fenneman of the United States Marine Corps. (*To* ANDY) And in six weeks Ah will be *Mrs.* First Lieutenant Burt Fenneman of the United States Marine Corps. (*To* NORMAN) And Ah intend to be happily married to him for the rest of mah natural life. (*She takes a step left*) Do you understand that?

NORMAN (*Goes right to her*)   Please lower your voice. I'm trying to hear your hair growing.

SOPHIE (*Goes right to* ANDY)   What is wrong with him? Does he have oral trouble?

ANDY   Oral trouble?

SOPHIE (*Points to her ears*)   With his ears. Hard of hearing.

ANDY   Yes, he has very bad orals.

SOPHIE   Ah thought as much. (*Goes back to* NORMAN) Ah could have you arrested, you know that? For loiterin', breakin' 'n' enterin', tamperin' with mah mailbox, pesterin', peepin' tom'n! Don't think Ah won't do it. (*She starts toward the door*)

NORMAN (*Stops her*)   Then I'll have *you* arrested. For creamy smooth skin, perfect teeth, a ridiculously small nose, insanely gorgeous earlobes and an indecently fantastic, unbelievable fragrance.
(*He inhales*)

SOPHIE (*Screams*)   Ah told you to stop smelling me! (*To* ANDY) Do something!

ANDY   Do you want me to hold his nose?

NORMAN (*Moves right to her*)   I'm sorry. A girl who looks like you shouldn't be allowed to walk the streets. (*Grabs her downstage arm*) This is a citizen's arrest!
(*He starts pulling her with him toward the steps*)

SOPHIE (*She pulls away. To* ANDY)   If he doesn't keep away from me, Ah'm going to arrange to have mah fiancé inflict bodily harm to him. Tell him that.

ANDY   Norman, her fiancé is going to inflict your body with harm.

NORMAN   Do you think that would stop me? Beatings? Flailings? Whippings? I welcome them. Tell her!

ANDY (*To* SOPHIE)   He says he welcomes beatings, flailings and whippings.

SOPHIE   Ah heard him!

ANDY   She heard you.

NORMAN (*On the stairs*)   If having a friend of yours punch me very hard is going to make you happy, my entire face is at your disposal.

SOPHIE Hey . . . Are we on one of those television programs or somethin'? If we are, Ah'd like to know. Otherwise Ah'm callin' Camp Pendleton.

ANDY Don't look at me. I'm just an innocent bystander.

SOPHIE So am I. Two years ago in Japan Ah represented mah country in the Olympic swimming competition. In order to be a member of the official United States Olympic swimming team, you must be in one hundred percent perfect physical condition. That's me. Ah was one hundred percent physically perfect. *Until* Ah moved next door. From the day Ah found that trail of little heart-shaped peanut brittles leading from mah door to his door, Ah have been a nervous wreck . . . Not only is it difficult to keep up with mah swimming, but Ah'm afraid to take a bath. Ah have found that when Ah brush mah hair, mah hair falls out. And the ones that fall out have not been replaced by new ones . . . Ah am twenty-three years old and that man is starting me on the road to total baldness. Ah intend to get married while Ah still have a full head of hair left. (*She goes to the door*) Ah am now going to have a dinner of good, basic American food, clean mah apartment and get ten hours' sleep. If Ah see him sittin' in that big tree outside mah window again, strummin' that ukelele and singin' those Spanish love songs, Ah'm gonna call for the United States Marines.
  (*She exits and slams the door.* NORMAN *and* ANDY *stand there for a brief second in silence. Then a wild gleam of uncontrolled happiness flashes across* NORMAN's *face*)

NORMAN (*Goes to the kitchen*) I'm getting to her, Andy . . . I tell you, I'm getting to her.

ANDY The only thing you're going to get is bayonet practice . . . She's engaged, Norman, forget about her.

NORMAN (*Coming out of the kitchen*) Forget about her? Did you see what was just in this room? Did you see?

ANDY I saw. It was a girl.

NORMAN (*Shocked. Comes down right to* ANDY) A girl? You call that a girl?? That's not a girl. *That* was one of God's creations made during His *best* period! Don't ever call her a girl in front of me again.
(*He storms back into the kitchen*)

ANDY Well, whatever that thing is, if it goes bald, you're in big trouble with our armed forces.

NORMAN (*Comes out of the kitchen with a mop*) I can handle Uncle Sam.

ANDY Where are you going with that?

NORMAN (*Crossing down left, he empties wastebasket on the floor*) You think I'm going to let her clean her apartment after she's been working all day?

ANDY (*Rises and goes to the bar. He gets the ukelele, and goes stage left menacingly*) All right, I've had just about as much of King Kong and Fay Wray as I can take . . . You move two steps away from that typewriter and for the rest of this week you'll be picking ukelele out of your head.

NORMAN Not unless you're capable of swallowing an entire mop.

ANDY Norman, what's happened to you? I've seen you panting over a girl before, but this is the first time I ever saw steam coming out of your ears . . . I'm worried about you.

NORMAN Don't you think I am too? I am definitely worried about me. I was up all last night rereading Krafft-Ebbing. In 1926 there was a case very similar to mine in Gutenburg, Germany. It involved a nun and a knockwurst salesman. (*He crosses to the door with the wastebasket and mop.* ANDY *then goes left, and leaves the ukelele on up left table*) But I can't help myself because I'm crazy about that girl. I'll do anything, including mopping her kitchen floor, to be with her every night for the rest of my life.

ANDY   In six weeks she's marrying the Marine.

NORMAN   What she does during the day is her business.
        (*He exits. The telephone rings.* ANDY *turns the tape
        recorder on to "record," and talks into the mike*)

ANDY (*In Chinese*)   Oh sing mah toh wan po soo chow
        moo ling. (*He turns the machine off. The telephone
        rings again. He quickly reruns the tape, then picks up
        the phone and speaks in his Chinese dialect*) Yes, please?
        Wo Ping's Chinese Gardens.
                (*He turns the machine on and we hear his voice
                from before*)

ANDY'S VOICE   Hey, Luigi, how about a little service?
        (*He quickly hangs up, and turns off the machine.
        The door flies open and* SOPHIE *storms in angrily*)

SOPHIE (*Shouts*)   Do you know what he's doing? Do you
        know what he's doing now?

ANDY   He's mopping your kitchen floor.

SOPHIE   *He is mopping mah kitchen floor!*

ANDY   And you don't want your kitchen floor mopped.

SOPHIE (*Screams*)   Ah don't want it mopped 'cause Ah
        waxed it last night and now *he's moppin' up all the wax!*

ANDY   I can hear you. I have perfect orals.

SOPHIE   Don't you understand? He has illegally entered
        mah apartment and criminally mopped mah floor. Aren't
        you going to do anything except stand there?

ANDY   If you'll calm down, maybe we can discuss this?

SOPHIE   Of course. (*Crosses to the desk*) Ah just have to
        make one call. May Ah use your phone?

ANDY   Certainly.

SOPHIE (*Dials once*) Thank you. Ah don't have one of mah own. (*Into the phone*) Hello? San Francisco Police.
      (ANDY *closes the door*)

ANDY You wouldn't.

SOPHIE Wouldn't I? (*Into the phone*) Ah'd like to report a demented man who's run amuck in mah kitchen.

ANDY (*Goes to* SOPHIE) Will you just listen to me for two minutes?

SOPHIE (*To* ANDY) In two minutes he will have mah wallpaper steamed off and sent out to be dry cleaned. (*Into the phone*) That's right, run amuck . . . No, not with a knife, with a mop.

ANDY (*He tries to restrain her by holding her shoulder*) Give me sixty seconds.

SOPHIE Take your hands off mah "ingaged" shoulder.

ANDY Give me that phone.
      (*He takes it from her*)

SOPHIE It's just gonna cost you another dime 'cause Ah'm gonna call them again.

ANDY Why won't you listen to me?

SOPHIE Why? Ah'll tell you why. (*She crosses and picks up a lamp. She crosses back to him and turns the lamp on, holding it up to her cheek right in front of his face.* ANDY *puts phone on desk*) Look at mah skin. Those big, ugly red blotches are hives. Do you know what causes me to get hives?

ANDY Holding a lamp to your face?

SOPHIE Nervous tension causes me to get hives. And having mah floor mopped causes nervous tension. Ah am breaking out in big red blotches and Ah am losing mah hair and Ah have a date (*Puts the lamp back on the*

desk) with mah fiancé tomorrow night and Ah'm going
to look like a little old man with the measles . . . And
you have the ultimate gall to ask me for time.
(*She goes right—upstage of* ANDY)

ANDY   I know exactly what you're going through. I've lived
with that nut for three years and he's turned my hair
grey.

SOPHIE (*Comes back downstage*)   Ah fail to notice it.

ANDY (*Goes to* SOPHIE)   Look at my eyelashes. All grey.
I used to have long, beautiful black eyelashes. Did you
ever see anything like that before? Grey! Grey! Grey!

SOPHIE (*Moves in close and scrutinizes*)   Grey eyelashes
are not as noticeable on a man as a receding hairline is
on a girl.
(*She goes downstage*)

ANDY (*Being solicitous*)   It's not receding. You have beautiful hair.

SOPHIE   Do you like it?

ANDY   Very much.

SOPHIE   I'm glad. Because a lot of it has fallen on your
floor. And if he's not out of there in five seconds, a lot
of his blood is going to be on mah floor . . . Ah'm gonna
start counting before Ah call again.

ANDY   No, you're not. You're going to sit down and listen
to me.
(*He gives her a gentle push toward a chair*)

SOPHIE (*Rises immediately*)   If you're threatening me
Ah'd advise you not to. You're tall and skinny and Ah'm
short and strong.

ANDY   Well, I'm glad you live next door. I have a lot of
trouble opening jars . . . Can I tell you about Norman
Cornell?

SOPHIE Why not? Ah'm not doin' anything but countin'
. . . One, two, three—

ANDY He is impulsive, compulsive, irrepressible and incorrigible . . . (SOPHIE *starts to interrupt, but* ANDY *continues*) but he is also one of the most talented, creative
and inspired young writers living in this country today.
Will you accept that?

SOPHIE Ah have never read anything of his except an
Italian mash note in mah grocery basket . . . Four, five—
(*Goes left, downstage of* ANDY, *to the desk*) Ah'm usin'.
the phone.

ANDY (*Rushes left*) Not until you hear me out. (*He takes
the phone*) In his freshman year at Dartmouth he wrote
a thesis on the economic growth of the Philippine Is-
lands since 1930 without any previous knowledge of eco-
nomics, the Philippines, or 1930.

SOPHIE There is no end to the talent of the mentally
warped. (*She starts to pick up the phone, but* ANDY's
hand is there to stop her again) If Ah have to scream,
Ah'll scream.

ANDY He's been offered jobs to write for every news
agency in the country, plus *Time, Look, Life,* the *Saturday Review* and the *Diners' Club Monthly.* (*He guides*
SOPHIE *into the chair. He goes left upstage of* SOPHIE,
and sits on the desk) Please believe me when I tell
you that Norman Cornell is not only one of the brightest
young men in America today, but he is also the hope and
promise of today's young generation and tomorrow's future.
(*And in the door with a mop comes the hope of
tomorrow's future*)

NORMAN I just knocked your cat in the toilet. It was an
accident. He's going to be all right.
(*He rushes back out, closing the door behind him*)

SOPHIE (*She rises and runs right, above the table, to the
landing*) Police! Somebody get the police!

333

*The COMEDY
of Neil Simon*

ANDY (*Running after her*)   All right, Miss Rauschmeyer, let's not panic.

SOPHIE (*On the steps leading to the landing*)   That's easy for you to say. He's not out flushin' your cat into the San Francisco Bay. (*She comes down the stairs*) Gimme that phone.

ANDY (*When he stops her, she starts kicking him*)   I promise the minute he comes back I'll thumbtack him to the wall. Stop kicking me. I have very thin socks.

SOPHIE   Either you let me call the police or Ah'll smash everything in your house, startin' with the dishes.
          (*She runs into the kitchen. We hear a loud crash*)

ANDY   Okay, if you want to play rough, then we'll play rough. (*We hear another crash. He charges into the kitchen after her. Now there is some yelling followed by dishes crashing, and pots and pans. Two seconds later he comes out, his arm twisted behind his back, followed by* SOPHIE, *who is doing the twisting*) All right, let go . . . I don't want to take advantage of you, so let go.

SOPHIE   Ah'm callin' the police and Ah don't want any trouble from you.

ANDY   I won't give you any trouble if you don't give me any trouble.

SOPHIE   Are you goin' to let me call the police?

ANDY (*In pain*)   Yes . . . Yes . . . (*She lets him go. He rubs his arm and goes left around the pole table.* SOPHIE *goes to the phone*) You ought to be ashamed of yourself, being stronger than a fellow.

SOPHIE   Physical fitness is as important as Godliness and Cleanliness.

ANDY   What about friendliness? And good neighborliness? Just hear me out and then if you're still upset we can go back to angriness and destructiveness. All right? (*She*

looks at him, then puts the phone back on the receiver)
Thank you . . . Have you ever heard of a monthly magazine called *Fallout?*

SOPHIE   Is it anything like the *Reader's Digest?*

ANDY   It is nothing like the *Reader's Digest.* It is a protest magazine. And one of the things it protests against
is the *Reader's Digest* . . . What *do* you read?

SOPHIE   Ah'm a religious follower of *Sports Illustrated.*

ANDY   Why did I ask? I'll try to explain what we do.
(*He points to a sign above the bulletin board on left
wall*) This is our credo—"A Remedy for a Sick Society"—
(*He goes left above the pole table*) We're not doctors,
we're diagnosticians. We point to the trouble spots. I'm
the editor and publisher. It's my job to get it printed and
sold. Norman is our staff. He is fourteen of the best
writers around today. Every word, from cover to cover,
is his. Besides Norman Cornell, he is sometimes Abbott
Kellerman, Professor O. O. Pentergast, Gaylord Heyer-
dahl, José Batista, Madame Pundit Panjab, Doctor Sydney Kornheiser, Major General Wylie Krutch and
Akruma Oogwana—the kid is versatile . . . Now we may
use assumed names, but we believe in what we write
and in what we publish. (*He gets a copy of* Fallout
from a pile of magazines under the left end of the desk)
When you go back to your room, I would like you to
read last month's issue, and then I want you to tell me
if you think we've spent three years and every penny we
have in the world for nothing. (*He goes right, with the
magazine, downstage of* SOPHIE *to below the center table*) Tell me if the things we protest against every month
in *Fallout* aren't the things you protest against every day
in your everyday life. (SOPHIE *starts to interrupt*) We
have a modest business here, Miss Rauschmeyer. We
don't make much money. If we sell every magazine we
print each month, we make just enough to buy a new
typewriter ribbon so we can get out the next month's issue. But we stay alive. And we love every minute of it.
And we'll continue doing it as long as there is an angry
breath in our body and as long as there is one single iota
of corruption left in our society that's worth protesting

about. (SOPHIE *makes a move to interrupt*) But, Miss Rauschmeyer, unless you smile at that talented lunatic in there and say, "Thank you for your little Budapest sausages," one of the great organs of free press will disappear from the American scene.
(*There is a pause as he waits for her reaction*)

SOPHIE Ah don't think we've been properly introduced.

ANDY My name is Hobart, Andrew Hobart.
(*He drops the magazine on the table*)

SOPHIE (*Goes right to* ANDY) How do you do. Ah'm Sophie Rauschmeyer. (*They shake hands*) Mr. Hobart, Ah appreciate the fact that you want to preserve the dignity of our nation. As Ah told you before, Ah had the privilege of representing the United States in the Tokyo Olympics.

ANDY I think that's wonderful. How did you do?

SOPHIE Well—Ah came in fifth. Not only was Ah beaten by the USSR and Poland, but Ah also trailed behind Turkey and Egypt.

ANDY I didn't know they swam in Egypt.

SOPHIE Then you can imagine how Ah felt representing the greatest nation on earth, coming in six seconds behind a little fat girl who was raised in the desert. (*She goes left a few steps*) Since the day Ah disgraced them, Ah have not been back to mah home in Hunnicut.

ANDY Hunnicut seems to disgrace quite easily.

SOPHIE (*She comes back to the center table*) You don't know Hunnicut. In our schools we sing all four stanzas of "The Star-Spangled Banner."

ANDY I thought there were only three.

SOPHIE Our principal wrote a new one. Since mah black day in Tokyo Ah have made a new life for mahself. One that Ah don't wish to jeopardize. (ANDY *goes upstage of center table to the desk, where he then sits.* SOPHIE *follows him*) Ah have found a nice job teachin' children to swim at the YWCA. (ANDY *starts licking the envelopes and then seals them*) It doesn't pay much, but it keeps me wet . . . My parents, bless 'em, come up to see me twice a year from Hunnicut. (*He nods and licks another envelope*) But most important, Ah have met, fallen in love with, and intend to marry—First Lieutenant Burt Fenneman of the United States Marines.

(*She grabs an envelope from* ANDY, *licks it, and puts it down on the desk*)

ANDY   I'm delighted you're going to marry a Marine. I hope you live happily ever after in the halls of Montezuma.

SOPHIE   Except he's not gonna marry me if he finds that wax-moppin', cat-drownin' lunatic in mah house.

ANDY   There's a very simple solution. (*Rises*) I'll save your marriage and you'll save my magazine.

SOPHIE   How?

ANDY (*He goes to the table and picks up a copy of* Fallout) I promise to keep Norman away from you as much as possible, if when you see him in the hall or on the stairs you'll just smile at him. One hello from you will keep him happy for a long time. It'll keep us all happy. Will you do it?

SOPHIE   No!

ANDY   Will you do it for me?

SOPHIE   No!

ANDY   Will you do it for America?

SOPHIE   Well, if you put it that way.

ANDY   And will you please read this tonight?

SOPHIE (*She goes upstage*)   All right, but you better keep him away from me.

ANDY (*Follows*) I promise you he'll never bother you again.
>   (NORMAN *reappears with the mop*)

NORMAN (*With a big smile*) All finished. And the cat is fine. I gave her artificial respiration.
>   (*He shows how with his two index fingers, then takes the mop to the kitchen*)

SOPHIE (*She looks at* ANDY, *then back to* NORMAN *as he comes back into the room and goes to the tape recorder*) Thank you.

NORMAN (*Moved*) Andy—she said "Thank you."

ANDY I heard.

SOPHIE Now if you'll excuse me . . .
>   (*She starts for the door*)

NORMAN Norman. Say my name . . . Norman.
>   (SOPHIE *looks at* ANDY)

ANDY (*Shrugs*) It's one little word. Norman.

SOPHIE (*Reluctantly*) Norman.

NORMAN (*He holds the mike from the tape recorder*) Would you say it in here? I'd like to have it to keep.

SOPHIE (*She glares at* ANDY, *who looks at her for a little understanding. She sighs.* NORMAN *turns the machine on and she speaks into the microphone*) Norman.

NORMAN (*He turns the machine off*) Oh, that was wonderful. Thank you, Sophie.

SOPHIE (*She turns and starts out. To* ANDY) Ah've kept mah promise. Live up to yours.
>   (*She exits. The instant she's gone,* NORMAN *rushes over to the window and opens it, then rushes back to the tape recorder*)

ANDY   All right, Norman, I've just made that girl a promise.
As long as you behave decently and normally and act
like a sensible hum . . . What are you doing?

NORMAN   I want the world to hear it. From her own lips.
(*Shouts out the window*) Norman loves Sophie and
someday Sophie will love . . .
        (*He turns the machine on*)

SOPHIE'S VOICE (*From the recorder*)   Norman.

ANDY (*Afraid* SOPHIE *will hear*)   Turn that thing off!

NORMAN (*He stops the machine, rewinds, and shouts out
the window again*)   Tell 'em again, Sophie! Who's the
one who drives you out of your mind?
        (*He turns the machine on*)

SOPHIE'S VOICE (*Again from the recorder*)   Norman.
        (SOPHIE *bursts into the room*)

SOPHIE (*She screams and goes to the pole table*).   Ah
heard that. He is using mah voice in vain. That's against
the law. Make him stop.

ANDY (*Runs after her*)   He was just kidding around. He
won't do it again.

NORMAN   I was just kidding around. I won't do it again.

SOPHIE   Stop embarrassin' me in front of mah neighbors.
And that's the last time Ah'm warnin' you. (*She points
her finger at him, and sees her fingernails*) Look at that.
Now mah nails are beginnin' to crack.
        (*She exits.* NORMAN *turns back to the tape recorder*)

ANDY (*He closes the door*)   If you turn that machine on
again, you'll be recording your own death.

NORMAN   I'll play it very low. She'll never hear me. (*To*

the machine) Whisper it, Sophie. Tell me and nobody else. Who do you love?
(*He turns the machine on, lowering the volume*)

SOPHIE'S VOICE (*Whispering from the recorder*)   Norman.
(NORMAN *falls to his knees as the curtain falls*)

Act Two

It is the next day, about 5 P.M. The room is in pretty much the same condition, though the bills have been cleaned up from the floor around the desk and the dirty cup and coffee pot have been removed from the center table. Two used coffee containers have replaced the stack of newspapers on the ratan stool. ANDY's *briefcase, the United Nations grocery bag, and the "bon voyage" basket are no longer in sight. The tape recorder is missing from the desk and the clippings as well, but the dummy magazine is still there to be finished. A recent copy of* Fallout *is on the center table. The ukelele is back on the kitchen bar. On the slant-top desk we now see two hairbrushes and an electric cordless razor. On the sofa down right is an empty coffee can. Both doors are closed on the balcony.*

There is no one on stage, but we can hear the slow, steady rhythm of a typewriter coming from NORMAN's *bedroom. It stops occasionally, then proceeds to plod on.*

The front door opens and ANDY *enters carrying a small bag, his bathing suit wrapped in a towel, and a terrycloth robe. In the other hand he carries a jar of Noxzema. He walks carefully and in pain, the result of an excruciating sunburn.*

ANDY Norman? (*The typewriter clicks away.* ANDY *looks up at* NORMAN's *room and nods in relief. He throws the bag, towel, and robe onto the sofa, and puts the Noxzema in his jacket pocket*) I'm back! I'm back from the beach . . . I have first degree burns on ninety-eight percent of my body—the other two percent is scorched. We went a half a mile out on the surfboard and there wasn't a goddamned wave for three hours . . . (*The typewriter continues*) The only time I had shade was when a bird flew over me . . . You can see his outline on my back. (*He starts up the stairs*) This is my eighth jar of Noxzema. (*The typewriter continues but no sound of* NORMAN)

. . . How's it going, Norm? (*Still no answer*) Norman . . . ? (*Now he's nervous. He starts up the stairs to* NORMAN's *room*) Norman, you hear me? (*He goes into* NORMAN's *room. The typing stops.* ANDY *returns carrying the tape recorder. He takes Noxzema out of his pocket, unscrews the top and puts a dab under his shirt at the back of his neck. He winces as the cold meets the hot. He picks up the phone gingerly, then starts to dial but winces in pain after the second dial. With his left hand he takes some more Noxzema and applies it to the dialing finger of his right hand and then continues to dial. He also puts a little on his ear before applying the phone to that spot. Then he talks, in pain and softly*) Hello, Mrs. Mackininee . . . ? It's me, Andy . . . I can't speak louder, my lips won't open all the way . . . No, the chattering stopped but now I have chills. I really don't think I'll be able to come down for that cocktail—do you mind? You *do* mind . . . Then I'll be down for that cocktail . . . (*He hangs up*) I sold my soul.
(*The door opens and* NORMAN *steps in. He holds one hand over his eye, and he seems to be in some pain.* ANDY *looks at him*)

NORMAN (*Calmly, looking at* ANDY *through his other eye*) Why did you hit me with an apple?

ANDY Why?

NORMAN Yes, why? Why did you hit me with an apple? (*He goes to the landing*) What were you trying to do, take my eye out?

ANDY I was trying to *kill* you but I'll take whatever I can get.

NORMAN (*Going up to the balcony*) I don't think it's funny. Do you know what the impact force is of an apple falling three-and-a-half stories? Forty-eight miles per hour. That apple was doing forty-eight miles an hour.
(*He goes into the room*)

ANDY You're lucky you didn't get a jar of Noxzema doing seventy-five . . . ! I'm not going to ask you where you were, Norman, because I think I know where. I'm just curious as to why you came back. (NORMAN *comes out of his room, his jacket off*) Because there is nothing left for you here except physical mutilation.

NORMAN (*Comes down the stairs*)   I came back because I have work to do. I believe we have a magazine to get out.
　　(*He goes left toward the desk*)

ANDY (*Goes right*)   Norman . . . Don't play with me. I'm in a fragile state of mind.

NORMAN   If you'll excuse me—
　　(NORMAN *puts a handkerchief in his pocket and sits. Next he puts a piece of paper in the typewriter*)

ANDY   Who are you kidding? What about the girl?

NORMAN (*Looks straight at him*)   What girl?

ANDY   That star-spangled cornpone next door! I think I know where you were this morning, Norman. You were down at the delicatessen having a life-sized statue of her made in potato salad.

NORMAN   You're wrong, Andy. I'm no longer interested. It's over. Done. Finished. Finito.

ANDY   Is that a fact?

NORMAN   That's a fact.

ANDY   Then who did I hear in your room at three o'clock this morning playing "Prisoner of Love" on tissue paper and comb?

NORMAN   Me! That was me! But that was last night. And last night is not today.

ANDY   Something's happened, Norman, and I'm afraid to ask what. What's happened, Norman? (NORMAN *turns*

away from ANDY. ANDY *goes upstage to* NORMAN's *left*)
Look at me and tell me what happened!

NORMAN (*Walking away, stage right*)   Nothing.

ANDY   You followed her this morning.

NORMAN   I don't want to talk about it.

ANDY   You waited for her outside the "Y."

NORMAN (*Right of the center table*)   I did not wait for her outside the "Y."

ANDY   You went *inside* the "Y"?

NORMAN (*He sits on the chair*)   I don't want to talk about it.

ANDY   You went inside and started yelling for Sophie.

NORMAN   I did not yell. I asked politely.

ANDY   Then you started to yell and they asked you to leave.

NORMAN   I don't want to talk about it.

ANDY (*He goes to the center table*)   You didn't go all over the YWCA looking for her, did you?

NORMAN   No, I did not go all over the YWCA looking for her.

ANDY   Where *did* you look?

NORMAN   Just the swimming pool.

ANDY (*He turns away*)   I don't want to talk about it.

NORMAN   They wear bathing suits, if that's what you're worried about.

ANDY That's what I was worried about. What did she do, threaten to call the police?

NORMAN She did *not* threaten to call the police.

ANDY What *did* she do?

NORMAN She *called* the police . . . They took me away in a patrol car.

ANDY I knew it. I knew it.

NORMAN (*He gets up*) You wanna hear my side?

ANDY I'm not through with *their* side yet.

NORMAN (*He sits*) We live in a police state, Andy. Did you know we are living in a police state?

ANDY (*Who can reason with this idiot*) I know. First they start burning books. Then they keep the men out of the women's pools.

NORMAN As we drove away I heard her screaming, "I hate you . . . I hate you, I loathe you, and I despise you. Hate, hate, hate, loathe, despise, and hate!" So I figured the best thing to do is forget about her.

ANDY I think you made a wise decision, Norman.

NORMAN I mean if she wants to play it cool, I don't have time to waste.

ANDY (*He may be serious*) Do you mean that, Norman?

NORMAN (*He gets up again*) I want to bury myself in work, Andy. Busy. I have to get busy again. (*He goes left, downstage of the table and* ANDY, *to the desk*) Just give me a typewriter and a lot of paper and then stand back, because you may get hurt.
(*He sits at the desk*)

ANDY I think you really mean it. That's wonderful! (*He

goes to the up left table, gets a pile of paper and hands it to NORMAN) Here. Type. No spaces, just lots of words.

NORMAN What did I see in her, Andy? She's not bright, you know. Do you think she's bright?

ANDY She has a native intelligence. Of a very remote country.

NORMAN We have absolutely nothing in common. And how long does physical attraction last?

ANDY An hour, an hour and a half the most.

NORMAN Say it again!

ANDY Sophie!

NORMAN Say the last part.

ANDY Rauschmeyer.

NORMAN Now the whole thing.

ANDY Sophie Rauschmeyer!

NORMAN You're boring me. I've got work to do.

ANDY (*Elated*) Ah ha! I'll knock out the mailing list. (*He goes to the up left table and gets the clipboard with pencil attached—he then goes to the chair right of the center table*) You just sit there and write. If you want to eat or drink or smoke or go to the bathroom, you sit there and I'll do everything. (NORMAN *starts to type and he goes at it furiously.* ANDY *sits and makes out the mailing list.* NORMAN *stops, looks at what he wrote, quickly tears it out of the typewriter, crumples it up, throws it away, puts another piece in and begins to type furiously. Then he stops, looks at what he wrote, tears it out of the machine, crumples it and throws it away. He then rises, paces right, sits, and puts in another sheet of paper and begins to type.* ANDY *looks up at this. The third time that* NORMAN *starts and stops typing is too much for* ANDY) Norman, if you're having trouble, maybe I can help you.

NORMAN (*Looks up at him*) What is today's date?

ANDY Norman, the date isn't important. Just write the article. I'll fill the date in later.

NORMAN (*He stares at the paper*) You're right . . . Who cares about the date? Boy, it's good to get back in harness again. (*He stares at the blank paper a moment*) And here we go . . . (*He adjusts the margin indicator*) You notice how I don't mention her name anymore?

ANDY You're not concentrating, Norman.

NORMAN You're right. You're right . . . You'd better get up on the roof because I'm opening the flood gates. Okay. We're all set . . . The paper is in—my fingers are poised . . . An idea is forming in my mind . . . Something is about to come out—

ANDY Norman, don't announce it. You're a writer, not a train conductor.

NORMAN Maybe if I just started typing, something'll come out.
　　(*He starts to type as* ANDY *looks at him incredulously*)

ANDY I don't think that's going to work, Norman.

NORMAN I can try, can't I? There's no harm in trying. (*He types. After doing a line, he stops and looks at it*) Andy!

ANDY (*Hopefully*) Yes?

NORMAN I think I'm going out of my mind.

ANDY You're stale, sweetheart. You haven't written anything in nearly five days.

NORMAN   Did you see what I just put down on this paper? Zizzivivizz! Second in my class at Dartmouth and I wrote zizzivivizz . . . ! You wouldn't accept work like that from a monkey.

ANDY   Don't get hysterical on me, Norman.

NORMAN (*He rips the sheet out of the typewriter and takes it to* ANDY)   Here. Read it for yourself. What does that say?

ANDY (*Resigned*)   Zizzivivizz!

NORMAN (*Crumples the paper, throws it on the table and goes back to the desk*)   Don't tell me not to get hysterical. Maybe if I called her at the "Y" and tried to apologize . . .

ANDY (*Rises and goes to a place above the table*)   She just had the police drag you away. Does it make sense for you to call her again?

NORMAN   You're talking to a man who just wrote zizzivizz . . . ! (*He picks up the phone*) I'll dial, you talk to her.

ANDY   Why should *I* talk to her?

NORMAN   Because my mouth dries up when I talk to her. No words come out, just little bla bla sounds. (*He demonstrates*) Bla bla bla—

ANDY   If you dial, Norman, you're going to bla bla to her yourself.

NORMAN (*Glares at him, the phone still in hand*)   You know what you are, Hobart? You're cold turkey. Cold turkey, lumpy stuffing, and watery cranberry sauce. You have all the romance and sensitivity of a used-car lot. (*He dials*) You know what else you are? You're a sexual snob. You don't get really excited unless the girl has a straight-A average . . . Tell the truth, Andy, the sexiest woman who ever lived was Madame Curie, right?

ANDY   Right. I dream of her leaning over a low-cut microscope.

NORMAN   I don't need you. I'll talk to Sophie myself. (*Into the phone*) Hello? Is this the YWCA . . . ? It is? Bla—bla—bla—bla . . .
          (*He quickly gives the phone to* ANDY *and goes stage center*)

ANDY   (*Reluctantly talks into the phone*) Miss Sophie Rauschmeyer, please . . . What? (NORMAN *hurries to* ANDY's *side to listen*) When . . . ? Why . . . ? Where?

NORMAN   (*Anxiously*) What - when - why - where - what? What's happening?

ANDY   I see. Thank you. (*He hangs up*) They just fired her! They said it's the *third* time this week a madman caused a commotion there.
          (*We hear a pounding on the door*)

SOPHIE'S VOICE (*Offstage*)   Open this door or so help me, Ah'll break it down.

NORMAN   Andy, help me. What'll I do?

ANDY   Get out of here. Let me talk to her.
          (*The doorbell buzzes furiously*)

NORMAN (*Starting upstairs*)   What will you say, Andy? What will you tell her?

ANDY   She's banging on the door. I can't audition for you now.
          (*Again the doorbell buzzes angrily*)

NORMAN (*Halfway upstairs*)   Just tell me one thing. Tell me one nice thing you're going to say about me.

ANDY   You never wear brown shoes with a blue suit. (*The doorbell again*) Get out of here . . . (NORMAN *is climbing the ladder to the roof*) Where are you going?

NORMAN On the roof. If everything is all right, call me and I'll come down. If not, I'll jump down.

(*He disappears through door at the top of ladder. The doorbell buzzes again.* ANDY *goes to the door and opens it.* SOPHIE *enters—wet. She carries a YWCA duffle bag and a copy of* Fallout)

SOPHIE (*She goes to the foot of the stairs*) Where is he? Where is that insane, crazy, trespassin' lunatic? (ANDY *closes the door*) Ah know exactly what Ah'm goin' to do to him. Ah planned it all as Ah sat there drippin' all over the bus.

ANDY (*Goes toward her*) He's up on the roof, miserable and eating his heart out.

SOPHIE Well, you can tell him not to bother. Ah'm gonna get a big dog to eat it out for him . . . Ah have been fired. They didn't even give me time to dry off.

ANDY I know. I just spoke to the "Y." But it wasn't your fault. Didn't you explain that to them?

SOPHIE Ah found it difficult gettin' their attention while a crazy man was chasin' me all through the YWCA . . . And that present of his is still pecking away at everyone in the buildin'.

ANDY What present?

SOPHIE The duck. He brought me a live duck. It's still there quackin' and snappin' at everyone. When Ah left, the gym teacher was a-hangin' from the basketball hoop and then that crazy bird chased a seventy-three-year-old arts and crafts teacher down to the swimmin' pool and off the high diving board.

ANDY I didn't know about that.

SOPHIE Well, did you know that Ah've been locked out of mah apartment until Ah pay mah rent which Ah can't do because Ah don't have a job.

ANDY Look, we'll make it up to you somehow. I'll get you another job. Just give me a couple of days.

SOPHIE (*Goes left, downstage of* ANDY) Ah don't have a couple of days. Ah have rent to pay and food to buy. What am Ah gonna do?

ANDY There must be someone in San Francisco who needs somebody young and healthy and strong . . . I don't suppose you've ever considered professional football?

SOPHIE (*She goes downstage to the phone on the desk and starts to dial*) Ah'm callin' my fiancé!

ANDY (*He goes toward* SOPHIE) Wait . . . I have an idea. I don't say you're going to love it, but how would you like to come to work for us?

SOPHIE Ah would rather get beaten in the Olympics by Red China.

ANDY Why not? It'll pay your rent and buy you your iron and steel, or whatever it is you eat.

SOPHIE (*She hangs up*) Ah believe you're serious. If you're serious, Ah suggest you make yourself available for our country's mental health program. Do you think Ah would work for that bomb aimed at the heart of America?

ANDY What bomb?

SOPHIE (*She goes a few steps right to* ANDY) Mr. Hobart, Ah don't know if you're a communist, or a fascist, or just a plain old-fashioned traitor—but you are certainly no American.

ANDY What are you calling me a traitor for?

SOPHIE (*She picks up the magazine from the pole table*) For this! For holding your country up to ridicule in black and white. All Ah read last night was the table of contents, but if you don't like the country that gave you your birth, why don't you go back where you came from?

ANDY I don't know what you're talking about, but writing

constructive criticism about the degenerating American way of life is certainly not treason.

SOPHIE   Ah don't know what is in your government-overthrowing mind, but do you expect me to work for a magazine that publishes an article entitled (*Goes right, upstage of* ANDY, *and looks through the pages*) . . . "Is LBJ on LSD?"

ANDY   We are not implying that he takes drugs. It's a symbolic alliteration meaning maybe the President in certain areas has gone too far.

SOPHIE   How about "Twenty-Seven Ways to Burn a Wet Draft Card"? Written from personal experience, Mr. Hobart?

ANDY   For your information, I happened to have served two years in the United States Army where I was interpreter for Brigadier General Walker Cooper.

SOPHIE   In what country?

ANDY   In *this* country. That idiot could hardly speak English! (*Tosses the magazine on the table*) My feelings about this country run just as deeply as yours, but if you'll turn down the national anthem for a few minutes, you'll be able to hear what some of the people are complaining about.

SOPHIE   Well, Ah am one of the people and *you* are one of the things Ah'm complaining about.

ANDY   Well, fortunately, you're not in much of a position to complain about *anything* . . . ! Look, if you don't work, you don't eat. If you don't eat, you get very skinny, you fall down and then you're dead. (*He goes left, upstage of the pole table*) If you think your Marine will be happy living with a dead, skinny lady, that's his business. Personally, I think you ought to accept the meager bread I'm offering you.

SOPHIE   First you take away my loaf and then you offer me your meager bread.

ANDY   Why does everything you say sound like it came out of the Bible?

SOPHIE   Thank goodness you heard of the book.

ANDY   Look, do you want the job or don't you? If you don't want it, *I'll* take it, 'cause I need the money.

SOPHIE   Unfortunately, so do Ah. Just tell me why . . . why do you want me around here?

ANDY   I'll tell you why. I *don't* want you around here. But that nut up on the hot tin roof wants you around here. You believe in your principles, I believe in mine. Mine is this magazine, and I'll do anything to keep it from going under water—that was an unfortunate choice of phrase.

SOPHIE   All right. That's your principle. Mah principle is breathin', eatin' and livin', just like any other animal on this earth.

ANDY   So much for your character references. Now about salary. What did you get at the "Y"?

SOPHIE   Seventy-two dollars.

ANDY   Norman and I both know how to swim; I'll give you fifty-five.

SOPHIE   For fifty-five dollars Ah will come in early and poison your coffee. Ah want what Ah got at the "Y." Seventy-two dollars.

ANDY (*Reluctantly*)   So be it, you're hired. Your hours will be from ten to six, half a day on Saturday. Can you type?

SOPHIE   No.

ANDY   Can you take shorthand?

SOPHIE   No.

ANDY   Can you do filing?

SOPHIE   No.

ANDY   Maybe you'd better come in at eleven . . . Can you cook?

SOPHIE   Mah cat seems to think so.

ANDY   Okay, you can make lunches and pretend to look busy. Let's say you have two main functions. First, to keep out of my way at all times, and second, to *smile* at Norman as much as is humanly possible.

SOPHIE   Yes, sir. The first Ah will do with the utmost dedication. And the second Ah will do over mah dead body.

ANDY   (*Goes right, downstage of* SOPHIE) Miss Rauschmeyer, it's evident you and I haven't gotten along since you came to work here . . . We're both trying to make the best out of an impossible situation. You need money, I need you to say goo-goo to my partner once in a while. Now I suggest you roll up your lips and smile so we can get to work.

SOPHIE   All right, Ah'll make mah bargain with the devil. Ah've never run from a fight. Ah'm ready to go to work. (*She extends her hand*)

ANDY   Am I supposed to shake that?

SOPHIE   No, you're supposed to put seventy-two dollars in it.

ANDY   We pay at the end of the week. Company policy.

SOPHIE   Then Ah'll start at the end of the week. Ah-don't-trust-you policy.

ANDY   All right, wait a minute. (*He gets the milk bottles filled with pennies*) There's seventy dollars in pennies. (*He gives her the two bottles, takes the third bottle and empties some of it in the can on the sofa)* Minus Federal withholding tax and social security.

(Curtain. While the curtain is down, we hear the sound of a typewriter over the house speakers)

354

The COMEDY
of Neil Simon

It is a few days later.

Missing from the room now is SOPHIE's *YWCA bag,
all the crumpled paper from the floor, the coffee can
seen on the sofa in the previous scene, the Noxzema jar,
and all of* ANDY's *beach equipment. Half a dozen books
are now occupying the shelf where the pennies were. The
left side of the center table is set for lunch. A copy of
Sports Illustrated is also on the table.*

NORMAN *is seated at the typewriter, his back to the front
door. He is pounding away like a man obsessed. To his
right, on the desk, is a pile of typed yellow pages. Despite
this display of frenetic labor,* NORMAN *seems to be a happy
man. Suddenly he stops as he seems stuck on something.
He thinks a moment, then picks up a bell that is on top
of his typed pages, and rings it with a flourish.*

SOPHIE *appears from the kitchen wearing a little apron
over a bright orange dress and holding a dish towel. She
looks at him.*

NORMAN Ubiquitous.

SOPHIE (*She goes left to the slanting desk where there
is a large dictionary. She looks up the word*) Ubiquitous. U-b-i-q-u-i-t-o-u-s. Ubiquitous.
(*She closes the dictionary and marches back to the
kitchen*)

NORMAN Thank you.

SOPHIE You're welcome.
(*She smiles, then exits. Once* SOPHIE *is in the
kitchen,* NORMAN *rises, goes to the slanting desk,
gets the dictionary and brings it to his desk. He sits*

at the typewriter again and rings the bell. SOPHIE
*returns, tired, carrying the bowl with the mixing
spoon)*

NORMAN Meretricious!
(*Wordlessly* SOPHIE *crosses left to the slanting desk,
but discovers that the dictionary has been moved to*
NORMAN's *left. She quickly runs through the pages,
stops and reads from the book, slowly and deliberately)*

SOPHIE Meretricious. M-e-r-e-t-r-i-c-i-o-u-s! Meretricious!
(*She puts the dictionary back on the desk, picks up her
mixing bowl and starts to exit. Once past him, she turns
and gives him a huge, forced smile baring all her teeth.
She continues to the kitchen. He picks up the bell again
and rings with a flourish. She turns around)* Stop ringin'
that bell, Ah'm not a cow!

NORMAN Well, you don't like it when I call you Sophie.

SOPHIE Ah'm an employee here, mah name is Miss Rauschmeyer . . . What is it, Mr. Cornell?

NORMAN What's for lunch, Miss Rauschmeyer?

SOPHIE Banana fritters, Mr. Cornell. Do you like them?

NORMAN I love them. What are they?

SOPHIE Fritters made with bananas.
(*She starts to go back into the kitchen, stops, turns
and smiles. Then exits.* NORMAN *rushes to the slant-
top desk and quickly combs his hair, looking in the
mirror on the wall above the desk. He quickly shaves
with an electric cordless razor. Then he goes toward
the kitchen)*

NORMAN Do you notice the way I've calmed down? (*He
looks in*) I'll never know how we got along without a
secretary all these—oh, let me help you with that.
(*He goes into the kitchen. We hear* SOPHIE *shout
and then a loud crash.* NORMAN *rushes out and goes
stage right)*

SOPHIE (*Following him, brandishing a pot*) You try that with your hands again and you'll have to learn to type with your nose.

NORMAN Your apron was slipping. I was just tying it in the back.

SOPHIE And stop trying to get me into corners.

NORMAN I'm not trying to get you into corners.

SOPHIE Then how come this mornin' for ten minutes we had our heads stuck in the oven?

NORMAN All right, don't be angry. Don't be mad at me. (*Goes back to the desk*) You go back into the kitchen and I'll go back to work. See? See? I'm working again. (*He types*) See? Working . . . (*She returns to the kitchen and after a moment of disgust, he resumes work. He is once more engrossed and does not hear or notice* ANDY *as he comes in the front door.* ANDY *looks exhausted from his outside activities. He looks over at* NORMAN, *whose back is to him, typing away feverishly.* ANDY *tiptoes behind him to get a better look at his work without disturbing him. He reads over* NORMAN's *shoulder a minute. He seems pleased with what he reads. To get a better look, he leans over and places his hands on* NORMAN's *shoulders.* NORMAN *closes his eyes upon feeling the hand on his shoulder. He turns his head and kisses* ANDY's *hand*) Forgive me! (*He notices that it is* ANDY's *hand and jumps out of his chair and turns angrily to* ANDY) Are you crazy? You wanna give me a heart attack? Don't ever sneak up on me like that again.

ANDY I didn't want to disturb y... You've really been working, heh?
          (*He picks up a stack of typewritten pages and begins to look them over*)

NORMAN I've been doing fine, fine.

ANDY (*Looks around*) Where's Esther Williams?
          (*He starts walking stage left, followed by* NORMAN)

NORMAN *(Following)* Shhh! I thought you were going to be gone all day.

ANDY I couldn't take anymore. *(Turns and now walks stage right, followed by* NORMAN*)* I just flew under the Golden Gate Bridge with a crazy landlady pilot. Actually she did very well for a woman who just got her license yesterday.
(He continues to read NORMAN's *pages)*

NORMAN Tell me all about it later. I want to finish this.

ANDY She made three passes at the bridge. On the third one we had to pay a toll. *(He starts up the stairs)* Norman, this is good. It's better than good. It's brilliant.

NORMAN I know . . . I know . . .
*(*ANDY *goes on up the stairs and into his room.* SOPHIE *comes out of the kitchen carrying a frying pan with a banana fritter)*

SOPHIE Come on! Here's your lunch. Eat it while it's hot.
*(*NORMAN *crosses and sits in a chair to the left of the table—he tucks a napkin in his shirt)*

NORMAN I like that. You're worried about me.
*(*SOPHIE *tosses the fritter onto the plate already set on the table and returns to the kitchen. She re-enters, taking off her apron)*

SOPHIE *(Standing above the table)* Would that be all now? If so, Ah'd like to go home.

NORMAN You could vacuum the rug.

SOPHIE Where's the vacuum?

NORMAN In that closet. *(*SOPHIE *leaves her apron on the kitchen bar en route to the closet)* I'll help you with it. It's very heavy.
(He goes into the closet after her and closes the door. We hear a loud crash. The closet door opens and SOPHIE *comes storming out. She slams the door behind her.* NORMAN *does not appear.* ANDY *rushes*

out of his room without his jacket and comes run-
ning down the stairs)

SOPHIE This time Ah'm pressin' charges.
(*She heads for the door*)

ANDY (*Carrying* NORMAN's *yellow pages*) What's the matter? Where's Norman?

SOPHIE You'll find him under the vacuum cleaner.
(*She storms out and slams the door.* NORMAN *comes
out of the closet, holding his head in pain and wearing the vacuum-cleaner hose around his neck*)

ANDY (*To* NORMAN) What did you do?

NORMAN I bit her earlobe! It was dangling right in front
of my mouth. What did you want me to do, ignore it?

ANDY (*He rushes to the door and goes out in the hall and
shouts*) Miss Rauschmeyer! Sophie! Wait a minute!

NORMAN (*Follows* ANDY *to the door*) Tell her I'm sorry.

ANDY Seventy-five dollars! I'll raise your salary to seventy-
five dollars a week. (*He comes back into the room and
leaves the door open*) She's coming back.

NORMAN (*Following* ANDY) Andy, you've got to square
me with her just one more time.

ANDY Norman, this has got to stop. She's becoming one
of the highest-priced secretaries in America—and she
can't even type.

NORMAN Tell her I've been working under a great strain
lately. That I haven't been myself. Help me! What am
I gonna do?

ANDY (*Removes the napkin and the vacuum hose from*
NORMAN's *neck and tosses them upstage of the kitchen
bar*) Go downstairs and buy a bottle of wine. We'll
have a party just for the three of us.

NORMAN (*He rushes to the front door*) That's a wonderful idea. I'll get a bottle of muscatel.

ANDY Not muscatel. Champagne. Girls love champagne.

NORMAN That's right. I'll take all my pennies and get a bottle of champagne.
(*He starts toward the shelf where the pennies were kept*)

ANDY (*He grabs* NORMAN, *stops him and shoves him toward the door*) No, you're right. Muscatel is better. Now get out of here.
(NORMAN *gets to the door just as* SOPHIE *returns.* NORMAN *hides his face with his hands*)

NORMAN Sophie, I just want to say. I know you hate me now, but—bla bla bla bla bla . . .
(*He runs down the corridor and disappears.* SOPHIE *ignores him*)

SOPHIE Where's mah three-dollar raise?

ANDY You'll be drinking it in ten minutes.

SOPHIE Ah knew Ah shouldn't have trusted you.
(*She turns to go*)

ANDY I thought you never run from a fight.

SOPHIE (*Turning back*) Ah don't. Ah just had one in the closet. Mah ear is pierced now and Ah don't even wear earrings.

ANDY I told you it wouldn't be easy. I should have known you didn't have the guts to stick it out.

SOPHIE Stick it out? Ah have been smiling at that idiot for three days. (*She gives a big, forced smile as she comes back into the room to the center table*) You see that? That's what Ah've been doing since ten o'clock this morning.

ANDY Well, cut it out. You look like a demented ventril-
oquist.
>   (*He picks up* NORMAN's *work and sits to the right
>   of the table—he takes a pencil from the mug*)

SOPHIE Look, this was not *mah* stupid idea. It was *your*
stupid idea.

ANDY Well, it's a very *smart* stupid idea because it's
working!
>   (*He flourishes* NORMAN's *papers in the air as proof*)

SOPHIE It's working for *you!* You're gettin' your magazine.
Ah'm gettin' holes in mah ears.

ANDY I happen to be paying through the nose for those
holes in your ears. It won't happen again . . . Now I've
got fifty pages to edit so I'd like a little quiet, please.

SOPHIE You won't even know Ah'm here—'cause Ah
won't be here!
>   (*She starts for the door*)

ANDY (*Turns and shouts*) You'll be here because I'm paying you to be here and he's coming back in ten minutes
and he *wants* you here.

SOPHIE (*Closes the door and comes downstage*) Then
here Ah will be!
>   (*She sits left of the table angrily, grabs a magazine,
>   crosses her legs, and reads*)

ANDY (*Looks at her*) This is not the Christian Science
Reading Room. It's an office. And there's work to be done.

SOPHIE Then do it.
>   (*She continues reading*)

ANDY I'm talking about you.

SOPHIE Would you like me to type a letter? Ah can have
it finished a year from September.

ANDY   You can sharpen some pencils—and be quiet.

SOPHIE   Yes, Boss!
(SOPHIE *glares at him, then gets up and goes to the* radiator *where there's a pencil sharpener. From a* bowl *she takes one, inserts it in the sharpener, and* grinds. *It makes a loud noise.* ANDY *looks up, then* goes over to her)

ANDY   What are you doing?

SOPHIE   What you told me to do.

ANDY   (*Pulls the pen from the sharpener*)   Thank you. I now have a ballpoint pen without a ballpoint. (*He goes to a tall vase on the kitchen bar and takes a feather duster from it. He goes back toward* SOPHIE) Do you see this?

SOPHIE   Ah see it.

ANDY   First let me tell you that it is not a dead chicken on a stick. It's a feather duster. By that I don't mean you dust feathers with it. You hold it on this end (*He demonstrates*)—and you flick it against the furniture, thus dusting it. Do you think you could do that?

SOPHIE   Lefty or righty?

ANDY   If you'd like, you can stick it in your pierced ear and shake your head. Just clean the room and be quiet. (*He puts the duster on the pole table, then goes back and sits in a chair to continue working.* SOPHIE *glares at him, holding the duster*)

SOPHIE   Yes, sir! (*She begins to dust the pole table, vigorously and angrily—she knocks magazines onto the floor. She dusts her way across the room to* ANDY'S *chair, dusts under it, making some noise. Then she moves back to the center table*) Ah think Ah'm gettin' the hang of it.

ANDY   Yes, you seem to be.

SOPHIE   (*She dusts bits of torn paper out of the ashtray, and sings as she goes up to the kitchen bar)*

"Yankee doodle went to town, riding on a pony,
Stuck a feather in his cap and called it macaroni . . ."
(Now she is dusting the steps leading to the landing)

ANDY You're not going to whistle the second chorus, are you?

SOPHIE Ah just work here. Ah do what Ah'm told.
(She starts to whistle. ANDY gets up and crosses to her. He takes her wrist, leads her to the desk)

ANDY All right. *(He takes some envelopes from the end of the desk and some stamps and places them before her)* Here are fifty addressed envelopes and fifty stamps. You have a tongue. Don't talk. Lick.
(He takes the duster from her and puts it on the pole table. He goes back to the chair and picks up the pages)

SOPHIE *(Seated at the desk, holding the envelopes)* Are these announcements for next week's cell meeting, Comrade?

ANDY No. Actually they're very thin bombs. You just add water. *(She laughs. Then she begins to lick the stamps and places them on the envelopes)* I get the impression that you don't approve of me as a person.

SOPHIE If that's what you are, that's what Ah don't.

ANDY Why not?

SOPHIE Because Ah don't approve of your character, your philosophy, your principles, your ideals, your vocation, your methods, your scruples—shall Ah continue?

ANDY Look, your opinions on anything have as much practical value as a 1939 calendar. I'm not paying seventy-five dollars a week to listen to a limited vocabulary. Be quiet and lick the stamps. I'm a busy man.
(He goes back to his pages)

SOPHIE   So was John Wilkes Booth the night he assassinated Lincoln.

ANDY (*Stops*)   Are you implying I was in on the Lincoln job?

SOPHIE   Ah'm talking about your present activities. But Ah wouldn't put it past you.

ANDY   Sorry, that night I was in Philadelphia cracking the Liberty Bell. (*He gathers his papers, rises, and starts up the stairs*) I can't concentrate in front of the Senate Investigating Committee.

SOPHIE   The truth is always difficult to face. (*She stands up*) Can mah tongue rest? The well has dried up.

ANDY (*He stops on the stairs*)   Look—if you're unhappy here, why don't you take a job as night watchman at the Statue of Liberty? Then you could swim around her at night checking to see if the torch went out.

SOPHIE (*Going upstage a few steps*)   "The enforcers of justice have always been the scapegoat of the enemies of freedom . . ." Do you know where Ah read that?

ANDY   On the back of a Patrick Henry bubble-gum card?

SOPHIE (*She walks stage left above the pole table*)   No— in the speeches of Socrates. Did you ever read the speeches of Socrates?

ANDY   I'm waiting for the paperback to come out.
(*He goes up to the balcony*)

SOPHIE (*Shouts up*)   It's out. That's where Ah read it . . . It would shock you, Mr. Hobart, to know the amount of political literature Ah have read.

ANDY   I would be nonplussed if you got into anything deeper than the names and addresses of the girls in the Miss America Contest. I notice that your tongue is functioning again. Go back and lick the stamps.
(*He goes into his room*)

SOPHIE   And Ah'm sure if it was left up to a *traitor* like you, no one would *win* the Miss America Contest.
  (*She goes back to the desk and stamp-licking—standing up.* ANDY *comes out of his room again, much angrier at the "traitor" remark*)

ANDY   You're right. I think a parade of pretty girls is fine. But listening to Miss North Dakota singing an aria from *The Barber of Seville* in the key of *M,* while baking an upside-down seven-layer cake in a hoop skirt she hooped herself, is beyond human endurance . . . I'll be very frank with you, Miss Rauschmeyer, up until now I'm not happy with your work.
  (*He goes back to his room*)

SOPHIE   (*She glares after him. She is murmuring to herself and what she says is almost inaudible*)   Ah suppose next he'll outlaw apple pie.

ANDY   (*He comes out of his room*)   I heard that. I happen to love apple pie. Which, for your information, originated in Bavaria, Germany.

SOPHIE   (*She goes stage left to above the pole table*)   That's a lie. Apple pie is as American as blueberry pie.

ANDY   The only truly indigenous American foods are Thanksgiving turkey and chicken chow mein. (*He starts down the stairs as she goes right to meet him*) You're deliberately distracting me from working on my magazine, aren't you?

SOPHIE   (*Returning left to the desk, and back to the stamps*) Each citizen must do what he can.

ANDY   Of all the bigoted things—you haven't read one word in it past the table of contents.

SOPHIE   You don't have to drink the poison if it says so on the label.

ANDY   I'm going in the closet to work. Call me when Norman gets back.
  (*He goes up center*)

SOPHIE (*She goes toward him*) All right, tell me. Is there *anything* about this country you do like?

ANDY I like almost everything about this country except people who like *absolutely everything* about this country.

SOPHIE Why don't you answer mah question?

ANDY Why don't you question my answer?

SOPHIE Why don't you talk like a person so Ah can understand which are the questions and which are the answers?

ANDY Would it be all right if I worked in your apartment?

SOPHIE It would not. If there's gonna be a fight, let's draw the battle lines on the field of the aggressor. And don't bother guessin' who said that 'cause Ah made it up mahself.

ANDY I had it narrowed down to you or Winston Churchill.
(*He goes right a few steps*)

SOPHIE (*Follows*) *And* for your information, did you know Winston Churchill's mother was born in the United States—*in Brooklyn!*

ANDY You'd never know it from the way he talked. (*Goes to the door, downstage of* SOPHIE) Why don't you go back to your apartment and make some chitlins or grits? Your cat must be hungry.
(*He opens the door for her*)

SOPHIE (*She sits right of the table*) Ah'm not leavin' until you admit you are snide, smug, and narrow-minded.

ANDY Will you settle for belligerent?

SOPHIE Ah will accept deceitful and treacherous.

ANDY (*He slams the door, and comes downstage to the bottom step*) Okay, I'm deceitful and treacherous. And *you* are provincial, and old-fashioned, antiquated, un-realistic, unimaginative, unenlightened, uninformed, and unbelievably unable to understand anything that isn't un-der water . . . (SOPHIE *rises*) Your big trouble in life is that you were born a hundred and fifty years too late. You should have been at Bunker Hill loading muskets, raising flags, and waiting for the British to show up with the whites of their eyes. Well, you may be shocked to learn that this is 1967 and this country has a whole new set of problems. But you wouldn't know about that be-cause I don't think you're a real person of flesh and blood with feelings and sensitivities. I don't think you could be capable of having a genuine emotional attachment for an-other human being unless it was first passed by Congress and amended to the Constitution and painted red, white, and blue. If you've been listening carefully, Miss Rausch-meyer, I have just made a point.

SOPHIE (*She walks to the door, opens it, then slams it shut*) All right, if you wanna make points, then Ah'm gonna make one. Ah'm gonna make the biggest point you ever heard.

ANDY (*He goes to the sofa and tosses the pages on it*) When you get to it, raise your right hand. With you it's hard to tell.

SOPHIE You'll *know* when Ah'm makin' it only you're not gonna like it. Are you listenin'?

ANDY With one ear. That's all I need with you.

SOPHIE Then here goes. (*She comes downstage to* ANDY) Ah don't like you for a lot of the reasons Ah already said. But the main reason Ah don't like you is because Ah am ingaged to Lieutenant Burt Fenneman of the United States Marines. And in a few weeks we're supposed to get married. But for some insane reason that only a Hun-garian psychoanalyst could explain, Ah have suddenly discovered—and here comes the part Ah was telling you about—that *Ah am physically attracted to you . . . !* Now how do you like *that* for a point? (*And she storms out slamming the door behind her.* ANDY *does not react. He just stands there. Suddenly the door flings open again and* SOPHIE *stands there glaring at him, hands on her hips*) Did you hear what Ah said?

ANDY (*Without emotion*) I heard. I heard what you said.

SOPHIE (*Slams the door*) Well, how do you like them apples?

ANDY *Those* apples.

SOPHIE (*She goes to stand above the center table*) *Them* apples. How do you like them?

ANDY Are you serious?

SOPHIE (*Yelling*) Of course Ah'm serious! There is something about your physical presence that appeals to me—and Ah am as repulsed by it as you are.

ANDY You couldn't possibly be.

SOPHIE There is no earthly reason why Ah should like *anything* about you. And Ah don't. But Ah do! What do we do about it?

ANDY If you're looking for another boost in salary, this is *not* the way to get it.
    (*He starts up the stairs*)

SOPHIE Where are you goin'?

ANDY To get Norman's copy of Krafft-Ebbing. You're a bigger nut than he is.

SOPHIE You don't believe me.

ANDY I *believe* you. I just don't *understand* you. (*Comes back down the steps*) What do you mean you're physically attracted to me?

SOPHIE Do you want a complete rundown of arms, legs,

hair, and teeth? Go get a pencil and paper and we'll take
.it item for item.

ANDY   You mean you like the way I look?

SOPHIE   Not terribly.

ANDY   You like the way I walk?

SOPHIE   Not really.

ANDY   You like the way I dress?

SOPHIE   Not remotely.

ANDY   Then what *do you like?*

SOPHIE   *Ah like the way you smell!!*
(ANDY *turns and looks to heaven or anyone else for
some help*)

ANDY   Oh, Sophie, Sophie, Sophie!

SOPHIE   And don't call me Sophie-Sophie-Sophie. Ah'm attracted to you but Ah still don't like you.

ANDY   That's impossible.

SOPHIE   Ah know. You are the most irritating, nauseating
man Ah have ever met in mah life—and if you tried to
kiss me right now Ah would not stop you. You wanna
work on that for a while?

ANDY (*He turns in despair and goes to the landing*)   No,
I think I need outside help.

SOPHIE   Ah suppose you wanna know what started it all?

ANDY (*Turns to a wall and just faces it*)   No, I don't.

SOPHIE   Yes, you do.

ANDY   Yes, I do. What started it all?

SOPHIE It was your grey eyelashes. Ah have never met a man in your age bracket with grey eyelashes. Ah think it's *dumb* to have grey eyelashes, but Ah'm very glad you have them . . . Now can Ah ask you a question?

ANDY Yes, you may ask me a question.

SOPHIE Do you have any desire whatsoever to touch me?

ANDY What does that mean?

SOPHIE Which is the part you don't understand, desire or touchin'?

ANDY (*Goes downstage*) I understand both parts, I just never thought about it.

SOPHIE (*Follows*) Well, *think* about it . . . Time's up! Do you want to touch me or don't you?

ANDY You've been spiking your fritters with bourbon, haven't you?

SOPHIE Ah am being honest with mah emotions because that's the only way Ah know how to deal with them. (*She moves closer to* ANDY) The plain disgustin' truth is Ah would like to stand very close to you and feel your breath somewhere on mah neck.

ANDY You shouldn't tell me that.

SOPHIE Ah know it but it just comes out. Is there any possibility of you havin' the same disgustin' feeling about me?

ANDY If I did it wouldn't be disgusting, and if I found it disgusting I wouldn't have the feeling.

SOPHIE Ah don't think Ah got that but touché anyway.

ANDY (*As he moves into the right corner*) And will you stop following me around the room.

SOPHIE Ah'm not followin' you. You're runnin' from *me!*

ANDY I'm running because you're following. Stay over there!

SOPHIE Ah can't *smell* you from over here!

ANDY (*Exasperated*) What am I going to do with you?

SOPHIE Ah gave you a suggestion, you didn't do it.

ANDY Listen, you, for an all-American girl with a complete set of Eagle Scout principles, how do you explain being engaged to one man and attracted to another man?

SOPHIE Very simple explanation. Ah can't explain it.

ANDY What about your fiancé?

SOPHIE He can't explain it either.

ANDY You mean you *told* him?

SOPHIE Certainly Ah told him. We're ingaged.

ANDY Oh, God, I'm afraid to ask what his reaction was.

SOPHIE You may well fear. He wants to kill you.

ANDY WHY? WHAT DID I DO?

SOPHIE What did Ah do when that lunatic friend of yours chased me all over the YWCA? It's nobody's fault. It's something that just happened.

ANDY (*He escapes from her by going left, between the right chair and the center table*) Well, make it *un*happen. If I'm going to get killed by a man in uniform, let it be the enemy.

SOPHIE Ah am tryin' just as hard as Ah can to make it un-happen. The minute you do anything physically repul-sive, we'll all be a lot better off. (ANDY *looks at her and then in an effort to be physically repulsive, he knocks over the director's chair and goes to her, grabs her and gives her a hard, vicious kiss. Then he pushes her back and returns to stage left. He looks at her)* Ah liked it. We're in big trouble.

ANDY   What do you mean, *we're* in big trouble? *I'm* the one who's in big trouble.

SOPHIE   Are you going to yell at me or are you going to do something about our predicament?

ANDY *(Yelling)*   I'm going to yell at you! You're going to ruin everything I ever worked for in my entire life! Why don't you go back into the ocean with the rest of the fish? *(She smiles)* What are you smiling at?

SOPHIE   Ah like it when you yell at me?

ANDY   I don't care what you like, WHAT ARE WE GOING TO DO?

SOPHIE   How should *Ah* know? But until we think of somethin', why don't you kiss me again?
        (ANDY charges at her with a threatening finger)

ANDY   You are without a doubt—the most—you—ah—oh, the hell with it.
        (He goes to her, takes her in his arms, and kisses her. He's not quite sure why, but at this point his common sense is beyond all reasoning. SOPHIE puts her arms around his neck and solidifies the kiss. The door flies open and NORMAN springs in happily, a bottle of muscatel in a brown paper bag in his hand)

NORMAN *(Singing)*   "She loves me, but . . ." *(He stops and freezes as he catches them in the embrace. He looks at ANDY and SOPHIE)* The least you could have done was chipped in for the wine!

Curtain

Act Three

It is the next day, early afternoon. There is one open suitcase, downstage of the kitchen bar. A duffle bag is on the sofa next to the portable typewriter, all ready to go. The luncheon dishes have been cleared and the feather duster returned to the kitchen bar. The stamped envelopes and the manuscript pages are no longer on the desk, but the dummy magazine is still there, unfinished. The telephone is back on the pole table along with a large pile of magazines near the pole. Upstage, unseen by the audience, is an eight-pack of empty Coke bottles. ANDY's *clipboard is on the center table.*

NORMAN *appears from his room at the top of the stairs, carrying a pile of books. He leans over the railing and drops the books like a load of bombs into the open suitcase below.*

The front door opens and ANDY, *in his raincoat, enters, a very morose-looking young man. He looks up at* NORMAN, *who tosses his head.* NORMAN *is trying to convey all his anger and bitterness in this one gesture.*

The telephone rings. ANDY *closes the door, crosses to the pole table and answers the phone.*

ANDY (*Into the phone*) Cavanaugh's Crematorium . . . Oh—Mrs. Mackininee—no, I'm not trying to avoid you. I have a little answering service on the side . . . Yes, I called you earlier because I was wondering if I could beg off tonight's karate party . . . Well, I'm sure the *Takoshimo's* are a lot of fun, but I'm awfully tired—I just don't think I'm up to an entire evening of being thrown against the wall . . .

> (NORMAN *comes out of his room carrying an enormous five-foot-square blowup photograph of Albert Einstein*)

NORMAN (*Not to* ANDY *directly*) Railway Express will pick it up in the morning.

> (*He leans the picture-face to the wall and goes back into his room*)

ANDY (*Back into the phone*) Mrs. Mackininee, I definitely don't think I can make it tonight. I have some urgent business here . . . No, I'm positive I can't—Mrs. Mackininee, I think this is hardly the time to discuss a rent increase . . . Well, for that matter, I couldn't even pay a fifteen percent *decrease* . . . ! All right, if that's how you feel about it, you can pick up your apartment in the morning.
(*He hangs up.* NORMAN *comes out of his bedroom carrying a flower box with a few tiny leaves starting to sprout. He carries it down the stairs*)

NORMAN I'm taking the marijuana plant.
(*He puts the plant on the kitchen bar. He starts for the stairs again*)

ANDY Is this your final decision?

NORMAN (*He crosses to the tape recorder, turns it on, picks up the speaker and switches on to record*) It's my final decision. This is a recording.
(*He switches it off and starts up right*)

ANDY Because I think you're making a mistake.

NORMAN (*He stops at the bottom of the stairs*) I've only made two mistakes in my life. One was trusting you as my friend—the other was going out for the muscatel.
(*He continues up the stairs*)

ANDY Norman, I've known you for eight years. Can you ever remember me lying to you *once* in all those eight years?

NORMAN Yes. I've known you for nine years.
(*He continues up the stairs*)

ANDY All right, *nine* years. I don't care what you saw yesterday, I'm telling you the truth. I cannot abide that girl and she finds me snide, smug, and repulsive.

NORMAN (*Stops*) I see. And I walked in just as she was sinking her fangs into your throat, and you fought off the attack with your mouth.

ANDY (*He goes up center*) No, she was kissing me.

NORMAN Kissing *you* . . . ? You're a foot taller than she is and you can't stand her. So the way I see it, the only way she could have kissed you against your wishes is for her to have nineteen-inch lips—and I just don't buy that.

ANDY I don't care what you're buying, I did not make an overt act toward her.

NORMAN In other words, she was the one who did the overting.

ANDY Correct.

NORMAN Why?

ANDY Well—that's beside the point.

NORMAN I think not. Why did she overt you right on the mouth?

ANDY You're gonna laugh.

NORMAN Try me.

ANDY She likes the way I smell.

NORMAN (*He looks at his watch*) It is now three o'clock. I will be hysterical until three-fifteen.
(*He continues up the stairs into the room*)

ANDY What's so insane about it? *You* like the way *she* smells.

NORMAN (*He storms out*) How can you even *mention* the two smells in the same breath?
(*He exits to his room*)

ANDY Norman . . . (*He takes off his raincoat and tosses it on a high stool up left between the table and stairs*) You mean to tell me that after nine years of a personal, meaningful relationship, you would let that flag-waving sea urchin come between us?

NORMAN (*He comes out of his room and goes down the stairs to the landing*) I can live with a slob, a sadist, a forger, or a junkie. I draw the line at finks.
(*He goes to the light-fixture on the landing and removes one bulb*)

ANDY (*He walks downstage to the desk*) And what about the magazine?

NORMAN (*He comes down the stairs to the suitcase*) The magazine is no longer my concern.
(*He puts the bulb in his suitcase and goes above the kitchen bar for the eight-pack of empty Coke bottles—takes half the bottles and packs them in the suitcase*)

ANDY You—hypocrite! You pretend to be devoted and dedicated to an ideal that we've literally starved for, and you can blithely toss it all aside because we're suddenly embroiled in a romantic triangle!

NORMAN (*He goes to* ANDY) *Now* I know why this magazine never made a cent. *Now* I know why we were starving. You, me, the girl and the Marine are a quadrangle, not a triangle!! You can't add!
(*He goes to the suitcase*)

ANDY And what do you think you're going to do once you leave here?

NORMAN In exactly thirty minutes I have an interview for a job with the A-P.

ANDY Working at the checkout counter?

NORMAN Not the A *and* P, you idiot. The A-P! The Associated-Press.

ANDY Doing what?

NORMAN I'm a writer. They'll pay me for writing . . . Just as, I imagine, you'll make your living by *finking!*
(*He goes to the closet*)

ANDY (*He goes left to upstage of the pole table*) A writer?
Without me to push you, prod you, and encourage you,
you couldn't hold down a job writing Rhode Island license plates.

NORMAN (*He comes out of the closet carrying two jackets
on wooden hangers and goes stage left to* ANDY)
No . . . ? LJ Seven-one-nine-six . . . ! And there's
plenty more ideas where that came from.
(*He gives the jackets to* ANDY *and takes the coat
hangers to the duffle bag*)

ANDY All right, so we don't get along. Gilbert and Sullivan didn't speak to each other for fourteen years and they
wrote twenty-three operettas together. Why can't we?

NORMAN (*At the sofa*) Gilbert never walked in and
caught Sullivan kissing Poor Little Buttercup.

ANDY (*He puts the jackets on the up left table and then he
goes right to the short wooden stool*) Okay, Norman,
if I have to fight for my magazine, I'll fight for it.

NORMAN (*Looks at him in disbelief*) You're joking, surely.

ANDY Surely not.

NORMAN Andy, I'm warning you. I'm not wiry, but I'm
thin. I'll cut you to ribbons.

ANDY I've already faced death with our paratrooper landlady. I'm not afraid of a skinny typist.
(*He takes the short stool to the door. He sits on it
and crosses his legs in a Gandhi fashion*)

NORMAN (*Looks at him*) What is that supposed to be?

ANDY What does it look like? It's a *sit-in!*

NORMAN (*He looks around to see if any sane person heard
this lunatic remark. Then he moves up to the door*) If
you don't get up from that sit-in, you're gonna see a
punch-down!

ANDY   Is that your answer to passive resistance?

NORMAN   No, my answer to passive resistance is active kicking . . . Get up! What do you think you're doing?

ANDY   The same as they did in Bombay in 1947 when twelve thousand Indians threw themselves across fifteen miles of railroad tracks.

NORMAN   (*Looks at his watch, goes to his suitcase, closes it and picks it up. Then he goes to* ANDY)   Well, Charley, in thirty seconds the five-fifteen is coming through.

ANDY   (*Steeling himself*)   Thou shalt not pass!

NORMAN   Thou shalt bleed from both ears!

ANDY   You would hit a man who wouldn't raise his arms in defense?

NORMAN   Actually I prefer it that way.

ANDY   Norman, if you go over to their side it's the end of free, creative thinking. They'll have you writing weather reports and shipping news.

NORMAN   In two minutes I bring in my first story about a dead man leaning against a door.

ANDY   (*Looks at him, then gets up*)   All right, Norman . . . (*He returns the stool to right of radiator*)   I had hoped to avoid bloodshed . . . (*He takes off his sweater*)   But you leave me no recourse. The pain I am about to inflict is done purely on request.

NORMAN   (*Looks at him in disbelief*)   Do you mean it is your intention to actually come to blows? Hard hitting and everything?

ANDY   (*At the pole table, rolling up his shirt sleeves*)   My fist right on your deviated septum.

NORMAN   Knowing full well that on July sixteenth I finish a three-year course in Oriental combat?

ANDY   I intend to compensate by fighting dirty.

NORMAN   (*He puts down his suitcase, takes off his jacket and puts it on the landing*)   Okay, Andy, as long as you know the score. I've been waiting six months to try this in a real-life situation. I had hoped my first victim would be a mugger, but you'll do nicely. (*Goes to the center table as he rolls up his shirt sleeves*) Oh, by the way. It's my legal obligation to warn you that karate may be hazardous to one's health.

ANDY   And let me warn you that I have never once in my life struck another human being in anger. (*Both* ANDY *and* NORMAN *pick up the center coffee table and carry it stage right*) I don't want to kill you, but I have no idea how strong I am. (*Goes left and takes the director s chair to the right of the desk*) If you feel yourself dying, just speak up.
        (NORMAN *tries to lift the right chair with one hand.* ANDY *comes to his rescue.* NORMAN *then carries the chair up right and puts it down near the table—he bows to the chair*)

NORMAN   Anytime you're ready.

ANDY   I'm ready if you are.
        (NORMAN *assumes a sort of professional pose while* ANDY *just tries to look menacing*)

NORMAN   (*Smirks*)   Is that the way you're going to stand? You don't know the first thing you're doing. You won't last ten seconds.

ANDY   When you're able to talk again, you can teach me.

NORMAN   Can I show you the four basic positions? I'm still going to break your neck, but at least you'll look better. (*He goes toward* ANDY, *who growls at him*) This is ridiculous. You have no defense at all. I'm not even enjoying this.
        (*He goes stage right*)

ANDY   If you want entertainment, turn on the television. If you want to fight, come over here.

NORMAN I want to fight . . .

> (*In true karate fashion,* NORMAN *takes a step towards* ANDY, *swipes at the air twice and grunts audibly in Japanese fashion. He repeats the move with the other hand and the sound*)

ANDY If you're gonna do that, why don't you put on those big white bloomers like the Japanese wear?

NORMAN You must be out of your mind. (*Holds up his poised right hand*) Don't you realize this is a lethal weapon? This hand is trained to kill. Once I start it in motion, it can't be stopped. It's been trained that way. All right, Andy, I'm through toying with you. I'm gonna give you one chop (*Looks at his watch*) . . . and then I've got to go. (NORMAN *approaches* ANDY. *He raises his hand.* ANDY *runs upstage of the pole table and goes right.* NORMAN *follows him*) Damnit, Andy, why don't you stand still and fight like a man?

ANDY Because I'm afraid, that's why.

NORMAN I told you that before we started.

ANDY Not of you, of myself. I am so seething, so fed up with your monumental stupidity and infantile behavior, that if I get within two inches of you, I swear by everything I believe in this world, I'll crack your head wide open.

NORMAN Then you'd better do it to me before I do it to you.

ANDY All right, damnit, here!! (*And in a karate-type swipe,* ANDY *swings at* NORMAN, *who simultaneously swings at him with an identical blow, but they succeed in landing both blows on each other's arms between the wrist and elbow, causing enormous pain to both. They both stop and rub their painful arms and moan together*) Oohhhh . . . Oh, boy, that hurts . . .

NORMAN (*Grimaces*) Oh, God, my arm, my arm.

ANDY (*Goes toward him*) Are you all right?

NORMAN (*Goes away to the pole table*) Let me alone. Why don't you look where you're hitting? In karate you hit the neck or the kidneys, not the arm. (*He looks at his wrist*) Ah, damn.

ANDY What's wrong?

NORMAN You broke my Benrus watch.

ANDY (*He takes a few steps left*) Let me see.

NORMAN It's broken. It's broken. There's nothing to see— it's my good watch, too.

ANDY I'm sorry.

NORMAN And I just put in a new crystal, and I had it cleaned.

ANDY Why didn't you take the watch off first?

NORMAN Because I didn't expect to get hit on the wrist. I told you you didn't know what you were doing . . . I don't want to fight anymore.
      (*He goes right, downstage of* ANDY)

ANDY Well, what are we gonna do?

NORMAN (*Putting on his jacket*) You can do whatever you want, I'm going.

ANDY For good?

NORMAN For good. I really don't like you anymore.

ANDY (*Turns away*) Okay, Norman, if you wanna go, then go. I think you're wrong, but if that's what you want (*Goes left to the desk*) I wish you the very best of luck.

NORMAN (*Looking at his watch again*) Boy, I really loved this watch, too.

ANDY (*He goes upstage of the pole table.* NORMAN *goes to his suitcase*) So, this is the end of *Fallout* magazine—you've got to admit it, Norm, for a while we had a good thing going here.

NORMAN (*Points to his watch*) If I knew what time it was, I'd hang around another ten minutes and watch you cry.

ANDY You don't think I'm sincere about our friendship.

NORMAN (*Picks up his suitcase*) For this magazine you would sell your own mother—who, incidentally, no one has seen for three years.

ANDY Norman, please believe me when I say I'd rather have a handshake from you right now—than the Pulitzer Prize. (*He extends his hand out to* NORMAN. NORMAN *looks at him, puts down his suitcase and goes left to* ANDY) What's the matter?

NORMAN I'm afraid you're going to grab me and handcuff me to the steampipe.

ANDY (*He extends his hand again*) Good-bye, Norman.

NORMAN Good-bye, Andy. (NORMAN *extends his hand to* ANDY, *who in a flash of dexterity pulls up a pair of handcuffs from the pole table. One handcuff has been affixed to the steampipe, the other one* ANDY *puts on* NORMAN's *wrist. The handcuffs had been hidden by a pile of magazines. It happened so fast* NORMAN *is dumbfounded and can only stare blankly at what* ANDY *has done.* ANDY *rushes to remove the telephone from the pole table, puts it on the floor. He replaces the director's chair left center, pulls back the round center table and resets the chair right of the table*) You dirty, no-good rat, I even have to write your lousy ideas!
(*He pulls on the handcuffs*)

ANDY That one was my own, sweetheart. I heard you on the phone this morning with the A-P. Now we have one article to finish, one more page. And we're down to the finish line, Norman, because in forty-five minutes, Mr. Franklyn's two Neanderthal sons will be here to pick up our completed magazine or their six hundred dollars. And if I can't give them either one, I'll give them you.

NORMAN (*Looks at him in disbelief*) You mean you're serious? You actually intend, in real life, to keep a human being chained to a steampipe?

ANDY (*He gets the typewriter from the sofa and takes it to the pole table*) Until tomorrow—when the police find an unidentified broken object dangling from a post.
(*He puts the typewriter on the table*)

NORMAN All right, Andy, I'm in no mood for the "Prisoner of Zenda." Open up!

ANDY Not until I see some paper work.
(*He starts for the kitchen*)

NORMAN Where are you going?

ANDY To the kitchen to get myself a tiny-kumquat sandwich.
(*He goes into the kitchen*)

NORMAN (*Shouts toward the window*) Help! Help! I'm being held prisoner! (*He looks out the window and shouts to someone*) Hey, lady! You wanna make a dollar? (*We hear a thunderous crash in the kitchen and a loud scream from* ANDY) What happened?
(*From the kitchen,* ANDY *staggers out holding his back in pain. He leans on the bar for support*)

ANDY Why did you wax the kitchen floor?

NORMAN Are you crazy? I didn't wax the kitchen floor.

ANDY (*Going toward a chair*) Well, the kitchen floor is waxed and if you didn't wax it, who did?
(*The front door opens and* SOPHIE *enters carrying a package in tin foil in one hand and a red suitcase in the other*)

SOPHIE (*Leaving the suitcase at the door*) Ah've come to
say good-bye. Ah froze a dozen fritters for you and be
careful in the kitchen, Ah just waxed the floor.
(*She puts the fritters on the kitchen bar*)

NORMAN Sophie, he's gone crazy. Look what he's done to
me. He's chained me to a steampipe!
(ANDY *sits in the chair*)

SOPHIE That won't be necessary anymore, Mr. Hobart.
My bus is leavin' for Hunnicut in fifteen minutes. Since
Ah only put in a three-day week Ah believe you have
some money comin' back to you.
(*She pours the pennies out of her purse onto the
center table and starts out*)

NORMAN Sophie, you don't have to leave because of me.
I'm not going to bother you anymore. I didn't even smell
you coming in here.

SOPHIE Ah'm glad, Norman. Ah'm not leavin' because of
you. Ah don't blame you for the crazy way you been
actin' lately. Ah understand it now. There are some
things in life we just can't control. For no reason at all
somethin' strange and mystifyin' hits us and there's
nothin' anybody can do about it except just sit and wait
and hope it goes away just as fast as it came. Unfortunately Ah don't see mine goin' away in the foreseeable
future and that's why Ah decided Ah can't marry Lieutenant Burt Fenneman and that's why Ah'm gettin' on
the bus to Hunnicut an' Ah can't say another word or
else Ah'll start cryin' all over this room.
(*She starts to cry and runs toward the door, picking
up her suitcase*)

ANDY Miss Rauschmeyer . . . Wait! (*She stops at the
door and waits*) I am in great physical pain. I have a
dislocated back from an overwaxed floor and a limp arm
from a misguided karate chop. (*He rises from the chair*)
But I just wanted you to know that I'm sorry—sorry that
some of us react to certain stimuli, and that others of us
don't. However, I have no wish to cause you any embarrassment or discomfort. Starting tomorrow I may be run-

ning this magazine myself. If you like, you can stay on— at half salary.

SOPHIE (*Puts her suitcase down outside the door and returns to the room*) You expect me to stay here with me feelin' the way Ah feel and you feelin' the way you don't . . . ? Mr. Hobart, if Ah wasn't afraid Ah'd miss mah bus, Ah'd really tell you somethin'. (*To* NORMAN) Do you have the time?

NORMAN (*Looks at his watch*) I don't even have a crystal.

SOPHIE (*To* ANDY) Well, Ah'll tell you anyway. You're right. Ah may be provincial and old-fashioned. Ah may believe in a lot of things like patriotism and the Constitution because that's the way Ah was brought up, and that's the way Ah feel. The trouble with you is you can't feel. You can't feel, you can't see, you can't hear and oh, boy, *you can't smell*. All you can do is think. But until you learn to use all those wonderful gadgets that nature has given you, you are only one-fifth of a man. Unfortunately by the time you get them all workin' and realize you are crazy about me, Ah will be back home in mah high school gymnasium gettin' in shape for next year's Olympics. If you want mah advice, Ah suggest you take those pennies and visit an eye, ear, nose and throat man. (*Starts for the door*) And maybe you ought to see a dentist too. Because mah former fiancé, not happy with the recent turn of events, is on his way over here to separate your teeth from your face.

NORMAN (*Jumps up and down happily*) Now you're gonna get it! *Now* you'll first get it!
(ANDY *sits*)

SOPHIE Did you hear what Ah said? There's an eight-foot Marine on his way here to chomp you up!

NORMAN (*Gleefully*) You hear that? The Yanks are coming! It's all over now, brother. (*Yells out the window*) Come on, Leathernecks. (*He sings the "Marine Hymn"*) I'm glad I'm chained to a pipe because I wouldn't miss this for anything.

SOPHIE (*With a big smile*)   Ah wish Ah could stay to see it.

ANDY   But you can't because you're leaving.

SOPHIE (*Goes to stairs leading to the front door*)   That's right, Ah'm leavin'! Ah'm leavin'! Back to Hunnicut. And startin' tomorrow Ah'm gonna swim a mile every day from now until next summer. (*She comes down the steps and walks toward the center table*) Every American has to do what he does best for his country, and Ah can swim! Ah'm gonna swim the United States right into a gold medal and this time Ah'm gonna beat the livin' nose plugs offa that little fat girl from the desert. (*She picks the phone off the floor*) Ah'm usin' your phone one more time. (*She dials*) Gimme Western Union! (*To* ANDY) And what you did to blacken America's good name with your protestin' magazine, Ah will whitewash with mah backstroke down in Mexico City. (*Into the phone*) Ah'd like to send a telegram, please. To Mr. Andrew Hobart, 217 Chestnut Hill, San Francisco. (*She looks at* ANDY) "Dear Mr. Hobart . . . Whether you like it or not, Ah pledge allegiance to the flag of the United States of America . . . And to the republic for which it stands, one nation, under God, indivisible, with liberty and justice for all." Sign that "A Patriot," and send it collect.
(*She hangs up, puts the phone back on the floor and exits with a flourish*)

NORMAN   You mean you're just going to sit there? She's going back to Hunnicut and you may never see her again!

ANDY   I'll see her again.

NORMAN   When?

ANDY   In 1972. I guarantee you she's the next President of the United States . . . Norman, I've had just about enough of you. Every man has his breaking point and my point just broke.

NORMAN   What are you gonna do?

ANDY Murder! I'm going to commit cold-blooded murder right in this room. (*He rises and goes stage left*) I'm going to kill the only thing in this world that really means anything to me—my magazine. (*He takes the key and unlocks* NORMAN's *handcuffs*) There! Go on, you're free. Now get out of here and let me bury the body. (*He goes to the bulletin board while* NORMAN *goes center.* ANDY *rips down the credo sign and breaks it over his knee*) Maybe you were right. Maybe you were both right. Maybe I am crazy. Maybe it was lunatic to try to hold on to one tiny, not very important, insignificant little voice-in-the-wilderness against such overwhelming odds as a girl-smelling mental case and a wetback Martha Washington. (*He picks up the magazines from the pole table and takes them right to the duffle bag on the sofa. Then he puts the magazines into the bag*) I'm sure she'll be very happy now. America is safe tonight. In tribute, to-morrow Howard Johnson's will add another flavor. (*He throws the duffle bag on the floor*) She's won, don't you see that, she's won. Divide and conquer, that's the way they do it. Well, we're divided and we're conquered. The war is over and we've surrendered. In reparations, she gets the Polish corridor, the free city of Danzig, three outfielders, two turtledoves and a partridge in a pear tree. (*He collapses into the chair right of the table*)

NORMAN Well—we can't always have what we want.

ANDY Go on, you were in such a hurry to go, why don't you go?

NORMAN (*Goes to the suitcase*) Yeah . . . Want me to help you straighten up before I go?

ANDY I wouldn't want you to be late for your appointment.

NORMAN (*He nods and picks up the suitcase*) One thing you were right about. Physical attraction isn't enough. It's like chewing gum. It starts off great, but the flavor doesn't last long.

ANDY   That's why they put five sticks in a pack. I'll see you, Norman.
(*He rises and goes up the steps to the landing*)

NORMAN   Any idea what you're gonna do now?

ANDY   I might go back to Philadelphia. Maybe work for my father.

NORMAN   I can't picture you in your father's business.

ANDY   I don't know. There's a lot of important work being done in the kitchen-cabinet field today.

NORMAN   Yeah. They say Formica is the hope of the future. (*He pauses*) I just want to say that if you decide not to go back to Philadelphia, that maybe someday, I don't know when, I'll be able to forget our differences, forget what's happened here the last few days, forget everything . . . And when I do, maybe someday I'll be back.

ANDY   I hope so, Norman . . . So long.
(NORMAN *nods and leaves. There is a moment's silence, then the door opens and* NORMAN *returns*)

NORMAN   I forgot everything; I'm back.

ANDY   What took you so long?

NORMAN   (*He puts his suitcase down near the kitchen bar*) I got stuck in traffic. (ANDY *comes down steps*) Hey, tell the truth! Were you really going back to Philadelphia?

ANDY   Of course not. I was going to marry Mrs. Mackininee and open up the only discothèque funeral parlor in California.
(*They break up laughing*)

NORMAN   And you'll be glad to know I'm Norman again. Norman the writer . . . (*He picks up the typewriter from the pole table*) Norman the man who's dedicated to this magazine.
(*He goes upstage to the left window*)

ANDY (*Closing the door*) And promise me you'll never go off the deep end over a girl like that again.

NORMAN (*At the window*) I'll promise tomorrow.

ANDY Why not today?

NORMAN 'Cause there's a gorgeous redhead across the street. (*Yells out*) Hey, beautiful redhead lady, I love you!

ANDY Norman, get back to that typewriter. (*He picks up the phone and puts it on the desk*) We've got a magazine to get out.

NORMAN (*Going to the desk. He sits*) All right. All right.

ANDY And promise me you won't get up from that chair until you finish.
(*He picks up the dummy magazine from the desk*)

NORMAN My fingers are glued to the keys.

ANDY No distractions?

NORMAN No distractions.

ANDY (*Going stage right*) No matter how much the smell in here is driving you crazy?

NORMAN What smell?

ANDY What do you mean, "what smell"? Her smell. Sophie.

NORMAN I don't smell Sophie.

ANDY Are you crazy? How can you not smell it? It's all over the room.

NORMAN This room?

ANDY Of course this room. She was just in here, wasn't she? I know the difference between a room-smell and a Sophie-smell and this is definitely—(*He drops the dummy magazine on the center table*) My God, what has happened to me?

NORMAN   You want me to chain you to the steampipe?

ANDY   It's not possible. These things don't happen to me. You were second in your class in Dartmouth, *but I was first*.

NORMAN   It's just physical attraction. That's not for us. It's for hippopotamuses.

ANDY (*Screaming*)   I know that, damnit!

NORMAN   What are you screaming for?

ANDY   Because I'm standing here talking to you, and my hippopotamus is getting on the bus. (*Rushes right to the window on the landing*) Sophie! Sophie!
(*The door flings open and* SOPHIE *rushes in but stops on the steps*)

SOPHIE   Ah been standin' out there just prayin' you'd say mah name. If you didn't say it in two more minutes, Ah was gonna come back in here and say it for you.

ANDY (*Comes down the stairs*)   You didn't get on the bus.

SOPHIE   Ah didn't get on the bus because Ah'm not goin' anywhere. Ah heard everything you said and if you were gonna give up this subversive magazine Ah was personally gonna come in here and tear you apart mahself. (*Comes down one step*) Ah may not agree with what you say, but if you stop sayin' it, then no one will disagree and that is not the idea of democracy. (*Down one more step*) We got free speech in this country and Ah'm here to see that it stays free and spoken.

ANDY   You really didn't get on the bus.

SOPHIE (*Goes right to* ANDY)   Of course Ah didn't get on the bus. 'Cause in the first place Ah'm crazy about you and in the second place Ah left mah bus fare on your table.

ANDY If you had gone back to Hunnicut, I'd have done something crazy like going after you on the next bus or the next train or the next plane or the next ship out of here.
(*The telephone rings.* NORMAN, *at the desk, picks it up*)

NORMAN (*Into the phone*) Thomas Cook Travel Agency . . . No, it's his friend, Norman.

SOPHIE Besides, Ah got a job here that pays me seventy-five dollars a week and Ah'm not about to give it up.

ANDY Seventy-*two* dollars. We've got to stick to the President's guide lines.

SOPHIE That's fine with me.

NORMAN (*On the phone*) That sounds wonderful. I'll be right there.
(*He hangs up and starts for the door*)

SOPHIE Where are you goin'?

NORMAN Skydiving with Mrs. Mackininee.

SOPHIE (*She takes a few steps to* NORMAN) You stay where you are and get back to work. We have a magazine to get out here. (*To* ANDY) Right?
(NORMAN *sits down again*)

ANDY Right! Only let me give you fair warning. It's not going to be easy. You start at eight and quit at seven.

SOPHIE That's fine with me!

ANDY I want pencils sharpened and papers stacked.

SOPHIE That's fine with me!

ANDY I want the books dusted, the floors cleaned and when I say hot coffee I mean hot coffee!

SOPHIE That's fine with me!

ANDY   Good. Now that you know what the rules are . . .
(*He goes to* NORMAN, *who is sitting at the desk*) Let's
you and I get back to ripping apart the degenerating
American way of life. Right?
(SOPHIE *follows*)

NORMAN   Right!

ANDY (*Turns to* SOPHIE)   And if you've got anything to
say, say it to yourself . . . Okay! Now that we all understand each other, maybe we'll finally get a little work
done around here.
(*Both* ANDY *and* SOPHIE *smell each other.* ANDY
*crosses downstage of her, goes to the chair right of
the center table and sits. He picks up the clipboard
and goes to work.* NORMAN *starts typing.* SOPHIE
*takes off her jacket and puts it on the back of the
director's chair. She goes to the kitchen bar for the
feather duster. As she starts dusting, she starts
singing*)

SOPHIE (*She dusts the up left table and pole table*)
"Mine eyes have seen the glory of the coming of the
Lord,
He is trampling out the vintage where the grapes of
wrath are stored,"
(*From the wings—no, from the heavens, we hear*
VOICES *joining* SOPHIE *in the stirring, building
strains of this, the most inspiring of all patriotic
hymns*)
"He hath loosed the fateful lightning of His terrible
swift sword:
His truth is marching on."
(*Curtain. The curtain goes back up immediately.*
SOPHIE *is busy dusting and singing. Both* ANDY *and*
NORMAN *look front incredulously. The curtain falls
—music rings out during the curtain calls*)
"Glory, glory, hallelujah!
Glory, glory, hallelujah!
Glory, glory, hallelujah!
His truth goes marching on."

Curtain

Promises, Promises

BOOK BY

Neil Simon

BASED ON THE SCREENPLAY

THE APARTMENT

by Billy Wilder & I. A. L. Diamond

MUSIC BY   LYRICS BY

Burt Bacharach   Hal David

Synopsis of Scenes

Act One

PROMISES,
PROMISES

CHUCK BAXTER *is at his desk working at an adding machine. He looks up and notices the audience.*

CHUCK The main problem with working as a hundred-and-twelve-dollar-a-week accountant in a seventy-two-story insurance company with assets of over three billion dollars that employs thirty-one thousand two hundred and fifty-nine people here in the New York office alone . . . is that it makes a person feel so God-awful *puny.* (*He resumes work, then stops*) Not that I don't have aspirations and ambitions. I definitely have aspirations and ambitions . . . As you can see it's five-forty and everyone else went home at five-thirty and I didn't go home at five-thirty because Mr. Sheldrake, the personnel manager, doesn't leave until five-forty and I thought it wouldn't hurt, promotion-wise, if he saw me working past five-thirty—(SHELDRAKE *enters, heading for the elevators; he rings the elevator bell*) Evening, Mr. Sheldrake . . . How are you, Mr. Sheldrake . . . You're looking well, Mr. Sheldrake . . . (SHELDRAKE *enters the elevator*) Nice seeing you again, Mr. Sheldrake. Good-by, Mr. Sheldrake. (SHELDRAKE *has gone. Crossing in front of the desk,* CHUCK *sits against it*) If you've noticed, I'm the kind of person that people don't notice . . . I wish I were sitting out there with you so I could take a look at me and figure out what's wrong. (*He sings "Half As Big As Life"*)

Did you ever stop, really stop, and take a look
Take a look, a really good look at yourself?

I just took a peek, really peeked, to tell the truth
Through my eyes, I don't look so good to myself.

Half as big as life, that's me
But that's not the way I always mean to be.

Half as big as life, that's small
But deep in my heart I can feel
That I'm ten feet tall—ten feet tall.

I know that
Inside of myself there's a man, the kind of man
You would like, if you were just willing to look.

I've got lots of dreams
And my dreams will take me far
Very far, a cover is not the whole book.

Half as big as life, they say
But they're gonna see how wrong they are
Someday.
Half as big as life, that's small
But I wasn't born to be looked at
As five feet tall—no, not me.

I want a lot
And I know that I'll get it all
Just like someone who's
Twice as big as life.

(*He crosses behind the desk and puts on his jacket*) Not that there aren't some people around here who've noticed I'm something more than a nine-to-five adding machine . . . Like this real pretty girl who works up in the Employees' Cafeteria, Fran Kubelik . . . *she* notices . . . Oh, Miss Kubelik . . . Working late too, I see.

FRAN   Oh, hello, Chuck. Yes, I had a few things to take care of in the cafeteria and I thought I'd just— Oh, what's the use, Chuck. I stayed late because I wanted to see you. I guess it's no secret that I'm enormously attracted to you but you never seem to pay any attention to me . . . Look, Chuck, can't we go somewhere and have a drink because—

CHUCK (*Raises his hand*)   Wait! Hold it a second! (FRAN *freezes,* CHUCK *turns to the audience*) It's not true. She never said that. I mean, I can kid myself but there's no point in lying to you. I'm not doing too well in this department either. So sometimes I dream up conversations . . . (*He looks at her, then back to the audience*)

Well, you can hardly blame me, can you? . . . No, what she actually said was—

FRAN Oh, hello, how are you, Frank?

CHUCK Chuck! Chuck Baxter.

FRAN Oh yes, I'm sorry.

CHUCK That's all right. How are things in the cafeteria?

FRAN Fine. I didn't see you there last week. Were you sick?

CHUCK No, I was there. You just didn't see me . . . Look, if you're not in a hurry to get home, I was wondering if—

FRAN Oh, excuse me, Chuck, I'm in a hurry to get home. Bye.
(She exits into the elevator)

CHUCK —if you'd like to have a drink? (To the audience.) How about you? You're not doing anything, are you? After work I usually like to unwind and have a friendly sociable drink at one of the bars on Second Avenue . . . where the young single set go . . . It could be any bar on Second Avenue . . . Your Mother's Hairnet, The Booze Boutique, Helen's Navel . . . As a matter of fact, my favorite Second Avenue bar is on First Avenue . . . It's owned by a friend of mine, Eddie Roth. (The lights hit a sign that reads "Grapes of Roth." A bar is revealed, smoke-filled and packed with people. A dance is beginning. CHUCK enters the bar, and calls to the bartender) Hi, Eddie. One beer!
(BARTENDER EDDIE draws a beer, which is passed from one customer to another, over the heads of the others, eluding CHUCK. When he finally gets it, a lady customer drops her cigarette in it. A well-dressed man in his early fifties fights his way through the crowd pulling an attractive girl with him)

DOBITCH Baxter! Baxter!

CHUCK   Oh, hello, Mr. Dobitch. (*To the audience*) Mr. Dobitch, an executive in the Mortgage and Loans Department, a very important man for me to know.

DOBITCH   Hya, Chuck. How are you?

CHUCK   Fine, Mr. Dobitch. What are you doing here? (*To the audience*) I'll tell you what he's doing here. Some married men between the ages of forty-five and fifty-five find single girls between the ages of twenty-one and thirty more attractive than some married women between the ages of forty-five and fifty-five, that's what he's doing here.

DOBITCH   Oh, just dropped in for a beer . . . Oh, Sylvia, I'd like you to meet a bright young man from our Accounting Department, Chuck Baxter. Chuck, I'd like you to meet Miss Gilhooley, a bright young girl from our Telephone Operating Department.

CHUCK   Hello.

SYLVIA   Pleased to make the connection. (*Aside to* DOBITCH) Mr. Dobitch, it's almost seven-thirty. Are we or aren't we?

DOBITCH (*Aside*)   We are, we are—I'm trying, honey. (*To* CHUCK) Baxter, can I speak to you for a second? Man to man?

CHUCK   Gee, Mr. Dobitch, I never thought you considered me that way.

DOBITCH (*Takes him aside*)   I've had my eye on you for a long time, Baxter . . . I understand you're a hard-working, dedicated, ambitious young man who has his own apartment on West Sixty-seventh Street. Is that true?

CHUCK   Well, I try, Mr. Dobitch.

DOBITCH   About the apartment?

CHUCK   Oh, that? Yes, it's true. I have a small place. One bedroom, nothing to speak about.

DOBITCH I'd like to speak to you about it . . . The young lady I'm with is not feeling very well.

CHUCK Oh, I'm sorry to hear that. Is there anything I can do?

DOBITCH Interesting you should ask. She'll be all right, you understand, but the thing is, she needs a place to lie down—for about forty-five minutes, an hour the most.

CHUCK Oh?

DOBITCH You see, she lives all the way up in the Bronx—

SYLVIA Brooklyn!

DOBITCH —all the way out in Brooklyn, and we have no place else to go . . .

CHUCK For what?

DOBITCH For her to lie down . . .

CHUCK I see what you mean, Mr. Dobitch. The thing is I was just going home. I'm learning to play tennis on Channel Thirteen and I was just getting to the point where my backhand . . .

SYLVIA (For CHUCK's benefit, but poorly done) Oh, God, am I feeling rotten.

DOBITCH She's feeling rotten.

CHUCK Well, I'm certainly not adverse to getting ahead, Mr. Dobitch, but you see, Mrs. Lieberman, the landlady, is very sensitive about bringing unattached young ladies up to the apartment—

DOBITCH She's not unattached. She's with me.

CHUCK Oh! And you say she's really feeling sick?

DOBITCH   I just touched her hand. She's hot as a pistol.

CHUCK (*Reaching in his pocket for the key*)   Well, if you think it won't be more than an hour.

DOBITCH   In her present condition, maybe only thirty minutes.

CHUCK (*Hands him the key*)   Here's the key. Nineteen West Sixty-seventh Street, second floor front.

DOBITCH (*Takes the key*)   I won't forget you for this, Baxter . . . advancement-wise.

CHUCK   There's some aspirins in the medicine cabinet and tea balls in the kitchen . . . Oh, and in case anything else develops, there's a doctor right next door.

DOBITCH   Bite your tongue, kid!
          (*He exits with* SYLVIA. *Music begins. Everything blacks out except for a lone spotlight on* CHUCK)

CHUCK (*Turning to the audience*)   As it turned out, he didn't need the doctor, the aspirin or the tea balls. He nursed her back to health with a bottle of vodka and my record player . . .

Fade Out

*The outside stoop of a brownstone building swings in
from the side.*

CHUCK   She was fine the next day but it must have been
a recurring ailment because she began feeling sick regularly every Tuesday night for the next month. But
things were looking up. Mr. Dobitch introduced me to
Mr. Kirkeby of Public Relations . . . (*Music to "Upstairs" begins*) . . . which meant that Wednesday nights
I sat out in the public while he was busy having relations
. . . (*He sings*)

> Upstairs—two flights up
> Looking out on the street
> For eighty-six fifty a month it's mine
> It may not be much but it's mine.
>
> You just go upstairs, two flights up
> Comfortable and complete
> For every-day living it works out fine
> It may not be much but it's mine.
>
> Except on Wednesday night
> It's walk, don't run.
> I just kill time till Mister Kirkeby's done
> With his Wednesday night fun
> Outside of that the place is mine.

> (*After* CHUCK *sings the first chorus,* GINGER *and*
> KIRKEBY *come out of the building.* CHUCK *hides
> behind the stoop*)

KIRKEBY   Come on, Ginger, let's go.

GINGER   Rush, rush, rush! First you rush me up here,
then you rush me out.

KIRKEBY (*Looking at his watch*) I'm sorry, but I've got to meet my wife at eight-thirty. Tonight's our night with the marriage counsellor.
(*Blackout; a spotlight turns on* CHUCK)

CHUCK Three weeks later, I still didn't have a promotion. However, I did meet Mr. Eichelberger of Research, who said he was looking for a bright young man for his department. He could have found one out on the stoop every Thursday night but he was busy doing research— upstairs, two flights up.
(*The lights black out on* CHUCK *and go up on the apartment.* MR. EICHELBERGER, *a very austere, controlled-looking middle-aged executive, sits on the bed, wearing an opened vest, his head rests on his hands.* VIVIEN, *a nifty-looking brunette, sits near him*)

EICHELBERGER Oh, God, what have I done? I'm a married man with children, what kind of animal am I? A cheat, a liar, a phony. A deceiving sneak. *I've lost all respect for myself.*

VIVIEN What about next Tuesday?

EICHELBERGER Tuesday's *fine* with me.
(*Blackout on the apartment; the lights go up on* CHUCK *in the vestibule outside his apartment*)

CHUCK And that's the way it went for a couple of months. Three nights a week I spend browsing through Doubleday's, Brentano's, Cinema I, Cinema II, and once in *great* desperation, a dance at Hunter College. (*He bends down, lifts up the mat and picks up the key. He inserts it in the door*) Now you may ask the question, "Didn't I think lending out my apartment in hopes of getting a promotion was morally wrong?" (*He opens the door*) Well, my answer is— "Yes, but I tried not to think about it." (*He goes in and turns on the lights. He looks around the apartment, disgusted at the mess*) You'd think they'd have the decency to clean up afterwards. (*He picks up an empty liquor bottle*) I'm beginning to feel like a chambermaid in a New Jersey motel.
(*He shakes his head angrily, then crosses to the*

door, opens it and puts out three empty bottles just as DR. DREYFUSS, *an affable middle-aged man, comes up the vestibule heading for his own apartment directly opposite* CHUCK'S. *He carries the usual black bag)*

DR. DREYFUSS (*Disapproving*) Hello, Baxter. And how is "Mr. Whoopee" today?

CHUCK Oh, hi, Doc. Just tidying up.

DR. DREYFUSS (*Looks at the bottles*) It's a wonder you can *stand* up. The garbage man told me the only place he picks up more empty bottles is the Copacabana.

CHUCK That's not me, Doc. It's just that once in a while I have some people in for a drink.

DR. DREYFUSS From what I hear through the walls, that's not all you have them in for. Three, four nights a week, you'll be dead by August.

CHUCK I'm sorry if it gets noisy—

DR. DREYFUSS I was telling the interns at the clinic about you. Three of them want to study you, four of them just want to shake your hand.

CHUCK I'm afraid they'd be disappointed, Doc.

DR. DREYFUSS Yeah. Well, slow down, kid. Take some of those sleeping pills I gave you.

CHUCK I'm not tired.

DR. DREYFUSS Me! Me! I haven't closed an eye in six weeks.
          (*He goes into his apartment.* CHUCK *goes back into his and closes the door)*

CHUCK Funny, isn't it? Everyone in the building thinks I'm the greatest lover in New York—and at Hunter I couldn't get a dance until "Goodnight, Sweetheart." (*Takes a pill*) Well, at least I'll get a night's sleep tonight.

(The doorbell rings. CHUCK *opens it.* MR. VANDER-HOF *stands there. He is another dapper middle-aged gentleman)*

VANDERHOF Baxter? C. C.?

CHUCK Yes?

VANDERHOF Hi there. Jesse Vanderhof, twenty-seventh floor, Claims Investigation. Ed Dobitch and Mike Kirkeby were talking about you the other day in the Executive Dining Room and I thought I'd just drop by to say hello.

CHUCK Oh, that's very nice of you, Mr. Vanderhof. Hello.

VANDERHOF Hello. (CHUCK *starts to close the door quickly.* VANDERHOF *grabs it)* Forty-five minutes, kid, that's all I need the place. I got very lucky this afternoon.

CHUCK *(Trying to shut the door)* Yeah, well, your luck ran out tonight because I just took a sleeping pill.

VANDERHOF Kid, you don't understand. This is a nurse. She works for my dentist. I only see him twice a year. I won't bother you again until April.

CHUCK I've heard that before.

VANDERHOF I just had a tooth pulled. Give me a break, kid, the Novocaine is wearing off.

CHUCK I've got my own health to think about. The last hot meal I had was a bag of roasted chestnuts.
    (He closes the door and leans his back against it)

VANDERHOF Baxter, there's a Junior Executive opening coming up in my department next month.

CHUCK *(Nothing doing)* Promises, promises, I'm sick and tired of promises.

VANDERHOF I'll put your name on top of the list.

CHUCK Is that a promise?

VANDERHOF It is not a promise, it's my bonded word of honor.

CHUCK (*Opens the door*) Well, as long as it's not a promise.

VANDERHOF (*Entering, circling from the sofa to the door*) You won't regret this, kid.

CHUCK You get the apartment just the way it is. I'm all out of liquor, all out of cheese, all out of crackers . . .

VANDERHOF Don't worry about it, I can't eat anything for an hour anyway.
> (*He goes into the hall and whistles, then returns to the apartment and starts to help* CHUCK *on with his raincoat*)

CHUCK (*Putting it on*) I don't know why you can't go to a motel.

VANDERHOF (*Softly*) Because no decent girl would go to a motel with a man she met three hours ago . . . A friend's apartment is different . . . Can't you put your coat on outside?
> (CHUCK *has an arm in one sleeve of his coat as* VANDERHOF *ushers him toward the door*)

CHUCK I don't know where you get your energy, Mr. Vanderhof. You should be home gargling with salt water. (*He steps to the hall and comes face to face with the willowy* NURSE) . . . Oh, hello.

NURSE I just dropped by to powder my nose.
> (*She slinks into the apartment.* VANDERHOF *comes out into the hall with* CHUCK)

CHUCK (*Whispers*) Well, tell her not to powder too loud. I've got neighbors, you know.
> (*He starts down the hall*)

VANDERHOF (*Calls after him*) If you can make it an hour and a half I'd appreciate it. (CHUCK *disappears as*

VANDERHOF *goes into the apartment, closing the door behind him. At that moment,* DR. DREYFUSS *opens his door, putting out empty milk bottles.* VANDERHOF *says to* NURSE) . . . And now, Miss Kreplinski, shall we have a little music while we discuss my bridgework.

(*He flips a record on the phonograph. Music comes on.* DR. DREYFUSS *listens, shakes his head and turns into his apartment*)

DR. DREYFUSS   Mildred! He's at it again!

(*The lights black out on* DR. DREYFUSS *and* VANDERHOF *and light up on* CHUCK *as he sits on the front stoop*)

CHUCK (*He is angry, but mostly with himself*)   No, I am not altogether proud of myself, if that's what you're thinking . . . But let me tell you this . . . Once I get to be a Junior Executive, I am going to work harder and later and with more dedication than any Junior Executive who ever lent out his apartment ever did before . . . (*He looks up*) . . . and some day *I'm* the one who's going to be . . . (*Singing*)

> Upstairs two flights up
> Looking out on the street
> For eighty-six fifty a month it's mine
> It may not be much but it's mine.

(*Lightning flashes, thunder rolls and* CHUCK *looks up as if to say "Wouldn't you know it." He lifts his collar up about his neck and sinks deeper into his coat*)

Fade Out

1ST GIRL (*On mike*) Good morning, Consolidated Life. I'm sorry, he's not in yet.

2ND GIRL (*On mike*) Good morning, Consolidated Life. No, he gets in at nine.

1ST GIRL (*On mike*) Good morning, Consolidated Life. Oh, hello, Ethel. Wasn't that some storm last night?
(CHUCK *appears on the right and crosses to the center*)

CHUCK They didn't leave until two-thirty in the morning. Don't come near me, I'm very sick. (*To* NURSE) Er, my name is Baxter. I'd like to see the Doctor, please.

NURSE Do you have an appointment?

CHUCK No, just a cold. It was unexpected. I didn't know it was coming.

NURSE Take a seat, the Doctor will be right with you.

CHUCK I hope so, I'm almost out of nasal spray . . . By the way, I have a 101.3 temperature. You can see it on my thermometer here.
(*He shows her the thermometer*)

NURSE The Doctor will take it.

CHUCK Oh. (*He starts to give it to her*) All right. If I can have it back when he's through. It's my only thermometer . . .

NURSE He has his own. Will you please sit down?
(*He sits as the* COMPANY DOCTOR *and* VANDERHOF *come out of the office*)

DOCTOR I'd leave the bandage on another day, Mr. Vanderhof.

VANDERHOF Right, Doc.

DOCTOR And I don't care what you say, they still look like teeth marks to me.
(*He exits*)

CHUCK Hi, Mr. Vanderhof.

VANDERHOF Oh, hi, kid.

CHUCK Don't "Hi, kid" me. Do you know I sat on a park bench until two-thirty in the morning in a snow storm in a London Fog coat? It's for fogs in London, not snow in New York!

VANDERHOF I'm sorry, kid. By the way, I intend to pay you for the broken ironing board. Kind of interesting the way it happened.

CHUCK And then you left the wrong key under the mat. I had to sleep in a Spanish Synagogue on Sixty-ninth Street.

VANDERHOF Think about your promotion, kid. I spoke to Mr. Sheldrake in Personnel, you should be hearing from him this morning.

CHUCK If I'm still alive.

VANDERHOF Now put me down for the apartment next Friday. And get in some new records, will you? It's not easy being sexy to Lithuanian Folk Dances.
(*Exits*)

CHUCK (*Shouts*) No one's using anything until I hear from Mr. Sheldrake! (*He holds his head*) Oh, God, I cracked a sinus.
(FRAN *enters*)

FRAN Excuse me, is the Doctor in?

CHUCK (*Rising*) Oh, Miss Kubelik, hello.

FRAN Oh, hello, er—

CHUCK Frank . . . er, Chuck. Chuck Baxter.

FRAN Yes, I know. How are you?

CHUCK Oh, just a little cold. How are you?

FRAN Oh, the same old problem. Can't eat, can't sleep, just thinking about you, dreaming about you, hoping you'll call me—

CHUCK (*Turns to the audience*) I'm sorry, I won't do that again. (*To* FRAN) And how are you?

FRAN Oh, just a mild case of the hiccups.

CHUCK I'm sorry, my Eustachian tubes are blocked up, I didn't hear what you said. (*She hiccups*) No, I heard that. I missed the part in front of it.

FRAN I said just a mild case of hiccups.

CHUCK Oh. (*He is stuck for a moment. To the audience*) I think I'm running out of conversation . . . I mustn't panic. If I keep talking I'll be all right. (*To* FRAN) So, you have a mild case of the hiccups, do you?

FRAN Yes.

CHUCK I see. (*To the audience*) That's it. I have no more thoughts, I'm finished.

FRAN By the way, they made me hostess in the Executive Dining Room.
　　　(*She hiccups*)

CHUCK I heard. Congratulations.

FRAN So I guess I won't be seeing you any more in the cafeteria.

CHUCK   Unless I become an executive, which isn't entirely remote. Excuse me, a terrible sneeze is coming.
(*He holds it in*)

FRAN   You really shouldn't suppress it, you know. You could blow out something internally. (*She hiccups*) Sneeze. (*He sneezes*) God bless you.

CHUCK   Thank you. (*She hiccups*) Hey, we had a nice rhythm going there.

FRAN   I don't know what brought these on.

CHUCK   I read that emotional distress can sometimes cause hiccups. Are your emotions by any chance distressed? I don't mean to pry.

FRAN   I don't think so.

CHUCK (*To the audience*)   I think so. There was talk she was involved with some man but it's over now . . . Don't say anything. (*To* FRAN) Listen, I'm not a doctor or anything, but why don't you try taking your mind off whatever it is that's distressing you.

FRAN   How?

CHUCK   Well, try thinking about something else—get involved with a new interest. (*To the audience*) Me, me! Please let it be me.

FRAN   Like what?

CHUCK   Like me! I mean, take a person like me. I have lots of interests . . . uh . . . walking . . . browsing . . . (*The music to "You'll Think of Someone" begins*) . . . Don't you have any hobbies?

FRAN   I don't like doing things alone.

CHUCK   Oh, well, I'm sure there are lots of interesting people who'd be interested in doing things with you . . . for example . . .

FRAN (*Singing*)
 I could take up knitting to feel better
 I'd make someone a hand-knit sweater
 But I just don't know who that someone should be.

CHUCK (*Singing*)
 If you can't think of anyone else
 How about maybe, someone
 Like for example, perhaps, someone
 Oh, you'll think of someone.

FRAN
 I could take up tennis to relax me
 A game of doubles wouldn't tax me
 But I just don't know who my partner should be.

CHUCK
 If you can't think of anyone else
 How about maybe, someone
 Like for example, perhaps, someone
 Oh, you'll think of someone

FRAN *and* CHUCK
 Who likes you and the things you like to do
 Happy little things like climbing hills
 And rowing boats on a lake
 Fun is something that is yours to take.

FRAN
 I could take up painting to amuse me
 A portrait picture might enthuse me
 But I just don't know who my model should be.

CHUCK
 You can bet that there's someone around

FRAN
 Someone to talk to, laugh with
 Like for example dance with, sing to . . .

CHUCK
 Cling to . . .
  (*The* NURSE *comes out of the office*)

NURSE Baxter? Mr. Sheldrake in Personnel wants to see you right away. You're next, miss.

CHUCK (*Excited*) Did you hear that? Did you hear? This is what I've been waiting for in the fog and the snow and the cold for two months.

FRAN Well, I wish you the best of luck. And I want to thank you for trying to help me. It was very nice of you, Chick.

CHUCK Chuck.

FRAN Oh, yes, I'm sorry . . . Well, I hope I'll be seeing you in the Executive Dining Room. Bye. (*She enters the office and the* NURSE *follows*)

CHUCK (*He looks after her and sings*)
       When you think about that someone
       Who it could be
       How about me?

Fade Out

The office of J. D. SHELDRAKE, *the Personnel Director. It is not an executive suite, but it is several pegs above the glass cubicles of the middle echelon.* MISS OLSON, *an attractive secretary, ushers* CHUCK *into the office.*

MISS OLSON If you'll take a seat, Mr. Sheldrake will be right with you.

CHUCK Thank you.
　　(*He sits*)

MISS OLSON And relax.

CHUCK I'm perfectly relaxed. (*She smiles and exits. He turns to the audience*) We know better, don't we? (SHELDRAKE *enters*) Mr. Sheldrake? I was told you wanted to see me . . . C. C. Baxter . . . (SHELDRAKE, *smiling at* CHUCK, *sits, picks up a folder of papers from the desk and studies them*) . . . Premium Accounting Division . . . Baxter . . . C. C.?
　　　　(SHELDRAKE *puts down the papers, sits back in his reclining chair, cups his hands under his chin and studies* CHUCK *in silence a moment.* CHUCK *fidgets nervously*)

SHELDRAKE So you're C. C. Baxter.

CHUCK (*Big smile*) Yes, sir. I am. I am C. C. Baxter.

SHELDRAKE Mmmm, hm.

CHUCK Yes, sir.
　　　　(SHELDRAKE *looks at the papers again;* CHUCK *sniffles*)

SHELDRAKE   Is that a cold you have there, Baxter?

CHUCK   Where? Oh, here . . . (*He touches his nose*)
Yes, sir, that's a cold. I haven't been sleeping much lately.

SHELDRAKE   Maybe you ought to go to bed early.

CHUCK   That certainly is wonderful advice, Mr. Sheldrake
. . . The thing is, I've been trying to catch up on extra
work in the office a couple of nights a week. (*Turns to the
audience*) I've sold out. God'll punish me.

SHELDRAKE   So you do have ambitions.

CHUCK   Yes, sir, I do . . . Ambitions and capabilities . . .

SHELDRAKE   Like "Loyal, resourceful, cooperative"?

CHUCK   Well, yes, those are good ones.

SHELDRAKE   (*He picks up the papers on his desk and
looks at them*) That's what Mr. Vanderhof thinks. This
is his report. He says you're loyal, resourceful, cooperative.

CHUCK   (*He twists his head to look at the report*) Mr.
Vanderhof said that? In that order? Imagine.

SHELDRAKE   And Mr. Dobitch told me that you've been
of immense help to him. And Mr. Kirkeby in Public
Relations thinks you're very bright.

CHUCK   Mr. Kirkeby thinks I'm bright?

SHELDRAKE   Yes, they're all keen on you. Vanderhof,
Kirkeby, Dobitch . . . even Mr. Eichelberger.

CHUCK   (*To the audience*) I think they overdid it. He's
going to want to know what makes me so popular.

SHELDRAKE   Tell me, Baxter, what makes you so popular?

CHUCK   Well, I imagine it's . . . Well, they probably
. . . I don't know.

SHELDRAKE Baxter, is it your impression that I'm stupid?

CHUCK No, sir, it is not. Have I given the impression that you give that impression, sir?

SHELDRAKE Well, I can tell you I'm anything but stupid. I know everything that goes on in this building. In every department, on every floor.

CHUCK (*To the audience*) All right, don't get nervous. Because if you get nervous, I'll get nervous. (*To* SHELDRAKE) On every floor?

SHELDRAKE In nineteen sixty-three we had an employee here named Fowler. Fowler was very popular too. Turned out he was running a bookie joint right in the Actuarial Department . . . tying up the switchboards, figuring the odds on our IBM machines. Used to pass the money back and forth on the coffee wagon. Winners paid off under the prune danish.

CHUCK Isn't that terrible?

SHELDRAKE It was for Fowler. I let him keep the prune danish because I knew he wouldn't be eating again for a long time.

CHUCK Sir, is there some point in this story that you're trying to point out to me? Because I'm not running any bookie joint.

SHELDRAKE (*He stops behind him and speaks into his ear*) What kind of joint *are* you running?

CHUCK I, sir? Me?

SHELDRAKE There's a certain key floating around the office, from Kirkeby to Vanderhof to Eichelberger to Dobitch back to Kirkeby, et cetera, et cetera, et cetera. That key I mentioned is to a certain apartment . . . And do you know who that key belongs to?

CHUCK (*To the audience*) You are looking at a young man in big trouble. (*To* SHELDRAKE) Do you?

SHELDRAKE Yes.

CHUCK (*To the audience*) See?

SHELDRAKE To "Loyal, Resourceful, Cooperative C. C. Baxter." Can I get you anything? Coffee? Prune Danish?

CHUCK Mr. Sheldrake, if you would just let me explain—

SHELDRAKE All right.

CHUCK Oh! . . . Well, you see one night about two months ago I was on my way home from work when I stopped in at the Grapes of Roth for a quick beer . . . that's all I drink, quick beers . . . when I met a certain executive from one of our departments, quite a decent gentleman, who was suddenly confronted with this very unusual problem—

SHELDRAKE The girl he was with was feeling sick.

CHUCK —the girl he was with was feeling sick. That's right! . . . Anyway, you could see she was hot as a pistol and all she needed was—

SHELDRAKE A place to lie down.

CHUCK —a place to lie down. You're right again. Anyway, he was in a tight spot because this girl—

SHELDRAKE Lived all the way up in the Bronx.

CHUCK No, as a matter of fact, she lived in Brooklyn.

SHELDRAKE Where did I make my mistake?

CHUCK That's all right. So what could I do but give him the key to my apartment? Then pretty soon I started getting calls from these other decent executives and that's pretty much how this whole thing sneaked up on me.

(*He takes out a spray bottle and quickly sprays both nostrils*)

SHELDRAKE Baxter, an insurance company can't afford to betray the public trust, you agree with that?

CHUCK (*Grimaces*) Ohhh.

SHELDRAKE You don't agree?

CHUCK I agree. I just sprayed my nose with eye drops. That can't hurt me, can it? I mean, you can't go blind in the nose.

SHELDRAKE Baxter, how many charter members are there in this little key club of yours?

CHUCK Just those four. Out of a total of 31,259 employees . . . so percentage-wise, we can be very proud of our personnel . . . (*He sniffs, then breathes freely*) Gee, the eye drops are better than the nose drops.

SHELDRAKE That's not the point. Four rotten apples in a barrel, no matter how large the barrel . . . You realize that if this ever leaked out—

CHUCK Oh, it won't, believe me. And I've decided from now on no more apples are going to use my barrel . . . apartment. (*He squints*) I wonder if the ear drops would work in the eyes.

SHELDRAKE Where is it?

CHUCK What?

SHELDRAKE Your apartment.

CHUCK West Sixty-seventh Street . . . But I'm changing the key, the lock, the door. I'd change my name but I don't know how else I'd get my mail.

MISS OLSON (*Entering*) Excuse me. Mrs. Sheldrake called and wants to know if you'll be home for dinner.

SHELDRAKE   No, tell her I'm taking the branch manager from Kansas City to the basketball game. I'll be home late.

MISS OLSON   Yes, sir.
   (*She exits*)

SHELDRAKE   Tell me something, Baxter. Do you like basketball?

CHUCK   Basketball? I love it. I was going to play in college . . . but I stopped growing in high school.

SHELDRAKE   How'd you like to see the Knicks' first game tonight?

CHUCK   You mean you and me? Well, won't the branch manager from Kansas City be disappointed . . . ?

SHELDRAKE   I made other plans for him . . . and me. You can have both tickets.

CHUCK   Well, that's very kind of you . . . but I thought I'd just go home and take some Excedrin, Bufferin, Contac, Dristan, Cope, a lot of that stuff . . .

SHELDRAKE   You don't understand, Baxter. I'm not just giving you these tickets . . . I want to *swap* them.

CHUCK   Swap them? What could I have that you would possibly want?

SHELDRAKE   (*He picks up* VANDERHOF's *report*)   It also says here that you are alert, astute and quite imaginative.

CHUCK   Well, I am but I just can't imagine— (*The dawn breaks*) Oh! (*He reaches into his pocket and takes out the key*) This?

SHELDRAKE   (*Smiles*)   . . . And I see what they mean . . . Next week there's going to be a shift in personnel around here, and as far as I'm concerned, do you know what I think you are?

CHUCK   Executive material?

SHELDRAKE We think alike. Now put down the key—
(CHUCK *quickly puts the key on the desk.* SHELDRAKE
pushes a pad toward CHUCK)—and put down the address.
(CHUCK *grabs the thermometer, lays the key on
the desk, unclips what he thinks is his pen and
starts to write on the pad*)

CHUCK It's the second floor front . . . my name's not on
the door . . . it just says 2A . . . and the "A" fell off
. . . (*Suddenly realizes he's writing with his thermometer*)
Oh, that's my thermometer . . . (*Looks at it*) 106? My
God . . . (*Then realizes*) Oh, that's just my pocket temper-
ature . . .

SHELDRAKE Relax, Baxter.

CHUCK Thank you, sir. I certainly will.
(*He replaces the thermometer with his pen and
resumes writing*)

SHELDRAKE Now remember, Baxter, what is tonight going
to be?

CHUCK Tonight, sir? (*Thinks*) A fun evening?

SHELDRAKE No, Baxter. Tonight is going to be our little
secret.

CHUCK Oh, of course. You didn't even have to say that.

SHELDRAKE You know how people talk.

CHUCK You don't have to remind me.

SHELDRAKE Not that there's anything wrong. This happens to be a nice girl.

CHUCK Listen, you didn't have to tell me. Besides, it's
none of my business. I mean, after all, four apples, five
apples, what's the difference?

SHELDRAKE That's where you're wrong, Baxter. From now
on there's only room for one apple in the basket, right?

CHUCK Right.

(CHUCK *and* SHELDRAKE *sing* "*Our Little Secret*")

CHUCK

All the other apples are spoiled and they're rotten
Out of the basket they'll go.

SHELDRAKE

Your loyalty is something that won't be forgotten.

CHUCK

And there's one thing I promise you
I can keep secrets, too.
Oh—

CHUCK *and* SHELDRAKE

It's our little secret
Little secret, little secret . . .

CHUCK

I'm gonna buy me a hat
And keep our secret under that.

CHUCK *and* SHELDRAKE

It's our little secret
Little secret, little secret . . .

CHUCK

I'll even stop counting sheep
To prove I don't talk when I sleep.

CHUCK *and* SHELDRAKE

We've got a little plot
That we can tell—just one another
There isn't anyone
That we can trust, except each other.

That's why we'll never tell a soul
What it's all about
They'll never get a chance
To find out.

SHELDRAKE

There'll be questions

CHUCK
    I won't answer

SHELDRAKE
    There'll be gossip

SHELDRAKE *and* CHUCK
    Let them gossip
    We don't care.

CHUCK
    Just put your trust in me.

CHUCK *and* SHELDRAKE
    It's our little secret
    And I'll keep it locked inside me
    'Cause it's no one else's business
    But our own anyhow . . .

        (MISS OLSON *enters.* CHUCK *and* SHELDRAKE *whistle four bars.* MISS OLSON *exits*)

    'Cause it's no one else's business
    But our own anyhow.

    Our little secret, oh yes, it's yours and mine
    Our little secret, for now and all the time
    We'll stick together
    'Cause we've got our little secret now.

        (*After the number is over there is a blackout on the set, except for a spot that stays on* CHUCK *as he steps out front and addresses the audience*)

CHUCK   Listen, I wouldn't be too quick to judge a decent executive like Mr. Sheldrake. . . . I wouldn't want to pin any labels on him like "hypocritical" or "unprincipled." No, sir, not me . . . Of course, *you're* free to make up your own minds.

Fade Out

CHUCK *waits in the lobby of Consolidated Life as other employees emerge, some posting letters on their way home.* FRAN *passes him on her way to the letter box.*

FRAN (*She passes* CHUCK) Good night.

CHUCK Good night . . . Oh, hey, Miss Kubelik, I've been waiting for you.

FRAN You have?

CHUCK I almost didn't recognize you without your hiccups. I don't hear them so I guess you cleared up your emotional distress.

FRAN Well, temporarily. Did you get your promotion?

CHUCK Table for one tomorrow in the Executive Dining Room. And I like my salad tossed from left to right.

FRAN Good. Congratulations.

CHUCK Thanks. (*She starts toward the revolving door*) Oh, Miss Kubelik. Look, is there a wild, way-out remote impossible possibility that you'd be interested in basketball?

FRAN Oscar Robertson led the N.B.A. in scoring last year with a twenty-nine-point-seven average.

CHUCK That's right! Even the point seven. How did you know that?

FRAN I live in three and a half rooms with a father, brother, and one television set.

CHUCK Well, how'd you like to see the Knicks play in actual, real-life seven-foot-tall flesh?

FRAN You mean tonight?

CHUCK (*He takes the tickets out*) Yes.

FRAN I'm sorry, I can't tonight. I'm meeting someone.

CHUCK   Oh. Exit the hiccups, heh? This date . . . is it just a date . . . or is it something serious . . . I'm sorry, you don't have to tell me that.

FRAN   It *used* to be serious . . . At least *I* was, he wasn't.

CHUCK   He must be crazy . . . So where does it stand now? You really don't have to answer that.

FRAN   I don't know where it stands. I'm just going to have a drink with him. He's been calling me all week.

CHUCK   He must be a nice fellow if you're interested in him.

FRAN   I'm not interested in him. I'm interested in you. I've always been interested in you. You're all I ever think about or dream about or—

CHUCK   (*He yells at himself*) All right, cut that out, Chuck. (FRAN *freezes*) No one's interested in what you *want* to hear. (*To the audience*) You're interested in what she *said*, right? And what she said was—

FRAN   (*Unfreezes*) Yes, he *is* very nice . . . Well, I'm late. Good night.

CHUCK   Good night. (*To the audience*) I really didn't expect her to go anyway.

FRAN   What time does the game begin?

CHUCK   Six-thirty. But it's a double header. We don't have to see the first game. We don't even have to see the whole second game. I mean we could come in at the half or the last quarter. All the action's in the last twelve minutes anyway—

FRAN   I could meet you at the entrance about nine.

CHUCK   Nine! Nine is the perfect time. You don't run into all those early rushers who want to see everything—

FRAN   Okay. Then I'll see you at nine.

CHUCK   (*He calls after her*) Hey! The *new* Madison Square Garden. The old one is torn down. . . . How about that. She likes basketball! (*He sings*)

She likes basketball, how about that?
We've got something in common to talk about . . .
Basketball.
She likes basketball, how about that?

I have someplace to take her
When we go out . . .
Basketball.
Who ever would have dreamed

Ever would have thought
That my favorite girl liked my favorite sport
Like any other kid I would make believe
With a ball in my hand.

I'd dribble right past
All the others real fast
And I'd be six-foot-eight
And my jump-shot was really great.

She likes basketball, isn't that wild?
It's an omen that good things are on their way.
Things to share . . .

We share basketball, couldn't you die?
From a simple beginning like this
We may get somewhere.

It's nice to dream
Someday it might be
Basketball and me.

Who ever would have dreamed
Ever would have thought
That my favorite girl
Liked my favorite sport.

Like any other kid
I would make believe
With a ball in my hand
I'd dribble right past

All the others real fast
And I'd be six-foot-eight
And my jump-shot was really great.

She likes basketball!
Isn't that wild?

It's an omen that good things
Are on their way
Things to share . . .

We share basketball
Couldn't you die?
From a simple beginning like this
We may get somewhere.

It's nice to dream
Someday it might be
Basketball and me.

Fade Out

Lum Ding's Chinese Restaurant. There are a number of booths and a couple of scattered tables. The place is a little less than half filled. A lone man sits at the corner table.

The HOSTESS enters and crosses to the exit at the other side. The WAITER then enters and crosses to the exit at the other side. FRAN enters and without looking around heads straight for the lone man at the corner table.

SHELDRAKE Fran . . . Fran, how've you been?

FRAN Fine, Mr. Sheldrake.

SHELDRAKE Mr. Sheldrake? Whatever happened to Jeff?

FRAN Yeah, whatever happened to him?

SHELDRAKE Let me take your coat.

FRAN I can't stay long.

HOSTESS Good evening, miss. (*Points to her head*) You changed your hair. Very pretty.

FRAN Thanks.

SHELDRAKE That's right. You have changed your hair.

FRAN I knew you'd be the first to notice.

SHELDRAKE Okay, I haven't called you in six weeks. I deserve a little hostility. Am I going to get the egg rolls in the face?

FRAN I'm waiting for the sauce.

SHELDRAKE Fran, I missed you.

FRAN And there it is.

SHELDRAKE I was going to call you one night last week.
I started dialing your number, then hung up in the middle.

FRAN It must have been Tuesday, the phone didn't ring
all night. Can I have a cigarette?

SHELDRAKE (*He looks at her, then takes out a pack*)
First time I ever saw you smoke.

FRAN I was saving it as a surprise. It's my new image.
Joan Crawford, older but wiser.

SHELDRAKE (*He smiles*) It needs work. You've got the
filter at the wrong end.

FRAN Yeah, well, in case you haven't noticed, I'm nervous
as hell about seeing you again.

SHELDRAKE (*Lighting her cigarette*) I've noticed. I like
it. You look great, Fran.

FRAN Thank you . . . How's the family?

SHELDRAKE You don't want to hear nice things from me,
do you?

FRAN Yeah, I think it's terrific. You do it better than
anyone I know. What'd you have in mind?

SHELDRAKE You know I haven't worked all day just
thinking about you?

FRAN (*She puts her cigarette out, looking down without
emotion*) Well, it's always a little slow before Christmas—

SHELDRAKE (*He grabs her wrist*) Damn it, Fran, look at
me.

FRAN (*She snaps back quickly*) How do you want me to

react, with a chill and a quiver? . . . I did that all summer. And the phone still didn't ring Tuesday night.

SHELDRAKE   Fran, you know neither one of us wanted it to go this far . . . That first night we did nothing but sit here and talk until two in the morning . . .

FRAN   Yeah, just a couple of innocent kids.

SHELDRAKE   What is there about you that makes everything I say so damned phony?

FRAN (*She shrugs*)   Everything you say. Hey, no kidding, Mr. Sheldrake, why did you call me? What do you want?

SHELDRAKE   To look at you . . . to talk to you . . . to see if I can get things started again.

FRAN   Well, that's honest enough . . . Sorry. Next summer I'm going to camp.

SHELDRAKE   It's only November, maybe I can talk you out of it. Fran, I want you back. I don't want to go another day without seeing you.

FRAN   You've already arranged that. Hostess in the Executive Dining Room. I've gone from "I love you, Fran" to "How are the scallops today?" in two short months.

SHELDRAKE   If you really believe that, Fran, get up and walk out that door right now. I swear, I'll never bother you again . . . Otherwise, sit there and be quiet and listen to me. Because I have something to tell you.

FRAN (*Shrugs*)   Go ahead and tell me. I'm just smoking and drinking.

SHELDRAKE   Damnit, I can't talk here. Can't we go someplace?

FRAN   No. I have a date at nine.

SHELDRAKE   Oh? Important?

FRAN Not very. But I'm going anyway.
      (*The* WAITER *approaches.* FRAN *takes out a compact and fixes her face*)

WAITER You like to order dinner now?

FRAN No. No dinner.

SHELDRAKE Bring us two more drinks.

FRAN No more drinks either.

WAITER Very good. That's no dinner and no more drinks.
      (*He leaves.* FRAN *fixes her hair in the compact's mirror*)

SHELDRAKE I see you still use my birthday present.

FRAN Don't I get to keep it?

SHELDRAKE (*Smiles*) You've got that same petulant look on your face. You had it that first night in Atlantic City.

FRAN Stop it, Jeff . . . Hey, could I have another cigarette? I don't know what to do with my hands.

SHELDRAKE (*Getting up*) I'll get a pack. I have to make a call anyway.

FRAN Do you need change? It's twenty cents to White Plains. (SHELDRAKE *looks at her. There's no point in answering that. He walks off.* FRAN *sits there alone. She picks the compact up from the table and looks at herself*) You know what you would do now if you were smart, don't you? (*She sings "Knowing When to Leave"*)

> Go while the going is good
> Knowing when to leave
> May be the smartest thing
> That anyone can learn.
> Go—
> I'm afraid my heart
> Isn't very smart
>
> Fly while you still have your wings.
> Knowing when to leave
> Won't ever let you reach

The point of no return.
Fly—foolish as it seems
I still have my dreams

So I keep hoping, day after day,
As I wait for the man I need
Night after night
As I wish for a love that can be
Though I'm sure that
No one can tell
Where their wishes and hopes will lead
Somehow I feel
There is happiness just waiting there for me.

When someone walks in your life
You just better be sure he's right
'Cause if he's wrong
There are heartaches and tears you must pay.
Keep both of your eyes on the door
Never let it get out of sight
Just be prepared
When the time has come for you to run away.
Sail when the wind starts to blow.
But like a fool I don't know when to leave . . .

> (*The lights fade on* FRAN *and the Chinese res-*
> *taurant, although the set stays on. As the lights*
> *go up on the right we see* CHUCK *waiting under a*
> *sign that says "The New Madison Square Gar-*
> *den"*)

CHUCK (*Looks at his watch*) She's probably having trouble getting crosstown . . . Gee, it must be rough on her trying to get rid of this other fella . . . In a way I feel sorry for the poor guy . . . (*He goes behind a poster looking for her again. The lights go up on* FRAN *as she sings*)

> . . . So I keep hoping day after day
> As I wait for the man I need
> Night after night
> As I wish for a love that can be
> Though I'm sure that
> No one can tell
> Where their wishes and hopes will lead
> Somehow I feel
> There is happiness just waiting there for me.

When someone walks in your life
You just better be sure he's right
'Cause if he's wrong
There are heartaches and tears you must pay.
Keep both of your eyes on the door
Never let it get out of sight
Just be prepared
When the time has come for you to run away.

Sail when the wind starts to blow.
But like a fool I don't know
When to leave—when to leave—when to leave
When to leave.

    (*The lights go up on* CHUCK)

CHUCK   Maybe I rushed her? Do you think I moved in too fast? I mean she's just a simple girl, doesn't get around much. Mostly watches basketball at home with her brother . . . Maybe a fast-talking rising young executive like me frightened her . . . Sure . . . That's it . . . (*Looks at his watch*) That's why it's ten-to-eleven . . .
    (*The lights go up on* SHELDRAKE *and* FRAN)

SHELDRAKE   (*Returning from his call*) Tommy's got a cold . . . nothing serious.

FRAN   Good. I'm glad everything's all right at home.

SHELDRAKE   You know it isn't, Fran. And it hasn't been for a long time. Remember what we talked about? My getting a divorce?

FRAN   We didn't talk about it, Jeff. You did.

SHELDRAKE   I called my lawyer this morning. I'm going through with it, Fran.

FRAN   Jeff, let's get something straight. I never asked you to leave your wife.

SHELDRAKE   It's my decision. It's what I want.

FRAN   Are you sure?

SHELDRAKE   I'm sure. If you'll just tell me you still love me.

FRAN   You know I do.

SHELDRAKE   (*Smiles*)   I never doubted it for a minute. Come on.

FRAN   Wait a minute. I had a date.

SHELDRAKE   You said yourself it wasn't important. (*He kisses her*) Come on.
   (*They exit. The lights go up on* CHUCK)

CHUCK   Maybe she caught my cold. Sure, I bet she's in bed as I'm standing here. So I guess I'll get the papers and go home. After all, I'm sure she tried. (*A* WATCHMAN *comes out and locks the door*) Who won?

WATCHMAN   Knicks lost one hundred twenty-nine to one hundred twenty-eight in double overtime . . .

CHUCK   Well, doesn't sound like we missed much . . .

Blackout

A single telephone in the lobby of Consolidated Life.
KIRKEBY *is on the phone talking in hushed tones while*
DOBITCH *paces nervously.* VANDERHOF *and* EICHELBERGER
join them.

VANDERHOF   Any luck with the kid?

DOBITCH   He won't budge. No key, no apartment, no
nothing. And the louse still has a box of my cheese
crackers.

VANDERHOF   That rotten kid is using his apartment for
his own selfish needs.

EICHELBERGER   Oh, my God, no apartment! What'll we
do?

DOBITCH   Will you stop panicking, you dirty old man.

VANDERHOF   I'd use my car but the nurse is five-foot-ten
and it's a Volkswagen.
         (KIRKEBY *comes out of the booth*)

KIRKEBY   Forget it. I just spoke to Hertz and they don't
rent trailers for the night.

VANDERHOF   Listen, I have a friend who has a liquor
store with a cot in the back. We can have it Sundays and
Election Day.

EICHELBERGER   But tonight was supposed to be my night.
What am I going to do?

DOBITCH   Why don't you take some hot Ovaltine and go
to bed?

KIRKEBY It serves us right. Never trust an ambitious kid with a one-bedroom apartment.

EICHELBERGER There must be somewhere, someplace— (*The music to "Where Can You Take a Girl?" begins*)

DOBITCH Where? Where? (*He sings*)

Where can you if you're a man
Take a girl if she's a girl
That you can't
Can't ever take home for a little drink
Like other guys who live alone can do?
That is the reason why
Most married men are true.

Aside from hotels
Where can you on Tuesday night
Take a girl who's out of sight
That you can't
Can't ever take home for a little fun
Chase her around the room until you win?
That is the reason why
Most single men stay thin.

Aside from motels
Where can you if you're alone
Take a girl who's on her own
That you can't
Can't ever take home on your one night out
One night to be a man and not a mouse?
Most married men play cards
Most single men play house
We'd like to play house too.

All we need is one place
A small apartment, a truck or trailer, old or new
Oh there must be some place
A baby carriage, a kiddy car will do
We aren't proud.
Where can you take a girl that you just
Can't take home?

(*The set changes to the Executive Dining Room*)

You know, if it were a little warmer I'd even take Sylvia
to Central Park.

VANDERHOF   And take a chance of being mugged?

DOBITCH   Nahh, she's a very nice girl. (*Singing*)

Where can you if you are free
Take a girl you'd like to see
That you can't
Can't ever take home on a weekday night
Put on some records and then go berserk?
Most single men we know
Work hardest after work.

Aside from rowboats
Where can you, a man that's true
Take a girl who gets to you
That you can't can't ever take home for a little whirl
Dance her around so fast she starts to shout?
Most married men just waltz
Most single men make out
We'd like to make out too.

All we need is one place
For sixty minutes or forty minutes more or less
Oh there must be some place
In twenty minutes we'll find happiness
We can be fast
In fact we always are.

Aside from rooftops
Where can you if you are free
Take a girl you'd like to see
That you can't ever take home?
What's there left to do
But to go home to
Our wives!

(*At the conclusion of the number,* CHUCK *enters
the room gaily. He is dressed a lot better now that
he is a Junior Executive. He crosses to his "usual"
table near the window, sits and looks at the menu.
He nods at the "boys" and gives them a little
wave with his fingers, then looks back at the menu.
They mumble obscenities under their breath*)

Look at him, calm, well-rested, the little fink.

> (FRAN *enters from the kitchen, wearing a pert hostess uniform. She carries a glass of sherry on a serving dish. She crosses to* CHUCK)

FRAN   Good afternoon, Mr. Baxter.
(*She puts down the drink*)

CHUCK   Oh, hello.

FRAN   A dry sherry before lunch, isn't it?

CHUCK   Yes. You have a wonderful memory.

FRAN   Not for some things.

CHUCK   Oh, you mean the basketball game? I've forgotten about that. I told you yesterday.

FRAN   You didn't wait outside all night, did you?

CHUCK   No . . . just about fifteen minutes, then I went in. It was a terrific game.

FRAN   I had no excuse.

CHUCK   Well, that's plenty good enough for me. After all, I'm sure you couldn't help yourself . . . How's the chicken pot pie?

FRAN   You shouldn't be so understanding. I'm not worth it.

CHUCK   Miss Kubelik, one doesn't get to be a Junior Second Administrative Assistant around here unless he's a pretty good judge of character . . . and as far as I'm concerned, you're tops. I mean decency-wise and other-wise-wise.

FRAN   Will that be all?

CHUCK   That'll be all . . . unless you're not busy Thursday night? I'm usually free on Thursdays.

FRAN   I'm usually not.

CHUCK (*Smiles*) Then I guess that'll be all. (*To the audience*) Cheers. (*The* FOUR EXECS *approach*) I know. I see them.

> (FRAN *nods and exits into the kitchen as the* FOUR EXECS *surround* CHUCK *at his table*)

DOBITCH Dry sherry dry enough for you, kid?

VANDERHOF Nice big table all for yourself.

KIRKEBY Hot food, warm plates, clean silverware.

EICHELBERGER This is the life, heh, Chuck, boy?

CHUCK (*Smiles*) Well, I'm not without contentment, no.

> (*He sips his sherry*)

DOBITCH You've got it all now, Baxter. Success . . . accomplishment . . . security . . .

VANDERHOF But there's one thing missing, kid.

CHUCK What's that?

KIRKEBY Gratitude. We don't see any gratitude, do we, boys?

> (*They all shake their heads "no"*)

CHUCK Well, I certainly don't want to seem ungrateful . . . How about four chicken pot pies?

> (*They gather around him*)

VANDERHOF Don't play with us, kid. Don't toy with angry middle-aged executives.

CHUCK Look, fellas, for your information, my apartment is private property, not a public playground. I don't understand what happens to men when they get to be your age.

DOBITCH Don't understand us. Help us!

> (*The* FOUR EXECS *sing*)

All we need is one place
For sixty minutes or forty minutes
More or less
Oh, there must be some place
In twenty minutes we'll find happiness
We can be fast
Where can you take a girl
That you just can't take home

(*They exit, singing*)

Where can you, if you're a man
Take a girl, if she's a girl . . .

(*The lights black out, leaving a spot on* CHUCK, *who steps out front to the audience*)

CHUCK In a way I sympathized with them. As middle-aged men they wanted to have occasionally what they thought young men like me have regularly. But I wasn't having it regularly. As a matter of fact, I wasn't even having what they have occasionally . . . it's something for you to think about. (*He crosses to* SHELDRAKE, *who is reclining on a sun deck chaise*) Oh, Mr. Sheldrake . . . they told me I'd find you here on the Executive Sun Deck.

SHELDRAKE Am I getting too red?

CHUCK Not for me, J.D. You have the kind of skin that bronzes nicely.

SHELDRAKE You've got your promotion. Don't butter me. I like you, Baxter, but let's understand each other. We may have a reciprocal arrangement that fulfills certain mutual needs, but in no way does it mean we're bosom buddies. I'm starting you on the very lowest rung of the executive ladder but you'll have to climb upward on your own initiative. I may have a private life to lead but I also have a department to run.

CHUCK Well, may I say you lead them and run them beautifully, sir. I just dropped up because I have something here I think belongs to you.
(*He reaches in his pocket*)

SHELDRAKE (*Puts down his reflector*) To me?

CHUCK I mean the young lady, whoever she may be. It was on the couch when I got home last night. It's a compact. (*He takes out* FRAN's *gold compact*) I'm afraid the mirror is broken.

SHELDRAKE I know. She threw it at me. Fortunately I ducked. Was thére any damage?
(*He takes the compact*)

CHUCK Oh, nothing much. A little hole in an old Van Gogh print on the wall. Luckily it went right through the sunset. (*Reaches in his pocket*) I have all the broken pieces of the mirror in my pocket if you care to put them together . . .

SHELDRAKE You know, Baxter, I envy you.

CHUCK Me? Why?

SHELDRAKE Your life is simple. A bachelor who can have an affair with no complications, no promises made that you can't possibly keep. You've got it made, right?

CHUCK If you say so, sir. (*He turns to the audience*) Why is it everyone envies me except me?
(CHUCK *exits.* SHELDRAKE *turns and looks out over the sun deck, then takes* FRAN's *mirror out of his pocket and looks at it. He sings "Wanting Things"*)

Tell me how long must I keep wanting things
Needing things, when I have so much?
There are many men who have much less than me
Day by day they make their way
And they find more in life than I can see.
Tell me

When will I learn to resist wanting things
Touching things that say
Do, do not touch.
People that I meet seem to think I am strong
They don't see inside of me
So they don't know I'm weak and often wrong.

Tell me why must I keep wanting things
Needing things that just can't be mine.
Oh wanting things that just can't be
Mine.

(He exits)

Blackout

The COMEDY
of Neil Simon

Outside the elevator. FRAN *appears and looks around.* MISS OLSON *comes out of an elevator, somewhat tipsy, holding a paper cup full of liquor.*

FRAN   Excuse me, can you tell me where the Christmas party is?

MISS OLSON (*Points up*)   One floor down.

FRAN (*Smiles*)   Thank you.
(*She starts to walk away*)

MISS OLSON   Hey, aren't you the branch manager from Kansas City?

FRAN   I beg your pardon.

MISS OLSON   I'm Miss Olson, Mr. Sheldrake's secretary.

FRAN   Yes, I know.

MISS OLSON   Four years ago I was the branch manager from Minneapolis.

FRAN   I'm sorry, I don't understand—

MISS OLSON   I know what you're going through, honey. I got the same routine, from a weekend in Atlantic City right through to Chinese food.

FRAN   I'm afraid I don't know what you're talking about.
(*She starts to turn away*)

MISS OLSON   Oh, come on, sugar, I know all about it. I'm very perceptive . . . and I also listen in on his telephone calls. (*She rocks a bit*) . . . You know I never drank before I met Jeff. I smoke now too . . . and I put on twelve pounds . . . Which is why I now smoke and drink and you're the new branch manager from Kansas City.

FRAN Miss Olson, if you'll excuse me . . .

MISS OLSON It's all right, honey, you're in good company. He only picks the cutest girls. Miss Rossi in Auditing, Miss Koch in Disability, Miss Della Hoya from Petty Cash—we thought we'd meet once a year for lunch at Schrafft's. When we get two more girls we're going to charter a boat ride to Bear Mountain.

FRAN Miss Olson, I don't know what you've heard, but I can assure you—

MISS OLSON What a salesman. If our affair lasted two more days I would have bought insurance from him. But you'll buy it too, sweetie. The same pitch about divorcing his wife, only by the time the papers come through, you'll be telling some cute receptionist what I'm telling you . . .
     (She raises her hand)

FRAN I'm sure you mean well, Miss Olson—

MISS OLSON (Shrugs) Some people give to the Heart Fund, I warn girls about Sheldrake . . . You want to be smart, honey? Take the compact he bought you that I picked out, trade it in for a pair of track shoes and run for your life. (Looks in her cup) Excuse me, my stupor is wearing off. I've got to re-stupe.

                    Blackout

The nineteenth floor. The floor is decked out in
Christmas trimming, the desks are all pushed together for
"Turkey Lurkey." DOBITCH *stands on a desk.*

DOBITCH And now, ladies and gentlemen, the Christmas
Party Committee has asked the Idea Committee to come
up with an idea for the Christmas Party. So without
further ado, I give you Miss Polansky of Accounts Re-
ceivable, Miss Wong of Mimeograph, and Miss Della
Hoya of Petty Cash.

(*They sing*)

It's Turkey Lurkey time
Tom Turkey ran away but he just came home.
It's Turkey Lurkey time
He's really come to stay never more to roam.
Let us make a wish
And may all your wishes come true.
A snowy blowy Christmas
A mistletoey Christmas
A Turkey Lurkey Christmas to you
A Turkey Lurkey Christmas to you.

It's Goosey Poosey time
She was a gadabout but she's back again.
It's Goosey Poosey time
Her time is running out and we all know when.
Let us make a wish
And may all your wishes come true.
A snowy blowy Christmas
A mistletoey Christmas
A Goosey Poosey Christmas to you
A Goosey Poosey Christmas to you.

Turkey Lurkey
Goosey Poosey

Some for Uncle Joe
And some for Cousin Lucy.
Everybody gather round the table
Dig in, dinner's being served
Eat all the turkey you are able
If you see a partridge in a pear tree
Climb up and bring it down for me
That's something I would like to see.

(*They dance a wild dance, urged on, and later joined by, all the employees. When the dance is over the girls again sing*)

A snowy blowy Christmas
A mistletoey Christmas
A Turkey Lurkey Christmas
To you-ou-ou.

Jingle Bells, Jingle Bells,
Jingle Bells, Jingle Bells,
Merry Christmas,
Merry Christmas.

DOBITCH   Listen, kid, did you get my note? I meant what I said. The keys to my Jaguar and my Diners Club card for the entire Christmas holidays.

CHUCK   Yeah, sure, Mr. Dobitch, anything you want. You just caught me at the right season.

DOBITCH   Good. You leave the keys under the doormat. I'll be there at four o'clock.

CHUCK   Hey, you didn't see Miss Kubelik around here, did you? (*She appears on the opposite side of the stage*) Never mind, I just felt her presence. (*He crosses to* FRAN, *who is glum*) Hi. Glad you could make it up to the nineteenth floor. I hear the eighteenth floor's already been arrested. (*He laughs*) Can I get you a drink?

FRAN (*Downhearted*)   No thanks.

CHUCK   Is anything wrong?

FRAN No, there are just too many people here.

CHUCK Funny how we're beginning to think alike. (*Takes her arm*) Miss Kubelik, I would like to show you something. (*They cross to the desk, where a couple is necking*) Ahem. (*The couple exits quickly*) Boy, are they drunk. Those two are married to each other. (*He takes a box from the desk drawer*) Miss Kubelik, I want your honest opinion. I've had this in my desk for a week. (*He shows her the hat*) Cost me twenty-three bucks, but I just couldn't get the nerve up to wear it. (*Puts on a gray homburg*) It's called "Young Exec" . . . comes with a free subscription to the *Wall Street Journal* . . . Remember, an honest opinion. (*He poses; she looks dumbly*) All right, I'll accept a dishonest opinion . . . You hate it. I look like Sidney Greenstreet in "The Maltese Falcon" . . . I agree. Well, there's a doctor in my building I owe a Christmas present . . .

FRAN No, I like it. Very distinguished.

CHUCK Really? Classy Distinguished or Trying Distinguished? I mean I don't want to get an Al Capone effect.

FRAN I like the way you look. I really do.

CHUCK How about that? Listen, maybe I'll try it out this afternoon on Fifth Avenue. I sure could use some moral support.

FRAN Oh . . . This is a bad day for me.

CHUCK I understand. Christmas, family and all that . . .

FRAN Well, I'd better get back to the Dining Room. They must be wondering where I am.

CHUCK Hey, you sure you like the hat? I mean, is the angle good for my face?

FRAN I think so. Here, look for yourself.
(*She takes out her compact and gives it to him*)

CHUCK After all, this is a conservative firm. I wouldn't want people to think I was a ward heeler or something . . .
> *(As he looks in the compact mirror his voice gives out. FRAN notices his peculiar expression)*

FRAN What's wrong?

CHUCK The mirror . . . it's broken.

FRAN I know. I like it this way . . . makes me look the way I feel. *(The phone rings. CHUCK doesn't hear it. He closes the compact, hands it back to FRAN)* . . . Your phone.

CHUCK Oh. *(He picks up the phone)* Yes? *(Throws a quick look at FRAN)* Just a minute. *(He covers the phone with his hand and speaks to FRAN)* If you don't mind, this is sort of personal.

FRAN All right. Have a nice Christmas.
> *(CHUCK nods. She exits. CHUCK takes his hand off the mouthpiece)*

CHUCK *(Every word hurts)* Yes, Mr. Sheldrake . . . No, I didn't forget . . . the tree is up and the Tom and Jerry mix is in the refrigerator . . . Yes, sir, the same to you.
> *(He hangs up and stands there for a moment, the new hat still on his head. He sits on the desk chair)*

Curtain

Act Two

SCENE 1

CHUCK *is sitting at a booth in Clancy's Lounge, a seedy Eighth Avenue bar. He looks up at the audience, obviously drunk.*

CHUCK I'd rather not talk about it if you don't mind . . . Just look at me . . . in some seedy bar . . . God knows where . . . cheaping up slop whiskey . . . slopping up cheap whiskey . . . I disgust me . . . I mean what did I expect? That she was some kind of pure, untouched, unblemished rose just waiting for me to come along? . . . Yes, that's what I expected . . . Listen, I don't want to talk to you any more . . . I'll call you next week . . . (*He crosses to the bar and* BARTENDER EUGENE. *He puts money on the bar*) Eugene, Eugene, I'd like twenty-two dollars' worth of cheering up.

(BARTENDER EUGENE *pours him a shot.* MARGE *crosses to* CHUCK *with her empty glass*)

MARGE (*Warm smile*) Hello, there. All alone I see.

CHUCK (*He looks at* MARGE, *then at the audience*) I think I'm gonna be all right. (*To* MARGE) Hello there yourself.

MARGE As it happens, I'm alone too.

CHUCK As what happens?

MARGE Ooh, fast with the repartee, aren't you? In point of fact, I'm just trying to be friendly. I mean the world is hostile enough, isn't it?

CHUCK Everywhere you turn.

MARGE And your name is?—

CHUCK (*Lifts his hat*) Baxter. C. C. Baxter.
(*He drops the hat back on his head*)

MARGE Ohh, initials. That's very fancy . . . I'm just plain Margie MacDougall.

CHUCK (*Looks her up and down*) I don't see anything plain about you, Margie.

MARGE Oh, touché! . . . (*She looks at her empty glass*) My goodness, have I finished that stinger already?

CHUCK (*To* BARTENDER EUGENE) Eugene, another stinger. Here.

MARGE Oh, isn't that sweet? That really isn't necessary. (*Quickly to* BARTENDER EUGENE) Double on the vodka, Eugene. (*To* CHUCK) By the by, before we go any further, I wouldn't want you to get the wrong idea about me. I'm *not* a pickup.

CHUCK Never crossed my mind.

MARGE Sociable maybe, but not a pickup . . . I'm just looking for a drink and some friendly conversation, that's all.

CHUCK Got you, Marge.

MARGE I mean I have no intention of going *any*where with *any*one for *any*thing.

CHUCK Good girl, Marge.

MARGE Why, do you have a place near here? . . . That's conversation, not curiosity. As I said, I'm not a pickup.

CHUCK Anyone could tell from the way you dress . . . Très chic.

MARGE (*Flattered*) Oh, gracias . . . You like this coat? It's owl. I actually swear on my mother's life, it's made from those birds with the big eyes that see in the dark and go "Hoo." A gift from my late husband, Jerome.

CHUCK Oh, a widow.

MARGE (*Takes a drink*) Well, I'm not dead certain I'm a widow, but when you don't hear from your husband in twenty-two months there's no point in keeping the roast warm. Sköl!
(*She drinks her vodka stinger*)

CHUCK Two years is a long time to be lonely.

MARGE I don't recall saying I was lonely. Have I indicated to you in any way whatever that I was lonely? Indeed not. So don't be getting any fancy ideas in that rather attractive head of yours.

CHUCK So you find me attractive, eh, Marge?

MARGE You catch everything, don't you . . . I don't mean to imply attractive in any sexual way. Nor do I wish to imply that you are *un*attractive in a sexual way . . . What I *do* want to imply is that I'm not thinking in a sexual way at all. Not to imply that I've *never* thought in a sexual way. But I am, technically speaking, still in a state of mourning. So can we just drop the subject of sex, Mr. Fast-on-your-feet?

CHUCK How's your stinger?

MARGE You *are* persuasive, aren't you? (*She hands her glass to* BARTENDER EUGENE *for a refill*) Question. You married?

CHUCK Answer. No!

MARGE Family?

CHUCK In Ohio.

MARGE Mm. A night like this, Christmas Eve and all, it's not much fun walking into an empty apartment, is it?

CHUCK I said I wasn't married. I didn't say I had an empty apartment.

MARGE It wouldn't make any difference because I have no intention of going there, as I previously indicated . . . So just get it right out of your mind, Mr. C. C. Baxter with the sweet-smelling after-shave cologne that just happens to be my favorite.

CHUCK You like Aqua Velva?

MARGE Oh, yes. Jerome used it by the gallon. He was quite masculine, you know. Used to shave three, four times a day.

CHUCK Boy . . . They don't make 'em like that any more.

MARGE I didn't mean to imply that you're *not* masculine. In your own off-beat way, I suppose you are. I mean with the light behind you and your chapeau at that jaunty angle, you remind me somewhat of Jerome, if I remember him correctly.

CHUCK —But Jerome isn't here.

MARGE (*She nods in agreement*) But Jerome isn't here.

CHUCK And "rather attractive" me is.

MARGE (*Nods*) And rather attractive you is.

CHUCK Those are facts we've got to face, Marge.

MARGE Well, you're definitely a fact . . . (*She sings*)
And a fact can be a beautiful thing
When the fact I am facing is you.

CHUCK (*Singing*)
A fact can be a terrible thing
When the dreams you've been dreaming fall through.

CHUCK *and* MARGE
Forget the past and think about the present
Right now is everything.
Forget the past and think about the present,

CHUCK
>   The present's very pleasant.

CHUCK *and* MARGE
>   Who cares what the future will bring?
>   There's just no predicting a thing.
>   Don't wait for a miracle
>   Because it's Christmas
>   Not a time to be alone with memories.
>   Christmas is supposed to be a happy holiday
>   Throw a little joy my way,

MARGE
>   You could really make my day,

CHUCK
>   Throw a little joy my way,

MARGE
>   And a fact can be a beautiful thing
>   When I can see what I'm seeing in you.

CHUCK
>   A fact can be a wonderful thing
>   When your hopes to be happy come true.

CHUCK *and* MARGE
>   What's gone is gone and don't you ever doubt it,
>   Wake up and start to live.
>   What's gone is gone so learn to live without it

CHUCK
>   And never think about it.

CHUCK AND MARGE
>   Who cares what the future will bring?
>   There's just no predicting a thing.
>   Don't wait for a miracle
>   Because it's Christmas
>   Not a time to be alone with memories.
>   Christmas is supposed to be a happy holiday
>   Throw a little joy my way.

MARGE
>   Do we really have to stay?

Throw a little joy my way . . .

(They start out, but are stopped by the singing of the PATRONS *and employees, who insist on having a drink with them)*

ALL

Forget the past and think about the present
Right now is everything.
Forget the past and think about the present,
The present's very pleasant.
Who cares what the future will bring?
There's just no predicting a thing.
Don't wait for a miracle
Because it's Christmas
Not the time to be alone with memories.
Christmas
Is supposed to be a happy holiday
Throw a little joy my way.

(An accidental rhythm occurs, caused by noises of a tray, two whiskey bottles, a laugh. CHUCK *improvises a dance step to the rhythm. The others join in, till all are dancing the Game, including a first-reluctant* MARGE)

Because it's Christmas
Just the perfect night
For us to dance and sing.
Christmas
Is supposed to be a happy holiday
Happy holiday
So throw a little joy my way.

*(*CHUCK *and* MARGE *exit. The* PATRONS *dance in couples and sing)*

Forget the past and think about the present
Right now is everything.
Forget the past and think about the present,
The present's very pleasant.
Who cares what the future will bring?
There's just no predicting a thing . . .

Blackout

CHUCK's *apartment. The living room is dark, except for a shaft of light from the kitchen, and the glow of the colored bulbs on a small Christmas tree in front of the phony fireplace.*

Hunched up in one corner of the couch is FRAN, *still in her coat and gloves, crying softly. Pacing up and down is* SHELDRAKE. *His coat and hat are on the chair, as are several Christmas packages. On the coffee table are an unopened bottle of Scotch, a couple of untouched glasses and a bowl of melting ice.*

SHELDRAKE (*Looking very upset as* FRAN *cries*) Come on, Fran, don't be like that. You just going to sit there, crying? (*No answer. He tries a new approach*) Look, I know you think I'm stalling you. But when you've been married to a woman for twelve years, you don't just sit down at the breakfast table and say, "Helen, can I please have the sugar and a divorce." (*He resumes pacing,* FRAN *keeps sobbing*) Anyway, this is the wrong time. The kids are home from school, the in-laws are visiting for the holidays. I can't bring it up *now*. (*Stops*) For God's sake, Fran, are you going to listen to me or are you going to keep crying?

FRAN (*Sobs*) I can do both.

SHELDRAKE You know, this isn't like you, Fran. You were always such a good sport, such fun to be with.

FRAN That's me, the Happy Idiot. Short on brains but a million laughs.

SHELDRAKE I didn't mean it that way . . .

FRAN It's true. I laugh easily. I even got a big chuckle

today out of your secretary, Miss Olson. You remember her, the branch manager from Minneapolis?

SHELDRAKE Is that what's bothering you? Miss Olson? For God's sakes, Fran, that's ancient history.

FRAN Well, she brought me up with more current events . . . like Miss Koch, Miss Rossi, Miss Della Hoya . . . How do you work it, Jeff, alphabetical order or one floor at a time?

SHELDRAKE Oh, come on, Fran . . .

FRAN It must have been rough when they switched to automatic elevators. All those cute little operators going to waste—

SHELDRAKE All right, Fran, I suppose I deserved that.

FRAN Try *definitely*.

SHELDRAKE Damnit, don't you understand that no one —*no one* means anything to me any more except you? Fran, I don't like to see you like this.

FRAN (*She takes a handkerchief from her purse*) Did I tell you I'm writing a book? *Affairs Can Be Fun.* (*Wipes her eyes*) Chapter One, Never Wear Mascara When You're in Love with a Married Man.

SHELDRAKE It's Christmas Eve, Fran. Let's not fight.

FRAN Merry Christmas.
        (*She throws a package to him*)

SHELDRAKE What is it?

FRAN A scarf. I knitted it the six nights a week I don't see you.

SHELDRAKE Fran, if it were possible I would *never* leave . . .

FRAN (*She takes out a small leather frame from her*

purse) And I had that picture we took on the boardwalk framed. I bought it as a gift from you to me. I know you don't have much time to do any shopping . . .

SHELDRAKE As a matter of fact, I wanted to get you something . . . But you never know who you run into in department stores . . . (*He takes out a money clip, detaches a bill*) . . . so here's a hundred dollars . . . go out and buy yourself something. (*He holds the money out but she doesn't move.* SHELDRAKE *slips the bill into her open bag*) . . . They have some nice alligator bags at Bergdorf's . . . (FRAN *gets up and slowly starts peeling off her gloves.* SHELDRAKE *looks at her, then nervously glances at his watch*) . . . Fran, it's a quarter to seven—and I mustn't miss the train tonight—if we hadn't wasted all that time—well, I have to get home and trim the tree . . .

FRAN (*Having started to remove her coat*) Oh. Okay. (*She shrugs, puts her coat back on*) I just thought as long as it was paid for—

SHELDRAKE (*He takes an angry step toward her*) Don't ever talk like that, Fran. Don't make yourself out to be cheap.

FRAN A hundred dollars? I wouldn't call that cheap. And you must be paying someone for the use of the apartment—

SHELDRAKE Fran, the last thing I want to do is to hurt you.

FRAN (*She stares at him*) You'll miss your train, Jeff.
      (SHELDRAKE *releases her, then hurriedly puts on
      his hat and coat, and gathers up his packages*)

SHELDRAKE Are you coming?

FRAN You run along—I want to fix what's left of my face.

SHELDRAKE (*Nods*) Don't forget to kill the lights . . . I'll see you next week.

FRAN (*With bite*) I have it marked on my calendar. I draw a little heart around all the Thursdays.

SHELDRAKE It won't always be like this, Fran . . . I love you, you know.

FRAN I never doubted it for a minute. (*He bends to kiss her; she pulls away*) Careful . . . lipstick.
　　(*He kisses her cheek, looks at her uncomfortably, and then goes, closing the door behind him. Music begins.* FRAN *crosses back to the sofa and sits a moment, then picks up the photograph she has placed down and looks at it. . . . She sings "Whoever You Are"*)

Sometimes your eyes look blue to me
Although I know they're really green.
I seem to see you differently
Changing as I'm treated kindly
Or treated meanly.
From moment to moment
You're two different people
Faithful and warm when I'm in your arms
And then when you leave, you're so untrue, but
However you are, deep down whatever you are
Whoever you are, I love you.

Sometimes I feel you're mine alone
And yet I'm sure it's just not so.
I get this feeling on my own
After I learn if you're staying
Or if you're going.
From moment to moment
You're two different people
Someone I know as the man I love
Or the man I wish I never knew, but

However you are
Deep down whatever you are
Whoever you are, I love you.

Sometimes your eyes look blue to me.

　　(*After the song, she suddenly starts to sob, then crosses to the bed. She takes a Kleenex and starts wiping off her mascara. Then she notices a vial*) *of pills on the table. She takes it. Then she sits back and stares at it. The lights in the apartment dim and go to black. Outside in the vestibule we see* CHUCK *and* MARGE)

CHUCK   Just five more steps to Paradise.

MARGE   I still haven't made up my mind if I'm going in there. I mean, can I trust you?

CHUCK   Not for a minute, Marge.

MARGE   Well, I guess a girl can't get hurt in a minute, can she? (*She laughs, then staggers*) Whoops . . . Don't push.

CHUCK   Hey, Marge, are you all right?

MARGE   So they tell me . . . Oh, heavens, you must think I'm awful.

CHUCK   (*Grins*) I think you're peachy.

MARGE   Oh, you're a smooth talker . . . I can see I'm going to have my hands full with you, Mr. Ready-for-Everything.

CHUCK   An apt description, Mrs. MacDougall. (*He opens the door*) Enter. (*Switches on the light*) Like it?

MARGE   (*Looks around*) Well, I'm not looking to rent it. (CHUCK *closes the door*) Just the one room, is it?

CHUCK   And there's a bed back there, in case you were wondering.

MARGE   One more remark like that and I'm going to ask you to leave the door ajar.

CHUCK   May I take your owl?

MARGE   Hoo! Not wasting any time, are you?

CHUCK   Not preliminary-wise. (*He takes her coat off*) You beginning to get the feeling, Mrs. MacDougall, you are in the clutches of a raving sex-pot?

MARGE I may as well warn you now, erotic language doesn't arouse me . . . So don't be so sure of yourself.

CHUCK I'm as cute as the dickens and you know it . . . You are looking at the only male rape victim in this neighborhood.

MARGE (*Smiles*) That's adorable. You are not totally without charm.

CHUCK And I haven't started yet. (*He crosses to the phonograph*) Why don't you bat those big blue eyes at the refrigerator and melt some ice, while I put on my theme song.

MARGE I wish you'd stop being so attractive. I'm beginning to think wicked thoughts.
(*She gives him a flutter of her eyes and goes into the kitchen.* CHUCK *takes off his hat and tosses it on a chair. He skips to the door and bolts it. He rubs his hands eagerly, then notices* FRAN's *bag on the coffee table. He takes it over to the screened area and tosses it over and onto the bed. He starts away when he realizes what he has just seen. He pushes the screen back revealing* FRAN *in the bed. She is still dressed but appears to be in a deep sleep, almost lifeless.* CHUCK, *annoyed, shakes her*)

CHUCK All right, Miss Kubelik, get up . . . It's past checkout time and the hotel management would appreciate it if you would check out! *Now!* (FRAN *doesn't stir*) Look, Miss Kubelik, I used to like you. I used to like you a lot—but it's all over between us—so beat it! O-U-T! *Out!* (*No reaction. He puts a hand on her shoulder and shakes her more vigorously*) Come on, wake up! You wanna sleep, go home! (*She doesn't respond. He notices something in her fist. He opens it and removes the vial which contained the sleeping pills, now empty. He shakes it upside down*) Oh, my God! (*For a second he is paralyzed. Then he drops the vial and grabs* FRAN, *and shakes her violently*) Miss Kubelik!! *Miss Kubelik!!* (FRAN's *head drops to one side like a rag doll.* CHUCK *lets go of her, then dashes into the living room. He rushes to the phone and dials quickly. He speaks into the phone*) Hello, operator, get me the police.

(*Thinks about that*) No! . . . No, don't get me the police.
    (MARGE *comes out of the kitchen with a bowlful of ice cubes*)

MARGE   Your ice cube tray isn't cooperating at all. You really ought to get a new refrigerator. (CHUCK *ignores her and runs out of the apartment*) . . . Hey, I didn't mean *right now!*
    (*She shrugs and goes back into the kitchen.* CHUCK, *in the vestibule, bangs on* DR. DREYFUSS's *door*)

CHUCK   Doctor Dreyfuss! Hey, Doc! (*He bangs on the door*) Come on, please, you've got to be home. (*The door opens and* DR. DREYFUSS *stands there sleepily, pulling on his bathrobe*) There's a girl in my place—she took some sleeping pills—you'd better come quick, I can't wake her up . . .

DR. DREYFUSS   Let me get my bag.
    (*He goes back into his apartment.* CHUCK *turns and goes back into his apartment as* MARGE *comes out of the kitchen holding a bottle*)

MARGE   Look what I found. Tom and Jerries. You sly dog!

CHUCK (*Takes her arm and pulls her*)   Come on. Let's go.

MARGE (*Smiling vacantly*)   Aren't we rushing things?

CHUCK   The party's over. Nothing personal.

MARGE (*Being pushed toward the door*)   I don't understand.

CHUCK   Come on.

MARGE (*Taking his arm off her*)   I'm going to ask you not to get physical.

CHUCK   It's an emergency. I'll see you some other Christmas.

MARGE (*Suddenly she hears* FRAN *moan. She looks and*

Who's that? Where did she come from? (DR.
DREYFUSS *comes in and looks at* MARGE) Who's he?

CHUCK (*To* DR. DREYFUSS) Not this one, Doc— (*Points
to the bed*) The other one!
    (DR. DREYFUSS *rushes in to* FRAN)

MARGE What's going on here? Who are these people?

CHUCK Please!

MARGE Oh, my God! *It's an orgy!*

CHUCK (*To* MARGE) Would you please go! Now!

MARGE An orgy—on Christmas Eve! It's the most disgusting thing I've ever run across.

CHUCK (*He hands her his last few dollars*) Here! Take
a taxi! Get another stinger, only please go!

MARGE (*Takes the money*) I should have known. The
minute I saw you walk in the bar with that dignified hat
I knew you were a pervert!

CHUCK Well, that's the way it is.
    (*He pushes her out in the hall and closes the
    door. She pulls her coat around her and starts out*)

MARGE Filthy, filthy perverts! (*She knocks on* DR.
DREYFUSS's *closed door and yells in*) They're having an
orgy on the second floor! . . . Oh, God, I think I'm going
to be sick!
    (*She runs out and disappears.* CHUCK *rushes back
    to* DR. DREYFUSS *who is examining* FRAN's *eyes
    with a flashlight*)

CHUCK Is she gonna be all right, Doc?

DR. DREYFUSS How many pills were in that bottle?
    (*He takes out a stomach tube from his bag*)

CHUCK Twelve. I only used one . . . Is that enough—
to do it?

DR. DREYFUSS Without even trying. Help me with her. (*They get* FRAN *into an upright position. They half-carry, half-drag* FRAN's *limp form toward the bathroom*)

CHUCK What are you going to do?

DR. DREYFUSS Get that stuff out of her stomach, if it isn't too late.
(*He takes* FRAN *himself*)

CHUCK (*Stepping back*) Oh, God . . . My God . . .

DR. DREYFUSS First put on some hot coffee . . . then you can ask your friend God for His help . . . (CHUCK *backs away as* DR. DREYFUSS *enters the bathroom with the limp* FRAN. *The lights fade. About fifteen minutes later:* DR. DREYFUSS *is placing* FRAN *on the sofa as* CHUCK *stands watching fearfully, the hot coffee pot in his hand*) Get my bag. (CHUCK *quickly gets him his bag, and looks bewildered.* DR. DREYFUSS *has taken out a needle and syringe and measures off the correct amount of c.c.'s from a medical bottle*) First put the coffee down, dummy. (CHUCK *puts down the pot.* DR. DREYFUSS *feels her arm for the right spot to inject*) Nice veins. You've seen them before, I guess.

CHUCK Huh?

DR. DREYFUSS (*He swabs a spot with alcohol and takes the hypodermic needle from* CHUCK) Want to tell me what happened?
(*He injects her arm*)

CHUCK I don't know . . . I wasn't here . . . I mean, we had some words earlier . . . nothing serious . . . what you might call a lovers' spat.

DR. DREYFUSS Some spat. Eleven pills worth.

CHUCK I didn't know she was so upset . . .

DR. DREYFUSS When did you pick up the other tootsie? *Before* she took the pills or *during*?

CHUCK I wouldn't have picked up the other one if I knew she was still here . . .

DR. DREYFUSS You know, Baxter, for a fink you got a lotta class.
  (*He starts to slap* FRAN *in the face. She moans and reacts*)

CHUCK (*Enormous relief*) Look, Doc, she's breathing . . .

DR. DREYFUSS If it annoys you, I can turn it off. (*He takes an ampule out of his bag*) A half hour later you'd have found some Christmas present. (*He breaks it under her nose. She winces*) Give me that coffee. (CHUCK *hands him the pot and mug*) Open those windows. Get some air in here. It smells from disillusionment. (CHUCK *quickly rushes to the windows, pulls up the shades and opens the windows wide.* DR. DREYFUSS *pours coffee into a mug and then tries to get* FRAN *to sip some. She coughs*) What's her name?

CHUCK Fran, Kubelik.
  (*He crosses back to them*)

DR. DREYFUSS Fran, I'm a doctor. I'm here because you took too many sleeping pills. Do you understand what I'm saying? (FRAN *mutters*) Come on, Fran, pay attention.
  (*He slaps her face again. She winces*)

CHUCK (*Winces too*) Doesn't that hurt her, Doc?

DR. DREYFUSS (*Scowling at him*) For deep concern, you got lousy timing. (*To* FRAN) Fran, do you know where you are? . . . Do you know whose apartment this is, Fran?

FRAN (*Sleepily*) No . . .

DR. DREYFUSS (*Pulls* CHUCK *over in front of her*) Do you know who this is, Fran? . . . Look at him!

FRAN (*Looks at him*) Mr. Baxter—

CHUCK   Hello, Miss Kubelik.

DR. DREYFUSS   Mister—Miss—pretty formal for a suicide.

CHUCK   Well, we work for the same company and we try to keep it quiet.

FRAN (*Puzzled, to* CHUCK)   What are you doing here?
   (CHUCK *looks at* DR. DREYFUSS *as if to say* "Her mind still isn't functioning")

CHUCK (*To* FRAN)   Don't you remember? We were at the office party together?

FRAN   The office party—Miss Olson—

CHUCK (*To* DR. DREYFUSS)   That's who we had the fight about—Miss Olson—you know, the other girl who just left—

DR. DREYFUSS   You ought to print programs.

FRAN (*Pushing the coffee away*)   I'm so tired. Please —just let me sleep.

DR. DREYFUSS   Not tonight, little girl. (*Shakes her*) Come on, Fran, open your eyes. You mustn't sleep now. (*To* CHUCK) All right, give me a hand. Now comes the dangerous part.

CHUCK (*Concerned*)   What do you mean, dangerous?

DR. DREYFUSS   We gotta walk her around a couple of hours. I have to be careful I don't get a heart attack. (*He lifts* FRAN *up on her feet*) All right, Fran, we're going for a nice little walk . . . all around the apartment. (CHUCK *stands there watching*) You're just going to stand there, God's gift to women?

CHUCK   What should I do?

DR. DREYFUSS   Take her other arm. In this neighborhood

I don't like to walk alone. (CHUCK *takes her other arm; they continue walking as the lights fade into a blackout. Five* A.M.: *Through the windows we can see the first faint light of dawn.* FRAN, *in her slip, is asleep on the bed.* DR. DREYFUSS *and* CHUCK, *both on the sofa, sit exhausted, their legs outstretched. Neither one seems to have the strength to speak*) If I charged you by the mile, I'd be a rich man today.

CHUCK   The color's come back to her cheeks. Don't you think she has better color?

DR. DREYFUSS (*He glances at her*)   If you happen to like green, yes.

CHUCK (*He gets up and looks at her*)   But she'll be okay, won't she?

DR. DREYFUSS   She'll sleep on and off for the next twenty-four hours. Then she'll have a headache so bad they'll complain on Sixty-fourth Street . . . This will be followed by a monumental depression because we saved her life . . . In between this there'll be constant throwing up . . . All in all, she won't make the perfect house guest . . . Hold on to the good china, I'm gonna try to stand up.
   (*He struggles to his feet*)

CHUCK   You okay?

DR. DREYFUSS   I'll have to wear braces the rest of my life. Fortunately I got a brother in surgical supplies . . . Let me have another cup of lousy coffee.

CHUCK (*He brings over the coffee*)   I don't know what I would have done without you, Doc.

DR. DREYFUSS (*Reaching in his bag*)   Probably you would have picked up a third girl and I'd be here pumping Miss Olson too. (*He takes out a pad and pen*)   How do you spell her last name?

CHUCK   Who?

DR. DREYFUSS (*Looks at him, then points to* FRAN) This one. Why, what have you got in the kitchen?

CHUCK   Oh. Kubelik . . . With two K's.
      (CHUCK *stares at him*)

DR. DREYFUSS   Where does she live?

CHUCK   You don't have to report this, do you, Doc?

DR. DREYFUSS   You ever hear of a thing called "police regulations"?

CHUCK   But she didn't mean it. It was . . . it was an accident.

DR. DREYFUSS (*Looking at him*) She tripped over the bottle and the pills fell in her mouth? What do you mean, an accident?

CHUCK   I mean, she had too much to drink . . . she didn't know what she was doing . . . there was no suicide note or anything . . . Believe me, Doc, I'm not thinking about myself . . .

DR. DREYFUSS (*Mockingly*) Perish the thought.

CHUCK   It's just that she's got a family . . . and there's the people in the office . . . the company . . . please, Doc, just look at her . . . She's really a wonderful girl . . .

DR. DREYFUSS (*He looks at* CHUCK, *then at the sleeping* FRAN) Well, as a doctor I guess I can't prove it *wasn't* an accident . . .

CHUCK   Thanks, Doc.

DR. DREYFUSS (*He closes the pad*) But as another human being, don't walk up the same staircase I'm walking down! (*He picks up his bag, puts it on the table, packs and closes it*) You kids today think you can get away with anything. You don't care who you hurt as long as you have yourself a good time . . . Well, life doesn't work that way, believe me.

CHUCK I found that out, Doc.

DR. DREYFUSS (*Stops at the door*) And don't think just because I'm the older generation, I don't know what's going on. Experimentally, I took a trip on LSD.

CHUCK You did?

DR. DREYFUSS I had a better time in Miami Beach when it rained for two weeks . . .
                    (*He exits and* CHUCK *closes the door behind him.* CHUCK *crosses back into the room, behind the bed where* FRAN *is fast asleep. He pulls the cover around her. Then he gets his coat, fishes out the Christmas card from* SHELDRAKE. *He turns and looks at the audience*)

CHUCK Look, I'd like to say something on her behalf . . . Aside from one tiny illicit affair and one very unprofessional suicide attempt . . . there lies one of the most decent girls it's been my privilege to meet.
                    (*He takes the phone to the coffee table, sits on the table and starts to dial. An overhead spotlight comes up as* CHUCK *dials his phone.* VOICES *sing in the orchestra pit*)

VOICES
          Christmas Day is here and so are we,
          Time for children and presents
          And Christmas tree happiness.

                    (VOICES *continue humming as* SHELDRAKE *steps into the spotlight answering a phone which he carries*)

SHELDRAKE Yes?

CHUCK (*On his own phone in his apartment. Softly*) It's me, Mr. Sheldrake. Chuck Baxter. I hate to disturb you but something important's come up . . . I think it would be a good idea if you could see me . . . at the apartment . . . as soon as possible . . .

SHELDRAKE On Christmas morning? What's this all about, Baxter?

CHUCK I didn't want to tell you over the phone . . . but that certain party. You know who I mean . . . I found her here last night . . . she'd taken an overdose of sleeping pills.

SHELDRAKE *What?*

HELEN SHELDRAKE (*Appears next to* SHELDRAKE) What is it, Jeff? Anything wrong?

SHELDRAKE (*He covers the phone*) One of our employees had an accident. Nothing serious. (*Into the phone*) How bad is it?

CHUCK Well, it was touch-and-go there for a while, but she's sleeping it off now . . . I thought you might like to be here when she wakes up . . .

SHELDRAKE Well—of course I would—but I just can't get away . . . Listen, do you think there'll be any er . . . problems . . . I mean, with a doctor?

CHUCK No, he's a friend of mine and I kept your name out of it . . . So I think you're in the clear, trouble-wise.

SHELDRAKE Don't think I don't appreciate that, Baxter.

CHUCK Well, you know me. Loyal and resourceful . . .

SHELDRAKE And if you need anything, medicines, well, you know, I'll pay for everything.

CHUCK Right. I'll just put it on the bill with the Tom and Jerries . . . Is there any sort of message you want me to give her?

SHELDRAKE A message. Like what?

CHUCK Never mind. I'll think of something . . . Goodby, Mr. Sheldrake. (*He hangs up; the lights black out on* CHUCK *but remain on* SHELDRAKE)

SHELDRAKE Good-by, Baxter . . . and I really apprecia—
(*He realizes* CHUCK *has hung up. He puts down*

the phone, stands for a second, then exits. The
VOICES sing)

VOICES
    If Christmas Day is really in your heart
    You don't have to save up all your love
    To give once a year.
    Try to give, learn to live
    Each day like Christmas Day.

    (*It is later that morning.* FRAN *moves in the bed.*
CHUCK *enters with a tablecloth to set the table.*
He looks at her)

CHUCK Good morning.
    (*He closes the door*)

FRAN (*She holds her hands over her eyes*) You wanna
bet?

CHUCK (*Looking out the window*) Actually good afternoon. You slept all day. It looks like snow.

FRAN I don't think I could stand the noise.
    (*She props herself a bit, not without discomfort*)

CHUCK Fresh Colombian coffee coming right up, each
bean carefully selected by El Exigente himself.

FRAN (*She looks at him*) I didn't know this was your
apartment . . . I'm sorry . . .

CHUCK You'll be a lot sorrier in a few minutes. I make
the world's worst coffee—

FRAN I'm so ashamed. Why didn't you just let me die?

CHUCK (*He moves toward her*) Hey, what kind of talk
is that? You were just emotionally distressed again. So
instead of getting hiccups, you took a few sleeping pills . . .
    (*He puffs up her pillow. The front door opens and*
DR. DREYFUSS *enters*)

DR. DREYFUSS Anything unusual?

CHUCK (*He turns to him*) No. She's resting.

DR. DREYFUSS I meant with you. I expected to find six naked dancing girls feeding you grapes. (*He crosses to* FRAN, *lifts her hand to take her pulse. She looks at him*) Good afternoon. Remember me?

FRAN (*She turns to him*) Yeah. You slapped me in the face last night.

DR. DREYFUSS (*To* CHUCK) A bedside manner I never had. (*Lets go* FRAN's *arm*) If that's your pulse, I'm not crazy about it.

FRAN I'm alive. Doesn't that make you happy? What do I owe you?

DR. DREYFUSS (*Looking at the thermometer*) For your recovery, nothing. For my recovery, you couldn't afford it.
       (*Shakes the thermometer*)

FRAN Sure I can. I'm rich. I've got a hundred dollars here someplace. Where's my bag? (*She reaches into her purse and takes out the one hundred dollar bill*) Take it, Doctor. A hundred dollars is the going price for me these days.

DR. DREYFUSS (*Putting a thermometer in her mouth and crossing to flick ashes on the coffee table*) Use it to stock up on Campbell's soup. What you need is hot food and plenty of rest.

FRAN What I need is to be left alone. What's the world coming to when a person can't get off whenever he wants?

DR. DREYFUSS (*Crossing to the foot of the bed*) Shame on you. Shame on you for being young and pretty and sorry you're alive. I'm a general practitioner. You want sympathy, go to a specialist.

CHUCK   She's just tired, Doc.

DR. DREYFUSS   I don't know. No one today can take heart-ache any more. Where I was brought up, as a kid we got *misery* as a reward. Like I tell the people with gallstones, live with it a few days. It'll pass.

FRAN (*Looks at* DR. DREYFUSS, *a faint smile*)   Thanks for the poetry, Doctor.

DR. DREYFUSS (*Mock heart attack*)   Don't tell me, is that the beginning of a smile I see? Well, don't let it lay there like a lump on your lips, give birth to it. Give me a full-grown, healthy smile. The way I walked for you last night I deserve it.

FRAN   I'm sorry, Doctor, it's the best I can do.

DR. DREYFUSS   Then take my advice. (*He sings "A Young Pretty Girl Like You"*)

> Put my glasses on on the top of your head
> On the top of your head—you won't see a thing
> And the less you see, the sooner you'll be
> Smiling, laughing, and happy.

CHUCK   (*Singing*)

> Oh yes, the less you see the better you feel
> The better you feel, the quicker you smile
> And the quicker you smile, the sooner you'll be happy
> Happy!

DR. DREYFUSS

> And a young pretty girl like you,

CHUCK *and* DR. DREYFUSS

> Pretty as she can be
> Really should be happy,

CHUCK

> Happy.

DR. DREYFUSS

> Try to
> Take my stethoscope, plug it into your ears
> Plug it into your ears—you won't hear a thing.

When there's too much noise, nobody enjoys
Smiling, laughing, be happy.

CHUCK *and* DR. DREYFUSS
Oh yes, the less you see, the better you feel
The better you feel, the quicker you smile
And the quicker you smile, the sooner you'll be happy
Happy!

And a young pretty girl like you,

Pretty as she can be
Really should be happy,

CHUCK
Happy.

DR. DREYFUSS
Try to
Open up your mouth, let me look at your throat
Let me look at your throat, don't you say a thing
'Cause the less you say the sooner you'll play
Lipstick, powder, and girl games.

CHUCK *and* DR. DREYFUSS
Oh yes, the less you see, the better you feel
The better you feel, the quicker you smile
And the quicker you smile, the sooner you'll be happy
Happy!

DR. DREYFUSS
And a young pretty girl like you

CHUCK
Why don't you take a look?

CHUCK *and* DR. DREYFUSS
Really should be happy,

CHUCK
Happy!

CHUCK *and* DR. DREYFUSS
Yes, a young pretty girl like you

With all you've been through
Really should be happy,

DR. DREYFUSS
Smiling,

CHUCK
Laughing,

DR. DREYFUSS
Giggling,

CHUCK *and* DR. DREYFUSS
Happy!
(*At the end of the song,* DR. DREYFUSS *and* CHUCK
*are standing, each with one foot on a chair, the
other on the table*)

CHUCK Hey, look, Doc. She's smiling.
(FRAN *covers her head*)

DR. DREYFUSS Now I know what Albert Schweitzer felt
like. (*He gets his stethoscope and glasses, and begins to
leave*) I'll look in again tonight. (*He clutches his heart,
breathing hard*) I can't catch my breath . . . Lucky for
me I have hospitalization.
(*He exits.* CHUCK *turns to* FRAN *and looks at her.
She looks back at him*)

FRAN You're not going to keep staring at me like that
all day, are you?

CHUCK (*Rising, he crosses to the bookcase*) I'm sorry. I
guess it's the practical nurse in me. Do you play gin?

FRAN Not well.

CHUCK Good. If there's anything I love it's a lousy gin
rummy player with a hundred dollars. Feet off my table,
please. Penny a point?
(DOBITCH *and* SYLVIA *enter the stage outside the
door of the apartment*)

FRAN Why do people have to love people anyway?

CHUCK (*Shrugs*) We just don't know any better, I guess.

FRAN I read in a science fiction magazine that in the future we won't need love any more. It's going to become an obsolete emotion.

CHUCK Well, we certainly have a lot to look forward to, don't we? (*Looks at a card*) Do you want that Jack?
  (*She shakes her head "no"*)

FRAN Maybe he does love me . . . only he doesn't have the nerve to tell his wife.
  (*She throws out another card*)

CHUCK I'm sure that's the explanation.
  (*He takes the card she threw out*)

FRAN You really think so?

CHUCK I really think so.
  (*She takes another card and throws it out without looking*)

FRAN I don't . . . Oh, God, I'm so fouled up . . . You're a smart person, Chuck, tell me what to do.

CHUCK Well—my personal advice is not to throw out that other Jack.

FRAN (*Distracted*) I really don't want it.

CHUCK In that case, I knock with three. You lose.
  (*He lays out his cards*)

FRAN Yeah . . . I guess I do.
  (*She turns her head away from him into the pillow and quietly begins to cry again. CHUCK looks at her, gets up and pulls the cover over her, knowing she will soon cry herself to sleep. DOBITCH and SYLVIA are at the door. DOBITCH rings. CHUCK crosses and opens the door*)

DOBITCH Four o'clock, kid, aren't you supposed to be in Radio City Music Hall?

CHUCK (*Trying to keep him out*) What do you want? You can't come in.

DOBITCH (*Pushes his way in*) What's the matter with you? I made a reservation for four o'clock. (CHUCK *closes the door, locking* SYLVIA *out*) "You caught me at the right season, Mr. Dobitch," don't you remember?
(*He sees* FRAN *in bed*)

SYLVIA Hey, what about me?

DOBITCH Well, well, well, who'd a thought it. Next time I'll know what to order in the Dining Room.
(DR. DREYFUSS *appears in the vestibule*. CHUCK *and* SYLVIA *speak together*)

CHUCK (*Points to the door*) Get out, Mr. Dobitch.

SYLVIA Hey, come on, what are we waiting for? Open up, willya?

DR. DREYFUSS Mildred, you'll never believe it.
(*He enters his apartment*)

CHUCK (*Crosses to the door*) Did you hear what I said, Mr. Dobitch? Get out!

DOBITCH Your problem, kid, is that you run this place like the Long Island Rail Road. You've got schedules but you don't keep to them. (*He hands him a champagne bottle*) Merry Christmas. (*He and* SYLVIA *exit. We hear* DOBITCH *in the vestibule*) Let's go to Central Park.

CHUCK (*Looking at* FRAN) Don't worry. I'll tell them at the office that you were in the neighborhood and you slipped in the snow and came up to dry off . . . and that's maybe the worst story I ever heard.

FRAN But very sweet . . . You know, if I had any brains, Chuck Baxter, I'd have fallen in love with someone nice like you.

CHUCK (*Turns*) Cut it out, Chuck, you'll drive yourself crazy.

FRAN   Did I say something wrong?

CHUCK   Oh, my gosh, that was really her talking. (*To* FRAN) No, no, you said the rightest thing in the whole world. You couldn't have said anything righter if you *tried*. (*There is a blackout on the set with a spot remaining on* CHUCK. *He speaks to the audience*) All right, you all heard that. Don't deny it, I was standing right here. She said, "If I had any brains I would have fallen in love with someone nice like you" . . . meaning someone nice like me . . . Oh, I realize the fact that she just tried to kill herself over someone else means my position is still a little shaky . . .

> (*Blackout. In a spotlight we see the* THREE EXECS *at a phone*)

KIRKEBY   (*On the phone*) Hello, Ginger! Listen, I think I found a spot . . . it's a deserted tug boat on Pier Twenty-three . . . But Ginger . . .
> (*He hangs up*)

EICHELBERGER   Can't you think of anyplace?

VANDERHOF   For crying out loud, will you stop whispering. It's like living with the Goddamned CIA.

EICHELBERGER   (*Grabs him*) But tonight was supposed to be my night. What'll we do?

VANDERHOF   Take your clammy, oversexed hands off me.

KIRKEBY   I don't know, fellas. I'm getting tired of all this. Why don't we just go to a steam bath?

EICHELBERGER   Are you crazy? They'd spot the girls there in a minute.

> (*Blackout.* FRAN *is in bed;* CHUCK *is helping her into his bathrobe*)

CHUCK   Listen, I don't want to seem gloomy, but what are you going to tell your family? About what happened?

FRAN   I thought I'd just tell my father. He's hard of

hearing . . . My brother's a problem. He's six-feet-six with a Polish temper.

CHUCK (*Starting to make the bed*) Well, if you need a character reference, I'm your man.

FRAN (*Looks at the guitar on the table*) Is this your guitar?

CHUCK I bought it second-hand three months ago, in another futile attempt to become the life of the party.

FRAN (*Picks it up*) Would you play something for me?

CHUCK In about two weeks. The blisters on my fingers haven't healed yet . . . Luncheon will be served as soon as I finish my housework.

FRAN (*At the sofa with the guitar*) Tell me, how come someone like you isn't married?

CHUCK Oh. Well, there was a girl I wanted to ask back home. Bertha Gosseman. I was so crazy about her I even thought her name was pretty.

FRAN What happened?

CHUCK She married Albert Mangassarian, my best friend. On their wedding day I tried to kill myself.

FRAN You?

CHUCK I was going to hang myself in the attic. My kid sister saved me.

FRAN She cut you down?

CHUCK No, she wanted to watch, I got embarrassed.
(FRAN *strums the guitar*)

FRAN Well. I guess there's a lesson in there we've both learned.

CHUCK What's that?

(FRAN *and* CHUCK *sing "I'll Never Fall in Love
Again"*)

FRAN

What do you get when you fall in love?
A guy with a pin to burst your bubble
That's what you get for all your trouble.
I'll never fall in love again
I'll never fall in love again.

What do you get when you kiss a guy?
You get enough germs to catch pneumonia
After you do he'll never phone ya.
I'll never fall in love again
I'll never fall in love again.

Don't tell me what it's all about
'Cause I've been there and I'm glad I'm out
Out of those chains
Those chains that bind you
That is why I'm here to remind you.

What do you get when you fall in love?
You only get lies and pain and sorrow
So for at least until tomorrow

FRAN *and* CHUCK

I'll never fall in love again
I'll never fall in love again.

CHUCK

What do you get when you give your heart?
You get it all broken up and battered
That's what you get—a heart that's shattered.
I'll
Never fall in love again,
I'll
Never fall in love again.
Don't tell me what it's all about
'Cause I've been there and I'm glad I'm out
Out of those chains
Those chains that bind you.

FRAN

That is why I'm here to remind you.

FRAN *and* CHUCK
> What do you get when you fall in love?
> You only get lies and pain and sorrow
> So for at least until tomorrow

FRAN
> I'll

FRAN *and* CHUCK
> Never fall in love again.

CHUCK
> I'll

FRAN *and* CHUCK
> Never fall in love again
> I'll never fall in love again.

FRAN   Are you still in love with Bertha Gosseman?

CHUCK   Well, since she moved to Canada, had six kids and put on forty pounds, my fervor has waned . . . But she sends me a fruit cake every Christmas. We're having it for dessert. And after dessert you know what we're doing?

FRAN   Well, how about going up to White Plains and letting the air out of Mr. Sheldrake's tires?

CHUCK   No, after dessert we're going to finish that gin game . . . (KARL *rings the doorbell;* CHUCK *crosses to the door*) . . . so I want you to keep a clear head. (*Opens the door*) Because I don't want to . . . take advantage of you the way I did yesterday in bed!

FRAN   Karl!

CHUCK   Your brother? . . . How do you do!
    (KARL *walks in menacingly*)

KARL   Get dressed, I got the car downstairs.

FRAN   Karl, how did you find me?

KARL   I went to the office looking for you. Four executives in the Dining Room said I'd find you up here . . . Who's this?

CHUCK (*Friendly*)   My name is C. C. Baxter, Mr. Kubelik, but you can call me Chuck. Can I call you Karl? . . . Ho, heh? . . . Okay . . . Well, Mr. Kubelik, let me say this—

KARL   Get your clothes and let's go.

CHUCK   Go where? . . . Oh, he wants you to get your clothes . . . Would Karl care for some coffee and fruit cake? . . .

KARL   My advice to you is to shut up. You still got your teeth in your face because I trust my sister. If she tells me nothing went on here, that's good enough for me.

CHUCK   Nothing went on here.

KARL   Are you my sister?

FRAN   Nothing went on here.

KARL   That's good enough for me.

FRAN   I'll get my clothes.
         (FRAN *goes into the bathroom and closes the door. There is an awkward moment as* CHUCK *tries to escape the contemptuous gaze of* KARL, *but* KARL *persists*)

CHUCK   May I say one thing? . . . Your sister is really *terrific!* (KARL *glares*) No, I think I said the wrong thing . . .
         (*The front door opens and* DR. DREYFUSS *steps in*)

DR. DREYFUSS   Hi. How's the patient.

CHUCK   Oh. *I'm fine*, Doc.

DR. DREYFUSS   I mean Miss Kubelik.

KARL   What's the matter with Miss Kubelik?

DR. DREYFUSS   Who are you?

KARL   Her brother.

DR. DREYFUSS   (*Takes a step back*)   Oh.

KARL   Who are you?

DR. DREYFUSS   Her doctor. *His* doctor. Just a doctor.

KARL   Why does she need a doctor?

DR. DREYFUSS   Er—ah! (*To* CHUCK) Tell him why she needs a doctor.

CHUCK   Er—fruit cake. Too much fruit cake.

DR. DREYFUSS   (*Nods*)   An overdose!

CHUCK   It comes from Canada. And it was a very bad year for Canadian fruit cake.

DR. DREYFUSS   One of their worst.

CHUCK   Oh, what's the use . . . She had an accident.

DR. DREYFUSS   These things happen.

KARL   What things? Hey, what kind of a doctor are you?

DR. DREYFUSS   (*Shrugs*)   General practice. Colds, virus—

CHUCK   He gave her a shot and pumped her stomach out.

KARL   What for?
(FRAN *comes out of the bathroom*)

FRAN   Because I took some sleeping pills. But I'm all right now. So let's go.

KARL   Not until I find out what went on here. Why did you take sleeping pills?

CHUCK   On . . . on account of me. (KARL *looks at him*) I jilted her. I threw her over. (*He smiles at* FRAN, *pleased with himself. Then turns to* KARL) You're going to hit me, aren't you?

KARL   You know it, brother.
           (KARL *smashes his fist into* CHUCK's *stomach*. CHUCK *groans and stands there doubled over*)

FRAN   Karl! (*Then* KARL *finishes the job, smashing his fist into* CHUCK's *jaw, who goes sprawling across the room, over a chair and onto the floor*) Stop it! Leave him alone.

DR. DREYFUSS (*Looking on*)   Tell me if you're going to do that again. I want my wife to watch.

FRAN (*Rushes to* CHUCK *on the floor*)   You idiot. You really are an idiot!

KARL (*Opens the door*)   Let's go.

FRAN   Good-by, idiot!
           (*She kisses him warmly on the cheek and exits*)

DR. DREYFUSS (*Bends down, looks at* CHUCK)   You know, Baxter, I was just thinking. If I had three more like you in the building, I could give up the rest of my practice.
           (FRAN *and* KARL *exit from the stoop. The* EXECS *emerge after them, dancing and singing*)

We did the right thing, the proper thing,
What else were we to do?

If it was your sister,
I'd do the same for you.

           (*A* YOUNG MAN *crosses in front of them*)

YOUNG MAN   Happy New Year, Mr. Vanderhof.

VANDERHOF Happy New Year, kid.
      (YOUNG MAN *continues off and exits*)

DOBITCH Who's that?

VANDERHOF A new boy in my department.

DOBITCH Single?

VANDERHOF Yeah.

DOBITCH With his own apartment?

VANDERHOF Yeah.
      (*They all look at each other, then dance off in
      the direction of the* YOUNG MAN *as they sing*)

We did the right thing, the proper thing,
What else was there to do?
      (*They exit*)

Blackout

SCENE 3

The lights go up on SHELDRAKE's *office at the left.*
SHELDRAKE *enters and crosses to his desk; he looks at the
papers and calls offstage.*

SHELDRAKE Miss Olson . . . (*No answer . . . a little
louder*) Miss Olson. (MISS OLSON *enters, carrying a sheet
of paper with a check attached. He seems perturbed*)
I'm not taking you away from anything, am I?

MISS OLSON I'm sorry, I was just typing this up. (*She
puts it on his desk*) It needs your signature. (*He looks
at it*) By the way, shall I tell the cashier to dock Miss
Kubelik's pay? She didn't come in today. (*He looks up at
her*) Virus, do you think?

SHELDRAKE I don't know what you're implying, but I've
been with my family for the past two nights. In addition
to which I don't think it's any of your business.
(*He signs the check and paper*)

MISS OLSON I know, just typing, filing, and reserving
you hotel space in Atlantic City . . . or is it West Sixty-
seventh Street now?

SHELDRAKE (*Glances at her*) I think that'll be all, Miss
Olson.

MISS OLSON You know what's going to happen to you
some day? You're going to use up all the girls in the
office . . . and you'll have to turn to IBM machines . . .
That means you'll have to get a bigger car, Mr. Sheldrake.

SHELDRAKE The Christmas party is over. I think you'd
better pull yourself together.

MISS OLSON   You know . . . somehow I could adjust to the end of our affair by telling myself I still had a good-paying job. But I think when you tell that kid your interoffice fling is over she's going to head for the nearest gas pipe. She's not made of concrete like me.

SHELDRAKE (*Gets up*)   I've got a conference now. I think we'd better finish this discussion later.

MISS OLSON   If you enjoy talking to yourself, because I won't be here. I'm quitting as a Christmas present to myself. (*She picks up the papers from his desk*) You just signed my two weeks' severance pay.

SHELDRAKE (*Looks at her*)   That's up to you, Peggy.
          (*He starts to go*)

MISS OLSON   Oh . . . In case you're worrying about anyone telling your wife about all this, I have one word of advice . . . worry.
          (*He glares at her; the lights go off on the office set. He turns and exits*)

Blackout

The lights go up on CHUCK *outside Lum Ding's Chinese Restaurant.* CHUCK *takes a note from his pocket, shows it, and addresses the audience.*

CHUCK (*Reads*) "Would like to have a drink with you five o'clock, Lum Ding's Restaurant . . . J. S. Sheldrake" . . . (*Puts the note in his pocket*) . . . Well, I can see a two-week vacation with pay coming up for being loyal, cooperative and pretty damned quiet about Christmas Eve . . . I wasn't going to come except I have something to say myself . . . How does this sound to you? Be honest. (*Clears his throat*) "Mr. Sheldrake, inasmuch as you seem to be in an inextricable position, to relieve you of any further pain or hardship, since you don't really want her anyway and I do, I would like to take Miss Kubelik off your hands . . . It would be the thing to do . . . solution-wise" . . . I like that—"inextricable"—(*He turns and goes into the restaurant, which lights up as he enters. It is decorated for New Year's Eve, although it's only about* 5:00 P.M. CHUCK *crosses to* SHELDRAKE *at the usual table*) Happy New Year, Mr. Sheldrake.

SHELDRAKE Hello, Baxter. Sit down. Can I get you anything?

CHUCK No, thanks. I'm on my way to someone's party.

SHELDRAKE Pretty?

CHUCK Well, if you like chunky middle-aged doctors. He's got a few interns that are anxious to meet me . . . Er, Mr. Sheldrake . . . inasmuch as you seem to be in an inextricable position—

SHELDRAKE But I'm not. At least not any more. If you were in the office about eight-fifteen this morning, you would have seen me arrive with two large suitcases.

CHUCK Going somewhere, sir?

SHELDRAKE Temporarily to the New York Athletic Club. Mrs. Sheldrake and I have split up—

CHUCK You mean—for good?

SHELDRAKE It's funny what can happen to a twelve-year-old marriage with one phone call from a jealous ex-secretary.

CHUCK Oh. I'm sorry.

SHELDRAKE So it looks like I'll be taking Miss Kubelik off your hands permanently. By the way, I'm not un-grateful for Christmas Eve. I was thinking about a two-week vacation, with pay.

CHUCK (*Empty*) Gee, I never expected that.

SHELDRAKE Anyway, I'm meeting Fran—Miss Kubelik—later tonight. I intend asking her to marry me.

CHUCK I see. Well, I guess you don't need any good luck, knowing how she feels about you. I'm sure you'll both be very happy.

SHELDRAKE I appreciate that, Baxter, especially after the way I must have sounded on the phone the other day. I imagine I impressed you as a Class A-One heel.

CHUCK Well, it's not my place—

SHELDRAKE It's all right. You can be honest.

CHUCK Okay. That was my impression. Class A-One heel.

SHELDRAKE I don't blame you, Baxter. My behavior that day was anything but admirable. But you understood, I couldn't help myself. My hands were tied.

CHUCK   Well, maybe it was the kicking with your feet that I objected to.

SHELDRAKE   I'll let that pass, Baxter. We've all been under a big strain this past week.

CHUCK   That's very charitable of you, sir. I'll try to keep my place from now on . . . So, when is the happy day?

SHELDRAKE   Well, I'm not sure.

CHUCK   I mean, this week? This month? This year?

SHELDRAKE   I said I'm not sure. You know, these things—

CHUCK   (Nods)   —usually drag out for months . . .

SHELDRAKE   That's right. They usually drag out for months.

CHUCK   There's always a million details—

SHELDRAKE   Exactly. All those damn details—

CHUCK   And in the meantime you have no place to go with Miss Kubelik, so you'd like the key to my apartment again.

SHELDRAKE   Well, I can't very well take her into the New York Athletic Club. And it's New Year's Eve, there's not a hotel room in town. So if I could just have it for tonight—

CHUCK   (Puts a key on the table)   Here you are, Mr. Sheldrake.

SHELDRAKE   (Picks it up)   Thanks, Baxter. (CHUCK gets up)   I'm sorry to ask on such short notice but I didn't know until last night that Mrs. Sheldrake—Hey, Baxter, wait a minute. You gave me the wrong key. This is for the Executive Bathroom.

CHUCK   Right, Mr. Sheldrake. I'm all washed up around here.

SHELDRAKE   What are you talking about?

CHUCK You're not going to bring anybody up to my apartment.

SHELDRAKE I'm not bringing anybody—I'm bringing Miss Kubelik.

CHUCK (*Leans forward, his voice rising*) *Especially* Miss Kubelik!

SHELDRAKE Just a minute, Baxter. I've been pretty damn nice to you. You were handing me that key fast enough when you were getting raises and promotions in the other hand.

CHUCK Mr. Sheldrake, I refuse to work for a man who would make a Junior Executive out of anyone whose only qualification is an available *eighty-six fifty a month apartment* . . . Especially when that Junior Executive is hypocritical, opportunistic, and an indiscriminate streetwalker *like me!* HAPPY NEW YEAR! (*He storms out of the restaurant into the street. Lights dim on the restaurant.* CHUCK *speaks to the audience*) I will NEVER—never, never, never, EVER get myself into a situation like that again. *That's* a promise! Oh, God, there's that word again! (*He sings*)

> Promises, promises,
> I'm all through with promises, promises now.
> I don't know how
> I got the nerve to walk out.
> If I shout
> Remember I feel free.
> Now I can look at myself and be proud
> I'm laughing out loud.
> Oh, promises, promises,
> This is where those promises, promises end.
> I won't pretend
> That what was wrong can be right.
> Every night I'll sleep now.
> No more lies.
> Things that I promised myself fell apart
> But I found my heart.
> Promises, their kind of promises
> Can just destroy your life.

Oh, promises, those kind of promises
Take all the joy from life.
Oh, promises, promises, my kind of promises
Can lead to joy and hope and love,
Yes, love.
   (*He exits*)

Blackout

The voices of TWO COUPLES *are heard as they climb the steps to the vestibule.*

INTERN   Hey, Doc, where are you. We're here! This is the place.

DR. DREYFUSS (*Appearing at the door*)   Mildred, they're here.
(*The* TWO COUPLES *enter* DR. DREYFUSS's *apartment*)

DR. DREYFUSS (*To the last* INTERN)   Where's the ice? You were supposed to bring ice.
(*Enters his apartment. In his apartment,* CHUCK *is packing his clothes into a suitcase. He looks up and sees the audience*)

CHUCK   I'll be leaving in a few minutes so I guess I won't be seeing you any more . . . You've been very patient . . . Listen, my rent is paid up for the next two weeks, so if you need a place to stay—you know where to find the key.
(DR. DREYFUSS's *door opens across the hall*)

INTERN (*Offstage*)   Where you going, Doc.

DR. DREYFUSS   Be right back. (CHUCK *continues packing.* DR. DREYFUSS *comes in*) Hello, Baxter. You were supposed to come to my party and we're running short of ice so I thought I'd come to a professional. (*Looks around, whispers*) Who's playing tonight?

CHUCK   It's okay, Doc. I'm alone.

DR. DREYFUSS On New Year's Eve? Don't kid me. Ten-to-twelve I'll be in here on another house call.

CHUCK (*Hands him a bottle*) There's no ice, Doc. I defrosted the refrigerator . . . Can you use a bottle of champagne?

DR. DREYFUSS Booze we don't need. Why don't you join us, Baxter? I got a psychiatrist, a cardiologist and a gynecologist, all right up your alley.

CHUCK Thanks, but I've got to finish packing. I'm moving out tonight.

DR. DREYFUSS Moving out? You mean giving up the apartment? Where are you going?

CHUCK I'm not sure yet. All I know is I got to get out of this place.

DR. DREYFUSS Mildred'll be sorry to hear it. Once you moved in, she gave up the Late Show . . .

CHUCK Doc, in case I don't see you again . . . I just want to thank you for taking care of that girl.

DR. DREYFUSS Forget it. She looked like a nice kid. I wouldn't trust her with a bottle of aspirins, but a nice kid. Whatever happened to her?

CHUCK Oh, you know me when it comes to women. Easy come, easy go . . . (*We see* FRAN *come down the vestibule toward* CHUCK's *apartment*) . . . Come on, Doc. Let's kill the bottle for old-time's sake.
    (*He pulls the cork, it pops with a loud bang.* FRAN *freezes at the door*)

FRAN Oh, my God! Mr. Baxter!! (*She rushes to the door*) Mr. Baxter!!! (*She opens the door and rushes into the apartment as* CHUCK *stands there pouring champagne into* DR. DREYFUSS's *glass* . . . CHUCK *looks up and sees* FRAN) Oh!

CHUCK Miss Kubelik . . . What's wrong?

FRAN   Nothing. I heard an explosion and I thought—well, I thought that—that you did something terrible.

CHUCK   Like what?

FRAN   Like leaving town without calling me.

CHUCK   I *am* leaving town and I didn't see much point in calling.

FRAN   Try me.

CHUCK   What's that?

FRAN   I said try me.

CHUCK   Hello? Is Miss Kubelik there? . . . I'd like to speak to Miss Kubelik, please . . . Fran?
        (*They just stare at each other, as if in a trance, almost oblivious to the fact that* DR. DREYFUSS *is standing there between them. He looks at* FRAN)

DR. DREYFUSS   It's for you.

FRAN   Yes, Chuck? . . .

CHUCK   I just wanted to say good-by . . . and wish you and Mr. Sheldrake all the happiness in the world.

FRAN   What was that name again? My Eustachian tubes are closing up.

DR. DREYFUSS   What did I tell you? It's not even ten-to-twelve yet.

CHUCK   Mr. Sheldrake told me he was meeting you tonight to ask you to marry him.

FRAN   He did?

CHUCK   . . . What did you say?

FRAN   What do you think I said?

DR. DREYFUSS (*Looks at* CHUCK, *then at* FRAN. *There is a pause*) I can't stand it! What did you say?

FRAN It suddenly hit me for the first time. Mr. Sheldrake and I don't have anything in common. He really doesn't like basketball.

CHUCK (*Big smile*) He doesn't?

DR. DREYFUSS Who could marry anyone who doesn't like basketball? (*To* CHUCK) I'm glad you're not moving out. I'm getting used to you. Happy New Year . . . I said Happy— (*He waves his arm in disgust and exits*) Forget it, Mildred, he's busy again.
> (DR. DREYFUSS *goes through the vestibule, into his apartment, and closes the door.* CHUCK *and* FRAN *have virtually been staring at each other all this time.* FRAN *picks up the deck of cards on the table, sits on the sofa and starts to deal as* CHUCK *stares at her*)

CHUCK (*Crosses to her right*) I love you, Miss Kubelik.

FRAN You'll have to speak louder. You want the Queen of Hearts?

CHUCK (*Sitting right of her, picks up his cards*) I said, Miss Kubelik, that I absolutely adore you.

FRAN I heard you. Now shut up and play cards.
> (*MUSIC swells*)

CURTAIN

Plaza Suite

Directed on Broadway by Mike Nichols

Synopsis of Scenes

VISITOR FROM MAMARONECK

A suite in the Plaza Hotel:—a late winter afternoon.

VISITOR FROM HOLLYWOOD

The same suite:—an early afternoon in spring.

VISITOR FROM FOREST HILLS

The same suite:—a Saturday afternoon in June.

VISITOR FROM MAMARONECK

A suite at the Plaza Hotel on the seventh floor, over-looking Central Park. The set is divided into two rooms. The room at stage right is the living room. It is a well-appointed room, tastefully furnished with an entrance door at the extreme right and windows that look out over the park. A door leads into the bedroom, which has a large double bed, etc., and a door that leads to the bathroom. The room also contains a large closet.

It is about four in the afternoon in mid-December. The door of the suite opens and a BELLHOP *enters and switches on the lights in the living room. He carries one small overnight bag.*

KAREN NASH *enters behind him. She wears a six-year-old mink coat which could use a bit of restyling, and a pair of galoshes. Underneath she wears an expensive suit which unfortunately looked better on the model in Bendel's than it does on* KAREN. KAREN *is forty-eight years old, and she makes no bones about it. C'est la vie. She is a pleasant, affable woman who has let weight and age take their natural course. A mink hat is plopped down on her head. She carries a box from Bendel's with her afternoon's purchases and a small bouquet of flowers.*

The BELLHOP *closes a half-open window in the living room, switches on the lights and puts the bag on the luggage tray.* KAREN *looks around the living room, crosses to the bedroom and puts her packages down on a chair. The* BELLHOP *goes to the bathroom and turns a light on in there.*

KAREN *follows him to the bathroom. The* BELLHOP *comes out of the bathroom, crosses the living room, opens the door to leave, and hesitates in the doorway.*

BELLHOP Everything all right, ma'am?

KAREN Wait a minute, I want to make sure this is the right room. (*She crosses back into the living room*) I know this is Suite 719, but was it always 719?

BELLHOP Yes, ma'am—719.

KAREN No, you don't understand. I know sometimes hotels change the numbers around, and this could have been 723 or 715. And it's very important I get 719.
(*She returns to the bedroom for the flowers*)

BELLHOP I'm here two years, it's always been 719.

KAREN Because you know about 826 at the Savoy-Plaza?

BELLHOP No, ma'am.

KAREN (*Unwrapping the flowers at a table behind the sofa in the living room*) Oh, well, they had a famous murder in 826. Then the next year there was a fire, and the year after that a husband and a wife committed suicide. Then no wanted 826. So they turned it into a linen closet. It's a fact, there is no more 826 at the Savoy-Plaza.

BELLHOP There's no more Savoy-Plaza either. They tore it down two years ago.

KAREN (*Looks at him incredulously, then goes to look out the window*) Oh, my God, look at that. There's no Savoy-Plaza . . . What's that monstrosity?

BELLHOP It's the new General Motors building.

KAREN (*Still looking out the window*) Shows you how often I get into the city. Well, listen, that's what they're doing today. If it's old and it's beautiful, it's not there in the morning . . .

BELLHOP (*Indicating the other windows*) Well, you still have a nice view from here.

KAREN (*Crosses to the other windows and looks out*) Mmmm, for how long? I guarantee you Central Park comes down in five years.

BELLHOP You think so?

KAREN (*Starts to put the flowers in a vase on the sofa table*) I *know* so. Five years from now you'll look out this window and you'll see one little tree and the world's largest A and P.

BELLHOP   I don't think I'll be working here five years from now.

KAREN   You mean the rumor is true?

BELLHOP   What rumor?

KAREN   That the Plaza is coming down too!

BELLHOP   *This* Plaza?

KAREN (*Puts the vase on the chest between the windows*) I don't want to worry you or anything. It's just a rumor. No one knows for sure . . . But it's definitely coming down.

BELLHOP   I didn't hear that.

KAREN (*Crossing to the bedroom, she takes a bag from the luggage rack and puts it on the dresser in front of the bedroom window*) Well, I'm sure they want to keep it quiet from the staff. The story is that they're going to tear down the Plaza and put up a fifty-two-story luxury hotel.

BELLHOP   Why? *This* is a luxury hotel.

KAREN   Yeah, but it's an *old* luxury hotel. Today it has to be new. Old is no good any more. (*Picks up the phone on the chest in the living room*) Well, all I really care about is tonight.

BELLHOP   Yes, ma'am. Is there anything else?

KAREN   Oh, wait a minute. (*She puts down the phone, runs to the bedroom for her purse and looks for change*) Don't tell me I don't have any change.

BELLHOP   That's all right, ma'am.

KAREN (*Crossing back into the living room*) It's not all right. This is your living. (*Takes out a dollar bill*) Here you are.

BELLHOP (*Taking it*) Thank you very much.

KAREN   I'll be very honest with you. I don't usually give dollar tips. But it's my anniversary. So I can be a sport.

BELLHOP (*With his hand on the door. He'd really like to go*) Oh, well, congratulations.

KAREN Thank you, dear. Twenty-four years ago tonight I spent my honeymoon in this room. This *is* 719, isn't it?

BELLHOP Yes, ma'am—719.

KAREN I bet you weren't even born twenty-four years ago, right?

BELLHOP No, I was born . . .

KAREN You know what I was? I was twenty-five. You know what that makes me today? . . . Some old lady.

BELLHOP Well, you certainly don't look like an old lady. (*Smiles*) . . . Well . . . have a pleasant stay, ma'am . . . and happy anniversary.
 (*He starts out the door*)

KAREN Thank you, dear . . . and take my advice. Don't rush . . . but look around for another job. (*The* BELL-HOP *nods and exits.* KAREN *crosses to the bedroom and looks at herself in the full-length mirror on the closet door. She takes off her hat and puts it on the dresser*) . . . You are definitely some old lady. (*She crosses to the phone on the night table next to the bed, takes it and sits on the bed, still wearing her mink coat*) . . . Room service, please. (*She groans as she bends over to take off the galoshes*) . . . Ohhhhh . . . (*Into the phone*) . . . No, operator. I was groaning to myself . . . (*Taking off her coat*) Hello, room service? . . . Listen, room service, this is Mrs. Sam Nash in Suite 719 . . . I would like a nice cold bottle of champagne . . . That sounds good, is it French? . . . Fine . . . with two glasses and a tray of assorted hors d'oeuvres . . . but listen, room service, I don't want any anchovies . . . They always give you anchovy patties with the hors d'oeuvres and my husband doesn't eat anchovies and I hate them, so don't give me any anchovies . . . Instead of the anchovies, give me some extra smoked salmon, or you can split them up . . . half smoked salmon and half caviars . . . That's right. Mrs. Nash. 719 . . . No anchovies . . . (*She hangs up*) They'll give me anchovies. (*She puts the phone back on the night table*) Look at that. No more Savoy-Plaza. (*Starts to take off the galoshes again. The telephone rings. There is one in each room. She gets up and picks up the one next to the bed*) Hello . . . (*The phone in the living room rings again. Hastily she hangs up the bedroom phone and rushes to answer it*) Hello? . . . Oh, Sam. Where are you? . . . Good. Come up. I'm here . . . . What room do you think? . . . 719 . . . Remember? 719? Suite 719 . . . That's right! (*She hungs up*) He doesn't remember . . . (*She rushes to the Bendel box and takes out a sheer negligée. She crosses to the mirror on the closet door and looks at herself with the negligée in front of her. She is not completely enchanted. The telephone rings. She puts down the negligée and rushes to the living room to answer it*) Hello . . . (*The phone in the bedroom rings again. She hastily hangs up the living room phone and rushes to answer it*) Hello? . . . Oh, hello, Miss McCormack. . . . No, he's not, dear. He's on his way up. Yes, I will . . . It's not important, is it? . . . Well, he seemed so tired lately, I was hoping he wouldn't have to think about work tonight. (*Glancing down at her feet*) . . . Oh, my God, I still have my galoshes on . . . All right, I'll tell him to call. Yes, when he comes in. Good-by. (*She hangs up and quickly bends over in an effort to remove her galoshes. She is having difficulty. The doorbell rings*) . . . Oh, damn it. (*Calls out*) Just a minute! (*The doorbell rings again. She is having much trouble with the right galosh*) . . . You had to wear galoshes today, right? (*She pulls her right galosh off but her shoe remains in it. The doorbell rings impatiently*) Oh, for God's sakes . . . (*She tries to pull her shoe out of the galosh but it is imbedded in there*) All right, all right, I'm coming (*She throws down the galosh with the shoe still in one galosh and her stockinged foot. She crosses into the living room*) Look at this, my twenty-fourth anniversary. (*She "limps" to the door and opens it. SAM NASH stands there. SAM has just turned fifty but has made every effort to conceal it. He is trim, impeccably neat. His clothes are well tailored, although a bit on the junior-executive side. He carries an attaché case, a fine leather Gucci product. Everything about SAM is measured, efficient, economic. She smiles warmly*) Hello, Sam.

(SAM *walks brusquely past her, surveying the room*)

SAM An hour and fifteen minutes I was in the god-damned dentist's chair . . .
> (*He puts down his attaché case on the chair downstage of the door to the bedroom, and takes off his coat*)

KAREN (*Closes the door, still warmly*) How do you feel, Sam?

SAM Between his lousy dirty jokes and WQXR-FM, I got some headache. (*He crosses to the mirror over the chest in the living room and looks at his teeth*) Did anyone call?

KAREN Sam, do you remember this room?
> (*Moving to him*)

SAM (*Still examining his teeth*) Well, two more caps and I'm through. (*He turns, baring his teeth at her*) What do you think?

KAREN (*Put her hands in front of her eyes to shield the glare*) Ooh, dazzling!

SAM You don't think they're too white, do you? (*Turns and looks in the mirror again*) Do they look too white to you?

KAREN No, no. Perfect. Very nice with the blue shirt.

SAM (*Still looking*) These don't stain, you know. A hundred years from now when I'm dead and buried, they'll be the same color.

KAREN Oh, good. You'll look wonderful. You don't remember this room, do you?

SAM (*Looks at his watch*) Four thirty already? The meeting must be over . . . Didn't anyone call?
> (*Takes his coat and attaché case into the bedroom, putting the coat on the chest and the case on the bed*)

KAREN Miss McCormack, from the office . . . She wants you to call back.

SAM (*Looks at her, annoyed*) Why didn't you tell me?

KAREN We were busy talking about your white teeth. Happy anniversary, Sam.
> (*Picks up a vase and crosses to the bedroom*)

SAM (*Not hearing her, into the phone*) Judson 6-5900
. . . What did you say? (*Sees her limp into the bedroom*) What's the matter with your leg?

KAREN (*Limps into the bathroom*) One is shorter than
the other. Didn't you ever notice that? I've had it for
years.

SAM (*Into the phone*) Lorraine? Mr. Nash. Let me
have Miss McCormack, please. (SAM *looks at himself
in the closet mirror*) . . . Well, that kills my barber's
appointment today. Oh, could I use five minutes under
the sun lamp. (*Into the phone.* KAREN *begins to sing
in the bathroom*) Miss McCormack? Did Henderson
call? . . . Did he send the contracts? (*Places his hand
over his ear to shut out* KAREN'S *singing*) . . . What
about Nizer? . . . I see . . . (*He quickly takes a note
pad from the night table and places it on the attaché
case on the bed in front of him. He can't find a pencil.
He snaps his fingers at* KAREN. *Still into the phone*)
What does it look like? . . . Ah huh . . . ah huh . . .
(*He snaps his fingers at* KAREN *again*) A pencil . . .
pencil . . . (KAREN, *rushing in from the bathroom,
searches through the night tables on both sides of the
bed and dresser.* SAM *is still on the phone*) Very good.
All right, give me the figures. (*He nods into the
phone.* KAREN *still can't find a pencil. She limps hurriedly over to her purse on the sofa table in the living
room.* SAM, *into the phone*) . . . It sounds right, but
I've got to go over the estimates . . . Tomorrow morning? That doesn't give us much time . . . Wait a
minute, give me those figures again . . . (*He puts his
hand over the phone, and whispers angrily*) Karen, for
God's sakes, a pencil! (KAREN *is frantically looking
through her purse.* SAM, *into the phone*) . . . One
seventy-five escalating up to three and a quarter . . .
(KAREN *takes a lipstick out of her purse and hobbles
quickly to* SAM. *She hands it to him*) Hold it. (*He
writes on the pad*) One seventy-five up to three and a
quarter . . . (*He stops writing and looks at* KAREN)
That's a lipstick.

KAREN (*Taking the empty Bendel box from the chair*)
I don't have a pencil.

SAM Then why do you give me a lipstick?

KAREN Because I don't have a pencil. It's shocking pink but it writes.
(*Puts the box into the wastebasket next to the dresser*)

SAM (*He glares at her. Into the phone*) All right, I'm going to go over my figures here. If Henderson calls or the contracts come in, bring them right over. What's that? (*He laughs*) Yes! Well, it's like we were saying the other night, it's the old badger game. (*He laughs again.* KAREN *mocks his private joke with* MISS MC-CORMAC *as she hobbles back into the bedroom*) . . . All right, I'll speak to you later. And thank you, Miss McCormack. (*He hangs up*) A hundred and seventy-five thousand dollar contract, you give me a lipstick.
(*Puts the lipstick down on the table next to the chair*)

KAREN (*Hobbles out of the bathroom with the vase*) I'd have given you blood but it isn't blue.

SAM All right, don't test me, because I've got enough of a headache. (*He rubs his eyes with his thumb and index finger, opens the case and takes out a bottle of aspirin. She limps into the living room and places the vase on the desk. He looks at her*) And for God's sakes, Karen, stop hobbling around. I don't feel like listening to thump, thump, thump!

KAREN (*She sighs*) And happy anniversary to you.

SAM What?

KAREN Forget it.
(*Sits at the desk and takes off her other galosh and shoe*)

SAM (*Moving to the bathroom with the aspirin*) What are you talking about? . . . It's not our anniversary.

KAREN Today is December fourteenth, isn't it?

SAM Yes.

KAREN So. We're married twenty-four years today.

SAM (*Looks at her incredulously*) Are you serious?

KAREN We're not married twenty-four years today?

SAM No.
(*Comes out of the bathroom with a glass of water and takes an aspirin*)

KAREN We're not married twenty-four years?

SAM No.

KAREN . . . We're not married?

SAM Tomorrow is our anniversary and we're married twenty-three years.
(*Puts the glass down on the dresser and moves into the living room*)

KAREN (*Looks at him*) . . . Are you sure?

SAM What do you mean, am I sure? I know when our anniversary is. December fifteenth, we're married twenty-three years. How can you make a mistake like that?

KAREN All right, don't get so excited, and it's not such a big mistake because I didn't get you a present . . . You're sure it's not the fourteenth?

SAM I go through this with you every year. When it comes to money or dates or ages, you are absolutely unbelievable. (*Turns, exasperated, and goes to the bedroom*) We were married December fifteenth, nineteen forty-five . . .

KAREN Then I'm right. Twenty-*four* years.

SAM Forty-five from sixty-eight is *twenty-three!*

KAREN Then I'm wrong. (*Shrugs*) Math isn't one of my best subjects.

SAM (*Hanging his jacket over the dresser chair*) This isn't math, this is people's *lives!* (*Moves back to* KAREN) How old are you?

KAREN What?

SAM It's a simple question. How old are you?

KAREN (*She's reluctant to answer and moves to the window*) I don't want to play.

SAM   I can't believe it. You really don't know how old you are.

KAREN   I know how old I am. But you get me nervous. Promise you won't leave me if I'm wrong . . . I'll be forty-nine in April. (SAM *stares at her in the disbelief, crosses back into the bedroom and wearily leans against the closet door.* KAREN *follows him*) . . . Isn't that right?

SAM   No, but you're close.

KAREN   I'm not going to be forty-nine?

SAM   Not *this* April. *This* April you're going to be forty-eight. How the hell can you make a mistake like that? Can't you add?
      (*Taking several contracts out of the attaché case*)

KAREN   All right, don't talk to me like I'm a child. I'm a forty-eight-year-old woman.

SAM   But the thing that infuriates me is that you make the mistake the wrong way. Why don't you make yourself younger instead of older, the way other women do?

KAREN   Okay, I'm forty-seven. (*Throws herself on the bed and poses sexily*) So how do I look to you now?

SAM   I've got work to do. I've got a very important meeting at eight o'clock in the morning.
      (*Crosses to the desk and sits*)

KAREN   (*Sitting up in bed*)   Oh, come on, Sam, where's your sense of humor? I think it's cute as hell that I don't know how old I am.

SAM   (*Starts to look over the papers*)   I can't even think straight. I've had five meetings this morning, four teeth capped, and I haven't even had my Metrecal. (*He crosses to the phone in the living room*) I'd better eat something.
      (*Picks up the phone*)

KAREN   I just ordered hors d'oeuvres.

SAM   Not for me. You know I'm on nine hundred calories a day. (*Into the phone*) Room service, please. (*He turns and looks in the mirror*) . . . My God, who the hell is that? Will you look at my eyes? I have no pupils left. (*He turns to* KAREN) Come here. Look at this. Do you see any pupils?

KAREN (*Crosses and looks into the mirror*) Yes, Sam. I see two gorgeous pupils . . .

SAM (*Still looking in the mirror*) Where? Where? I don't have a pupil in my head. Would you get my eye drops out of the case . . .

KAREN (*Crossing to the case on the bed*) I think you've been overworking, Sam. I haven't seen you two nights this month.

SAM (*Stretches his arms*) I really could use some sun. And about a month of sleep.

KAREN (*Searching through the case*) Hey, why don't we go down to Jamaica for a couple weeks? Just the two of us. We haven't done that in years.

SAM (*Into the phone, pacing*) Oh, hello, room service, where were you? . . . Listen, I'd like a plate of cold roast beef, medium rare, very lean. You know what very lean is? . . . No, it doesn't mean no fat . . . It means *absolutely* no fat . . . and I want a salad, *no dressing*, a half grapefruit and a pot of black coffee . . . And I'd appreciate it as soon as possible . . . Wait a second. (*To* KAREN, *who has entered the living room with eye drops*) Where are we again?

KAREN 719, Plaza Hotel, New York, twenty-three, New York.

SAM (*Into the phone*) 719 . . . As soon as you can. (*He hangs up, moves down to* KAREN *at the couch*) What's wrong with you today?

KAREN You wouldn't believe it, but fifteen minutes ago I was the happiest woman on earth . . . Sit down, I'll put your pupils back in.

SAM (*Hand extended*) I can do it myself.

KAREN I know you can, Sam, but I like to put your eye drops in. (*He lies down on the sofa with his head on the arm and she moves to look down at him from*

the side of the sofa) It's the only time lately you look at me.
　　(*She poises the eye dropper*)

SAM (*Looks up at her*)　. . . I'm sorry.

KAREN　You are?

SAM　I haven't been nice to *anyone* the past couple of weeks.

KAREN　You sounded swell to Miss McCormack.

SAM　Put the eye drops in.

KAREN (*Bending down over the arm of the sofa*)　First give an old lady a kiss.
　　(*He gives her a soft, gentle kiss*)

SAM　I give you my permission to hate me.

KAREN (*Straightens up*)　I'll save it for later. Open your gorgeous pupils.
　　(KAREN *fills the dropper with fluid*)

SAM　Eight months I've been working on this deal and suddenly today my two top men in the office come down with the flu and I've got to do everything myself. (*She puts the drops in his eye. He jumps up*) Aaghh!
　　(*He grabs his eye in pain*)

KAREN　What's the matter?

SAM (*Sitting up*)　You *drop* them in, you don't *push* them in.

KAREN　I'm sorry, you moved your head.

SAM　I moved my head because you were stabbing my eyeball. (*Gets up and peers in the mirror over the fireplace*) Oh, damn it!

KAREN　All right, don't panic, Sam, I'm sorry.

SAM　Why do you think they call it a dropper? If they wanted you to stab people, they would call it a stabber. (*Grabs it from her*) Give it to me, I'll do it myself.
　　(*Lies back down on the sofa and begins to put drops in both eyes*)

KAREN You mean that's the end of being nice to each other?

SAM I don't know what we're doing in a hotel anyway.

KAREN What's the Plaza got to do with my stabbing your eyeball?

SAM Because it's insane being here, that's why. I've got work to do tonight, I don't know how I'm going to concentrate.

KAREN You've got to sleep *some*place tonight. The painter says it's going to take two days for the house to dry.

SAM Yes, but why *now*? Do it in the spring. This is my busy time of the year.
> (SAM *puts the eye drops on the coffee table and crosses to the bedroom*)

KAREN I know, but it's not the painter's busy time of the year. In the spring he doesn't want to know you.

SAM Why didn't you ask me first?
> (KAREN *follows him into the bedroom*)

KAREN I never see you . . . I saw the painter.

SAM You could have checked with my secretary.
> (*He goes into the bathroom*)

KAREN I did. She said go ahead and paint the house.
> (*She takes his coat from the bed and hangs it in the closet*)

SAM'S VOICE Of all times of the year. Did you bring my things? Toothbrush? Pajamas?

KAREN I brought your toothbrush.

SAM'S VOICE You forgot my pajamas?

KAREN (*Plops down on the bed*) I didn't forget them, I just didn't bring them.
> (SAM *comes out of the bathroom wiping his eyes on the towel*)

SAM Why not?

KAREN   Because this is Suite 719 at the Plaza and I just didn't think you'd want your pajamas tonight.

SAM   You know I can't sleep without pajamas.
(*He returns to the bathroom*)

KAREN (*Yelling after him*)   I took that into consideration . . .

SAM   What?

KAREN   Never mind. They've got shops in the lobby. (*Gets up and picks up the phone next to the bed*) Should I send for their catalog or will you take pot luck?

SAM   Heh. You know what a pair of pajamas would cost at the Plaza? Forty, fifty dollars.

KAREN   You want me to send a bellhop to Bloomingdale's? (*Hangs up the phone*)

SAM (*Comes out of the bathroom*)   I don't understand you. One lousy little bag is all you had to pack.

KAREN   Forgive me. It's my busy time of the year.

SAM   Karen, do me a favor. Don't get brittle. (*Crosses to the desk in the living room*) I'm very shaky right now and one good crack and I go right to the dry cleaner's . . . Boy, could I use a nice, big, cold double martini.
(*He sits and begins to examine the contracts*)

KAREN (*Follows him into the living and leans on the chest of drawers*)   Don't get angry, but can I make a suggestion? Why don't you have a nice, big, cold double martini?

SAM   Are you serious? You know how many calories are in a double martini?

KAREN (*Shrugs*)   Four or five million?

SAM   You know my metabolism. One double martini, and right in front of your eyes I get flabby.

KAREN   You used to get sexy.
(*She takes a sheet from a pile of stationery in the chest*)

SAM (*Gets up with the papers to sit in more comfort on the sofa*)   Well, now I get flabby. Unless I watch my-

self like a hawk . . . (*As he passes the fireplace mirror, he pauses, admiring his waistline*) which I think I manage to do.
    (*Sits on the sofa*)

KAREN (*She starts to fold the piece of stationery*) I like you flabby.

SAM What does that mean?

KAREN (*Still folding the paper*) It means I like you flabby. I admit you look like one of the Pepsi generation, but it seems a little unnatural to me. A man of your age ought to have a couple of pounds of skin hanging over his belt.

SAM Well, I'm sorry to disappoint you.

KAREN I'm not disappointed, I'm uncomfortable. I watch you when you get undressed at night. Nothing moves. You're vacuum packed. When you open your belt I expect it to go like a can of coffee—Pzzzzzz!
    (*She continues folding*)

SAM Do you think it's easy with my metabolism to keep my weight down? Do you know what it's like to have a business luncheon at the Villa Capri and watch someone slop down a bowl of spaghetti and I'm munching on a hearts of lettuce salad?

KAREN My compliments to your restraint.

SAM I go through torture to maintain my weight.

KAREN I have nothing but admiration for your waistline.
    (*She is through folding*)

SAM But you like me flabby.

KAREN We all have our little perversions.

SAM Can we drop the subject?

KAREN Like a baked potato.

SAM Thank you.

KAREN You're welcome.
    (*She aims her finished paper airplane across the room and lets it fly*)

SAM (*Gets up and paces angrily*) . . . Why do you like me flabby?

KAREN Is the floor open again?

SAM No. Forget it.

KAREN It's forgotten.

SAM What was I just doing?

KAREN Watching yourself like a hawk.
(*She crosses to the bedroom and begins to fold her negligée at the dresser.* SAM *returns to the sofa. There is a silence. Finally*)

SAM Look, I just want to say one more thing and then the discussion is closed. (KAREN *puts down the negligée and crosses back to the sofa in the living room*) I'm at the athletic club three, four times a week watching men at least ten years younger than me huffing and puffing trying to sweat off a couple of ounces that goes right back on after the cocktail hour. Now maybe you don't consider it a monumental achievement, but my weight hasn't changed in six years. I'm still one seventy-seven on the scale.

KAREN So am I. (*Crosses to the bedroom and puts the negligée away in the chest*) Now you know why I like you flabby . . . The subject is closed.
(*She crosses to the chair and sits.* SAM, *upset, remains in the living room. They contemplate the floor a few seconds*)

SAM . . . Hey, Karen.

KAREN Yah, Sam . . .

SAM Let's not fight.

KAREN It's all right with me, Sam.

SAM . . . Let's be nice to each other.

KAREN Okay . . . Who goes first?
(SAM *gets up and starts for the bedroom. He stops at the door . . . trying to find words*)

SAM Karen . . .

KAREN (*Looks up*) Yes, Sam?

SAM (*This doesn't seem to be the time to bring up what-*

ever is on his mind) Nothing . . . I'm going to do a little work, okay?

> (*He goes back into the living room and sits on the sofa*)

KAREN (*Still sitting. Without malice*) You don't even remember this room, you louse.

SAM What's that?

KAREN (*Gets up and crosses into the living room*) I may not know how old I am, but I sure as hell remember we spent our honeymoon night in Suite 719 at the Plaza Hotel and this is definitely 719 because I just tipped the bellhop an entire dollar.

SAM (*Looks at the room for the first time*) Was this the room?

KAREN Oh, Christ.

> (*She sits on the arm of the sofa*)

SAM (*Gets up and looks about*) Wait a minute, I think you're right. (*He looks into the bedroom*) Sure, this looks like the suite. Only it was decorated differently. This room was blue.

KAREN (*Going into the bedroom*) That was you. You were in the Navy. The bedroom was green.

SAM I think you're mistaken. The bedroom was blue.

KAREN You're probably confusing it with some other honeymoon . . . (*Sitting on the bed*) Hey, Sam, remember we had dinner here in the bedroom?

SAM. No

KAREN Yes. We had dinner here in the bedroom. Do you remember what we had?

SAM For dinner? Twenty-three years ago?

KAREN *I* remember. You remember too. Take a guess.

SAM Karen, I don't remember.

KAREN Yes, you do. Think about it a second.

SAM I thought about it. I don't remember.

KAREN We had a bottle of champagne and a tray full of hors d'oeuvres. And we left all the anchovies in the drawer.
  (*Indicates the night table*)

SAM Oh.
  (*Crosses and looks out the living room window*)

KAREN See. It's coming back to you. (*Notices him looking out the window*) If you're looking for the Savoy-Plaza, it's not there.
  (*She goes to the bedroom window and follows his gaze*)

SAM (*Looking out the window*) I'm looking at the Pierre.

KAREN There it is.

SAM . . . Karen.

KAREN What?

SAM (*Still looking out the window*) It was 819. (KAREN *Steps back from the window and looks at* SAM. SAM *turns and looks at her*) We were in 819, not 719.

KAREN (*She glares at him and grits her teeth with hostility*) You're wrong!

SAM I'm not wrong, I'm right. We were in 819. I'm right.

KAREN (*Angry*) Don't keep saying you're right like you're right. You're wrong. We were in 719.

SAM I'll prove it to you. Come here. (KAREN *joins him at the living-room window*) Remember, I had my binoculars, we were watching that couple getting undressed in the Pierre? They were on the eighth floor. I remember because we were looking for them the next night. We called them "The Couple on the Eighth Floor."

KAREN I don't know what you called them, I called them "The Couple on the Seventh Floor."
  (*She walks away angrily into the bedroom*)

SAM Look, it's pointless to argue about it. It's not important.

KAREN (*From the bedroom*) If it's pointless, then why are you pointing it out?

SAM Because you made an issue of it.

KAREN (*Crossing to the bedroom door*) Maybe I made an issue of saying we were in 719, but *you* made an issue of proving to me we *weren't* in 719.

SAM All right, Karen.
(*He walks away to the fireplace*)

KAREN Don't tell me, "All right, Karen." If I thought it was 719, why didn't you have the decency to let me just go on in my ignorance and think it was 719?

SAM Okay. Okay. I'm sorry. It was 719.

KAREN Aw, forget it. It was 819.
(*Moves back into the bedroom*)

SAM (*Rushing into the bedroom*) No, no. As a matter of fact, you're right. I just remembered. It really was 719.

KAREN I don't want it 719. I want it 819 . . . Look, why don't you go inside and lose some weight? (*That was a nasty remark.* SAM *glares at* KAREN, *then goes into the living room, reassures himself with a glance at his waistline in the fireplace mirror, picks up his work papers and sits.* KAREN *realizes what she's done. She crosses to the living room and embraces him*) I'm sorry, Sam. (SAM *nods his head and looks at his papers.* KAREN *moves around the sofa*) . . . We're some lousy couple, aren't we? . . . Aren't we?

SAM. (*Doesn't look up*) Mmm.

KAREN Mmm what?
(*Sitting on the arm of the sofa*)

SAM (*Looks up*) Mmm, yes, we're some lousy couple.

KAREN (*Without malice*) That's what I said. First thing we agreed on today.

SAM Look, Karen, I really don't mean to be rude, but I *must* work on these estimates tonight. You understand.

KAREN Sure, I understand.

SAM I explained to you that Sid and Walter suddenly came down with the flu—

KAREN It's all right, Sam. You're excused . . . (*She wanders aimlessly about the room. Catching sight of herself in the mirror over the chest, she examines her figure and then decides to do some exercises, which she quickly gives up. She sits on the arm of the sofa next to* SAM) Do you have any good estimates for me to read?

SAM Isn't there anything to read in the bedroom?

KAREN (*Shrugs*) "Check-out time is three o'clock." That's all I could find . . . Don't worry about me. I'll find something to do.

> (SAM *goes back to his papers.* KAREN *puts her arms around his shoulders and rocks him play-fully from side to side, much to* SAM's *displeasure. Suddenly she releases him, goes to the front door, opens it and goes into the hall*)

SAM What are you doing?

KAREN (*Coming back into the room*) Looking for the waiter.

SAM Call him up.

KAREN I thought I'd look in the hall first. Gives me something to do. (*She goes back out into the hall*) Nope, don't see him. (*Comes back in and closes the door*) In five minutes I'll call. See? I'll alternate them.

SAM Karen, please.

KAREN (*Crosses to him and takes his arm*) Oh, come on. Forget your crummy old papers and take me to a dirty movie. (*Tries to pull him out of the sofa*) Come on,. Sam. Let's go.

SAM Stop it, Karen.

KAREN You know what's playing on Sixth Avenue? *Cat House Confidential* and *Ursula the Slut*. I passed it in the cab, I swear on my mother's life.

SAM Don't be ridiculous.

KAREN (*Kneeling by the sofa*) Are you afraid we'll be recognized? We'll buy beards in the five-and-ten.

SAM If you want to go, go yourself.

KAREN What happens if I get picked up?

SAM Call me and I won't wait up for you.

KAREN (*Hugging him*) Oh, good, you've got your sense of humor back. All right, just take a walk with me. A ten-minute walk and I'll leave you alone.

SAM Maybe later. We'll see.

KAREN (*Getting up and pacing*) No movies . . . no walk. (*She sits on top of the chest of drawers and picks up* What to Do in New York *magazine and skims through it. There is a silence. Finally*) Feel like going back to the house and watching the paint dry? (SAM, *at the end of his patience, gets up with the papers and moves into the bedroom*) . . . I'm just trying to think of something we can do together.
    (*The doorbell rings*)

SAM (*Pacing in the bedroom*) Shall I get it, or is that something you'd like for us to do together?

KAREN Listen, I'll even take nastiness. It's not much, but it's a start.
    (KAREN *crosses to the door and opens it. It's the* WAITER *with the food on a roller table. He is a middle-aged Puerto Rican*)

WAITER Good evening.

KAREN (*Smiles*) Hello.
    (*The* WAITER *rolls the table in*)

WAITER Would you like the table near the window?

KAREN (*Moves toward the bedroom*) Sam, would you like the table near the window?

SAM (*Disinterested*) It doesn't make any difference.

KAREN (*Sweetly, to the* WAITER) It doesn't make any difference.

WAITER (*Leaving the table up near the window*) Shall I leave it here?

KAREN Sam, should he leave it there?

SAM (*Throwing the contract on the bed and moving to the doorway*) Here, there, anywhere, it doesn't make any difference.

KAREN (*Shrugs, smiles at the* WAITER) Here, there, anywhere. It doesn't make any difference.

WAITER (*Takes a chair from the desk and puts it to the right of the table*) Yes, Ma'am.
        (*He gets the armchair from the right of the sofa and brings it to the table*)

SAM (*To the* WAITER) You don't have to set up the chairs.

KAREN (*To the* WAITER) You don't have to set up the chairs.

WAITER Yes, Ma'am.
        (*He starts to put the armchair back*)

SAM All right, leave them, you've done it already.

KAREN Yes, why don't you just leave the chairs. They're all set up.
        (*The* WAITER *puts the chair back at the table*)

SAM Can I have the bill, please?

WAITER Yes, sir.
        (*Takes the bill and a pencil to* SAM. KAREN *looks at the tray of hors d'oeuvres on the table*)

KAREN (*Sweetly*) Oh, look at all the anchovies.

SAM (*Signing the bill*) Didn't you tell them you didn't want anchovies?

WAITER (*To* KAREN) You didn't want anchovies?

KAREN (*Doesn't want more trouble*) No, no. I asked for anchovies. I'm a very big fan of anchovies.

SAM (*Hands the bill to the* WAITER) That'll be all, thank you.

KAREN Yes, that'll be all, thank you.

WAITER And thank you.
        (*Crosses to the door*)

KAREN (*Looks at the table*) Wait a minute. The champagne. Where's the champagne?

WAITER No champagne? (*Looks at the check*) You're right. They forgot the champagne.

KAREN But the anchovies they remembered.

SAM (*Returning to the bedroom*) I can't drink anything now, I've got work to do. What do you need a whole bottle of champagne for?

KAREN It's our anniversary. (*To the* WAITER) It's our anniversary.

WAITER Oh, congratulations.

KAREN (*Sitting on the arm of the chair at the table*) Thank you. We're married twenty-three or twenty-four years today or tomorrow.

WAITER Then you want the champagne?

KAREN With two grown children in college.

WAITER Oh? That's wonderful.

KAREN (*Shrugs*) You think so? He's flunking out and she's majoring in dirty clothes.

SAM (*Greatly irritated, moves back to the living room*) He's not flunking out. Why do you say he's flunking out? (*Controls himself. To the* WAITER) That'll be all, thank you.

WAITER If you don't want the champagne, I'll cross it out of the bill.

SAM She doesn't want the champagne. Cross it off the bill.
(*Crosses back to the bedroom*)

KAREN (*To the* WAITER) I *want* the champagne. Don't cross it off the bill. Bring me a bottle and *one* glass.

WAITER Yes, Ma'am.

SAM (*From the bedroom*) That'll be all, thank you.

KAREN Yes, that'll be all, thank you.

WAITER (*Opening the door*) When you want me to take the table, just ring.

KAREN (*Moving to the* WAITER)   Yes, I'll ring when I want you to take the table.

WAITER   Thank you . . . And again, congratulations. (*He exits.* SAM *crosses to the table and takes the cover off a dish*)

KAREN   (*At the mantel*)   . . . Did you hear that, Sam? We're being congratulated on being married to each other.

SAM (*Disgusted, slams the cover back on the dish*)   I asked for lean roast beef. That is not lean roast beef. (*Moves to the sofa and sits, taking a contract from the coffee table*)

KAREN (*Contemplatively*)   You know how many people we know who are still married as long as us? One other couple. The Shelley's . . . The most boring people I ever met.

SAM (*Cannot contain himself any more*)   Why do you talk to the waiter like that?

KAREN   Like what?
(*Sits at the table and begins to serve herself*)

SAM   Like you've known him for twenty years. You just met him. He walked in here two minutes ago with fatty roast beef. It's none of his business how our son is doing in school.

KAREN   I was just having a conversation. I get lonely, I like to talk to people.

SAM   He's a waiter. Talk to him about food.

KAREN   I did something wrong again. I'm sorry, Sam. When he brings the champagne I'll hide behind the drapes.

SAM   You don't have to hide. Just don't tell him our personal problems, that's all.

KAREN   What should I do, lie?

SAM   Certainly, lie. Everybody else does. Tell them you have a beautiful and devoted daughter. Tell them you have a brilliant son who's on the dean's list. Tell them you're only forty-two years old.

KAREN   There's no point to it. In two years I'll be fifty. Who's going to like me better if I'm only forty-two?

SAM   You don't have to revel in it like it's some kind of an accomplishment.

KAREN   I'm not insane about getting older. It happens to everyone. It's happened to you. You're fifty-one years old.

SAM   (*Nods his head in exasperation*) That's the difference between us. I don't accept it. I don't have to accept being fifty-one. (*Getting up and moving to her*) I don't accept getting older.

KAREN   Good luck to you. You'll be the youngest one in the cemetery.

SAM   We can't even have a normal discussion any more. (*He stalks into the bedroom, closes the door and stretches out on the bed*)

KAREN   Accept being fifty-one and I'll have a normal discussion. (*Stops as* SAM *closes the door*) . . . Aren't you going to have your dinner? (*Gets up and examines the plate of meat. Holds up a piece to the bedroom door and calls to* SAM) Sam, I found some very lean roast beef. (*She nibbles on a piece*) Come inside and see how thin I'm getting. (*The doorbell rings*) . . . Hey, come on. The champagne is here. (*She opens the door to the bedroom and calls in*) If you don't come out, I'll tell the waiter you wear dentures. (*She crosses and opens the front door.* JEAN MCCORMACK *stands there. She is* SAM's *secretary. She is a trim, attractive woman about twenty-eight. She is neatly dressed, bright, cheerful and smilingly efficient*) . . . Oh! Hello, Miss McCormack.

JEAN   Hello, Mrs. Nash. I hope I'm not disturbing you.

KAREN   No, no, not at all. Mr. Nash and I were just sitting around, joking. Come in.
(*Still holding the roast beef in her hand*)

JEAN   Thank you. (*She enters the room, closing the door behind her*) I hate to barge in this way, but I have some papers that need Mr. Nash's signature immediately.

KAREN Certainly. (*Calls out*) Sam. It's Miss McCormack. (*To* JEAN) It is *Miss* McCormack now, isn't it?

JEAN (*Taking several contracts out of her brief case*) It *was* Mrs. Colby last year. This year it's Miss McCormack again.

KAREN (*Sitting on the arm of the sofa*) Oh. You're lucky you can remember. I've been married so long, if I got divorced, I'd have to make up a maiden name . . . Have you had your dinner yet?
(*Indicates the roast beef in her hand*)

JEAN (*Laying out some contracts on the coffee table in front of the sofa*) I don't have dinner, thank you.

KAREN No dinner? Ever?

JEAN (*Getting her glasses and a pen from her purse on the console table behind the sofa*) I have a large breakfast, a moderate lunch and a snack before going to bed. On this job I've worked late so often, I had to readjust my eating routine. Now I'm used to it.
(SAM *gets up from the bed and moves into the living room*)

KAREN Oh. Well, I can understand that. I miss a lot of dinners with Mr. Nash too.

SAM Oh, hello. You got them, huh?
(*Sits on the sofa and examines a contract*)

JEAN Just came in. All ready for signature.

KAREN (*To* JEAN) How about some black coffee? Or would that fill you up?

JEAN Black coffee would be fine, thank you

KAREN One black coffee coming up. Sam, would you like some black coffee?

SAM No.

KAREN That's no black coffee and one black coffee.
(KAREN *crosses to the table;* SAM *is looking over the contracts.* JEAN *sits next to him.* KAREN *pours coffee*)

SAM　Why is there an adjustment on this figure?

JEAN　(*Looks at it*)　There was a clerical omission on the Cincinnati tabulations. It didn't show up on the 1400 but I rechecked it with my own files and made the correction. (*Points to respective pages of the contract*) So that item 17B should read three hundred and twenty-five thousand and disregard the figure on 17A.

KAREN　Cream and sugar?

JEAN　No, thank you.

SAM　But this should have been caught on the IBM.

JEAN　It should have, but it wasn't. Obviously it wasn't fed properly.

KAREN　No cream and no sugar or no cream and yes, sugar?

JEAN　No cream and *no* sugar.

KAREN　So it's yes, no cream and no sugar.

SAM　Did you call this to Purcell's attention?

KAREN　(*Handing a cup to* JEAN)　Would you like some pastry or cookies? I could call down. They have beautiful pastry and cookies here.

JEAN　This is fine thank you. (*To* SAM)　Mr. Purcell says this happened once before this month. He can't pin it down until he rechecks the whole 66 file.

KAREN　(*Leaning on the console table behind the sofa*)　You're sure? A sandwich? A Welsh rarebit?

JEAN　No, I'm really quite happy, thank you. (*Takes saccharine from her purse and puts it in the coffee*)

SAM　Well, I'm just going to have to go over this whole thing tonight with Howard. If we give Henderson any room for doubt, we can blow our entire presentation.

JEAN　(*Sips the coffee*)　I told him there was a possibility of this, so he made plans to stay in town tonight.

SAM　Damn! Of all nights to have this happen. (*Putting down the contract*) What time is it now?

JEAN (*Looks at her watch*) Ten past five.

KAREN (*Looking over* JEAN's *shoulder*) Ten past five.

SAM All right, you tell Howard I'll meet him in the office between six fifteen and six thirty. Tell him I want to see every one of last year's 1400 forms.

KAREN (*Moving around the sofa to* SAM) You're going to the office? Tonight?

SAM It can't be helped, Karen. (JEAN *puts her coffee cup down*) We're having that same damned trouble with the computer again.

KAREN I could go with you. Maybe all it needs is a little dusting.

SAM Something in that office sure as hell needs dusting. (*Getting up and moving to the bedroom.* JEAN *gathers up the contracts and moves to put them in the brief case at the console table*) All right, Miss McCormack, why don't you hop in a cab now and get started on these figures with Howard? I just want to clean up and I'll meet you in about twenty minutes.

JEAN Yes, sir.

SAM I hope I'm not ruining any plans you had for to-night.

JEAN When I saw the figures this morning, I expected it. (*Closes the case.* SAM *takes a bottle of pills from his attaché case and crosses to the bathroom*) Mrs. Nash, thank you very much for the coffee.

KAREN You really should eat something. You'll faint right over the IBM machine.

JEAN (*Opening the front door*) I'll be all right.

KAREN (*Moving to her above the sofa*) It's a pity you can't stay two more minutes. I just ordered champagne. Can I tell her why, Sam?

SAM (*Returns from the bathroom, having taken pills. Throws the pills back into his case*) What's that?
    (*Drinks from a glass on the dresser. Takes his jacket from the back of the chair and puts in on*)

KAREN   Well, I'm not supposed to go around blurting these things out, but it's our twenty-third anniversary . . .

JEAN   Oh? I didn't know. Congratulations.

KAREN   (*To* JEAN, *but for* SAM's *benefit*)   Thank you . . . Yes, life has been very good to me. I have a beautiful and devoted daughter, a brilliant son who's on the dean's list, I'm forty-two years old, what more can I ask?

SAM   (*Moving into the living room*)   Karen, Miss Mc-Cormack has to get back to the office.
(SAM *goes back into the bedroom, takes hairbrushes from an overnight bag and brushes his hair in front of the closet mirror*)

KAREN   Oh, I'm sorry. (*To* JEAN) Don't let him work you too late.

JEAN   It's all right. I'm used to it now. Best wishes again, Mrs. Nash.

KAREN   (*As* JEAN *starts out*)   Thanks, dear. And see that he buys me a nice gift.

JEAN   (*Smiles*)   I definitely will.
(*Closes the door*)

KAREN   (*To* SAM)   What a sweet girl. That's a very sweet girl, Sam.

SAM   Karen, listen, I'm very sorry about tonight. It just can't be helped.
(*Puts the brushes back*)

KAREN   That's a sweet, young, skinny girl.

SAM   (*Takes a cordless electric razor from his attaché case and crosses to the bathroom*)   The thing is, if I leave now maybe I can still get back in time for us to have a late dinner.

KAREN   (*Enters the bedroom and sits in the armchair*)   Oh, don't worry about me, Sam. (SAM *begins to shave*) I understand. I just feel badly for you. You could have really relaxed tonight, and instead you'll be cooped up in that stuffy office until all hours working over some boring contracts with your smooth-shaven face.

SAM (*Still shaving, moves into the bedroom*) Well, I can't very well walk through the lobby of the Plaza Hotel with a stubbly chin.
    (*Returns to the bathroom*)

KAREN They wouldn't let you into the elevator. Don't forget your Jade East.

SAM'S VOICE My what?

KAREN Your sexy cologne. The doorman will never get you a cab if you don't smell nice.

SAM (*Enters the bedroom. Looks at* KAREN *for a moment and then shuts the razor off*) What are you doing, Karen?

KAREN Oh, I'm just joking. Can't you tell when I'm kidding around any more, Sam?

SAM No, I can't.
    (*Crosses around the bed and puts the razor back in the case*)

KAREN (*Playfully pats his fanny, and then sits on the bed*) Well, of course I am. I'm just teasing you by intimating you're having an affair with your secretary.

SAM I see.
    (*Takes his overcoat from the top of the bureau and puts it on*)

KAREN Are you, Sam? Is sweet, skinny Miss McCormack your mistress?

SAM For God's sakes, Karen, what kind of a thing is that to say?

KAREN If you're not, it's a lousy thing to say. If you are, it's a hell of a question.

SAM I'm not even going to dignify that with an answer.

KAREN (*On her knees, bouncing up and down like a child*) Oh, come on, Sam, dignify it. I'm dying to know. Just tell me if you're having an affair with her or not.

SAM And you'll believe me?

KAREN   Of course.

SAM   No, I'm not having an affair with her.

KAREN   (*Giving a big smile*)   Yes, you are.

SAM   Curses, trapped again. (*Looks out the window*)
It looks like snow. I hope I can get a cab.

KAREN   (*Starting to take off her hairpiece*)   Even if you're
not, Sam, it's all right if you do. I approve of Miss
McCormack. She's a nice girl.

SAM   (*Getting his attaché case from the bed*)   Thank
you. She'll be pleased to know. Look, I could call
downstairs and get you a ticket for a show tonight.
There's no reason for you to sit alone like this. Is
there something you'd like to see?

KAREN   (*Smiles*)   Yeah. What you and Miss McCormack
will be doing later.

SAM   Really, Karen, I find this in very poor taste.
(*Moving to the living room, puts the attaché case
down on the console table behind the sofa*)

KAREN   (*Getting a brush from the overnight case*)   Why?
I'm just being honest again. I'm saying that if at this
stage of your life you wanted to have a small, quiet
affair with a young, skinny woman, I would understand.
(*Sits back on the bed and begins to brush out her
hairpiece*)

SAM   (*Stops abruptly in his gathering of the contracts
from the coffee table and returns to the bedroom*)
What do you mean, at this stage of my life?

KAREN   (*Continues her brushing*)   Well, you're blankety
years old. I would say the number but I know you
don't accept it. And I realize that when a man becomes
blankety-one or blankety-two, he is feeling insecure,
that he's losing his virility (*Smiles broadly at* SAM),
and that a quiet fling may be the best thing for him.
I know, I read the New York *Post*.

SAM   I'm glad to know I have Rose Franzblau's permission.

KAREN   And mine if you really want it.

SAM (*Yells*)   Well, I don't want it and *I'm not having an affair!*

KAREN   Then why are you yelling?

SAM (*Crosses to the living room*)   Because this is an idiotic conversation.

KAREN (*Collapses on the bed*)   Oh, Sam, I'm so glad.

SAM (*Takes the contracts from the coffee table and puts them in his case*)   Now you're happy? You're happy because *now* you don't think I'm having an affair?

KAREN   Well, of course I'm happy. You think I'm some kind of a domestic mental case? I don't want you having an affair. I'm just saying that if you *are* having one, I understand.

SAM (*Crosses to the bedroom and picks up a contract from the bed*)   Karen, I have a hard night's work ahead of me. I'll be back about twelve.
(*Starts to leave*)

KAREN   Sam, stay and talk to me for five minutes.

SAM   They're waiting for me at the office. I've got work to do.

KAREN   You've got help in the office. I've been with the firm longer than all of them . . . (*After a moment,* SAM *sits on the edge of the bureau*) Sam, I know we haven't been very happy lately. I know you've been busy, you may not have noticed it, but we have definitely not been very happy.

SAM   Yes, Karen, I've noticed it.

KAREN (*Continues to brush her hairpiece*)   What's wrong? We have a twelve-room house in the country, two sweet children, a maid who doesn't drink. Is there something we're missing?

SAM   I—don't know.

KAREN   Can you at least think about it? I need hints, Sam . . . (*Quoting*) "Is there something else you want?" (SAM *doesn't answer*) "Is there something I can give you that I'm not giving you?" (*Again no answer*) . . . Could you please speak up, we're closing in ten minutes.

SAM It's me, Karen, not you.
(*Crosses to the living room, puts the contract in his case, closes it*)

KAREN (*Puts her hair and brush on the dresser and follows him into the living room*) I'll buy that. What's wrong with you, Sam?

SAM (*There is a long pause*) I don't know . . . (*Moves to the mantel and then paces in front of the sofa*) I don't know if you can understand this . . . but when I came home after the war . . . I had my whole life in front of me. And all I dreamed about, all I wanted, was to get married, and to have children . . . and to make a success of my life . . . Well, I was very lucky . . . I I got it all . . . Marriage, the children . . . more money than I ever dreamed of making . . .

KAREN (*Sitting on the sofa*) Then what is it you want?

SAM (*Stopping by the fireplace*) I just want to do it all over again . . . I would like to start the whole damned thing right from the beginning.

KAREN (*Long pause*) I see. Well, frankly, Sam, I don't think the Navy will take you again.

SAM (*Smiles ruefully*) Well, it won't be because I can't pass the physical. (*Takes his case and starts for the door again*) I told you it's stupid talking about it. It'll work itself out. If not, I'll dye my hair.
(*He opens the door*)

KAREN You know what I think? I think you want to get out and you don't know how to tell me.

SAM (*Stops in the door. Turns back to* KAREN) That's not true.

KAREN Which isn't? That you want to get out or that you don't know how to tell me?

SAM Why do you always start the most serious discussions in our life when I'm halfway out the door?

KAREN If that's what you want, just tell me straight out. Just say, "Karen, there's no point in going on." I'd rather hear it from you personally, than getting a message on our service.

SAM Look, we'll talk about it when I get back, okay? (*He starts out again*)

KAREN (*Can no longer contain herself. There is none of that "playful, toying" attitude in her voice now. Jumping up*) No, goddamnit, we'll talk about it now! I'm not going to sit around a hotel room half the night waiting to hear how my life is going to come out ... If you've got something to say, then have the decency to say it before you walk out that door.
    (*There is a moment's silence while each tries to compose himself ... SAM turns back into the the room and closes the door*)

SAM ... Is there any coffee left?

KAREN It's that bad, huh? ... All right, sit down, I'll get you some coffee. (*She starts to cross to the table and stops, looking at her hands. SAM crosses to the sofa. He puts down his attaché case by the coffee table and sits*) Look at this. I'm shaking like a leaf. Pour it yourself. I have a feeling in a few minutes I'm not going to be too crazy about you.
    (*KAREN crosses and sits on the ottoman next to the sofa, hands clasped together. SAM finds it difficult to look at her*)

SAM ... No matter what, Karen, in twenty-three years my feelings for you have never changed. You're my wife, I still love you.

KAREN Oh, God, am I in trouble.

SAM It has nothing to do with you. It's something that just happened ... It's true, I am having an affair with her ... (*SAM waits for KAREN to react. She merely sits and looks at her hands*) ... It's been going on for about six months now ... I tried stopping it a few times, it didn't work ... After a couple of days I'd start it again ... And then—well, what's the point in going on with this? You wanted honesty, I'm giving it to you. I'm having an affair with Jean, that's all there is to it.

KAREN (*Looks up*) Who's Jean?

SAM Jean! Miss McCormack.

KAREN Oh. For a minute I thought there were two of them.

SAM I'm not very good at this. I don't know what I'm supposed to say now.

KAREN Don't worry about it. You're doing fine. (*She gets up and moves to the table*) You want that coffee now? I just stopped shaking.

SAM . . . What are we going to do?

KAREN (*Turns back to* SAM) Well, you're taken care of. You're having an affair. I'm the one who needs an activity.

SAM Karen, I'll do whatever you want.

KAREN Whatever *I* want?

SAM I'll leave. I'll get out tonight . . . Or I'll stop seeing her. I'll get rid of her in the office. I'll try it any way you want.

KAREN (*Moves to the sofa*) Oh. Okay. I choose "Stop Seeing Jean" . . . Gee, that was easy. (*Snaps her fingers*) Now we can go back to our old normal life and live happily ever after. (*Starts to pour coffee, but stops and puts the pot down*) It's not my day. Even the coffee's cold.

SAM Oh, come on, Karen, don't play "Aren't we civilized." Call me a bastard. Throw the coffee at me.

KAREN You're a bastard. You want cream and sugar?

SAM It's funny how our attitudes have suddenly changed. What happened to "I think a man of your age *should* have an affair"?

KAREN It looked good in the window but terrible when I got it home.

SAM If it's any solace to you, I never thought it would go this far. I don't even remember how it started . . .

KAREN Think, it'll come back to you.

SAM Do you know she worked for me for two years and I never batted an eye at her?

KAREN Good for you, Sam.

SAM (*Angry*) Oh, come on.
(*Crosses to the bedroom and stretches out across the bed*)

KAREN (*She follows him into the bedroom*) No, Sam, I want to hear about it. She worked for you for two years and you didn't know her first name was Jean. And then one night you were both working late, and suddenly you let down your hair and took off your glasses and she said, "Why, Mr. Nash, you're beautiful" . . .

SAM (*Takes a pillow and places it over his head*) That's it, word for word. You must have been hiding in the closet.

KAREN (*Tears the pillow away and throws it back down on the bed*) All right, you want to know when I think the exact date your crummy little affair started? I'll tell you. It was June nineteenth. It was your birthday, and you just turned fifty years old. Five-oh, count 'em, folks, and you were feeling good and sorry for yourself. Right?

SAM Oh, God, here comes Doctor Franzblau again.

KAREN And the only reason you picked on Miss McCormack was because she was probably the first one you saw that morning . . . If she was sick that day, this affair very well could have been with your elevator operator.

SAM Wrong. He's fifty-two and I don't go for older men.

KAREN (*Breaks away and crosses to the living room*) You were right before, Sam. Let's discuss this later tonight.

SAM (*Sitting up on his side on the bed*) No, no. We've opened this up, let's bring it all out. I've told you the truth, I'm involved with another woman. I'm not proud of it, Karen, but those are the facts. Now what am I supposed to do about it?

KAREN (*Moves back to the bedroom doorway*) Well, I *would* suggest committing suicide, but I'm afraid you might think I meant *me* . . . (*Goes back to the living room*) I have one other suggestion. Forget it.

SAM (*Sharply*) Forget it?

KAREN (*Pacing above the sofa*) I understand it, Sam. It's not your fault. But maybe I can live with it until it's over. What else can I do, Sam, I'm attached to you. So go out, have a good time tonight and when you come home, bring me the *Daily News*, I'm getting sick of the *Post*.
  (*Sits on the sofa*)

SAM If I lived with you another twenty-three years, I don't think I'd ever understand you.

KAREN If that's a proposition, I accept.

SAM (*Gets up and moves to* KAREN) Damn it, Karen, stop accepting everything in life that's thrown at you. Fight back once in a while. Don't understand me. Hate me! I am *not* going through a middle-aged adjustment. I'm having an affair. A cheating, sneaking, sordid affair.

KAREN If it helps you to romanticize it, Sam, all right. I happen to know better.

SAM (*Crossing above the sofa to the fireplace*) You don't know better at all. You didn't even know I was having an affair.

KAREN I suspected it. You were working three nights a week and we weren't getting any richer.

SAM (*Leaning on the mantelpiece*) I see. And now that you know the truth I have your blessings.

KAREN No, just my permission. I'm your wife, not your mother.

SAM That's indecent. I never heard such a thing in my life. For crying out loud, Karen, I'm losing all respect for you.

KAREN What's the matter, Sam, am I robbing you of all those delicious guilt feelings? Will you feel better if I go to pieces and try to lash back at you?

SAM *(Crosses below the sofa)* At least I would understand it. It's normal. I don't know why you're not having hysterics and screaming for a lawyer.

KAREN *(Getting up to confront him)* All right, Sam, if it'll make you happier . . . I think you stink. You're a vain, self-pitying, deceiving, ten-pound box of rancid no-cal cottage cheese. How'm I doing?

SAM Swell. Now we're finally getting somewhere.

KAREN Oh, you like this, don't you? It makes everything nice and simple for you. Now you can leave here the martyred, misunderstood husband. Well, I won't give you the satisfaction. I take it back, Sam. *(Sits on the sofa. Pleasantly, with great control)* You're a pussycat. I'll have milk and cookies for you when you get home.

SAM *(Sits on the ottoman)* No, no. Finish what you were saying. Get it off your chest, Karen. It's been building up for twenty-three years. I want to hear everything. Vain, self-pitying, what else? Go on, what else?

KAREN You're adorable. Eat your heart out.

SAM *(Furious)* Karen, don't do this to me.

KAREN I'm sorry, I'm a forgiving woman. I can't help myself.

SAM *(Gets up, takes his case and crosses to the door)* You're driving me right out of here, you know that, don't you?

KAREN There'll always be room for you in my garage.

SAM If I walk out this door now, I don't come back.

KAREN I think you will.

SAM What makes you so sure?

KAREN You forgot to take your eye drops.
   (SAM storms to the coffee table, snatches up the drops and crosses back to the door. He stops)

SAM Before I go I just want to say one thing. Whatever you think of me is probably true. No, not probably, *definitely*. I have been a bastard right from the beginning. I don't expect you to forgive me.

KAREN But I do.

SAM (*Whirling back to her*) Let me finish. I don't expect you to forgive me. But I ask you with all conscience, with all your understanding, not to blame Jean for any of this.

KAREN (*Collapses on the couch. Then pulling herself together*) I'll send her a nice gift.

SAM (*Puts down his case beside the sofa*) She's been torturing herself ever since this started. *I'm* the one who forced the issue.

KAREN (*Moving away from him on the sofa, mimics* JEAN) "It didn't show up on the 1400 but I rechecked it with my own files and made the correction on the 640" . . . You know as well as I do that's code for "I'll meet you at the Picadilly Hotel."

SAM (*Kneeling beside the sofa*) You won't believe me, will you? That she's a nice girl.

KAREN Nice for you and nice for me are two different things.

SAM If it's that Sunday supplement psychology you're using, Karen, it's backfiring, because you're just making it easier for me.

KAREN Well, you like things easy, don't you? You don't even have an affair the hard way.

SAM Meaning what?

KAREN (*Getting up*) Meaning you could have at least taken the trouble to look outside your office for a girl . . . (*Picks up an imaginary phone*) "Miss Mc-Cormack, would you please come inside and take an affair!" . . . Honestly, Sam.
(*Moves above the sofa*)

SAM Karen, don't force me to say nice things about her to you.

KAREN I can't help it. I'm just disappointed in you. It's so damned unoriginal.

SAM What did you want her to be, a fighter pilot with the Israeli air force?

KAREN *Everyone* cheats with their secretary. I expected more from *my* husband!

SAM (*Shaking his head*) I never saw you like this. You live with a person your whole life, you don't really know them.

KAREN (*Crossing below the sofa to the bedroom*) Go on, Sam, go have your affair. You're fifty-one years old. In an hour it may be too late.
    (*Sits at the dresser and brushes her hair*)

SAM (*Getting up and crossing to her in the bedroom*) By God, you are something. You are really something special, Karen. Twenty-three years I'm married to you and I still can't make you out. You don't look much different than the ordinary woman, but I promise you there is nothing walking around on two legs that compares in any way, shape or form to the likes of you.

KAREN (*Drops the brush and turns to him. Laughing*) . . . So if I'm so special, what are you carrying on with secretaries for?

SAM I'll be goddamned if I know . . .
    (*They look at each other. He turns and starts to the front door, taking his attaché case*)

KAREN (*Following him into the living room*) Sam! (SAM stops) Sam . . . do I still have my two choices? (*He turns and looks at her*) Because if I do . . . I choose "Get rid of Miss McCormack." (*He looks away*) I pick "Stay here and work it out with me, Sam." (KAREN *turns her back to him and leans against the arm of the sofa*) . . . Because the other way I think I'm going to lose. Don't go to the office tonight, Sam . . . Stay with me . . . Please.

SAM (*Leaning on the console table, he looks at her*) I swear, I wish we could go back the way it was before. A couple of years ago, before there were any problems.

KAREN Maybe we can, Sam. We'll do what you said before. We'll lie. We'll tell each other everything is all right . . . There is nothing wrong in the office tonight, there is no Miss McCormack and I'm twenty-seven goddamned years old . . . What do you say, Sam?

SAM (*Moves about indecisively*) . . . Maybe tomorrow, Karen . . . I can't—tonight! I'll—I'll see you.

KAREN When? (*He exits, leaving the door open*) Never mind. I love surprises.
(*As* SAM *leaves, the* WAITER *appears with a tray with an ice bucket filled with a bottle of champagne and two glasses*)

WAITER The champagne . . . I brought two glasses just in case. (*He closes the door and places the ice bucket and glasses on the desk. He glances back*) Is he coming back?

KAREN (*Remains leaning on the sofa*) . . . Funny you should ask that.
(*He begins to open the bottle*)

Curtain

Suite 719 at the Plaza. It is about three in the afternoon on a warm, sunny spring day.

The WAITER *is just finishing setting up some fresh glasses and bottles of liquor on top of the bureau between the windows in the living room.*

The telephone in the bedroom rings. JESSE KIPLINGER *emerges from the bathroom.* JESSE *is about forty, a confident, self-assured man. He is applying after-shave lotion to his face. He is dressed in "Hollywood mod," with a tan turtleneck sweater and tight blue suede pants. His shoes are highly polished and buckled. He has the latest-style haircut, with bangs falling over his forehead. He crosses to the phone and picks it up.*

JESSE Hello? . . . Oh, just a minute. (*He drops the phone and crosses to the* WAITER) I'll take that. (*He indicates the check, which the* WAITER *hands him. He signs it and returns it to the* WAITER, *who nods and crosses to the door.* JESSE *picks up the phone and holds his hand over the phone until the* WAITER *is gone, closing the door behind him. Then into the phone*) Put her on . . . (*Waits, then in a much softer, romantically persuasive tone*) Hello? . . . Muriel? Where are you? . . . Well, come on up . . . Yes, I'm positive it's all right . . . (*More insistently*) . . . Muriel, do you want me to come down and get you? . . . All right, then, take the elevator and come to Suite 719 . . . And stop being so silly, I'm dying to see you. (*He hangs up, thinks a second, then picks up the phone again*) Hello, operator? This is Mr. Kiplinger in Suite 719. Would you please hold all local calls for the next hour, I'm going to be in conference . . . (*Checks an appointment book on the night table*) Make that an hour and a half . . . Thank you. (*He hangs up and begins to clear the bed of a collection of scripts, trade papers and galley proofs. Kneeling, he pushes them under the bed. Rising, he carefully smoothes the spread. He snatches up a section of colored comics from the*

*arm of the armchair and throws it into the waste-
basket. Taking a blue button-down sweater from the
back of a chair at the dresser, he puts it on with a great
flair and carefully examines himself in the mirror on
the closet door. Satisfied with his appearance, he crosses
to the living room and checks the bar set-up on the
bureau. The front doorbell rings.* JESSE *crosses to
answer it, checking his hair in the mirror over the
mantel as he does. He is finally ready. Taking a deep
breath, he opens the door.* MURIEL TATE *stands there.*
MURIEL *is in her late thirties and is extremely attractive. She wears a bright-yellow spring coat and a simple, demure, high-necked gray dress which shows off
her svelte, still girlish figure. Her hair falls simply to
her shoulders, held back by a wide white band.* MURIEL
*is a warm, easy, smiling woman who seems as naïve
and vulnerable as the day she graduated from Tenafly
High School. When the door opens, the two of them
greet each other with enormous smiles.* JESSE *throws
out his arms)* Muriel!

MURIEL (*Smiles, cocks her head*) Jesse?

JESSE   It's not.

MURIEL   It is.

JESSE   Muriel, I can't believe it. Is it really you?

MURIEL   It's me, Muriel.

JESSE   Well, come on in, for pete's sakes, come on in.

MURIEL (*Enters with a rush and crosses to the far side
of the sofa*)   I can only stay for a few minutes.

JESSE (*Closes the door and follows her to below the
near side of the sofa*)   My God, it's good to see you.
(*They stand and confront each other*)

MURIEL   I just dropped in to say hello. I really can't stay.

JESSE   You sounded good on the phone, but you look
even better.

MURIEL   Because I've got to get back to New Jersey.
I'm parked in a one-hour zone. Hello, Jesse, I think
I'm very nervous.

JESSE   Hey! Hello, Muriel.

MURIEL   Same old Muriel, heh?

JESSE   What do you mean, same old Muriel? You look fantastic (*Arms outstretched, he moves to her*) Come here, let me take a good look at you.

MURIEL (*Evading him, crosses below the coffee table*) Oh, don't, Jesse. Don't look at me. I've been stuck in the Holland Tunnel for two hours. What time is it? Tell me when it's three o'clock. I can't stay.
(*Sits in the armchair*)

JESSE (*Moves toward her*)   Muriel, I can't get over it. You look absolutely wonderful.

MURIEL   Well, I *feel* absolutely wonderful.

JESSE (*Sitting on the arm of the sofa*)   I really, sincerely mean that. You simply look incredibly fantastic.

MURIEL   Well, I *feel* incredibly fantastic.

JESSE   Well, you look it.

MURIEL   Well, I *feel* it.

JESSE   And how are you?

MURIEL (*Without enthusiasm*)   I'm all right . . . I don't know why I'm so nervous, do you?
(*She shrugs her coat off her shoulders and arranges it over the back of the chair*)

JESSE   No. I can't imagine why you should be so nervous.

MURIEL   Neither can I. I just am . . . Should I be here?

JESSE   Why not? Is there anything wrong in it?

MURIEL   Oh, no. No, of course not. There's nothing wrong in it. My God, no. I don't see anything wrong. I just dropped by from New Jersey to say hello. What's wrong with that? . . . I just don't think I should be here. (*Getting up and moving toward the mantel*) Is it three o'clock yet?

JESSE (*Moving toward her*)   Little Muriel Tate, all grown up and married. How many kids you got now?

MURIEL   Three.

JESSE   No kidding? Three kids . . . What are they?

MURIEL   A boy and a girl.

JESSE   A boy and a girl?

MURIEL   (*Breaking away to the other side of the sofa*)
And another boy who's away in camp. I can't even
think straight. Isn't this terrible?

JESSE   (*Moving to the sofa. Good-naturedly*)   What's
wrong?

MURIEL   I don't know, I can't catch my breath. Well,
it's *you*, that's the simple explanation. I'm nervous
about meeting you.

JESSE   Me? Me? Jesse Kiplinger, your high school boy
friend from Tenafly, New Jersey. Ohh, Muriel.

MURIEL   You know what I mean, Mr. "Famous Hollywood Producer" staying at the Plaza Hotel.

JESSE   Mr. Famous Hollywood Producer. (*Sitting on the
sofa*) Muriel, you know me better than that. I haven't
changed. I made a couple of pictures, that's all.

MURIEL   (*Moving to the sofa*)   A couple of pictures? The
Easter show at the Radio City Music Hall? I stood
on line with my children for three hours in the rain.

JESSE   What did you do that for? You could have called
my office in New York. My girl would have gotten you
right in. Any time you want to see one of my pictures . . .

MURIEL   Oh, I couldn't do that.

JESSE   Why not?

MURIEL   I couldn't. I couldn't impose like that.

JESSE   You're *not* imposing.

MURIEL   I am.

JESSE   I *want* you to.

MURIEL   What's the number?

JESSE   I'll give it to you before you go. (*Getting up*)

But first you're going to sit down and have a drink.
There's a million things I'm dying to ask you.

MURIEL Oh, no drinks for me.

JESSE One little drink.

MURIEL No, no, no. You go ahead and have a drink.
I have a five-o'clock hairdresser's appointment.

JESSE You don't drink?

MURIEL Oh, once in a great while. Anyway, I've got
to get home. I shouldn't even be in the city. The kids
will be home from school soon and I've got to make
dinner for Larry and I haven't even done my shopping
in Bonwit's. No, no, I just dropped by to say hello.

JESSE What'll you have?

MURIEL A vodka stinger.

JESSE Coming right up.
(He crosses to the bar set-up)

MURIEL (Sitting on the sofa) And then I've got to go
. . . Whoooo, I finally took a breath. That felt good.

JESSE (Pouring liquor into a shaker) Will you relax?
Will you, Muriel? Come on now. I want you to stop
being so silly and relax.

MURIEL (Chiding) Is that how you talk to your stars
when they're nervous? Is that what you say to Elke
Sommer?

JESSE I don't talk to the stars. I have directors for
that . . . For God's sakes, Muriel, what are you so
nervous about?

MURIEL Oooh, there's that famous Hollywood temper
I read about . . . You want me to be frank?

JESSE Please.

MURIEL I feel funny sitting here drinking in a hotel
room . . . I mean, I'm a married woman.

JESSE (Having finished making and pouring drinks, he
moves to her) Would you feel better if we had our
drinks down in the Palm Court?

MURIEL   We're here, we might as well stay.

JESSE (*Handing her the drink*) Okay. Then will you
sit back and relax?
    (*Sits down next to her on the sofa*)

MURIEL   Just for a few minutes. I've got a six-o'clock
hairdresser's appointment.

JESSE   I thought it was at five?

MURIEL   It's flexible . . . Is it warm in here?
    (*Putting down her drink on the coffee table*)

JESSE   Why don't you take off your gloves?

MURIEL (*Shaking a finger at him*) Oh, no! Let's not
have any of *that*, Mr. Jesse Kiplinger of Hollywood,
California . . . My gloves will stay where they belong,
if you please.

JESSE (*Putting his drink down on the coffee table*)
Muriel, you are delightfully and incredibly unchanged.
How long has it been now? Fifteen, sixteen years?

MURIEL   Since our last date? It'll be seventeen years on
August sixth.

JESSE   You remembered that?

MURIEL   I still have the swizzle sticks from Tavern on
the Green.

JESSE (*Leaning toward her*) No, time hasn't changed
you, Muriel. You're still so fresh and clean. (*Sniffs about
her*) You even smell the same way.

MURIEL   Ohhh?

JESSE (*Sniffs her ear*) Like cool peppermint . . . Clear,
cool peppermint.

MURIEL (*Pushes his nose away with her finger*) Now,
you and your nose just behave yourself . . . I did not
come to the Plaza Hotel to be smelled.

JESSE   And now you've blossomed and matured . . .
only in reverse . . . You look younger and fresher and
. . . well, you know what I mean. I just think you look
absolutely fantastic.

MURIEL (*Pulls herself together. Clears her throat. Very businesslike*) You going to be in New York long, Jesse?

JESSE Possibly just till the weekend. I've got to sign a director for my new picture.

MURIEL John Huston?

JESSE Yes. How did you know that?

MURIEL Oh, we keep up on things in Tenafly . . . Mr. Famous Hollywood Producer, staying at the Plaza Hotel, signing up John Huston for his next picture. (*Playfully pushing his leg*)

JESSE I might stay over another few days. It depends . . . on what develops.
(*He looks down at his leg. She gets up nervously*)

MURIEL I've never been in the Plaza before. It's beautiful. (*Stops near the door to the bedroom, which is opened*) What's in there?

JESSE The bedroom. You can go in.

MURIEL (*Shying away, moves back to the sofa*) It's all right, I take your word for it . . . Is this where you meet with John Huston? I mean, does he sit in here and the two of you talk and then he signs the contract? Is that how you do it?

JESSE (*Lolling back on the sofa*) In this very room . . . Will you stop with the celebrity routine. Aside from a couple of extra pounds, I'm still the same boy who ran anchor on the Tenafly track team.

MURIEL And is living in the old Humphrey Bogart house in Beverly Hills.

JESSE How did you know that?

MURIEL (*Moving to the ottoman*) Never mind, I know, I know . . . Maybe I haven't seen you in seventeen years, but I know an awful lot about you, Mr. Jesse Kiplinger . . . (*Sits*) Pootch!

JESSE Pootch?

MURIEL Isn't that what they call you in Hollywood? Your nickname? Pootch?

JESSE Gootch!

MURIEL I thought it was Pootch.

JESSE No. No, no, it's Gootch.

MURIEL I thought I read that you have all your shirts
specially made by Pucci in Florence, so they call you
Pootch.

JESSE No, no. I have all my shoes made by Gucci in
Rome so they call me Gootch.

MURIEL Oh.

JESSE (*Deprecatingly*) It's a silly thing. I don't know
why they print stories like that.

MURIEL Because people like me like to read them. Are
those Gucci shoes you're wearing now, Gootch?

JESSE These? (*To display his shoes, he puts one foot
up on the coffee table, the other over the arm of the
sofa*) No. These are the one pair I had made in
England. You can't get this leather in Italy. No, I
have a man in Bond Street makes them for me . . .
MacCombs.
(MURIEL *reacts to the sight of his widespread legs
and turns away in embarrassment*)

MURIEL (*Attempting to make a joke*) Well, they're
beautiful shoes, *MacCootch!*

JESSE MacCootch! That's very good. (*He laughs*) Hey,
can we stop talking about me for a while?

MURIEL (*Turns back to him*) Why? I think you're
very interesting to talk about.

JESSE Well, I don't. I'm very bored with me. I'm much
more interested in you . . . (*Sits up and hands her a
drink*) But first let's have our drinks.

MURIEL And then I've got to go.
(*Takes the glass*)

JESSE Let's say, to renewing old acquaintances.

MURIEL You drink to that. (*Moves to the sofa*) I'll
drink to your new picture winning the Academy
Award.

JESSE   Muriel, it's not going to win the Academy Award. It's not even going to get nominated. (*Beginning to laugh*) As a matter of fact, it's a piece of crap . . . (*Catches himself*) Excuse me, Muriel.

MURIEL   (*Sitting on the sofa*) Be that as it may, it's going to gross over nine million. Domestic.

JESSE   That's beside the point . . . How did you know that?

MURIEL   I know, I know, Mr. "Gootch" Kiplinger . . . I've been following your career very closely, if you please.

JESSE   (*Moving closer*) Muriel, it is so exciting seeing you again. The minute you walked in that door, I got a—a tingle, all over, the way I used to . . . You know what I mean.

MURIEL   (*Trying to remain matter-of-fact*) I'm sure I don't. I have three children and I'm very happy and I have a wonderful life and I have no business being in a hotel room in New York at three o'clock in the afternoon with a man I haven't seen since Tavern on the Green seventeen years ago. (*He kisses her on the lips. She looks at him*)—Any particular reason you did that?

JESSE   (*Still leaning toward her*) I wanted to. Desperately.

MURIEL   Do you always blithely go ahead and do whatever you want to?

JESSE   If I can get away with it . . . As a matter of fact . . . if you don't object too strenuously, I'm going to kiss you again.

MURIEL   . . . And then I've got to go. (JESSE *kisses her again tenderly on the lips. She lets him kiss her for a moment. Then jumps up and moves away*) Woo . . . That'll be enough of that, Mr. Do-Whatever-You-Want-to Kiplinger. Wow, that vodka stinger has really gone to my head.

JESSE   (*Noncommittally*) It's even better when you drink it.

MURIEL   (*Takes her drink from the coffee table and*

crosses to the chair) Now, don't confuse me. I'm nervous enough as it is. Cheers. *(Drinks)* Was it good?

JESSE *(Taking his drink)* What? The drink?

MURIEL The kiss.

JESSE The kiss? Yes, the kiss was very good.

MURIEL What did it feel like?

JESSE What do you mean, what did it feel like?

MURIEL *(Sitting in the chair)* Was it a good kiss or a medium kiss or a waste-of-time kiss? I'm interested in knowing your reaction.

JESSE Why? You never asked me that when I kissed you in Tenafly.

MURIEL You weren't a famous Hollywood producer living in Humphrey Bogart's house signing John Huston for your next picture in Tenafly. Can I please have your reaction to my kiss?

JESSE It was a superb kiss.

MURIEL *(Puts her drink down on the floor next to the chair. Takes a compact from her purse on the chair)* It wasn't superb. I don't kiss superbly. It was an average, inexperienced, everyday New Jersey kiss . . . I don't know why I let you kiss me anyway, "Mr. Famous Hollywood Kisser."
(Powdering her face)

JESSE *(Smiles warmly)* Is it possible that you are the last, sweet, simple, unchanged, unspoiled woman living in the world today?

MURIEL I'm sure I don't know what you're talking about. *(Looking in the compact mirror)* Oh, God, look at my lips. I'd never get past the house detective. What time is it?

JESSE *(Looks at his watch)* Twenty after.

MURIEL Three? Already? I've got to go.
(Puts the compact back in her purse, gets up and begins to gather her purse and coat from the chair)

JESSE   Not yet.

MURIEL   I must.

JESSE   Ten more minutes?

MURIEL   I can't . . .

JESSE   Please!

MURIEL   I'll stay five.
   (*Sits back down in the chair*)

JESSE   Good.

MURIEL   Why did you call me yesterday?

JESSE (*Smiles*)   I called you because, believe it or not, I've been thinking about you.

MURIEL   For seventeen years?

JESSE   On and off.

MURIEL   In Humphrey Bogart's old house? I don't believe you, "Mr. International Liar." And I don't trust you. (*She gets up and again begins to gather her belongings*) And I'm not staying.

JESSE (*Quietly*)   Good-by.

MURIEL (*Stops in surprise*)   Do you mean that?

JESSE   I don't want to force you to stay here. You know what's best for you.

MURIEL (*Looks at him*)   I'll just finish my drink.
   (*She puts her things back on the chair and picks up her drink*)

JESSE   Muriel, you must believe me when I tell you I have no ulterior motives in asking you here today. I just wanted to see you. I'm trying to impress you with the fact that you are the only, solitary, real, honest-to-goodness, unphoney woman that I have been with since the day I arrived in Hollywood seventeen years ago.

MURIEL   What about your mother?

JESSE   She's the worst one.

MURIEL (*Sitting next to him on the sofa*) Well, your mother must be very proud to have such a famous son.

JESSE (*Edges closer to her*) Do you know, in my own quiet way, I was crazy about you?

MURIEL (*Puts the drink down on the table*) As a matter of fact, everyone in Tenafly is proud of you. Even Larry, my husband, talks about you all the time. He always says, "Jesse Kiplinger, Jesse Kiplinger, that's all I ever hear around this house."
    (*Stops and thinks about what she has just said*)

JESSE I remember exactly what you looked like the day I left for California. You were wearing a tan raincoat, a tweed skirt and a brown sweater. And a little locket that your grandmother had given you. (*Traces a locket on her chest*) Do you remember?

MURIEL I remember when your first picture came to Tenafly, that's what I remember. Everybody went. Do you know it was the only Jeff Chandler picture that ever played two weeks at the Hillside Drive-In?

JESSE Even then, you had a quality about you, Muriel, that was sort of—well, untouched. (*Puts his hand on the outside of her leg and caresses her*) You were the only girl that gave me pleasure in just holding her hand.

MURIEL (*Determinedly ignoring* JESSE'S *actions*) You know a lot of the girls from school still kid me about you. I mean when they see your name in a column or something like that.

JESSE I didn't expect to see it any more, Muriel, that quality of honesty . . . and frankness . . . that ability to cut through deceit (*Moves his hand, and going underneath her skirt, puts it between her legs*) and phoniness with just one look through those big, unsuspecting, wide-open eyes. I really did not expect to see it again in my lifetime.

MURIEL They always kid me and say, oh, if I married you instead of Larry, I'd be living in Hollywood now, going to parties with James Garner and Otto Preminger, running around with the Rat Pack.

JESSE You don't know what you are. You really don't
. . . Well, I'll tell you what you are. You're something very special. I *know*, Muriel.

MURIEL . . . I mean I wouldn't even know what to
say to Otto Preminger.

JESSE Don't change, Muriel. Don't ever change the
sweet, simple way you are.
      (*He kisses her neck, deeply. For a minute she is
      lost in the embrace and then, without changing
      her mood*)

MURIEL Do you know Frank Sinatra?

JESSE (*Slowly comes out of her neck and looks at her*)
Who?

MURIEL Frank Sinatra. Did you ever meet him?

JESSE (*Slightly shaken, pulls back, takes his hand away
and sits back on the sofa*) Yes. Yes, I know Frank.

MURIEL What's he like?

JESSE Frank? . . . I . . . I don't really know him that
well, we had dinner a few times.

MURIEL Where? In his house?

JESSE Once in a restaurant, once I think in his house.
I don't remember.

MURIEL Was Mia there?

JESSE Uh . . . no. This was before he met Mia.

MURIEL So in other words, you never met Mia?

JESSE Yes, I did meet Mia, but she wasn't married to
Frank then.

MURIEL I see. They say he's very generous. Is that
true? Is he as generous as they say?

JESSE Yeah, I guess so. He served very large portions
. . . I don't know. Christ, who cares about Frank
Sinatra?

MURIEL (*Hurt*) I'm sorry—I was just curious. I didn't
mean to pry into your personal life. Well, I've got to
be going.
      (*She gets up and moves to the chair*)

JESSE (*Apologetic*) Wait, Muriel . . .

MURIEL (*Getting her belongings from the chair*) No, I've got to leave before the traffic starts. If I get stuck in the Holland Tunnel again and I'm late for Larry's dinner, he'll want to know where I was, and I don't lie very well, and oh, God, I don't know why I came here in the first place . . . (*Drops her things back in the chair. Becoming more and more upset*) What have I done?

JESSE You haven't done anything, Muriel.

MURIEL (*Pacing*) Haven't done anything? I'm sitting there letting you kiss me and smell me . . .

JESSE Muriel, if I've done anything to offend you, I'm sorry.

MURIEL (*Moving toward the windows*) I must have been out of my mind, coming to the Plaza Hotel in the middle of the week.

JESSE There is no reason to get yourself upset. I didn't do anything worse than give you a friendly kiss.

MURIEL (*Coming back to the sofa*) I happen to enjoy a wonderful reputation.

JESSE I'm glad you enjoy it . . . Now stop being so silly. Sit down and finish your drink.

MURIEL I suppose you'll go back to Hollywood and have a big laugh with Otto Preminger over this.

JESSE I wouldn't dream of it.

MURIEL Promise.

JESSE I promise.

MURIEL Say it. Say, "I will not have a big laugh with Otto Preminger over this."

JESSE I don't even *talk* to Otto Preminger. Why would I laugh at you? I have nothing but respect and the warmest of feelings for you.

MURIEL You do? God's truth?

JESSE God's truth. You're an angel.

MURIEL Really? (*She hesitates a moment, then sits on the arm of the sofa*) Would I fit in with your crowd?

JESSE No, you would not fit in with my crowd. You're too good for them. You're too sweet and honest for the whole slimy bunch.

MURIEL . . . But which ones would I fit in with?

JESSE Muriel, I don't know what kind of distorted image you have of these people, but they're not what you think they are. *I'm* not what you think I am. All these things you read in the paper about me being witty, charming, the boy genius, that's only part of the story. Do you know what kind of a life I really lead in Hollywood?

MURIEL Are you going to tell me?

JESSE Yes, I'll tell you. Why did I call you yesterday? After seventeen years? Okay, let's start with, "Yes, I'm a Famous Hollywood Producer. Yes, I never made a picture that lost money. Yes, I got that magic touch, call it talent, whatever you want, I don't know" . . . The fact is, ever since I was old enough to sneak into the Ridgewood Theatre in Tenafly, I've been a movie nut. (*Getting up, stands by the sofa*) Not only have I seen every Humphrey Bogart movie he ever made at least eight times, I now own a print of all those pictures. Why do you think I was so crazy to buy his house? (*Moves slowly to the window*) . . . So I went to Hollywood and was very lucky and extremely smart and presto, I became a producer. (*Unobtrusively pulls down the shade*) I love making movies. Some are good, some are bad, most of them are fun. I hope I can continue doing it for the next fifty years. That's one half of my life. The other half is that in the last fourteen years I've been married three times—to three of the worst bitches you'd ever want to meet.
　　(*Gets a bottle of vodka and a glass from the bar*)

MURIEL Jesse, you don't have to tell me any of this if you don't want to.

JESSE   Maybe you're right. (*Moves to the front door and locks it*) Maybe I shouldn't be telling you about my sordid Hollywood past.
(*Leans on the mantel*)

MURIEL (*Settling down on the sofa, she picks up her drink*) . . . So you married these three bitches, then what happened?

JESSE (*Moves to* MURIEL) What happened . . . I gave them love, I gave them a home, I gave them a beautiful way of life—and the three bitches took me for every cent I got. (*Refills her glass, then sits on the floor by the armchair*) But I don't even care about the money, screw it—excuse me, Muriel. What hurts is that they took the guts out of me. They were phony, unfaithful, all of them. Did you know I caught my first wife, Dolores, in bed with a jockey? A jockey! (*Indicates the man's size, holding his hand a foot off the floor*) Do you know what it does to a man's self-respect to find his wife in the sack with a four-foot-eight shrimp, weighs a hundred and twelve pounds? But as I said before, screw it. Tell me if I'm shocking you, Muriel.
(*Refills his own drink*)

MURIEL   I'll let you know.
(*She drinks*)

JESSE   All right . . . My second wife, Carlotta . . . She was *keeping* her Spanish guitar teacher . . . *Keeping him!* . . . I never caught her, but she didn't fool me. *No one* takes twenty-seven thousand dollars' worth of guitar lessons in one year . . .

MURIEL   Is Carlotta the one you met at Kirk Douglas's house?

JESSE   Yes, as a matter of fact. Was that in the paper too?

MURIEL   Sheilah Graham's column. It was a big party for the Ukrainian Folk Dancers and the Los Angeles Rams.

JESSE (*Getting up, replenishes her drink*) Muriel, forget the Los Angeles Rams...(*Putting the bottle and his glass down on the console table, he crosses behind the sofa*) Listen to what I'm saying to you. I am in a very bad way. I've been through three hellish, miserable marriages. I don't want to go that route again. I am losing my faith and belief that there is anything left that resembles an uncorrupt woman . . . (*Sighs*) So last week my mother, who still gets the Tenafly newspaper, shows me a picture of the PTA annual outing at Palisades this year, and who is there on the front page, coming in first in the Mother and Daughter Potato Race, (*Leans in to* MURIEL *over the side arm of the couch*) looking every bit as young and lovely and as sweet as she did seventeen years ago, was my last salvation . . . Muriel Tate. (*Gradually moving to the bedroom door*) That's why I had to see you, Muriel. Just to talk to you, to have a drink, to spend five minutes, to reaffirm my faith that there *are* decent women in this world . . . even if it's only one . . . even if you're the last of a dying species . . . if somebody like you exists, Muriel . . . then maybe there's still somebody for me . . . *That's* why I called you yesterday.

(JESSE *has finished his speech. He is somewhat spent, emotionally. He moves to the bed and sits*)

MURIEL (*Getting up and moving toward the bedroom door*) Well . . . well . . . well . . .

JESSE (*From the bedroom*) I hope whatever I said didn't embarrass you, Muriel . . . but hell, if you expect honesty from another person you can't be anything less than honest yourself.

MURIEL (*Still at the doorway*) I'm not embarrassed, I'm flattered. To think a famous person like you wants to confide in a plain person like me . . .

JESSE (*Gets up and moves to her in the living room*) Now you finish your vodka stinger and then I'm going to let you go.

MURIEL (*Pouring herself a drink at the bar*) Oh, I've got plenty of time. Larry's never home till seven. (*She holds up the drink*) Cheers. (*She drinks.* JESSE *crosses to* MURIEL, *touches her*)

JESSE   How are you, Muriel? Are you happy?

MURIEL   Happy? . . . Oh, yes. I think if I'm anything, I'm happy.
   (*Moves down to the sofa*)

JESSE   I'm glad. You deserve happiness, Muriel.

MURIEL   Yes, Larry and I are very happy . . . (*She drinks*) I would have to say that Larry and I have one of the happier marriages in Tenafly.
   (*She drinks again*)

JESSE   That's wonderful.

MURIEL   I mean, we've had our ups and downs like any married couple, but I think in the final analysis what's left is . . . that we're happy.

JESSE   (*Moves down to her*)   I couldn't be more pleased. Well, listen, it's no surprise. Larry's a wonderful guy.

MURIEL   Do you think so?

JESSE   Don't you?

MURIEL   Yes, *I* do. But no one else seems to care for him. (*Sits on the sofa*) Of course, they don't know him the way *I* do. I'm out of stinger again.
   (*Holds her glass out to* JESSE)

JESSE   (*Takes her glass*)   Are you sure you're going to be all right? I mean, driving?

MURIEL   (*Gradually feeling the effects of the drinks, she slowly exposes a whole, new, unexpected* MURIEL) If I had to worry about getting home every time I had three vodka stingers, I'd give up driving. (*JESSE crosses to the bar, looking back at her in puzzlement*) . . . Yes, I'd say that in spite of everything, Larry and I have worked out happiness . . . or some form of it.

JESSE   Is he doing well in business?
   (*Fills her glass once again*)

MURIEL   Oh, in business you don't have to worry. In that department he's doing great. I mean, he's really got a wonderful business there . . . Of course, it was good when my father had it. (*JESSE hands her a drink*) Ooh, cheers.

JESSE (*Sitting on the arm of the sofa*) In what department isn't he doing well?

MURIEL He's doing well in *every* department.

JESSE Are you sure?

MURIEL I'm positive.

JESSE Then I'm glad.

MURIEL Why, what do you hear?

JESSE I haven't heard a thing except what you're telling me.

MURIEL Well, I'm telling you that we have a happy marriage. Are you trying to infer we don't have a happy marriage?

JESSE No . . .

MURIEL Well, you're wrong. We have a happy marriage. A goddamned happy marriage. (*Tries to put the glass down on the table, misses and nearly slips off the sofa*) Oh, I'm sorry. I should have had lunch.

JESSE (*Steadies her and picks up the glass from the floor and puts it on the table*) Shall I order down for some food?

MURIEL No, I can't stay. Larry'll be home about five.

JESSE I thought he comes home at seven.

MURIEL If he comes home at all . . . Please forgive me, Jesse, I seem to be losing control of myself.

JESSE You drank those too quickly. Didn't you have anything to eat all day?

MURIEL Just an olive with the two stingers I had downstairs . . . I'll be all right.

JESSE Do you want to lie down for a while?

MURIEL What's the point? You're going back to Hollywood in a few days . . . Oh, I see what you mean . . . Oh, God, I'm sorry, Jesse, I seem to be running off at the mouth.

JESSE (*Sits down next to her*) What is it, Muriel? What's with you and Larry?

MURIEL Nothing. I told you, we're very happy. We have tiny, little differences like every normal couple, but basically we're enormously happy together. I couldn't ask for a better life ... (*And she throws her arms around* JESSE *and gives him a full, passionate kiss on the lips . . . then she pulls away*) . . . Oh, you shouldn't have done that, Jesse. I'm very vulnerable right now and you mustn't take advantage . . . I'm going. I've got to go.
    (*Gets up and moves away*)

JESSE (*Taking her hand*) Muriel, I didn't know.

MURIEL (*Pulling away*) No, Jesse, don't.

JESSE Why didn't you let me know?

MURIEL (*Crying, crosses to the chair for her things*) Who knew you were interested? You were always at a party with the Los Angeles Rams.

JESSE I never suspected for a minute. Why didn't you write to me?

MURIEL (*Crying*) Where? I don't know where Humphrey Bogart lived. (*Rushes to* JESSE *where he sits on the sofa and throws her arms about him*) I've got to go. Let me go.

JESSE (*With his arms about her waist*) God, how I thought about you on the plane all the way to New York.

MURIEL Please, Jesse. I've got to buy something in Bonwit's and get dinner for Larry. (*He munches on her neck*) Don't bite my neck, it'll leave marks.

JESSE You're different, Muriel. I know you are. You're not like any of the others.
    (*Caressing her*)

MURIEL I'm not different, Jesse. I'm a woman. A happily married woman with normal desires and passions. Please don't rub me.
    (*Pulls away from him*)

JESSE (*Reaching out for her*) My life is empty, Muriel. Empty. But you can fill it for me. You can.
    (*Gets up and moves to her*)

MURIEL (*Retreating behind the chair*) I can't fill your
life for you, Jesse, I've got to get home. Larry'll kill me.

JESSE (*Catching her hands*) Stay! An hour. Just one
hour, that's all.

MURIEL No, no. Tomorrow I'll be alone with my regrets and you'll be out there with Dino and Grou-
cho . . .

JESSE (*Pulling her above the sofa in the direction of the
bedroom*) One hour, Muriel. Live my life with me
for one hour.

MURIEL No, please, Jesse. I've got to pick up my lamb
chops.

JESSE One hour, Muriel. The world can change for
one hour.

MURIEL (*Stopping above the sofa*) Can it, Jesse? Can
it really?

JESSE (*Moving behind her*) It can for me, Muriel. It
can for you.

MURIEL I don't know, Jesse. I just don't know.

JESSE All right, we'll just talk. (*Reaches around her
waist from behind her, and places his hand on her
stomach. Soothingly*) No one ever got hurt just talking, did they?

MURIEL . . . I suppose not.

JESSE Of course they didn't.
(*Rubbing her stomach*)

MURIEL (*Under the spell of his soft voice*) What'll
we talk about?

JESSE Whatever you say. Whatever you want.

MURIEL . . . Did you go to the Academy Awards dinner
last year?

JESSE (*Resignedly*) Certainly. I go every year.

MURIEL Oh, God, really?

JESSE Really.
(For a moment, they rock gently back and forth,
but slowly, almost as in a dance step, he leads her
into the bedroom)

MURIEL Who did you sit next to?

JESSE (As if to a child) In the theatre, I sat next to
Steve McQueen on one side and Liza Minelli on the
other.

MURIEL She's adorable, isn't she?
(They move into the bedroom)

JESSE A real pixie.

MURIEL And who did you sit with at the dinner?

JESSE (Leading her to the bed) Well, let's see, at my
table there was Charlton Heston and his wife, Joseph
E. Levine, the producer, Eva Marie Saint, Marge and
Gower Champion . . .
(Sits down on the side of the bed)

MURIEL Oh, they're cute . . . All at your table?

JESSE (Drawing her down on his knee) All at my
table. And at the next table—there was Anthony
Quinn and Virna Lisi, Paul Newman and Joanne . . .
(Searches for the name)

MURIEL Woodward . . .

JESSE Woodward . . . (He begins to unzip her dress)
And there was Dean Jones and Yvette Mimieux . . .

MURIEL Together . . . ?

JESSE Yes, together . . . (He gently forces her back
down on the bed, at the same time pulling the dress
off her shoulders) Then behind us there was Troy
Donahue and Stella Stevens, Sammy Davis, Jr., and
Margot Fonteyn . . .
(They are both lying on the bed. The lights have
faded out)

Curtain

VISITOR FROM FOREST HILLS

Suite 719 at the Plaza. It is three o'clock on a warm Saturday afternoon in spring.

The living room is bedecked with vases and baskets of flowers. In the bedroom one opened valise containing a young woman's street clothes rests on the floor. A very large box, which had held a wedding dress, rests on the luggage rack, and a man's suit lies on the bed. A fur wrap and gloves are thrown over the back of the sofa. Telegrams of congratulation and newspapers are strewn about. The suite today is being used more or less as a dressing room, since a wedding is about to occur downstairs in one of the reception rooms.

As the lights come up, NORMA HUBLEY *is at the phone in the bedroom, impatiently tapping the receiver. She is dressed in a formal cocktail dress and a large hat, looking her very best, as any woman would want to on her daughter's wedding day. But she is extremely nervous and harassed, and with good cause—as we'll soon find out.*

NORMA *(On the phone)* Hello? . . . Hello, operator? . . . Can I have the Blue Room, please . . . The Blue Room . . . Is there a Pink Room? . . . I want the Hubley-Eisler wedding . . . The Green Room, that's it. Thank you . . . Could you please hurry, operator, it's an emergency . . . *(She looks over at the bathroom nervously. She paces back and forth)* Hello? . . . Who's this? . . . Mr. Eisler . . . It's Norma Hubley . . . No, everything's fine . . . Yes, we're coming right down . . . *(She is smiling and trying to act as pleasant and as calm as possible)* Yes, you're right, it certainly is the big day . . . Mr. Eisler, is my husband there? . . . Would you, please? . . . Oh! Well, I'd like to wish you the very best of luck too . . . Borden's a wonderful boy . . . Well, they're *both* wonderful kids . . . No, no. She's as calm as a cucumber . . . That's the younger generation, I guess . . . Yes, everything seems to be going along beautifully . . . Absolutely beautifully . . . Oh, thank you. (*Her husband has obviously just come on the other end, because the expression on her face changes violently and she screams a rasping whisper filled with doom. Sitting on the bed*) Roy? You'd better get up here right away, we're in big trouble . . . Don't ask questions, just get up here . . . I hope you're not drunk because I can't handle this alone . . . Don't say anything. Just smile and walk leisurely out the door . . . and then get the hell up here as fast as you can. (*She hangs up, putting the phone back on the night table. She crosses to the bathroom and then puts her head up against the door. Aloud through the bathroom door*) All right, Mimsey, your father's on his way up. Now, I want you to come out of that bathroom and get married. (*There is no answer*) Do you hear me? . . . I've had enough of this nonsense . . . Unlock that door! (*That's about the end of her authority. She wilts and almost pleads*) Mimsey, darling, please come downstairs and get married, you know your father's temper . . . I know what you're going through now, sweetheart, you're just nervous . . . Everyone goes through that on their wedding day . . . It's going to be all right, darling. You love Borden and he loves you. You're both going to have a wonderful future. So please come out of the bathroom! (*She listens; there is no answer*) Mimsey, if you don't care about your life, think about mine. Your father'll kill me. (*The front doorbell rings.* NORMA *looks off nervously and moves to the other side of the bed*) Oh, God, he's here! . . . Mimsey! Mimsey, please, spare me this . . . If you want, I'll have it annulled next week, but please come out and get married! (*There is no answer from the bathroom but the front doorbell rings impatiently*) All right, I'm letting your father in. And heaven help the three of us!

> (*She crosses through the bedroom into the living room. She crosses to the door and opens it as* ROY HUBLEY *bursts into the room.* ROY *is dressed in striped trousers, black tail coat, the works. He looks elegant but he's not too happy in this attire. He is a volatile, explosive man equipped to handle*

*the rigors of the competitive business world, but
a nervous, frightened man when it comes to the
business of marrying off his only daughter)*

ROY   Why are you standing here? There are sixty-
eight people down there drinking my liquor. If there's
gonna be a wedding, let's have a wedding. Come on!
(*He starts back out the door but sees that* NORMA
*is not going anywhere. She sits on the sofa. He comes
back in)* . . . Didn't you hear what I said? There's
another couple waiting to use the Green Room. Come
on, let's go!
      (*He makes a start out again*)

NORMA   (*Very calm*)   Roy, could you sit down a minute?
I want to talk to you about something.

ROY   (*She must be mad*)   You want to talk *now*? You
had twenty-one years to talk while she was growing
up. I'll talk to you when they're in Bermuda. Can we
please have a wedding?

NORMA   We can't have a wedding until you and I have
a talk.

ROY   Are you crazy? While you and I are talking here,
there are four musicians playing downstairs for seventy
dollars an hour. I'll talk to you later when we're
dancing. Come on, get Mimsey and let's go.
      (*He starts out again*)

NORMA   That's what I want to talk to you about.

ROY   (*Comes back*)   Mimsey?

NORMA   Sit down. You're not going to like this.

ROY   Is she sick?

NORMA   She's not sick . . . exactly.

ROY   What do you mean, she's not sick exactly? Either
she's sick or she's not sick. Is she sick?

NORMA   She's not sick.

ROY   Then let's have a wedding! (*He crosses into the
bedroom*) Mimsey, there's two hundred dollars' worth

of cocktail frankfurters getting cold downstairs . . . (*He looks around the empty room*) Mimsey? (*He crosses back to the living room to the side of the sofa. He looks at* NORMA) . . . Where's Mimsey?

NORMA Promise you're not going to blame me.

ROY Blame you for what? What did you do?

NORMA I didn't do anything. But I don't want to get blamed for it.

ROY What's going on here? Are you going to tell me where Mimsey is?

NORMA Are you going to take an oath you're not going to blame me?

ROY *I take it! I take it!* NOW WHERE THE HELL IS SHE?

NORMA . . . She's locked herself in the bathroom. She's not coming out and she's not getting married.
(ROY *looks at* NORMA *incredulously. Then, because it must be an insane joke, he smiles at her. There is even the faint glint of a chuckle*)

ROY (*Softly*) . . . No kidding, where is she?

NORMA (*Turns away*) He doesn't believe me. I'll kill myself.
(ROY *turns and storms into the bedroom. He crosses to the bathroom and knocks on the door. Then he tries it. It's locked. He tries again. He bangs on the door with his fist*)

ROY Mimsey? . . . Mimsey? . . . *MIMSEY?* (*There is no reply. Girding himself, he crosses back through the bedroom into the living room to the sofa. He glares at* NORMA) . . . All right, what did you say to her?

NORMA (*Jumping up and moving away*) I knew it! I knew you'd blame me. You took an oath. God'll punish you.

ROY I'm not blaming you. I just want to know what *stupid* thing you said to her that made her do this.

NORMA I didn't say a word. I was putting on my lipstick, she was in the bathroom, I heard the door go click, it was locked, my whole life was over, what do you want from me?

ROY And you didn't say a word?

NORMA Nothing.

ROY (*Ominously moving toward her as* NORMA *backs away*) I see. In other words, you're trying to tell me that a normal, healthy, intelligent twenty-one-year-old college graduate, who has driven me crazy the last eighteen months with wedding lists, floral arrangements and choices of assorted hors d'oeuvres, has suddenly decided to spend this, the most important day of her life, locked in the Plaza Hotel john?

NORMA (*Making her stand at the mantel*) Yes! Yes! Yes! Yes! Yes!

ROY (*Vicious*) YOU MUSTA SAID SOMETHING!
(*He storms into the bedroom.* NORMA *goes after him*)

NORMA Roy . . . Roy . . . What are you going to do?

ROY (*Stopping below the bed*) First I'm getting the college graduate out of the bathroom! Then we're gonna have a wedding and then you and I are gonna have a big talk! (*He crosses to the bathroom door and pounds on it*) Mimsey! This is your father. I want you and your four-hundred-dollar wedding dress out of there in five seconds!

NORMA (*Standing at the side of the bed*) Don't threaten her. She'll never come out if you threaten her.

ROY (*To* NORMA) I got sixty-eight guests, nine waiters, four musicians and a boy with a wedding license waiting downstairs. This is no time to be diplomatic. (*Bangs on the door*) Mimsey! . . . Are you·coming out or do we have the wedding in the bathroom?

NORMA Will you lower your voice! Everyone will hear us.

ROY (*To* NORMA) How long you think we can keep this a secret? As soon as that boy says "I do" and there's no one standing next to him, they're going to suspect something. (*He bangs on the door*) You can't stay in there forever, Mimsey. We only have the room until six o'clock . . . *You hear me?*

(*There is still no reply from the bathroom*)

NORMA   Roy, will you please try to control yourself.

ROY (*With great display of patience, moves to the foot of the bed and sits*)   All right, I'll stay here and control myself. You go downstairs and marry the short, skinny kid. (*Exploding*) *What's the matter with you?* Don't you realize what's happening?

NORMA (*Moving to him*)   Yes I realize what's happening. Our daughter is nervous, frightened and scared to death.

ROY   Of what? OF WHAT? She's been screaming for two years if he doesn't ask her to marry him, she'll throw herself off the Guggenheim Museum . . . What is she scared of?

NORMA   I don't know. Maybe she's had second thoughts about the whole thing.

ROY (*Getting up and moving to the bathroom door*) Second thoughts? This is no time to be having *second thoughts.* It's costing me eight thousand dollars for the *first* thoughts. (*He bangs on the door*) Mimsey, open this door.

NORMA   Is that all you care about? What it's costing you? Aren't you concerned about your daughter's happiness?

ROY (*Moving back to her below the bed*)   Yes! Yes, I'm concerned about my daughter's happiness. I'm also concerned about that boy waiting downstairs. A decent, respectable, intelligent young man . . . who I hope one day is going to teach that daughter of mine to grow up.

NORMA   You haven't the faintest idea of what's going through her mind right now.

ROY   Do you?

NORMA   It could be anything. I don't know, maybe she thinks she's not good enough for him.

ROY (*Looks at her incredulously*) . . . Why? What is he? Some kind of Greek god? He's a plain kid, nothing . . . That's ridiculous. (*Moves back to the door and bangs on it*) Mimsey! Mimsey, open this door. (*He turns to* NORMA) Maybe she's not in there.

NORMA She's in there. (*Clutches her chest and sits on the side of the bed*) Oh, God, I think I'm having a heart attack.

ROY (*Listening at the door*) I don't hear a peep out of her. Is there a window in there? Maybe she tried something crazy.

NORMA (*Turning to him*) That's right. Tell a woman who's having a heart attack that her daughter jumped out the window.

ROY Take a look through the keyhole. I want to make sure she's in there.

NORMA She's in there, I tell you. Look at this, my hand keeps bouncing off my chest.
(*It does*)

ROY Are you gonna look in there and see if she's all right or am I gonna call the house detective?

NORMA (*Getting up and moving below the bed*) Why don't *you* look?

ROY Maybe she's taking a bath.

NORMA Two minutes before her own wedding?

ROY (*Crossing to her*) What wedding? She just called it off.

NORMA Wouldn't I have heard the water running?

ROY (*Making a swipe at her hat*) With that hat you couldn't hear Niagara Falls! . . . Are you going to look to see what your daughter's doing in the bathroom or do I ask a stranger?

NORMA (*Crossing to the door*) I'll look! I'll look! I'll look! (*Reluctantly she gets down on one knee and looks through the keyhole with one eye*) Oh, my God!

ROY What's the matter?

NORMA (*To him*) I ripped my stockings.
>   (*Getting up and examining her stocking*)

ROY Is she in there?

NORMA She's in there! She's in there! (*Hobbling to
the far side of the bed and sitting down on the edge*)
Where am I going to get another pair of stockings
now? How am I going to go to the wedding with torn
stockings?

ROY (*Crossing to the bathroom*) If *she* doesn't show
up, who's going to look at *you*? (*He kneels at the door
and looks through the keyhole*) There she is. Sitting
there and crying.

NORMA I *told* you she was in there . . . The only one
in my family to have a daughter married in the Plaza
and I have torn stockings.

ROY (*He is on his knees, his eye to the keyhole*)
Mimsey, I can see you . . . Do you hear me? . . . Don't
turn away from me when I'm talking to you.

NORMA Maybe I could run across to Bergdorf's. They
have nice stockings.
>   (*Crosses to her purse on the bureau in the bed-
room and looks through it*)

ROY (*Still through the keyhole*) Do you want me to
break down the door, Mimsey, is that what you want?
Because that's what I'm doing if you're not out of
there in five seconds . . . Stop crying on your dress. Use
the towel!

NORMA (*Crossing to* ROY *at the door*) I don't have
any money. Give me four dollars, I'll be back in ten
minutes.

ROY (*Gets up and moves below the bed*) In ten minutes
she'll be a married woman, because I've had enough
of this nonsnse. (*Yells in*) All right, Mimsey, stand
in the shower because I'm breaking down the door.

NORMA (*Getting in front of the door*) Roy, don't get
crazy.

ROY (*Preparing himself for a run at the door*)   Get out of my way.

NORMA   Roy, she'll come out. Just talk nicely to her.

ROY (*Waving her away*)   We already had nice talking. Now we're gonna have door breaking. (*Through the door*) All right, Mimsey, I'm coming in!

NORMA   No, Roy, don't! Don't!
(*She gets out of the way as* ROY *hurls his body, led by his shoulder, with full force against the door. It doesn't budge. He stays against the door silently a second; he doesn't react. Then he says calmly and softly*)

ROY   Get a doctor.

NORMA (*Standing below the door*)   I knew it. I knew it.

ROY (*Drawing back from the door*)   Don't tell me I knew it, just get a doctor. (*Through the door*) I'm not coming in, Mimsey, because my arm is broken.

NORMA   Let me see it. Can you move your fingers?
(*Moves to him and examines his fingers*)

ROY (*Through the door*)   Are you happy now? Your mother has torn stockings and your father has a broken arm. How much longer is this gonna go on?

NORMA (*Moving* ROY's *fingers*)   It's not broken, you can move your fingers. Give me four dollars with your other hand, I have to get stockings.
(*She starts to go into his pockets. He slaps her hands away*)

ROY   Are you crazy moving a broken arm?

NORMA   Two dollars, I'll get a cheap pair.

ROY (*As though she were a lunatic*)   I'm not carrying any cash today. Rented, everything is rented.

NORMA   I can't rent stockings. Don't you even have a charge-plate?
(*Starts to go through his pockets again*)

ROY (*Slaps her hands away. Then pointing dramatically*) Wait in the Green Room! You're no use to me here, go wait in the Green Room!

NORMA   With torn stockings?

ROY   Stand behind the rented potted plant. (*Takes her by the arm and leads her below the bed. Confidentially*) They're going to call from downstairs any second asking where the bride is. And *I'm* the one who's going to have to speak to them. *Me! Me! Me!* (*The phone rings. Pushing her toward the phone*) That's them. *You* speak to them!

NORMA   What happened to *me me me?*
        (*The phone rings again*)

ROY (*Moving to the bathroom door*)   Answer it. Answer it.
        (*The phone rings again*)

NORMA (*Moving to the phone*)   What am I going to say to them?

ROY   I don't know. Maybe something'll come to you as you're talking.

NORMA (*Picks the phone up*)   Hello? . . . Oh, Mr. Eisler . . . Yes, it certainly is the big moment.
        (*She forces a merry laugh*)

ROY   Stall 'em. Stall 'em. Just keep stalling him. Whatever you do, stall 'em!
        (*Turns to the door*)

NORMA (*On the phone*)   Yes, we'll be down in two minutes.
        (*Hangs up*)

ROY (*Turns back to her*)   Are you crazy? What did you say that for? I told you to stall him.

NORMA   I stalled him. You got two minutes. What do you want from me?

ROY (*Shakes his arm at her*)   You always panic. The

minute there's a little crisis, you always go to pieces
and panic.

NORMA (*Shaking her arm back at him*) Don't wave
your broken arm at me. Why don't you use it to get
your daughter out of the bathroom?

ROY (*Very angry, kneeling to her on the bed*) I could
say something to you now.

NORMA (*Confronting him, kneels in turn on the bed*)
Then why don't you say it?

ROY   Because it would lead to a fight. And I don't want
to spoil this day for you. (*He gets up and crosses back
to the bathroom door*) Mimsey, this is your father
speaking . . . I think you know I'm not a violent man.
I can be stern and strict, but I have never once been
violent. Except when I'm angry. And I am really
angry now, Mimsey. You can ask your mother.
      (*Moves away so* NORMA *can get to the door*)

NORMA (*Crossing to the bathroom door*)   Mimsey, this
is your mother speaking. It's true, darling, your father
is very angry.

ROY (*Moving back to the door*)   This is your father
again, Mimsey. If you have a problem you want to
discuss, unlock the door and we'll discuss it. I'm not
going to ask you this again, Mimsey. I've reached the
end of my patience. I'm gonna count to three . . . and
by God, I'm warning you, young lady, by the time
I've reached three . . . *this door better be open!*
(*Moving away to below the bed*) All right—One!
. . . Two! . . . THREE! (*There is no reply or movement from behind the door.* ROY *helplessly sinks down
on the foot of the bed*) . . . Where did we fail her?

NORMA (*Crosses to the far side of the bed, consoling
him as she goes, and sits on the edge*)   We didn't
fail her.

ROY   They're playing "Here Comes the Bride" downstairs and she's barricaded in a toilet—we must have
failed her.

NORMA (*Sighs*)   All right, if it makes you any happier,
we failed her.

ROY You work and you dream and you hope and you save your whole life for this day, and in one click of a door, suddenly everything crumbles. Why? What's the answer?

NORMA It's not your fault, Roy. Stop blaming yourself.

ROY I'm not blaming myself. I know *I've* done my best.

NORMA (*Turns and looks at him*) What does that mean?

ROY It means we're not perfect. We make mistakes, we're only human. I've done my best and we failed her.

NORMA Meaning *I* didn't do my best?

ROY (*Turning to her*) I didn't say that. I don't know what your best is. Only *you* know what your best is. Did you do your best?

NORMA Yes, I did my best.

ROY And I did my best.

NORMA Then we *both* did our best.

ROY So it's not our fault.

NORMA That's what I said before.
     (*They turn away from each other. Then*)

ROY (*Softly*) Unless one of us didn't do our best.

NORMA (*Jumping up and moving away*) I don't want to discuss it any more.

ROY All right, then what are we going to do?

NORMA I'm having a heart attack, *you* come up with something.

ROY How? All right, I'll go down and tell them.
     (*Gets up and moves to the bedroom door*)

NORMA (*Moving to the door in front of him*) Tell them? Tell them what?
     (*As they move into the living room, she stops him above the sofa*)

ROY I don't know. Those people down there deserve some kind of an explanation. They got all dressed up, didn't they?

NORMA What are you going to say? You're going to tell them that my daughter is not going to marry their son and that she's locked herself in the bathroom?

ROY What do you want me to do, start off with two good jokes? They're going to find out *some* time, aren't they?

NORMA (*With great determination*) I'll tell you what you're going to do. If she's not out of there in five minutes, we're going to go out the back door and move to Seattle, Washington! . . . You don't think I'll be able to show my face in this city again, do you? (ROY *ponders this for a moment, then reassures her with a pat on the arm. Slowly he turns and moves into the bedroom. Suddenly, he loses control and lets his anger get the best of him. He grabs up the chair from the dresser, and brandishing it above his head, he dashes for the bathroom door, not even detouring around the bed but rather crossing right over it.* NORMA *screams and chases after him*) ROY!

(*At the bathroom door,* ROY *manages to stop himself in time from smashing the chair against the door, trembling with frustration and anger. Finally, exhausted, he puts the chair down below the door and straddles it, sitting leaning on the back.* NORMA *sinks into the bedroom armchair*)

ROY . . . Would you believe it, last night I cried. Oh, yes. I turned my head into the pillow and lay there in the dark, crying, because today I was losing my little girl. Some stranger was coming and taking my little Mimsey away from me . . . so I turned my back to you—and cried . . . Wait'll you hear what goes on *tonight!*

NORMA (*Lost in her own misery*) I should have invited your cousin Lillie. (*Gestures to the heavens*) She wished this on me, I know it. (*Suddenly* ROY *begins to chuckle.* NORMA *looks at him. He chuckles louder, although there is clearly no joy in his laughter*) Do you find something funny about this?

ROY Yes, I find something funny about this. I find it

funny that I hired a photographer for three hundred dollars. I find it hysterical that the wedding pictures are going to be you and me in front of a locked bathroom! (*Gets up and puts the chair aside*) All right, I'm through sitting around waiting for that door to open.

(*He crosses to the bedroom window and tries to open it*)

NORMA (*Following after him*) What are you doing?

ROY What do you think I'm doing?
(*Finding it impossible to open it, he crosses to the living room and opens a window there. The curtains begin to blow in the breeze*)

NORMA (*Crosses after him*) If you're jumping, I'm going with you. You're not leaving *me* here alone.

ROY (*Looking out the window*) I'm gonna crawl out along that ledge and get in through the bathroom window.
(*He starts to climb out the window*)

NORMA Are you crazy? It's seven stories up. You'll kill yourself.
(*She grabs hold of him*)

ROY It's four steps, that's all. It's no problem, I'm telling you. Now will you let go of me.

NORMA (*Struggling to keep him from getting out the window*) Roy, no! Don't do this. We'll leave her in the bathroom. Let the hotel worry about her. Don't go out on the ledge.
(*In desperation, she grabs hold of one of the tails of his coat*)

ROY (*Half out the window, trying to get out as she holds onto his coat*) You're gonna rip my coat. Let go or you're gonna rip my coat. (*As he tries to pull away from her, his coat rips completely up the back, right up to the collar. He stops and slowly comes back into the room.* NORMA *has frozen in misery by the bedroom door after letting go of the coat.* ROY *draws himself*

up with great dignity and control. He slowly turns
and moves into the bedroom, stopping by the bed.
With great patience, he calls toward the bathroom)
Hey, you in there . . . Are you happy now? Your
mother's got torn stockings and your father's got a
rented ripped coat. Some wedding it's gonna be. (*Exploding, he crosses back to the open window in the
living room*) Get out of my way!

NORMA (*Puts hand to her head*) I'm getting dizzy. I
think I'm going to pass out.

ROY (*Getting her out of the way*) . . . You can pass
out *after* the wedding . . . (*He goes out the window
and onto the ledge*) Call room service. I want a
double Scotch the minute I get back.

> (*And he disappears from view as he moves across
> the ledge. NORMA runs into the bedroom and
> catches a glimpse of him as he passes the bed-
> room window, but then he disappears once more*)

NORMA (*Bemoaning her fate*) . . . He'll kill himself.
He'll fall and kill himself, that's the way my luck's
been going all day. (*She staggers away from the
window and leans on the bureau*) I'm not going to
look. I'll just wait until I hear a scream. (*The telephone rings and NORMA screams in fright*) Aggghhh!
. . . I thought it was him . . . (*She crosses to the phone
by the bed. The telephone rings again*) Oh, God,
what am I going to say? (*She picks it up*) Hello? . . .
Oh, Mr. Eisler. Yes, we're coming . . . My husband's
getting Mimsey now . . . We'll be right down. Have
some more hors d'oeuvres . . . Oh, thank you. It
certainly *is* the happiest day of my life. (*She hangs
up*) No, I'm going to tell him I've got a husband
dangling over Fifty-ninth Street. (*As she crosses back
to the opened window, a sudden torrent of rain begins
to fall. As she gets to the window and sees it*) I knew
it! I knew it! It had to happen . . . (*She gets closer
to the window and tries to look out*) Are you all right,
Roy? . . . Roy? (*There's no answer*) He's not all right,
he fell. (*She staggers into the bedroom*) He fell,
he fell, he fell, he fell . . . He's dead, I know it. (*She
collapses onto the armchair*) He's laying there in a

puddle in front of Trader Vic's . . . I'm passing out. This time I'm really passing out! (*And she passes out on the chair, legs and arms spread-eagled. The doorbell rings; she jumps right up*) I'm coming! I'm coming! Help me, whoever you are, help me! (*She rushes through the bedroom into the living room and to the front door*) Oh, please, somebody, help me, please!

    (*She opens the front door and* ROY *stands there dripping wet, fuming, exhausted and with clothes disheveled and his hair mussed*)

ROY (*Staggering into the room and weakly leaning on the mantelpiece. It takes a moment for him to catch his breath.* NORMA, *concerned, follows him*) She locked the window too. I had to climb in through a strange bedroom. There may be a lawsuit.
    (*He weakly charges back into the bedroom, followed by* NORMA, *who grabs his coattails in an effort to stop him. The rain outside stops*)

NORMA (*Stopping him below the bed*) Don't yell at her. Don't get her more upset.

ROY (*Turning back to her*) Don't get her *upset?* I'm hanging seven stories from a gargoyle in a pouring rain and you want me to worry about *her?* . . . You know what she's doing in there? She's playing with her false eyelashes. (*Moves to the bathroom door*) I'm out there fighting for my life with pigeons and she's playing with eyelashes . . . (*Crossing back to* NORMA) . . . I already made up my mind. The minute I get my hands on her, I'm gonna kill her. (*Moves back to the door*) Once I show them the wedding bills, no jury on earth would convict me . . . And if by some miracle she survives, let there be no talk of weddings . . . She can go into a convent. (*Slowly moving back to* NORMA *below the bed*) . . . Let her become a librarian with thick glasses and a pencil in her hair, I'm not paying for any more canceled weddings . . . (*Working himself up into a frenzy, he rushes to the table by the armchair and grabs up some newspapers*) Now get her out of there or I start to burn these newspapers and smoke her out.

(NORMA *stops him, soothes him, and manages to get him calmed down. She gently seats him on the foot of the bed*)

NORMA (*Really frightened*) I'll get her out! I'll get her out! (*She crosses to the door and knocks*) Mimsey! Mimsey, please! (*She knocks harder and harder*) Mimsey, you want to destroy a family? You want a scandal? You want a story in the *Daily News?* . . . Is that what you want? Is it? . . . Open this door! *Open it!* (*She bangs very hard, then stops and turns to* ROY) . . . Promise you won't get hysterical.

ROY What did you do?
(*Turns wearily to her*)

NORMA I broke my diamond ring.

ROY (*Letting the papers fall from his hand*) Your good diamond ring?

NORMA How many do I have?

ROY (*Yells through the door*) Hey, you with the false eyelashes! (*Getting up and moving to the door*) . . . You want to see a broken diamond ring? You want to see eighteen hundred dollars' worth of crushed baguettes? . . . (*He grabs* NORMA's *hand and holds it to the keyhole*) Here! Here! *This* is a worthless family heirloom (*Kicks the door*)—and *this* is a diamond bathroom door! (*Controlling himself. To* NORMA) Do you know what I'm going to do now? Do you have any idea? (NORMA *puts her hand to her mouth, afraid to hear.* ROY *moves away from the door to the far side of the bed*) I'm going to wash my hands of the entire Eisler-Hubley wedding. You can take all the Eislers and all the hors d'oeuvres and go to Central Park and have an eight-thousand-dollar picnic . . . (*Stops and turns back to* NORMA) I'm going down to the Oak Room with my broken arm, with my drenched rented ripped suit—and I'm gonna get blind! . . . I don't mean drunk, I mean totally blind . . . (*Erupting with great vehemence*) because I don't want to see you or your crazy daughter again, if I live to be a thousand.
(*He turns and rushes from the bedroom, through*

*the living room to the front door. As he tries to
open it,* NORMA *catches up to him, grabs his tail
coat and pulls him back into the room)*

NORMA   That's right. Run out on me. Run out on your
daughter. Run out on everybody just when they need
you.

ROY   You don't need me. You need a rhinoceros with
a blowtorch—because no one else can get into that
bathroom.

NORMA   *(With rising emotion)*   I'll tell you who can
get into that bathroom. Someone with love and understanding. Someone who cares about that poor kid
who's going through some terrible decision now and
needs help. Help that only *you* can give her and that
I can give her. *That's* who can get into that bathroom
now.
     *(*ROY *looks at her solemnly . . . Then he crosses
     past her, hesitates and looks back at her, and then
     goes into the bedroom and to the bathroom door.*
     NORMA *follows him back in. He turns and looks
     at* NORMA *again. Then he knocks gently on the
     door and speaks softly and with some tenderness)*

ROY   Mimsey! . . . This is Daddy . . . Is something
wrong, dear? . . . *(He looks back at* NORMA, *who nods
encouragement, happy about his new turn in character. Then he turns back to the door)* . . . I want
to help you, darling. Mother and I both do. But how
can we help you if you won't talk to us? Mimsey can
you hear me?
     (There is no answer. He looks back at NORMA)

NORMA   *(At the far side of the bed)*   Maybe she's too
choked up to talk.

ROY   *(Through the door)*   Mimsey, if you can hear me,
knock twice for yes, once for no. *(There are two
knocks on the door. They look at each other en-
couragingly)* Good. Good . . . Now, Mimsey, we
want to ask you a very, very important question. Do
you want to marry Borden or don't you?
     *(They wait anxiously for the answer. We hear
     one knock, a pause, then another knock)*

NORMA (*Happily*) She said yes.

ROY (*Despondently*) She said no.
(*Moves away from the door to the foot of the bed*)

NORMA It was two knocks. Two knocks is yes. She wants to marry him.

ROY It wasn't a double knock "yes." It was two single "no" knocks. She doesn't want to marry him.

NORMA Don't tell me she doesn't want to marry him. I heard her distinctly knock "yes." She went (*Knocks twice on the foot of the bed*) "Yes, I want to marry him."

ROY It wasn't (*Knocks twice on the foot of the bed*) . . . It was (*Knocks once on the foot of the bed*) . . . and then another (*Knocks once more on the foot of the bed*) . . . That's "no," twice, she's not marrying him.
(*Sinks down on the side of the bed*)

NORMA (*Crossing to the door*) Ask her again. (*Into the door*) Mimsey, what did you say? Yes or no? (*They listen. We hear two distinct loud knocks.* NORMA *turns to* ROY) . . . All right? There it is in plain English . . . You never *could* talk to your own daughter.
(*Moves away from the door*)

ROY (*Getting up wearily and moving to the door*) Mimsey, this is not a good way to have a conversation. You're gonna hurt your knuckles . . . Won't you come out and talk to us? . . . Mimsey?

NORMA (*Leads* ROY *gently to the foot of the bed*) Don't you understand, it's probably something she can't discuss with her father. There are times a daughter wants to be alone with her mother. (*Sits* ROY *down on the foot of the bed, and crosses back to the door*) Mimsey, do you want me to come in there and talk to you, just the two of us, sweetheart? Tell me, darling, is that what you want? (*There is no reply. A strip of toilet paper appears from under the bathroom door.* ROY *notices it, pushes* NORMA *aside, bends down, picks it up and reads it*) What? What does it say? (ROY *solemnly hands it to her.* NORMA *reads it aloud*) "I would rather talk to Daddy."

> (NORMA *is crushed. He looks at her sympathetically. We hear the bathroom door unlock.* ROY *doesn't quite know what to say to* NORMA. *He gives her a quick hug*)

ROY   I—I'll try not to be too long.

> (*He opens the door and goes in, closing it behind him, quietly.* NORMA, *still with the strip of paper in her hand, walks slowly and sadly to the foot of the bed and sits. She looks glumly down at the paper*)

NORMA (*Aloud*)   ... "I would rather talk to Daddy" ... Did she have to write it on this kind of paper? (*She wads up the paper*) ... Well—maybe I didn't do my best ... I thought we had such a good relationship ... Friends. Everyone thought we were friends, not mother and daughter ... I tried to do everything right ... I tried to teach her that there could be more than just love between a mother and daughter ... There can be trust and respect and friendship and understanding ... (*Getting angry, she turns and yells toward the closed door*) Just because *I* don't speak to my mother doesn't mean *we* can't be different!

> (*She wipes her eyes with the paper. The bathroom door opens. A solemn* ROY *steps out, and the door closes and locks behind him. He deliberately buttons his coat and crosses to the bedroom phone, wordlessly.* NORMA *has not taken her eyes off him. The pause seems interminable*)

ROY (*Into the phone*)   The Green Room, please ... Mr. Borden Eisler. Thank you.

> (*He waits*)

NORMA (*Getting up from the bed*)   ... I'm gonna have to guess, is that it? ... It's so bad you can't even tell me ... Words can't form in your mouth, it's so horrible, right? ... Come on, I'm a strong person, Roy. Tell me quickly, I'll get over it ...

ROY (*Into the phone*)   Borden? Mr. Hubley ... Can you come up to 719? ... Yes, now ... (*He hangs up and gestures for* NORMA *to follow him. He crosses into the living room and down to the ottoman where he sits.* NORMA *follows and stands waiting behind him. Finally)* She wanted to talk to me because she couldn't bear to say it to both of us at the same time . . . The reason she's locked herself in the bathroom . . . is she's afraid.

NORMA   Afraid? What is she afraid of? That Borden doesn't love her?

ROY   Not that Borden doesn't love her.

NORMA   That she doesn't love Borden?

ROY   Not that she doesn't love Borden.

NORMA   Then what is she afraid of?

ROY   . . . She's afraid of what they're going to become.

NORMA   I don't understand.

ROY   Think about it.

NORMA   (*Crossing above the sofa*)   What's there to think about? What are they going to become? They love each other, they'll get married, they'll have children, they'll grow older, they'll become like us (*Comes the dawn. Stops by the side of the sofa and turns back to* ROY) —I never thought about that.

ROY   Makes you stop and think, doesn't it?

NORMA   I don't think we're so bad, do you? . . . All right, so we yell and scream a little. So we fight and curse and aggravate each other. So you blame me for being a lousy mother and I accuse you of being a rotten husband. It doesn't mean we're not happy . . . does it? . . . (*Her voice rising*) Well? . . . Does it? . . .

ROY   (*Looks at her*)   . . . She wants something better. (*The doorbell rings. He crosses to open the door.* NORMA *follows*) Hello, Borden.

BORDEN   (*Stepping into the room*)   Hi.

NORMA   Hello, darling.

ROY   (*Gravely*) Borden, you're an intelligent young man,

I'm not going to beat around the bush. We have a serious problem on our hands.

BORDEN   How so?

ROY   Mimsey—is worried. Worried about your future together. About the whole institution of marriage. We've tried to allay her fears, but obviously we haven't been a very good example. It seems you're the only one who can communicate with her. She's locked herself in the bathroom and is not coming out . . . It's up to you now.
(*Without a word,* BORDEN *crosses below the sofa and up to the bedroom, through the bedroom below the bed and right up to the bathroom door. He knocks*)

BORDEN   Mimsey? . . . This is Borden . . . Cool it! (*Then he turns and crosses back to the living room. Crossing above the sofa, he passes the Hubleys, and without looking at them, says*) See you downstairs!
(*He exits without showing any more emotion. The Hubleys stare after him as he closes the door. But then the bathroom door opens and* NORMA *and* ROY *slowly turn to it as* MIMSEY, *a beautiful bride, in a formal wedding gown, with veil, comes out*)

MIMSEY   I'm ready now!
(NORMA *turns and moves into the bedroom toward her.* ROY *follows slowly, shaking his head in amazement*)

ROY   *Now* you're ready? *Now* you come out?

NORMA (*Admiring* MIMSEY)   Roy, please . . .

ROY (*Getting angry, leans toward her over the bed*)   I break every bone in my body and you come out for "Cool it"?

NORMA (*Pushing* MIMSEY *toward* ROY)   You're beautiful, darling. Walk with your father, I want to look at both of you.

ROY (*Fuming. As she takes his arm, to* NORMA)   That's how he communicates? That's the brilliant understanding between two people? "Cool it"?

NORMA (*Gathering up* MIMSEY's *train as they move toward the living room*) Roy, don't start in.

ROY What kind of a person is that to let your daughter marry?
(*They stop above the sofa.* MIMSEY *takes her bridal bouquet from the table behind the sofa, while* NORMA *puts on her wrap and takes her gloves from the back of the sofa*)

NORMA Roy, don't aggravate me. I'm warning you, don't spoil this day for me.

ROY Kids today don't care. Not like they did in my day.

NORMA Walk. Will you walk? In five minutes he'll marry one of the flower girls. Will you walk—
(MIMSEY *takes* ROY *by the arm and they move to the door, as* NORMA *follows*)

ROY (*Turning back to* NORMA) Crazy. I must be out of my mind, a boy like that. (*Opens the door*) She was better off in the bathroom. You hear me? Better off in the bathroom . . . (*They are out the door . . .*)

Curtain

Last *of the* RED HOT Lovers

Synopsis of Scenes

The action takes place in an apartment in New York's East Thirties.

ACT I: A late afternoon in December.
ACT II: A late afternoon in August.
ACT III: A late afternoon in September.

Act One

The scene is a one-and-a-half-room apartment in the
Turtle Bay section of Manhattan. It's a new building, not
more than five or six years old. At first glance we can see the
incongruity of the apartment and its furnishings. The room
has a built-in air conditioner, modern parquet floors and the
sleek, trim lines of modern-day apartments. The furniture,
however, is another story. The pieces are all about thirty
years old; good stuff, extremely well taken care of, but clearly
from another generation. Pictures abound of family, children and grandchildren. An older person obviously lives
here and, probably, judging from the size of the apartment,
alone.

The room is empty. The doorbell is ringing as the curtain
rises. There is a pause, then a key is heard in the lock, and
the door opens. BARNEY CASHMAN sticks in his head and calls
out.

BARNEY Hello? . . . Mom? . . . (There is no answer, so he
quickly enters the apartment and closes the door. BARNEY
CASHMAN is forty-seven years old, neatly dressed in blue
suit, blue topcoat and gray felt hat. After removing the
key from the lock, he places it on the shelf by the door. He
carries an attaché case with him, which he puts down
immediately on the floor. He takes the rubbers off his
shoes, spreads out a newspaper he is carrying, puts it in
a corner of the room and puts his rubbers on the newspaper. He removes his hat and coat and puts them neatly in
the closet, which contains a fur coat and other feminine
apparel. He crosses to a large window, trying to stay out
of sight as much as possible, and reaches out and closes the
Venetian blind. He then moves to the other two windows
and closes the drapes. The room is plunged into darkness
despite the fact that outside is a bright December afternoon. He then goes to the light switch by the front door
and touches it to turn on all the lamps in the room. He

picks up the attaché case and crosses to the dining table to open it. He takes out a bottle of J&B Scotch and places it on the table. He then takes out a Bloomingdale's bag, removes one tissue-wrapped glass, unwraps it and puts it on the table. Then he takes out a bottle of aftershave lotion, opens it, and administers it to his face lavishly. He rubs his fingers vigorously with lotion and smells them. He goes to the sofa, checks his watch, slides the coffee table to one side, throws the sofa cushions over the back and pulls out the convertible bed. He looks at his watch again, closes the bed, replaces the cushions, and slides the coffee table back into place. He returns to the dining table and pours himself a drink, which he carries to the telephone. He dials the phone, puts the receiver on the desk and takes a drink, wincing. He then quickly picks up the receiver, presumably just as the other party has come on. Into the phone, hardly above a whisper) Hello? . . . Harriet? . . . Mr. Cashman . . . Everything all right? . . . Did Pepito come in? . . . Pepito, the busboy . . . All right, Pietro—whatever his name is . . . Didn't come in, heh? . . . Did you try the agency again? . . . Well, listen, there's nothing I can do right now—*(Looks at his watch)*—I'll be in about five o'clock . . . I'm still in Bloomingdale's. It's just murder in here with all the Christmas shoppers . . . Did my wife call? And you told her Bloomingdale's? . . . Good. Good . . . Listen, I gotta run. I see an opening on the escalator . . . I'll be back at five-thirty the latest . . . Thank you, Harriet. *(He hangs up the phone; thinks for a second)* What the hell am I doing here? *(He quickly goes to the closet. The doorbell rings. He freezes, looking around for an exit. There is, of course, none. He rushes to the door and peers out the minuscule peephole. Satisfied, he opens the door.* ELAINE NAVAZIO *enters. She is in her late thirties, somewhat attractive, and modestly dressed. There is an air of desperation about* ELAINE. BARNEY *looks at her nervously)* Hello. (ELAINE *smiles and nods)* I was in the kitchen. I didn't hear the bell. (ELAINE *walks past him into the apartment)* Come on in.
        (He closes the door)

ELAINE *(Turns; looks at him)*   I'm in.

BARNEY   How are you?

ELAINE Very nice.

BARNEY Well, you look very nice.

ELAINE You look surprised. Didn't you think I'd come?

BARNEY I wasn't sure . . . but I was hoping.

ELAINE I wasn't sure either . . . but I came.

BARNEY I'm glad.

ELAINE *(Smiles)* Good.

BARNEY I'd have been disappointed if you didn't come . . . Would you?

ELAINE Be disappointed if I didn't come? No, I'd know I wasn't coming, so there'd be no disappointment.

BARNEY Anyway, hello . . . My God, I'm sorry. I forgot your name.

ELAINE *(With sincerity)* You're forgiven. Elaine Navazio.

BARNEY Really?

ELAINE Don't tell me I'm wrong?

BARNEY You just don't look like an Elaine Navazio to me.

ELAINE No? What then?

BARNEY I don't know. For some reason you looked like an Irene to me.

ELAINE Irene? You think I look like an Irene? *(She turns and looks at the wall mirror)* No, I look like an Elaine Navazio.
     (She continues examining the apartment)

BARNEY Are you of Italian origin? Navazio?

ELAINE No, I'm of Polish persuasion. Mr. Navazio is of Italian origin. What extraction are you of?

BARNEY Actually I'm part Russian and part Lithuanian. My real name isn't Cashman. It's Czernivekoski. When my grandfather came to this country someone told him if he has any trouble with the immigration office at Ellis Island he should give the *man* some *cash*. So when they asked my grandfather his name and they couldn't understand him, he gave the *man* some *cash*. So that's the name they gave him. Cashman.

ELAINE *(Looks at him)* That's an extremely interesting story.

BARNEY I'm sorry. I was just making conversation. *(She passes the kitchen)* That's the kitchen.

ELAINE *(Nods)* No bedroom?

BARNEY No. Well, the sofa opens into a bed. It's a convertible.

ELAINE *(Not much enthusiasm)* Yippee! *(She turns and stares at* BARNEY. *He doesn't quite know what to do, so he looks around awkwardly. Then, after a few moments)* You like it quiet like this? I mean, no talking?

BARNEY I'm sorry. I guess I just ran out of conversation for a minute.

ELAINE Are you nervous?

BARNEY The truth? . . . Yes. Are you?

ELAINE *(Smiles)* The truth? . . . No.
        (She turns and examines the room again)

BARNEY Good. No sense in *both* of us being nervous. You mentioned *Mr.* Navazio. So I assume you're married.

ELAINE *Mr.* Navazio assumes I'm married. I assume what I want.

BARNEY I didn't see a marriage ring so I was wond— *(*ELAINE *interrupts by turning her head away and coughing. It's a small cough at first. She tries to suppress it to no avail. All at once she is having a coughing spasm, coughing violently and uncontrollably. She holds on to the desk chair for support as the fit finally subsides. She sits there gasping for air. Then, to* BARNEY*)*

ELAINE   Can I have a cigarette?

BARNEY   A cigarette? Wouldn't you rather have some
water?

ELAINE   I can't smoke water.
(She pants heavily)

BARNEY   You're not sick, are you?

ELAINE   In what way?

BARNEY   In a sick way. I mean, that's a terrible cough.

ELAINE   If it bothers you, I won't do it again.

BARNEY   It doesn't bother *me.* I thought it would bother
you.

ELAINE   If it bothered me, I wouldn't do it, would I?
. . . You're not going to give me that cigarette, are
you?

> (BARNEY *feels pointlessly in his pockets, as though
> to prove he doesn't carry them)*

BARNEY   I don't smoke.

ELAINE   Then what are you feeling your pockets for?

BARNEY   I don't know. It was just a reflex action.

ELAINE   You mean you always feel your pockets when
you don't offer someone a cigarette?

BARNEY   No. I don't know why I did it.

ELAINE   You don't keep any in the apartment?

BARNEY   It's not my apartment.

ELAINE   I see. *(She takes a deep breath and regains her
composure)* You just borrow it once in a while.

BARNEY   No, nothing like that. As a matter of fact, it's
my mother's apartment.

ELAINE   You're not actively serious?

BARNEY   I am. I'm very serious. It's my mother's apartment. This is where my mother lives.

ELAINE   Is she gonna join us?

BARNEY   She works two days a week for Mount Sinai Hospital. She doesn't get home until five.

ELAINE   Well, that'll make things interesting.

BARNEY   My mother is always doing charity work. She likes to help out needy people.

ELAINE   Like us.

BARNEY   *(Shrugs)*   I didn't know where else to come.

ELAINE   Listen, I always say, Keep it in the family.

BARNEY   Er . . . Would you like a drink?

ELAINE   Desperately.

BARNEY   *(He crosses to his attaché case)*   I'm sorry. I should have offered you one right away. I have J&B Scotch. Is that all right?

ELAINE   *(Opens her coat)*   What else have you got?

BARNEY   That's it. Just J&B Scotch.

ELAINE   I'll have a J&B Scotch.

BARNEY   I never noticed you drink at the restaurant, so I figured a plain Scotch . . .

          (He takes a glass out of the paper bag)

ELAINE   You brought glasses too?

BARNEY   I picked them up in Bloomingdale's. I was thinking of getting them for the restaurant.

ELAINE   You were afraid if you dirtied your mother's glasses she'd know someone was here.

BARNEY   *(Caught, he smiles)*   Well, she's a very meticulous woman. And if anything looked different when she came home I'd have to explain to her and it would get very complicated.

ELAINE   I think you did the smart thing. How many ice cubes did you bring?

BARNEY   *(Smiles)*   Well, I didn't go quite that far. Why, would you like some ice? I'll get some ice for you.

ELAINE   Forget it. We'd spend the rest of the afternoon wiping fingerprints off the tray.

> (BARNEY *pours the Scotch into* ELAINE*'s glass.* ELAINE *watches him*)

BARNEY *(Pouring)* My mother's very typical, you know. She remembers exactly how high the pillows were puffed when she left.

ELAINE   Is that why you put your rubbers on the newspaper? So it wouldn't leave telltale slush?

BARNEY   I'm beginning to feel very foolish about all this.

ELAINE   Forget it. Meeting on the sly is not without its drawbacks.

BARNEY *(Hands her the drink)* Well, here you are.

ELAINE *(Takes it)* I *would* like to ask you one question though.

BARNEY   Yes?

ELAINE   Are you going to talk soft like that all afternoon?

BARNEY   Was I talking soft?

ELAINE   I know that's not your natural voice because I hear you yelling a lot in the restaurant— *"The lady wants boiled halibut not baked halibut!"* Are you talking soft because you think that's sexier? Because I don't find it sexy. I find it hard to hear.

BARNEY   I'm sorry. It's just that these new buildings have paper-thin walls and, you know, I was afraid— I mean my mother has this high squeaky voice and there's this old lady next door who's home all day, and if she were to hear deep voices she'd start to wonder—

ELAINE   So what's the plan? You whisper and I clean the house in a high squeaky voice?

BARNEY   No, no. There's no plan. We'll both talk natural.

ELAINE   You got a pencil and paper? We could pass notes.

BARNEY   I didn't mean to inhibit you. *(Talks louder)* Look. Look. I'm talking loud and clear in my natural voice. Is that better? Does that make you feel more comfortable?

ELAINE *(Smiles, nods)*   Much.

BARNEY   I really feel like an idiot. I want you to relax and say anything and do anything you want. *(He smiles)* Okay?

ELAINE   Do you know you have a nice smile?

BARNEY *(Slightly embarrassed)*   Me? No!

ELAINE   That's not your smile? It looked like your smile.

BARNEY   Well, thank you.

ELAINE   Don't thank me. It's your smile.

BARNEY   I never know when you're kidding me.

ELAINE *(With sincerity)*   I was just kidding you. Don't pay attention to me.

BARNEY   Anyway, you're not supposed to say nice things to me, I'm supposed to say nice things to you.

ELAINE   All right. Say nice things to me.

BARNEY *(Looks at her)*   You're an attractive woman.

ELAINE   That's it? You came off better than I did. Cheers.

BARNEY   Cheers!

(They both drink. She, a healthy slug; he, just a sip and he winces)

ELAINE   Is that your wife I see once in a while in the restaurant? The tall blond woman with the mink coat and the space shoes?

BARNEY   That's right. How did you know?

ELAINE   I figured the only person who'd come in and take money out of the cash register and leave without saying a word is either a mute crook or a wife.

BARNEY. She does that once a week. She goes to the bank on Fridays.

ELAINE *(Nods)* How long are you and the depositor married?

BARNEY *(Shrugs)* A long time.

ELAINE How long? Five years? Ten years? What?

BARNEY Twenty-three years.

ELAINE *(Nods)* Oh. Professionals . . . So here it is Friday, and your wife's at the bank with her space shoes, and your mother's rolling bandages at Mount Sinai . . . and you are all alone with an attractive woman with an empty glass.

BARNEY *(Takes it)* Oh, I'm sorry. *(He goes back to the bottle. He surreptitiously smells his fingers and then starts to pour Scotch into her glass)* You sure you don't want ice?

ELAINE Positive. You just did it again.

BARNEY Did what?

ELAINE Smelled your fingers. That's the third time you smelled your fingers since I'm here.

BARNEY Did I do that? I wasn't even conscious of it.

ELAINE Is that an occupational hazard? Owning a fish restaurant and always worrying how your fingers smell?

BARNEY Well, it's opening those clams and oysters. I enjoy doing it. I do about eight dozen every morning. That's for the last twenty years. I use soap, perfume, aftershave lotion, turpentine . . . They're all right for a few hours, then about four in the afternoon—it comes back in just like the tide.

ELAINE I wouldn't worry about it if I were you.

BARNEY Well, it's not the suavest thing in the world. I mean sitting here in a nice blue suit with an attractive woman, smelling my fingers.

ELAINE The smelly fingers don't bother me as much as the blue suit. You never wear anything else, do you?

BARNEY Not in the restaurant. My father always taught me, a business man should always wear a dignified blue suit. I wear them in the summer, too, only in a cooler fabric.

ELAINE Good. I was concerned.

BARNEY What do they call a person like me? A creature of habit?

ELAINE Yes, I think that's what they call a person like you. Didn't you ever have a wild, crazy desire for a brown sports jacket?

BARNEY I have sports jackets in my closet at home. I have a brown sports jacket and a gray checked sports jacket . . .

ELAINE Is that where you wear them? In your closet at home?

BARNEY I wear them all the time. I'm not as staid as you think.

ELAINE Yes, you are. Staid is a very staid word. You own a car?

BARNEY Yes.

ELAINE A Buick, right?

BARNEY My God, how did you know?

ELAINE *(Shrugs)* It goes with blue suits.

BARNEY You're a very unusual woman, Elaine. Like the way you came to my restaurant. I've never seen you there before and suddenly you come back for lunch eight days in a row. What is it, a special high-protein diet?

ELAINE I get cravings.

BARNEY You mean to eat?

ELAINE To eat, to touch, to smell, to see, to do . . . A

sensual, physical pleasure that can only be satisfied at *that* particular moment.

BARNEY   You mean like after an hour of handball, a cold Pepsi?

ELAINE *(She looks at him)*   I'm going to have trouble with you, right? . . . I have a craving for another Scotch.

BARNEY   Coming right up.
     (He takes her glass and starts to go over to the bottle, when his hand passes in front of his face)

ELAINE *(Chidingly)*   Eh, eh. Caught you again.

BARNEY   I wasn't smelling my fingers. I was looking at my watch.

ELAINE   Oh. Is it time to smell your fingers yet?

BARNEY   I was just thinking about my mother. We have plenty of time.

ELAINE   What time is it?

BARNEY   Ten after three.

ELAINE   And Mount Sinai lets out at five. We've got an hour and fifty minutes. Okay, you want to make the first move?

BARNEY   Boy, you're very *open* about things, aren't you?

ELAINE   In other words, you're not going to make the first move.

BARNEY   Sure I am. Certainly. I just thought we'd finish our drink.

ELAINE *(Shrugs)*   It's your schedule. Listen, you think there's a chance the little old lady next door smokes? All I need is one cigarette.

BARNEY   I wouldn't think so.

ELAINE   I could ring her bell. I could say I'm collecting for the Red Cross.

BARNEY   I'm sorry I didn't bring any. You don't think you could wait until five o'clock?

ELAINE   I could wait until August if you were a hypnotist. Forget it, I'll take shorter breaths.

BARNEY   Can I say something? ... This isn't going very well, is it?

ELAINE   It's had its ups and downs.

BARNEY   You know, Mrs. Navazio, you really are ...

ELAINE   If you're going to keep calling me Mrs. Navazio, you'd better get out a deck of cards.

BARNEY   I'm sorry ... Irene.

ELAINE   Try Elaine. You'll get a better response.

BARNEY   Elaine. Why do I think you're Irene?

ELAINE   Is your wife Irene?

BARNEY   No, my wife is Thelma.

ELAINE   Well, let *her* worry about Irene.

BARNEY   The thing is, Elaine—

ELAINE   Yes, Barney?

BARNEY   Barney. That's right. Please call me Barney.

ELAINE   What else have I got to do?

BARNEY   The thing is, Elaine —

ELAINE   Yes, Barney?

BARNEY   The thing is—I find you an extremely attractive woman.

ELAINE   I heard. Thank you.

BARNEY   I know, I said it before. And I said it in the restaurant, didn't I? Wasn't it the first thing I said to you?

ELAINE   No. The first thing you said to me was "Try the scallops."

BARNEY   I mean after I got to know you. Once we got to talking. On a personal basis.

ELAINE   The first *personal* thing you said to me was "I have never seen such beautiful fingers in my finger bowls."

BARNEY   Well, listen, I'm not George Bernard Shaw. For me, I thought it was clever . . . It was corny, right?

ELAINE   I'm not in George Bernard Shaw's mother's apartment, am I?

BARNEY   Not that I don't dabble a little in writing myself.

ELAINE   Oh? You dabble?

BARNEY   Nothing serious, but I get a kick out of it. You read some of my stuff.

ELAINE   I did? Where?

BARNEY   In the menu. "Sweet savory swordfish steak swimming in salivary succulence." That's mine.

ELAINE   Very catchy. It has a nice beat.

BARNEY   That's the idea. It's what they call alliteration.

ELAINE   Do they? You take that in college?

BARNEY   I didn't go to college. I went from the army right into the "Queen of the Sea." My father started the restaurant in 1931. We used to be in Sheepshead Bay. That's where I grew up. I was always hoping to be a radio writer. Orson Welles and the Mercury Theater, that was my dream. But then came the war, and then my father died and left me the restaurant, and then television killed radio. And I never thought my kind of writing would go on television. I don't write visual. I write for the ear. "Sweet succulent savory swordfish steak" . . . Anyway, I still get a kick out of doing the menus. Did you see the one I did on Flaming Florentine Flounder?

ELAINE   I browsed through it . . . What time is it now?

BARNEY   *(Looks at his watch)*   Twenty after three.

ELAINE   That's another ten minutes shot. So what's it going to be?

BARNEY   My God, you really come right to the point, don't you?

ELAINE   Look, did you ask me to come up here with the intentions of having an affair or not?

BARNEY   Well, in a manner of speaking—

ELAINE   Yes or no?

BARNEY   *(A pause)*   Yes.

ELAINE   And that we've got to be out by five?

BARNEY   I don't think I put it that bluntly.

ELAINE   What time do we have to be out?

BARNEY   *(Shrugs)*   Five.

ELAINE   *(Has made her point)*   All right?

BARNEY   Look, I don't deny my intentions were of a romantic nature—

ELAINE   *Romantic?*   In your mother's clean apartment with two glasses from Bloomingdale's and your rubbers dripping on the newspaper?

BARNEY   It was my belief that romance is inspired by the participants and not the accouterments.

ELAINE   That's beautifully worded. You ought to use it on the Cherrystone Clams. What's the matter, is "having an affair" a dirty expression?

BARNEY   Certainly not. "Having an affair." What's wrong with that?

ELAINE   I mean people talk that way today, you know. Maybe not Buick drivers, but a lot of people I know.

BARNEY   I admitted I was a creature of habit, not a prude.

ELAINE   The hell you're not. I bet I could say three words right now that would turn your blue suit into a glen plaid.

BARNEY   Look, Elaine, this is really silly . . .

ELAINE   I'm gonna say it. I'm going to say a word now. You want to put your hands over your ears?

BARNEY   Hey, come on, Elaine, I don't think this is funny . . .

ELAINE   I'm saying it . . . Screw!

BARNEY *(Looks at her)*   Asshole! I can do it too. I don't understand the point of this.

ELAINE   The point is we've got a time problem and you're reading me fish poetry.

BARNEY   I realize we have a time problem but there's also the business of human communication. Of talking to someone, getting to know someone . . . I'm sorry, maybe my whole approach to you is a little too old-fashioned.

ELAINE *(Throws up her hands)*   Okay. All right. I'm flexible. I'll try things your way . . . What did you want to see me about, Mr. Cashman?

BARNEY   Ohh, Elaine, don't be like that.

ELAINE   Well, maybe I just don't understand you. I've got a two-hundred-and-ten-pound husband who'd break my arms and legs if he caught me up here and you're telling me about your sweet succulent childhood in Sheepshead Bay.

BARNEY   I just thought you might be interested in knowing a little bit more about me. I mean until you walked in here ten minutes ago—

ELAINE   *Twenty* minutes ago—

BARNEY   Twenty minutes ago, I was just a restaurant owner who admired your fingers and you were an attractive woman who has a craving for fish.

ELAINE   Look, *you* were the one who wrote down an address and apartment number on the back of a dollar-eighty check. Then I come here and find out we've got an hour and fifty minutes before your social-working mother with the high squeaky voice comes home to examine the puffed pillows. Now, if we had two weeks in Nassau I'd gladly look at color pictures of your tonsils—

BARNEY   I explained that. I thought a motel was a little sordid . . . And I would gladly have picked up your check but my cashier's very nosey and if she saw me paying for some woman—

ELAINE   Forget it. You got a lot of courage. I was surprised you took a chance giving me an extra shrimp in the shrimp cocktail.
(She finishes her drink)

BARNEY   I don't know how we got started on this—

ELAINE   It's cigarette nerves, pay no attention. (Indicating the Scotch) Is that bottle just going to sit up there or are you going to turn it into a lamp?

BARNEY   You finished the other one already?

ELAINE   I didn't finish it, it evaporated.

BARNEY   Elaine . . . Can I ask you a very honest question?

ELAINE   Yes, I've done this before.

BARNEY   (Looks at her)   That wasn't what I was going to ask.

ELAINE   All right, you got one for free. What were you going to ask?

BARNEY   I'm still not over that answer. You mean you have—on other occasions—?

ELAINE   I have on other occasions—in other places— with other men—done the unthinkable. If it'll help your vanity any, you are the first owner of a fish restaurant I've ever been with. In that respect, I'm still a virgin.

BARNEY   I gather then you're not very happy with Mr. Navazio?

ELAINE   What the hell kind of a question is that, am I happy with Mr. Navazio?

BARNEY   I'm sorry. It's none of my business.

ELAINE   I didn't come up here to get reformed. It's bad enough you got me to quit smoking; leave my sex life alone.

BARNEY   I drop the subject.

ELAINE   What was your question?

BARNEY   What question? Oh, before . . . Well, I was just
wondering, I mean, I told you I thought you were
attractive . . . I know why *I* asked you to come here.
Did you come because . . . er . . . Isn't it funny? I find
it hard to just come out and say it.

ELAINE   Would you like me to wait in the kitchen?

BARNEY   Am I appealing to you?

ELAINE   Yes.

BARNEY   I am?

ELAINE   *Now* you appeal to me.

BARNEY   What do you mean, now? Do you mean possibly not tomorrow?

ELAINE   I mean possibly not in fifteen minutes. I have
a short span of concentration.

BARNEY   You mean with you it can change from day to
day?

ELAINE   By tonight I may hate filet of sole.

BARNEY   I'm not talking about sea food. I'm talking
about people.

ELAINE   Yes, with me it can change from day to day.

BARNEY   Oh. Well, I find that disturbing.

ELAINE   *(An edge of sarcasm)*   Do you really?

BARNEY   Yes, I do. I find it disturbing, and a little sad,
that your attitude towards people is so detached.

ELAINE   You'll get over it. Can I ask you a question?

BARNEY   Yes?

ELAINE   Are you writing some kind of research book?
Is that really why you got me up here? *Sexual Secrets
of Seafood Sufferers?* You got a little tape recorder
going on in the candy dish?

        (She leans over and lifts the top of the candy dish)

BARNEY   I'm sorry, it's very hard keeping up with you.
One minute we're having a nice conversation, and the
next minute you turn on me.

ELAINE   Listen, it's really been terrific, Mr. Cashman. I don't know when I've had a better time. You certainly pour a beautiful glass of Scotch and my compliments to your mother's housekeeping.

BARNEY   Where are you going?

ELAINE   Outside to look for cigarette butts. And then home. Don't worry, no one will notice me leaving the building. I'll walk out backwards.

BARNEY   What did I say? Why are you so upset?

ELAINE   *I* disturb *you?* *I* make *you* sad? I have been called a lot of things by a lot of people in a lot of places but I have *never* been called a depressant. *(She starts for the door)*

BARNEY   I didn't say that. I didn't even mean that.

ELAINE   You got some nerve getting me up here in a 1938 furnished apartment in your shiny blue suit and your thimbleful of Scotch, sitting there smelling your fingers and telling me *I* give *you* the blues.

BARNEY   When did I say that? I'm not depressed. I'm not blue. I'm very happy.

ELAINE   No kidding? How about two fast choruses of "Let a Smile Be Your Umbrella"? . . . Look, let me have a dollar-fifty. I'll be goddamned if I'm going to pay for the lunch *and* the taxi.

BARNEY   Elaine . . . Elaine, please . . . please sit down. Let me just say something.

ELAINE   *Say* something? You've already talked away half our allotted time. Now you'll have to use the other half to wipe my lip prints off the glass, puff the pillows, and get the hell out of here.

BARNEY   *(Softly)*   Elaine, if you could just lower your voice a little—

ELAINE *(Screams)*   LOWER MY VOICE?

BARNEY   Shhh . . .

ELAINE *(Crosses to the wall and yells at it)*   *Mr. Cashman is using his mother's apartment to bring broads!*

BARNEY   What's the sense in that?

ELAINE   Don't tell me I depress you! "Flaming Florentine Flounder"—Holy Christ!

BARNEY   Elaine, you're getting yourself unduly upset.

ELAINE   Unduly upset? I'm risking a bullet between the eyes and I can't even get a lousy cigarette . . .
(This starts her coughing. It gradually worsens into the same violent coughing fit as before. As she coughs, he rushes into the bathroom for a glass of water. Her fit gradually subsides and then turns into just heavy, deep breathing. He returns to her side with the water)

BARNEY   Your chest sounds all congested. Have you ever tried sleeping with a vaporizer?

ELAINE   No, but don't worry, I'll get around to everyone.

BARNEY   I don't want to seem gloomy, but that's a very bad cough. Have you gone to a doctor?

ELAINE   There is nothing wrong with my lungs or my chest. I cough because I have nothing better to do in the afternoons.

BARNEY   *(Still with the glass in his hand)*   Don't you want the water?

ELAINE   Keep it as a memento of this wonderful afternoon.

BARNEY   Boy, oh boy, I sure bungled this whole thing, didn't I?

ELAINE   You want it straight?
(She makes a circle sign with three fingers)

BARNEY   I'm sorry. I really am sorry.

ELAINE   All right, forget it.

BARNEY   No, I am. I really am. I'm sorry I wasted your time. I'm sure you could have found something more interesting to do than sitting here talking to me.

ELAINE   If I rush I can still make the second show at the Hayden Planetarium. Don't get wistful, will you, please? I can't stand wistful forty-five-year-old men.

BARNEY   Is that how old I look to you? Forty-five?

ELAINE *(She looks at him)*   Cut right down to the marrow, heh? No, actually you look like a college kid, twenty-one, twenty-two . . .

BARNEY   Aw, come on.

ELAINE   It's your black socks with the clocks on them that threw me off.

BARNEY   Anyway, I'm flattered, because I'm forty-seven. Does that surprise you?

ELAINE   It's a good thing I was sitting when you told me.

BARNEY   You're still upset, aren't you? About what I said before.

ELAINE   Forget it.

BARNEY   No, you're still upset, I can tell.

ELAINE   I'm not upset, I'm not angry, I'm not mad. If you want the plain, heartbreaking truth, I'm a little bored. But there was no harm done, no one got hurt. The worst that'll happen is that from now on I'll get the same five shrimps as everyone else. *(She gets up)* It's been a glorious and memorable thirty minutes. Good-bye, Mr. Cashman.

BARNEY   Don't go.

ELAINE   It happens to the best of us.
        (She crosses to the door)

BARNEY   Elaine . . . Do you know what I wish?

ELAINE *(Warding him off with her hand)*   Don't tell me, it won't come true.
        (She opens the door)

BARNEY   I wish that you would go out, close the door, then ring the bell and come back in again. I wish we could start this whole thing over, from the beginning.

ELAINE *(Turns at the door; looks at him)* Yeah . . .Well
. . . That's life . . . Good-bye, Barney. *(She goes and
closes the door.* BARNEY *shrugs, then goes over to the table
and picks up the two glasses. Then he crosses back to his
attaché case with the glasses and puts one of them away.
The doorbell rings. He looks up, dabs some more after-
shave lotion on his fingers and crosses back to the door. He
opens it.* ELAINE *walks into the room, surveys it as if for
the first time, then turns and smiles at* BARNEY. *Sweetly,
almost girlish)* I just happened to be in the neighborhood and I thought I'd drop by . . . (BARNEY *looks at
her, then wordlessly he moves toward her.* ELAINE *looks
at him expectantly, seeing a new* BARNEY, *one that she
hoped to find in the first place. He is beside her. He pulls
her firmly to him and then kisses her—solidly and passionately. Then, still with his lips on her, he tries to
maneuver her back toward the couch.* ELAINE *trips and
falls backwards onto the sofa.* BARNEY *falls on top of her)*
Oh, Christ!

BARNEY   Are you all right?

ELAINE   My goddamn lip is bleeding.

BARNEY   I'm sorry, Elaine.

ELAINE   If you wanted me on the sofa, why didn't you
just point to it?

BARNEY   I didn't want you on the sofa. I'm very sorry.
Let me see your lip.

ELAINE   It's a bleeding lip, you've seen them before.

BARNEY   Let me put some cold water on it.

ELAINE   It's all right, it'll heal. It's only royal families
that have to worry. Give me a handkerchief.
(He gives her a handkerchief. She dabs)

BARNEY   Damned stupid idiot. I don't know why I
kissed you so hard.

ELAINE   It was a terrific kiss. A little pointy maybe, but
very nice. Help me up.
(He pulls her up)

BARNEY   Can I put a little ice on it?

ELAINE   Just your worrying about it is enough for me. It stopped. *(Hands him the hanky)* Here. You'd better burn this.
    (He takes it)

BARNEY   How about a little more Scotch?

ELAINE   How about a lot more? *(He nods, goes back to the attaché case and takes out the glass. She looks at him)* You packed the glasses already? You didn't wax the floors too, did you?

BARNEY *(Pours another drink)*   Some klutz, heh? That's me. World's Olympic Champion klutz.

ELAINE   Listen, it was the best two minutes we had. I'm not one to knock a little physical contact.

BARNEY   Yeah, but I mean it was right out of high school. If we missed the sofa, I could have fallen on top of you and broken your back.
    (He hands her drink)

ELAINE *(Smiles)*   That's an interesting picture. You want to take another shot at it?

BARNEY *(Smiles back)*   You mean I'm forgiven? You really are something, Elaine. I never saw anyone who can change moods as quickly as you.

ELAINE   It's a talent. It's not as good as tap dancing, but what the hell.

BARNEY   I don't think you're as tough as you like to sound.

ELAINE   I'll bet you're going to hold my hand next.

BARNEY   Yes, I am. How do you like that? *(Holds her hand)* Don't you like having a man hold your hand in his?

ELAINE   Well, it depends what he's doing with the other hand.

BARNEY   I wish I could figure you out. I wish I knew what was going on in that brain of yours right now.

ELAINE We're not going to get on a *talking* thing again, are we? Without cigarettes?

BARNEY Elaine, what were you like when you were a girl?

ELAINE Fat and pimply. Don't you even smoke a pipe? A couple of drags is all I really need.

BARNEY My God, is that all you can think of? Is that the most important thing in your life right now? Is there nothing else on your mind but a lousy god-damned mentholated filtered cigarette?

ELAINE Well, what are you offering that's more enjoyable?

BARNEY I'm trying to talk to you, to know what you're like as a human being. Is there anything wrong with that?

ELAINE Not if we didn't have to be out by five. If you wanted information I could have filled out a form in the restaurant.

BARNEY Tell me the truth—the honest truth. Would you be a lot happier if I started ripping off your clothes and jumping all over you? No hello, no nothing. Just the pure, physical animal act. Is that what you would prefer?

ELAINE Well, it *would* be a way of breaking the ice.

BARNEY Because if that's what you want I certainly could accommodate you. I mean there's no problem in that area, is there?

ELAINE If you say so.

BARNEY I say so. There is *no* problem in that area.

ELAINE Then what *is* the problem?

BARNEY There's *no* problem . . . yes, there is. I'm sorry, I just happen to think that's crude. Look, I admit I don't know you very well, but I was hoping to start off this relationship with at least mutual *respect* for each other . . .

ELAINE If you don't know me how can you respect me?

BARNEY   Because you're a human being, a woman. And I respect that.

ELAINE   Hey, listen, no offense, but I'm getting a bad headache. How much do you get for a couple of aspirin?

BARNEY   I suppose I did that. As you said, I'm boring you to death, right?

ELAINE   Barney, you're simply too overconfident for me. I'm just putty in your hands. Can I pour it myself? I promise I won't go past the pencil mark. *(She pours a drink)*

BARNEY *(Watches her)*   Elaine . . . Is it possible you really are as cold as you sound?

ELAINE   I need gloves to take off my underwear.

BARNEY   Flippant, wise, cold . . . You won't permit yourself to be sincere and honest for a minute, will you?

ELAINE *(She drinks)*   Barney, I'm going to give you one free hint so the afternoon isn't a total write-off. If you want undying love and romance, take a guitar and go to Spain. *(She puts down her glass)* I am leaving for good now. My peak has ebbed.

BARNEY   Cold, callous and unemotional.

ELAINE   *(Starting for the door)*   Those are my attorneys. You know where to get in touch with me.

BARNEY   Forgive me for saying so, but it's a pretty frightening way to go through life.

ELAINE *(At the door)*   You're forgiven.

BARNEY   . . . frightening, sad and pitiful.
(ELAINE *is just about to step out when she stops at this last remark. She stands there for a moment. Then she takes a step back and turns to* BARNEY, *in a rage)*

ELAINE   You hypocrite! You soul-searching, finger-smelling, hypocritical son of a bitch! Who are you to tell anybody how to go through life? What would you have done if I came in here all fluttery and blushing and "Ooh, Mr. Cashman, don't put your hand there, I'm a married woman"? Were you going to tell me how much you respect me, admire me and, at the moment of truth, even love me? You know damn well tomorrow you'd be back behind that counter opening clams and praying to Christ I'd never come back in your restaurant. And you know something? That's the way it should be. Forgive me for the terrible, sinful thing I'm about to say but I happen to like the pure physical act of making love. It warms me, it stimulates me and it makes me feel like a woman— but that's another ugly story. That's what I came up here for and that's what you were expecting. But don't give me, "When I was nine years old my mother ran off with the butcher and I've been looking for someone to love me ever since." I don't know your problems and I don't care. Keep your savory swordfish succotash stories to yourself. No one really cares about anything or anyone in this world except himself, and there's only one way to get through with your sanity. If you can't taste it, touch it or smell it, forget it! If you want a copy of that speech, send fifty cents and self-addressed envelope—

BARNEY Please don't go yet.

ELAINE It's getting late . . . and I have to feed the lion at six.

BARNEY But I don't want you to leave like this. I want you to hear me out. Stay five more minutes. You can do that, can't you?

ELAINE Don't waste your time. We're incompatible. You need Joan Fontaine and I need a box of lozenges. *(She opens the door)*

BARNEY *(He goes to the door and closes it)* All right, if I have to lock you in, I'll lock you in. *(He bolts the door)* You saw me opening the clams, you know I'm stronger than you.

ELAINE *(Looks at him; smiles)* Wouldn't you know it? We've only got forty minutes left and finally you show me some brute force.

BARNEY Will you please sit down? I'm asking nicely.

ELAINE You want to really get me crazy? Push me! *(He suddenly grabs her arm, pulls her and shoves her onto a chair. She falls into it, stunned, and looks up at him with great surprise. He is shaking with anger, and points a threatening finger at her)*

BARNEY Just sit there! Don't talk, don't cough, don't even breathe. Just sit there and shut up until I tell you you can go. If I get nothing else from you this afternoon it's going to be your undivided goddamned attention! Excuse me! *(He crosses to the bottle, pours himself a drink, and gulps it down. She looks at him incredulously but silently. He does not look at her)* I'm sure it will come as no great shock to you, but you are the first "attempted" extramarital affair for me in twenty-three years of marriage. I've never even kissed another woman. In twenty-three years. I got married to my high-school sweetheart—and when have you heard that expression last—at the age of twenty-four, having gone steady with her since I was sixteen. And how many experiences with other women do you think I've had prior to getting married? ... One! I had one shot at it. When I was eighteen my brother took me to an apartment in Newark, New Jersey, where I consorted with a forty-four-year-old woman who greeted me lying naked on a brass bed reading a newspaper. It cost me seven dollars and I threw up all night. I don't smoke, I don't gamble, and you've had more to drink this afternoon than I've had in my whole life. I've never had a car accident, never had a fistfight, never had a broken bone, never had a temperature over a hundred and two ... Life has not only been very kind to me, it goes out of its way to ignore me ... I've got three kids I'm very proud of, a house I've worked very hard for and a wife who is not extraordinary, not what you would call an exciting, vivacious woman, but one who is kind, considerate, devoted and that I happen to love. So why after twenty-three years do I write my mother's address on the back of a check, buy a bottle of Scotch with two glasses and pray to God I never get caught? Why? I'll tell you why . . . I don't know. I've never had the urge before . . . Not true. I started getting the urge about five years ago. Two years ago seriously. About a year ago I decided to give in to it, and the last six months conscientiously. I'm forty-seven years old and for the first time in my life I think about dying. The thought of death has now become a part of my life. I read the obituaries every day just for the satisfaction of not seeing my name there. I constantly think about how it's going to come and how I'm going to bear up to it. Do you know I even practice dying? I lie in bed at night trying to feel myself slipping away . . . and then I let my head drop off to the side . . . and then I let out my last gasp of air . . . then I go in and take two sleeping pills because I'm up the rest of the night scared out of my wits. But it's inevitable, it's going to happen someday, maybe sooner than I think. And I ask myself, "Have you enjoyed it, Barney? Was it a really terrific forty-seven years?" And you know what my answer is? "Well, I wouldn't say terrific. It was nice." . . . The sum total of my existence is nice. I will go to my grave having led a nice life. And I will have a nice funeral and they will bury me in my nice blue suit. And my wife will weep for me and mourn for me and in six months she will marry another nice fellow . . . maybe even give him my brown sports jacket. And I wouldn't condemn her for it. It's the natural order of things. Life must go on . . . But while it's going on, shouldn't it be better than just "nice"? Shouldn't there be something else besides opening the restaurant eleven o'clock every morning? Shouldn't there be something better than those three weeks every August in Saratoga Springs where I stand in a pool with fifty fat middle-aged people, wishing I were home opening the restaurant at eleven o'clock in the morning? Couldn't I just once give in to my fantasies, my secret dreams, experiencing things, emotions, stimulants I've never experienced before . . . I wanted to know what it was like with another woman. Would I be successful, would she like me, would I like the touch of her? A thousand questions that I'd never know the answer to if suddenly my name were in that obituary column tomorrow morning. So I decided to indulge myself, just once. I don't pretend I'm being fair to my wife. If she indulged herself the same way I'd never forgive her. So I started looking around . . . and, I promise you, with all intentions of having one affair, one day of pleasure and that's all. But if it was just going to be one day I wanted it to be memorable—an experience so rewarding and fulfilling that it would last me the rest of my life . . . not cheap, not sordid. And then I'd go back to opening the restaurant at eleven o'clock in the morning—but knowing that for one brief afternoon I had changed the pattern of my life, and for once I didn't just exist—I lived!

(There is a long silence)

ELAINE   And that's why you wanted to get laid?

BARNEY   I said I'd let you know when you can go. *Now* is a good time.

ELAINE   I was going to cry in the middle, but I didn't want to wet your mother's carpeting.

BARNEY   I had hoped you'd understand, but I didn't expect it.

ELAINE   No, listen, it was terrifically entertaining. I really enjoyed it. There's one or two reasons, though, why I couldn't feel too sympathetic for the hero . . . In the first place, there is a very good possibility that that forty-four-year-old woman in Newark, New Jersey, was my mother. That'll give you some idea of my background. In the second place, any man who expects to have a beautiful, memorable and enchanting day of honest love with a woman he picks up in a fish restaurant is either sexually retarded or a latent idiot! And in the third place, no one gives a good crap about you dying because a lot of people discovered it ahead of you. We're all dying, Mr. Cashman. As a matter of fact, I myself passed away about six months ago. I'm just hanging around to clean up some business affairs

. . . Together, Barney, we blew one of the very few free afternoons we have allotted to us in this life. But I'm not putting the blame on you. It serves me right. If I had a craving for corned beef and cabbage I'd be in some big Irishman's apartment right now having the time of my life . . . *C'est la vie! (At the door)* Good luck, Barney, in your quest for the Impossible Dream. *(Opens the door)* Oh, please God, let there be a machine in the lobby . . .

> *(And she is gone.* BARNEY *stands there a moment, still shaken from his experience. Then he crosses slowly and opens the drapes. He looks at his watch, then goes to the phone, picks it up and dials. Then, into the phone)*

BARNEY   . . . Hello, Harriet? . . . Mr. Cashman . . . The busboy show up? . . . Well, call the agency again . . . I'll be there in about twenty minutes. I'm leaving Bloomingdale's now . . . No, I didn't get anything . . . I looked, I shopped around, but I didn't get anything . . . Well, that's the way it goes . . . I'll see you, Harriet . . . *(He hangs up. He looks around the room, then sits. He buries his head in his hands and is silent a moment)* I'll never do that again! . . . Never never never never never . . . never . . . never . . .

Curtain

Act Two

The scene is the mother's apartment. It is the following August, about three in the afternoon. A key fits in the latch; the door opens, and BARNEY *sticks his head in.*

BARNEY   Mom? *(He waits; there is no answer. He enters the apartment, puts the key on the shelf, and closes the door. He puts his straw hat on the railing post. He carries the attaché case, wears the summer version of his blue suit, in a lighter fabric, of course. He crosses to the dining table and puts down the attaché case. He goes to the large window and lowers the Venetian blind, crosses to the smaller windows, turns down the air conditioner and closes the blinds. He opens the attaché case and this time he has* two *bottles, Scotch and vodka. He takes them out, places them on the table. Then from the case he takes three packs of cigarettes and puts them on the coffee table. He goes over to the phone and dials, puts the receiver on the desk, takes a small mouth spray from his pocket and sprays mouth and fingers. He picks up the receiver, and into the phone, in a soft voice)* . . . Hello, Harriet? . . . Mr. Cashman . . . *(The doorbell rings)* I can't talk now, I'm at the dentist. *(He hangs up.* BARNEY *turns quickly and moves to the door. He looks out the peephole, then opens the door.* BOBBI MICHELE *stands there, a pretty girl of about twenty-seven. Despite the oppressive heat outside,* BOBBI *looks cool and fresh. She carries a large leather portfolio and a make-up bag.* BARNEY *smiles)* Well, hello.

BOBBI   Oh, thank God, air conditioning. Do you know it's a hundred and forty degrees outside? I swear. I mean it gets hot in California but nothing like this. Hi. Bobbi Michele?

BARNEY   Yes, yes. Come in, I'll close the door. It's cooler.

(She comes in: he closes the door)

BOBBI   I was wandering up and down the hall. All these

apartments look alike. *(Looks quickly)* Oh, this is nice. I like this. I'm not disturbing you now, am I? I mean you're not busy or anything?

BARNEY   No, no, I was expecting you. Remember I said—

BOBBI   I wasn't sure I'd be here on time. I just got through with my audition.

BARNEY   No, you're fine. Remember I said three o'clock—

BOBBI   It's got to be a hundred and ten, right? *(Crosses to the air conditioner)* I mean forget about breathing, it's over. *(Stands with her back to the air conditioner)* You sure I'm not disturbing you? I could come back later.

BARNEY   No, I'm positive. I'm clear till five. *(He smells his fingers)* Can I get you a cool drink?

BOBBI   I love this neighborhood. I knew this street looked familiar. I once had a girl friend who lived on this block. Forty-seventh between First and York.

BARNEY   This is Thirty-seventh.

BOBBI   Thirty-seventh. Of course. Then she couldn't have lived on this block. Ohh, that's better. The Shubert Theatre was a sauna bath. Oh, listen, my accompanist *did* show up, which I have you to thank for because you were so sweet in the park yesterday and I want you to know I have not forgotten it, but here I am talking and talking and I really haven't said hello yet. Hello.

BARNEY   Hello.

BOBBI   Hello. Here I am.

BARNEY   So I see.

BOBBI   Oh, God, I talk a lot when I get nervous. Have you noticed that? I'll try and stop it if I can. You'll have to forgive me.

BARNEY   Are you nervous?

BOBBI   Well, I'm not nervous now. I was nervous

before. I just had a terrible experience with a cab driver. Well, I don't want to go into it. Ohh, God, I just wilt in the heat. If I pass out on the floor, I'm just going to have to trust you.

BARNEY *(Smiles)*   You don't have to worry.

BOBBI   Well, you're not a cab driver. You wouldn't try something like that.

BARNEY   Like what?

BOBBI   He wanted to make it with me under the Manhattan Bridge during his lunch hour. Listen, can we forget about it, it's over now. I must look awful.

BARNEY   Not at all. You look lovely.

BOBBI   Oh, poof, I don't.

BARNEY   You do. You do.

BOBBI   Give me three minutes, I'll dazzle you. Did you get shorter?

BARNEY   Shorter? Since yesterday?

BOBBI   Why do you look shorter?

BARNEY   I can't imagine why I should look shorter.
(He sits next to her)

BOBBI   Oh, flats.

BARNEY   Flats?

BOBBI   I was wearing flats yesterday. I put on heels for the audition today. I got taller. Actually, you're not really short. Well, you know that.

BARNEY   Yes, well, sometimes when a person has large bones—

BOBBI   You know, I couldn't make out your handwriting. I thought I had the wrong address. 432 East Thirty-seventh?

BARNEY   No, that's the right address.

BOBBI   Well, I should hope so. Otherwise where am I and who are you? *(She laughs; he tries to)* Oh, that's silly. If I'm goofy today, it's the heat.

BARNEY   You're not goofy at all.

BOBBI   I am. I'm goofy, let's face it.

BARNEY   I think you're charming.

BOBBI   Oh, I know I'm charming but I'm also goofy which I think is part of my charm. That's a terrible thing to say, isn't it?

BARNEY   Not at all. Sometimes frankness can be—

BOBBI   It's terrible, I can't help it. I'm so open about things. That's why I'm always getting myself into trouble, you know what I mean?

BARNEY   What kind of trouble do you get—

BOBBI   My God, I didn't even notice it. You shaved your moustache.

BARNEY   What moustache?

BOBBI   Didn't you have a moustache yesterday?

BARNEY   Me? No.

BOBBI   You *never* had a moustache?

BARNEY   Never. I don't look good in a moustache. It doesn't grow in thick on the left side.

BOBBI   Who am I thinking of? Who did I meet yesterday with a moustache?

BARNEY   That I couldn't tell you.

BOBBI   Well, I can't think straight. I'm still a nervous wreck over that cab incident. I've been back in New York three days and look what happens. I just want to forget about it.

BARNEY   Certainly. How about a drink? I have J&B Scotch, Wolfschmidt vodka . . .

BOBBI   I wrote the cabbie's name down. Max Schoenstein. I was going to report him to the police but he started to cry. Tears pouring down his face, I thought his cigar would go out. Then he pleaded with me he's married twenty-seven years with one son in Vietnam and another son in medical school and that he didn't mean any harm and I felt sorry for him and I said all right, I wouldn't report him, so he thanked me and asked me to reconsider going under the Manhattan Bridge. *(Brushes her hair and poses)* How do I look? Better?

BARNEY   Marvelous. Gee, that's terrible.

BOBBI   Oh, it happens to me all the time. Coming in on the plane from California. The man sitting next to me kept feeling me up all during the movie. Well, I don't want to go into that. *(Looks around)* This is the kind of place I'm looking for. Does it have a terrace?

BARNEY   No, no terrace. He was *feeling* you?

BOBBI   Well, he said he was looking for the dial to turn up the volume but he didn't even have the headset plugged in his ears . . . Nice view.

BARNEY   Why didn't you say something to him?

BOBBI   Well, he was Chinese, I didn't want to seem bigoted. Then he has the nerve to call me, in the middle of the night. Some strange Chinaman.

BARNEY   How'd he get your number?

BOBBI   I don't know. I must have given it to him or something. What's the difference? Look, it's over, let's forget it. Am I talking too much? I haven't given you a chance to say anything.

BARNEY   I'm fascinated. Those are incredible stories.

BOBBI   How do you mean incredible? You don't believe them?

BARNEY   I do. I do believe them.

BOBBI   Because they're true.

BARNEY   That's the fascinating part.

BOBBI   Maybe to you. They were terrifying to me.

BARNEY   To me too.

BOBBI   Could I have a drink?

BARNEY   What a good idea. J&B? Vodka?

BOBBI   I don't provoke these things. They just happen.

BARNEY   I'm not surprised. You're such a pretty girl.

BOBBI   I don't know why they single me out. I'm always getting these obscene telephone calls.

BARNEY   Well, there's an awful lot of that going on.

BOBBI   I get them wherever I go. Once I wasn't home, he left an obscene message.

BARNEY   My goodness.

BOBBI   *(Looking at the photos on the table)*   And the language. I never heard such filth. I once got a call where this psycho actually described vile and indecent acts for over fifteen minutes.

BARNEY   FIFTEEN MINUTES!

BOBBI   Listen, if you don't shut me up I'll never stop talking. What time is it?

BARNEY   A quarter after three.

BOBBI   Oh, God, I've got to make a call. May I? I don't have one on me.

BARNEY   Yes, certainly.

BOBBI   Is this where you write those sea stories you were telling me about?

BARNEY   Yes, I work here during the day. Actually it's my mother's apartment.

BOBBI   I knew this writer in California. A registered weirdo. He used to write these underground movies you see on Eighth Avenue. You know, *Sex Family Robinson, Tom Swift and His Incredible Thing* . . . I thought I was in love with him until I found out he was deranged. I mean the things he wanted me to do.

BARNEY   Like what?

BOBBI   Oh, God, I couldn't repeat them.

BARNEY That's all right. You can repeat them.

BOBBI *(Dials the phone and listens)* She hears the phone. She's just a lazy bitch.

BARNEY But like what? What kind of things did he want you to do?

BOBBI I couldn't tell you. I told my analyst, he went into cardiac arrest . . . Can you believe this? I could wait here twenty minutes.

BARNEY You mean things together or alone? What kind of things?

BOBBI If I tell you this man had his teeth sharpened, can you fill in the rest?
          (She inspects the photos on the table)

BARNEY His teeth? My God!

BOBBI The man was psychotically inclined. *(Smiles at a photo)* This is adorable. Your mother?

BARNEY *(Shakes his head)* No, it's me. But did you ever do any of them? These things he wanted?

BOBBI Me? No! Never! Of course not . . . Some. I had to do some otherwise I was afraid he would kill me. Is this you and your father?

BARNEY Yes . . . He actually forced you to do these things?

BOBBI You don't play it cool with a man who had his teeth sharpened. *(Indicating a picture)* Were you both in the Navy?

BARNEY No, if you look close it says "Queen of the Sea" on the sailor caps. I can't imagine what kind of things he made you do.

BOBBI Please forgive me for what I'm about to say, but the man was a shit. Am I forgiven?

BARNEY Certainly. How'd you get hooked up with a guy like that?

BOBBI By sheer chance. He was living with my room-mate and she moved out. Hey, did I tell you about my audition?

BARNEY   No, you didn't.
          (He looks at his watch)

BOBBI   Do you have to go somewhere?

BARNEY   Me? No. I'm here till five. What happened at the audition?

BOBBI   I was fabulous. David Merrick thought I was the end.

BARNEY   No kidding? David Merrick?

BOBBI   Well, it was dark, but it was someone with a moustache. Anyway, they went absolutely ape over me. They really loved me. I would have gotten the part except they wanted a Negro girl. That's how it is in the theater today. If you're not black, you're nowhere. Anyway, it was my best audition thanks to this groovy accompanist I was telling you about—which brings us to why I'm here, doesn't it? I owe you twenty dollars.

BARNEY   There's no hurry.

BOBBI   What do you mean? You were nice enough to lend me twenty dollars for an accompanist—a stranger you met in the park. I told you I would pay you back today, didn't I? I insist.

BARNEY   Well, all right.

BOBBI   The thing is, I don't have the money. I'm good for it, though. If I don't get a show in New York I may go do a series of one-night concerts in New Zealand . . . *(Takes out some photos)* I just wanted to show you some stills from this movie I was in so you'll believe I'm really an actress. That's me on location in Malibu. And those are the stars, Frankie Avalon, Annette Funicello and the Beach Boys.

BARNEY   Oh, yes.

BOBBI   It was a cute picture. They used the basic story of *Wuthering Heights* and worked in surfriders.

BARNEY   What a good idea.

BOBBI   And that's me with Fabian—

BARNEY   Fabian?

BOBBI   —who, and I say this with deep sincerity, is one of the great human beings I've ever met. He was unbelievably kind to me when I had my accident.

BARNEY   What kind of accident?

BOBBI   I was beaten up by some Mexican in a motel. *(She puts pictures back)* How I got there or who the Mexican was I'll never know. And the police'll never give you any information.

BARNEY   My God, the things that happen to you.

BOBBI *(Zipping up her portfolio)*   Well, I certainly don't look for it. Goodness, you must think I'm some sort of bizarre *femme fatale. (Picks up the phone and listens)* Can you believe this?

BARNEY   Who are you calling?

BOBBI   My answering service! At least she promised she'd take messages for me. I have the worst damn luck with roommates.

BARNEY   You live with someone now?

BOBBI   Heinrich Himmler. I can't afford my own place yet so in the meantime I'm living with this Nazi vocal teacher. She's not just German, she's actually Nazi. Wears black shirts, boots, the whole thing.

BARNEY   My God.

BOBBI   Great vocal coach, though—if you don't mind getting whipped.

BARNEY   You're not serious?

BOBBI   Oh, Wilhelmina Weirdo. She paid four hundred dollars to have a three-inch scar put on her face. My suspicion is she's sexually—er—what's the word?

BARNEY   Aberrated?

BOBBI   No, worse than that.

BARNEY   Worse than aberrated?

BOBBI   She's got this queen-size bed in her room with a *leather* bedspread. Does that seem funny to you?

BARNEY   Well, you live with her, you'd know better.

BOBBI   Goodness, how would I know? I'm no lesbian. I'm only staying there because she's a damned good vocal teacher and she's not taking any rent.

BARNEY   How come?

BOBBI   Because she thinks I'm going to make it very big in this business and she wants to get in on the ground floor! . . . Oh! Finally! *(Into the phone)* Hello, Hilda? Vas nicht gessen? Auf lichter shein bister? . . . *(To* BARNEY, *smiling)* I make up German, she gets hysterical . . . *(Back into the phone)* . . . Nowhere . . . With a friend . . . Did the Merv Griffin Show call? . . . Well, how would you know? Where were you for twenty minutes, downstairs in the bunker? . . . *(Smiles at* BARNEY. *Into phone)* I already told you, just a friend . . . It's *not* another girl . . . No, I don't think I'll be home for dinner . . . I *won't* be home for dinner . . . Just a minute . . . *(To* BARNEY) Are we going to have dinner?

BARNEY   I don't think I can tonight.

BOBBI   *(Into the phone)* Yes, I'll be home for dinner . . . About six . . . I promise . . . I said I promise, didn't I? . . . Then *auf Wiedersehen. (She hangs up)* Do you know, if they'd won the war she'd be choral director at Radio City Music Hall?

BARNEY   If you're so uncomfortable, why do you stay with her?

BOBBI   You know, you're the second person who's accused me of being homosexual.

BARNEY   I never said you were hom—

BOBBI   My goodness, the thought of it makes my skin crawl. That's the one thing in life I find revolting. I mean I sleep so far away from her in that bed she'd have to take a taxi to get near me. People can be so vicious sometimes . . .

BARNEY   I never for a minute suggested—

BOBBI   Are you married?

BARNEY   Yes. Yes. I'm married.

BOBBI   The other person who suggested it was this kinky writer who would stoop to anything because I wouldn't do these "terrible things" I told you about before . . . I mean not *all* of them.
(She opens the make-up box and takes out a brush)

BARNEY   Listen, you sure you wouldn't want a drink?

BOBBI   *(Brushing her hair again)* I didn't mean *you* when I said people can be vicious sometimes.

BARNEY   That's all right.

BOBBI   You're not vicious. You're married. Married men are rarely vicious. They're too guilty.

BARNEY   Do you find that?

BOBBI   Without exception. Except for this one married man I knew. Was he ever vicious. *(She stops brushing, and puts the brush back)* Goodness, I'm letting you in on everything. Whatever happened to the Woman of Mystery? Do you mind terribly if I smoke?

BARNEY   No, no. Please smoke *(Rushes to the cigarettes on the table)* I have plenty of cigarettes. Filters, mentholated, super king, whatever you want.

BOBBI   *(Takes out a small case from her make-up box)* I have my own, thanks. *(She opens the box)* Promise me you won't ask me about this married man because it's one episode in my life I'd rather not discuss.
(She takes out a thin cigarette and holds it out. BARNEY opens a box of cocktail matches he just bought for the occasion)

BARNEY   Certainly. I understand that.

BOBBI   If I tell you, it'll go no further than this room?

BARNEY   You don't have to discuss it if it's painful.
(He lights her cigarette. She takes a long drag)

BOBBI   For obvious reasons, I can't reveal his identity. Let's just call him Mr. H. That's all I'll divulge about him. Mr. H.

BARNEY   *(Puts out the match)* I understand.

BOBBI   *(Takes another drag)* Arnold H. He lives in Palm

Springs, California, and is in the hotel business. *(She takes a long breath)* You've heard of him, I'm sure. He had a big spread in *Time* magazine.

BARNEY When was that?

BOBBI I'm sorry, I can't betray any confidences. I don't think we should talk about it. Would you like one of these?

BARNEY I don't really smoke.

BOBBI I don't either. I mean, not cigarettes. Anyway, I met Mr. H. about two years ago in Arizona. I was a house guest of this very short movie producer and one ni—

BARNEY Excuse me. I don't want to interrupt. Is that—
        (He mouths the word "marijuana")

BOBBI *(Looks at him, puzzled)* I didn't catch the last word.

BARNEY *(Looks around nervously)* I didn't want to say it too loud. There's an old lady next door who listens to everything. Is that . . . *(He leans in and whispers)* marijuana?

BOBBI *(Nods)* Mmm.

BARNEY Pot?

BOBBI Yes. Change your mind?

BARNEY No.

BOBBI You sure?

BARNEY I'm trying to cut down.

BOBBI Actually it's a blend. Half Turkish tobacco, half grass. It's prescribed by my doctor in Beverly Hills. I take it instead of a tranquilizer because I have this inability to swallow pills. *(Holds out the box)* You sure? They're not strong. They're a twenty-minute freak-out at the most.

BARNEY Maybe later.

BOBBI   I take it for medicinal purposes, but you can get high if you like. By the way, you have a nice smile.

BARNEY   Other people have told me that.

BOBBI   You're a very basic person, no crap. Am I right?

BARNEY   Well . . .

BOBBI   Sincere . . . sweet . . . You meet so damn few in my business . . . Well, anywhere for that matter . . .

BARNEY   Well, most people that I've run across . . .

BOBBI   *(She sits back, and suddenly begins to sing)*
     What the world needs now is love, sweet love
     That's the only thing that there's just too
       little of . . .*
   That's what I'm going to do if I get the Merv Griffin show. If the Beast of Berlin ever takes my messages. *(Looks around)* I like the color of these walls. I am so sick of white walls . . . Is the door locked?

BARNEY   The door? Yes. Is it all right?

BOBBI   I just wanted to make sure. I thought I saw somebody following me outside. Probably not . . . Is this a rent-controlled building?

BARNEY   *(Nervously)*   What do you mean? Who would follow you?

BOBBI   Who indeed? That's a good question. I'm just being silly. *(Takes another drag)* Why don't you just check the lock?

BARNEY   *(Starts toward the door)*   It's locked, I checked . . . You mean it's possible someone knows you're here with me? Now?

BOBBI   *(Smiles)*   Oh, that's sweet. You're worried some jealous nut is going to rush in here and blow our brains out. Wouldn't that be a kick, a regular blood bath . . .

BARNEY   Oh, jeez—

---

*From "What the World Needs Now is Love," by Burt Bacharach and Hal David. Copyright © 1965 by Blue Seas Music, Inc. and Jac Music Co., Inc. All rights reserved.

BOBBI   Well, it's *one* way of getting your name in the papers. *(Reassuring him)* No, I think we're okay . . . *(She takes another drag)*

BARNEY *(Nods without listening)*   Look, er, Bobbi. You understand, of course, that my intention in asking you here today was merely one of convenience. I mean you wanted to pay me back the twenty dollars and I thought this was as good a place as any—

BOBBI   My goodness, that was understood. I certainly didn't think I was coming here to be seduced. *(She puts the "stick" out in the ashtray)* All gone. Finished my pot like a good little girl. *(Points to the ashtray)* Don't forget to get rid of this. Tear the paper, scatter the ashes and flush the toilet twice. You can't imagine the number of people who are serving time today because they only flushed once.

BARNEY   Flush twice . . . That's a good thing to remember. *(He takes the ashtray and walks toward the bathroom. Waves the air with his hand)* It leaves a slight odor, doesn't it?
 (He enters the bathroom)

BOBBI   You want me to open the window?

BARNEY *(Offstage)*   You understand, of course, when I spoke to you in the park *(Toilet flushes)* it was only because I thought you were in trouble. I mean I never do things like that, it's very rare for me. The thing is you looked so all alone *(Toilet flushes)* and you had this sad look on your face—so troubled, so distraught . . .
 (He comes out of the bathroom)

BOBBI *(Peering through the blinds)*   Did you ever see that man before?

BARNEY   What man?
 (BOBBI *beckons him with her finger.* BARNEY *moves quickly to the window and peers out)*

BOBBI   The one across the street. In front of that building. Have you ever seen him standing there?

BARNEY   All the time. He's the doorman.

BOBBI   I was just wondering. *(Looks at* BARNEY*)* Do you think I'm being silly?

BARNEY   No . . . Well, I'm not sure. You certainly seem worried about something . . . Even when you were sitting in the park.

BOBBI   Can I trust you? I mean absolutely trust you?

BARNEY   I'd—like to be your friend.

BOBBI   *(She pours Scotch into a glass)*   I'm not crazy or anything, so what I tell you you must accept as the gospel truth. Do you know he had my dog kidnapped?

BARNEY   Who?

BOBBI   Mr. H. . . . of Palm Springs, California . . . He had my thirteen-month-old Lhasa Apso kidnapped. You promised I could trust you.

BARNEY   I wouldn't tell that to anyone. Why would he kidnap your dog?

BOBBI   Do you think I'm making that up?

BARNEY   No. You tell me a man kidnapped your dog, I accept it.

BOBBI   I mean the dog is gone. He loves me and he knows his way home, so he's obviously being held against his will.
       (She pours the Scotch back into the bottle)

BARNEY   Your Lhasa Apso? Did you call the police?

BOBBI   What's the point? They're in on it too.

BARNEY   The police are in on the kidnap of your Lhasa Apso?

BOBBI   Mr. H. is also one of the biggest political bigwigs in California. Who would you say the police are more likely to cooperate with? *(Takes off her shoes)* Listen, the things I could tell about men I've met. Some day I'm going to write a book naming names, dates and places. I wouldn't leave a *single* man out.

BARNEY *(Nervously)* Well, I'm sure once in a while you must have met some *nice* men.

BOBBI Oh, you wouldn't be in the book. You have sensitive hands. *(She takes his hand)* That's how I knew you were nice in the park. I can tell everything about a person by just looking at his hands. You have such long, delicate fingers . . .

BARNEY I knew a girl in school who was able to determine a person's character by—

BOBBI *(Singing)*
What's it all about, Alfie? Is it just for the moment we live?
What's it all about, when you sort it out—*
I smell oysters.

BARNEY What?

BOBBI What could that be?

BARNEY *(Moves his hand away)* I can't imagine. Look, Bobbi, the reason I asked you up here today . . .

BOBBI God, how I miss my dog. He kidnapped him because he was jealous of anyone or anything I cared about. He didn't want me to have a dog or a car or a career. Especially a career. He knows I'm enormously talented and he's afraid of losing me. Well, that's his problem because nothing's going to stop me. I'm going to make good no matter how many opportunities he tries to block. I've got it, I know that. Ask anyone on the Coast. The talent's there, it's just a question of time. Do you know he had me fired from the Cocoanut Grove? Did you hear about that?

BARNEY Er, no, I didn't.

BOBBI On opening night. After the first show. And I was fabulous. You could ask my agent, he'll give you an unbiased rave . . . Did you ever stop to wonder why I was never on the *Hollywood Palace?*

BARNEY I . . . er . . . really can't say that I did.

*From "Alfie," by Burt Bacharach and Hal David. Copyright ©
1966 by Famous Music Corporation.

BOBBI   I had a two-week contract at the Cocoanut
Grove. They had to pay me off. But I wasn't allowed
to sing the second show. Who would you say was
responsible for that?

BARNEY   Sure sounds like Mr. H. to me.

BOBBI   Because he knew the producers of the *Hollywood
Palace* were coming for the second show. And let me
ask you another question. I had the best orchestrations
for any night club singer on the West Coast, right?

BARNEY   Right.

BOBBI   Then who stole the trumpet parts five minutes
before show time?

BARNEY   Could it have been the same ones who were in
on the Lhasa Apso job?

BOBBI   *(Stares at him)*   Are you trying to put me on?

BARNEY   I'm not. I swear I'm not. I think I'll have a
drink.

BOBBI   That's why I had to leave the Coast. He blocked
every move I made. (BOBBI *laughs)* You know he once
tried to have me committed to a hospital?

BARNEY   No. Why?

BOBBI   Obviously to keep tabs on me. Actually it was
my own fault. I was faking a nervous breakdown so
he'd leave me alone. I made believe I went crazy in
a department store one day and the police came with
an ambulance. He must have had me followed because the ambulance was there in five minutes. Who
else could have sent them?

BARNEY   *(Nods)*   What did they do?

BOBBI   Oh, they just held me for observation.

BARNEY   And sent you home?

BOBBI   In twelve weeks. He must have paid them off.
Otherwise why would they keep me there? It wasn't
too bad, I wasn't working anyway. I ask you, is that
some experience?

BARNEY   *(Nods)*   Some experience.

BOBBI   Hey, have you ever heard of Babylon Revisited?

BARNEY   Who?

BOBBI   Babylon Revisited. It's a rock group. They want me to record with them. But once you do the Janis Joplin scene your voice is gone in two years. Don't you think I'm better off taking the David Merrick show ?

BARNEY   I thought they turned you down?

BOBBI   Where did you hear that?

BARNEY   *You* told me before.

BOBBI   I didn't say they turned me down. I said they took the black girl.

BARNEY   But you didn't get the part.

BOBBI   What are you trying to say?

BARNEY   I'm not trying to say anything. Hey, listen, don't get angry with me.

BOBBI   *(Tensely)*   I'm not angry with anyone.

BARNEY   Well, you seem upset.

BOBBI   I am not upset. I am not angry. I am not uptight. I am not anything . . . I'm turning on again.

BARNEY   *(Nervously)*   Listen, I'm not sure that's a good idea. Anyway, the thing is . . . it's getting kind of late, you know?

BOBBI   And you want me to leave.

BARNEY   No, I don't *want* you to leave—

BOBBI   But you'd be happier if I left.

BARNEY   Happier? No, not happier—

BOBBI   Don't worry. I'm not going to try anything.

BARNEY   Try what? Like what? What would you try?

BOBBI   Nothing. I thought you were looking at the scars on my wrist. You're wrong about them.

BARNEY   I wasn't even looking at them. I didn't even

know you had them. Listen, your scars are your business.

BOBBI   I was watering plants and the window fell on my wrists.

BARNEY   That happens so often. I know people who have the same scars.

BOBBI   Please forgive me. I'm suspicious of everyone. I really have to run.

BARNEY   Oh, that's too bad. Just when we were getting acquainted. *But*—if you have to rush off.

BOBBI *(Opens the box)*   I just have to have a few drags before I face the world again.

BARNEY   Now? Now? Wouldn't you be better off facing the world first and then relaxing when you get home?

BOBBI   Doctor's orders.

BARNEY   Well, I wouldn't want you to go without your medicine but *(She takes out two sticks)* as I said before, I'm way behind in this story— *(She holds one out to him)* What's that?

BOBBI   You said you'd have one with me later.

BARNEY   I said "maybe" later. *Maybe* . . .

BOBBI   You said "later."

BARNEY   No, no. I said "maybe later." I remember saying the maybe just before the later. We were talking about that incident with the Mexican in the motel.

BOBBI   I think it's very impolite of you. I'm not going unless you have one with me . . . if I have to stay all night.

BARNEY   Two puffs. Two quick puffs and then I really have to get back to work.
        (He puts it in his mouth and takes the matches)

BOBBI   I like the way you hold it in your mouth. You

can tell a lot about a man by the way he holds pot in his mouth.

BARNEY   Here we go.
     (He lights both)

BOBBI   Good?

BARNEY   Oh, yeah. Mm, man, that's pot.

BOBBI   It's better when you close your eyes.

BARNEY   Oh, listen, don't I know. But I really don't have time to close my eyes. I'm just taking one more puff and then I've got to get to work. *(He takes another quick drag)* Okay. Finished. Really terrific. My best pot this week.
     (He starts to put it out in the ashtray)

BOBBI   Let me see you get it in your lungs and hold it there.

BARNEY   You don't want to see that. There's nothing to see. A man with pot in his lungs. You must have seen it a hundred times.

BOBBI   Why won't you inhale it?

BARNEY   I will. I will. Watch. I promise.
     (He takes another drag)

BOBBI   Swallow it.

BARNEY   Hmm?

BOBBI   Swallow it! (BARNEY *swallows)* Okay, now exhale.
     (BARNEY *exhales; nothing comes out)*

BARNEY   Oh, my God, it didn't come out. It's still in there.

BOBBI   In a few minutes your mouth will feel numb and your toes will start to tingle.

BARNEY   Good, good. I can't wait.

BOBBI   What do you feel now?

BARNEY   Outside of sharp pain, nothing very much.

BOBBI   Is your mouth getting dry?

BARNEY   A little. *(Tests his mouth)* It's drying now. *(Tests it again)* There it goes, it's all dried up.

BOBBI   This is quality grass. You can tell, can't you? It's from South America.

BARNEY   Well, you know what they say: "You can take pot out of the country, but you can't take the—"

BOBBI   Toes tingling yet?

BARNEY *(Nods)*   Toes tingling.

BOBBI   Relaxed?

BARNEY   Relaxed . . . Oh, my God, my tongue is paralyzed. I just lost the use of my tongue. I'll never talk again.

BOBBI   You're high, baby, just sit back and enjoy it.

BARNEY   I'll try, I'll try . . . Everything is slowing down. Do you feel everything slowing down?

BOBBI   Mm-hmmm.

BARNEY *(Puts his hand on his chest)*   Oh, God, I don't feel my heart. What the hell happened to my heart?

BOBBI   Relax . . . Don't fight it, honey.

BARNEY   I'm not. I'm not fighting it. I'm letting it do whatever it wants.

BOBBI   Hang it out for the world to see, honey.

BARNEY   I'm hanging it out. Here I go. I don't know where I'm going, but I'm going . . .

BOBBI   Just let yourself go.

BARNEY   Oh, boy, what's that? What is that?

BOBBI   What?

BARNEY   I hear my eyes blinking—thump, thump— There it goes again, thump!

BOBBI   If you got it, baby, flaunt it.

BARNEY   I'm flaunting it, I'm flaunting it. *(A big, enormous smile spreads across his face)* Wheeeee!

BOBBI   God, the things that have happened to me.

BARNEY   I heard, I heard. I can't wait to read the book.

BOBBI   Did I tell you about this man in California?

BARNEY   The dognapper or the teeth-sharpener?

BOBBI   Well, I was in love with him. You know about love, I can tell . . . You must have suffered plenty, didn't you?

BARNEY   Many years ago I was involved with an older woman in Newark, New Jersey.

BOBBI   Oh, yeah, I know that scene. How long did it last?

BARNEY   About fifteen minutes.

BOBBI   You got to make it alone in this world. All I need is one show. The talent's there, it's just a question of time.

BARNEY   That's all it is, Bob.

BOBBI   People don't want to see you make good . . . they're all jealous . . . they're all rotten . . . they're all vicious.

BARNEY   So many things I wanted to do . . . but I'll never do 'em. So many places I wanted to see . . . I'll never see 'em. Trapped . . . we're all trapped . . . Help! Help!

BOBBI   *(After a moment's quiet she begins to sing)*
What the world needs now, is love, sweet love

    (BARNEY *joins her, humming along)*
    That's the only thing that there's just too
    little of . . .

Curtain

Act Three

It is the following September; the usual hour again, about three in the afternoon. The key in the lock; the door opens. BARNEY'S *head peers in. He enters.*

No aark blue business suit for BARNEY *this time. He wears a gay glen-plaid sports jacket, tan slacks, a blue shirt and a joyful tie. The attaché case, however, is standard equipment. He puts the key on the shelf, closes the door, places the attaché case on the dining table and opens it.* BARNEY *is a bit more inspired this time. He takes out a bottle of champagne and walks to the kitchen, humming as he goes, and pausing to hit the light switch on his way past. We hear the refrigerator door open and close, and* BARNEY *returns with a glass of water which he leaves on the sideboard as he goes to the attaché case. He takes out two champagne glasses, and as he is attempting to remove the label from one of them the doorbell rings. He straightens his hair, adjusts his tie and goes to the door. He again peers out the peephole, then opens the door.* JEANETTE FISHER *stands there. She is about thirty-nine years old, a woman of no discernible physical attributes. There is only one distinguishable quality about* JEANETTE FISHER. *She is probably the singularly most depressed woman on the face of the Western Hemisphere. She wakes up to gloom and goes to bed with gloom. She fills the in-between hours with despair. She wears a beige dress and matching stole.*

She looks at BARNEY, *and then nervously glances around the room.*

BARNEY *(With some sincerity)* Hello, Jeanette! *(He extends his hand and leads her into the room, closing the door behind him)* Any trouble finding the place? *(She shakes her head "no")* It's not raining yet, is it? *(She shakes head "no" again)* Good. Good. *(He starts to walk around to her front but she turns away, her back to him, not looking at anything in particular)* Jeanette, there's nothing wrong, is there? *(Another wordless shake of her head. He goes over and takes her hand)* Well, then, come here and sit down . . . Hey, come on, Jeanette, look at me. *(She finally picks her head up and looks at him)*

You okay? *(She finally manages a small smile and nods "yes")* Come here. *(He leads her to the sofa; they both sit)* Listen, there's no sense in denying this is a little awkward. But that's why I respect you, Jeanette. If you weren't nervous, if you just barged in here, cold and callous like some women could, or if you were some—some *nut* I met in the park, that would be one thing. But you're not, Jeanette. You are the only one in our circle, the *only* one of Thelma's friends that I have ever had any respect or feeling for. That's why I was so happy the other night when we were having dinner at your place, when you indicated to me— *(Suddenly JEANETTE begins to sob quietly)* Oh, Jeanette, don't. It's all right. *(She grabs a handkerchief out of her pocketbook and cries quietly into it)* Hey, come on, Jeanette. None of that now . . . *(She is sobbing. He starts to put his arm around her shoulder to comfort her)* Listen, it's all right. It's just me. Barney. *(She pushes him away. He looks around, not knowing what to do)* Jeanette, you're not going to sit here crying until five o'clock, are you? . . . *Are* you? *(JEANETTE suddenly jumps up and rushes into the bathroom, still sobbing. BARNEY gets up)* Jeanette! . . . Jeanette? *(But she's in the bathroom. He goes over and listens to her through the door. Then he walks away and throws his arms up in dismay)* Oh, Christ! *(He talks to himself)* Boy, can you pick 'em. Can you pick 'em!

> *(The door suddenly opens and JEANETTE stands there. She has stopped crying. BARNEY looks at her in anticipation. She smiles at him)*

JEANETTE   Why am I here, Barney?

BARNEY   What was that?

JEANETTE   Why am I here? I've known you and Thelma for twelve years. She's been a good friend to me. I wouldn't hurt her for the world. You and Mel are closer than brothers. So why am I here?

BARNEY   Why? Because I *asked* you here, that's why. I'm very fond of you. Look, why don't you put your pocketbook down, Jeanette, and relax, and I'll go inside and get us a drink, okay?
(He starts for the kitchen)

JEANETTE I don't find you physically attractive. You knew that, didn't you?
(That stops him)

BARNEY No! No, I didn't know that . . . It doesn't surprise me . . . I mean it's not mandatory . . .

JEANETTE I think you're sweet . . . I think you're basically a good person. I do not think you're physically attractive.

BARNEY *(Cheerfully)* Listen, you can't win 'em all.

JEANETTE I can be honest with you, Barney, can't I? I think we've known each other long enough for that, haven't we?

BARNEY *(The good sport)* Hell, yes.

JEANETTE So I can just come out and say it, can't I? I do not find you physically attractive.

BARNEY *(Smiling)* Fine, fine. Listen, I think we've covered that ground pretty good, Jeanette. So why don't I go get the drinks and you put down your pocketbook and relax and then—

JEANETTE Don't misunderstand me. It's not the weight. The weight thing doesn't bother me. I have never been repelled by obesity.

BARNEY I'm glad to hear that, Jeanette. Actually I was a skinny kid. I blew up in the army. I was a mess sergeant in Fort Totten for about two years and I would constantly—

JEANETTE I am attracted to you emotionally, intellectually—

BARNEY Isn't that funny? I always felt that you and I had a certain rapport—

JEANETTE But not physically.

BARNEY *(Nods)* Not physically. We established that a number of times. Would you excuse me one second, Jeanette. I want to get the champagne.
(He starts again)

JEANETTE Barney, do you know I haven't slept with Mel in eight months?

BARNEY *(That stops him again)* No, I didn't. Eight months, my God. I knew Mel had a bad back but I had no idea—

JEANETTE *Have not* slept with him in eight months.

BARNEY Well, listen, Jeanette, that's none of my business, really. That's between you and Mel . . .

JEANETTE He's slept with me. I haven't slept with him.

BARNEY *(Looks at her, puzzled)* How does that work out?

JEANETTE I don't particularly enjoy sex, Barney.

BARNEY Is that right? Ever?

JEANETTE It was important to me once. Nothing is very important to me any more.

BARNEY You're just tense, Jeanette. You're going through a dry period right now. Eight months, my God, no wonder . . .

JEANETTE Has Mel indicated in any way there was any trouble between us?

BARNEY None. Mel is not a talker.

JEANETTE I know you see him all the time.

BARNEY I play handball with him on Saturday mornings. We never discuss personal problems. He serves, I hit it back.

JEANETTE He didn't seem upset?

BARNEY No. Can I take your pocketbook, Jeanette?

JEANETTE *You* wouldn't talk, would you, Barney?

BARNEY Me, Jeanette? I'm surprised that you would even think—

JEANETTE Then I don't have to worry about my name ever coming up in a cocktail party—

BARNEY May God strike me dead! May I never live to

see my oldest girl married, if I ever mentioned even casually—

JEANETTE Swear!

BARNEY I just swore. May I become totally paralyzed from the hips down—

JEANETTE It was not easy for me to come here today.

BARNEY May my hands get crippled with arthritis. I'm surprised that you would even think . . .

JEANETTE I'm not very good at this sort of thing, Barney.

BARNEY Who *is*, Jeanette?

JEANETTE I don't even know what I'm supposed to do.

BARNEY I'd put my pocketbook down first if I were you . . .

JEANETTE *(She gets up)* My only concern is that whatever happens between us will never go beyond these four walls.
    (She crosses to the window)

BARNEY May my restaurant be destroyed by fire, Jeanette. You'll never have to worry as long as you live. I told you that the other night.

JEANETTE Did Mel ever mention being involved with another woman?

BARNEY No.

JEANETTE Would you tell me if he did?

BARNEY Yes. Yes, I would tell you.

JEANETTE You would?

BARNEY Yes.

JEANETTE Why would you tell me?

BARNEY I don't know why. You asked me if I would; I'm trying to be polite, that's all.

JEANETTE I see.

BARNEY Can I take your pocketbook, Jeanette?

JEANETTE   What do you think about all this, Barney?

BARNEY   About all what?

JEANETTE   About all this that's going on.

BARNEY   *Nothing's* going on, Jeanette. I can't even get your pocketbook.

JEANETTE   You're not appalled by the times we live in, by all the promiscuity you find everywhere?

BARNEY   I don't find it anywhere. I *hear* a lot about it, I haven't found any. You want to sit down a few minutes? You're here, you might as well sit.

JEANETTE   Let me ask you a question, Barney. Do you have any guilt about asking me here today?

BARNEY   Do I have any guilt?

JEANETTE   Don't repeat the question, just answer it.

BARNEY   What? Do I have any guilt? . . . No, I do not.

JEANETTE   In other words, you don't care who you hurt?

BARNEY   I'm not hurting anyone.

JEANETTE   Really? You want to think about that answer?

BARNEY   Not necessarily . . . Why probe deeply into everything?

JEANETTE   Exactly. That's the attitude we live with today. Don't think about it. Well, I'm not going to think about it, Barney. I'm going to become like everyone else in the world. That's why I'm here today.
        (She opens her purse, takes out a pillbox and puts a pill in her mouth)

BARNEY   Somehow I think we've gotten off on a tangent, Jeanette . . . What are you doing? What's that?

JEANETTE   Digilene. It's for depression.

BARNEY   Don't you want any water?

JEANETTE   I couldn't wait.

BARNEY Until I brought the water? You're *that* depressed?

JEANETTE Isn't that how we cope with our problems today, Barney? With pills, drugs . . . Do you know how many people in this country take pills because they cannot cope with emotional problems? Do you know the number in this country? It was in *Look* magazine.

BARNEY I didn't get a haircut this week, I missed the new *Look*.

JEANETTE Sixty million.

BARNEY That many?

JEANETTE Do you know the alternative to taking pills?

BARNEY Was this in the same issue?

JEANETTE Melancholia. Do you know what that is? Melancholia?

BARNEY Brooding, isn't it? Heavy brooding?

JEANETTE I'll tell you what melancholia is, Barney, because I've had it for the last eight months. It's total and complete despair. It's waking up each morning of your life not wanting anything, not hoping, not caring, not needing. You don't pray for happiness because you don't believe it exists, and you don't wish for death because if you don't exist, then death is meaningless. All that's left is a quiet, endless, bottomless, relentless, eternal, infinite gloom. That's melancholia.
> *(There is a long, awkward pause as* BARNEY *thinks about how to retrieve the afternoon)*

BARNEY Hey, how about a nice, cool drink? I bet that would pick you up?

JEANETTE What do you want with me anyway, Barney, a good time? You're not going to have a good time with me.

BARNEY I think we could have an interesting afternoon if we got off the gloom and the brooding, I really do,

Jeanette. Why don't I get the champagne while you put down your pocketbook and relax—

JEANETTE   You mean Mel never mentioned another woman to you?

BARNEY   As God is my judge. You seem so different from the other night, Jeanette, so tense. I don't know, you had such a zest and spirit about you.

JEANETTE   It was not easy for me to come here today.

BARNEY   I understand that.

JEANETTE   If anyone knew or even suspected—

BARNEY   May I become deformed in all my vital organs —stop it already, Jeanette, no one's going to know. I'm going to get the wine and I want you to sit back and relax. *(He starts out, and stops at the table)* You see this table?

JEANETTE   Yes.

BARNEY   *(Taps it)*   Good spot for your pocketbook. *(He starts off)*

JEANETTE   Barney, do you know I can't taste food?

BARNEY   Oh, now wait a minute, Jeanette. I can't believe that. I can well understand your being in a state of depression most of the time but you can certainly taste food.

JEANETTE   I can *not* taste food.

BARNEY   It may not taste *good* to you, but you can taste it.

JEANETTE   Can *not* taste food.

BARNEY   What are you saying, Jeanette? You had two pieces of pot roast the other night, I saw you.

JEANETTE   I eat what's in front of me. It doesn't make too much difference.

BARNEY   It wasn't in front of you, you got up and took a second piece. Well, what's the difference. It's how you feel that's important.

JEANETTE   And how do *you* feel, Barney? About being here with Mel's wife?

BARNEY   Why do you put it that way? You're Jeanette, I'm Barney. Why do you complicate everything?

JEANETTE *(Gets up, goes to the phone and picks up the receiver)*   What do you think Mel's reaction would be if I called him now and told him what was going on here?

BARNEY *(Gets up and crosses to her)*   Big! I think his reaction would be big! *(He takes the phone away from her)* With a lot of killing and murder. *(He moves across the room with the phone)* Don't test him, Jeanette. It's not good for a marriage to test it too much.
(He pushes the phone behind the lamp)

JEANETTE   Do you think death is so terrible, Barney?

BARNEY   Death? I do. I think death is terrible. I think *violent* death is the worst . . . Jeanette, I think we're getting a little morbid here . . .

JEANETTE   You don't think there are worse things than death?

BARNEY   Like suffering and pain? They're bad, but they're second and third after death. Death is first . . . Jeanette, I really think you should have some champagne.

JEANETTE   You mean you enjoy your life? You like living?

BARNEY   I *love* living. I have some problems with my *life,* but living is the best thing they've come up with so far . . . Look, Jeanette, I know you're going through analysis right now, but I don't think this is a good time to talk shop. *(He reaches for her pocketbook)* Why don't you let me take your pocketbook and—

JEANETTE *(Pulls it aside away from him)*   Tell me what you like about living, Barney.

BARNEY   What I like? I like all of it.

JEANETTE   *All* of it?

BARNEY   A lot of it. A lot of it is very nice.

JEANETTE   For example.

BARNEY   For example? You mean like what are my favorite things? Is that what you mean? Your pocketbook is really getting me crazy. Put it on the floor, nothing'll happen to it.

JEANETTE *(She doesn't, of course)*   What makes life worth getting up for? Name emotions for me, feelings . . . What gives you the strength to go on, Barney?

BARNEY   Well, that takes in such a wide area, Jeanette. I don't think I could cover it in one statement. Do you mean single items like love or sex or family? *(He has been staring at her pocketbook, and finally leaps at her)* Let me have that goddamned pocketbook! *(He grabs it from her)* Nothing'll happen to it, I'll leave it right here! *(He puts it on the desk and sinks into a chair)* I'm sorry, Jeanette, I couldn't stand it any more. Oh, I feel so much better.

JEANETTE   How much of life do you actually enjoy, Barney?

BARNEY   You're still on that, Jeanette?

JEANETTE   Give me a number, a percentage.

BARNEY   A percentage? How much of a percentage of life do I enjoy? I couldn't answer that, Jeanette. It would be meaningless . . . Half! About half. Fifty-one, fifty-two percent, something like that. I'm just giving you a figure off the top of my head.

JEANETTE   Do you know what *my* percentage is? Do you know what Doctor Margolies estimated *my* percentage of happiness is?

BARNEY *(Thinks)*   Low. I would imagine it was low.

JEANETTE   Eight point two percent.

BARNEY   I estimated something like that.

JEANETTE   I'm thirty-nine years old, Barney. I've enjoyed eight point two percent of my life.

BARNEY   You actually sat down with a pencil and paper and figured that out? No wonder you're so depressed.

I mean I depressed myself with the fifty-one percent.
I can understand how you feel with an eight point
two.

JEANETTE   Do you think that people are basically good?

BARNEY   Another question?

JEANETTE   Do you think the world is populated with
decent, loving, gentle human beings?

BARNEY *(He'd better think about that)*   . . . Not all of
them. There's no question about that, Jeanette. Certainly not all of them.

JEANETTE   In other words, you think there are *some.*
Some people are decent—

BARNEY   Right.

JEANETTE   —loving—

BARNEY   Right.

JEANETTE   —gentle—human beings.

BARNEY   Right.

JEANETTE   Name some.

BARNEY   I knew that was your next question. I would
have bet my life on it.

JEANETTE   Name ten, Barney.

BARNEY   Name ten. There's a point to all this. I don't
see it yet but I know there's a point.

JEANETTE   Name *five.* Five people you think are decent, gentle and loving. Name *three.*

BARNEY   Three? Three people out of the whole world?
That's ridiculous. I can name three hundred, three
thousand . . .

JEANETTE   Just three.

BARNEY   Living or dead?

JEANETTE   Three people, Barney, three fellow human beings—who are gentle, loving and decent.

BARNEY   You think I can't do it. No one can be that cynical, Jeanette. No one could be *that* contemptuous of the world. Okay. I'll play. Here we go. At the top of my list, I pick, in the number-one spot . . . this one's going to surprise you . . . Are you ready?

JEANETTE   I'm ready.

BARNEY   Thelma. My wife Thelma.

JEANETTE   That's one.

BARNEY   You agree with Thelma? I mean relatives are not prohibited?

JEANETTE   Thelma is certainly a gentle and loving woman.

BARNEY   Oh, good. You agree. Thank you. So I need two more and I'm in.

JEANETTE   So far you have Thelma.

BARNEY   I've *said* that already. I'm thinking, I want to be selective . . . For second I would pick—I don't know, is John F. Kennedy acceptable to you?

JEANETTE   If he's acceptable to you.

BARNEY   Certainly he's acceptable to me. He's acceptable to *everyone*. I'll tell you the truth, Jeanette, when you told me in the kitchen the other night that you were willing, even *anxious* to meet me here today, I had no idea it was to play this game.

JEANETTE   I'm trying to prove to you why I'm here. All right, let's forget it, we'll have the champagne.

BARNEY   One second. Let me finish my list first. *(Enumerates on his fingers)* Thelma, my wife, John F. Kennedy . . . and, I don't know, Christ—oh, yes. Him. Christ! All right? Three?

JEANETTE   Three. You did it, Barney. You actually

found three people who you consider gentle, loving and decent. I congratulate you.

BARNEY   You don't have to congratulate me, it wasn't so hard. I just picked the Big Three—Kennedy, Christ and Thelma. For God's sakes, Jeanette, if anyone heard this conversation . . .

JEANETTE   I couldn't do it, Barney. I couldn't pick three people. Not in this world.

BARNEY   In thirty-nine years, you have never met—

JEANETTE   Never!

BARNEY   During your eight point two percent of happiness, surely there were three people—

JEANETTE   There weren't.

BARNEY   Not even a close friend or a girl you went to school with?

JEANETTE   Who?

BARNEY   I don't know who you went to school with! All right, what about Christ? Are you going to tell me Jesus Christ was not a decent, gentle, loving man? or John F. Kennedy?

JEANETTE   Mention people I know.

BARNEY   All right, Thelma. Will you agree with Thelma?

JEANETTE   I told you before. I consider Thelma a gentle and loving woman.

BARNEY   Wait a minute. Hold it a second. What about decent? That's the second time you left out decent. The first time I thought it was an oversight, this time I'd like to discuss it. Why did you leave out decent?

JEANETTE   Do you consider her decent?

BARNEY   Thelma? My wife Thelma? What's the matter with you? She's the most decent human being on earth. Ask anyone. Thelma is the epitome of decency. My God, Thelma Cashman is synonymous with the word "decent."

JEANETTE   That's wonderful.

BARNEY   Why, have you heard something?

JEANETTE   Of course not.

BARNEY   Then why did you leave out decent?

JEANETTE   She's on *your* list. It's not important if she's on mine.

BARNEY   What are you trying to do, Jeanette? Are you making inferences concerning the decency of my wife Thelma?

JEANETTE   I'm not making inferences, Barney. *You're* indicating some doubt.

BARNEY   *Doubt? Doubt?* About Thelma? *(Laughs)* Good God, what the hell is there to doubt about Thelma?

JEANETTE   How would I know, Barney?

BARNEY   Well, I'll tell you. NOTHING! THERE IS NOTHING TO DOUBT ABOUT THELMA!

JEANETTE   As long as you're sure.

BARNEY *(Shouting)*   Don't tell me "as long as I'm sure" because I'm sure. I have lived with the woman my whole life. I grew up with her. I know every nerve fiber in her body, every thought that's ever been in her head. The woman is without malice, without jealousy. Thelma Cashman is *beyond* reproach. She is as totally incapable of an act of deception as *you* would be or *I* would be or—oh, my God!
(He slumps in his seat. She stares at him)

JEANETTE *(A long pause)*   So you have Kennedy and Christ! You have one more pick.

BARNEY   It's not true! Not Thelma, it's not true. She's not like other people. She's gentle and loving and decent.

JEANETTE   In other words, you agree that other people are *not* gentle and loving and decent?

BARNEY   For God's sakes, Jeanette, why are you doing this? Is there something about Thelma you know that I don't? Is there something about her I should know that you're not telling me? I'll find out sooner or later, so you might as well tell me now. *(He points a threat-ening finger at her)* You hear me, Jeanette? *I demand to know about Thelma!*

JEANETTE *(Stares at* BARNEY *a few seconds)* Thelma is the only gentle, loving and decent woman I've ever met. She is unreproachable and incapable of decep-tion. She is the epitome of decency. And the fact that you could doubt her is an act of indecency on your part. You are not a decent human being. Neither am I because I'm here with you, knowing what Thelma is. Neither is Mel, because he drove me to it. We are not decent people, Barney. Only Thelma is. But she thinks you're the most decent one of us all, so that makes her an idiot in my eyes. There are only inde-cent people or idiots in this world because that's all I ever see. And that's how I spend most of my day, thinking about things like that. Is it any wonder I take Digilene?

BARNEY *(Falls back in his chair, exhausted. He shakes his head)* I swear, I have never been so depressed in all my life.

JEANETTE I think my analyst has an opening Thursday afternoon.

BARNEY Is it true, Jeanette? Am I really so terrible? Are we *all* so terrible?

JEANETTE Do you know what the rate of literacy is in the United States? Eighty-six percent. Do you know how many married people have committed adultery? Eighty-seven percent. This is the only country in the world that has more cheaters than readers.

BARNEY I never thought of myself like this. I never thought of anybody like this.

JEANETTE You should see what it's like *without* Digi-lene.

BARNEY No. No, listen, Jeanette. I don't buy it. We're not indecent, we're not unloving. We're human. That's what we are, Jeanette. *human!*

JEANETTE   If I were to tell you stories about people you know, people you respect, you would get sick to your stomach right here on this carpet.

BARNEY   I'm not interested in other people. It's no concern of mine.

JEANETTE   You don't see what's going on around you? The lies, the deceit. The stinking, sordid affairs that are going on in motels, in offices, in little German cars.

BARNEY   Jeanette, you can't go on like this. You've got to look at the brighter side.

JEANETTE *(Fighting back tears)*   Do you know Charlotte Korman, big, red-headed, buxom woman, her husband is the Mercedes-Benz dealer in Wantagh? (BARNEY *nods)* Mel doesn't like her. He doesn't want me to see her. He doesn't want her to be my friend, doesn't want her to come to our house; he can't stand Charlotte Korman.

BARNEY   So?

JEANETTE   He's been having an affair with her for eight months! I had to stop seeing her three times a week so *he* could see her four times a week. These are the times we live in, Barney.

BARNEY   Listen, Jeanette, maybe you're wrong. Maybe it's just your imagination. Your whole outlook's a little distorted lately. You must admit you're even having trouble tasting food.

JEANETTE   You know what my proof is? He told me. Two o'clock in the morning, he leans over, taps me on the shoulder and says, "I've had an affair with Charlotte Korman." Who asked him? When he tapped me on the shoulder in the middle of the night I thought he wanted *me!* You know what it is to wake up from a sound sleep with no eyelashes and a dry mouth and hear that your husband is getting it from a woman you're not allowed to see for lunch? And you know why he told me, Barney? He explained it to me. We're living in a new guiltless society. You can do anything you want as long as you're honest about it. Aren't we lucky to be living in such a civilized age? In the old days I would have gone to my grave *ignorant* of the wonderful and beautiful knowledge that my husband was spending his afternoons humping Charlotte Korman! . . . When he told me, I didn't say a word. I went down to the kitchen and made myself a cream cheese and jelly sandwich on date-nut bread. And that was the last time in eight months that I tasted food . . . I estimate, going four times a week, I should be through with Doctor Margolies in another year. And then, when we both think I'm ready, I'm going to get in my car and drive off the Verrazano Bridge. In the meantime, I'm very depressed. Excuse me, Barney. Nothing personal, but I don't think we're going to have our affair.

BARNEY   Where are you going?

JEANETTE   Where's anyone going?

BARNEY   Please, not yet.

JEANETTE *(Walks over to the desk and gets her pocketbook)* Some good time you had, heh, Barney? A barrel of laughs, right? I think my eight point two is down to a three or a four.

BARNEY   I'm not indecent, Jeanette.

JEANETTE   Don't start again, Barney. I only got one Digilene left.
     (She's at the door)

BARNEY   Foolish, stupid, maybe, but I'm not indecent.

JEANETTE *(Hand on the door)*   Have it your way.

BARNEY   *Don't leave!* Don't leave until you say I am not indecent. It's important to me, Jeanette.

JEANETTE   You want me to lie? You're not indecent. We're a terrific bunch of people.

BARNEY *(Begins to fume)*   All right! All right, we're all no good. We're all indecent, unfeeling, unloving, rotten human beings. Sick, monstrous, disgusting people, all of us. You don't know the half of it. You haven't the slightest idea how filthy and ugly I really am deep inside. You think you're the first woman I ever had up here? Ha! You want to hear about Elaine, a woman of Polish persuasion I picked up in my own restaurant? A drinking, smoking, coughing, married woman who practically begged me to rip her clothes off . . . And you know what happened? *Nothing,* Jeanette. Nothing happened. Because I was looking for something beautiful, something decent. You want to hear about Bobbi, a psycho unemployed night club singer who had her dog kidnapped by the Beverly Hills police and sleeps with a Nazi vocal coach? I sat there with her smoking marijuana and singing popular songs of the day . . . And you know what happened? Nothing, Jeanette. Nothing happened. Because I was looking for something beautiful, something decent . . . And then I invited you. A woman who grabbed me in her kitchen last Thursday night and physically pinned me down on the table. I had mayonnaise stains on my back when I got home. And when you get here, what do you do? You sit there taking pills and holding on to your goddamned pocketbook all day. And again, *nothing* happened, Jeanette. Nothing. Because I was looking for something beautiful, something decent. Well, I'm through, dammit. I'm through looking for something beautiful and decent because *it doesn't exist.* You're right, Jeanette, we're no damned good, all of us. There are no decent, gentle, loving people left in the world. *(He advances toward her)* We're depraved, lustful, disgusting monsters, all of us. *(He pushes a chair out of his way)* But if we're guilty, Jeanette, then let's at least commit the crime. If we're depraved, let's see a little depravity. *(He is moving toward her; she backs away)* If we're indecent, then let's see a couple of terrific indecencies! *COME HERE, JEANETTE!*

JEANETTE   Barney, get out of my way.

BARNEY   Who do you think you're fooling around with here, Jeanette? Some kid? Some scared amateur? I'm a pro, baby, I know the ropes.

JEANETTE Barney, stop it, I don't think this is funny.

BARNEY *(Stalking her)* I could tell you stories that happened in a motel with a Mexican that would make your teeth curl.

JEANETTE Get away from me, Barney, I'm not kidding.

BARNEY You want to hear language? You want to hear words? SCREW! ASSHOLE! Come on, Jeanette, let's hear a few!

JEANETTE Barney, stop it. Get away from me, I want to go, Barney. I'm not kidding.

BARNEY Kidding? Who the hell is kidding? I'm *dead serious*, Jeanette! Who do you think you are, coming on like that in the kitchen the other night and then coming up here to tell me your troubles. I'm not interested in your troubles. I want your flesh, not your heartbreaking stories.

JEANETTE Oh, my God, you must be out of your head. What's the matter with you, Barney?

BARNEY Nothing's the matter with *me*, sweetheart. I'm with it! I'm *now!* I'm here where it's happening, Jeanette, where the hell are you? Now, are you going to take off that dress or do I rip it off with my fingers?

JEANETTE Barney, stop it, I'm scared to death. You're not like this, Barney, I know you're not like this.

BARNEY No? Then tell me. Tell me what I'm really like.

JEANETTE You're quiet. You're intelligent.

BARNEY Really? And what else? Let me hear it, Jeanette, what else?

JEANETTE *(Backing away as BARNEY tosses furniture aside)* You're not mean. I've never seen you do a mean thing in your life. *(She begins to whimper)* Barney, you're scaring me.

BARNEY   Quiet, intelligent . . . More, more. I wanna hear more.

JEANETTE   You're kind. You're the kindest man I know. Please let me go, Barney.
            (She is crying)

BARNEY   It's not enough, dammit. You'll stay in this room until your pocketbook rots. I want to hear the rest, Jeanette.

JEANETTE   You're kind and good and intelligent . . .

BARNEY   *(A real Gestapo officer)*   You *said* intelligent. I already *heard* intelligent. No repeats allowed, Jeanette. I want to hear a *new* word. One you haven't said yet. Come on, Jeanette, you can say it! What else am I?

JEANETTE   Decent! You're decent! You *are*, Barney!

BARNEY   Aha! Decent. That's the one I wanted. Decent and what else?

JEANETTE   . . . and gentle.

BARNEY   And gentle. And what else?

JEANETTE   . . . and loving . . .

BARNEY   *Loving!* Decent and gentle and loving? But how can I be, Jeanette? You said no one is.

JEANETTE   You are, Barney. Just you.

BARNEY   And Thelma?

JEANNETTE   And Thelma.

BARNEY   That's two. So if there's two there could be more, wouldn't you say that, Jeanette?

JEANETTE   I don't know. I don't know.

BARNEY   Think, Jeanette. Think. There's gotta be one more. Can't you think of one more?

JEANETTE   No. No, I can't. There are no more. *(She is sobbing)* Mel! Mel! I want Mel . . .

BARNEY   Why? Why do you want Mel?

JEANETTE   I want him, I need him . . .

BARNEY   Because you love him, Jeanette?

JEANETTE   Yes! . . . Yes!

BARNEY   How can you love anyone who isn't decent and gentle and loving?

JEANETTE   He is. He is. I don't care what he's done. He is! Mel! Mel!

BARNEY *(With sincerity)*   That's three. I knew you could come up with it, Jeanette.
(She sits there awhile, quietly sobbing. BARNEY *puts his arm around her)*

JEANETTE   What's happened to us, Barney? What's happened to the world? . . . I can't keep up with it.

BARNEY *(Shrugs)*   There's no sense denying it, Jeanette. It's changing.

JEANETTE *(Looks at him)*   In London, I've read about it. In New York, I've seen it. I never expected it in Great Neck.

BARNEY   You okay? *(She nods. He helps her up)* You want to compose yourself again?

JEANETTE   It'll take me the rest of my life. Barney, swear to me that you'll never breathe a word to a living soul—

BARNEY   May I have a coronary occlusion in my doctor's office. Stop worrying, Jeanette. You want me to get you a taxi?

JEANETTE *(Shakes her head "no")*   Someone'll see us together—probably Charlotte Korman.

BARNEY   I feel like such a louse. Do you hate me for what I've done, Jeanette?

JEANETTE *(Looks at him)*   *Hate* you . . . No, Barney.

BARNEY   See you Thursday night for dinner?

JEANNETTE   You really believe it, don't you, Barney? That we're not all sick and rotten. You actually believe that some of us are decent, gentle and loving.

BARNEY   I do. And deep down, so do you.

JEANETTE   Maybe . . . but at two o'clock in the morning I think I'm going to tap Mel on the shoulder and tell him I've had an affair . . . Let *him* be depressed for a while.

> *(She leaves.* BARNEY *closes the door. He turns back into the room and surveys the wreckage of strewn furniture. He begins to replace the chairs and things in their proper places, when he stops and looks at his watch. An idea strikes him. He crosses to the phone and puts his hand on the receiver. He thinks a moment, decides to go through with it, and picks up the receiver and dials. He waits, then)*

BARNEY   *(Into the phone)*   . . . Hello, Thelma? . . . What are you doing? . . . You busy? . . . Listen, honey, I was thinking, why don't you meet me this afternoon, we could do something . . . Sure, now, it takes you ten minutes to get here . . . No, not in the restaurant . . . In my mother's apartment . . . No, she didn't invite us to dinner, I just want you to meet me here . . . Thelma, don't be so stubborn, can't you meet me in my mother's apartment . . . ?

> *(The curtain begins to fall)*

Curtain